If you're wondering why you need this new edition of *Texas Government*, here are eight good reasons!

1. The text features full coverage of the 2008 election and 2010 spring primaries in Texas. Chapter 4 includes updated voter turnout rates from the 2008 election and changes the turnout basis from voting age population to voting eligible population; Chapter 6 looks at the demographic trends that may well bring the Democratic Party back into power sometime between now and 2020; and Chapter 7 discusses the Texas Two-Step and its role in the 2008 Democratic presidential nomination contest between Hillary Clinton and Barack Obama. Chapter 13 examines the effect of the new federal healthcare reform law on the Texas Medicaid program.

2. "Around the Nation" features have been updated throughout the text to reflect current hot topics in state politics across the nation. Topics include the Massachusetts healthcare program as an example of a state serving as a "laboratory of democracy"; the cash-for-grades student incentive program in Washington, D.C.; campaign finance reform in Arizona; party politics in Kansas; healthcare reform in San Francisco; and toll road privatization in Indiana.

3. New material on social issues has been incorporated throughout the text. Chapter 1 discusses how religion impacts public policy in Texas; Chapter 14 examines sobriety checkpoints as a way to reduce drunk driving; and throughout the text updated data on death penalty verdicts and executions looks at the national trends and compares them to the Texas criminal justice system.

4. Chapter 2 explores the issue of expanding legalized gambling to raise revenue. It also analyzes the Texas Constitution's role in the policymaking process. Chapter 10 looks at the Texas Supreme Court decision in the *Perry Homes v. Cull* court case.

5. The new Chapter 3 opener discusses Governor Rick Perry's rejection of federal stimulus money earmarked to shore up the state's unemployment insurance fund.

6. Legislative politics and processes are analyzed in Chapter 8 by examining the fate of environmentally friendly legislation in the 81st session of the Texas legislature.

7. Chapter 9 discusses insurance regulation in the Lone Star State, focusing on the role of the TDI. The section on the SBOE discusses the recent debate over the state's high school science and social studies curricula.

8. Chapter 13 discusses the state budget crisis that Texas will soon be facing.

PEARSON

LONGMAN STUDY EDITION

Texas Government

POLICY AND POLITICS

Eleventh Edition

NEAL TANNAHILL
Houston Community College

Longman

Boston Columbus Indianapolis New York San Francisco Upper Saddle River
Amsterdam Cape Town Dubai London Madrid Milan Munich Paris Montreal Toronto
Delhi Mexico City São Paulo Sydney Hong Kong Seoul Singapore Taipei Tokyo

Editor-in-Chief: Eric Stano
Editorial Assistant: Elizabeth Alimena
Supplements Editor: Corey Kahn
Senior Marketing Manager: Lindsey Prudhomme
Production Manager: Bob Ginsberg
Project Coordination, Text Design, and Electronic Page Makeup:
   S4Carlisle Publishing Services
Cover Design Manager/Cover Designer: Wendy Ann Fredericks
Cover Photo: © Steve Vidler/Superstock
Visual Researcher: Julie Tesser
Senior Manufacturing Buyer: Roy L. Pickering, Jr.
Printer and Binder: RR Donnelley, Crawfordsville
Cover Printer: RR Donnelley, Crawfordsville

For permission to use copyrighted photographs, grateful acknowledgment is made to the copyright holders on p. 412, which is hereby made part of this copyright page.

Library of Congress Cataloging-in-Publication Data
Tannahill, Neal, 1949-
   Texas government : policy and politics / Neal Tannahill. — 11th ed.
      p. cm.
   Includes bibliographical references and index.
   ISBN-13: 978-0-205-82540-0 (alk. paper)
   ISBN-10: 0-205-82540-0 (alk. paper)
   1. Texas–Politics and government–1951—Textbooks. 2. Local government–Texas–Textbooks.
   3. Political planning–Texas–Textbooks. I. Title.
    JK4816.T36 2010
    320.4764--dc21

                                                                    2010007218

1 2 3 4 5 6 7 8 9 10—DOC—13 12 11 10

Longman
is an imprint of

www.pearsonhighered.com

ISBN-13: 978-0-205-82540-0
ISBN-10:   0-205-82540-0

Contents

CHAPTER 3 • The Federal Context of Texas Policymaking   57

CHAPTER 4 • Political Participation   79

Preface

Textbooks should be designed with students in mind. I have written this textbook in a clear, straightforward fashion so students can easily understand concepts even if they have little background knowledge of Texas government and politics. I have also done my best to present the subject in an interesting fashion. Texas government is not boring; Texas government textbooks should not be boring, either.

NEW TO THIS EDITION

This edition of *Texas Government* includes a number of changes designed to reflect recent political developments, take account of the latest developments in scholarly research, and respond to requests for changes from faculty using the textbook.

- **Introduction** Did Texas execute an innocent man? The Introduction's opener features an examination of the execution of Cameron Todd Willingham for setting a fire that killed his three children. Experts now believe that the fire was likely accidental. The Introduction chapter updates information on capital punishment to note the national decline in juries assessing the death penalty and states carrying out executions. To some extent, the trend carries over to Texas.
- **Chapter 1** This chapter has added information on religious faith and practice in Texas and discusses how religion impacts public policy in the state.
- **Chapter 2** The new chapter opener focuses on the issue of expanding legalized gambling in the state to raise revenue. Because the Texas Constitution prohibits gambling, the expansion of gambling would require the adoption of a constitutional amendment. This example illustrates the role of the Texas Constitution in structuring the policymaking process.
- **Chapter 3** The new chapter opener discusses Governor Rick Perry's rejection of federal stimulus money earmarked to shore up the state's unemployment insurance fund because he opposed expanding program eligibility, which he said would eventually drive up taxes on employers. The chapter's "Around the Nation" feature highlights the Massachusetts healthcare program as an example of a state serving as a "laboratory of democracy."
- **Chapter 4** The chapter opener examines the debate over the adoption of a photo ID law in the legislature. It updates voter turnout rates to include 2008

and changes the turnout basis from voting age population to voting eligible population.

- **Chapter 5** The opener shifts the focus from medical malpractice insurance reform to tort reform in general. The chapter's "Around the Nation" feature concerns campaign finance reform in Arizona.

- **Chapter 6** The chapter opener focuses on the outcome of the 2008 presidential election in Texas, noting that although John McCain handily carried the state, Barack Obama and the Democrats made some inroads. The main theme of the chapter is that demographic trends may well bring the Democratic Party back into power sometime between now and 2020. The chapter's "Around the Nation" feature spotlights party politics in Kansas.

- **Chapter 7** The chapter opener discusses the Texas Two-Step and its role in the 2008 Democratic presidential nomination contest between Hillary Clinton and Barack Obama.

- **Chapter 8** The chapter opener illustrates both legislative politics and the legislative process in Texas by examining the fate of environmentally friendly legislation in the 81st session of the legislature.

- **Chapter 9** The chapter opener discusses insurance regulation in the Lone Star State, focusing on the role of the TDI. The section on the SBOE discusses the recent debate over the state's high school science and social studies curricula.

- **Chapter 10** The chapter opener discusses the Texas Supreme Court decision in the case of *Perry Homes v. Cull*, which pitted an ordinary couple against Perry Homes, which is owned by the most prolific campaign contributor in the state. Guess who won? The chapter also includes a discussion of the 2009 decision of the U.S. Supreme Court over whether a West Virginia Supreme Court justice should have recused himself from a case involving a major campaign contributor.

- **Chapter 11** The chapter opener discusses the 2009 mayoral election in Houston as an illustration of contemporary big-city politics in Texas. The chapter's "Around the Nation" feature focuses on healthcare reform in San Francisco.

- **Chapter 12** Does money motivate teacher performance? How about student performance? The chapter opener discusses merit pay, whereas the chapter's "Around the Nation" feature looks at a cash-for-grades student incentive program in Washington, DC.

- **Chapter 13** The chapter opener discusses the state budget crisis that Texas will soon be facing. The chapter's new "Around the Nation" feature deals with toll road privatization in Indiana. The chapter also considers the impact of the new federal healthcare reform law on the Texas Medicaid program.

- **Chapter 14** The chapter opener examines sobriety checkpoints as a way to reduce drunk driving.

FEATURES

The text includes a number of features designed to help students learn and instructors teach.

- **What We Will Learn** Each chapter begins with questions that focus on the topics covered in the chapter and then concludes with a What We Have Learned section that presents the answers to each of the questions.

- **Key Terms** Words and phrases that have a specific meaning in the context of the subject matter appear in bold type, followed by a clear, straightforward definition. Students should not memorize the definition of the terms, but rather learn what they mean in the context of the chapter and be able to define and explain them in their own words. The list of terms at the end of each chapter helps students study by focusing their attention on important concepts.

- **Internet Research** A major goal of this textbook is to equip students with tools they can use to learn about Texas government and politics well after this course is over. The Internet is one of those tools. Each chapter includes an exercise requiring students to learn about Texas government through Internet research.

- **Multiple-Choice Questions** A set of 25 multiple-choice questions is provided for each chapter. Students can use them to help master course material.

- **Around the Nation** Each chapter includes a short essay about politics and government in another state. By reviewing these essays, students will better understand Texas government and politics in comparison with other state governments.

- **Getting Involved** Each chapter includes a feature telling students how they can get involved in their communities, the college, and their government by doing volunteer work, joining an interest group, or becoming a court-appointed special advocate.

- **Glossary** The textbook contains a glossary that includes the definitions of the key terms listed in the text. If students forget what a term means, they can look it up quickly in the glossary without having to search for it in the text.

- **What Is Your Opinion?** The text includes a number of questions asking students their opinion about some of the political controversies discussed in the text. The questions are designed to be interesting and thought provoking.

- **Instructor's Manual/Test Bank** The Instructor's Manual includes chapter outlines, chapter summaries, teaching suggestions, ideas for student projects, and discussion questions. The Test Bank contains hundreds of challenging multiple-choice, short answer, and essay questions with an answer key.

- **TestGen-EQ 2.0** The printed Test Bank is also available electronically through our computerized testing system, TestGen-EQ 2.0. This fully networkable test-generating software is now available on a cross-platform CD-ROM. TestGen-EQ 2.0's friendly graphical interface enables instructors to view, edit, and add questions; transfer questions to tests; and print tests in a variety of fonts and forms. Search and sort features allow instructors to locate questions quickly and arrange them in preferred order. Six question formats are available, including short answer, true/false, multiple-choice, essay, matching, and bimodal.

- **Study Guide** The Study Guide helps students reinforce the themes and concepts they encounter in the text. It includes learning objectives, chapter outlines, chapter summaries, case studies, key terms, and practice tests for each chapter.

- **Companion Website** A website is available to provide both students and instructors with additional resources. The website includes practice test questions, a syllabus builder, links to relevant websites on the Internet, and more. It can be accessed at www.ablongman.com/tannahilltexas.

ACKNOWLEDGMENTS

Many persons contributed significantly to the writing and production of this book. Eric Stano, Donna Garnier, Elizabeth Alimena, and the other professionals at Pearson Longman gave me sympathetic and professional help from the edition's beginning to its completion. I am also grateful to the scholars who reviewed the manuscript. Their comments proved invaluable in preparing the final text.

I am grateful to the government faculty at Houston Community College for their friendship and support. I have learned most of what I know about teaching from them. Thank you Ghassan Abdallah, Cecile (Cammy) Artiz, Evelyn Ballard, Max Beauregard, Harold "Hal" Comello, Dale Foster, Larry Gonzalez, Mark Hartray, Thomas Haymes, Edmund "Butch" Herod, Brenda Jones, Aaron Knight, Heidi Lange, Gary LeBlanc, Raymond Lew, Joe C. Martin, Vinette Meikle Harris, David Ngene, Carlos Pierott, Donna Rhea, John Speer, Jaye Ramsey Sutter, John Ben Sutter, R. Mark Tiller, Steven Tran, Linda Webb, and Celia Wintz.

Finally, I wish to dedicate this book to Anup Bodhe, Anderson Brandao, Jason Orr, Ron Rueckert, Kim Galle, and Hal Stockbridge.

NEAL TANNAHILL
Houston Community College
neal.tannahill@hccs.edu

Introduction

The Policymaking Process

WHAT WE WILL LEARN

After studying the Introduction, students should be able to answer the following questions:

▸ What are the stages of the policymaking process?

▸ What are the political dynamics of the policymaking process?

▸ Why is it important to study state and local government in Texas?

1

Did Texas execute an innocent man? In 2004, Cameron Todd Willingham was executed for setting the 1991 fire that killed his three children. Since Willingham's conviction, the science of arson investigation has changed considerably. Much of what investigators once thought they understood about arson has not held up under scientific investigation. Some fires that were once thought to be arson are now considered accidental under the new standards.[1] The Texas Forensic Science Commission hired Craig Beyler, a nationally known arson expert, to review the evidence in the Willingham case. He concluded that the state fire marshal who investigated the fire had a limited understanding of fire science and that the evidence did not support the finding that Willingham intentionally set the fire that killed his children. The deadly fire was likely accidental.[2]

Texas leads the nation in executions. Between 1982 and March 2010, the state of Texas put to death 450 convicted murderers. This total represents more than any other state and more than one-third of the total executions carried out nationwide.[3] In March 2010, 320 men and 10 women awaited execution on death row at the Allan B. Polunsky Unit of the state prison system in Livingston.[4] Only California has more people on death row than Texas.[5]

The death penalty is controversial. Death penalty advocates contend that criminals who take a life should pay for their crime with their own life. The death penalty also protects law-abiding citizens by permanently removing violent criminals from society. The fear of the death penalty deters potential criminals from committing murder. Death penalty proponents believe that an execution enables the family members of a murder victim to reach closure and go on with their lives. In contrast, death penalty opponents call capital punishment a barbaric relic of the nineteenth century, pointing out that the United States is the only Western democracy that still uses the death penalty against criminal defendants. Instead of deterring crime, they say, the death penalty may increase the violent crime rate by cheapening the value of human life. The opponents of capital punishment also charge that it is biased because a large majority of the persons who are sentenced to death and actually executed are poor, uneducated members of racial and ethnic minority groups.

THE STAGES OF THE POLICYMAKING PROCESS

Policymaking process A logical sequence of activities affecting the development of public policies.

The **policymaking process** is a logical sequence of activities affecting the development of public policies. The death penalty is an example of a **public policy,** an action government officials choose to do or not to do regarding public problems. Texas and 34 other states have responded to the problem of violent crime by adopting **capital punishment,** also known as the death penalty. No state carries out the policy more aggressively than Texas. A study of capital punishment in Texas from a policy perspective examines the context for making a policy to address the issue of violent crime. It considers how and why violent crime became an issue of public concern and the process through which the state formulated and adopted a policy on capital punishment. The study discusses the actions taken by public officials to ensure that the

Public policy The response, or lack of response, of government decision makers to an issue.

Capital punishment The death penalty.

policy is perceived as legitimate. It examines the implementation of the death penalty, evaluates its effectiveness at reducing violent crime, and assesses its impact on the state. Finally, the study discusses policy change.

The Context of Policymaking

The policymaking process takes place within a cultural, socioeconomic, legal, and political context. The policymaking context is not one of the stages of the policymaking process; rather, it is the background in which the policymaking process takes place. It helps determine the problems that government attempts to solve, the set of policy alternatives that government decision-makers will be willing to consider, the resources available to government to address the problem, and the relative strength of the political forces involved in the policymaking process.[6]

The most important contextual factors influencing capital punishment in Texas are (1) the legal and constitutional setting and (2) public attitudes toward violent crime and the death penalty. The state's death penalty statute must meet the constitutional standards set by federal and state courts. Because of the high stakes involved, defendants sentenced to death typically appeal their convictions through the state and federal court systems. Frequently, Texas has changed its capital punishment policy to conform to state and, especially, federal court rulings. The U.S. Supreme Court recently ruled, for example, that the execution of persons who are mentally retarded violated the U.S. Constitution, forcing Texas to commute the sentences of several death row inmates.[7] The state's death penalty policy also reflects public opinion. Texas is the nation's death penalty leader because capital punishment is more popular in Texas than it is in most other states. According to public opinion polling data, 78 percent of Texans support the death penalty, compared with only about 18 percent who oppose it. The rest are undecided.[8]

Agenda Setting

Agenda setting The process through which issues become matters of public concern and government action.

Agenda setting is the process through which issues become matters of public concern and government action. Those problems that government officials actively consider how to resolve are part of the **official policy agenda.** Not all problems become the object of government action, however. In short, agenda setting is the process through which issues become part of the official policy agenda.

Official policy agenda Those problems that government officials actively consider how to resolve.

Capital punishment has been part of the official policy agenda in Texas for decades. More than 40 years ago, state policymakers rewrote the state's capital punishment law to satisfy the objections of the U.S. Supreme Court. In subsequent years, state officials have considered a broad range of death penalty issues, including streamlining the appeals process and providing post-conviction DNA analysis for death row inmates. In 2005, for example, the Texas legislature amended the state's death penalty statute to give juries the option of sentencing convicted capital murderers to either death or life in prison without the possibility of parole. The latter punishment replaced the option of life in prison with the possibility of parole after 40 years.

At any one time, the official policy agenda contains a relatively small number of major issues. In recent years, the official policy agenda for Texas state government has included the following issues:

- **Funding public education**—How can the state ensure that local school districts have adequate revenues to provide a quality education to the state's school children and that the money is collected fairly?
- **Educational accountability**—How can taxpayers be sure that they are getting their money's worth for the school taxes they pay?
- **Property tax reform**—How can the state protect property owners from rapidly rising property taxes without undermining the ability of local governments to fund the essential services they provide?
- **Insurance reform**—What steps can the state take to ensure that Texas homeowners are able to purchase home insurance at affordable rates?
- **Healthcare**—What actions can the state take to reduce the number of Texans without health insurance?
- **Transportation**—What steps should state government take to address the state's transportation needs?
- **Electricity deregulation**—How can the state ensure that consumers will have an adequate supply of electricity at affordable rates?
- **Border security**—What actions can state government take to limit the flow of illegal aliens into Texas?

As students of Texas government, we ask how each of these issues became part of the official policy agenda. Who raised each issue? What actions did individuals and groups take to get their issues addressed by government? Did other individuals and groups attempt to keep these issues off the official policy agenda? Why did the former succeed and the latter fail?

Agenda setting not only identifies problems for government attention but also defines the nature of the problems and, therefore, the eventual thrust of a policy solution. Capital punishment, for example, can be defined in different terms. Death penalty advocates prefer to focus on the seriousness of violent crime and the length of delay between a death sentence and its imposition. In contrast, the opponents of capital punishment emphasize racial disparities in sentencing, the risk of executing an innocent person, and the relative cost of capital punishment compared with the expense of life in prison without parole. Whether state government attempts to streamline the appeals process to make it easier to carry out the death penalty, adopts reforms to protect against bias, or even eliminates capital punishment altogether depends on the way the issue is defined.

 WHAT IS YOUR OPINION?

Do you support the death penalty? Why or why not?

Policy Formulation

Policy formulation is the development of strategies for dealing with the problems on the official policy agenda. Once an issue becomes part of the official policy agenda, individuals and groups—both inside and outside of government—develop and propose approaches for addressing the problem. Defense attorneys, victims' rights organizations, legislators, prison officials, criminologists, prosecuting attorneys, civil rights activists, prison reformers, and the news media may all be involved in formulating policies affecting the death penalty.

Scholars who study public policymaking identify two models of policy formulation. The **rational comprehensive model of policy formulation** assumes that policymakers establish goals, identify policy alternatives, estimate the costs and benefits of the alternatives, and then select the policy alternative that produces the greatest net benefit. In contrast, the **incremental model of policy formulation** assumes that policymakers, working with imperfect information, continually adjust policies in pursuit of policy goals that are subject to periodic readjustment.[9] Most political scientists believe that the rational comprehensive model is an unrealistic approach to policy formulation except when dealing with technical questions of limited scope. They believe that the incremental model of policy formulation more closely reflects the real world of public policymaking in which political actors disagree about policy goals, information about policy alternatives is imperfect, and resources to achieve goals are limited. At least for major issues, policy formulation involves policymakers developing strategies to achieve short-term goals, with both strategies and goals subject to modification. Furthermore, some scholars believe that the incremental approach is not only more realistic than the rational comprehensive model but also a more effective model for decision-makers because it allows policymakers greater flexibility in modifying policy approaches to account for new information, changes in resource availability, and variation in political support.[10]

Consider the death penalty. Policymakers and other participants in the debate over the death penalty disagree about the goals of capital punishment and its effectiveness. Some participants in the policymaking process favor the death penalty in order to deter crime, whereas others seek to punish offenders. Still others hope to minimize the application of the death penalty or eliminate it altogether. They argue that life in prison without possibility of parole achieves societal goals without the state taking life.

Scholars also disagree about the effect of capital punishment on the murder rate and its impact on society. The nature of the death penalty makes it difficult, if not impossible, to assess its impact with precision. How do we place a value on the life of a convicted murderer or the murder victim? In practice, current death penalty policy reflects a compromise developed by policymakers with different personal values, working with imperfect information, and facing conflicting political pressures on an emotional issue.

Policy Adoption

Policy adoption is the official decision of a government body to accept a particular policy and put it into effect. For example, the legislature passes, and the governor signs, a bill. The Texas Supreme Court issues a major ruling. A city council passes an

---

Policy formulation The development of strategies for dealing with the problems on the official policy agenda.

Rational comprehensive model of policy formulation An approach to policy formulation that assumes that policymakers establish goals, identify policy alternatives, estimate the costs and benefits of the alternatives, and then select the policy alternative that produces the greatest net benefit.

Incremental model of policy formulation An approach to policy formulation that assumes that policymakers, working with imperfect information, continually adjust policies in pursuit of policy goals that are subject to periodic readjustment.

Policy adoption The official decision of a government body to accept a particular policy and put it into effect.

ordinance. In practice, major government policies frequently reflect adoption decisions made at different points in time by different units of government. The legislature and the governor enacted the state's basic death penalty statute in 1973. They subsequently adopted amendments changing the method of execution from the electric chair to lethal injection, expanding the list of capital crimes, modifying appeals procedures, and providing juries with the sentencing option of life in prison without possibility of parole as an alternative to the death penalty.

Policy Legitimation

Policy legitimation
The actions taken by government officials and others to ensure that most citizens regard a policy as a legal and appropriate government response to a problem.

Policy legitimation refers to the actions taken by government officials and others to ensure that most citizens regard a policy as a legal and appropriate government response to a problem. In Texas, the governor, members of the Texas legislature, and judges defend capital punishment as an appropriate policy in light of the state's murder rate. They discuss the issue from the perspective of the victims of crime rather than the possibility that the state may have executed innocent persons. Rather than risk the possibility that the Texas Forensic Science Commission might conclude that the fire that killed Todd Willingham's children was accidental, Governor Rick Perry replaced three members of the commission and named a new chairman who immediately postponed consideration of the Willingham case.

Policy Implementation

Policy implementation
The stage of the policy process in which policies are carried out.

Policy implementation is the stage of the policy process in which policies are carried out. Implementation involves government officials as well as individuals and groups outside of the government. A number of political actors participate in the implementation of the state's death penalty policy:

- District attorneys determine whether to ask for the death penalty in a particular capital murder case.
- Juries and judges decide whether to sentence a convicted defendant to death or life in prison without parole.
- State and federal judges hear appeals.
- Lawyers from the office of the attorney general represent the state in court during the appeals process.
- Private defense attorneys represent the defendant during the appeals process.
- The Board of Pardons and Paroles entertains requests for clemency.
- The governor may grant a 30-day reprieve on the execution of a death sentence and must concur with a decision of the Board of Pardons and Paroles to grant clemency.
- Officials in the Texas Department of Corrections carry out death sentences.

Implementation is an essential part of the policy process. Sometimes policymakers misjudge the nature of a problem or underestimate the resources needed for its solution. As a result, the policy may evolve far differently in operation than what its architects intended or expected. Consider the implementation of capital punishment in Texas. Because of the length of the appeals process, the average stay on death row in Texas is 10.3 years.[11] In 2010, the death row inmate with the longest tenure was Ronald Chambers of Dallas County, who was first sentenced to death in 1975.[12] The opponents of the death penalty argue that appeals are necessary to ensure that inno-cent people are not put to death. In contrast, critics charge that the current system is unfair to the relatives of murder victims and inhumane to people awaiting execution.

 WHAT IS YOUR OPINION?

Do convicted murderers spend too much time on death row before their sentences are carried out?

The implementation of the state's capital punishment statute varies from county to county. Many small counties rarely, if ever, send anyone to death row because they cannot afford the expense of conducting a capital murder trial, which can cost the county $225,000 in immediate trial expenses, not including the cost of subsequent mandatory appeals.[13] In contrast, Harris County (which includes the city of Houston) has sentenced more people to death than any other county in the United States. Figure I.1 depicts the number of Texas death row offenders sentenced from

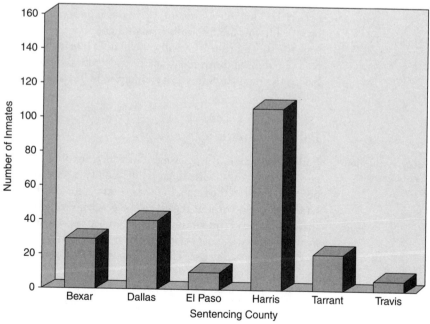

FIGURE I.1   Death Row Inmates, 2010.

the six largest Texas counties—Bexar County (San Antonio), Harris County, Dallas County, El Paso County, Tarrant County (Fort Worth), and Travis County (Austin). As the figure shows, Harris County has sent more convicted murderers to death row than the other five counties combined.

The national trend is toward fewer death sentences and fewer executions. In 2008, juries nationwide gave 111 defendants the death penalty, the smallest number of death sentences issued in decades. Texas juries are handing down fewer death sentences as well. In 2009, no one was added to death row in Texas, a remarkable development considering that just a decade earlier Texas juries sentenced 48 convicted murderers to death. Although the number of executions nationwide is in decline, Texas continues to carry out 18 to 26 executions a year, a rate that has held fairly steady over the last seven years.[14]

Juries nationwide are giving fewer death sentences because of a decline in support for the death penalty. In the mid-1990s, national opinion surveys found that death penalty supporters outnumbered opponents by a lopsided margin of 80 percent to 16 percent. Although recent national polls indicate that capital punishment remains popular, the ratio of supporters to opponents is closer, with a 64 percent to 30 percent margin.[15] Some observers believe that public support for capital punishment has fallen because of publicity surrounding the release of prison inmates, including some on death row, after DNA testing proved their innocence.[16]

Texas juries are assessing the death penalty less frequently not because of public opinion, but because of the impact of the life without parole option and a reduction in the murder rate. Richard Dieter, the head of the Death Penalty Information Center, believes that life without parole gives Texas jurors a more attractive sentencing option than life imprisonment. "When you present life without parole to juries," he says, "it lifts any confusion they might have about whether someone is ever going to walk the streets again."[17] Finally, the murder rate in Texas has declined, reducing the pool of potential death row inmates. According to the Texas Department of Public Safety, the number of murders committed in Texas fell from 2,149 in 1993 to 1,373 in 2008.[18]

Policy Evaluation

Policy evaluation
The assessment of policy.

Policy evaluation, the assessment of policy, involves questions of equity, efficiency, effectiveness, and political feasibility. Equity is the concept that similarly situated people be treated the same. In other words, is the death penalty assessed in an even-handed fashion without regard to the gender, race, ethnicity, or financial status of the criminal and the victim? Death penalty opponents charge that capital punishment is assessed against persons with little status in society who cannot afford to hire an effective legal defense. They also contend that the race of the crime victim affects the likelihood of a jury sentencing a convicted killer to die because people convicted of murdering whites are more likely to be given the death penalty than are people convicted of killing African Americans. In Texas, people charged with murder in urban counties, especially Harris County, are more likely to face a death sentence than people charged in other counties.

Efficiency is a comparison of a policy's costs with the benefits it provides. Because of the cost of trials and appeals in death penalty cases, capital punishment is actually several times more expensive than imprisoning a criminal for 40 years or more. Nonetheless, the supporters of capital punishment believe that the costs of the legal process need to be balanced against the benefits of permanently eliminating a violent criminal from society.

Effectiveness is the extent to which a policy achieves its goals. In this context, the question is: Does the death penalty deter violent crime? Researchers at Sam Houston State University and Duke University recently published a study of the effect executions carried out in Texas between 1994 and 2005 had on the murder rate. The study concluded that the number of murders in Texas declined by 0.5 to 2.5 during the month following each execution. Consequently, as many as 60 people may be alive because of the Texas death penalty.[19] Critics of the study argue that studies evaluating the effect of capital punishment are suspect because executions are relatively rare and a large number of factors influence the murder rate.

Political feasibility pertains to a policy's ability to obtain public support. The Texas legislature will never repeal the death penalty as long as public opinion in the state supports capital punishment as strongly as it does today. Furthermore, the interest groups that defend the death penalty are more influential than the groups opposed to capital punishment.

Evaluation can be either empirical or normative. An **empirical analysis** is a method of study that relies on experience and scientific observation. Empirical research on capital punishment finds that Texas juries are no more likely to sentence convicted murderers to death than are juries in other states. Rather, Texas is the national capital punishment leader because it is a populous state with a relatively high murder rate and because state authorities are willing to carry out executions.[20] In contrast to an empirical study, a **normative analysis** is a method of study that is based on certain values. A normative analysis of the death penalty might consider the morality of the policy and the fairness of its implementation. It examines whether the death penalty is right or wrong, good or bad, fair or unfair.

Policy evaluation sometimes highlights the distinction between policy outputs and policy outcomes. Whereas **policy outputs** are actual government policies, **policy outcomes** are the situations that arise as a result of the impact of policy in operation. Consider the distinction between policy outputs and outcomes as far as capital punishment is concerned. Thirty-five states have capital punishment laws on the books (a policy output). In practice, however, many states seldom, if ever, carry out executions (a policy outcome). In 2009, only 11 states conducted executions. No state enforces the death penalty as aggressively as Texas, which carried out 24 of the 52 executions nationwide in 2009.[21]

Policy Change

Policy change refers to the modification of policy goals and means in light of new information or shifting political environments. Policy change is frequently the result of policy evaluation. Programs that are successful may no longer be needed; likewise,

---

Empirical analysis A method of study that relies on experience and scientific observation.

Normative analysis A method of study that is based on certain values. A normative analysis of the death penalty might consider the morality of the policy and the fairness of its implementation.

Policy outputs Actual government policies.

Policy outcomes The situations that arise as a result of the impact of policy in operation.

Policy change The modification of policy goals and means in light of new information or shifting political environments.

unsuccessful programs may be eliminated because of their failure. However, partially successful programs or programs with unintended negative consequences may be modified in hopes of improving their operation. The number of death row sentences is declining in Texas because the murder rate is falling and jurors now have the option to give convicted murderers a life sentence without the possibility of parole.

THE DYNAMICS OF THE POLICY PROCESS

Policymaking is more complex than the policy process would suggest at initial glance.

Policy Cycles

Policy cycle The passage of an issue through the policy process from agenda building through policy evaluation.

The term **policy cycle** refers to the passage of an issue through the policy process from agenda setting through policy change. Issues do not always travel smoothly through the policy cycle, moving from one stage to the next. No clear lines of separation can be drawn among the five stages of the policy process; therefore, the agenda setting and policy formulation stages sometimes overlap. For example, a number of religious leaders in Texas have called for a moratorium on executions in Texas to allow time to review death penalty convictions because they believe that the capital punishment process is seriously flawed. The religious leaders are attempting to both raise an issue (the danger that the state may execute an innocent person) and propose a solution (a moratorium on the implementation of the death penalty to allow time to review questionable convictions). Similarly, policy implementation often has an aspect of policy adoption to it as agencies fill in the details of policies adopted by legislative bodies. Policy evaluation occurs throughout the policy process, not just at its end.

Not every issue completes the policy cycle. Issues may be raised to the official policy agenda and policies formulated but then forgotten as the attention of the general public and government officials turns to other, more pressing problems. Sometimes public officials, interest group spokespersons, or individual citizens succeed in keeping an issue in the public eye until a policy solution is adopted and implemented. A triggering mechanism, such as a dramatic event, a news media report, or a scandal, is often necessary to force a public policy response to an issue.

Finally, some issues—particularly major, controversial issues, such as the death penalty—travel through the policy process again and again over an extended period of time. The issue of capital punishment has arisen repeatedly because of court rulings, controversies over the guilt or innocence of particular death row inmates, public concern over crime rates, publicity about the length of time between sentencing and execution, and political campaigns. As long as the public remains deeply divided over capital punishment, the death penalty is likely to be a recurring item on the state's official policy agenda.

Issue Networks

The policymaking process involves a broad range of political actors, including government officials, the institutions of government, individual policy activists, political parties, the news media, and interest groups. Political scientists use the term

Issue network
A group of political actors that is concerned with some aspect of public policy.

issue network to describe a group of political actors that is concerned with some aspect of public policy. District attorneys, victims' rights organizations, defense attorneys, organizations opposed to capital punishment, legislators concerned with criminal justice issues, state and federal judges, the governor, and the members of the Board of Pardons and Paroles constitute the issue network for capital punishment in Texas. Issue networks vary from issue to issue. Although not all participants in an issue network are equally influential, no one individual or group is usually able to dominate policymaking on the issue. Instead, policy reflects the result of conflict (and occasionally compromise) among the participants.

Policymaking and Politics

Politics The process that determines who will occupy the roles of leadership in government and how the power of government will be exercised.

Politics is the process that determines who will occupy the roles of leadership in government and how the power of government will be exercised. Politics exists because individuals and groups have different interests and different views about public policy. For example, the decision of county government officials to widen and extend a road might please land developers who hope to build a shopping center alongside the road but displease area homeowners who do not want additional traffic in their neighborhoods. The developers and the homeowners would oppose each other on this issue because their interests clash. Individuals and groups may also disagree on policy questions because their values differ. Whereas some people believe that the death penalty is morally wrong, other individuals think that it is morally just.

Political actors compete to shape public policy in ways that conform to their interests and values. Individuals and groups attempt to push issues to the forefront of the official policy agenda on which they want government action while diverting attention from matters on which they prefer that the current policy remain unchanged. Once an issue is part of the official policy agenda, political actors seek to influence the policy formulation process in ways that further their interests. Individuals and groups who support the policy work for its adoption, whereas those who oppose the policy try to defeat it. Conflict continues during implementation, with competing interests attempting to shape implementation in ways beneficial to them. Finally, individuals and groups evaluate policies in accordance with their own perspectives, creating feedback designed to support the policy's continuance, encourage its revision, or urge its repeal.

WHY STUDY TEXAS GOVERNMENT?

Public opinion polls show that many Americans are cynical about government and uninterested in the way it works. Less than half of the public trusts the government to do what is right most of the time.[22] Many people question the relevance of government to their daily lives and express little interest in public affairs. College students often tell their professors that they have registered for a course in Texas government only because it is required. They frankly admit that they have little interest in the subject and doubt that they will learn anything beneficial. International students, in particular, question the value of a class in Texas government.

Nonetheless, Texas government is profoundly important to the lives of Texas residents, regardless of their ages, backgrounds, and careers. State and local government in Texas provides a broad range of essential services, including law enforcement, fire protection, education, highways, mass transportation, welfare, job training, parks, airports, water and sewage treatment, libraries, and public hospitals. Students attending public colleges and universities benefit directly from state-supported higher education. Everyone living in Texas needs to understand state and local laws and regulations concerning such matters as driver's licenses, automobile purchases, and renters' rights.

Laws and regulations adopted by state and local governments affect all Texans. Cities enact and enforce zoning ordinances, fire codes, and building codes to regulate land use and construction within city limits. Federal and state regulations affect air and water quality. The state criminal law governs many aspects of personal behavior. State agencies establish educational and technical requirements that must be fulfilled before individuals can engage in certain occupations and professions. College students take courses in Texas government because the Texas legislature requires that public college and university students complete six semester-hours in American national, state, and local government, including study of the Texas Constitution.

 WHAT IS YOUR OPINION?

Do you agree with the legislative requirement that college students must complete six semester-hours in political science?

Texans pay for government through taxes and fees. State government and many local governments levy sales taxes on the retail purchase of a broad range of items. Property owners pay property taxes to municipalities, school districts, counties, and some other units of local government. Texans also pay fees to state and local governments in order to drive an automobile, operate a business, practice their profession, sell liquor, obtain a marriage license, and go hunting or fishing.

State and local government impacts not just individuals but society as a whole. In general, the actions of state and local governments affect the business climate in Texas, which in turn helps determine whether new companies relocate to the state and whether firms already here expand their operations. Education, healthcare, welfare assistance, good roads, public transportation, sanitation, recreation facilities, law enforcement, environmental regulations, and fire protection make the state a better place to live and work. Tax rates and the impact of individual taxes on different income groups affect the distribution of wealth in society and influence the state's economy.

Students benefit from courses in Texas government because they can learn not just how state and local governments affect their lives but also how they can influence public policy in the state. The essence of American democracy is that citizens govern themselves through their elected officials. Texans have the right (some would say *obligation*) not just to vote but also to communicate their policy preferences to their representatives. Government officials are responsive to the demands and requests of their constituents, especially officials at the state and local levels who work directly with individual citizens on a regular basis.

WHAT WE HAVE LEARNED

1. **What are the stages of the policymaking process?**

   The policymaking process is a logical sequence of activities affecting the development of public policies. The policymaking process takes place within a context of factors, including the social, economic, political, governing, and cultural contexts. It includes seven stages: agenda setting, policy formulation, policy adoption, policy legitimation, policy implementation, policy evaluation, and policy change.

2. **What are the political dynamics of the policymaking process?**

   Policymaking is more complex than the policy process would suggest at initial glance. Policy cycles, issue networks, and politics all play a role in the process. The passage of an issue through the policy process from agenda setting through policy change is a policy cycle. The policymaking process involves a broad range of political actors, including government officials, the institutions of government, individual policy activists, political parties, the news media, and interest groups.

   Political scientists use the term *issue networks* to describe this phenomenon. The policymaking process also involves politics, which is the process that determines who will occupy the roles of leadership in government and how the power of government will be exercised.

3. **Why is it important to study state and local government in Texas?**

   Texas government is profoundly important to the lives of Texas residents, regardless of their ages, backgrounds, and careers. State and local governments provide a wide range of services. Laws and regulations adopted by state and local governments affect all Texans. Texans pay for government through taxes and fees. State and local government impacts not just individuals but society as a whole by affecting the business climate and the quality of life for people living in the state. Students benefit from courses in Texas government because they can learn not just how state and local governments affect their lives but also how they can influence public policy in the state.

KEY TERMS

agenda setting

capital punishment

empirical analysis

incremental model of policy formulation

issue network

normative analysis

official policy agenda

policy adoption

policy change

policy cycle

policy evaluation

policy formulation

policy implementation

policy legitimation

policymaking process

policy outcomes

policy outputs

politics

public policy

rational comprehensive model of policy formulation

NOTES

1. Christy Hoppe, "Are Texas Arsons a Case of Bad Science? Some Experts Think So," *Dallas Morning News*, September 13, 2009, available at www.dallasnews.com.

2. "Burning Question: Did Texas Execute an Innocent Man?" *Texas Observer*, September 4, 2009, p. 7.

3. U.S. Census Bureau, "Prisoners Executed Under Civil Authority by State," *The 2009 Statistical Abstract*, available at www.census.gov.

4. "Offenders on Death Row," Texas Department of Criminal Justice, available at www.tdcj.state.tx.us.

5. California Department of Corrections, available at www.cdcr.ca.gov.

6. Michael E. Craft and Scott R. Furlong, *Public Policy: Politics, Analysis, and Alternatives*, 3rd ed. (Washington, DC: CQ Press, 2010), pp. 10–15.

7. *Atkins v. Virginia*, 536 U.S. 304 (2002).

8. Jim Henson, "The Polling Center: Voter Empathy," *Texas Tribune*, February 23, 2010, available at www.texastribune.org.

9. Christine H. Rossell, "Using Multiple Criteria to Evaluate Public Policies: The Case of School Desegregation," *American Politics Quarterly* 21 (April 1993): 155–184.

10. David Braybrooke and Charles E. Lindblom, *A Strategy of Decision* (New York: Free Press, 1970).

11. "Execution Statistics," Texas Department of Criminal Justice, available at www.tdcj.state.tx.us/stat/annual.htm.

12. "Offenders on Death Row," Texas Department of Criminal Justice, available at www.tdcj.state.tx.us/.

13. Robert Tharp, "Is the Death Penalty Losing Capital?" *Dallas Morning News*, December 30, 2005, available at www.dallasnews.com.

14. Texas Execution Information Center, "Year-by-Year Death Row Statistics," available at www.txexecutions.org.

15. Lydia Saad, "Americans Hold Firm to Support for Death Penalty," November 17, 2008, available at www.gallup.com.

16. Max B. Baker, "Texas Still Leads in Executions, but the Numbers Are Down Here and Across the Nation," *Fort Worth State Telegram*, December 11, 2008, available at www.star-telegram.com.

17. Quoted in John Moritz, "The Life Penalty," *Texas Observer*, November 28, 2008, p. 16.

18. Texas Department of Public Safety, "The Texas Crime Report," various years, available at www.txdps.state.tx.

19. Michael Graczyk, "Texas Study: Death Penalty Deters Killers," *Houston Chronicle*, January 7, 2010, p. B2.

20. Adam Liptak, "Study Revises Texas's Standing as a Death Penalty Leader," *New York Times*, February 14, 2004, available at www.nytimes.com.

21. Death Penalty Information Center, available at www.deathpenaltyinfo.org.

22. "Trust in the Federal Government, 1958–2004," *The ANES Guide to Public Opinion and Electoral Behavior*, available at www.electionstudies.org.

Chapter 1

The People, Economy, and Political Culture of Texas

WHAT WE WILL LEARN

After studying Chapter 1, students should be able to answer the following questions:

• How is the population of Texas described in terms of size, diversity, distribution, and religious beliefs?

• How does the economy of Texas compare with the economies of other states in terms of household income, poverty rates, and health insurance coverage?

• How do political scientists describe the political culture of Texas?

Education is the key to the future of Texas. In 2007, the average annual income of men 25 years of age and older with a bachelor's degree was $57,397 compared with annual earnings of $32,435 for men with only a high school education. Male high school dropouts, meanwhile, made just $22,602 a year. On average, women with bachelor's degrees earned $38,628, whereas the average earnings for a woman with a high school diploma were $21,219. Female high school dropouts earned $14,202.[1] Educated citizens pay more in taxes than people without degrees because they earn more money, whereas high school dropouts cost the state money because they are more likely than their educated counterparts to collect unemployment, receive welfare benefits, and go to prison. A study conducted by the Bush School of Government and Public Services at Texas A&M University estimates that students in the class of 2012 who drop out of high school will cost the state and its economy $6 to $10.7 billion over their lifetimes in lost tax revenues, welfare payments, and prison costs.[2] Furthermore, an educated population is critical to the state's economic future because business needs highly skilled workers capable of functioning effectively in a global economy. Every U.S. state in the top tier in terms of personal income has a highly educated population. Connecticut, New Jersey, Massachusetts, Maryland, Colorado, and Virginia lead the nation in both personal income and educational attainment. In contrast, Mississippi, West Virginia, Arkansas, Louisiana, Kentucky, and Alabama are both the poorest states in the nation and the least well educated.[3]

Unfortunately, Texas trails the national average in educational attainment and is falling further behind. Texas has the second lowest high school graduation rate in the nation (after Mississippi). In 2007, 79.1 percent of Texans 25 years of age and older had graduated from high school compared with a national high school graduation rate of 84.5 percent. Texas also trailed the national average in the proportion of adults holding bachelor's degrees, 25.2 percent to 27.5 percent.[4] Only 5.4 percent of Texas residents are currently enrolled in higher education compared with 6.6 percent of the residents of California, 6.3 percent in Illinois, and 5.9 percent in New York.[5] To make matters worse, the rate of college enrollment in Texas is dropping. State officials estimate that the proportion of Texans attending college will fall to 4.6 percent or less by 2015.[6]

The fastest growing segment of the Texas population is also the least well educated. Latino and African American Texans as a group are less well educated and have lower incomes than whites and Asian Americans. In 2007, Latinos and African Americans made up 48 percent of the state's population but comprised only 39 percent of college and university enrollment.[7] Furthermore, the high school dropout rates for Latino and African American youngsters are higher (43 percent and 38 percent, respectively) than they are for white students (20 percent).[8] Population experts project that the state's population will be 46 percent Latino and 10 percent African American by the year 2030. If the educational, occupational, and income status of Hispanic and African American Texans does not improve significantly, a majority of the state's working-age population will be poorly educated, low-income minority residents. As a result, personal income per capita (per person) in Texas will decline from $19,663 in 2000 to $18,708 in 2020.[9] Business and industry will be reluctant to relocate to the state, tax collections will fall, and the state budget will be strapped trying to provide social services for a large population of low-income residents.[10]

The complex relationships among race and ethnicity, income and education, and public policy illustrate the importance of demographic, economic, and cultural factors to policymaking in Texas. This chapter examines some of the more significant factors shaping the Texas policymaking environment. The first section of the chapter profiles the people of Texas, considering the size of the state's population, population growth, population diversity, and the geographic distribution of the state's people. It also examines the religious faith and practice of the people of the state. The second section of the chapter examines the state's economy, looking at economic trends, personal income, poverty, and healthcare. The final section of the chapter deals with the subject of political culture.

THE PEOPLE OF TEXAS

The population of Texas is one of the largest and most diverse of any state in the nation.

Population Size and Growth

In July 2009, the U.S. Census Bureau estimated that the population of Texas was 24.8 million. That number made Texas the nation's second most populous state. Only California, with 37 million people, had a larger population.[11]

Figure 1.1 traces the growth of the state's population decade by decade from the 1970s through 2009 and compares the population growth rate of Texas with the growth

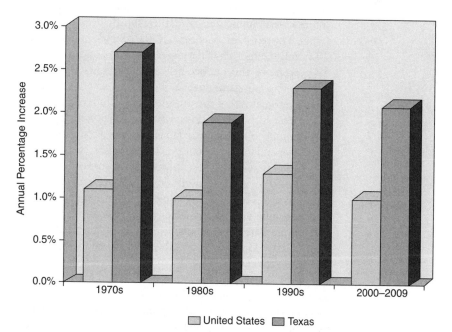

FIGURE 1.1   Average Annual Population Growth.

rate for the United States as a whole. As the figure shows, the state's population expanded the most rapidly between 1970 and 1980, growing at an annual rate of 2.7 percent. The state's population growth rate fell just below 2 percent a year in the 1980s before rebounding to grow at a rate of 2.3 percent a year in the 1990s. The growth rate between 2000 and 2009 was 2.0 percent. Throughout the period, the population of the **Lone Star State,** which is a nickname for Texas, increased more rapidly than did the population of the nation as a whole.

Lone Star State
Nickname for Texas.

Both natural population increase and immigration contribute to population growth in Texas. **Natural population increase** is the extent to which live births exceed deaths. The birthrate in Texas is the second highest in the nation. In 2006, the birthrate in Texas was 17 babies for every 1,000 people. Only Utah had a higher birthrate.[12] Because the state's population is relatively young (a median age of 32.3 compared with a national average of 35.3),[13] the proportion of women of childbearing age is relatively high. The state's ethnic composition also contributes to rapid population growth. The birthrate for Mexican American women, particularly recent immigrants, is more than 50 percent higher than the birthrates for Latino women who are not of Mexican origin and for women who are African American or white.[14] The relatively high birthrate for Hispanic Texans also reflects the average age for Latinos in the state, which is 27, compared with the average age of the state's white population, which is nearly 40, just past the prime childbearing years.[15]

Natural population increase The extent to which live births exceed deaths.

The state's population also grows because of immigration. Between April 1, 2000, and July 1, 2009, Texas recorded a net gain of 1.8 million residents from international and domestic immigration combined (933,083 residents from international immigration and 848,702 people from domestic immigration).[16] Many international immigrants enter the country illegally. According to a study conducted by the Pew Hispanic Center, 1,450,000 undocumented residents lived in Texas in 2008; only California had a larger number of undocumented residents. Of that total, 59 percent of the undocumented immigrants were from Mexico, with another 22 percent coming from the Caribbean and other Latin American countries. The Pew Center estimates that unauthorized immigrants constitute 7.9 percent of the Texas workforce. Although undocumented workers work in all sectors of the economy, the largest numbers are employed in agriculture, grounds keeping and maintenance, construction, and food preparation and serving.[17]

Illegal immigration is controversial. Critics charge that undocumented workers take jobs from American citizens while overcrowding schools and hospital emergency rooms. They add to traffic congestion and contribute to the crime problem. In contrast, immigration advocates contend that the United States benefits from immigration, even illegal immigration. They argue that undocumented workers fill jobs that citizens do not want and that they pay more in taxes than they receive in government services.

Both sides of the debate offer studies to bolster their position on illegal immigration. The Immigration Reform Coalition of Texas, a group opposed to illegal immigration, has published a report concluding that unauthorized immigrants cost the state $4.5 to $5 billion a year, mostly to educate their children and pay for their healthcare.[18] In contrast, Americans for Immigration Reform, an organization formed by business interests that benefit from immigration, released a study estimating that the complete elimination of undocumented workers from Texas would cost the state's economy more than $220 million a year along with 1.1 million jobs.[19]

The Texas Comptroller of Public Accounts, meanwhile, has published a relatively balanced report assessing both the costs and benefits of illegal immigration in Texas. On one hand, the report finds that undocumented workers add to the state's economy and pay more money in state taxes than they receive in services. Illegal immigrant workers and their families boost the Texas economy by $17.7 billion a year through their purchases of goods and service. They also pay more taxes to state government than they receive in state services—$1.58 billion in sales, excise, and motor vehicle taxes paid compared with $1.16 billion in state services for education, healthcare, emergency medical services, and incarceration. On the other hand, illegal immigrants are a drain on local governments because of the cost to provide healthcare services and law enforcement. The report found that illegal immigrants pay $513 million a year in local sales and property taxes while receiving $1.44 billion in local services.[20]

Because of immigration, Texas has a large and diverse foreign-born population. The 3.8 million foreign-born residents in Texas make up 16 percent of the state's

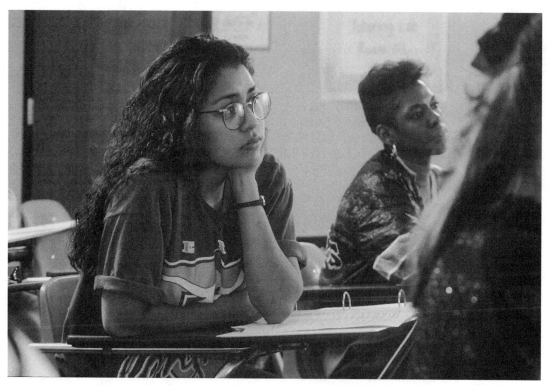

Education is key to the future of Texas, especially of the state's growing Latino and African American populations.

population.[21] This foreign-born population of Texas is younger, poorer, and less well educated than are the state's native-born residents. More than three-fourths of the state's foreign-born residents are not American citizens.[22]

Rapid population growth presents both opportunities and challenges for policymakers. On the one hand, population growth has led to greater representation for Texas in Congress, a bigger share of federal grant money, and an enlarged tax base. Because the number of seats in the U.S. House of Representatives each state receives is based on its population, relatively rapid population growth in the Lone Star State translates into more representation in Congress. For example, Texas gained three House seats after the 1990 Census and two more after the 2000 Census, giving the state 32 seats in the U.S. House. Election Data Services, a political consulting firm, projects that Texas will gain three seats in the House after the 2010 Census.[23] Population growth also means an increase in federal financial aid because funding for many grant programs is based on population. Furthermore, population growth has generally meant a larger tax base for state and local governments. With more consumers to buy products, sales tax receipts have risen. On the other hand, population growth also presents policy challenges. Rapid population growth has placed a considerable strain on public services in Texas. More people mean more automobiles on city streets and freeways, more garbage to be collected and disposed, more children to be educated, and more subdivisions for local law enforcement agencies to police.

Population Diversity

The population of Texas is quite diverse. In fact, a majority of Texans (53 percent) are members of racial and ethnic minority groups. The U.S. Census Bureau estimates that the population of Texas in 2008 was 47 percent white (not Hispanic), 36 percent Latino, 12 percent African American, 3 percent Asian American, and 2 percent other.[24] Although most Latino residents of Texas are Mexican American, the state's Hispanic population includes significant numbers of people who trace their ancestries to Cuba, El Salvador, or other Latin American countries. Similarly, the state's Asian population includes Vietnamese, Chinese, Indian, Filipino, Korean, and Japanese Americans. One-third of the state's population speaks a language other than English at home.[25]

The ethnic communities in Texas are distributed unevenly across the state. Most African Americans live in the rural areas and small towns of East Texas, along the Gulf Coast, and in the state's metropolitan areas. Houston and Dallas are home to one-third of the state's African American population. Although Latinos live in every part of the state, they are more numerous in South Texas and West Texas, especially along the Mexican border. San Antonio, El Paso, Corpus Christi, Brownsville, McAllen, and Laredo all have Hispanic majorities.[26] Asians are clustered in the Gulf Coast region, whereas many Texans of German and Czech descent live in the Hill Country in Central Texas. More than 90 percent of the state's foreign-born residents, regardless of racial/ethnic origin, live in metropolitan areas.[27]

INTERNET RESEARCH

Foreign-Born Residents

U.S. Census Bureau data show that Texas has a large and growing population of foreign-born residents. Go to the website of the U.S. Census Bureau: **www.census.gov**. Scroll to the bottom of the page to the area labeled "Special Topics" and look for the link to the online version of the *Statistical Abstract of the United States*, which is an excellent reference source. Point your mouse to the population section and click on the link to "Native and Foreign Born Populations." Study the table and answer the following questions:

1. In 2006 (or the most recent year available), what percentage of Texas residents was born abroad? How does that percentage compare with the national average?
2. What percentage of the foreign-born population in Texas entered the country in 2000 or later? How does that percentage compare with the national average?
3. Why does Texas have a larger foreign-born population than most other states?
4. What are some of the public policy issues that are affected by Texas having a relatively large foreign-born population?

Population Distribution

The population of Texas is not evenly distributed across the state. The most populous regions are Central, South, North, and East Texas and the Gulf Coast region. The most rapidly growing areas of the state are the San Antonio-Austin corridor in Central Texas, the Dallas-Fort Worth region in North Texas, the Houston area in Southeast Texas, and the strip along the border with Mexico. In contrast, the Panhandle region in Northwest Texas and far West Texas (with the exception of the border area near El Paso) are sparsely populated and growing slowly, if at all. Many of the rural counties in West Central Texas and the Panhandle lost population during the 1990s.[28]

Texas is an urban state, with 85 percent of its population living in metropolitan areas. Table 1.1 identifies the largest cities in the state, showing their population in 2007 and their rate of population growth since the 2000 Census. Three Texas cities—Houston, San Antonio, and Dallas—are among the ten largest cities in the United States. Houston is the fourth largest, San Antonio the seventh, and Dallas the eighth. Many Texas cities are also growing rapidly. As Table 1.1 shows, Houston, San Antonio, Austin, Fort Worth, Arlington, and Plano grew by 10 percent or more between 2000 and 2008.

Much of the growth in metropolitan areas has taken place in the suburbs. During the 1990s, eight of the ten most rapidly growing counties in Texas were suburban counties. Collin County, which is north of Dallas, grew by 86 percent. Montgomery County and Fort Bend County, which are part of the Greater Houston metropolitan area, grew by 61 percent and 57 percent, respectively.[29]

In contrast, the state's rural areas are growing slowly or, in some cases, losing population. Less than 10 percent of the 3.9 million residents added to the state's population during the 1990s lived in rural areas. The two most important industries for

TABLE 1.1   Population and Growth Rates for Texas Cities

City	2008 Population Estimate	Rate of Population Increase Since 2000 Census
Houston	2,242,000	13.6%
San Antonio	1,351,000	16.5%
Dallas	1,280,000	7.7%
Austin	758,000	15.0%
Fort Worth	703,000	29.9%
El Paso	613,000	8.7%
Arlington	374,000	12.4%
Corpus Christi	286,000	3.2%
Plano	267,000	20.3%
Garland	219,000	1.3%

Source: U.S. Census Bureau, available at www.census.gov.

rural Texas, agriculture and oil, have changed to require fewer workers than before. Consequently, many rural areas have been losing population. During the 1990s, more than one-third of the state's rural counties lost population, whereas every metropolitan county grew.[30]

 WHAT IS YOUR OPINION?

If you could afford to live anywhere, would you prefer to live in the city, the suburbs, or the countryside?

RELIGIOUS BELIEF AND PRACTICE

Texans are more religious than people in the nation as a whole. According to the U.S. Religious Landscape Survey conducted by the Pew Forum on Religion & Public Life, the state's residents are more likely to say that religion is important in their lives and to participate in religious activities than are Americans as a whole. Considering the following data:

- 77 percent of Texans are "absolutely certain" of their belief in God compared with a national figure of 71 percent;
- 67 percent of Texans say that religion is "very important" in their lives compared with a national figure of 56 percent;
- 47 percent of Texans attend religious services at least once a week compared with a national figure of 39 percent; and
- 66 percent of Texans indicate that they pray at least once a day compared with a national figure of 58 percent.

In terms of religious affiliation, evangelical Protestants (Southern Baptists, Assemblies of God, etc.) are more numerous in Texas than they are nationally

(34 percent in Texas compared with 26 percent in the nation as a whole). Mainline Protestants (Presbyterians, Methodists, Episcopalians, etc.) are less numerous (15 percent in Texas versus 18 percent nationally). At 24 percent, the presence of Catholics in Texas is the same as their presence nationwide. Finally, fewer Texans (12 percent) are religiously unaffiliated than are people in the nation as a whole (16 percent).[31]

THE TEXAS ECONOMY

The Texas economy is an important part of the policymaking context.

An Economy in Transition

For most of Texas's history, the state's economy was based on the sale of agricultural commodities and raw materials. In the nineteenth century, cotton and cattle formed the basis of economic activity. Unfortunately for the state, neither product provided the necessary foundation for a manufacturing boom. Texas exported most of its ginned cotton for clothing production to other states or countries. Meanwhile, cattle ranchers drove their herds to railheads in Kansas for shipment to stockyards in the Midwest.

In 1901, oil was discovered at Spindletop near Beaumont. Subsequently, oil and gas deposits were found throughout the state and Texas became the nation's leading

East Texas oil fields in 1903.

producer of oil and gas. In contrast to other commodities, oil spawned huge process-ing industries, including pipelines and refineries. The growth of petroleum-related businesses helped move the majority of Texans into urban areas by the 1950s.

Having an economy built on agriculture and oil had a major impact on the state's development. In the nineteenth century, Texas's economic health depended on the prices of cotton and cattle. For much of the twentieth century, the state's economy rose and fell in line with oil prices. Because commodity prices tend to fluc-tuate widely, Texas's economic history was one of booms and busts as prices for Texas products soared or collapsed. The state's economy boomed in the 1970s and early 1980s, for example, as oil prices rose to around $40 a barrel. The economy sagged in the mid-1980s as the price of oil dipped to less than half its earlier level.

The nature of the state's economy has contributed to a relatively lopsided distri-bution of income. Even though Texas has been a rich state, most Texans have not been wealthy. Although agriculture and oil were sources of significant wealth for the state's major landowners and big oil producers, more Texans were farm workers and oil-field roughnecks than large landowners or oil producers. Workers in these indus-tries historically were poorly organized and poorly paid, at least in comparison with workers in the auto assembly plants or steel mills of the northern states. Because peo-ple employed in industrial plants work together in close proximity, it is easier for them to organize and form unions to demand higher wages and better working conditions than farm workers and oil-field roughnecks who are dispersed while working outdoors.

The Texas economy is changing. As Figure 1.2 demonstrates, Texas oil produc-tion has been falling sharply and fairly steadily for years. Natural gas production has fallen as well. In 2007, the oil and gas business provided only 0.8 percent of the state's

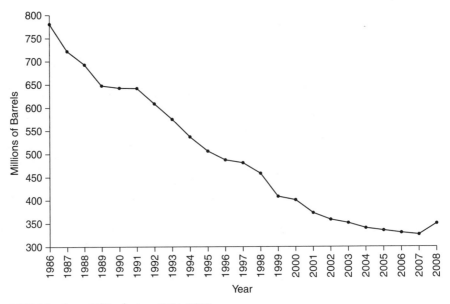

FIGURE 1.2   Texas Oil Production, 1986–2008.

Severance tax A tax imposed on the extraction of natural resources, such as oil, coal, or gas.

non-farm payroll, down from 7.3 percent in the early 1980s.[32] As oil and gas production have fallen, so have severance tax revenues. (A **severance tax** is a tax imposed on the extraction of natural resources, such as oil, coal, or gas.) Since the early 1970s, the proportion of state revenues generated by severance taxes on oil and gas production has declined from more than 20 percent to less than 3 percent in 2009.[33]

Declining oil and gas production and stagnant farm prices have forced state leaders, both in government and in private enterprise, to take steps to diversify the Texas economy. Although agriculture and petroleum are still important features of the state's economic picture, other industries are playing a greater role. Today, the state's economy is more diverse than ever before, resembling the national economy.

High-technology industries Industries that are based on the latest in modern technology.

The economic changes that are taking place in the state affect the Texas workforce. The most rapidly growing components of the state's economy involve healthcare and **high-technology industries,** those industries based on the latest in modern technology, such as telecommunications and robotics. These fields employ workers with technical knowledge and a capacity to learn new skills as technology changes. Texans who meet these criteria have a bright economic future. In 2009, medical professionals, engineers, and computer programmers in Texas enjoyed annual salaries in excess of $70,000.[34] In contrast, unskilled workers were lucky to find jobs that paid much more than **minimum wage,** which is the lowest hourly wage that an employer can pay covered workers.

Minimum wage The lowest hourly wage that an employer can pay covered workers.

Wealth, Poverty, and Healthcare

Gross State Product (GSP) The total value of goods and services produced in a state in a year.

Texas is a big state with a big economy. In 2009, the Texas **Gross State Product (GSP),** which is the total value of goods and services produced in a state in a year, stood at $1.2 trillion.[35] Only California had a larger state economy than Texas.[36] If Texas were an independent nation, it would have the ninth biggest economy in the world, larger even than Mexico, Brazil, Russia, India, and the Netherlands.[37]

The Texas economy has been growing at a more rapid pace than the national economy. Figure 1.3 compares the annual growth rate of the Texas economy with the rate of economic growth for the entire nation from 1990 through 2009. As the figure indicates, Texas economic performance generally parallels that of the national economy except that the Texas economy consistently outperforms the national economy. The economic slumps were not as deep in Texas, whereas the economic booms were more robust. In particular, the Texas economy significantly outperformed the American economy in 2008 and 2009, a time period during which the national economy suffered a serious **recession** (an economic slowdown characterized by declining economic output and rising unemployment).

Recession An economic slowdown characterized by declining economic output and rising unemployment.

Nonetheless, Texas is a relatively poor state, at least in terms of individual and family income. The median annual household income in Texas in 2007–2008 was $45,157 compared with a national figure of $51,233. Texas ranked thirty-fifth among the 50 states in this category.[38]

Household income varies with race and ethnicity. The median income for white families nationwide in 2008 was $55,530 compared with $37,913 for Latino households, $34,218 for African American households, and $65,637 for Asian households.[39] Professor Stephen Klineberg, a Rice University sociologist, attributes the income disparity

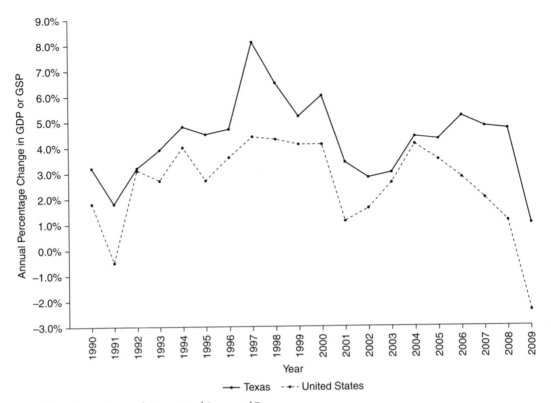

FIGURE 1.3   Economic Growth Rate, United States and Texas.

among ethnic and racial groups to a historic lack of access to quality education for African Americans and Latinos compared with whites and Asian Americans. Because the economy is changing, relatively few high-paying jobs are now available for people with weak job skills. "The good jobs that used to pay good money for unskilled or semi-skilled work are much harder to find these days," he explains.[40] As we discussed in the introduction to this chapter, the future economic health of Texas hinges on the socio-economic progress of its large and growing minority populations, especially the Latino and African American populations. That progress depends on education.

The income differential among the rich, the poor, and those in the middle in Texas is relatively large. According to a report jointly published by the Center on Budget and Policy Priorities and the Economic Policy Institute, the top one-fifth of Texas families has an annual income of $118,971, whereas the middle one-fifth of Texas families earns $41,015 a year. The average annual income for the bottom one-fifth of families is $14,724. The income gap between the top and the middle is greater in Texas than in any other state, whereas the gap between the top and the bottom is second only to that in the state of New York.[41] Analysts attribute the income gap to Texas having a large population of poorly educated people, including many immigrants from Mexico, who are unable to find good-paying jobs.[42]

? WHAT IS YOUR OPINION?

Should the government adopt policies designed to narrow the wealth and income gaps between the poorest and wealthiest segments of the population?

Poverty line The amount of money an individual or family needs to purchase basic necessities, such as food, clothing, health care, shelter, and transportation.

The poverty rate is relatively high in Texas. The government measures poverty on the basis of subsistence. By the official government definition, the **poverty line** is the amount of money an individual or a family needs to purchase basic necessities, such as food, clothing, healthcare, shelter, and transportation. The actual dollar amount varies with family size and rises with inflation. In 2009, the poverty line stood at $22,050 for a family of four.[43] The poverty rate in Texas was 16.9 percent compared with a rate of 13.3 percent for the United States as a whole. Texas had the seventh highest poverty rate among the 50 states.[44]

Poverty is concentrated among racial minorities, single-parent families headed by women, and the very young. In 2008, the national poverty rate for whites was 8.6 percent, compared with 24.7 percent for African Americans, 23.2 percent for Latinos, and 11.8 percent for Asians and Pacific Islanders. In addition, 19 percent of the nation's children under age 18 lived in poor families, whereas 28.7 percent of families headed by women with no husband present earned incomes below the poverty line.[45]

Texas has the highest percentage of residents without health insurance in the nation. More than 25 percent of Texas adults lack health insurance coverage compared with a national average of 15.4 percent.[46] Texas also trails the national average in the percentage of children without health insurance coverage (15.4 percent in Texas compared with a national average of 9.9 percent).[47] Most Texans without insurance are employed in low-wage jobs that do not provide health coverage. They and their families must do without healthcare, pay for health services out of pocket, or go to hospital emergency rooms.[48] A recent study found that Texas leads the nation in the percentage of residents who avoid physicians because they cannot afford care. The state is in the bottom tier of states in preventive care for diabetics and dental checkups.[49] Texas has the second lowest percentage of immunized children (75 percent), just above Nevada (which has an immunization rate of 71 percent).[50] It also has the third highest teen birthrate in the nation, behind Mississippi and New Mexico. The teen birthrate in Texas is 63.1 births for every 1,000 teenage girls compared with a national teen birthrate of 41.9 per 1,000.[51] Moreover, 23 percent of teen mothers in Texas are having their second, third, or even fourth child, giving the state the highest percentage of repeat teenage mothers in the nation.[52]

These sorts of data on health insurance, poverty rates, and income distribution trigger lively policy debates. Some policy analysts believe that the government should adopt policies designed to improve the lives of ordinary Texans. They favor government-sponsored health insurance programs, increased spending for education, and legislation to raise the state minimum wage. In contrast, other policy analysts argue that government programs hurt poor families by damaging the economy and thus limiting job growth. The best way to improve conditions for low- and middle-income people, they say, is to allow the market to work.

The state's high teen birthrate has sparked debate about sex education in the state. A number of observers believe that the high teenage birthrate is an indication that the state's abstinence-preferred approach to sex education is a failure. School districts in Texas are not required to teach sex education at all; however, if they do, they must present abstinence as the preferred choice for unmarried persons of school age. If a school district chooses to teach about contraception, it must allow parents to remove their children from the class and it must teach that contraception methods have failure rates. Critics of the state's sex education policy favor a balanced approach that combines information about contraception with an emphasis on abstinence. They believe that students need to know about birth control because abstinence-only is not a realistic approach for everyone. They point to research indicating that Texas teenagers are more likely to have sex and less likely to use condoms than their counterparts in states with comprehensive sex education programs.[53] In contrast, the defenders of the state's sex education policy stress that abstinence is the only foolproof way to prevent pregnancy. They oppose teaching youngsters about contraception because they do not want to give the impression that the state condones premarital sex. Furthermore, the Texas legislature apparently agrees with the proponents of abstinence-based sex education, and consistently defeats legislative efforts to require Texas public schools to include information about contraception in their sex education curricula.[54]

 WHAT IS YOUR OPINION?

Is abstinence-preferred education the correct approach in Texas?

POLITICAL CULTURE

Political culture The widely held, deeply rooted political values of a society.

Individualistic political culture An approach to government and politics that emphasizes private initiative with a minimum of government interference.

Political culture refers to the widely held, deeply rooted political values of a society. Professor Daniel Elazar identifies three strains of political culture found in the United States: individualistic, moralistic, and traditionalistic.[55] The **individualistic political culture** is an approach to government and politics that emphasizes private initiative with a minimum of government interference. This political culture stresses the importance of the individual and private initiative. In this view of society, the role of government should be limited to protecting individual rights and ensuring that social and political relationships are based on merit rather than tradition, family ties, or personal connections. Elazar says that individualistic political culture developed from the eighteenth- and nineteenth-century business centers in New York, Philadelphia, and Baltimore and spread westward through the central part of the nation. Immigrants from areas dominated by the individualistic political culture settled in the northern and central parts of Texas in the mid-nineteenth century.

AROUND THE NATION

Legal Prostitution in Nevada

Nevada is the only state in the nation with legal prostitution. State law allows every county except Clark County (where Las Vegas is located) to license and regulate brothel prostitution. However, street prostitution is illegal throughout the state. Eight of 16 Nevada counties license brothels to operate in designated areas. As of January 2009, 28 legal brothels employed 300 prostitutes in the state.* Prostitutes must use condoms during sex acts and state law requires weekly checks for certain sexually transmitted diseases and monthly HIV tests.

Prostitutes are independent contractors, living and working for several weeks at a time in a brothel. They seldom leave the premises and cannot have non-paying guests during their contract period. The brothel typically collects half the fee charged by the prostitutes for their room and board. Both the brothel owner and the prostitutes pay taxes to the government.

The Nevada legislature frequently debates whether to outlaw prostitution. Casino operators and business groups favor banning brothel prostitution in order to improve the state's image, whereas religious groups oppose prostitution on moral grounds. In contrast, the Brothel Owners' Association argues that the issue should be left to local government and that it is safer for prostitution to be legal and regulated rather than illegal and unregulated. Lawmakers from rural areas typically oppose efforts to outlaw the brothels because they provide jobs in poor counties and local tax revenue. In a good year, legal brothels generate $50 million in total revenue and contribute an estimated $400 million to the state's economy.† Some members of the Nevada legislature would like to expand legalized prostitution to Las Vegas and assess a state tax (currently, only counties tax the brothels) in order to generate revenue for the state.‡

Public opinion in Nevada is split on the issue. Newcomers to Nevada generally favor outlawing prostitution, whereas long-time residents endorse the status quo. In the meantime, politicians typically play both sides of the issue—they say they are against prostitution but believe that the counties, rather than the state legislature, should decide the issue.

QUESTIONS TO CONSIDER

1. If you were in the Nevada legislature, would you vote to outlaw the brothels? Why or why not?
2. Which political culture do you think is dominant in Nevada—moralistic, individualistic, or traditionalistic? What is the basis of your answer?
3. Do you think the Texas legislature will ever seriously consider legalizing brothel prostitution? Why or why not?

---

*"Prostitution in Nevada," available at www.answers.com.

†Jessica Ramirez, "Feeling the Pinch: Nevada's Brothels Hit Hard Times," *Newsweek*, June 18, 2008, available at www.newsweek.com.

‡Nick Gillespie, "Paying with Our Sins," *New York Times*, May 16, 2009, available at www.nytimes.com.

The **moralistic political culture** is an approach to government and politics in which people expect government to intervene in the social and economic affairs of the state, promoting the public welfare and advancing the public good. Participation in political affairs is regarded as one's civic duty. Elazar says the moralistic political culture developed from Puritanism (a religious reform movement) and New England town meetings and spread westward through the northern part of the nation and down the West Coast. Texas has received relatively little immigration from areas where the moralistic political culture was important.

Moralistic political culture An approach to government and politics in which people expect government to intervene in the social and economic affairs of the state, promoting the public welfare and advancing the public good.

Traditionalistic political culture An approach to government and politics that sees the role of government as the preservation of tradition and the existing social order.

Civic culture A political culture that is conducive to the development of an efficient, effective government that meets the needs of its citizens in a timely and professional manner.

The **traditionalistic political culture** is an approach to government and politics that sees the role of government as the preservation of tradition and the existing social order. Government leadership is in the hands of a social elite, and the level of participation by ordinary citizens in the policymaking process is relatively low. The government's role is to protect and preserve the existing social order. Elazar says that the traditional form of political culture developed from the plantation society of the South and spread westward through the southern states. Many immigrants from areas where the traditionalistic political culture was strong settled in East Texas.

Elazar believes that the political culture of Texas is a hybrid, including both traditionalistic and individualistic elements, and he identifies some aspects of state politics that reflect these two strains of political culture. Texas's traditionalistic political culture, Elazar says, is represented in the state's long history as a one-party state, low levels of voter turnout, and social and economic conservatism. Elazar identifies the state's strong support for private business, opposition to big government, and faith in individual initiative as reflections of Texas's individualistic political culture.

Political scientists Tom W. Rice and Alexander F. Sundberg take a different approach to political culture. They focus on the concept of **civic culture,** a political culture that is conducive to the development of an efficient, effective government that meets the needs of its citizens in a timely and professional manner. States with a civic culture have innovative and effective governments, they say, whereas states in which the culture is less civic have governments that are less responsive to citizen demands.

Rice and Sundberg identify four elements of a civic culture:

- **Civic engagement:** Citizens participate in the policymaking process in order to promote the public good.
- **Political equality:** Citizens view each other as political equals with the same rights and obligations.
- **Solidarity, trust, and tolerance:** Citizens feel a strong sense of fellowship with one another, tolerating a wide range of ideas and lifestyles.
- **Social structure of cooperation:** Citizens are joiners, belonging to a rich array of groups, from recreational sports teams to religious organizations.

Texas is forty-third among the 50 states in its level of civic culture. Rice and Sundberg found that most of the civic states are located in the north, running from New England to the Northwest. In contrast, most southern states are low in civic culture.[56]

Political culture is a useful concept for students of public policy because it leads them to focus on a state's history and development as important factors influencing politics and policy. Scholars who study the American states recognize variations in political behavior and beliefs among different regions of the country that can be explained on the basis of political culture. The concepts developed by Elazar and the team of Rice and Sundberg are useful tools for understanding policy differences among states that cannot be explained simply on the basis of socioeconomic factors.

GETTING INVOLVED

Volunteering

Everyone should do volunteer work, especially college students. Volunteering is a way to give back to the community for the kindness of others. People who volunteer develop an attachment to their community by learning about the problems in their area and helping solve them. Furthermore, volunteer work is a rewarding experience.

Your community has many fine organizations that welcome volunteers, including hospitals, schools, nursing homes, and animal shelters. Your college may have a service-learning program that matches volunteers with organizations needing help. Contact the organization of your choice and find out the procedures for volunteering. Even if you are able to put in only a few hours between semesters or on an occasional weekend, you will benefit from the experience.

It's your community—get involved!

WHAT WE HAVE LEARNED

1. How is the population of Texas described in terms of size, diversity, distribution, and religious belief?

Texas is the second most populous state in the nation behind California and one of the fastest growing states. Both natural population increase and immigration—legal and illegal—fuel the state's population growth. The population of Texas is quite diverse with no one racial/ethnic group in the majority. Central, South, North, and East Texas, as well as the Gulf Coast region of Texas, are growing rapidly whereas the Panhandle and most of West Texas are growing slowly or even losing population. Most Texans live in cities. Metro areas, including cities and (especially) suburban counties, are growing more rapidly than rural and small town Texas. Texans are more religious than people in the nation as a whole.

2. How does the economy of Texas compare with the economies of other states in terms of household income, poverty rates, and health insurance coverage?

Historically, the Texas economy has been based on the sale of agricultural commodities and raw materials. Cotton and cattle were king in the nineteenth century; oil and gas in the twentieth century. Fluctuating commodity prices meant the Texas economy alternated between boom and bust. The nature of the state's economy has contributed to a relatively lopsided distribution of income. Today, the most rapidly growing segments of the economy are healthcare and high-tech industries. Although the Texas economy generally grows at a faster pace than the national economy, Texas is a relatively poor state with a median household income below the national average. African Americans and Latinos have lower average incomes and higher poverty rates than do whites and Asians. The income differential among the rich, the poor, and those in the middle in Texas is relatively large. Texas also has the highest percentage of residents without health insurance in the nation.

3. How do political scientists describe the political culture of Texas?

Political culture refers to the widely held, deeply rooted political values of a society. Professor Elazar identifies three strains of political culture found in the United States: individualistic, moralistic, and traditionalistic. He believes that the political culture of Texas is a hybrid, including both traditionalistic and individualistic elements. Political scientists Rice and Sundberg focus on the concept of civic culture, a political culture that is conducive to the development of an efficient, effective government that meets the needs of its citizens in a timely and professional manner. Texas is forty-third among the 50 states in its level of civic culture.

KEY TERMS

civic culture
Gross State Product (GSP)
high-technology industries
individualistic political culture
Lone Star State

minimum wage
moralistic political culture
natural population increase
political culture
poverty line

recession
severance tax
traditionalistic political culture

NOTES

1. U.S. Census Bureau, "Median Earnings in the Past 12 Months of Workers by Sex and Women's Earnings as a Percentage of Men's Earnings by Selected Characteristics for the United States: 2007," available at www.census.gov.

2. Kate Alexander, "Study: Dropouts Costing Texas Billions," *Austin American-Statesman*, August 23, 2009, available at www.statesman.com.

3. Texas Higher Education Coordinating Board, "Report on the Select Commission on Higher Education and Global Competitiveness," January 2009, available at www.thecb.state.tx.us.

4. U.S. Census Bureau, "Educational Attainment by State," *The 2009 Statistical Abstract*, available at www.census.gov.

5. Governing, "State and Local Sourcebook," available at http://sourcebook.governing.com.

6. Michael Arnone, "Texas Falls Behind in Plan to Enroll More Minority Students," *Chronicle of Higher Education*, January 17, 2003, p. A23.

7. Texas Higher Education Coordinating Board, "Closing the Gaps by 2015: 2006 Progress Report," available at www.thecb.state.tx.us.

8. McNelly Torres, "High Schools Losing 1/3rd of Their Students," *San Antonio Express News*, March 7, 2005, available at www.mysanantonio.com.

9. Patrick McGee, "College Ethnic Gaps May Hit Economy, Report Says," *Fort Worth Star-Telegram*, November 9, 2005, available at www.dfw.com.

10. Martin Basaldua, "Closing the Gaps: Texas Higher Education Plan," Texas Higher Education Coordinating Board, 2000, available at www.thecb.state.tx.us.

11. U.S. Census Bureau, "Annual Estimates for the Population of the United States, Regions, States, and Puerto Rico: April 1, 2000 to July 1, 2008," available at www.census.gov.

12. National Center for Health Statistics, "Number of Births, Birth Rates, Fertility Rates, Total Fertility Rates, and Birthrates for Teenagers 15–19 Years by Age of Mother: United States, Each State and Territory 2006," available at www.cdc.gov.

13. U.S. Census Bureau, "Profile of General Demographic Characteristics for Texas: 2000," available at www.census.gov.

14. National Center for Health Statistics, "Fertility Rates and Birthrates by Age of Mother, Live-birth Order, and Hispanic Origin of Mother and by Race for Mothers of Non-Hispanic Origin: United States, 2006," available at www.cdc.gov.

15. Jim Getz, "Census: Texas Adds Almost 2 Million Hispanics Since 2000," *Dallas Morning News*, May 1, 2008, available at www.dallasnews.com.

16. U.S. Census Bureau, "Cumulative Estimates of the Components of Population Change for the United States, Regions, and States: April 1, 2000 to July 1, 2009," available at www.census.gov.

17. Pew Hispanic Center, "A Portrait of Unauthorized Immigrants in the United States," April 14, 2009, available at http://pewhispanic.org.

18. Elaine Ayala, "Study: Illegal Immigration Costs State Billions," *Houston Chronicle*, April 24, 2009, available at www.chron.com.

19. Brandi Grisson, "Report Says Loss of Undocumented Workers to Cost Trillions," *El Paso Times*, May 21, 2008, available at www.elpasotimes.com.

20. Texas Comptroller of Public Accounts, "Undocumented Immigrants in Texas: A Financial Analysis of the Impact to the State Budget and Economy," December 2006, available at www.window.state.tx.us.

21. U.S. Census Bureau, "Native and Foreign Born Population by Place of Birth and State: 2007," *The 2010 Statistical Abstract*, available at www.census.gov.

22. U.S. Census Bureau, "Profile of the Foreign-Born Population in the United States: 2000," available at www.census.gov.

23. Election Data Services, "New Population Estimates Show Slight Changes for 2008 Congressional Apportionment," December 22, 2008, available at www.electiondataservices.com.

24. U.S. Census Bureau, "Resident Population by Race, Hispanic or Latino Origin, and State, 2008" *The 2010 Statistical Abstract*, available at www.census.gov.

25. *Texas Observer*, March 7, 2008, p. 4.

26. U.S. Census Bureau, "Percent of Population by Race and Hispanic or Latino Origin, for States, Puerto Rico, and Places of 100,000 or more Population: 2000," available at www.census.gov.

27. U.S. Census Bureau, "Profile of the Foreign-Born Population in the United States: 2000."

28. Texas State Data Center and Office of the State Demographer, "Texas Population Growth in Texas Counties, 1850–2040," available at http://txsdc.tamu.edu/maps/thematic/popgrowth.php.

29. "Texas Population Growth in Texas Counties, 1850–2040."

30. U.S. Census Bureau, "Census 2000 Geographic Definitions," revised November 16, 2000, available at www.census.gov.

31. Pew Forum on Religion & Public Life, "Religious Landscape Survey," available at http://religions.perforum.org.

32. Texas Workforce Commission, "Current Employment Statistics for Texas, April 2009," available at www.tracer2.com.

33. Texas Comptroller of Public Accounts, *Fiscal Notes*, April 2009, p. 15.

34. Texas Workforce Solutions, "Wage Information Network," available at www.texasindustryprofiles.com.

35. Texas Comptroller of Public Accounts, "Texas Ahead: Gross State Product and Income," available at www.texasahead.org.

36. U.S. Census Bureau, "Gross State Product in Current and Real (2000) Dollars by State," *The 2009 Statistical Abstract*, available at www.census.gov.

37. U.S. Census Bureau, "Gross National Income by Country," *The 2009 Statistical Abstract*, available at www.census.gov.

38. U.S. Census Bureau, "Income, Poverty and Health Insurance in the United States: 2008," available at www.census.gov.

39. Ibid.

40. David Plesa, "Racial Income Gap Widens," *Houston Post*, April 16, 1993, p. A-1.

41. Center on Budget and Policy Priorities, "Income Inequality Grew Across the Country Over the Past Two Decades," available at www.cbpp.org.

42. Asher Price and Claire Osborn, "Texas Leads Nation in Upper and Middle Income Gap," *Austin American-Statesman*, January 28, 2006, available at www.statesman.com.

43. U.S. Department of Health and Human Services, "The 2009 HHS Poverty Guidelines," available at www.hhs.gov.

44. U.S. Census Bureau, "Individuals and Families Below Poverty Level—Number and Rate by State," *The 2009 Statistical Abstract*, available at www.census.gov.

45. U.S. Census Bureau, "Income, Poverty, and Health Insurance Coverage in the United States: 2008."

46. Ibid.

47. National Center for Health Statistics, "National Health Interview Survey," available at www.cdc.gov.

48. Carlos Guerra, "Private Group's Count Reveals Many More Uninsured Texans," *San Antonio Express News*, June 17, 2004, available at www.mysanantonio.com.

49. Richard S. Dunham and Lynsi Burton, "Health Care Debate Highlights Texas Paradoxes," *Houston Chronicle*, October 16, 2009, p. A19.

50. Corrie MacLaggan, "Report: Texas Ranks in Bottom 10 States for Percentage of Children in Poverty," *Austin American-Statesman*, June 27, 2006, available at www.statesman.com.

51. "State Teen Birth Ranking No Cause for Celebration," *San Antonio Express News*, January 13, 2009, available at www.mysanantonio.com.

52. Robert T. Garrett, "Dallas Leads Nation in Repeat Teen Births, Study Finds," *Dallas Morning News*, September 1, 2009, available at www.dallasnews.com.

53. Melissa Mixon, "Sex Education: Does Teaching Abstinence Work?" *Austin American-Statesman*, July 13, 2008, available at www.mysanantonio.com.

54. Michelle de la Rosa, "Sex Education Bill Going Nowhere," *San Antonio Express-News*, May 6, 2009, available at www.mysanantonio.com.

55. Daniel Elazar, *American Federalism: A View from the States*, 2nd ed. (New York: Crowell, 1972), pp. 84–126.

56. Tom W. Rice and Alexander F. Sundberg, "Civic Culture and Government Performance in the American States," *Publius: The Journal of Federalism* 27 (Winter 1997): 99–114.

Chapter 2

Texas Constitution

WHAT WE WILL LEARN

After studying Chapter 2, students should be able to answer the following questions:

▸ How do state constitutions compare and contrast with the U.S. Constitution?

▸ What is the historical background of the Texas Constitution?

▸ What were the goals of the majority of delegates at the state constitutional convention of 1875 and how did those goals affect the document they drafted?

▸ What are the principal features of the Texas Constitution?

▸ What are the means through which the Texas Constitution changes?

▸ What role do Texas courts and the Texas Constitution play in the protection of individual rights?

Is gambling the solution to the state's budget problem? Many state leaders believe that Texas is heading for a budget crisis. In 2006, the Texas legislature shifted some of the cost of public education from local government to the states to enable school districts to reduce their property tax rates. Because of this, the legislature increased the cigarette tax and created a new business tax in order to raise sufficient money to make up for the revenue lost because of the property tax reduction. Unfortunately, the new taxes have generated more than a billion dollars a year less than anticipated, leaving the state with a long-term budget shortfall.[1] Gambling proponents contend that the introduction of casino gambling in Texas along with the addition of slot machines (called video lottery terminals) at horse and dog tracks would more than make up for the revenue shortfall in school funding, generating perhaps as much as $3 billion a year. Gambling is a voluntary tax, they argue; no one pays unless he or she chooses to play. Legalized gambling creates jobs and attracts visitors with money to the state. It also provides a local alternative for Texans who have been traveling to neighboring states to visit casinos. In contrast, the opponents of legalized gambling argue that it creates a morally corrupting climate that is associated with social problems, such as crime, bankruptcy, and gambling addiction. Furthermore, the introduction of casinos and other gambling establishments to an area hurts small businesses because people spend their money gambling rather than purchasing goods and services.[2]

Gambling proponents have made little headway so far, despite the state's difficult budget picture, because the Texas Constitution prohibits gambling. The expansion of gambling in the state takes more than passage of ordinary legislation; instead, it requires the adoption and ratification of a constitutional amendment, and that is more difficult to achieve. Ordinary legislation requires majority vote approval of the Texas House and Texas Senate. After the measure passes the legislature it goes to the governor, who can sign it into law or allow it to become law without signature. If the governor issues a veto, the legislature can override the veto by a two-thirds vote of the House and Senate. In contrast, the adoption of a constitutional amendment requires a two-thirds vote by the Texas House and Texas Senate and then ratification by a majority of voters in a special constitutional amendment election.

The Texas Constitution sets the ground rules for policymaking by defining the process for policy adoption. It creates the branches of government and establishes processes for passing ordinary legislation and adopting constitutional amendments. Because the Constitution prohibits gambling, legislators who want to expand legalized gambling in the state to increase revenues will have to round up two-thirds majorities in the Texas House and Texas Senate and then persuade a majority of voters to approve the measure as well.

This chapter examines the Texas Constitution as an important element of the context for policymaking in the Lone Star State. The chapter begins with a discussion of the role of state constitutions in general. It explores the background of the Texas Constitution, describes the constitutional convention of 1875, and presents an overview of the document. The chapter discusses constitutional change and the role the Texas Constitution plays in protecting individual rights.

STATE CONSTITUTIONS

Constitution
A fundamental law by which a state or nation is organized and governed.

Bicameral legislature
A legislative body with two chambers.

Separation of powers The division of political authority among legislative, executive, and judicial branches of government.

Plural executive
The division of executive power among several elected officials.

Unicameral legislature
A legislative body with one chamber.

A **constitution** is the fundamental law by which a state or nation is organized and governed. The U.S. Constitution is the fundamental law of the United States. It establishes the framework of government, assigns the powers and duties of governmental bodies, and defines the relationship between the people and their government. Similarly, a state constitution is the fundamental law for a state. The U.S. Constitution and the state constitutions together provide the total framework for government within the United States.

State constitutions resemble the U.S. Constitution in some respects but differ in others. The framers of the U.S. Constitution based the document on the principle of separation of powers, with a strong chief executive, a **bicameral legislature** (a legislative body with two chambers), and a judiciary appointed for life. Although every state constitution provides for the **separation of powers** (the division of political authority among the legislative, executive, and judicial branches of government), many state documents differ from the national constitution in important details. A number of state constitutions, including the Texas Constitution, give their governor fewer official powers than the U.S. Constitution grants the president. Indeed, the constitutions of Texas and several other states weaken their governors through means of the **plural executive,** which is the division of executive power among several elected officials. Most state constitutions, including the Texas Constitution, provide for the election of judges. One state, Nebraska, has a **unicameral legislature,** which is a legislative body with one chamber.

Some state constitutions reflect a different approach to democracy than the U.S. Constitution embodies. The U.S. Constitution creates a **representative democracy** or a **republic,** which is a political system in which citizens elect representatives to make policy decisions on their behalf. The framers of the

GETTING INVOLVED

Joining a Student Club or Organization

If you join a student organization, you will enjoy college more and probably earn better grades as well. Joining a club will give you the chance to make new friends with similar interests and become acquainted with a faculty advisor outside the classroom setting. In addition, because you will be better connected to the school, you will be more likely to stay in college and finish your education.

Colleges and universities typically offer a range of student clubs and organizations. Students at your school may participate in such organizations as an international student association, Campus Crusade for Christ, chess club, Young Democrats, Young Republicans, choir, gay/lesbian/bisexual student association, black student union, bridge club, Muslim student association, computer science club, Jewish life organization, Latino student association, karate club, pre-medical society, Catholic Student Union, math club, and Asian student association. The student life office at your college will have a list of student groups active on your campus.

It's your college—get involved!

Representative democracy or **republic** A political system in which citizens elect representatives to make policy decisions on their behalf.

Direct democracy A political system in which the citizens vote directly on matters of public concern.

Initiative process A procedure whereby citizens can propose the adoption of a policy measure by gathering a prerequisite number of signatures. Voters must then approve the measure before it can take effect.

U.S. Constitution believed that elected representatives were needed to act as a buffer between the people and government policies. In contrast, some state constitutions include certain elements of **direct democracy,** which is a political system in which the citizens vote directly on matters of public concern. Almost half the states (but not Texas) provide for the **initiative process,** a procedure whereby citizens can propose the adoption of a policy measure by gathering a prerequisite number of signatures. Voters must then approve the measure before it can take effect. State officials then place the measure on the ballot for approval by the voters. Citizens can use the initiative process either to adopt measures or to repeal legislation enacted through the legislative process. Voters in California, Oregon, and other states with the initiative process have used it to make policy decisions concerning such issues as state tax rates, bilingual education, gay and lesbian rights, insurance rates, term limits for elected officials, and the provision of public services to illegal immigrants.

In contrast to the U.S. Constitution, state constitutions have a quality of impermanence to them. Although the present state constitution of Massachusetts was written in 1780, only six state constitutions now in effect were drafted before 1850. The average state constitution lasts for 70 years.[3] Nonetheless, about one-fourth of the states have adopted new constitutions since World War II. Furthermore, most states have changed constitutions several times. Louisiana, for example, has had 11 constitutions; Georgia has had ten.[4]

Most state constitutions have more amendments than the U.S. Constitution, which has only 27. In contrast, the average state constitution has been amended nearly a hundred times. At the high end, the Constitution of South Carolina has been changed formally more than 450 times.[5] The California Constitution has more than 500 amendments.[6]

Finally, state constitutions are on average four times longer than the U.S. Constitution. The Alabama Constitution, at 310,000 words, is the longest constitution in the nation, compared with only 7,400 words in the U.S. Constitution. The Texas Constitution is 93,000 words.[7] The length of state constitutions reflects the broader scope of state policy responsibilities compared with those of the national government. State constitutions deal with some matters not discussed at all in the U.S. Constitution, such as the structures, functions, and finances of local governments. State constitutions consider other issues, such as elections and land management, in greater detail than they are covered in the national document.

State constitutions also generally include numerous miscellaneous provisions that might be called "super legislation." These measures are the same quality and type as **statutory law** (law made by a legislature) but for historical or political reasons are upgraded to **constitutional law,** which is law that involves the interpretation and application of the constitution.[8] The South Dakota Constitution, for example, provides for state hail insurance; the Oklahoma Constitution requires that home economics be taught in public schools.[9] Some critics of the Texas Constitution believe that issues such as the expansion of legalized gambling should be addressed through the legislative process rather than addressed in the state constitution.

Statutory law Law made by a legislature.

Constitutional law Law that involves the interpretation and application of the constitution.

Because the Texas Constitution prohibits gambling, Texas legislators who want to legalize casino gambling in the state have to push for a constitutional amendment rather than just the passage of ordinary legislation.

BACKGROUND OF THE TEXAS CONSTITUTION

Jacksonian democracy The philosophy (associated with President Andrew Jackson) that the right to vote should be extended to all adult male citizens and that all government offices of any importance should be filled by election.

Suffrage The right to vote.

Texans adopted their first state constitution in 1845, when the Lone Star State joined the Union. As with most other state constitutions written in the first half of the nineteenth century, the Texas Constitution of 1845 was patterned after the U.S. Constitution. Following the national model, it created a government with legislative, executive, and judicial branches. Similar to the U.S. Constitution, the Texas Constitution of 1845 was a document of broad, general principles that allowed state government leeway to deal with policy problems as they arose. The voters would select the governor, lieutenant governor, and members of the legislature. The governor would then appoint other state executive officials and members of the state judiciary.

In 1850, Texas amended the state constitution to provide for the election, rather than appointment, of state judges and most executive officeholders. The change reflected the principle of **Jacksonian democracy,** the philosophy (associated with President Andrew Jackson) that suggested the right to vote should be extended to all adult male citizens and that all government offices of any importance should be filled by election. The advocates of Jacksonian democracy believed that government is made responsive to the people through broad-based **suffrage** (the right to vote) and the **long ballot** (an election system that provides for the election of nearly every public official of any significance).

Long ballot An election system that provides for the election of nearly every public official of any significance.

When Texas joined the Confederacy in 1861, the state changed its constitution. The new document pledged the state's allegiance to the Confederacy and included a strong prohibition against the abolition of slavery. Otherwise, the Constitution of 1861 closely resembled its predecessor.

In 1866, with the war lost, Texas rewrote its constitution once again in hopes of rejoining the Union under President Andrew Johnson's reconstruction plan. This new constitution repealed secession, repudiated the war debt, and recognized the supremacy of the U.S. Constitution. Although the document abolished slavery it fell short of granting full equality to former slaves. African Americans could not testify in court cases unless other African Americans were involved, and they were denied the right to vote. In most other respects, though, the Constitution of 1866 simply reenacted provisions of the 1845 document.

The Texas Constitution of 1866 was short lived. By the time of its adoption, the Radical Republican majority in Congress had taken control of Reconstruction from President Johnson. The **Radical Republicans** were members of the Republican Party who wanted sweeping social change to take place in the South after the Civil War. Congress passed legislation over President Johnson's veto declaring that Texas and the other states of the Confederacy could not reenter the Union until they granted African Americans the right to vote, ratified the Thirteenth and Fourteenth Amendments to the U.S. Constitution, and drafted new state constitutions acceptable to Congress.

Radical Republicans Members of the Republican Party who wanted sweeping social change to take place in the South after the Civil War.

Because Union troops occupied Texas, the state had little choice but to accept the demands. Ninety Texans, representing a broad range of political factions, gathered in convention in June 1868 to draft another state constitution. The convention was a stormy one, with the delegates unable to agree on a document. In 1869, the military commander of Texas intervened to gather the bits and pieces the convention had been working on into a single document. The U.S. Congress accepted this new constitution and Texas was readmitted to the Union in 1870.

The Texas Constitution of 1869 created an active state government. Reverting to the procedure established in the original state constitution of 1845, it provided for the gubernatorial appointment rather than election of judges and most executive branch officials. It established annual sessions of the legislature and authorized increased salaries for state officials. The constitution also included a compulsory school attendance law and provided for state supervision of education.

For most white, ex-Confederate Texans, the Constitution of 1869 represented defeat and humiliation. Many Texans regarded the document not as a Texas constitution at all but a document imposed on them by outside forces. Radical Republican Governor E. J. Davis held office under this constitution and the two were closely linked in the minds of the ex-Confederate Texans who considered Davis arrogant and corrupt. In particular, Democrats criticized the Davis administration for excessive spending, taxation, and borrowing.

Defenders of the Davis administration argued that the policies adopted by the governor and the Republican legislature were an appropriate effort to help the state recover from the Civil War. Under Davis, the state undertook programs to promote railroad construction, build an extensive network of roads, and construct a free public school system. Furthermore, Democratic Governor Richard Coke and the Democratic majority

Budget deficit
The amount of money by which annual budget expenditures exceed annual budget receipts.

in the legislature who succeeded the Republicans in office were no more successful at dealing with the state's financial problems than their predecessors. The state **budget deficit,** the amount of money by which annual budget expenditures exceed annual budget receipts, was higher in 1875 and 1876 under Coke than it had been in 1872 and 1873 under Davis.[10]

Nonetheless, the association of the Texas Constitution of 1869 with Reconstruction guaranteed strong Democratic support for a new document. When Democrats regained control of state government in 1872 and 1873, their first priority was to draft a new constitution for Texas. Governor Coke and Democratic legislative leaders initially proposed that a new constitution be written by the state legislature. When legislators deadlocked over a new document, however, the governor and the Democratic leaders had no choice but to call for the election of delegates to a state constitutional convention.

 WHAT IS YOUR OPINION?

Do you agree with the political philosophy underlying the concept of Jacksonian democracy?

CONSTITUTIONAL CONVENTION OF 1875

Grange An organization of farmers.

In the fall of 1875, 90 Texans gathered in Austin to draft a new constitution for the state. Although a number of Republicans, including several African Americans, served as convention delegates, a majority of the delegates were white Democrats. Farmers, ex-Confederate officers, and lawyers were all well represented at the convention. The largest organized group of delegates was the Texas Patrons of Husbandry, better known as the **Grange,** an organization of farmers. Indeed, "retrenchment and reform," the Grangers' slogan, became the watchword of the convention.

"Retrenchment and reform" embodied two basic goals: to restrict the size and scope of state government and to control the excesses of big business. Most of the delegates at the convention wanted to restrain a state government that they believed was too large and expensive. To accomplish this task, the delegates abandoned one constitutional tradition while reinstating another. On the one hand, the authors of the new constitution turned away from the pattern initially established in the Texas Constitution of 1845 of a general document phrased in broad terms, favoring instead a restrictive constitution of great length and detail. On the other hand, the delegates returned to the tradition of Jacksonian democracy, reinstating the long ballot and shortening the terms of office for elected officials.[11]

The convention restricted the authority of every branch and unit of Texas government. The new constitution weakened the office of governor by cutting the governor's salary and reducing the term of office from four to two years. It restricted the governor's power of appointment by creating a plural executive, which divided executive power among several elected officials, including a lieutenant governor, an attorney general, a comptroller, a treasurer, and a land commissioner. Executive officials elected independently from the governor would owe no allegiance to the governor. Indeed, they might be political rivals. The governor could appoint a number of lesser officials, but they would have little incentive to follow the governor's lead because the governor had no power to remove them before the end of their terms.

The constitution's framers reduced the power of the legislature by cutting its meeting time and restricting the scope of its policymaking authority. They limited regular sessions of the legislature to 140 calendar days, every other year. They reduced legislative salaries and required that the legislature adopt a balanced budget unless four-fifths of the membership agreed to deficit spending. Furthermore, by including long, detailed sections on education, finance, railroad regulation, and similar matters in the constitution, the framers forced legislators to propose constitutional amendments if they wanted to adopt policy changes in many areas.

The authors of Texas's new constitution employed several devices for reducing the power of the judicial branch of state government. They divided the state's court system into two segments, limiting the types of cases individual courts would be authorized to hear. In the best tradition of Jacksonian democracy, they provided for the election of judges to relatively brief terms. The framers also reduced judicial discretion by writing a long, detailed constitution that left relatively little room for judicial interpretation.

The framers of the Texas Constitution didn't overlook local government, either. They specified the forms local governments must take and restricted local authority to levy taxes, provide services, adopt regulations, and go into debt. In many instances, local officials would have to ask the state legislature for permission to adopt even relatively minor policies. Changing local political structures would frequently necessitate a constitutional amendment.

Another major goal of the Granger-dominated convention was to control the excesses of big business. Consider the constitutional provisions dealing with banking. Many of the convention delegates were small farmers, used to living on the financial edge. They distrusted big, impersonal banks, which might be inclined to foreclose on their property during hard times. Instead, they preferred smaller, locally owned banks whose managers would be more understanding. Consequently, the convention prohibited **branch banking,** a business practice whereby a single, large bank conducts business from several locations. This provision ensured that banks would be locally owned rather than branches of large banks headquartered in Dallas or Houston.

Branch banking A business practice whereby a single, large bank conducts business from several locations.

The constitution's deference to local values is reflected in its provisions dealing with liquor regulation as well. Although the constitution empowered the legislature to regulate the manufacture, packaging, sale, possession, and transportation of alcoholic beverages, it left the decision to legalize the sale of alcoholic beverages to local voters. **Local-option elections** (also known as **wet-dry elections**) were held to determine whether an area could legalize the sale of alcoholic beverages. The voters living in a city, a county, or even an area as small as a justice of the peace precinct could vote to keep their area dry, that is, to prohibit the sale of alcoholic beverages. Once an area goes dry, it cannot go wet unless the voters approve. Of the 254 counties in Texas, 51 are totally dry and 39 are entirely wet. The other 164 counties are partially wet, which means that they include some areas where alcohol cannot be sold.[12]

Local-option (wet-dry) elections Elections held to determine whether an area legalizes the sale of alcoholic beverages.

The delegates at the constitutional convention believed in the old adage that a family's home is its castle, and they set about to protect it. They provided that a

Homestead
Legal residence.

family **homestead** (that is, legal residence) could not be seized and sold in payment of debt except for delinquent taxes and mortgage payments on a loan taken out to purchase the home itself. The framers also added a measure to the constitution requiring that both spouses must give written consent before the homestead could be sold. The constitution also prohibited the garnishment of wages for payment of debt. (A modern constitutional amendment provides an exception—garnishment for the enforcement of court-ordered child support or spousal maintenance.)

In the 1870s, it was common for states to adopt restrictive constitutions. Although the Texas Constitution written in 1875 reflected the political concerns of rural-oriented Texans, the document was not far out of step with other state constitutions adopted in the late nineteenth century. Many states provided for the election of judges and a broad range of executive-branch officials. Short terms of office for governors and judges were also common. Furthermore, Texans were not the only Americans who distrusted public officials and worried about the corrupting influences of big banks, corporations, and railroads.[13]

The delegates finished their work in less than three months and, in early 1876, the voters approved the new constitution by a margin of two to one. With amendments, the Constitution of 1876 remains the fundamental law of the state of Texas today.

Because the Texas Constitution prohibited branch banking, the legislature and the voters had to adopt a constitutional amendment to allow ATM machines.

OVERVIEW OF THE TEXAS CONSTITUTION

To students familiar with the U.S. Constitution, the most striking feature of the Texas Constitution is its length. At 93,000 words, the Texas Constitution is one of the longest state constitutions in the nation. It can be found in most reference libraries, in the *Texas Almanac*, and online.

The Texas Constitution shares a number of features with the U.S. Constitution: a bill of rights, separation of powers with checks and balances, and the creation of a bicameral legislature. A **bill of rights** is a constitutional document guaranteeing individual rights and liberties. As with other provisions of the Texas Constitution, the Texas Bill of Rights is long, considerably longer than its counterpart in the national constitution. The Texas document contains 29 sections and includes most of the guarantees found in the national Bill of Rights, such as the protection of free speech and a free press, the guarantee of the right of trial by jury, and a safeguard against "unreasonable searches and seizures."

Bill of rights
A constitutional document guaranteeing individual rights and liberties.

INTERNET RESEARCH   The Freedom of Worship Provision of the Texas Constitution

Both the U.S. Constitution and the Texas Constitution include provisions dealing with religious liberty. The state's Freedom of Worship Provision—Article I, Section 6, of the Texas Constitution—can be found online at the following Internet addresses: **www.statutes.legis.state.tx.us/** or **http://tarlton.law.utexas.edu/constitutions/text/IART01.html**. Read it from the perspective of comparing and contrasting it with the First Amendment of the U.S. Constitution, which can be found at the following website: **www.law.cornell.edu/constitution/constitution.overview.html**. Complete the assignment by answering the following questions:

1. "Congress shall make no law respecting an establishment of religion." This provision from the First Amendment of the U.S. Constitution is known as the Establishment Clause. Does Article I, Section 6, of the Texas Constitution include equivalent language? What passage or passages in the Texas document are comparable to the Establishment Clause of the U.S. Constitution?

2. "Congress shall make no law . . . prohibiting the free exercise [of religion.]" This provision from the First Amendment of the U.S. Constitution is known as the Free Exercise Clause. Does Article I, Section 6, of the Texas Constitution include equivalent language? What passage or passages in the Texas document are comparable to the Free Exercise Clause of the U.S. Constitution?

3. The framers of the Texas Constitution were familiar with the wording of the U.S. Constitution and could have chosen simply to duplicate it in the Texas document. Why do you think they decided to take a different approach?

4. Do you think that the wording in the Texas Bill of Rights provides individuals with greater protection for religious liberty than the First Amendment of the U.S. Constitution? Why or why not?

5. Suppose a Texas resident believed that a unit of state or local government had violated her freedom of religion. She filed suit in federal court under the U.S. Constitution but lost her case. Could she also seek relief in a Texas court based on the Texas Constitution? Explain the basis of your answer.

6. Would it be possible for the Texas resident referenced in Question 5 to win her case in Texas court even though she lost in federal court? Why or why not?

The Texas Bill of Rights does more than merely restate the guarantees found in the U.S. Constitution. The Texas document phrases the protection of rights positively rather than negatively. Consider the issue of freedom of expression. The First Amendment to the U.S. Constitution prohibits the abridgement of free expression: "Congress shall make no law . . . abridging the freedom of speech, or of the press." In contrast, the Texas Bill of Rights guarantees free expression: "Every person shall be at liberty to speak, write or publish his opinions on any subject . . . and no law shall ever be passed curtailing the liberty of speech or of the press" [Art. 1, Sect. 8]. Professor James C. Harrington believes that the provision in the Texas Constitution is potentially a stronger guarantee of free expression than the First Amendment to the U.S. Constitution. Whereas the U.S. Bill of Rights identifies rights the national government *may not infringe*, the Texas Bill of Rights lists rights state government *must protect*.[14]

The Texas Bill of Rights includes a number of measures not found in the national Bill of Rights. Whereas the U.S. Constitution provides for the right to a jury trial only if defendants face more than six months in jail, the Texas Constitution guarantees the right to trial by jury for persons charged with any offense, even minor traffic violations. The Texas Constitution also contains two guarantees of equal rights more explicit and detailed than any comparable measure included in the U.S. Constitution. Both provisions are found in Article I, Section 3. The first measure is fairly broad: "All free men . . . have equal rights." The second guarantee, which was added in 1972, is known as the **Texas Equal Rights Amendment (ERA).** It is a provision in the Texas Constitution that states the following: "Equality under the law shall not be denied or abridged because of sex, race, color, creed, or national origin" [Art. I, Sect. 3a.].

The Texas Constitution establishes a separation of powers system with checks and balances. Similar to the national government, Texas state government has three branches: an executive branch headed by the governor; a bicameral legislature, including the Texas House of Representatives and the Texas Senate; and a judicial branch. **Checks and balances** refers to the overlapping of the powers held by the different branches of government, so that public officials limit the authority of one another. The governor's appointments, for example, must be confirmed by a two-thirds vote of the Texas Senate. Legislation must pass both the House and the Senate before it has passed the Texas legislature. The governor can veto bills passed by the legislature, but the legislature can override the veto by a two-thirds vote of each house.

The Texas Constitution includes features not found in the U.S. Constitution. Some of these provisions involve policy matters of primary concern to state government. One section, for example, deals with voter qualifications and elections. Other sections outline the structures and responsibilities of local governments. Much of the length and detail of the Texas Constitution, though, can be attributed to the inclusion of long sections dealing with substantive policy areas. The framers of the constitution devoted thousands of words to such matters as railroad regulation, education, welfare, and taxation. Subsequent amendments have added thousands of additional words.

Texas Equal Rights Amendment (ERA) A provision in the Texas Constitution that states the following: "Equality under the law shall not be denied or abridged because of sex, race, color, creed, or national origin."

Checks and balances The overlapping of the powers of the branches of government so that public officials limit the authority of one another.

CONSTITUTIONAL CHANGE

Constitutions change by means of formal amendment, practical experience, and judicial interpretation. The U.S. Constitution is a relatively brief document of general principles. Although it has been amended 27 times, scholars believe that practical experience and judicial interpretation have been more important means of constitutional change than written amendments. State constitutions are usually longer and more detailed than the national document, providing less opportunity for constitutional growth through practical experience and judicial interpretation. State constitutional change generally occurs through the means of written amendments. This is certainly true for the Texas Constitution.

Change Through Amendment

Constitutional amendment
A formal, written change or addition to the nation's governing document.

A **constitutional amendment** is a formal, written change or addition to the state's governing document. The detailed style of the Texas Constitution has led to numerous amendments as each successive generation of Texans has attempted to adapt its features to changing times. Some amendments have been trivial, such as an amendment to allow city governments to donate surplus firefighting equipment to rural volunteer fire departments. Other amendments have dealt with weighty policy matters, such as an amendment authorizing the legislature to cap noneconomic damages for pain and suffering awarded in lawsuits. The voters approved both amendments in 2003.

Through the years, amendments have produced several major changes in the Texas Constitution. The legislature and the voters have amended the constitution to strengthen the authority of state officials, especially the governor. Amendments have increased the governor's term of office, as well as those of the state's other elected executive officials, from two years to four years and have empowered the governor to remove his or her own appointees, pending Senate approval. The constitution has also been amended to give the governor limited **budget execution authority,** which is the power to cut agency spending or transfer money between agencies during the period when the legislature is not in session.

Budget execution authority The power to cut agency spending or transfer money between agencies during the period when the legislature is not in session.

The legislature and the voters have amended the Texas Constitution to enable state government to promote economic development. Amendments have eliminated the constitutional prohibition against branch banking, allowed local governments to give tax breaks to businesses relocating to Texas, and provided money for the development and conservation of the state's water resources. Other amendments have provided funds for highway construction, student loans, and college expansion.

General obligation bonds
Certificates of indebtedness that must be repaid from general revenues.

The legislature and the voters have periodically approved amendments to enable the state to go into debt by issuing **general obligation bonds,** which are certificates of indebtedness that must be repaid from general revenues. Borrowing enables the state to spread the cost of major projects, such as prison construction and water development, over a period of time. Because the Texas Constitution prohibits the state from incurring debt that must be repaid from general revenues, the legislature has had to propose constitutional amendments to authorize borrowing. In 2009, the bonded indebtedness of the state of Texas was $15.4 billion, with the state paying $461 million a year in principal and interest out of general revenues.[15]

The process of amending the Texas Constitution is fairly straightforward. An amendment must first be proposed by a two-thirds vote of each house of the legislature. Then, it must be ratified by a majority of the voters in an election. Through 2009, the voters had approved 467 amendments to the Texas Constitution out of 643 proposed by the legislature.[16]

However, the amendment process is time-consuming and the electorate apathetic. Even in the most favorable circumstances, the interval between the formulation of a proposed amendment and its ultimate approval or rejection by the voters is measured in years. Furthermore, elections to ratify constitutional amendments generate relatively little voter interest. As Figure 2.1 indicates, the number of Texas voters who decided the fate of the 16 proposed constitutional amendments on the ballot in 2009 was considerably less than the number of Texans who participated in the 2008 presidential election or the 2006 governor's election.

Nearly every state allows its citizens to vote on constitutional amendments, and defenders of the process say that the people should have a voice in the adoption of changes in their state's fundamental law. They frame the issue in terms of democracy. Although the legislature can propose constitutional change, the voters should have the final word on whether changes are adopted.

In contrast, critics argue that most citizens are not well enough informed to make reasonable judgments about the details of state constitutional law. For example, Texas voters have twice rejected efforts to repeal a provision in the Texas Constitution requiring companies that seek investment from the Texas Growth Fund to disclose whether they do business with the white-minority governments of South Africa and Namibia. With the introduction of democratic, black majority-rule governments in those countries, the original rationale for the requirement no longer applies. Even

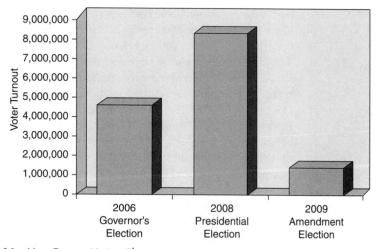

FIGURE 2.1 Voter Turnout, Various Elections.

though there is no organized opposition to repeal the measure, the voters, apparently confused by the issue, have failed twice to ratify amendments repealing the provision.

The Texas legislature sometimes words amendments with an eye toward deceiving the voters. The Texas Constitution requires that the state publish a summary and a brief explanation of proposed constitutional amendments in newspapers at least twice before Election Day. In 1989, the summary for one proposed amendment clearly explained that the amendment would increase the pay for members of the Texas legislature from $7,200 to $23,358 a year. It would raise the salaries of the Speaker of the House and the lieutenant governor even more. On the ballot, however, the description of the measure began as follows: "The constitutional amendment to *limit* the salary. . . ." Poorly informed voters might well have voted to raise legislative salaries while believing they were doing the opposite. In this instance, at least, the legislature's effort at deception failed because the amendment was defeated.

The legislature even manipulates the timing of amendment ratification elections to influence their outcome. In 2003, for example, the legislature passed a constitutional amendment to clarify that the legislature had the constitutional authority to limit the amount of noneconomic damages that a jury could award in a personal injury lawsuit. The legislature adopted the amendment to head off legal challenges against laws limiting the right of individuals to sue over faulty products, personal injuries, or medical malpractice. Instead of scheduling the ratification election for November, when amendment ratification elections are typically held, the legislature set the vote for a Saturday in September. Critics charged that legislative leaders reasoned the amendment would be more likely to pass if it were held in a low-turnout special election in September than it would in November when a Houston city election would bring large numbers of minority voters to the polls that might vote against it. The plan apparently worked because the amendment passed.

Change Through Practice and Experience

Not all constitutional changes result from the adoption of formal amendments. Many of the fundamental features of American national government have developed through practice and experience. Consider the military powers of the president. The U.S. Constitution declares that the president is the commander in chief of the armed forces. To determine what this important constitutional power really entails, however, one must look to its practical application by actual presidents, such as Lincoln during the Civil War or Franklin Roosevelt during World War II. When President George W. Bush commanded the American armed forces to attack Iraq to overthrow the regime of Saddam Hussein, for example, no one seriously questioned the president's constitutional authority to order the military into combat, despite the lack of a congressional declaration of war, because previous presidents had taken similar action.

Because of its detail and specificity, the Texas Constitution has not grown as much through practice and experience as the U.S. Constitution, but some informal changes have occurred. For example, the office of lieutenant governor of Texas, as outlined in the state constitution, resembles that of the vice president of the United

States, which, historically, has been a relatively weak office. In practice, however, the lieutenant governor has become one of the most important policy leaders in the state, far more important in state government than the vice president has been on the national scene. This is an important development in the fundamental structures of Texas government that resulted not from formal amendment but through the informal processes of practice and experience.

Change Through Judicial Interpretation

Many scholars believe that the most important mechanism through which the U.S. Constitution has changed has been judicial interpretation. Federal court rulings have defined constitutional principles in such key policy areas as school integration, voting rights, freedom of expression, freedom of religion, and the rights of persons accused of crimes. Because of the more detailed nature of state constitutions, judicial interpretation has historically been a less significant means for constitutional change at the state level than it has been at the national level. Today, however, this situation may be changing. State courts have begun to play an increasingly important policy-making role through the interpretation of state constitutions, addressing such issues as education funding and gay marriage.

Dedicated funds
Constitutional or statutory provisions that set aside revenue for particular purposes.

Dedicated Highway Fund
A constitutionally earmarked account containing money set aside for building, maintaining, and policing state highways.

Permanent University Fund (PUF) Money constitutionally set aside as an endowment to finance construction, maintenance, and some other activities at the University of Texas, Texas A&M University, and other institutions in those two university systems.

? WHAT IS YOUR OPINION?

Are constitutional amendment ratification elections in Texas so complicated that ordinary citizens cannot make intelligent choices?

Constitutional Revision

Many critics of the Texas Constitution believe that Texas should have a new state constitution. The League of Women Voters, the Texas Bar Association, some public officials, and many political scientists (including most textbook authors) contend that the document is so long and detailed, and so often amended, that most citizens (and even many public officials) do not understand it. A simpler, more straightforward document, they say, would increase respect for, and understanding of, state government.

The most telling criticism of the Texas Constitution is that it hinders the formulation, adoption, and implementation of sound public policy. The legislature is periodically forced to deal with serious budget shortfalls, necessitating spending cuts, tax increases, or a combination of the two. The legislature's ability to set spending priorities, however, is limited by constitutionally **dedicated funds,** which are constitutional or statutory provisions that set aside revenue for particular purposes. For example, the **Dedicated Highway Fund** is a constitutionally earmarked account containing money set aside for building, maintaining, and policing state highways. The **Permanent University Fund (PUF)** is money constitutionally set aside as an endowment to finance construction, maintenance, and some other activities at the University of Texas, Texas A&M University, and other institutions in those two university systems. In preparing the budget, legislators did not have the option of cutting highway funds to avoid a tax increase or diverting construction money from the

The Dedicated Highway Fund is a constitutionally earmarked account containing money set aside for building, maintaining, and policing state highways.

University of Texas and Texas A&M University systems to other colleges and universities because the constitution would not allow it. Similarly, the legislature is limited in its ability to raise revenues by constitutional provisions that prohibit a state property tax, outlaw gambling, and limit the basis for adopting an income tax.

Critics of the Texas Constitution charge that it is loaded with provisions that hinder the operation of efficient government. The governor has insufficient power, they say, to manage the state bureaucracy, the legislature meets too briefly and infrequently to resolve the state's policy problems, and the election of judges makes for a judiciary excessively dependent on interest-group campaign contributions. The critics believe that many of the problems facing the state will not be resolved until the Texas Constitution is significantly revised or rewritten entirely.

Constitutional revision The process of drafting a new constitution.

The most recent efforts at **constitutional revision** (the process of drafting a new constitution) have failed. In 1972, Texas voters approved a constitutional amendment to call a state constitutional convention with members of the legislature serving as convention delegates. The ground rules for the convention required a two-thirds vote of approval for a new constitution, but two-thirds of the legislator-delegates could not agree on a new document. Three years later, the legislature tried to make the best of the situation. After dropping the most controversial items, the legislature divided the rest of the document into a series of amendments to submit to the voters. If the voters approved all of the amendments, the state would effectively have a new constitution.

The campaign for the new constitution was hard fought, with state officials, interest groups, local officeholders, and a host of others getting involved. The proponents—including many state officials, newspaper editorial writers, and scholars—argued that the revision would produce a more efficient and effective state government. In response, the opponents—including many local officials and a number of interest groups—warned that the new constitution would increase the power of state government too much and might well lead to the adoption of a state income tax. In the end, the opponents of the new constitution won big as voters rejected all of the amendments by an overwhelming margin.

In the late 1990s, two respected members of the legislature once again raised the issue of constitutional revision. They proposed a new constitution of only 19,000 words that would be a more general statement of fundamental law than the document it would replace. Their proposed constitution would strengthen the powers of the governor, reorganize the executive branch to reduce the number of elected officials, replace the election of judges with a merit selection process, and reorganize the judicial branch of government. The idea never came to a vote in the legislature, however, because most legislators wanted to avoid having to address controversial issues.

Civil union
A legal partnership between two men or two women that gives the couple all the benefits, protections, and responsibilities under law as are granted to spouses in a traditional marriage.

AROUND THE NATION

Gay Marriage in Massachusetts

Gay couples have been able to marry legally in Massachusetts since May 2004. Gay marriage is the result of a ruling by the Massachusetts Supreme Judicial Court (SJC) holding that the state cannot discriminate against same-sex couples when it issues marriage licenses. The SJC, which is the state's highest court, acted in response to a lawsuit filed by seven same-sex couples. The court ruled that the state lacked a rational basis for denying the couples a marriage license simply based on their desire to marry a person of the same gender. "The Massachusetts Constitution affirms the dignity and equality of all individuals," declared the court. "It forbids the creation of second class citizens."*

The opponents of the decision immediately began an effort to amend the Massachusetts Constitution to overturn the SJC's ruling. The most commonly used procedure for amending the state constitution begins with the legislature passing an amendment by majority vote in two consecutive legislative sessions. The amendment then goes to the voters for approval. In 2004, the Massachusetts legislature voted 105–92

in favor of a state constitutional amendment that would ban gay marriage and establish civil unions. A **civil union** is a legal partnership between two men or two women giving the couple all the benefits, protections, and responsibilities under law as are granted to spouses in a marriage. A year later, however, the legislature rejected the amendment by a lopsided 157–39 vote. Over the preceding year, 6,600 same-sex couples had married uneventfully and the elected officials who supported gay marriage had generally won reelection. In short, the sky had not fallen. A legislator who initially opposed gay marriage but changed his mind to support it explained his decision as follows: "When I look in the eyes of the children living with these couples, I decided that I don't feel at this time that same-sex marriage has hurt the [state] in any way. In fact, I would say that in my view it has had a good effect for the children in these families."†

With the failure of the constitutional amendment in the legislature, the opponents of gay marriage turned to the initiative process. An organization called

Goodridge et al. v. Department of Public Health, SJC-08860 (2003).
†Pam Belluck, "Massachusetts Rejects Bill to Eliminate Gay Marriage," *New York Times*, September 15, 2005, available at www.nytimes.com.

continued on next page

VoteonMarriage.org gathered more than 150,000 signatures to put on the ballot a constitutional amendment to limit future marriages to one man and one woman. (The measure would not annul the same-sex marriages that had already been performed.) The procedure for approving the voter-initiated amendment required that it receive the votes of at least 50 lawmakers in two consecutive legislative sessions, then voter approval in a referendum. The measure won the votes of 61 legislators in early 2007, but it received only 45 votes in the next session held later in the year. Massachusetts opponents of gay marriage would have to start all over if they hoped to amend the state constitution.‡

Gay marriage opponents outside of Massachusetts have proposed an amendment to the U.S. Constitution that would declare that marriage in the United States is limited to the union of a man and a woman. The amendment would overrule any action taken at the state level, including the decision of the SJC. The procedure for amending the U.S. Constitution involves the U.S. House and U.S. Senate voting to propose an amendment by a two-thirds vote. Three-fourths of the states must then agree to ratify the amendment. In 2004 and 2006, the marriage amendment fell well short of the two-thirds margin needed in both the House and the Senate. Gay marriage is now well established in Massachusetts and has spread to several other states, either by state court order or through the legislative process. In 2010, same-sex couples could legally wed in Massachusetts, Connecticut, Maine, Vermont, New Hampshire, Iowa, and the District of Columbia.

QUESTIONS TO CONSIDER

1. The process for amending the Massachusetts Constitution is different from the process for amending the Texas Constitution. Which process do you prefer? Why?
2. Which level of government should decide the issue of gay marriage—the national government or the states? What is the basis of your answer?
3. Do you think gay men and women should be able to marry legally in Texas?

‡Pam Belluck, "Massachusetts Gay Marriage to Remain Legal," *New York Times*, June 15, 2007, available at www.nytimes.com.

INDIVIDUAL RIGHTS AND THE TEXAS CONSTITUTION

Historically, people who believe that their rights have been violated have turned to the federal courts for relief under the U.S. Constitution. During the 1950s and 1960s, in particular, the U.S. Supreme Court acted to protect individuals from racial discrimination, guarantee freedom of expression, and expand the rights of people who were accused of crimes. In *Brown v. Board of Education of Topeka* (1954), for example, the U.S. Supreme Court ruled that state laws that required racial segregation in the public schools violated the U.S. Constitution.[17]

Over the last 40 years, state courts have increasingly become a forum for disputes over individual rights lawsuits filed under the provisions of state constitutions. In America's federal system of government, states must grant their residents all the rights guaranteed by the U.S. Constitution (as interpreted by the Supreme Court). If state governments so choose, however, they may offer their residents *more* rights than those afforded in the U.S. Constitution.[18] Since 1970, state courts around the nation have issued hundreds of rulings providing broader rights than those recognized by the U.S. Supreme Court. The areas in which state courts have been most active are abortion rights, criminal procedures, church/state relations, and gender discrimination.[19]

Equal protection of the law The legal principle that state laws may not arbitrarily discriminate against persons.

In Texas, state courts have relied on the Texas Constitution to expand individual rights in several policy areas involving **equal protection of the law,** the legal principle that state laws may not arbitrarily discriminate against persons. The Texas Supreme Court has held that "similarly situated individuals must be treated equally under [state law] . . . unless there is a rational basis for not doing so."[20] In *Edgewood v. Kirby* (1989), for example, the Texas Supreme Court ruled that the state's system of financing public education violated the Texas Constitution because it resulted in unequal treatment for school children residing in different school districts.[21]

The emergence of the Texas Constitution as an instrument for the protection of individual rights is a relatively recent development. Whether it is a lasting development will depend on the state's judges and the voters who elect them. Will the justices serving on the state's two highest courts, the Texas Supreme Court and the Texas Court of Criminal Appeals, dare to make controversial decisions, considering that they must stand periodically for reelection? Election-minded justices may be eager to rule in favor of school children, but will they be just as willing to uphold the rights of gay men and lesbians, atheists, illegal immigrants, persons accused of crimes, or other individuals and groups who may not be popular with the average Texas voter? Because voters are generally uninformed about judges, a single, highly publicized case can have a major import on a judge's electoral fortunes. Research shows that as Election Day approaches judges bring their rulings in line with public opinion.[22]

WHAT WE HAVE LEARNED

1. **How do state constitutions compare and contrast with the U.S. Constitution?**

State constitutions resemble the U.S. Constitution in some ways, but they differ in other ways. All state constitutions resemble the U.S. document in that they establish a separation of powers system with checks and balances. All but Nebraska are similar to the U.S. Constitution in that they create bicameral legislatures. In contrast to the U.S. Constitution, many state constitutions provide for the election of judges and create a plural executive system. Some state constitutions also include elements of direct democracy. Most state constitutions are younger than the U.S. Constitution. They are also more frequently amended and longer than the federal document. State constitutions also generally include numerous miscellaneous provisions that might be called "super legislation."

2. **What is the historical background of the Texas Constitution?**

Texas has had several constitutions, adopting the first in 1845 and the last, the current document, in 1876. The first Texas Constitution resembled the U.S. Constitution in that it was a general document of basic principles, but other constitutions diverged from the national model. In 1850, Texas amended its constitution to provide for the election of judges, a development that reflected the philosophy of Jacksonian democracy. The Reconstruction era constitution of 1869, the immediate predecessor to the current document, provided for an active government. The Texas Constitution of

1876 was written in reaction to that constitution and Governor E. J. Davis, who served under it.

3. **What were the goals of the majority of delegates at the state constitutional convention of 1875 and how did those goals affect the document they drafted?**

Most delegates at the constitutional convention of 1875 were white Democrats. Many were former Confederates; many were members of the Grange. The delegates wanted to limit the size and scope of state government and to control the excesses of big business. The constitution they wrote restricted the authority of every branch and unit of government. It limited legislative session length and frequency, diluted the power of the governor with the plural executive, and checked the power of the courts by electing judges and creating two supreme courts. The constitution restricted the authority of local government as well. The Texas Constitution included a number of provisions limiting the power of big business, such as a prohibition against branch banking. The framers of the constitution also provided that a family's homestead could not be seized and sold in payment of debt except for delinquent taxes and mortgage payments on a loan taken out to purchase the home itself.

4. **What are the principal features of the Texas Constitution?**

The Texas Constitution, similar to the U.S. Constitution, has a bill of rights, uses separation of powers with checks and balances, and creates a bicameral legislature. The Texas Constitution is far longer than the U.S. Constitution and includes items not included in the latter document, including details about elections and local government.

5. **What are the means through which the Texas Constitution changes?**

Constitutions change by means of formal amendment, practical experience, and judicial interpretation. The Texas Constitution has been amended many times more than the U.S. Constitution. Amendments to the Texas Constitution have strengthened the office of governor, enabled the state to promote economic development, and approved the state going into debt. Amendments are proposed by a two-thirds vote of the Texas House and Texas Senate and then ratified by the voters. The means of constitutional change other than amendment have been less important for the Texas Constitution than they are for the U.S. Constitution. Although many critics of the Texas Constitution favor constitutional revision, efforts to write a new constitution for Texas have not been successful.

6. **What role do Texas courts and the Texas Constitution play in the protection of individual rights?**

Historically, people who believe that their rights have been violated have turned to the federal courts for relief under the U.S. Constitution. Over the last 40 years, state courts have increasingly become a forum for disputes over individual rights lawsuits filed under the provisions of state constitutions. In Texas, state courts have relied on the Texas Constitution to expand individual rights in several policy areas including education in the case of *Edgewood v. Kirby*.

KEY TERMS

bicameral legislature	budget deficit	civil union
bill of rights	budget execution authority	constitution
branch banking	checks and balances	constitutional amendment

constitutional law

constitutional revision

dedicated funds

Dedicated Highway Fund

direct democracy

equal protection of the law

general obligation bonds

Grange

homestead

initiative process

Jacksonian democracy

local-option (wet-dry) elections

long ballot

Permanent University Fund (PUF)

plural executive

Radical Republicans

representative democracy or republic

separation of powers

statutory law

suffrage

Texas Equal Rights Amendment (ERA)

unicameral legislature

NOTES

1. Robert T. Garrett, "Cloud Looms over Texas Budget," *Dallas Morning News*, March 26, 2009, available at www.dallasnews.com.

2. Kelly Shannon, "Casino Supporters Renew Efforts in Texas," *USA Today*, January 19, 2007, available at www.usatoday.com.

3. Christopher W. Hammons, "Was James Madison Wrong? Rethinking the American Preference for Short, Framework-Oriented Constitutions," *American Political Science Review* 93 (December 1999): 837.

4. Lawrence W. Friedman, "An Historical Perspective on State Constitutions," *Intergovernmental Perspective* (Spring 1987), pp. 9–13.

5. Data collected by Janice May, quoted in David C. Saffell and Harry Basehart, *State and Local Government: Politics and Public Policies*, 8th ed. (New York, NY: McGraw-Hill, 2005), pp. 24–26.

6. Alan Greenblatt, "Too Broke to Fix," *Governing*, July 2009, p. 12.

7. Ibid.

8. Friedman, "An Historical Perspective on State Constitutions," pp. 9–13.

9. Hammons, "Was James Madison Wrong?" p. 840.

10. John Walker Mauer, *Southern State Constitutions in the 1870s: A Case Study of Texas*, Ph.D. Thesis, Rice University, Houston, Texas, 1983, p. 152.

11. Ibid.

12. Glenda Taylor, "Going Wet," *Kerrville Daily Times*, February 12, 2005, available at www.dailytimes.com.

13. Friedman, "An Historical Perspective on State Constitutions," pp. 9–13.

14. James C. Harrington, "The Texas Bill of Rights and Civil Liberties," *Texas Tech Law Review* 1487 (1986).

15. Comptroller of Public Accounts, "The 2009 Comprehensive Annual Financial Report of the State of Texas," available at www.windows.state.tx.us.

16. Legislative Reference Library of Texas, "Constitutional Amendments," available at www.lrl.state.tx.us/legis/constAmends/lrlhome.cfm.

17. *Brown v. Board of Education of Topeka*, 347 U.S. 483 (1954).

18. *Pruneyard Shopping Center v. Robins*, 447 U.S. 74 (1980).

19. Jim Kincaid and Robert F. Williams, "The New Judicial Federalism: The States Lead in Rights Protection," in Thad L. Beyle, ed., *State Government: CQ's Guide to Current Issues and Activities 1993-94* (Chapel Hill: University of North Carolina Press, 1993), p. 183.

20. *Whitworth v. Bynum*, 699 S.W.2d 194 (1985).

21. *Edgewood v. Kirby*, 777 S.W.2d 391 (1989).

22. Gregory A. Huber and Sanford C. Gordon, "Accountability and Coercion: Is Justice Blind When It Runs for Office?" *American Journal of Political Science* 48 (April 2004): 247–263.

Chapter 3

The Federal Context
of Texas Policymaking

WHAT WE WILL LEARN

After studying Chapter 3, students should be able to answer the following questions:

▶ What role do states play in the federal system?

▶ How have the U.S. Constitution and the federal courts affected policymaking in Texas, especially concerning the following cases: *Brown v. Board of Education of Topeka, Ruiz v. Estelle,* and *Roe v. Wade?*

▶ How do federal preemptions and federal mandates affect policymaking in Texas?

▶ What are the various kinds of grant programs, and what are the various types of conditions that the federal government places on the receipt of federal funds?

▶ How important are federal programs and federal dollars to state and local governments in Texas?

Recession
An economic slowdown characterized by declining economic output and rising unemployment.

S tate officials rarely turn down federal money, but that is exactly what Texas Governor Rick Perry did when he rejected $555 million in federal funds designed to shore up the state's unemployment compensation system. The money was part of the $787 billion economic stimulus package passed by Congress and signed into law by President Barack Obama in early 2009. The measure contained tax cuts and spending initiatives aimed at helping the economy recover from a serious **recession** (an economic slowdown characterized by declining economic output and rising unemployment). Perry refused the federal money because he said that accepting the money would force the state to change how it calculates worker eligibility and make it extend benefits to more people. "We do not want you in Washington telling us how to run our business here in the state of Texas," Perry exclaimed.[1] If Texas accepted the federal stimulus money, the governor warned, the state would eventually be forced to increase premiums charged to Texas employers after the federal money ran out.

Critics accused Perry of being more interested in scoring political points than he was at helping Texas employees and employers. The changes in the Texas unemployment compensation program required by the federal stimulus program would simply bring the Texas program into line with that of most other states. Furthermore, they said, without the federal stimulus money, Texas would have to increase unemployment insurance contributions paid by employers immediately. Finally, critics charged Perry with hypocrisy because Texas already accepted billions in federal money, including more than $12 billion in federal stimulus dollars for purposes other than unemployment compensation, which it used to balance the 2009–2011 state budget without raising taxes. The critics said that Perry only rejected federal dollars when it suited him politically.[2]

Federal grant program
A program through which the national government gives money to state and local governments to spend in accordance with set standards and conditions.

Unemployment compensation is a **federal grant program,** which is a program through which the national government gives money to state and local governments to spend in accordance with set standards and conditions. Congress established the unemployment compensation program in 1935 when it passed the Social Security Act and President Franklin Roosevelt signed it into law. The purpose of unemployment compensation is to provide financial assistance to people who lose their jobs through no fault of their own. The program also helps maintain consumer spending during a recession. Unemployment compensation is funded through a combination of federal and state taxes assessed on employers. The tax revenues generated in each state go into a fund for that state from which benefits are paid. If the fund runs low, tax rates must be increased to make up the shortfall. After turning down the federal stimulus money in 2009, Texas borrowed $160 million from the federal government so it would have enough money to pay unemployment benefits through the end of the year. The state would begin paying back the federal funds in 2010 after raising the tax rate it charges employers. Had Governor Perry been willing to accept the stimulus money, which did not have to be paid back, Texas would not have had to borrow money and the tax increase imposed on the state's employers would have been smaller.[3]

Unemployment compensation is similar to other federal grant programs in that it allows states the flexibility to administer their own programs within federal guidelines. As a result, unemployment compensation tax rates, eligibility criteria, and benefit levels vary from state to state. The Texas unemployment compensation program is among the stingiest in the country in terms of the number of unemployed workers who can qualify, the level of benefits they receive, and the length of time they can draw benefits. Only 20 percent of unemployed workers in Texas qualify for benefits, compared with an average 37 percent nationwide.[4] By keeping benefit levels low, Texas is able to keep taxes on employers low as well.

However, the recession of 2008–2009 created a financial problem for unemployment compensation programs in Texas and other states. Rising unemployment rates increased the amount of unemployment compensation benefits paid while reducing tax revenues coming into the program. Congress earmarked money to shore up state unemployment compensation programs in the stimulus package it passed in early 2009, but required that states meet certain minimum benefit standards in order to qualify for the money. If Texas accepted the federal money, it could avoid a short-term unemployment compensation tax increase. However, as Governor Perry noted, the changes it would have to make in eligibility standards would drive up the cost of the program in the long run and force a future tax increase on employers.

The controversy over Governor Perry's rejection of federal stimulus money to support the state's unemployment compensation program illustrates the importance of the federal system to state government and introduces this chapter on the federal context of policymaking in Texas. The chapter identifies the role of state and local governments in the federal system of American government. It also explores the impact of the U.S. Constitution and federal courts on state and local governments by examining three important cases in constitutional law. The chapter studies the influence of federal law on state and local policymaking, considering federal preemption of state authority and federal mandates. The chapter describes federal grant programs and examines their influence on the state and local policymaking process. The chapter concludes with a discussion of the impact of federal programs and the federal money on Texas.

ROLE OF THE STATES IN THE FEDERAL SYSTEM

Federal system or federation A political system that divides power between a central government, with authority over the whole nation, and a series of state governments.

Policymaking in Texas takes place within the context of America's federal system of government. A **federal system** or **federal federation** is a political system that divides power between a central government, with authority over the whole nation, and a series of state governments. In a federal system, both the national government and the states enjoy **sovereignty,** which is the authority of a state to exercise legitimate powers within its boundaries, free from external interference. The national government and the states derive their authority not from one another but from the U.S. Constitution. Both levels of government act directly on the people through their officials and laws, both are supreme within their proper sphere of authority, and both must consent to constitutional change.

Sovereignty The authority of a state to exercise legitimate powers within its boundaries, free from external interference.

The national government is constitutionally the dominant partner in the federal system. Article VI of the U.S. Constitution includes a provision known as the **National Supremacy Clause,** which declares that the U.S. Constitution, the laws made under it, and the treaties of the United States are the supreme law of the land. In short, the National Supremacy Clause states that the legitimate exercise of national power supersedes state action when the two conflict. When state and local government policies conflict with the U.S. Constitution or U.S. law, the latter takes precedence.

National Supremacy Clause
A constitutional provision that declares that the Constitution, the laws made under it, and the treaties of the United States are the supreme law of the land.

Local governments
Subunits of states.

Nonetheless, state and **local governments,** which are subunits of states, enjoy considerable policymaking authority. States and localities provide their residents with a wide range of services. The major budget items for state and local governments in Texas and around the nation are education, healthcare, public safety (police and fire protection), and transportation. State and local governments build and repair roads, put out fires, educate young people, spray mosquitoes, vaccinate children, provide parks and recreation facilities, police neighborhoods, operate hospitals, provide water and sewage service, collect garbage, and provide healthcare services for low-income people and persons with disabilities.

State and local governments regulate a wide range of industries, including insurance, finance, oil and gas, and utilities. State governments require business owners to obtain licenses and follow state guidelines in operating their establishments. They license a wide range of professions, including doctors, lawyers, realtors, accountants, nurses, and hairstylists. Cities regulate land use, establish construction codes, and inspect food vendors.

States and localities levy taxes. The most important tax sources for state and local governments nationwide are sales, property, excise, and income taxes. All of these taxes, except the income tax, are important in Texas. Texas is one of only a handful of states that do not levy a personal income tax.

State governments are sometimes called "laboratories of democracy" because they have the ability to adopt innovative solutions to policy problems. If a creative policy approach adopted by one state is deemed successful, other states—and perhaps the national government—will likely adopt similar programs. Since 2006, for example, Massachusetts has been experimenting with a state universal healthcare system. The lessons of the Massachusetts approach, both its successes and failures, helped guide the U.S. Congress as it considered the adoption of a national healthcare reform program in 2009 and 2010.

AROUND THE NATION   Healthcare Reform in Massachusetts

Massachusetts is implementing a healthcare program aimed at providing universal health insurance coverage. The plan, which was passed by the legislature and signed into law by Governor Mitt Romney in 2006, uses a series of penalties and incentives to close the insurance gap. People who can afford health insurance are required to purchase it much the way drivers in Texas and most other states are required to have automobile liability insurance. Individuals who fail to get health insurance must pay a penalty through the state income tax system. In 2009, the penalty for failing to purchase health insurance was a little more than $1,000.* Businesses with at least ten employees are required to provide them with health insurance coverage or face a fine as well. State government subsidizes the cost of health insurance for lower income people based on a sliding scale. A single person earning $40,000 a year is expected to pay no more than 9 percent of his or her income (about $300 a month), whereas a person making $25,000 a year is expected to pay a smaller

*Kevin Sack, "Massachusetts Faces Cost of Big Health Care Plan," *New York Times,* March 15, 2009, available at www.nytimes.com.

percentage, a little more than 3 percent of his or her income ($70 a month).[†]

The Massachusetts plan has succeeded in expanding healthcare coverage but failed to control healthcare costs. It has also produced at least a temporary shortage of physicians. The program has reduced the proportion of Massachusetts residents without insurance to less than 3 percent of the population, the lowest uninsured rate in the nation.[‡] As a result, Massachusetts physicians, especially family physicians, have been inundated with new patients. An American Medical Association (AMA) survey finds that people in Boston face the longest wait time to see a physician among people living in metropolitan areas nationwide.[§] Furthermore, the Massachusetts plan has failed to control healthcare costs. Between 2007 and 2009, the cost of the program to the state increased from $630 million to $1.3 billion, a rate of increase that cannot be sustained over the long run. Massachusetts government is considering a new round of reforms aimed at controlling healthcare costs.[**]

QUESTIONS TO CONSIDER

1. Who should be responsible for providing individual health insurance coverage—the individual, private employers, or the government?
2. Is it right for the government to force healthy young people who do not think they need health insurance to purchase coverage?
3. Should the U.S. Congress adopt a national health insurance program modeled on the Massachusetts plan? Why or why not?

[†]Sharon K. Long and Paul B. Masi, "Access and Affordability: Update on Health Reform in Massachusetts, Fall 2008," available at www.consumerwatchdog.com.

[‡]Massachusetts Division of Health Care Finance and Policy, *Health Care in Massachusetts: Key Indicators,* February 2009, available at www.mass.gov/Eeohhs2/docs/dhcfp/r/pubs/09/key_indicators_02-09.pdf.

[§]Susan J. Landers, "Long Appointment Waits May Signal Doctor Shortage," *American Medical News,* June 1, 2009, available at www.ama-assn.org.

[**]Sack, "Massachusetts Faces Cost of Big Health Care Plan."

STATES, THE COURTS, AND THE CONSTITUTION

The U.S. Constitution is the supreme law of the land. It takes legal precedence over state constitutions, state laws, state administrative procedures, and the actions of local government. State and local officials pledge to uphold the U.S. Constitution and most of them take that responsibility quite seriously. When the legislature considers changes in the state's capital punishment law, for example, the debate frequently centers on the likelihood that any proposed revision will survive a constitutional challenge. Individuals and groups who believe that the policies of state and local government violate the U.S. Constitution may file suit in federal court, asking the court to intervene. We can illustrate the importance of federal court rulings on policymaking in Texas by examining three historic cases: *Brown v. Board of Education of Topeka, Ruiz v. Estelle,* and *Roe v. Wade.*

School Desegregation

Brown v. Board of Education of Topeka (1954) dealt with the constitutionality of state laws requiring racially segregated schools. The Brown family, residents of Topeka, Kansas, wanted their daughter, Linda, to attend a public school near their home.

However, Kansas state law required separate schools for white and African American youngsters. Because the school nearest the Brown home was for whites only, Linda, who was African American, would have to travel across town to another school. With the legal support of the **National Association for the Advancement of Colored People (NAACP),** which is an interest group organized to represent the interests of African Americans, the Browns filed suit against the state. They charged that the law requiring a racially segregated public school system violated the **Equal Protection Clause,** the constitutional provision found in the Fourteenth Amendment of the U.S. Constitution that declares "No State shall . . . deny to any person within its jurisdiction the equal protection of the laws."

The U.S. Supreme Court ruled that the state law was unconstitutional because it denied equal educational opportunities to African American students. "Segregation of white and colored children in public schools has a detrimental effect upon the colored children," wrote Chief Justice Earl Warren in the Court's opinion. "A sense of inferiority affects the motivation of the child to learn."[5]

Brown v. Board of Education of Topeka ultimately had a profound impact on policymaking in Texas. Even though the case involved a state law in Kansas, the precedent set by the Supreme Court in its ruling applied to all similar statutes throughout the United States. As was true for most southern states, Texas had a **dual school system,** that is, separate sets of schools for white and African American youngsters. Because of the *Brown* case, the state was eventually forced to dismantle its dual school system and adopt policies aimed at achieving racial integration of public schools.

Prison Overcrowding

Ruiz v. Estelle (1972) addressed the issue of living conditions in the Texas Department of Corrections (TDC). In 1972, a group of prison inmates filed suit in federal court, claiming that living and working conditions in Texas prisons constituted "cruel and unusual punishment," forbidden by the Eighth Amendment to the U.S. Constitution. They charged that the state's prison system was severely overcrowded, the prison staff was too small to maintain security, working conditions were unsafe, disciplinary procedures were severe and arbitrary, and medical care was inadequate.

In 1980, Federal District Judge William Wayne Justice ruled against the state of Texas, ordering sweeping changes in the Texas prison system. Although an appeals court later overturned part of Judge Justice's ruling, it upheld the key points of his decision. Eventually, the state settled the suit by agreeing to limit the inmate population to 95 percent of prison capacity, separate hardcore offenders from inmates convicted of nonviolent crimes, improve the guard-to-inmate ratio, and upgrade inmate medical treatment.[6]

The *Ruiz* case forced Texas to limit its prison population. Initially, the state responded with early release, turning offenders out on **parole,** which is the conditional release of convicted offenders from prison to serve the remainder of their sentences in the community under supervision. In the long run, the state complied with the court's decision to reduce overcrowding by dramatically increasing the capacity of its prison system.

Linda Brown and her family were the plaintiffs in the *Brown v. Board of Education of Topeka* case, in which state laws requiring racial segregation in public schools were ruled to be unconstitutional.

Abortion

Roe v. Wade (1973) dealt with the issue of abortion. "Jane Roe," an anonymous woman living in Dallas, challenged the constitutionality of a Texas law prohibiting abortion except to save the life of a woman. The U.S. Supreme Court found the Texas statute unconstitutional, saying that a woman's right to personal privacy under the U.S. Constitution included her decision to terminate a pregnancy within six months of conception.

The Supreme Court explained the ruling by dividing a pregnancy into three trimesters. During the first trimester (a three-month period), state governments could not interfere with a physician's decision, reached in consultation with a pregnant patient, to terminate a pregnancy. In the second trimester, a state could regulate abortion only to protect the health of the woman. In the third trimester, after the fetus had achieved viability (the ability to survive outside the womb), the Court

GETTING INVOLVED

Contacting Your Representative in Washington, DC

In America's federal system of government, individuals are citizens of the United States and citizens of the state in which they live. If you live in the Lone Star State, for example, you are both an American citizen and a citizen of Texas. You receive services, pay taxes, and are subject to the laws and regulations of both the national government and the state of Texas.

American citizens have the constitutional right to participate in the policymaking process of both the national government and their state government. They may vote in both national and state elections and contact their elected representatives at both levels of government to make their policy preferences known.

The names, postal addresses, and e-mail addresses of the people who represent you in Congress are available online. The website for the U.S. Senate is www.senate.gov, and the website for the U.S. House is www.house.gov. Each site has an interactive window that enables you to identify the name of your representatives. You can also find contact information. Write or e-mail your U.S. senators and U.S. representative, expressing your point of view on any federal or national issue about which you have an opinion.

It's your country—get involved!

---

ruled that states could choose to prohibit abortion except when necessary to preserve the life or health of the woman.[7]

In subsequent cases, the Supreme Court modified its ruling in *Roe v. Wade* to allow states greater leeway to limit abortion rights. Although the Court reaffirmed a woman's right to choose to abort a fetus before viability, it ruled that a state could regulate access to abortion as long as the regulations did not place an "undue burden" on a woman's right to choose. The Court's majority defined an undue burden as one that presented an "absolute obstacle or severe limitation" on the right to decide to have an abortion. State regulations that simply "inhibited" that right were permissible.[8]

The Texas legislature and the governor have taken advantage of the Supreme Court's flexibility on state abortion regulation by adopting the following measures:

- **Parental consent for minors**—A physician may not perform an abortion on an unmarried girl younger than 18 without the written permission of a parent or guardian. However, the consent requirement can be waived if a judge determines that involving a parent could put the minor at risk of physical or emotional abuse or that the girl seeking an abortion is sufficiently mature to make the decision herself.

- **24-hour waiting period**—Before performing an abortion, a physician must provide a pregnant patient with a state-created packet that includes information on the health risks associated with abortion, alternatives to terminating a pregnancy, and color images of fetal development. The woman must then wait 24 hours before having the abortion.

- **Late-term abortion prohibition**—A physician may not perform an abortion on a woman who has carried a fetus more than 26 weeks unless the woman's life is in jeopardy or the fetus has serious brain damage.

Roe v. Wade and other court cases dealing with abortion rights affected Texas law by restricting the state's ability to adopt policies controlling access to abortion. Before *Roe*, the state was free to adopt any policy ranging from legalization of abortion in most circumstances to the prohibition of abortion in almost all circumstances. Because of *Roe*, abortion is now legal in every state, including Texas, whether legislators and governors like it or not. In 2007, Texas physicians performed 81,079 abortions compared with 405,376 live births.[9]

The data indicate that the Texas parental consent requirement may be reducing the number of abortions performed on minors. After Texas began enforcing the consent requirement, the abortion rate fell by 11 percent for 15-year-olds, 20 percent among 16-year-olds, and 16 percent among 17-year-olds. Ironically, the second-trimester abortion rate increased for 18-year-olds who became pregnant within six months of their eighteenth birthday, suggesting that some 17-year-olds were waiting to seek abortion services until they were no longer covered by the parental consent requirement.[10]

 WHAT IS YOUR OPINION?

Do you agree with the Texas law that forces a minor to have the written permission of a parent before she can have an abortion? Why or why not?

STATES AND FEDERAL LAW

Federal laws apply to state and local governments as long as Congress acts within the scope of its powers under the U.S. Constitution. Article I, Section 8, of the Constitution grants Congress authority to legislate in a range of policy areas, including trade, immigration, patent and copyright law, and national defense. In practice, Congress has made frequent use of the Interstate Commerce Clause as a basis for legislation affecting the states. The **Interstate Commerce Clause** is the constitutional provision giving Congress the authority to "regulate commerce . . . among the several states." Congress has used this constitutional provision as a basis for legislation dealing with such diverse subjects as cable television regulation, agricultural price supports, and racial discrimination.

Interstate Commerce Clause The constitutional provision giving Congress authority to "regulate commerce . . . among the several states."

The federal laws and regulations that have the greatest impact on state and local policymaking take the form of federal preemption and federal mandates. Federal preemption *prevents* states from adopting their own policies in selected policy areas, whereas federal mandates *require* certain state policy actions.

Federal Preemption

Federal preemption of state authority An act of Congress adopting regulatory policies that overrule state policies in a particular regulatory area.

The federal government prevents state and local governments from making policy in some policy areas. An act of Congress adopting regulatory policies that overrule state policies in a particular regulatory area is known as a **federal preemption of state authority.** Congress has passed more than a hundred laws preempting state regulation, including preemption of state policies dealing with cellular phone rates, nuclear power safety, pension plans, automobile safety standards, and trucking rates.[11]

Preemption is controversial, however. The proponents of preemption believe that uniform national regulatory standards are preferable to state-by-state regulation. In contrast, critics of preemption contend that congressional efforts to override state authority violate states' rights principles that hold that state officials know best what policies are most appropriate for their states.

Ironically, business interests, which often oppose regulation in general, frequently support the federal preemption of state regulations. Firms doing business nationwide would rather adapt to a uniform national policy than conform to 50 different state regulations. As one state official put it, "A lot of . . . companies feel it is easier to work with Congress than 50 state legislatures."[12] Business interests would also prefer that Congress adopt a relatively mild nationwide regulatory standard than deal with tough regulations at the state level.

Federal Mandates

Federal mandate
A legal requirement placed on a state or local government by the national government requiring certain policy actions.

A **federal mandate** is a legal requirement placed on a state or local government by the national government requiring certain policy actions. The **Americans with Disabilities Act (ADA),** a federal law intended to end discrimination against persons with disabilities and to eliminate barriers preventing their full participation in American society, imposes a broad range of federal mandates. The ADA mandates that, when a new building goes up or an old building undergoes a major renovation, it must be made accessible to people with disabilities, and accommodations must be made for employees with disabilities. Because of the ADA, colleges and universities typically provide special assistance to students with disabilities, such as sign-language interpreters for students who have hearing impairments and additional time to take exams for students with learning disabilities.

Americans with Disabilities Act (ADA)
A federal law intended to end discrimination against disabled persons and eliminate barriers preventing their full participation in American society, imposes a broad range of federal mandates.

State and local government officials often resent federal mandates because they are sometimes so detailed that they force states to abandon their own policy approaches in favor of a one-size-fits-all federal prescription. Consider the **Real ID Act,** a federal law designed to ensure that states issue driver's licenses only to people who are in the country legally. Congress passed, and President George W. Bush signed, the measure in 2005 to combat terrorism and reduce identity theft. The Real ID Act establishes national standards for state-issued driver's licenses and identification cards for non-drivers. To get or renew a license, applicants must provide state officials with the following:

Real ID Act
A federal law designed to ensure that states issue driver's licenses only to people who are in the country legally.

- A photo ID with their full legal name and date of birth;
- Documentation of their date of birth, such as a birth certificate;
- Documentation of legal status and Social Security number, such as a visa, naturalization papers, or an original Social Security number card; and
- Documentation showing their name and the address of their principal residence.

States are required to verify the authenticity of every document and store the information they gather in a database linked to the databases of other states.[13]

The ADA mandates that public buildings be made accessible to persons with disabilities.

State officials nationwide are worried that the requirements of the Real ID Act will overwhelm their capacity to issue driver's licenses. State residents, who will be required to apply in person for license renewals every five years, will likely face long lines and increased cost. If the state passes along the expense of complying with the Real ID Act to consumers, the cost of a license renewal could exceed $100.[14] Every state, including Texas, has requested and been granted an extension for complying with the act until May 11, 2011.[15] States that fail to create databases and link them to other states by the deadline will lose federal funding. Furthermore, state residents who do not have an ID that meets federal standards by May 2013 will be unable to board an airplane, enter a federal building, get a job, or do banking business.

State officials complain about cost shifting from the federal government to the states. The war on terror, for example, has become a major drain on the finances of state and local government. Because the nation's cities, power plants, bridges, refineries, and monuments are potential targets for terrorists, state and local authorities have been forced to increase security. They have also had to invest millions of dollars in training and equipment for police officers, fire fighters, and other emergency responders, so that they will be ready in case of an attack. State officials believe that the cost of homeland security should be borne by the national government because national security has historically been a federal function. Nonetheless, the federal government has shifted most of the cost of homeland security to the states.

The National Conference of State Legislatures (NCSL) estimates that federal mandates cost the states $33.7 billion in 2008.[16] The most expensive programs for the states were the Disabilities Education Act, No Child Left Behind, prescription drug costs for people eligible for Medicaid or Medicare, the Help America Vote Act, federal environmental protection requirements, and the cost to states of incarcerating illegal immigrants.[17] The federal government projects the cost to states of implementing the Real ID Act at $23 billion spread over several years.[18] Texas officials anticipate that Real ID will cost the state $107 million.[19]

FEDERAL GRANT PROGRAMS

Federal grant programs are a major component of state and local government finances. In 2009, the federal government distributed $537 billion in federal grant money to state and local governments, which made up 15.3 percent of federal outlays.[20] Nearly 90 percent of the funds went directly to state governments rather than localities, although much of that money was passed on by the state to local agencies for health and human services, housing and urban development, transportation, and education.[21]

Program Adoption

Congress and the president adopt federal grant programs through the legislative process. Both houses of Congress must agree to establish a program and the president must either sign the legislation or allow it to become law without signature. If the president vetoes the measure, it can become law only if Congress votes to override the veto by a two-thirds margin in each house.

Authorization process
The procedure through which Congress legislatively establishes a program, defines its general purpose, devises procedures for its operation, specifies an agency implementation, and indicates an approximate level of funding.

Appropriation process
The procedure through which Congress legislatively provides money for a particular purpose.

Federal programs must be authorized and funds appropriated for their operation. The **authorization process** is the procedure through which Congress legislatively establishes a program, defines its general purpose, devises procedures for its operation, specifies an agency for implementation, and indicates an approximate level of funding. However, the authorization process does not actually allocate money for the program. Congress sometimes specifies that programs be reauthorized periodically. The **appropriation process** is an annual procedure through which Congress legislatively provides money for a particular purpose.

The adoption of the Help America Vote Act of 2002 illustrates the distinction between authorization and appropriation. Congress passed, and President George W. Bush signed, the measure to reform state election systems after the debacle of the Florida presidential election controversy in 2000. The law requires states to maintain a database of registered voters, provide voting systems with minimum error rates, set voter identification requirements, provide access for people with disabilities, and adopt procedures for resolving voter complaints.[22] Although the measure authorized $4 billion to cover the cost of new voting machines and other improvements, Congress failed to include the money in the annual appropriation bill, leaving the states to bear the cost of the measure on their own.[23]

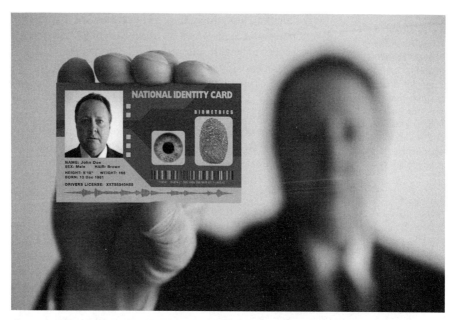

The Real ID Act establishes national standards for state-issued driver's licenses and identification cards for nondrivers.

Types of Federal Programs

Federal programs come in a variety of forms.

Categorical and Block Grants A **categorical grant program** is a federal grant-in-aid program that provides funds to state and local governments for a fairly narrow, specific purpose, such as removing asbestos from school buildings or acquiring land for outdoor recreation. In this type of program, Congress allows state and local officials little discretion as to how money is spent. Categorical grants comprise more than 90 percent of all federal grants and provide nearly 90 percent of federal grant money to state and local governments.[24]

A **block grant program** is a federal grant-in-aid program that provides money for a program in a broad, general policy area, such as elementary and secondary education or transportation. State and local governments have more discretion in spending block grant funds than they have for categorical grant money. For example, **Temporary Assistance for Needy Families (TANF)** is a federal block grant program that provides temporary financial assistance and work opportunities to needy families. The goal of the program is to move welfare families into the workforce. States have considerable leeway in designing their own programs, but if they fall short of federally mandated goals, such as the requirement that half of single parents receiving benefits must participate in a work activity program, they lose some federal funding.

Over time Congress tends to attach conditions to the receipt of block grant funds, thus reducing the flexibility of state and local officials. When Congress and

Categorical grant program
A federal grant-in-aid program that provides funds to state and local governments for a fairly narrow, specific purpose, such as removing asbestos from school buildings or acquiring land for outdoor recreation.

Block grant program
A federal grant-in-aid program that provides money for a program in a broad, general policy area, such as elementary and secondary education, or transportation.

Temporary Assistance for Needy Families (TANF)
A federal block grant program that provides temporary financial assistance and work opportunities to needy families.

the president created the Surface Transportation Program in 1991, for example, they gave states a lump sum of money to spend on highways and other transportation projects in accordance with statewide objectives. Subsequently, Congress and the president have added restrictions requiring that 10 percent of the funds be used to improve the safety of state highways and that 10 percent be spent on "transportation enhancement" activities, such as hike and bike trails.[25]

Policymakers disagree about the relative merits of categorical and block grants. The proponents of categorical grants argue that they enable Congress to identify particular policy problems and ensure that the money that Congress provides targets those problems. Categorical grants, they say, allow Congress to set national goals and apply national standards to achieve those goals. If local officials are given too much discretion, they may use grant money to reward campaign supporters or pay back political debts. In contrast, the proponents of block grants contend that state and local officeholders know better what their residents want and need than do officials in Washington, DC. Block grants enable the officials closest to the people to direct the federal dollars to where they will do the most good.

 WHAT IS YOUR OPINION?

If you were a member of Congress, would you prefer block grants or categorical grants?

Entitlement programs
Government programs providing benefits to all persons qualified to receive them under law.

Entitlement Programs Some federal programs, such as Medicaid and the School Lunch Program, are **entitlement programs.** These government programs provide benefits to all persons qualified to receive them under law. Congress sets eligibility standards based on such factors as age, income, and disability. Individuals who meet the criteria are entitled to receive the benefits. **Medicaid** is a federal program designed to provide health insurance coverage to low-income persons, people with disabilities, and elderly people who are impoverished. The **School Lunch Program** is a federal program that provides free or reduced-cost lunches to children from poor families.

Medicaid
A federal program designed to provide health insurance coverage to low-income persons, people with disabilities, and elderly people who are impoverished.

Spending for entitlement programs does not go through the appropriation process. The amount of money the federal government spends each year on Medicaid and other entitlement programs depends on the number of eligible recipients who apply for benefits and the cost of providing those benefits. If Congress and the president want to reduce (or increase) spending for an entitlement program, they must pass legislation to change the program.

School Lunch Program
A federal program that provides free or reduced-cost lunches to children from poor families.

Entitlement programs are controversial. The proponents of entitlement programs say that they represent a national commitment to address certain important policy issues, including healthcare for the poor and for people with disabilities (Medicaid) and nutritious lunches for low-income school children (the School Lunch Program). Program recipients do not have to depend on Congress and the president to appropriate money each year for their benefits because they are entitled to them by law. In contrast, the critics of entitlement programs charge that they are budget busters. Spending for entitlement programs goes up each year automatically as the number of beneficiaries rises and the cost of providing services increases, regardless of the budgetary situation. For example, state governments are hard pressed to keep up with the rapidly rising costs of the Medicaid program.

Project and Formula Grants Federal grants differ in the criteria by which funding is awarded. A **project grant program** is a grant program that requires state and local governments to compete for available federal money. State and local governments present detailed grant applications, which federal agencies evaluate in order to make funding decisions. The Department of Education, for example, administers project grants dealing with a range of educational initiatives, such as teacher training, math and science education, and the preparation of students for the demands of today's workforce. Public schools, colleges, and universities make application to the agency, which then decides which grant proposals merit funding.

A **formula grant program** is a grant program that awards funding on the basis of a formula established by Congress. In contrast to project grants, formula grants provide money for every state and/or locality that qualifies under the formula. The Clean Fuels Formula Grant Program, administered by the Department of Transportation, allocates money to transit authorities to assist in the purchase and use of low-emissions buses and related equipment. The program awards funds based on a formula that includes area population, the size of the bus fleet, the number of bus passenger miles, and the severity of the area's air pollution problem.[26]

Grant Conditions

Federal grants usually come with conditions. A **matching funds requirement** is a legislative provision that the national government will provide grant money for a particular activity only on the condition that the state or local government involved supply a certain percentage of the total money required for the project or program. The **State Children's Health Insurance Program (SCHIP),** a federal program designed to provide health insurance to children from low-income families whose parents are not poor enough to qualify for Medicaid, gives money to states based on a 75–25 match. The federal government picks up 75 percent of the cost, leaving only 25 percent to the states.[27] Even federal programs that do not require financial participation by state and local governments often require contributions in-kind. The national government covers the entire cost of the Supplemental Nutrition Assistance Program, which was once called the Food Stamp Program. This federal program provides vouchers to low-income families and individuals that can be used to purchase food; however, state governments must administer its operation.

Congress imposes legislative mandates on the recipients of federal funds. Some mandates apply to grant recipients in general. These include provisions in the area of equal rights, equal access for people with disabilities, environmental protection, historic preservation, and union wage rates for construction workers on federally funded projects. Furthermore, many individual programs have particular strings attached. For example, in order to receive money from the Violent Crime Control and Enforcement Act of 1994 to construct, expand, and operate correctional facilities,

Project grant program
A grant program that requires state and local governments to compete for available federal money.

Formula grant program
A grant program that awards funding on the basis of a formula established by Congress.

Matching funds requirement
A legislative provision that the national government will provide grant money for a particular activity only on condition that the state or local government involved supply a certain percentage of the total money required for the project or program.

State Children's Health Insurance Program (SCHIP)
A federal program designed to provide health insurance to children from low-income families whose parents are not poor enough to qualify for Medicaid.

states have to adopt "truth in sentencing" laws that accurately show the amount of time persons convicted of crimes spend behind bars. States must ensure that violent criminals serve at least 85 percent of their prison sentences. The federal government also requires states to impose stiff penalties for criminal offenders and adopt programs to protect the rights of crime victims.[28]

Congress sometimes uses federal grant money to compel states to adopt policies favored in Washington, although not necessarily in state capitals. In 1987, for example, Congress threatened states with the loss of federal highway grant money unless they adopted the 55 miles-per-hour speed limit and raised their minimum legal drinking age to 21. Although Congress dropped the speed limit requirement in 1995, it now requires that states ban open containers in vehicles and revoke the driver's licenses of repeat DUI offenders. If states fail to comply with these requirements, the federal government transfers a portion of their highway construction money into a fund that can be used only for highway safety.[29]

The School Lunch Program is a federal program that provides free or inexpensive lunches to children from poor families.

Congress initially took an incentive approach to setting a national blood-alcohol content standard of 0.08 for determining whether a driver is legally intoxicated. Although some states already followed the 0.08 standard, most states, including Texas, set the drunk-driving level at a blood-alcohol content of 0.10. Instead of penalizing states that failed to adopt the 0.08 standard with the loss of federal money, Congress established a fund to pay a cash bonus to states that voluntarily adopted the tougher blood-alcohol standard. Two years later, however, Congress decided that the incentive plan was not working well enough, so it adopted legislation mandating the loss of highway funds for states that failed to adopt the 0.08 standard. Although most states (including Texas) complied with the federal requirement rather than risk the loss of highway funding, state officials complained about Congress forcing its policy preferences on the states. "If states want 0.08, that's fine," said an Iowa legislator, "[but] if Congress says you have to have it, they've [sic] overstepped their bounds."[30]

Environmental Protection Agency (EPA)
The federal agency responsible for enforcing the nation's environmental laws.

States that fail to follow federal rules risk the loss of federal funds. The **Environmental Protection Agency (EPA),** the federal agency responsible for enforcing the nation's environmental laws, says that both the Houston and Dallas-Fort Worth metropolitan areas fail to meet federal air-quality standards for ozone, which is the principal ingredient of smog. Regions that fail to meet federal deadlines for ozone standards—which fall between 2013 and 2030, depending on the severity of the problem in an area—can lose funding for transportation projects.[31]

FEDERAL MONEY AND TEXAS

State and local governments in Texas receive billions of dollars in federal funds annually. In 2009, federal grant money represented one-third of total state revenue ($28 billion out of nearly $83 billion in revenue generated from all sources), despite Governor Perry's rejection of federal money designed to bolster the unemployment compensation system. Federal dollars helped fund healthcare, highway construction, welfare, and education.[32] Billions of federal dollars flowed to local governments for special education programs, school lunches, urban transit projects, parkland acquisition, neighborhood revitalization, sewage treatment plants, and other purposes. Furthermore, Congress included billions of dollars worth of special projects for states and localities in the annual appropriation bill.

Pork barrel spending
Expenditures to fund local projects that are not critically important from a national perspective.

Critics call these projects **pork barrel spending,** which are expenditures to fund local projects that are not critically important from a national perspective. The 2009 appropriation bill contained more than $2 billion in special projects for Texas, including money for a fitness center at Fort Bliss, Houston Ship Channel improvements, and state cultural programs.[33]

Figure 3.1 documents the growth in federal aid to state government in Texas between 1990 and 2009. The relative importance of federal funding to state government in Texas grew from 1990 through 2003, increasing from less than 26 percent in 1990 to 36 percent in 2003. Since then, the relative importance of federal money has somewhat declined to about one-third of total state revenue. Growth in the Medicaid program accounted for more than 40 percent of the increase in federal grant funds in the 1990s and early years of the twenty-first century, but it was not the only federal program to grow. Funding for three-fourths of federal programs increased during the 1990s, including money for programs dealing with natural resources and the environment, transportation, community and regional development, income security, and education and training.[34]

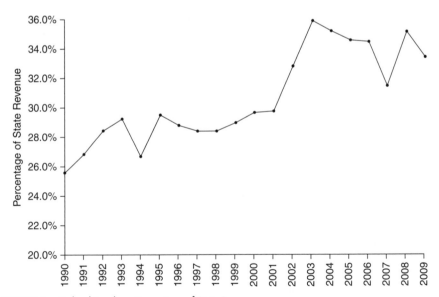

FIGURE 3.1   Federal Funds as Percentage of State Revenue.

WHAT WE HAVE LEARNED

1. **What role do states play in the federal system?**

   Texas is part of the federal system, which is a political system that divides power between a central government, with authority over the whole nation, and a series of state governments. Although the national government is the dominant partner in the federal system, state and local governments enjoy considerable policymaking authority to provide services, enact regulations, and levy taxes.

2. **How have the U.S. Constitution and the federal courts affected policymaking in Texas, especially concerning the following cases: *Brown v. Board of Education of Topeka*, *Ruiz v. Estelle*, and *Roe v. Wade*?**

   The U.S. Constitution takes legal precedence over state constitutions, state laws, state administrative procedures, and the actions of local government. Individuals and groups who believe that the policies of state and local government violate the U.S. Constitution may file suit in federal court, asking the court to intervene. *Brown v. Board of Education of Topeka* (1954) dealt with the constitutionality of state laws requiring racially segregated schools. Because of it, Texas was forced to dismantle its dual school system and racially integrate its public schools. *Ruiz v. Estelle* (1972) addressed the issue of living conditions in the Texas Department of Corrections (TDC). Because of it, Texas was forced to alleviate overcrowding in the state prison system. *Roe v. Wade* (1973) dealt with the issue of abortion. It restricted Texas's ability to adopt policies controlling access to abortion.

3. **How do federal preemptions and federal mandates affect policymaking in Texas?**

   Federal laws apply to state and local governments as long as Congress acts within the scope of its powers under the U.S. Constitution. Federal preemption *prevents* states from adopting their own policies in selected policy areas, whereas federal mandates *require* certain state policy actions. Congress has passed more than a hundred laws preempting state regulation, including preemption of state policies dealing with cellular phone rates, nuclear power safety, pension plans, automobile safety standards, and trucking rates. The ADA and the Real ID Act are examples of federal mandates.

4. **What are the various kinds of grant programs, and what are the various types of conditions that the federal government places on the receipt of federal funds?**

   Congress and the president adopt federal grant programs through the legislative process. Programs must be authorized and money appropriated for their operation. Federal programs may come in the form of categorical grants or block grants. Some federal programs, such as the School Lunch Program, are entitlement programs. Programs may be project grant programs or formula grant programs. Federal programs also come with strings attached, including matching funds requirements. States that fail to meet federal standards, such as air quality standards, may lose federal funding.

5. **How important are federal programs and federal dollars to state and local governments in Texas?**

   State and local governments in Texas receive billions of dollars in federal funds annually. Federal dollars help fund healthcare, highway construction, welfare, and education. The importance of federal funding to state and local budgets has been increasing despite some high profile rejections of federal dollars by Governor Rick Perry.

KEY TERMS

Americans with Disabilities
Act (ADA)

appropriation process

authorization process

block grant program

categorical grant program

dual school system

entitlement programs

Environmental Protection
Agency (EPA)

Equal Protection Clause

federal grant program

federal mandate

federal preemption of state
authority

federal system or federation

formula grant program

Interstate Commerce Clause

local governments

matching funds requirement

Medicaid

National Association for the
Advancement of Colored
People (NAACP)

National Supremacy Clause

parole

pork barrel spending

project grant program

Real ID Act

recession

School Lunch Program

sovereignty

State Children's Health
Insurance Program (SCHIP)

Temporary Assistance for
Needy Families (TANF)

NOTES

1. Quoted in Jason Embry and Kate Alexander, "Perry Will Fight Stimulus Dollars for Unemployment," *Austin American-Statesman*, March 13, 2009, available at www.statesman.com.

2. Dave Mann and Susan Peterson, "The Governor's Job Con," *Texas Observer*, April 17, 2009, pp. 16–18.

3. R. G. Ratcliffe, "State Gets Jobs Loan from Feds," *Houston Chronicle*, June 13, 2009, pp. A1, A8.

4. Mann and Peterson, "The Governor's Job Con," p. 17.

5. *Brown v. Board of Education of Topeka*, 347 U.S. 483 (1954).

6. *Ruiz v. Estelle*, 503 F. Supp 1265 (S.D. Tex 1980); 679 F 2d 115 (5th Cir. 1982).

7. *Roe v. Wade*, 410 U.S. 113 (1973).

8. *Planned Parenthood of Southeastern Pennsylvania v. Casey*, 505 U.S. 833 (1992).

9. Texas Department of State Health Services, "Vital Statistics," available at www.dshs.state.tx.us.

10. Theodore Joyce, Robert Kaestner, and Silvie Colman, "Changes in Abortions and Births and the Texas Parental Notification Law," *New England Journal of Medicine* 354 (March 2006): 1031–1038.

11. Joseph F. Zimmerman, "The Nature and Political Significance of Preemption," *PS: Political Science & Politics*, July 2005, p. 361.

12. Idaho Attorney General Jim Jones, quoted in Martha M. Hamilton, "On Second Thought, We'd Prefer the Feds on Our Backs," *Washington Post National Weekly Edition*, December 14, 1987, p. 32.

13. Public Law 109-13.

14. State Senator Leticia Van de Putte, Media Advisory, available at www.vandeputte.senate.state.tx.us.

15. Department of Homeland Security, "Real ID: States Granted Extensions," available at www.dhs.gov.

16. National Conference of State Legislatures, "Mandate Monitor," available at www.ncsl.org.

17. Molly Stauffer and Carl Tubbesing, "The Mandate Monster," *State Legislatures*, May 2004, pp. 22–23.

18. Suzanne Gamboa, "Senators Call for Real ID Overhaul," *Dallas Morning News*, March 27, 2007, available at www.dallasnews.com.

19. Peggy Fikac, "Delaying Fed Read ID Program Drops Cost in Texas," *Houston Chronicle*, March 12, 2008, available at www.chron.com.

20. Office of Management and Budget, "Summary Comparison of Total Outlays for Grants to State and Local Governments: 1940–2015," *The Budget for Fiscal Year 2011, Historical Tables*, available at www.omb.gov.

21. "Federal Aid to States and Localities," *Governing State and Local Source Book, 2006*, p. 32.

22. Public Law 107-252.

23. Alan Greenblatt, "Squeezing the Federal Turnip," *Governing*, March 2003, p. 29.

24. Larry N. Gerston, *American Federalism: A Concise Introduction* (Armonk, NY: M.E. Sharpe, 2007), p. 69.

25. Transportation Equity Act for the Twenty-first Century, available at www.fhwa.dot.gov.

26. Department of Transportation, "Fact Sheet: Clean Fuels Formula Grant Program," available at www.fhwa.dot.gov/tea21/factsheets/clnfuel.htm.

27. Colleen M. Grogan and Elizabeth Rigby, "Federalism, Partisan Politics, and Shifting Support for State Flexibility:

The Case of the U.S. State Children's Health Insurance Program," *Publius: The Journal of Federalism* 39 (Winter 2009): 47–69.

28. Public Law 103-322.

29. Lilliard E. Richardson, Jr. and David J. Houston, "Federalism and Safety on America's Highways," *Publius: The Journalism of Federalism* 39 (Winter 2009): 117–137.

30. Anya Sostek, "Slow to Toe the DUI Line," *Governing*, May 2003, p. 42.

31. Matthew Tresaugue, "EPA's Smog Rules to Get Stiffer," *Houston Chronicle*, March 12, 2008, available at www .chron.com.

32. Texas Comptroller of Public Accounts, "Biennial Revenue Estimate, 2010–2011," available at www.windows.state.tx.us.

33. Bennett Roth and Patrick Brendel, "Texas Reaps $2.2 Billion in Earmarks," *Houston Chronicle*, March 23, 2008, pp. A1, A6.

34. Robert J. Dilger, "The Study of American Federalism at the Turn of the Century," *State and Local Government Review* 32 (Spring 2000): 100.

Chapter 4

Political Participation

WHAT WE WILL LEARN

After studying Chapter 4, students should be able to answer the following questions:

▶ What is the history of voting rights for women, Latinos, and African Americans in Texas?

▶ What are the ways that individuals can participate in the policymaking process?

▶ How do voter participation rates in Texas compare with rates in other states, and what is the explanation for the difference?

▶ How do political participation rates vary based on income, age, race/ethnicity, and gender?

▶ How does the Texas electorate compare with the state's total population in terms of income, education, and age?

Should Texans be required to prove their identities with a photo identification card before being allowed to cast a ballot? Almost every Republican member of the Texas legislature answers that question with a resounding "YES!!!" The state needs a voter ID law, they say, to prevent fraud and enhance public confidence in the integrity of elections. The Republicans point out that people are routinely asked for a photo ID when they pay bills with a check, complete a bank transaction, or board an airplane. Why not require similar identification for something as important as voting?

In contrast to the Republicans who enthusiastically embrace voter ID, almost every Democratic member of the Texas legislature adamantly opposes the idea. The Democrats believe that the Republicans are pushing the adoption of a photo identification law in order to suppress Democratic voter turnout. Many elderly low-income people, especially minority citizens who typically vote Democratic, do not have a driver's license or other forms of picture identification and may lack the means to travel to a Texas Department of Public Safety office to apply for a state-issued photo ID card. A voter ID law would turn them away from the polls. Furthermore, the Democrats point out that the Republicans have failed to establish that voter impersonation is a problem in Texas elections. They note that both Attorney General Greg Abbott and the district attorney of Bexar County conducted extensive criminal investigations into possible voter fraud without uncovering more than a handful of isolated cases, most of which involved absentee balloting, which would not be addressed by a voter ID law.[1] Ironically, the only criminal charges brought as a result of the Bexar County investigation were filed against two U.S. citizens who lied about their citizenship status to get out of jury duty.[2]

The controversy over voter ID introduces this chapter, the first of four chapters dealing with participation in the policymaking process in Texas. Each chapter considers who participates in the policymaking process, how participation takes place, and what effect participation has on policy. This chapter examines individual political participation in Texas, focusing primarily on voting and voting rights. The chapter considers forms of participation, rates of participation, patterns of participation, and compares the electorate with the general population. Chapter 5 looks at interest groups, Chapter 6 considers political parties, and Chapter 7 deals with elections.

 WHAT IS YOUR OPINION?

If you were a member of the Texas legislature, would you vote in favor of a voter ID law? Why or why not?

VOTING RIGHTS AND MINORITY PARTICIPATION

Only white males enjoyed the right to vote when Texas joined the Union in 1845. Much of the subsequent history of the state is the story of the efforts of women and the members of racial and ethnic minority groups to gain the right to vote and participate meaningfully in Texas politics.

Women's Suffrage

In the nineteenth century, politics was a man's world, not just in Texas but in the entire United States. The women's rights movement emerged in the northern states in the 1840s as an offshoot of the abolition movement, a political reform effort in early nineteenth century America whose goal was the elimination of slavery. In Texas, the weakness of the abolition movement hindered the cause of women's rights. The drive for women's **suffrage** (the right to vote) did not begin to pick up steam in Texas until 1903 with the founding of the Texas Woman Suffrage Association. In 1915, the state legislature narrowly rejected an amendment to the Texas Constitution calling for women's suffrage. Three years later, the legislature approved a law allowing women to vote in primary elections. Finally, in 1919, the U.S. Congress proposed a constitutional amendment granting women the right to vote nationwide. Texas was the first state in the South to ratify the Nineteenth Amendment, which became law in 1920, giving women in Texas and across America the right to vote.[3]

Suffrage The right to vote.

Minority Voting Rights

Winning the right to vote and having that vote counted was a more elusive goal for Texans of African and Hispanic descent than it was for women.

African American Enfranchisement After the Civil War Before the Civil War, nearly all African Americans who lived in Texas were slaves; none could vote or hold public office. Slavery ended with the Confederate defeat, but the state's white political establishment refused to enfranchise former slaves. (**Franchise** is the right to vote; to **enfranchise** means to grant the right to vote.) The Texas Constitution of 1866, written under President Andrew Johnson's Reconstruction plan, denied African Americans the right to vote and hold public office. The U.S. Congress, however, refused to accept the Johnson plan for Reconstruction. In 1867, Congress passed legislation over Johnson's veto that placed the South under military rule and forced southern states to grant African Americans the right to vote.

Franchise The right to vote.

Enfranchise To grant the right to vote.

African Americans registered to vote for the first time in Texas in 1867. The following year, they cast ballots in an election to select delegates to a state constitutional convention. Of the 90 delegates chosen, nine were African American men, all of whom were Republicans. In 1869, African American voters helped elect E. J. Davis governor. In the same election, 11 African Americans won seats in the state legislature.

After the early 1870s, Texas politics began to return to the pattern in place before the Civil War. The Democratic Party regained control of the legislature in the 1872 election and recaptured the governor's mansion in the following year. Meanwhile, some white Texans organized chapters of the Ku Klux Klan to threaten and intimidate African American leaders. The Klan sometimes even resorted to violence to assert white control.

Nonetheless, African Americans continued to participate in Texas politics. Six African Americans were among the delegates elected to the constitutional convention of 1875. Furthermore, with the exception of the legislature elected in 1887, all legislatures chosen from 1868 through 1894 included African American members. All told, 41 African Americans served in the Texas legislature between 1868 and 1900.[4]

Minority Disfranchisement In the early twentieth century, the white establishment in Texas restricted the voting rights of minorities in order to maintain political power. After Reconstruction, Texas was a one-party state. The Democratic Party, which was controlled by wealthy economic interests, held virtually every elective office in the state. The political establishment used **disfranchisement,** the denial of voting rights, as a response to the Populist Party's attempt to win power by uniting lower-income voters of all races against the wealthy economic interests that controlled state politics. Conservative political leaders in Texas (and throughout the South) used racial issues to divide the working class along racial lines. They hoped to ensure their long-term control of state government by disfranchising African Americans (as well as many poor whites and Latinos).[5]

Disfranchisement
The denial of voting rights.

The poll tax and the white primary were the main instruments of disfranchisement. The **poll tax,** a tax prospective voters had to pay in order to register to vote, kept low-income people of all races from voting. In 1902, the Texas legislature proposed, and the voters approved, a state constitutional amendment requiring a poll tax of $1.50 or $1.75 a year (depending on the county), not an insignificant sum in early twentieth-century Texas. (In today's value, the poll tax would be $36 or $41.) Before the implementation of the poll tax, more than 60 percent of voting-age Texans typically participated in presidential elections. In contrast, once the poll tax went into effect, election turnout dipped to 30 percent of voting-age adults in 1904.[6]

Poll tax A tax that prospective voters had to pay in order to register to vote.

The **white primary,** an election system that prohibited African Americans from voting in Democratic primary elections, ensured that white voters would control the Democratic Party. In 1903, the state Democratic Party executive committee suggested that all county party committees exclude African Americans from party primary elections. A **primary election** is an intra-party election during which a party's candidates for the general election are chosen. By the 1920s, most counties with significant African American populations were using the white primary, and in 1924 the Texas legislature adopted the procedure statewide. Because the Democratic Party dominated Texas politics in those days, the Democratic primary was the most important election in the state. Whoever won the primary election invariably won the general election. Consequently, the exclusion of African Americans from participation in the Democratic primary barred them not only from having an influence in Democratic Party politics but also from meaningful participation in Texas politics in general.

White primary
An election system that prohibited African Americans from voting in Democratic primary elections, ensuring that white voters would control the Democratic Party.

Primary election
An intra-party election during which a party's candidates for the general election are chosen.

Boss Control in South Texas Although the white primary did not keep Latinos from the ballot box, political bosses often controlled their votes. In heavily Hispanic South Texas, in particular, ranch owners (some of whom were Latino) controlled both local economies and local politics. The boss would pay the poll tax for his workers (most of which were Latino) and then instruct them how to vote. With their jobs depending on it, the workers had little choice but to do as they were told.

Texans once had to pay a poll tax in order to register to vote.

Many Texans know the story of George Parr, the so-called Duke of Duval County, which is located in South Texas just west of Corpus Christi. For years, Parr ran Duval County as his own political kingdom. The most famous example of Parr's influence occurred in 1948 when a young member of Congress named Lyndon B. Johnson ran for the U.S. Senate against former governor Coke Stevenson. Parr supported Johnson, but the day after the election it appeared that Stevenson had won the statewide vote by a razor-thin margin. One ballot box remained uncounted, however, Box 13 in neighboring Jim Wells County, where Parr's influence extended. Johnson won Box 13 almost unanimously and "Landslide Lyndon" became an 87-vote winner. Remarkably, 200 voters at Box 13 arrived to cast their ballots in alphabetical order. The affair still inspires deathbed confessions.[7]

The Struggle for Minority Voting Rights African Americans in Texas turned to the federal courts for help in regaining the right to vote. Lawrence A. Nixon, an El Paso physician, challenged the constitutionality of the Texas White Primary Law in federal court. In 1927, the U.S. Supreme Court unanimously struck down the law as a "direct and obvious infringement" of the Equal Protection Clause of the Fourteenth Amendment to the U.S. Constitution.[8]

The Texas legislature responded to the ruling by repealing the White Primary Law and replacing it with a statute allowing the executive committee of each political party to "prescribe the qualifications of its own members." The executive committee of the Texas Democratic Party then declared that only whites could vote in

Democratic primary elections. Dr. Nixon again carried the fight to the U.S. Supreme Court and once again the Court invalidated the Texas law. The vote on the Court was close, however—five to four.[9]

Next, the legislature repealed all laws dealing with primary elections, and the Texas Democratic Party declared itself a private organization whose membership was exclusively white. Only party members could vote in Democratic primary elections. African Americans again turned to the federal courts, with Richard R. Grovey, a Houston barbershop owner, filing suit. This time, however, the courts refused to help. In 1935, the U.S. Supreme Court unanimously upheld the white primary on grounds that the state of Texas was not involved. The Court ruled that the Fourteenth Amendment did not apply to the Democratic Party because the party was a private organization.[10]

The white primary survived until 1944 when the U.S. Supreme Court decided *Smith v. Allwright*, reversing its earlier ruling. This case involved a suit brought by Lonnie Smith, a Houston dentist who was an African American community leader and political activist. The Court ruled eight to one that the Democratic Party acted as an agent of the state when it conducted primary elections. Consequently, the Court declared, the exclusion of African Americans from the Democratic primary was an unconstitutional violation of the Fifteenth Amendment to the U.S. Constitution, which grants African Americans the right to vote.[11]

Although the white primary was history, other forms of voting discrimination persisted. In Fort Bend County, for example, white officials arranged a whites-only pre-primary called the Jaybird primary. White voters would cast their ballots for the winner of the Jaybird primary in the regular Democratic primary, thus minimizing the impact of the African American vote. The U.S. Supreme Court overturned this procedure in 1953.[12]

The poll tax was the next barrier to fall. In 1962, the U.S. Congress proposed a constitutional amendment to prohibit poll taxes in elections for the presidency or Congress. When it was ratified as the Twenty-fourth Amendment in 1964, the Texas poll tax could be collected only for state and local elections. Two years later, the U.S. Supreme Court struck that down as well as a violation of the Equal Protection Clause of the Fourteenth Amendment.[13] The poll tax was thus just as dead as the white primary.

The Texas legislature and the governor responded to the loss of the poll tax by establishing the most difficult and restrictive system of voter registration in the nation. Prospective voters had to register between October 1 and January 31 each year. Anyone who lacked the foresight to sign up three months before the spring primaries and nine months before the November general election was out of luck. In practice, this system worked against poor persons of all races. It survived until 1971 when, as with so many other Texas election procedures, it was struck down by the federal courts.[14]

Many Texas Democrats believe that the Republican push to enact a voter ID law represents an attempt to return to the bad old days of minority voter suppression, but their concerns may be overblown. Political scientists have researched the effect of voter ID laws in other states that have adopted legislation similar to that proposed in Texas. Although one study finds that voter ID reduces turnout by 3 to 4 percent, most studies find that the laws have no impact on voter participation. They also indicate that voter ID laws have no effect on reducing fraud or enhancing confidence in election procedures. Ironically, voter ID laws apparently have little impact on the electoral process despite the emotion surrounding their adoption.[15]

FORMS OF PARTICIPATION

Individual Texans can participate in the policy process in a number of ways: voting, campaigning, joining political groups, contacting public officials, and participating in protest demonstrations and unconventional political acts.

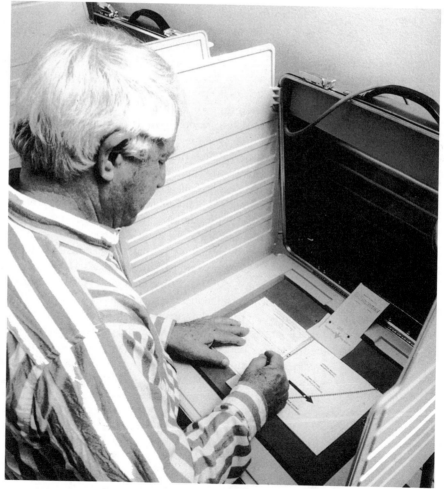

Voting is the most common form of political participation.

Voting

To vote in Texas, individuals must be 18 years of age as of the next election, American citizens (native-born or naturalized), and residents of Texas. Newcomers need not wait to establish residency; anyone who has a Texas home address is eligible to vote, including students who may be living in the state temporarily to attend college. Persons who have been declared mentally incapacitated by the final judgment of a court of law are disqualified from voting. Individuals who have been convicted of serious crimes (felonies) lose the right to vote as well, at least temporarily. Convicted criminals in Texas are eligible to vote again after they have fully completed their sentences, including time served on probation or parole. (**Probation** is the suspension of a sentence, permitting the defendant to remain free under court supervision, whereas **parole** is the conditional release of convicted offenders from prison to serve the remainder of their sentences in the community under supervision.)

Individuals must register before they can vote. Registration becomes effective 30 days after an application is received, so prospective voters must apply at least a month before the election in which they want to cast a ballot. Either the county tax assessor-collector's office or, in smaller counties, the county clerk or an election administrator handles voter registration. Voter registration applications are readily available in driver's license offices, libraries, and other government offices and public places. They are printed in both English and Spanish, easy to complete, and require only a person's name, gender, birth date, address, court of naturalization (if applicable), and signature. Voter registration applications are available online as well at the following Internet address: **https://webservices.sos.state.tx.us/vrapp/index.asp**.

Voter registration is permanent as long as citizens keep their addresses current with county election officials. People who change addresses within the same county may return to their old polling place to vote for 90 days after their move. Every two years, however, county election officials mail out new voter registration certificates and purge the voter rolls of the names of people who are no longer at their listed addresses. Consequently, people who move must take the initiative to report changes of address in order to remain registered. Texans who relocate from one county to another must register again in their new county of residence. People who lose their voter certificates can request replacements from county election officials.

Voters cast their ballots in **election precincts** (voting districts) near their homes. Rural counties may have only a handful of precincts, but urban counties have hundreds. Harris County, the state's most populous county, has more than 850 election precincts. Precinct polling places are typically located in public buildings, such as schools or fire stations. Newspapers usually print a list of polling locations a day or so before an election. Prospective voters can also learn the polling place for their election precinct by telephoning the county clerk's office or checking a county website.

Texas is one of 27 states that permit **early voting,** which is a system that allows citizens to cast ballots before Election Day.[16] State law once limited early voting (formerly called absentee voting) to individuals who planned to be out of town on the day of the election or at least *said* they planned to be out of town—some people voted absentee in order to avoid election-day lines. In 1987, the legislature revised the election code to allow people to vote early without having to give an explanation,

Probation The suspension of a sentence, permitting the defendant to remain free under court supervision.

Parole The conditional release of convicted offenders from prison to serve the remainder of their sentences in the community under supervision.

Election precinct An election district.

Early voting A system that allows citizens to cast ballots before Election Day.

and many Texans now take advantage of no-excuse early voting. The period for early voting begins 17 days before an election and ends 4 days before. Locations for early voting may be limited to the county clerk's office at the courthouse or a handful of branch offices located throughout the county.

It is also possible to vote early by mail. Individuals who expect to be out of the county on the day of the election and during the early voting period may write the county clerk's office and request a mail ballot. People age 65 and older and those who are disabled or ill may vote by mail as well. Students away at school have the option of voting by mail or registering and voting in the county where they attend classes. Two-thirds of Texans who voted in the 2008 presidential election cast their ballots early or in absentee voting, up from 51 percent who voted early in 2004.[17]

Early voting affects both the composition of the electorate and the strategy of election campaigns. Research shows that early voting increases election turnout by less physically active older adults who might have difficulty getting to the polls on Election Day.[18] With so many people casting their ballots early, early voting has turned Election Day into an election period, forcing candidates to advertise earlier and perhaps longer than they did before the popularity of early voting.[19] Candidates can also take advantage of early voting by organizing early get-out-the-vote (GOTV) drives. Because state law requires election officials to keep a running list of who has voted early and who has not, campaigns can concentrate on getting people to the polls who are most likely to be their supporters. Politically active people are more likely to take advantage of early voting than people who are less involved politically.[20]

Campaigning

People take part in politics by working on election campaigns. Although this is the age of television campaigns and the Internet, volunteers still have a place in election campaigns. Under-financed campaigns can often compensate for a lack of money with well-organized volunteer efforts. Many local election contests rely almost exclusively on volunteers. Even well-funded campaigns can put volunteers to good use in contacting prospective voters and encouraging them to go to the polls.

Campaigns ask volunteers to do work that demands energy and attention to detail. Volunteers often help with mass mailings. Although campaign professionals believe that direct mail is an effective means for getting a candidate's message across, sending letters and campaign literature to thousands of potential voters is a huge job. Computers can do the work, but that approach is expensive. Consequently, many campaigns use volunteers to flare envelopes, fold literature, stuff the literature into envelopes, seal the envelopes, affix address labels, and bundle the envelopes for mailing.

There is almost no end to the work volunteers perform in an election campaign. They assemble yard signs and distribute them to the candidate's supporters. They answer office telephones and deliver soft drinks and snacks to other volunteers. (One of the cardinal rules of a successful campaign is to feed the volunteers.) They build and develop candidate Internet sites and Facebook pages for the candidate. They may even compose Twitter messages on the candidate's behalf. On Election Day, volunteers drive people who lack transportation to the polls and pass out campaign literature outside polling places.

Some Texans participate in political campaigns by giving money to support the political party and the candidates they favor. Money is critical to electoral success. Although the best-funded candidates do not always win, poorly funded candidates almost always lose. Candidates can raise the money they need to compete successfully by soliciting small contributions from thousands of individuals or huge sums of money from a few contributors. Wealthy individuals can become major players in Texas politics by giving generously to candidates they favor. In 2006, for example, Houston homebuilder Bob Perry of Perry Homes contributed more than $7 million to various candidates for statewide office and the legislature. San Antonio businessman James Lieninger gave $5.5 million. Houston attorney John O'Quinn contributed more than $1 million to one candidate, Chris Bell, the Democratic nominee for governor.[21]

Other Forms of Participation

Voting and campaigning are not the only ways individuals take part in politics. People participate by working through a group. One person casting a single ballot or working alone for a candidate is not as effective as a group of people working together. Many Texans make their voices heard by taking part in such political organizations as the National Rifle Association (NRA), Mothers Against Drunk Driving (MADD), and the League of United Latin American Citizens (LULAC). The **National Rifle Association (NRA)** is an interest group organized to defend the rights of gun owners and defeat efforts at gun control. **Mothers Against Drunk Driving (MADD)** is an interest group that supports the reform of laws dealing with drunk driving. The **League of United Latin American Citizens (LULAC)** is a Latino interest group.

People participate in the policy process by contacting government officials. Citizens may send e-mail messages to their state legislators or telephone city council members. Individuals may speak before the board of trustees of the local school district or community college.

Some Americans participate in politics by engaging in protest demonstrations, rallies, and marches. Some Texans participate in political rallies and demonstrations such as those organized by the **Tea Party movement,** a loose network of conservative activists organized to protest high taxes, excessive government spending, and big government in general. The activists take their inspiration from the Boston Tea Party of 1773 when American colonists protested the British tax on tea by dumping three shiploads of tea into Boston harbor. TEA is also an acronym for "taxed enough already." As long as protestors do not break the law (by blocking traffic, for example), they are acting legally within the spirit and the letter of the U.S. Constitution.

Finally, some people go beyond peaceful protest to engage in acts of political violence, including the bombing of abortion clinics and the destruction of property. Although political violence will draw attention to a cause, it is often counterproductive because it provokes a backlash. Most mainstream anti-abortion groups, for example, dissociate themselves from individuals who advocate violence against abortion providers because they believe that violence undermines their cause with mainstream voters. Furthermore, people who commit violent acts or destroy property may face criminal prosecution as ordinary criminals.

National Rifle Association (NRA) An interest group organized to defend the rights of gun owners and defeat efforts at gun control.

Mothers Against Drunk Driving (MADD) An interest group that supports the reform of laws dealing with drunk driving.

League of United Latin American Citizens (LULAC) A Latino interest group.

Tea Party movement A loose network of conservative activists organized to protest high taxes, excessive government spending, and big government in general.

AROUND THE NATION

Mail Voting in Oregon

Oregon conducts all of its primary and general elections by mail. Election officials mail ballots to registered voters from 18 to 14 days prior to the election. A voter marks the ballot in blue or black ink and places it in an unmarked envelope; the voter then places the first envelope in a second envelope. The voter signs the outer envelope and either mails it or drops it off at the county election office. Voters have until the day of the election to return their ballots.*

Oregon election officials believe that mail balloting has increased voter participation. In 1996, approximately 1.4 million Oregon voters cast ballots for president the old-fashioned way, in person and by traditional absentee ballot. The figure represented 71 percent of the state's registered voters. In contrast, the 2008 presidential election turnout was 1.8 million, 86 percent of registered voters.†

Mail balloting is popular with Oregon voters. Nearly three-fourths of the state's voters tell survey researchers that they prefer voting by mail to traditional in-person voting. Younger adults and voters over the age of 50 are the biggest supporters of the new system. They like mail balloting not only because it is

convenient, but also because it gives them time to discuss races with their friends and family before deciding how to vote.‡ Voting by mail also saves the state from having to hire hundreds of poll workers.§

Research on the impact of mail voting in Oregon finds that it has increased participation by about 10 percent in congressional and presidential elections, without affecting the partisan profile of the electorate.** Women, young people, persons with disabilities, and homemakers report that they are more likely to take part in elections with mail voting than they were using traditional voting methods because they find the new system more convenient. The reform has had no apparent effect on the party balance in the electorate or on candidate preferences.††

QUESTIONS TO CONSIDER

1. Do you see any disadvantages to voting by mail?
2. Would you like to vote by mail rather than in person?
3. Do you think Texas and other states will adopt a mail voting system like the Oregon procedure?

*Don Hamilton, "The Oregon Voting Revolution," *The American Prospect*, May 2006, pp. A3–A7.

†Oregon Secretary of State, available at www.sos.state.or.us.

‡Dave Scott, "Ways to Turn Out Voters," *State Government News*, February 2000, pp. 18–19.

§Josh Goodman, "Pushing the Envelope," *Governing*, May 2008, pp. 40–41.

**Sean Richey, "Voting by Mail: Turnout and Institutional Reform in Oregon," *Social Sciences Quarterly* 89 (December 2008): 902–915.

††Priscilla L. Southwell, "Five Years Later: A Re-Assessment of Oregon's Vote by Mail Electoral Process," *PS: Political Science & Politics* (January 2004): 89–93.

PARTICIPATION RATES IN TEXAS

Voting age population (VAP)
The number of state residents who are 18 years of age or older.

Many adult Texans do not vote, even in high profile elections. Figure 4.1 summarizes participation in the 2008 presidential election in Texas. The Texas **voting age population (VAP),** which is the number of state residents who are 18 years of age or older, was 17.7 million people in 2008. The VAP is not the best basis for measuring voter turnout, however, because it includes non-citizens, prison inmates, and others

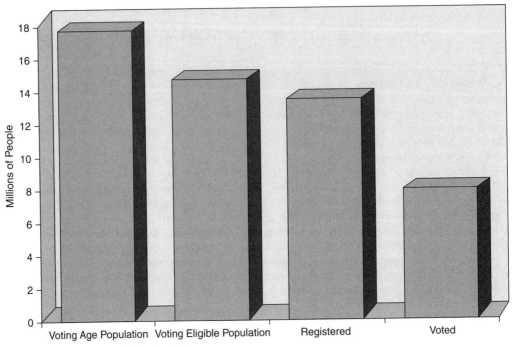

FIGURE 4.1   Participation in 2008 Election in Texas.

Voting eligible population (VEP)
The number of state residents who are eligible to vote.

who are not eligible to vote. A better measure is the **voting eligible population (VEP),** which is the number of state residents who are eligible to vote. Professor Michael McDonald estimates that the Texas VEP was 14.8 million people in 2008. Of that number, 13.6 million (92 percent of the voting-age population) were registered to vote. Voter turnout, meanwhile, was 8.1 million (55 percent of voting-age adults). Turnout in lower profile contests is less than it is in presidential races. Voter participation in the 2007 constitutional amendment election, for example, was only 7 percent of the VEP.[22]

Compared with other states, the level of political participation in Texas is relatively low, at least in terms of voter turnout. Although voting is not the *only* form of participation, it is the most common form and the most easily measured. Figure 4.2 traces voter turnout in Texas and the United States as a percentage of the VEP in the 2000, 2004, and 2008 presidential election years. Voter turnout increased in 2004 and 2008 in Texas and the United States as a whole, but in each year voter turnout in Texas lagged behind the national average by five to seven percentage points. In 2008, Texas had the fifth lowest turnout in the nation.[23]

Political scientists identify several factors that may account for the relatively low rate of political participation in the state. High levels of participation are associated with older, better-educated populations with relatively high incomes. Compared with other states, income levels in Texas are lower, the age distribution is

FIGURE 4.2   Voter Turnout, United States and Texas, 2000–2008.

younger, and levels of educational achievement are below average. All of these factors are related to lower levels of political participation.

The weakness of political parties and labor unions in Texas may be associated
with relatively low levels of voter turnout. Strong parties and unions are able to educate citizens about politics and motivate them to participate politically.[24] They recruit voters. Political parties in Texas are generally less well organized than parties in
many other states. Furthermore, labor unions in Texas are weaker than unions in the
Northeast and Midwest.

The relatively high percentage of recent immigrants to Texas may help account
for the state's low participation rates. In general, newcomers to an area need a few
years to settle into their new communities before becoming active in state and local
political affairs. People vote because they are concerned about their communities,
and new residents take time to identify with their new communities.[25] Newcomers
to an area must also take the time to register to vote. Furthermore, many of the state's
immigrants are not yet American citizens and therefore are ineligible to vote.

Finally, in recent presidential elections, Texas has not been a **battleground state,**
which is a swing state in which the relative strength of the two major party presidential candidates is close enough so that either candidate could conceivably carry the
state. In 2008, for example, neither the Barack Obama nor the John McCain presidential campaigns devoted resources to turning out the vote in Texas because they
both acknowledged that McCain would carry the state, which he did. Many Texans
were caught up in the excitement of the campaign because they followed it in the media. However, unlike the residents of battleground states, they were not subjected to
aggressive get-out-the-vote (GOTV) efforts by the major campaigns.

Battleground state
A swing state in which
the relative strength
of the two major
party presidential
candidates is close
enough so that either
candidate could
conceivably carry
the state.

GETTING INVOLVED

Become a Volunteer Deputy Voter Registrar

You can do more to influence the policymaking process than registering to vote and casting your own ballot. By becoming a volunteer deputy voter registrar, you can register other people to vote—your friends, family, and fellow students; members of your religious group; and even strangers walking through a shopping mall. If you are 18 years old and have never been convicted of failing to deliver a voter application to a voter registrar, you are qualified to become a deputy voter registrar. Visit the voter registrar in your county (whose location can be found online at: **www.sos.state.tx.us/elections/voter/votregduties.shtml**) and ask to become a deputy registrar. The clerk will give you voting application materials, swear you in

as an official deputy voter registrar, issue you a certificate of appointment, and give you a receipt book. You may then distribute and collect a voter registration application from any resident of the county who is eligible to vote. You may also accept updated registration information from registered voters who have changed addresses. Once you have collected completed voter registration applications, you must deliver them to the voter registrar within five days of receiving them. A conscientious deputy voter registrar can register hundreds of potential voters, more than enough to change the outcome of a close local election.

It's your government—Get involved!

PATTERNS OF PARTICIPATION

Exit polls Surveys based on random samples of voters leaving the polling place.

Participation rates vary among individuals based on income, age, and race/ethnicity. Middle- and upper-income groups participate at a higher rate than lower-income groups. According to **exit polls,** which are surveys based on random samples of voters leaving the polling place, 64 percent of Texas voters in 2008 had annual household incomes in excess of $50,000. Nearly half of the Texas electorate earned more than $75,000 a year.[26] In contrast, the median household income in the state is less than $45,000 a year.[27]

Political participation increases with age until advanced age and ill health force the elderly to slow down.[28] National surveys show that voter participation rates among younger adults are 20 or 30 percentage points lower than those for older citizens.[29] Young people have fewer resources and are less interested in the policy process than are older adults. As adults mature, their incomes increase and their skills develop. In addition, older adults establish roots in their communities that increase their interest and awareness of the political process.

The overall participation rates for blacks and whites are similar, whereas the participation rates for Latinos are substantially lower than they are for other racial and ethnic groups. According to the U.S. Census Bureau, the population of Texas is 48 percent white, 36 percent Latino, and 12 percent African American.[30] In contrast, the 2008 electorate in Texas was 63 percent white, 20 percent Latino, and 13 percent African American.[31] Whites are significantly over-represented at the ballot box, whereas Latinos are dramatically underrepresented.

Racial/ethnic patterns of participation reflect the importance of recruitment to political participation. We would expect that participation rates for African American and Latino citizens would be lower than participation rates for whites because of

Minority voters made up a third of the Texas electorate in 2008.

income and age differences. As a group, minority citizens are less affluent and younger than whites. Nonetheless, participation rates for African Americans exceed expectations because of the effectiveness of organizations in the African American community, such as churches and political groups, at stimulating participation. Latino voter turnout, meanwhile, increases when Latino candidates are on the ballot.[32]

Although men and women are equally likely to vote, men are more likely than women to engage in other forms of political participation. Women comprised 53 percent of the Texas electorate in 2008, reflecting the gender distribution of the state's adult population.[33] Women and men are also equally likely to participate in election campaigns. In contrast, women are less likely than men to contribute money to political campaigns, to contact public officials, and to join political organizations.[34]

INTERNET RESEARCH

Tracking Election Turnout

The Texas electorate is shifting from the state's big cities to the suburbs. Students can research turnout patterns using data available at the website of the Texas Secretary of State: **http://www.sos.state.tx.us/**. Point your mouse at the "Elections and Voter Information" link. Scroll down to "Election Returns" and click. Then, select the link, "Voter Registration Figures—County History." Your assignment is to research voter turnout

continued on next page

figures in the presidential election years of 1992 and 2008 for five Texas counties—the two largest counties in the state (Harris and Dallas) and three of the state's more rapidly growing suburban counties (Collin, Montgomery, and Fort Bend). Use the data to complete the following table:

County	Voter Turnout in 1992 (no. of voters)	Voter Turnout In 2008 (no. of voters)	Pct. Increase 2008 over 1992
Harris Co.			
Dallas Co.			
Collin Co.			
Montgomery Co.			
Fort Bend Co.			

Figure the percentage increase by subtracting the voter turnout in 1992 from turnout in 2008 to find the number of additional voters in the latter year. Then divide that number by turnout in 1992 to find the percentage increase between 1992 and 2008. Once you have completed the table, answer the following questions:

1. Did voting participation increase more rapidly in the urban counties (Harris and Dallas) or the suburban counties (Collin, Montgomery, and Fort Bend) between 1992 and 2008?
2. Does the growth of voter turnout in suburban counties reflect recent population growth patterns in the state?
3. Would you expect the residents of suburban counties to have different policy preferences than the residents of urban areas? On what sorts of issues would they differ?

PARTICIPATION AND REPRESENTATION

Political scientists Robert A. Jackson, Robert D. Brown, and Gerald C. Wright have published research comparing the population of each state with those people who vote. To what degree, they ask, does the electorate resemble the adult population of the state in terms of income, education, and age? Jackson, Brown, and Wright use a 100-point scale to show the results of their study. If the state's electorate has the same proportion of poor people as its population, the income score for that state is 100. A score of 75 indicates that the state's electorate includes only 75 percent as many low-income people as the state's population.

Table 4.1 compares the scale scores for Texas with the national mean for the 50 states. Voters as a group are wealthier, better educated, and older than the state's adult population. This is true not only in the Lone Star State but also in other states. The Texas electorate, however, is less representative of the state population than the average state electorate, especially in terms of income and education. The proportion of poor people in the electorate in Texas is only 50 percent as large as it is in the state's adult population. The comparable figure for the average state is 67 percent. In

TABLE 4.1   Representation Based on Income, Education, and Age

Population Characteristic	Texas	Mean of 50 States
Income	50	67
Education	46	58
Age	43	47

Source: Robert A. Jackson, Robert D. Brown, and Gerald C. Wright, "Representation, Turnout, and the Electoral Representativeness of U.S. State Electorates," *American Politics Quarterly* 26 (July 1998): 259–287.

sum, the poor are underrepresented among voters in all states, but they are more underrepresented in Texas than in the average state.[35]

The overrepresentation of older whites and underrepresentation of younger Latinos is even greater in low-turnout contests than it is in presidential elections. Professor Bob Bezdek, a political scientist at Texas A&M University-Corpus Christi, studies political participation in Corpus Christi. He has found that the electorate for relatively low participation races, such as a city election, is not just smaller than it is for presidential contests but also older and more likely to be white. According to the U.S. Census Bureau, the average resident of Corpus Christi is a low-income 33-year-old Hispanic woman, probably with a high school education. In contrast, Bezdek estimates that the average voter in a Corpus Christi city election is a 58-year-old white man, probably a property owner with at least a few years of college.[36]

The underrepresentation of Texans who are poor and minority is the legacy of the state's long history of public policies designed to limit the right to vote to middle-class and upper-income white people. The white primary, poll tax, and restrictive voter registration requirements all discouraged or prevented poor Texans from registering to vote. Although federal intervention has forced the state to expand its electoral system to broad-based participation, the legacy of exclusion still affects voter turnout today. For example, parents who could not vote were unable to serve as participation role models for their children. Adult Texans who grew up in households with adults who could not vote are less likely to participate politically than are citizens who were raised in families that participated in the political process.

The disparity between voters and the electorate impacts public policy. The electorate in Texas is significantly more conservative than the population as a whole. Because elected officials respond to the policy preferences of voters rather than non-voters, the result is that public policies in Texas are more conservative than they would be if the electorate mirrored the state's population.[37] In 2003, for example, state government faced a significant budget shortfall because of a **recession**, an economic slowdown characterized by declining economic output and rising unemployment. The state's chief budget officer estimated that tax revenues would fall more than $10 billion short of the funds necessary to maintain state services at their

Recession An economic slowdown characterized by declining economic output and rising unemployment.

current levels. The governor and legislature chose to address the shortfall by cutting spending, even though public services in Texas were already among the most poorly funded in the nation. They cut spending for school textbooks, higher education, and healthcare for children in low-income families. All of the cuts disproportionately impacted low-income Latino and African American families. Similarly, in 2005, when the governor and legislature debated school funding, they focused on cutting school property taxes rather than increasing state funding for public education. Their focus on property tax relief reflected the policy preferences of well-to-do white suburbanites and business owners rather than low-income Latino and African American Texans whose children attended public schools. In 2007, strong economic growth created a sizable budget surplus, a near mirror image of the shortfall of 2003. Nonetheless, instead of using the surplus to address the state's needs for better healthcare and education, the governor and the legislature left billions of dollars unspent in anticipation that the money would be needed later to fund future property tax reductions. Once again, the state's budget priorities reflected the policy priorities of middle- and upper-income whites rather than those of low-income minority residents. Finally, in 2009, the governor and legislature used billions of dollars in federal stimulus not to improve education and healthcare, but to fund basic services without increasing taxes.

Lupe Valdez was elected Dallas County Sheriff in 2004 and reelected in 2008. As the state's electorate has grown more diverse, the number of Latino and African American officeholders has increased.

WHAT WE HAVE LEARNED

1. **What is the history of voting rights for women, Latinos, and African Americans in Texas?**

Texas history records the struggle of women and minorities to gain full participation rates in the state's political process. Women won the right to vote in 1920 with the ratification of the Nineteenth Amendment. Although African American men voted for, and even won, elective office in Texas in the years following the Civil War, they were disenfranchised in the late nineteenth and early twentieth centuries by the poll tax and the white primary. The poll tax affected low-income citizens of all races. Meanwhile, boss control in South Texas limited the effectiveness of Latino participation. The U.S. Supreme Court eventually overturned the white primary, and a constitutional amendment (along with another court ruling) eliminated the poll tax. Nonetheless, other forms of voting discrimination persisted. They too were eventually struck down by federal court rulings and, ultimately, the enforcement of the Voting Rights Act.

2. **What are the ways that individuals can participate in the policymaking process?**

Individual Texans can participate in the policymaking process in a number of ways: voting, campaigning, joining political groups, contacting public officials, and participating in protest demonstrations and unconventional political acts. To vote in Texas, individuals must be 18 years of age as of the next election, American citizens (either native-born or naturalized), and residents of Texas. People can participate politically by working on election campaigns. Some Texans also participate in political rallies and demonstrations, such as those organized by the Tea Party movement.

3. **How do voter participation rates in Texas compare with rates in other states, and what is the explanation for the difference?**

In 2008, Texas had the fifth-lowest voter turnout in the nation. Compared with other states, income levels in Texas are lower, the age distribution is younger, and levels of educational achievement are below average. All of these factors are related to lower levels of political participation. Political parties and labor unions, which are associated with high levels of voter turnout, are relatively weak in Texas. Texas has a high percentage of recent immigrants and they are less likely as a group to register and vote than more established residents. Finally, neither political party has campaigned heavily in Texas in recent presidential elections because it has not been a battleground state.

4. **How do political participation rates vary based on income, age, race/ethnicity, and gender?**

Participation rates vary among individuals based on income, age, race/ethnicity, and gender. Middle- and upper-income groups participate at a higher rate than lower-income groups. Political participation increases with age until advanced age and ill health force the elderly to slow down. The overall participation rates for African Americans and whites are similar, whereas the participation rates for Latinos are substantially lower than they are for other racial and ethnic groups. Men and women are equally likely to vote, but men are more active than women in other forms of participation.

5. **How does the Texas electorate compare with the state's total population in terms of income, education, and age?**

Texas voters, as a group, are wealthier, better educated, and older than the state's adult population. The Texas electorate, however, is less representative of the state population than the average state electorate, especially in terms of income and education. Consequently, the electorate in Texas is significantly more conservative than the population as a whole.

KEY TERMS

battleground state

disfranchisement

early voting

election precinct

enfranchise

exit polls

franchise

League of United Latin
American Citizens (LULAC)

Mothers Against Drunk
Driving (MADD)

National Rifle Association
(NRA)

parole

poll tax

primary election

probation

recession

suffrage

Tea Party movement

voting age population
(VAP)

voting eligible population
(VEP)

white primary

NOTES

1. Chandler Davidson, "The Historical Context of Voter Photo-ID Laws," *PS: Political Science & Politics* 42 (January 2009): 93–96; Wayne Slater, "Texas AG Fails to Unravel Large-Scale Voter-Fraud Schemes in his Two-Year Campaign," *Dallas Morning News*, May 18, 2008, available at www.dallasnews.com.

2. Jaime Castillo, "Dems Winners as GOP Senators Push to Pass Voter ID Bill," *San Antonio Express-News*, January 18, 2009, available at www.mysanantonio.com.

3. Elizabeth A. Taylor, "The Woman Suffrage Movement in Texas," *Journal of Southern History* 17 (May 1951): 194–215.

4. Merline Pitre, *Through Many Dangers, Toils and Snares: Black Leadership in Texas, 1868–1900* (Austin, TX: Eakin Press, 1985).

5. V. O. Key, Jr., *Southern Politics in State and Nation* (New York, NY: Alfred A. Knopf, 1949).

6. *Historical Statistics of the United States* (Washington, DC: U.S. Government Printing Office, 1975), pp. 1071–1072.

7. Dudley Lynch, *Duke of Duval* (Waco, TX: Texian Press, 1978).

8. *Nixon v. Herndon*, 273 U.S. 536 (1927).

9. *Nixon v. Condon*, 286 U.S. 73 (1932).

10. *Grovey v. Townsend*, 295 U.S. 45 (1935).

11. *Smith v. Allwright*, 321 U.S. 649 (1944).

12. *Terry v. Adams*, 345 U.S. 461 (1953).

13. *United States v. Texas*, 384 U.S. 155 (1966).

14. *Beare v. Smith*, 321 F. Supp. 1100 (1971).

15. Stephen Ansolabehere, "Effects of Identification Requirements on Voting: Evidence from the Experience of Voters on Election Day," *PS: Political Science & Politics* 42 (January 2009): 127–130.

16. Paul Gronke, Eva Galanes-Rosenbaum, and Peter A. Miller, "Early Voting and Voter Turnout," *PS: Political Science & Politics* 40 (October 2007): 639.

17. Kelly Shannon, "Texas' Early Vote Increased, Sets Record," *Austin American-Statesman*, November 12, 2008, available at www.statesman.com.

18. William Lyons and John M. Scheb II, "Early Voting and the Timing of the Vote: Unanticipated Consequences of Electoral Reform," *State and Local Government Review* 31 (Spring 1999): 148.

19. Gronke, Galanes-Rosenbaum, and Miller, "Early Voting and Voter Turnout," pp. 639–645.

20. Ibid., pp. 639–645.

21. Texans for Public Justice, "Texas' 2006 Election Cycle '$100,000 Club,'" available at www.tpj.org.

22. Texas Secretary of State, "Turnout and Voter Registration Figures (1990–present)," available at www.sos.state.tx.us; Michael P. McDonald, United States Election Project, available at http://elections.gmu.edu.

23. McDonald, United States Election Project.

24. G. Bingham Powell, Jr., "American Voter Turnout in Comparative Perspective," *American Political Science Review* 80 (March 1986): 17–43; Benjamin Radcliff and Patricia Davis, "Labor Organization and Electoral Participation in Industrial Democracies," *American Journal of Political Science* 44 (April 2000): 132–141.

25. André Blais, *To Vote or Not to Vote?* (Pittsburgh, PA: University of Pittsburgh Press, 2000), p. 13.

26. "Exit Polls for Texas," available at www.cnn.com/elections/2008.

27. U.S. Census Bureau, "Household Income—Distribution by Income and State: 2006," *The 2009 Statistical Abstract*, available at www.census.gov.

28. M. Kent Jennings and Gregory B. Markus, "Political Involvement in the Later Years: A Longitudinal Survey," *American Journal of Political Science* 32 (May 1988): 302–316.

29. U.S. Census Bureau, "Reported Voting and Registration, by Race, Hispanic Origin, Sex, and Age, for the United States, November 2004," available at www.census.gov.

30. U.S. Census Bureau, "Texas Becomes Nation's Newest 'Majority-Minority' State," August 11, 2005, available at www.census.gov.

31. "Exit Polls for Texas."

32. Matt A. Barreto, "¡Sí Se Puede! Latino Candidates and the Mobilization of Latino Voters," *American Political Science Review* 101 (August 2007): 425–441.

33. "Exit Polls for Texas."

34. Sidney Verba, Kay Lehman Schlozman, and Henry E. Brady, *Voice and Equality: Civic Volunteerism in American Politics* (Cambridge, MA: Harvard University Press, 1995), p. 255.

35. Robert A. Jackson, Robert D. Brown, and Gerald C. Wright, "Representation, Turnout, and the Electoral Representativeness of U.S. State Electorates," *American Politics Quarterly* 26 (July 1998): 259–287.

36. Sara Foley, "Average Voter Isn't Average Resident," *Corpus Christi Caller*, March 29, 2009, available at www.caller.com.

37. John D. Griffin and Brian Newman, "Are Voters Better Represented?" *Journal of Politics* 67 (November 2005): 1,214.

Chapter 5

Interest Groups

WHAT WE WILL LEARN

After studying Chapter 5, students should be able to answer the following questions:

‣ What types of interest groups are active in American politics and what are their goals?

‣ What strategies and tactics do interest groups use to achieve their goals?

Tort reform The revision of state laws to limit the ability of plaintiffs in personal injury lawsuits to recover damages in court.

Texas Medical Association (TMA) A professional organization of physicians.

Punitive damages Monetary awards given in a lawsuit to punish a defendant for a particularly evil, malicious, or fraudulent act.

class action lawsuit A suit brought by one or more people on behalf of themselves and others who are similarly situated.

Texas Trial Lawyers Association (TTLA) An organization of attorneys who represent plaintiffs in personal injury lawsuits.

Interest groups An organization of people who join together voluntarily on the basis of some interest they share for the purpose of influencing policy.

The issue of tort reform features some of the most powerful interest groups in Texas politics. **Tort reform** is the revision of state laws to limit the ability of plaintiffs in personal injury lawsuits to recover damages in court. The **Texas Medical Association (TMA),** a professional organization of physicians, supports tort reform as a way to hold down the high cost of medical malpractice insurance. Hospitals, nursing homes, pharmaceutical companies, and the manufacturers of medical devices favor tort reform to protect them from lawsuits that drive up the cost of doing business. Home builders and construction companies want to force home purchasers to resolve their complaints through arbitration or other complaint resolution processes before filing lawsuits. Insurance companies in general favor laws designed to limit their financial liability.

Tort reform advocates support caps on the amount of money a jury can award in noneconomic damages and favor restrictions on class action lawsuits. Noneconomic damages include money to compensate for disfigurement, loss of companionship, pain, suffering, and **punitive damages,** which are monetary awards given in a lawsuit to punish a defendant for a particularly evil, malicious, or fraudulent act. In the meantime, a **class action lawsuit** is a suit brought by one or more people on behalf of themselves and others who are similarly situated. For example, a class action lawsuit could be filed against a company that manufactured a defective product on behalf of everyone who purchased the product and was harmed by it. Tort reformers believe that lawyers abuse the class action process by seeking out large numbers of people who have purchased a defective product or used a drug that has been shown to be harmful. The lawyers sue on behalf of the people harmed, seeking millions of dollars in damages. If the case is won, the attorneys collect millions in fees whereas each of the individuals listed in the suit receives a tiny amount of damages.

Tort reformers believe that lawsuit abuse harms the general public by driving up the cost of doing business in the state. The TMA claims that high medical malpractice insurance premiums force physicians to abandon their practices, especially doctors with high-risk specializations, such as obstetrics. The fear of lawsuits drives up healthcare costs because doctors practice defensive medicine, ordering every conceivable test for their patients in order to guard against a future lawsuit. Home builders and product manufacturers declare that jury awards in product liability cases increase their cost of doing business, which is then passed on to consumers.

The **Texas Trial Lawyers Association (TTLA),** an organization of attorneys who represent plaintiffs in personal injury lawsuits, and consumer groups, such as Public Citizen and Texas Watch, oppose tort reform. They believe that tort reform is anti-consumer because it limits the consumer's ability to seek compensation for the harm caused by drunk drivers, incompetent physicians, poor builders, or sloppy product manufacturers. Furthermore, the opponents of tort reform believe that it reduces the incentives that physicians, hospitals, nursing homes, builders, pharmaceutical companies, and others have to protect the general public from defects and errors.

The controversy over tort reform illustrates the role of interest groups in the policymaking process. **Interest groups** are organizations of people who join together voluntarily on the basis of some interest they share for the purpose of influencing policy. Groups on either side of the tort reform controversy attempt to influence the policymaking process by contributing to the election campaigns of candidates for governor, the legislature, and judicial office. They conduct public relations campaigns to sway public opinion and lobby lawmakers and other officials to formulate, adopt, and implement the policies they favor. Finally, groups attempt to influence policy evaluation by interpreting the impact of tort reform policies already in place in a light favorable to their interests.

This chapter is the second in a series of four chapters examining the political environment for policymaking. Chapter 4 discussed political participation in Texas. Chapters 6 and 7 will focus on political parties and elections. This chapter studies the role of interest groups in the policymaking process. It identifies the major interest groups active in the state, identifies their goals, and discusses the strategies and tactics they employ to achieve their goals.

 WHAT IS YOUR OPINION?

Do you favor or oppose tort reform? What is the reasoning behind your position?

INTEREST GROUPS IN TEXAS POLITICS

Although most Texans are interested in the policies of state and local government in Texas, not all Texans have organized to promote and defend their interests. As an analogy, compare and contrast the position of college students with that of the people who manage large energy companies, such as Reliant Energy and TXU Energy. Both groups have an interest in state and local government. Public policies dealing with college funding, university admissions, course transfer, tuition, and the availability of scholarships and financial aid affect college students. In the meantime, energy company executives have an interest in electricity deregulation, property taxes, alternative energy development, and government regulations dealing with environmental pollution, electric power transmission, and workplace safety. College students and energy company executives are not equally well organized. College students have little, if any, interest group representation. Although student organizations exist at many of the state's colleges and universities, their primary focus is not political. In contrast, energy company executives are organized both by firm and by industry group. They are widely regarded as being among the most influential voices in state and local government.

We begin our study of interest groups by identifying the most important organized interests in Texas politics. Who are the interests, how well are they organized, what do they want from state and local government, and how effective are they at achieving their goals?

Business Groups and Trade Associations

Business groups and trade associations are the most powerful interest groups in Texas politics. Other groups may be influential at particular levels of government, on certain issues, and at certain points in the policy process, but business interests are important everywhere, from the county courthouse to the governor's mansion. Whereas other interests focus on one issue or a narrow range of issues, business voices are heard on virtually every major policy issue, whether education finance, insurance regulation, water development, immigration, or transportation.

Business interests pursue their political goals both as individual firms and through trade associations. Comcast, Reliant Energy, AT&T, State Farm Insurance, and other large business enterprises are major players in state politics. Business groups also work through **trade associations,** which are organizations representing the interests of firms and professionals in the same general field. The **Texas Association of Business (TAB)** is a trade association for business firms ranging from giant corporations to small neighborhood business establishments. The TAB, which includes local chambers of commerce in its organizational structure, is perhaps the single most powerful interest group in the state. Other trade associations include the Texas Association of Builders, which is a trade association representing the interests of building contractors; the Mid-Continent Oil and Gas Association, which is a trade association that speaks for the concerns of the major oil producers; and the Insurance Council of Texas, which is a trade association representing insurance companies.

Business groups and trade associations are effective because they are well organized, well financed, and skilled in advocating their positions. Business people usually know what they want from government and have the financial and organizational resources to pursue their goals aggressively. Furthermore, business groups as a whole enjoy a relatively favorable public image. Although the alcohol, gambling, and tobacco industries have public relations problems, most Texans have a favorable image of business in general, especially small business.

Business groups and trade associations generally agree on the need to maintain a **good business climate,** which is a political environment in which business prospers. Business people believe that tort reform is an important element of a good business climate because it reduces the premium costs to business of insurance against lawsuit judgments. In general, a good business environment includes low tax rates on business, laws that restrict union influence, and regulation favorable to business growth. Business interests also support education to train the skilled, well-educated workforce needed for high-technology development.

Texas business interests have largely achieved their goal of promoting the adoption of public policies conducive to business growth. *Chief Executive*, a magazine for corporate executives, conducts an annual survey, asking business executives to evaluate the business climate of each state. For four years in a row, chief executives nationwide have rated Texas as the best state in the nation in which to do business. The factors most responsible for the state's high ranking were transportation, access to capital, technology, and innovation. Texas also scored highly on tax policy, regulation, and quality of living. The survey ranked North Carolina, Florida, Georgia, and Tennessee just behind Texas for being business friendly. In contrast, California and New York were ranked as the worst and second worst states to do business, respectively.[1]

When business groups and trade associations are united, they usually get what they want in Texas. The battle over tort reform illustrates the power of business interests united behind a particular policy objective. During the 1990s, the Texas

Trade associations Organizations representing the interests of firms and professionals in the same general field.

Texas Association of Business (TAB) A trade association for business firms ranging from giant corporations to small neighborhood business establishments.

Good business climate A political environment in which business would prosper.

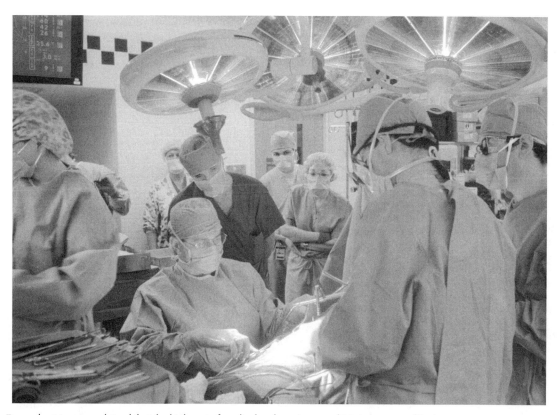

Texas physicians complained that the high cost of medical malpractice was driving them out of business.

legislature passed, and the governor signed, legislation enacting the following tort reform measures:

- **Frivolous lawsuits:** The legislature and the governor adopted legislation allowing judges to punish plaintiffs for filing lawsuits that the court determined to be without merit. (A **plaintiff** is the party initiating a civil suit.) The judge could fine the plaintiff or order the plaintiff to pay the defendant's attorney fees.

- **Punitive damages:** The legislature and the governor made it more difficult for plaintiffs to recover punitive damages and capped the amount of punitive damages that could be awarded to twice the economic damages suffered by the plaintiff.

- **Forum shopping:** The legislature and the governor limited the locations in which a plaintiff could file a personal injury lawsuit to the county of the principal office of the defendant, the site where the injury occurred, and the residence of the defendant.

- **Joint and several liability reform:** The legislature and the governor limited the applicability of **joint and several liability,** which is the legal requirement that a defendant with "deep pockets" held partially liable for a plaintiff's injury

Plaintiff The party initiating a civil suit.

Joint and several liability The legal requirement that a defendant with "deep pockets" held partially liable for a plaintiff's injury must pay the full damage award for those defendants unable to pay.

must pay the full damage award for those defendants unable to pay. In most personal injury lawsuits, a defendant cannot be held 100 percent responsible for a judgment unless the defendant is deemed at least 50 percent responsible for the injury.[2]

- **Lawsuit immunity:** The legislature and the governor passed legislation sheltering some potential defendants from liability suits, including medical providers who volunteer their help to charitable organizations. The state also prevents city governments from filing product liability lawsuits against firearms manufacturers.

In 2003, the legislature and governor adopted an additional set of tort reform measures:

- **Caps on noneconomic damages in medical malpractice suits:** Patients injured by medical malpractice can recover no more than $250,000 in noneconomic damages from a physician or another healthcare provider. If a hospital, clinic, or nursing home is also found liable, the patient can recover a maximum $250,000 each from two additional parties for a total cap of $750,000.

- **Protection against product liability suits:** The manufacturers of defective products are shielded from liability if they follow federal standards or regulatory requirements.

- **Joint and several liability:** Juries may allocate fault among all responsible parties, including parties with no financial assets. In cases involving automobile accidents, when apportioning liability juries may also be informed whether the injured party was wearing a seatbelt or was in a car seat.

The legislature and the governor adopted additional tort reform measures in 2005. They passed a measure that limited the number of lawsuits for asbestos- and silica-related exposure, allowing only people with serious illness to file suit. They added another measure to prohibit lawsuits against restaurants and food makers for obesity-related health problems.

Business groups also enjoy considerable influence with the judicial branch of Texas government, which is responsible for implementing tort reform legislation. Business interests that lose personal injury lawsuits or consumer fraud cases are more than twice as likely to win on appeal as are individual consumers who appeal.[3] Business groups are especially successful before the Texas Supreme Court. According to a study conducted by the Texas Watch Foundation, a consumer research and education organization, corporate and governmental defendants won 70 percent of the cases decided by the Texas Supreme Court between 1997 and 2006.[4]

Business interests are more influential in Texas politics than they are in national politics because they have fewer competitors in Texas than they do at the national level or in many other states. Organized labor, consumer groups, environmental organizations, and other groups that often oppose business interests on various policy issues are relatively weak in the Lone Star State. The best that the organizations opposed to tort reform have been able to accomplish, for example, has been to limit the extent of their defeat. The TTLA, the major organization against tort reform, enjoys considerable financial resources, but it has been outspent and out-organized by business interests.

Professional Associations

Professional associations are politically influential because of the relatively high socioeconomic status of their members. Doctors, dentists, lawyers, realtors, teachers, and other professionals generally have the financial resources to make their voices

INTERNET RESEARCH   Profile of an Interest Group

Many of the state's interest groups have websites that publicize mission statements, issue positions, news, and contact information.

- Lone Star Chapter of the Sierra Club (environmental group): **http://texas.sierraclub.org/**
- Texas Right to Life Committee (anti-abortion group): **www.texasrighttolife.com/**
- Public Citizen (consumer rights and environmental group): **www.citizen.org/texas/**
- Texas Public Interest Research Group (public interest advocacy group founded by students): **www.texpirg.org/**
- Children's Defense Fund of Texas (advocacy group for children): **www.cdftexas.org/**
- Texas Eagle Forum (interest group focusing on traditional values): **http://texaseagle.org/**
- NARAL Pro-Choice Texas (pro-choice group): **www.prochoicetexas.org/**
- Texas Freedom Network (interest group focusing on opposition to religious conservatives): **www.tfn.org/**
- Texas Civil Liberties Union (interest group focusing on civil liberties issues): **www.aclutx.org/**
- Texas League of United Latin American Citizens (Latino rights organization): **http://www.tx-lulac.org/**
- League of Women Voters of Texas (non-partisan group focusing on voter education): **www.lwvtexas.org/**
- Texas State Conference of NAACP Branches (African American rights organization): **www.texasnaacp.org/**
- Common Cause Texas (non-partisan group focusing on campaign finance reform and ethics in government): **www.commoncause.org**
- Texas Watch (consumer group): **www.texaswatch.org**
- Texas State Rifle Association (group supporting the rights of gun owners): **www.tsra.com/**
- The Metropolitan Organization (faith-based non-partisan organization focusing on civic education): **http://tmohouston.net/**
- National Organization for Women chapters in Texas (women's rights organizations): **http://www.nowtexas.org/**

Browse the website of one of the groups and answer the following questions:

1. What issues does the group stress in its website?
2. Does it appear that the group is more interested in raising money, recruiting volunteers, or influencing public policy?
3. Would you describe the group's website as organized and informative? Why or why not?

heard. The TMA, TTLA, Texas Association of Realtors (TAR), Texas State Teachers Association (TSTA), Texas Dental Association, and Texas Pharmacy Association are among the major campaign contributors in Texas politics.[5] Professional associations enjoy an added advantage in that many elected officials come from the ranks of professionals, especially lawyers. Public officials who happen to be lawyers, for example, are more likely to understand and sympathize with the policy perspectives of attorneys than are officials who lack legal training.

Professional associations concern themselves with public policies that affect their members. Doctors and lawyers battle one another over medical damage award caps in malpractice lawsuits. Real estate professionals are primarily concerned with public policies affecting real estate transactions, such as home equity lending and professional licensure. Teacher organizations focus on teacher pay and pensions as well as the whole range of education issues.

Organized Labor

Organized labor is relatively weak in Texas. State laws make it difficult for unions to organize workers and easy for business to use non-union labor. Texas is a right-to-work state because it has a **right-to-work law,** which is a statute prohibiting a union shop. A **union shop** or **closed shop** is a workplace in which every employee must be a member of a union. In states without right-to-work laws, the employees in a particular workplace may vote whether to create a union shop. If a majority of the workers agree, everyone employed in the plant must join the union and pay union dues. Union membership thus becomes mandatory. In a right-to-work state, union organizers are forced to recruit members individually.

Nationally, labor unions are strongest in the large, industrialized states of the Northeast and Midwest. In 2008, one-fourth of the workforce in New York belonged to unions; likewise, the unionization rate in Michigan was 19 percent. In contrast, organized labor is not nearly as well established in the states of the South and Southwest. Only 4.5 percent of Texas workers belonged to unions in 2008. That's less than half the national unionization rate of 12.4 percent. Texas ranked forty-sixth among the 50 states in the rate of unionization.[6] Labor unions in Texas are too small and too poorly organized to compete effectively against business groups in state politics. In 2008, labor interests contributed $6 million to candidates for various legislative and executive offices, a figure representing just 5 percent of interest group spending.[7]

In Texas, labor unions are strongest in the state's more heavily industrialized areas, such as the Texas Gulf Coast and the Dallas-Fort Worth area. Organized labor has political influence in Houston, Dallas, and Fort Worth, and labor unions may be the single most important political force in Pasadena, Deer Park, and the Golden Triangle area of Beaumont, Port Arthur, and Orange. Unions also have influence within the organization of the state Democratic Party.

Most Texas unions belong to the **American Federation of Labor–Congress of Industrial Organizations (AFL–CIO),** which is a national association of labor unions. The Texas AFL–CIO represents 220,000 workers and includes Texas affiliates of the Communications Workers of America; International Brotherhood of

Right-to-work law A statute prohibiting a union shop.

Union shop or **closed shop** A workplace in which every employee must be a member of a union.

American Federation of Labor–Congress of Industrial Organizations (AFL–CIO) A national association of labor unions.

Electrical Workers; Fire Fighters; American Federation of Government Employees; National Association of Letter Carriers; International Association of Machinists; Oil, Chemical, and Atomic Workers Union; American Federation of State, County, and Municipal Employees (AFSCME); and the Texas Federation of Teachers. The fastest growing unions are those representing service sector workers and government employees.[8] In Houston, for example, the Service Employees International Union (SEIU) and AFSCME have been aggressively organizing janitors, city hall workers, security guards, and medical workers.

Private-sector unions are concerned with employee compensation, working conditions, job availability, job training, and state laws affecting the ability of unions to organize. The Texas AFL–CIO supports increasing the state minimum wage, which covers farm workers and other employees not covered by the federal minimum wage. The **minimum wage** is the lowest hourly wage that an employer can pay covered workers. Unions also favor public education, job training, and other social programs that benefit working class families.

Minimum wage
The lowest hourly wage that an employer can pay covered workers.

Public employee organizations, such as the Fort Worth Firefighters and Houston Police Officers Union, are similar to private-sector unions in that they want higher wages, secure jobs, salaries based on seniority rather than merit, attractive fringe benefits, and good working conditions. Fire and police unions are concerned with state civil service rules for municipal fire and police employees. Public employee organizations also address issues related to the professional concerns of their members. Police organizations take positions on proposals to revise the state's criminal laws. Employees of the Texas Department of Corrections oppose efforts to privatize the state's prison system.

Agricultural Groups

Agricultural interests have long been powerful in Texas politics. In the nineteenth century, the most influential political voices in the state were those of major landowners, and the rural population was large enough to overwhelm the city vote in statewide elections. Even after Texas became an urban, industrial state, rural interests continued to exercise disproportionate power. Rural areas were overrepresented in the legislature and farm groups were politically skillful.

Although urbanization has weakened rural interests in Texas, farm groups still retain influence. Farmers and ranchers are politically astute, organized, and knowledgeable about how to exert influence in state politics. A great deal of agriculture in Texas has become agribusiness, run by corporations that possess all the political skills and advantages of big business in general. Also, many of the policy goals of agricultural interests have long since been achieved and entrenched in law or the state constitution. As a result, agricultural interest groups have the advantage of defending ground already won rather than pushing for new policies.

Agriculture is a tenuous business and farmers are well aware that government actions can frequently determine whether they make a profit or go broke. Taxes are an area of concern. Farmers on the outskirts of metropolitan areas, for example, can be hurt by rising property taxes. As the big city sprawls in their direction, the value

GETTING INVOLVED

Joining a Group

People who want to influence policy in a particular issue area should join a group. The Internet Research feature on page 107 includes the websites of a number of interest groups active in Texas politics. Each of these groups is a membership organization in that it invites the participation of ordinary citizens.

Contact the group whose values and viewpoints most nearly reflect your own and find out how you can join the group and contribute to its work. Add your name to the group's mailing list, give money to the organization, attend meetings, and volunteer.

It's your government—get involved!

League of United Latin American Citizens (LULAC)
A Latino interest group.

National Association for the Advancement of Colored People (NAACP) An interest group organized to represent the interests of African Americans.

Hate crimes legislation
Legislative measures that increase penalties for persons convicted of criminal offenses motivated by prejudice based on race, religion, national origin, gender, or sexual orientation.

Racial profiling
The practice of a police officer targeting individuals as suspected criminals on the basis of their race or ethnicity.

of their land goes up and, consequently, so do their property taxes. Their crops, though, are worth no more. Farm groups, such as the Texas Farm Bureau, have lobbied successfully to have farmland taxed on its value as farmland, not on its value as the site of a future subdivision. Agricultural interests have also won tax breaks on the purchase of farm machinery, seed grain, and fertilizer.

Agricultural groups have other interests as well. They are concerned with state laws and regulations affecting agriculture, such as livestock quarantine requirements and restrictions on the use of pesticides. They support generous state funding for agricultural research conducted at Texas A&M University. Water development and conservation are important for agricultural interests needing water for their livestock and irrigation for their crops.

Racial and Ethnic Minority Groups

Racial and ethnic minority groups enjoy some political influence in Texas. The two best-known minority rights organizations in the state are affiliates of prominent national organizations. The Texas **League of United Latin American Citizens (LULAC)** is a Latino interest group, whereas the Texas chapter of the **National Association for the Advancement of Colored People (NAACP)** is an interest group organized to represent the interests of African Americans.

Minority groups are interested in the enforcement of laws protecting the voting rights of minority citizens, the election and appointment of minority Texans to state and local office, college and university admission policies, public services for low-income residents of the state, inner-city development, and, for Latino groups in particular, economic development in South Texas. In recent sessions of the legislature, Latino and African American members have pushed for the passage of legislation concerning hate crimes and racial profiling. **Hate crimes legislation** refers to legislative measures that increase penalties for persons convicted of criminal offenses motivated by prejudice based on race, religion, national origin, gender, or sexual orientation. **Racial profiling** is the practice of a police officer targeting individuals as suspected criminals on the basis of their race or ethnicity. Most Latino and African American legislators also support funding for public education and healthcare

State Children's Health Insurance Program (SCHIP)
A federal program designed to provide health insurance to children from low-income families whose parents are not poor enough to qualify for Medicaid.

programs targeting low-income residents, such as the **State Children's Health Insurance Program (SCHIP),** a federal program designed to provide health insurance to children from low-income families whose parents are not poor enough to qualify for Medicaid.

Racial and ethnic minority groups are considerably more influential in Texas politics today than they were in the early 1960s. More African American and Latino Texans are registered to vote than ever before. In 2008, Latino, African American, and Asian Texans constituted more than one-third of the statewide vote.[9] Therefore, no serious candidate for statewide or municipal office in the state's big cities can afford to ignore minority concerns. Latino and African American legislators have also become an important voting bloc in the state legislature.

Nonetheless, racial and ethnic minority groups are not as powerful as the more established interest groups in the state. Racial and ethnic minority groups are sometimes divided among themselves and are almost always short of funds. Many minority residents are not registered to vote; others stay home on Election Day. Furthermore, African American and Hispanic voters do not necessarily follow the political lead of groups such as LULAC and the NAACP.

Religious Groups

Religious right
Individuals who hold conservative views because of their religious beliefs.

Churches and other religious institutions provide the foundation for a number of political organizations. Roman Catholic and Protestant churches in poor and minority areas have helped organize political groups to support healthcare, education, and neighborhood improvement for the state's poor people. These organizations include Communities Organized for Public Service (COPS) in San Antonio, Interfaith Alliance in the Rio Grande Valley, the Metropolitan Organization (TMO) in Houston, and the El Paso Inter-religious Sponsoring Organization (EPISO). They favor expanding SCHIP coverage, increasing funding for public education, and protecting the rights of immigrant workers.

CALVIN AND HOBBES

Source: Calvin and Hobbes copyright © 1999 Watterson. Distributed by Universal Press Syndicate. Reprinted with permission. All rights reserved.

Citizen groups
Organizations created to support government policies that they believe will benefit the public at large.

Advocacy groups
Organizations created to seek benefits on behalf of persons who are unable to represent their own interests.

Cause groups
Organizations whose members care intensely about a single issue or a group of related issues.

Texas Right to Life Committee
An organization that opposes abortion.

NARAL Pro-Choice Texas An organization that favors abortion rights.

Sierra Club
Environmental organization.

National Rifle Association (NRA)
An interest group organized to defend the rights of gun owners and defeat efforts at gun control.

National Organization for Women (NOW) A group that promotes women's rights.

The most active, and probably most influential, religiously oriented political groups are associated with the **religious right,** individuals who hold conservative social views because of their religious beliefs. Focus on the Family, Eagle Forum, and the American Family Association are national organizations with branches in Texas. Conservative religious organizations oppose abortion, pornography, stem cell research, gay marriage, and the teaching of evolution in public schools. They favor abstinence-based sex education, prayer in schools, home schooling, and family values in general. Some conservative religious groups also take positions on issues that do not have an obvious family values connection, such as tax rates, immigration, and the United Nations.

Conservative Christian groups are an important part of the base of the Texas Republican Party and that alliance has enabled them to win some important legislative victories. In recent sessions, the Texas legislature passed a constitutional amendment to outlaw gay marriage, adopted a measure to require couples to attend premarital counseling or pay higher marriage license fees, and defeated efforts to expand legalized gambling in the state. The legislature has also adopted a number of restrictions on access to abortion, including a parental consent requirement for minors.[10]

Citizen, Advocacy, and Cause Groups

Citizen groups are organizations created to support government policies that the members believe will benefit the public at large. For example, Texans for Public Justice (TPJ) and Common Cause are organizations that work for campaign finance reform, ethics regulations for public officials, and other good government causes. Texas Public Interest Research Group (Tex-PIRG) and Texas Watch are consumer rights organizations.

Advocacy groups are organizations created to seek benefits on behalf of persons who are unable to represent their own interests. The Children's Defense Fund, for example, is an organization that attempts to promote the welfare of children. The Texas AIDS Network represents the interests of people with HIV/AIDS.

Cause groups are organizations whose members care intensely about a single issue or a group of related issues. The **Texas Right to Life Committee,** for example, opposes abortion, whereas **NARAL Pro-Choice Texas** favors abortion rights. The **Sierra Club** is an environmental organization. Other cause groups include the **National Rifle Association (NRA), National Organization for Women (NOW),** and **AARP.** The NRA is an interest group organized to defend the rights of gun owners and defeat efforts at gun control. NOW is a group that promotes women's rights. The AARP, which was once the American Association of Retired Persons but now just goes by the acronym, is an interest group representing the concerns of older Americans.

Citizen, advocacy, and cause groups vary in political influence, depending on the strength of their organization, the power of the opposition, and the popularity of their cause. **Mothers Against Drunk Driving (MADD),** which is an interest group

AARP An interest
group representing
the concerns of older
Americans.

**Mothers Against
Drunk Driving
(MADD)** An interest
group that supports the
reform of laws dealing
with drunk driving.

that supports the reform of laws dealing with drunk driving, has been able to
overcome the opposition of the liquor industry and DWI defense attorneys because
it is well organized and its cause enjoys considerable popular support. In contrast, the
Sierra Club and other environmental organizations have been relatively unsuccessful. Even though the environment is a popular cause, environmental organizations
in Texas have been no match against the political influence of the oil and gas
industry or electric utilities.

INTEREST GROUP STRATEGIES AND TACTICS

Interest groups employ a variety of tactics in an effort to achieve their goals.

Electioneering

Interest groups attempt to affect public policy by participating in the electoral
process. Groups with a large membership and/or influence beyond their ranks try to
affect election outcomes by endorsing favored candidates and delivering a bloc vote
on their behalf. Unions, racial and ethnic minority groups, and some citizen groups
regularly use this strategy. In 2010, for example, the Texas Right to Life Committee
endorsed Republican Rick Perry for governor, whereas the Texas AFL–CIO threw its
support behind Bill White, the Democratic Party nominee.

**Political action
committees (PACs)**
Organizations
created to raise and
distribute money in
political campaigns.

The most effective tool interest groups have for affecting election outcomes is
money. Interest groups contribute to candidates they support through their **political
action committees (PACs),** which are organizations created to raise and distribute
money in political campaigns. People associated with the interest group such as
union members and business executives contribute money to the group's PAC,
which in turn gives money to candidates for office. Executives with Reliant Energy,
for example, contribute to the Reliant Energy PAC. Texas physicians give money to
the TMA PAC and trial lawyers contribute to the TTLA PAC.

Texas law does not limit the amount of money individuals, businesses, or PACs
can contribute in election campaigns, and some interest groups take advantage of
the opportunity to give large amounts of money to the candidates of their choice
through their PACs. As Figure 5.1 indicates, PAC spending has increased steadily
since the 2004 election. In 2008, 1,209 Texas PACs reported spending almost
$120 million, an increase of 21 percent over 2006 expenditures. Some of the best-
funded PACs were affiliated with forces on either side of the tort reform debate. Texans for Lawsuit Reform ($4.3 million), TMA PAC ($1.4 million), and HillCo PAC
($960,000), which is almost entirely funded by home builder Bob Perry, all support
tort reform legislation and gave most of their money to Republican candidates. In
contrast, Texans for Insurance Reform ($2.7 million), First Tuesday ($972,000),
Blue Texas PAC ($920,000), and the TTLA PAC ($866,000) were all heavily
funded by trial lawyers and contributed primarily to Democratic candidates.[11]

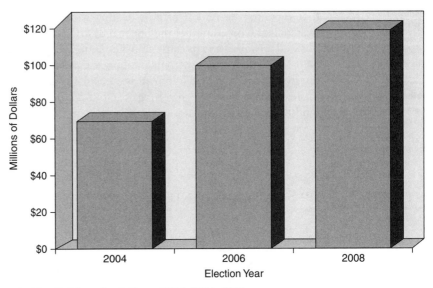

FIGURE 5.1   PAC Spending in Texas, 2004, 2006, 2008.

Interest groups consider several factors in determining which candidates to support. Groups typically back candidates who are sympathetic with their policy preferences. The Texans for Lawsuit Reform PAC supports candidates favoring tort reform, mostly Republicans, whereas the TTLA PAC gives its money to tort reform opponents, mostly Democrats. Interest groups also consider the likelihood of a candidate's winning the election because groups want to back winners. Interest group leaders would rather give to a strong candidate who is only somewhat supportive of their group than throw their money away on an almost certain loser who is completely behind the group's cause. Consequently, interest groups typically contribute more generously to incumbents than to challengers because they know that an **incumbent,** that is, a current officeholder, is more likely to win than is a challenger. Finally, interest groups prefer giving to incumbent officeholders who hold important policymaking positions, such as the members of the key policymaking committees in the legislature. Elected officials who hold important posts, such as the chairs of key committees in the legislature, are in a better position to return favors than are officeholders who have little power.

The political money game can be hazardous to the health of an interest group that winds up on the losing side of an election contest. Consider the experience of the Texas Automobile Dealers Association (TADA). Automobile dealers are business people who are traditionally allied with the Republican Party. In 2001, however, Governor Perry angered the automobile dealers by vetoing both of their top legislative priorities. One measure would have allowed dealers to increase the documentary fee they charge on new car sales from $50 to $75; the other would have allowed dealers to sell "gap insurance" to cover the shortfall when an outstanding loan exceeds the value of a new car that is totaled.[12] The car dealers retaliated against the governor by throwing their support to his Democratic opponent in the 2002 election. When

Incumbent Current officeholder.

AROUND THE NATION

Campaign Finance Reform in Arizona

Arizona has adopted a campaign finance reform measure designed to limit the role of interest group money in election campaigns. In 1998, Arizona voters approved the Citizens' Clean Elections Act, a voluntary campaign finance system that provides near full public funding for candidates seeking executive offices elected statewide or seats in the Arizona legislature. To qualify for the program a candidate must raise $5 each from 210 registered voters who live in the state (for candidates running statewide) or the district legislative candidates wish to represent. In 2008, candidates for the Arizona legislature received $12,921 for their primary election. Candidates who won their primary elections qualified for an additional $19,382 for the general election. However, candidates who accept the money must forego raising and spending additional money.*

An important feature of Arizona's Clean Election System is that it shelters candidates who participate in the program from being outspent by candidates who choose to raise funds privately. Assume that Candidate A and Candidate B are running against one another for a seat in the Arizona legislature. Candidate A participates in the Clean Election System, but Candidate B does not. The program gives Candidate A $19,382 to spend. Candidate B, meanwhile, raises money from individuals and interest groups. If Candidate B is able to raise and spend more than $19,382, Candidate A gets a matching amount of public money to level the playing field. Consequently, candidates who do not participate in the Clean Election program have a disincentive to raise large amounts of money because their opponents receive an equivalent amount of money without having to spend time fundraising.[†]

Arizona's Clean Elections program is controversial. Proponents argue that public funding reduces the role of interest groups by freeing candidates and elected officials running for reelection from having to raise money. Interest groups are free to endorse candidates they prefer and to lobby elected officials, but they can no longer buy access with their financial contributions. Public funding also relieves candidates from having to spend time fundraising, giving them more time to communicate with the voters about their qualifications and issue positions.[††] Studies indicate that the Clean Elections program has increased electoral competition by increasing the number of candidates, both in open seat races and in contests involving incumbents.[§] In contrast, critics of Clean Elections believe that it is unfair for candidates who are able to raise money on their own to have to face opponents who receive government funds. Candidates who cannot raise money on their own are not serious candidates, the critics claim, and should not be encouraged to run by public funding. Furthermore, taxpayers should not have to pay campaign expenses for politicians, especially in tough economic times. The money spent on campaigns can better be spent addressing the state's needs.[**]

QUESTIONS TO CONSIDER

1. If you were creating an advertising campaign calling for the repeal of the Arizona Clean Elections Act, what arguments would you stress?
2. If you were preparing an advertising campaign to defend the Clean Elections Act, what points would you raise in its favor?
3. Do you think the Texas legislature will ever adopt a similar program for Texas? Why or why not?

---

*Arizona Secretary of State, available at www.azsos.gov.

†Michael Miller, "Gaming Arizona: Public Money and Shifting Candidate Strategies," *PS: Political Science & Politics* 61 (July 2008): 527–532.

††Arizona's Clean Elections Institute, available at http://library.publicampaign.org.

§Neil Malhotra, "The Impact of Public Financing on Electoral Competition: Evidence from Arizona and Maine," *State Politics and Policy Quarterly* 8 (Fall 2008): 263–281.

**Andrea Woodmansee, "Clean Elections Are an Upside-Down Fairy Tale," Goldwater Institute, Center for Constitutional Government, available at www.goldwaterinstitute.org.

Catching the late train The practice of giving campaign contributions to a candidate after an election is over and the candidate has won.

Perry won anyway, the automobile dealers moved quickly to try to repair relations with the governor by contributing $50,000 to the Perry campaign, matching the amount they had earlier given to his unsuccessful Democratic opponent.[13] Giving campaign contributions to a candidate after an election that the candidate has already won is known as **catching the late train.** The group also hired a former top aide to Governor Perry as a lobbyist.

Lobbying

Lobbying The communication of information by a representative of an interest group to a government official for the purpose of influencing a policy decision.

Lobbying is the communication of information by a representative of an interest group to a government official for the purpose of influencing a policy decision. More than 1,600 registered lobbyists represent group interests in Texas.[14] Although some interests hire a single lobbyist to represent them, big companies often employ a small army of high-priced lobbyists. In 2007, AT&T, the communications giant, spent as much as $10.2 million on 126 lobby contracts. TXU, an energy company, spent up to $5.7 million on lobby expenses.[15] (State reporting requirements make it impossible to know the exact amount of lobby expenditures.)

Social lobbying The attempt of lobbyists to influence public policy by cultivating personal, social relationships with policymakers.

The traditional approach of lobbyists in Texas was called **social lobbying,** which is the attempt of lobbyists to influence public policy by cultivating personal, social relationships with policymakers. Cynics referred to the practice as "booze, bribes, and babes." Lobbyists would ply their trade by meeting legislators and executive branch officials at a local barbecue restaurant for an evening of ribs, beer, and storytelling.[16] Even though today's lobbyists are more professional than their predecessors, social lobbying continues to be a big part of the way they do business. In contrast to the national government and 22 other states, Texas places no limit on the amount of money interest groups can spend on meals and entertainment for public officials. Between 2005 and 2009, lobbyists spent nearly $13 million entertaining Texas lawmakers and members of their staffs, spending money on meals, entertainment, golf outings, and trips to conferences.[17]

Professional lobbyists are skilled technicians, knowledgeable both in how to approach public officials and in the subject matter vital to their groups. The basic stock in trade of the skilled lobbyist is information. In fact, interest groups are sometimes the main source of information on a piece of legislation. "We have 140 days to deal with thousands of bills," said one state senator. "The lobbyists are providers of information about those issues. I don't know how we could operate without them."[18]

The most effective lobbyists build personal relationships with members of the legislature. Many lobbyists are actually former members of the legislature or former staff members hired by interest groups to lobby their former colleagues over policy issues that they had worked on together in a previous legislative session. Unlike many states, Texas law allows former members of the legislature and employees of the executive branch to begin work as lobbyists the day after they resign their government positions. For example, two days after Pat Haggerty ended his 20-year career as a member of the Texas legislature, he went to work as a lobbyist, making as much as $300,000 in 2009, substantially more money than the $7,200 he earned as a member of the Texas House of Representatives in 2008.[19]

Legislative access
An open door
through which an
interest group hopes
to influence the
details of policy.

Although legislators all deny that campaign contributions influence their votes, most will admit that groups that give generously to political campaigns enjoy access to lawmakers that other interests do not share. **Legislative access** is an open door through which an interest group hopes to influence the details of policy. Lobbyists for interest groups that contribute heavily to political campaigns usually have the opportunity to make their case to lawmakers. Legislators return their calls, invite them into their offices, and respond to them more quickly than they do for ordinary citizens who are not major campaign contributors.

Interest groups back their legislative lobbyists by mobilizing group members in the home districts of legislators to contact their representatives. The TMA, for example, asks its physician members to personally contact public officials who happen to be their patients. Even though the doctors who make the contacts with policymakers are not professional lobbyists, they are particularly effective because they already have a personal relationship with the public official.

Public Relations Campaigns

Interest groups attempt to influence policy by building public support for their points of view. They recognize that public officials, especially elected officials, are unlikely to jeopardize their political futures by publicly supporting an unpopular cause, regardless of PAC money and lobbying. Interest groups understand that their lobbying efforts will be more effective if policymakers know that group goals enjoy public support.

The groups supporting tort reform have conducted a sophisticated public relations campaign to win support for their point of view. They have purchased billboards and run television and radio advertisements against what they call "lawsuit abuse." They have also used radio talk shows and other media to publicize examples of what they consider unreasonable jury judgments, such as the story of a woman who sued McDonald's restaurant chain after hot coffee spilled in her lap.

Groups without substantial membership or financial resources sometimes employ public relations as their primary strategy for influencing public policy. For example, consumer groups, such as Texas Watch, produce research reports on consumer-related issues, such as tort reform and utility rates. They publish the reports on their websites and hold press conferences to call attention to their findings and recommendations.

Litigation

Sometimes interest groups use litigation (i.e., lawsuits) to achieve their goals. In 2009, for example, Shell Oil Company settled a lawsuit filed by Environment Texas and the Sierra Club by agreeing to reduce emissions at its Deer Park refinery.[20] Shell also promised to pay a $5.8 million penalty. The lawsuit was filed under a provision of the federal Clean Air Act that allowed private citizens to enforce the act in federal court. The environmental groups filed suit against Shell because they were dissatisfied with what they considered lax enforcement by the Texas Commission on Environmental Quality (TCEQ), which had only issued small fines against Shell and had failed to force the refinery to halt the emissions.[21]

Protest Demonstrations

Groups also use protest demonstrations to influence public opinion. Civil rights groups used this technique in the 1960s. Today, it is occasionally employed by a variety of groups pursuing many different goals, ranging from anti-nuclear groups opposing the construction of a nuclear power plant to anti-pornography crusaders picketing convenience stores that sell *Playboy* magazine. In general, protest demonstrations are a tactic used by groups unable to achieve their goals through other means. Sometimes the protest catches the attention of the general public and pressure is brought to bear on behalf of the protesting group. In most cases, though, protests have only a marginal impact on public policy.

Political demonstrations sometimes backfire. Immigrant rights supporters lost ground when high school-aged demonstrators waved Mexican flags rather than American flags. In Houston, meanwhile, protestors organized by the SEIU had to pay fines as large as $2,000 and spend several days in jail after illegally blocking intersections in support of a union strike against janitorial companies.[22]

Political Violence

Occasionally, frustrated groups go beyond peaceful protest to violent, illegal activities. For example, during the 1960s some groups opposed to the war in Vietnam took over college administration buildings or burned Reserve Officer Training Corps (ROTC) offices on campus. The Ku Klux Klan has also been linked to violence in the state. Although political violence usually produces a violent response from the political establishment, violence can occasionally succeed in calling the public's attention to an issue that might otherwise be ignored.

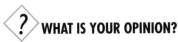 **WHAT IS YOUR OPINION?**

Is violence on behalf of a political cause ever justified?

Alliances

Interest groups find power in alliances with other interest groups and political parties. The battle over medical malpractice reform in particular, and tort reform in general, pitted two powerful interest group-political party alliances against one another. The TMA, business groups as a whole (especially insurance companies and construction companies), and the Republican Party lined up in favor of tort reform, whereas trial lawyers, consumer groups, and the Democratic Party were opposed. The tort reformers got most of what they wanted out of the legislature because their interest group alliance was better funded and better organized than were their opponents. Furthermore, the Republican Party had won electoral control of all three branches of state government, including both chambers of the Texas legislature.

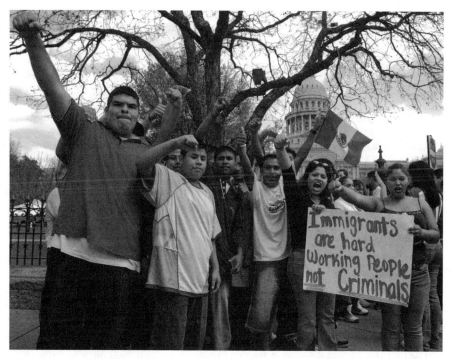

Immigrant rights supporters lost ground when high school-aged demonstrators waved Mexican flags rather than American flags.

WHAT WE HAVE LEARNED

1. **What types of interest groups are active in American politics and what are their goals?**

Business groups, such as Comcast and Reliant Energy, and trade associations, such as the Texas Association of Business, are the most powerful interest groups in Texas politics because they are well organized, well financed, and skilled in advocating their positions. Business groups and trade associations generally agree on the need to maintain a good business climate. Professional associations, such as the TMA and TTLA, are politically influential because of the relatively high socioeconomic status of their members. They are concerned with public policies that affect their members, such as medical malpractice insurance reform. Organized labor is relatively weak in Texas because of the state's right-to-work law and, in general, its anti-union climate. Unions, such as the Texas AFL-CIO, are concerned with employee compensation, working conditions, job availability, job training, and state laws affecting the ability of unions to organize. Agricultural interests have long been powerful in Texas politics. Farm groups, such as the Texas Farm Bureau, are concerned with taxes on farm land, state laws and regulations affecting agriculture, and agricultural research supported by the state. Racial and ethnic minority groups, such as LULAC and the NAACP, enjoy some political influence in Texas. Minority groups are interested in the enforcement of laws protecting the voting rights of minority citizens, the election and appointment of minority Texans to state and local office, college and university admission policies, public services for low-income residents of the state, inner-city development, and, for Latino groups in particular, economic development in South Texas. Churches and other religious institutions provide the foundation for a number of political organizations, including religiously liberal groups such as COPS, Interfaith Alliance, TMO, and EPISO, and religiously conservative organizations such as Focus on the Family, Eagle Forum, and the American Family Association. The religious liberals favor expanding SCHIP coverage, increasing funding for public education, and protecting the rights of immigrant workers; the religiously conservative groups oppose gay marriage and abortion while supporting abstinence-based sex education and prayer in schools. Citizen groups (such as Texans for Public Justice), advocacy groups (such as the Children's Defense Fund), and cause groups (such as the Sierra Club and the NRA) focus on a single issue or a group of related issues. Their influence varies, depending on the strength of their organization, the power of the opposition, and the popularity of their cause.

2. **What strategies and tactics do interest groups use to achieve their goals?**

Interest groups attempt to affect public policy by participating in the electoral process. They endorse candidates, encourage their members to support and vote for them, and, through their PACs, contribute money to them. Interest groups employ lobbyists to shape the content of legislation and influence the actions of the executive branch of state government. Interest groups attempt to affect policy by building public support for their points of view through public relations campaigns. Some interest groups file lawsuits to achieve their goals. Interest groups attempt to advance their goals through protest demonstrations and even political violence. Groups can also promote their interests by forming alliances with other interest groups and political parties.

KEY TERMS

AARP

advocacy groups

American Federation of Labor–Congress of Industrial Organization (AFL–CIO)

catching the late train

cause groups

citizen groups

class action lawsuit

good business climate

hate crimes legislation

incumbent

interest groups

joint and several liability

League of United Latin American Citizens (LULAC)

legislative access

lobbying

minimum wage

Mothers Against Drunk Driving (MADD)

NARAL Pro-Choice Texas

National Association for the Advancement of Colored People (NAACP)

National Organization for Women (NOW)

National Rifle Association (NRA)

plaintiff

political action committees (PACs)

punitive damages

racial profiling

religious right

right-to-work law

Sierra Club

social lobbying

State Children's Health Insurance Program (SCHIP)

Texas Association of Business (TAB)

Texas Medical Association (TMA)

Texas Right to Life Committee

Texas Trial Lawyers Association (TTLA)

tort reform

trade associations

union shop or closed shop

NOTES

1. "Best and Worst States—2009," *Chief Executive*, available at www.chiefexecutive.net.

2. Texas Department of Insurance, "Tort Reform Statutes," available at www.tdi.state.tx.us.

3. Janet Elliott, "Defendants Fare Better on Appeal, Study Finds," *Houston Chronicle*, Nov. 6, 2003, p. 27A.

4. Texas Watch Foundation, *A Decade of Watching and Waiting*, March 2007, available at www.texaswatch.org.

5. Texans for Public Justice, "Texas PACs: 2008 Election Cycle Spending," available at www.tpj.org.

6. Bureau of Labor Statistics, "Union Affiliation of Employed Wage and Salary Workers by State," available at www.bls.gov.

7. Texans for Public Justice, "Texas PACs: 2008 Election Cycle Spending."

8. Texas AFL–CIO, available at www.texasaflcio.org.

9. "Exit Polls for Texas," available at www.cnn.com/elections/2008.

10. Emily Ramshaw, "Christian Right Faring Well at Capitol," *Dallas Morning News*, May 16, 2007, available at www.dallasnews.com.

11. Texans for Public Justice, "Texas PACs: 2008 Election Cycle Spending."

12. Terry Box and Pete Slover, "Car Dealers Make U-Turn to Sanchez," *Dallas Morning News*, July 18, 2002, available at www.morningnews.com.

13. National Institute on Money in Politics, available at www.followthemoney.com.

14. Texas Ethics Commission, available at www.ethics.state.tx.us.

15. Texans for Public Justice, "Austin's Oldest Profession: Texas' Top Lobby Clients and Those Who Service Them," September 2008, available at www.tpj.org.

16. Keith E. Hamm and Charles W. Wiggins, "Texas: The Transformation from Personal to Informational Lobbying," in Ronald J. Hrebenar and Clive S. Thomas, eds., *Interest Group Politics in the Southern States* (Tuscaloosa, AL: University of Alabama Press, 1992), p. 163.

17. Matt Stiles, "$12.8 Million Spent Wooing Legislators," *San Antonio Express-News*, January 25, 2009, available at www.mysantantio.com.

18. Brent Manley, "Texas Lobbyists' Big Bucks Get Bigger," *Houston Post*, March 18, 1984, pp. 1A, 18A.

19. Christy Hoppe, "Texas Has No Law to Limit Revolving Door for Lawmakers to Become Lobbyists," *Dallas Morning News*, February 18, 2009, available at www.dallasnews.com.

20. "Short Arm of the Law," *Houston Chronicle*, May 5, 2009, available at www.chron.com.

21. Environmental Groups and Shell Oil Company Propose Landmark Settlement of Clean Air Act Lawsuit, available at http://lonestar.sierraclub.org.

22. L. M. Sixel, "Union Protesters Pay Price in City," *Houston Chronicle*, March 25, 2007, pp. D1–D4.

Chapter 6

Political Parties

WHAT WE WILL LEARN

After studying Chapter 6, students should be able to answer the following questions:

- What is the party system in the United States?

- How are the two major parties organized at the national and state level in Texas?

- What is the history of political party competition in Texas?

- How do the Texas Democratic and Republican Parties compare with one another in terms of voter support and offices held?

- What groups of voters generally support each of the major political parties in terms of income,

race and ethnicity, age, gender, region, and place of residence?

- What interest groups are allied with each of the state's major political parties?

- How do the issue orientations of the state's two major political parties compare and contrast with one another?

- What factors are most likely to affect the future of party politics in Texas and what are the challenges facing both major parties in the state?

In 2008, Texas was John McCain country. Although Democrat Barack Obama made history nationwide by winning the presidency, he did not carry Texas, losing the Lone Star State to the Republican McCain by 55 percent to 44 percent. Furthermore, the Texas Republican Party won every statewide office on the ballot as it has in every election since 1994. Republicans held onto their majorities in the Texas House of Representatives, the Texas Senate, and the State Board of Education (SBOE).

The election news was not all good for the Republican Party, however, because demographic trends are working in favor of the Democrats. Obama carried the segments of the electorate that are growing, winning both the Latino vote (63 percent to 35 percent) and the African American vote (98 percent to 2 percent for McCain).[1] Since 1992, the share of the vote cast by Latinos in Texas has doubled from 10 percent to 20 percent while the percentage of African Americans in the electorate has risen from 11 percent to 13 percent. Obama also won a majority of Texas voters under the age of 30. In contrast, McCain won the white vote (73 percent to 26 percent) and outpolled Obama among older voters. The share of the votes cast by Texas whites has fallen from 79 percent in 1992 to 63 percent in 2008. In the years ahead, the percentage of minority voters in the Texas electorate will inevitably grow while the number of older white voters will decline. Unless current voting patterns change dramatically, Texas will become Democratic country sometime between now and 2020.[2]

This chapter on political parties is the third in a series of four chapters examining the political context for policymaking. Chapter 4 discussed political participation in Texas, whereas Chapter 5 dealt with interest groups. Chapter 7 focuses on elections. This chapter begins by describing the party system in Texas and the United States. It traces the state's party history and examines party organization at the national and state levels. The chapter compares the state's major parties in terms of strength, base of support, interest-group alliances, and issue positions. It concludes by exploring the challenges facing both major parties.

THE PARTY SYSTEM

Political party A group of individuals who join together to seek public office in order to influence public policy.

A **political party** is a group of individuals who join together to seek public office in order to influence public policy. Parties are similar to interest groups in that both types of political organizations attempt to affect the policymaking process and both are interested in election outcomes. The difference is that political parties attempt to win control of the machinery of government by nominating candidates for elected office to run under the party label. If they are successful, they identify with the party while in office. The Republican Party, Democratic Party, Texas Association of Business (TAB), and Texas Trial Lawyers Association (TTLA) all participate in the election process and attempt to influence public policy. However, only the Republicans and the Democrats actually put forward candidates for office under their organizational name. They are political parties, whereas the other two organizations are interest groups.

Two-party system
The division of voter loyalties between two major political parties, resulting in the near exclusion of minor parties from seriously competing for a share of political power.

Throughout most of its history, the United States has had a **two-party system,** which means voter loyalties are divided between two major political parties, resulting in the near exclusion of minor parties from seriously competing for a share of political power. Since the Civil War era, the Democrats and the Republicans have been the two dominant parties in American national politics. Minor parties, such as the Libertarian, Green, and Reform Parties, have tried to have an impact in Texas politics. However, except for the election of a small number of Libertarian candidates at the local level, minor party candidates have had little success in the Lone Star State. After the 2008 election, every member of the Texas legislature and every member of the congressional delegation from Texas were either Republicans or Democrats.

Despite a national two-party system, many states have experienced periods of one-party dominance. The most significant example of one-party control took place in the South after the end of the Civil War era, during which the Democratic Party dominated southern politics for nearly a century. Political conflicts still occurred in the South, but they took place within the Democratic Party between factions divided over issues or personalities. A **party faction** is an identifiable subgroup within a political party.

Party faction An identifiable subgroup within a political party.

PARTY ORGANIZATION

The Democratic and Republican Parties have both national and state party structures.

National Party Organization

A national committee and a national committee chair head the national party organization. The national committee consists of a committeeman and committeewoman from each state and the District of Columbia, chosen by their state or the district party organization. The national committee elects the national chair. When the party controls the White House, the national chair is usually chosen by the president.

The national political party organizations support party candidates at the state level by spending money on their behalf and providing them with various services. Although federal law limits the amount of money a national party organization can contribute directly to a candidate, the national party organizations can spend unlimited amounts of money on behalf of candidates as long as they do not coordinate directly with a candidate's campaign. In 2008, for example, the Democratic Congressional Campaign Committee ($1.6 million) and the National Republican Congressional Committee ($1 million) invested heavily in the race between Democratic Congressman Nick Lampson and his Republican opponent, Pete Olson, in the race to represent the Twenty-second Congressional District of Texas, which included Fort Bend County and some suburban areas south of Houston. Olson won the race.[3] The national party organizations provide candidates and state parties with polling data and conduct get-out-the-vote efforts. Furthermore, individuals interested in running for state or national office can attend candidate training sessions sponsored by the national party organizations at which they can learn how to build a campaign organization, raise money, deal with the media, identify issues, and present themselves to voters.

Texas Party Organization

Political parties in Texas have both temporary and permanent party organizations. Figure 6.1 depicts the various structures.

Temporary Party Organization The temporary party organization of each party assembles for a few hours or days in general election years (even-numbered years—2010, 2012, etc.) to allow rank-and-file party supporters a chance to participate in the party's decision-making process. On the evening of the March primary after the polls have closed, Texans have the opportunity to attend precinct conventions, usually in the same location as the polling place, with Republicans gathering in one area and Democrats in another. Citizens who voted in a certain party's primary election are eligible to participate in that party's precinct convention. The turnout at precinct conventions is usually light, especially in non-presidential years, although turnout was heavy for the Democratic Party precinct conventions in 2008 because of the spirited presidential contest between Hillary Clinton and Barack Obama. The main business of precinct conventions is to elect delegates to the county or state senatorial district conventions, which are held on the second Saturday after the primary.

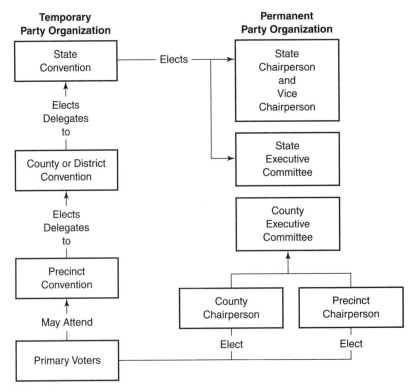

FIGURE 6.1 Texas Party Structures.

In counties with more than one state senatorial district (Bexar, Brazoria, Chambers, Collin, Dallas, Denton, El Paso, Galveston, Fort Bend, Harris, Hidalgo, Jefferson, Montgomery, Smith, Tarrant, and Travis), delegates elected at precinct conventions attend state senatorial district conventions. In other counties, they attend a county convention. The number of delegates an election precinct may send to the county or district convention depends on the size of the vote in that precinct for the party's candidate in the last governor's election.

The county and district conventions are larger and more formally organized than precinct conventions, and they generally last longer, sometimes a full day. The convention usually includes speeches by party leaders and officeholders, and the delegates will likely debate and vote on a number of resolutions. Once again, the main business of the meeting is to select delegates to the next highest level—in this case, the state convention. The number of delegates each county or district convention sends to the state convention depends on the size of the vote for the party's candidate in the last governor's election in the county or district.

The Republican and Democratic Parties hold their state conventions in June. This meeting is the largest, most formal, and longest of all, generally lasting most of a weekend. The state convention certifies party nominees for the fall general election, adopts a state **party platform** (a statement of party principles and issue positions), elects the state party chairperson and vice-chairperson, chooses members of the state executive committee, and selects individuals to serve on the national party executive committee. The state convention also gives the party the opportunity to showcase itself and its candidates for the upcoming general election.

In presidential election years, the state party convention selects delegates to the national party convention. State law provides that delegates to the national party conventions be pledged to support presidential candidates in rough proportion to the candidates' strength in the spring presidential preference primary. In addition to selecting delegates to the national party convention, each state party convention also names a slate of potential presidential electors to cast the Electoral College votes for Texas should the party's presidential candidate carry the state in the November general election. The **Electoral College** is the system established in the U.S. Constitution for the selection of the president and vice president of the United States.

Permanent Party Organization   Each party has a permanent party organization, which operates year-round. Forming the base of the permanent party organization are the precinct chairpersons, elected by party voters in each of the state's precincts, except in those areas where one party is so weak that no one can be found to accept the job. Precinct chairpersons conduct primary elections by staffing the polling place on Election Day. They may also work to organize the precinct for their party.

The county executive committee is the next highest level of permanent party organization. It includes all the precinct chairpersons in the county and the county chairperson, who is elected by party voters countywide. The county executive committee receives filing petitions and fees from primary election candidates for countywide offices and is responsible for placing candidate names on the ballot. The county executive committee also arranges for county and district conventions.

Party platform A statement of party principles and issue positions.

Electoral College The system established in the U.S. Constitution for the selection of the president and vice president of the United States.

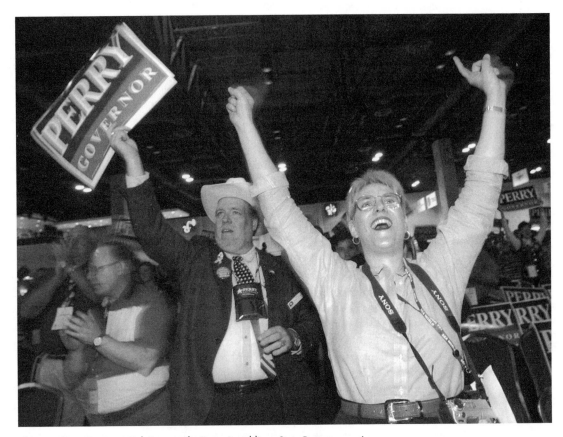

Delegates cheer Governor Rick Perry at the Texas Republican State Party convention.

The state executive committee is the highest level of party organization in the state. It includes the party chair, vice chair, and a committeeman and committee-woman representing each of the 31 state senatorial districts. The State Democratic Executive Committee (SDEC) includes a party treasurer as well. The main duties of the SDEC and the State Republican Executive Committee (SREC) are to certify statewide candidates for the March primary, arrange state party conventions, raise money for party candidates, and, in general, promote the party. In particular, state party chairs serve as media spokespersons for their party.

History of the Texas Party System

Grand Old Party (GOP) Nickname for the Republican Party.

The Civil War and Reconstruction produced the one-party Democratic South. Most native white southerners hated the Republican Party because of its associa-tion with the Union during the Civil War era. In Texas, the **Grand Old Party (GOP),** as the Republican Party was known, could only count on the loyalty of African Americans, German Americans living in the Hill Country who had

GETTING INVOLVED

Volunteer to Support Your Political Party

Political parties are a means for individuals to influence the policymaking process. The Internet Research feature found on page 130 includes the websites of the five most important political parties in Texas politics. Each party website includes information on how Texans can contact the party and get involved in its work. Contact the party of your choice and offer to help. Volunteers support their party by registering voters, helping out in the local office, raising money, and researching issues. People who get involved with their party may eventually win the opportunity to attend the county, state, or national convention. Some may even decide to run for office and get elected.

It's your country—get involved!

Solid South the usual Democratic sweep of southern state electoral votes in presidential election years between the end of the Civil War era and the current party era.

Conservatism The political view that seeks to preserve the political, economic, and social institutions of society against abrupt change. Conservatives generally oppose most government economic regulation and heavy government spending while favoring low taxes and traditional values.

New Deal program The name of President Franklin Roosevelt's legislative program for countering the Great Depression.

opposed secession before the Civil War, and a few others. With the Republican Party in disrepute, the Democrats were the dominant party not only in Texas but also throughout the South—so much so, in fact, that political commentators coined the term **"Solid South"** to refer to the usual Democratic sweep of southern state electoral votes in presidential election years. In Texas, Democrats won nearly every statewide race, most seats in Congress and the state legislature, and the overwhelming majority of local and judicial contests, frequently without Republican opposition.

Large landowners and industrialists controlled the Democratic Party of the late nineteenth and early twentieth centuries. The public policies they favored reflected a political philosophy of **conservatism,** the political view that seeks to preserve the political, economic, and social institutions of society against abrupt change. Conservatives generally oppose most government economic regulation and heavy government spending while favoring low taxes and traditional values.

By the 1930s, an identifiable liberal faction had emerged to challenge conservative dominance of the Democratic Party. **Liberalism** is the political view that seeks to change the political, economic, or social institutions of society to foster the development of the individual. Liberals believe that the government can (and should) advance social progress by promoting political equality, social justice, and economic prosperity. Liberals usually favor government regulation and high levels of government spending for social programs. They also value social and cultural diversity and defend the right of individual adult choice on issues such as access to abortion. Liberal Democrats in the Lone Star State supported Democratic President Franklin Roosevelt and his **New Deal program,** which was the name of Roosevelt's legislative program for countering the Great Depression. Liberal Democrats called for a more active role for state government in the fields of education, job training, healthcare, and public assistance to the poor. To pay for these programs, liberal Democrats proposed higher taxes on business and industry, as well as on people earning substantial incomes. Liberal Democrats in Texas called for the elimination of the white primary and the poll tax. They also supported an end to discrimination against African Americans and Latinos.

Liberalism The political view that seeks to change the political, economic, or social institutions of society to foster the development of the individual. Liberals believe that the government can (and should) advance social progress by promoting political equality, social justice, and economic prosperity. Liberals usually favor government regulation and high levels of government spending for social programs. Liberals value social and cultural diversity and defend the right of individual adult choice on issues such as access to abortion.

The liberal wing of the Texas Democratic Party achieved some political success during the 1930s as the Great Depression caused many Texans to question the wisdom of the state's conservative public policies. The highpoint for the liberals was the election of James Allred as governor in 1935 and 1937. During the Allred administration, the legislature and the governor enacted several liberal programs designed to combat the Great Depression. Support for the liberal Democrats came primarily from a loose coalition of unemployed persons, working-class whites, labor union members, Jews, university people, some professionals, Latinos, and African Americans. The latter were now beginning a wholesale change of allegiance from the GOP to the party of Franklin Roosevelt.

The conservative Democrats reestablished themselves as the dominant wing of the Democratic Party during the 1940s. With the Great Depression over, the economic issues raised by liberal Democrats were less effective. Conservative Democrats claimed that the return of economic prosperity proved the correctness of their philosophy. Another advantage for conservatives was that they enjoyed easier access to the financial resources needed to wage a modern political campaign in a large and rapidly growing state than did the liberal Democrats. Furthermore, working-class and minority voters who made up the core of support for the liberal Democrats were less likely to vote than the middle- and upper-income white supporters of the conservative Democrats.

The period running from the early 1950s through the late 1970s was a time of transition for party politics in the Lone Star State. By the 1950s, the liberal wing

INTERNET RESEARCH

Political Parties in Texas

The Texas Democratic, Green, Libertarian, Reform, and Republican Parties all have homepages. Learn more about the state's political parties by checking out their websites.

Democratic Party: **www.txdemocrats.org/**

Texas Green Party: **www.txgreens.org/**

Texas Libertarian Party: **www.tx.lp.org/**

Texas Reform Party: **www.texasreformparty.org/**

Texas Republican Party: **www.texasgop.org**

Review each of the websites and answer the following questions:

1. Which website is the most visually attractive? Why?

2. Which website is the least visually attractive? Why?

3. Pick out one website and write a short review, discussing its main features, strong points, and weaknesses.

of the Texas Democratic Party had become a formidable political force. Although conservative Democrats still held the upper hand, liberal challengers had to be taken seriously. Liberal Democrats scored a major breakthrough in 1957 when Ralph Yarborough, a liberal Democrat, won a special election to the U.S. Senate. He held the seat through 1970. Liberal Democrats also captured a few seats in Congress, won a number of positions in the state legislature, and ran credible races for the party's gubernatorial nomination.

Liberal Democrats gained strength because the electorate was changing. The legal barriers that had kept many African Americans, Latinos, and poor whites from the polls were coming down, primarily because of the intervention of the federal courts and the U.S. Congress. The liberal wing of the party also benefited from the defection of some conservative voters to the GOP. A poll taken in the mid-1960s found that 37 percent of Texans who said they were once conservative Democrats had left the party to become either Republicans (23 percent) or independents (14 percent).[4] The exodus of conservative voters from the Democratic Party made it easier for liberal candidates to win Democratic primary elections.

In the meantime, the Texas Republican Party was coming to life. The presidential candidacy of General Dwight D. Eisenhower in 1952 brought a flood of new faces into the Republican camp, many of which were former Democrats. Furthermore, many conservative Democrats, including Governor Allan Shivers, deserted their party's presidential nominee, Governor Adlai Stevenson of Illinois, to openly support the Republican presidential candidate. Eisenhower carried the state in both 1952 and 1956.

Texas Republicans built their party throughout the 1960s and 1970s. They elected candidates to the U.S. Congress and the Texas legislature and won a number of local races, particularly in urban areas. Perhaps their most important victory came in 1961, when Republican John Tower, a young college professor at Midwestern State University in Wichita Falls, won a special election to serve the remainder of Lyndon Johnson's U.S. Senate term after Johnson resigned to become vice president. Tower won reelection in 1966, 1972, and 1978.

Surveys of party identification among voters traced the Republican surge. For decades, the most common political animal in the Lone Star State was the Yellow Dog Democrat. This was a Texan, it was said, who would vote for a yellow dog if the dog were the Democratic candidate. In other words, a **Yellow Dog Democrat** was a loyal Democratic Party voter. In 1952, 66 percent of Texans called themselves Democrats, whereas only 6 percent declared allegiance to the Republican Party. Twenty years later, the margin was a bit closer, 57 percent to 14 percent.[5] By 1984, however, Democrats outnumbered Republicans by only 33 percent to 28 percent (with the rest independent).[6]

What accounted for the rise of the GOP as a significant electoral force in Texas? First, the legacy of the Civil War finally began to diminish in importance, especially for younger Texans. Surveys showed that younger voters were more likely to identify with the GOP than were older people.[7] Second, many conservative white Democrats became disenchanted with what they saw as an increasingly liberal national Democratic Party. Whereas some conservative

Yellow Dog Democrat A loyal Democratic Party voter.

southern Democrats openly defected to GOP ranks, other conservatives remained nominal Democrats but supported Republicans in statewide and national races whenever the Democratic nominee seemed too liberal for their taste. Finally, the Texas Republican Party benefited from the migration of white-collar workers from outside the South. Many of these Republican newcomers identified with the GOP in their old states and simply took their party loyalties with them to their new homes in Texas.

The 1978 election signaled the emergence of a competitive two-party system in Texas. The spring primary produced the most significant development for the Democrats when Attorney General John Hill, a liberal Democrat, defeated incumbent Governor Dolph Briscoe, a conservative. Hill's victory demonstrated that liberal Democrats could compete with conservative Democrats on an equal footing. The determining political event in 1978 for the GOP came in the fall general election, when Bill Clements defeated Hill to become the first Republican governor in more than a century. The election of Clements demonstrated that well funded Republican candidates could win statewide elections in Texas, especially against Democrats from the liberal wing of the party.

From 1978 to 1994, Texas party politics was more competitive than ever before. The GOP enjoyed an advantage at the top of the ballot, winning most races for governor and U.S. senator. The Republican presidential nominee also carried the state every time during the period. In contrast, Democrats were considerably more successful in contests below the top of the ballot. Throughout the period,

John McCain won 61 percent of the suburban vote in 2008.

Democrats won most statewide executive offices below the level of governor, enjoyed majorities in the Texas House and Texas Senate, elected most of the state's judges, and held most county offices.

The Republican Party became the clear majority party in the state in 1994 when Republican gubernatorial nominee George W. Bush defeated incumbent Democratic Governor Ann Richards and the GOP won a majority of seats in the Texas Senate. Since that point, no Democrat has won a statewide election for any office. The Democrats lost their last hold on power at the state level in 2002 when the GOP captured a majority of seats in the Texas House. Although Democrats clung to office at the county level in many areas of the state, especially in South Texas, the GOP made significant inroads in the state's urban centers, capturing every local office and judgeship elected countywide in Harris, Dallas, and Tarrant Counties.

The 2002 election was the zenith of Republican Party success. Although the Texas GOP remains the majority party in state politics, the Democratic Party has begun making inroads. Democrats have picked up seats in the legislature, especially in the Texas House, and made gains at the local level, winning every contested race in Dallas County in 2006 and 2008 and capturing a majority of contested countrywide races in Harris County in 2008.

THE PARTY BALANCE

The Texas electorate is almost evenly divided among Democrats, Republicans, and independents. A Gallup analysis of survey data during the first six months of 2009 showed roughly the same percentage of Democrats and Republicans in Texas.[8] Similarly, exit polls taken on Election Day in 2008 revealed that the makeup of the electorate was 33 percent Democrat, 33 percent Republican, and 34 percent independent.[9] Both sets of data showed Texas more Republican/less Democratic than the nation as a whole.

Although party identification is an important predictor of an individual's vote, the overall party identification balance does not necessarily forecast election outcomes. People typically vote for the candidates of their preferred political party. In 2008, for example, 89 percent of Texas Democrats backed Obama, whereas 93 percent of Texas Republicans voted for McCain.[10] The party identification balance does not necessarily match the vote because Democrats and Republicans are not equally likely to go to the polls. In Texas (and around the nation), Democratic turnout is typically lower than Republican turnout because Democrats as a group are lower income and lower-income people are less likely to go to vote than middle- and upper-income individuals. Furthermore, people who call themselves independents may tip the election to one party or the other. In 2008, independents nationwide backed Obama over McCain by a 52 percent to 44 percent margin.[11] In Texas, however, independents lined up solidly behind McCain, 62 percent to 32 percent for his Democratic opponent.[12] Finally, the Texas Republican Party benefits from the general political climate in the state. Surveys show that self-described conservatives outnumber people who call themselves liberal by a 44 to 17 percent margin, making Texas the thirteenth-most conservative state in the union.[13] Conservatives tend to vote

TABLE 6.1   Party Affiliation of Elected Officials in Texas, 2009

Office	Total Number of Officials	Democrats	Republicans
U.S. Senate	2	0	2
U.S. House	32	12	20
State Executives*	6	0	6
Texas Senate	31	12	19
Texas House	150	74	76
Texas Supreme Court	9	0	9
Texas Court of Criminal Appeals	9	0	9
Texas Railroad Commission	3	0	3
Texas State Board of Education	15	5	10

*Governor, lieutenant governor, attorney general, comptroller, agriculture commissioner, and land commissioner.

Republican, especially in national elections, giving the Texas GOP a decided advantage over their Democratic opponents.

Table 6.1 compares the electoral strength of the Texas Republican and Democratic Parties. After the 2008 election, the three highest profile elective officeholders in the state were Republicans: Rick Perry was governor, whereas Kay Bailey Hutchison and John Cornyn represented Texas in the U.S. Senate. The Republican Party held 20 of 32 seats in the U.S. House of Representatives. Every member of the Texas Railroad Commission, Texas Supreme Court, and Texas Court of Criminal Appeals was Republican. A majority of the members of both houses of the Texas legislature and the State Board of Education (SBOE) were Republican as well.

An analysis of 2008 election returns suggested that the baseline Republican vote statewide was around 54 percent of the electorate. Contests for the Texas Court of Criminal Appeals are a good measure of party strength because the individual candidates are not well known and seldom raise enough money to mount the media-based campaign necessary to build name recognition. Without information about the individual candidates, voters typically base their choices on party affiliation. When the Democratic Party dominated Texas politics, Democrats routinely swept races for the Court of Criminal Appeals. For more than a decade, however, the GOP has won every race for the Texas Court of Criminal Appeals. In 2008, the two Republican candidates facing Democratic opponents in races for seats on the Court of Criminal Appeals averaged 54 percent of the vote.[14]

After years of trailing the Republican Party in fundraising and organization, Texas Democrats have caught up with their GOP opponents. In 2008, the Texas Democratic Party and its allied campaign organizations raised $7.6 million to support its campaign activities. In contrast, the Texas Republican Party and its allied committees took in $4.8 million. Whereas trial lawyers were the most generous contributors to the Democratic cause, business interests provided most of the money for the Republicans, especially oil and gas, telecommunications, and agricultural interests.[15] The Texas Democratic Party has also enhanced its organizational structure, moving into a new headquarters office in Austin and more than doubling its political staff.[16]

VOTING PATTERNS

Voting patterns in Texas reflect differences in income, race and ethnicity, age, gender, region, and place of residence.

Income

Voting patterns are related to income, with higher-income citizens generally supporting Republican candidates and lower-income voters backing Democrats. Exit polls taken during the 2008 presidential election showed a clear relationship between income and voter choice. The Democratic nominee, Obama, led the Republican nominee, McCain, by a 56 percent to 42 percent margin among voters with family incomes under $50,000 a year. In contrast, 63 percent of voters with annual family incomes over $50,000 backed McCain compared with 36 percent for Obama.[17]

Race and Ethnicity

Voting patterns vary based on race and ethnicity. Minority voters, especially African Americans, support the Democrats. In 2008, African Americans in Texas supported Obama by an overwhelming margin of 98 percent to just 2 percent for McCain. The Latino vote went for Obama as well, with 63 percent compared with 25 percent for his Republican opponent. In contrast, the white vote in Texas is heavily Republican. In 2008, 73 percent of white voters backed McCain compared with only 26 percent who supported Obama.[18]

Age

Texas Democrats are stronger with younger voters; in contrast, Republicans do better with older voters. In 2008, Obama led McCain among people under the age of 30 by 54 percent to 45 percent. McCain edged Obama among voters in the 30 to 44 age group, 52 percent to 46 percent, and won older voter groups by wider margins, taking two-thirds of the votes of people over the age of 65.[19] The figures provide encouragement to Texas Democrats because the natural turnover of the electorate should produce Democratic gains at the ballot box.

Gender

gender gap A term that refers to differences in party identification and political attitudes between men and women.

Texas has a **gender gap,** a term that refers to differences in party identification and political attitudes between men and women. Although McCain carried both the women's vote and the men's vote in 2008, his margin was considerably closer with women than with men. McCain outpolled Obama among male voters by 20 percentage points (59 percent to 39 percent). In contrast, McCain only carried the women's vote by 5 percentage points (52 percent to 47 percent).[20]

Region

Texas voting patterns have a regional flavor. For example, Republicans are strongest in West Texas and East Texas. In 2008, McCain took 77 percent of the vote in West Texas and 62 percent in East Texas. In the meantime, Democrats are strongest in South Texas. Obama won 60 percent of the South Texas vote in 2008 compared with 38 percent for his Republican opponent. The other three geographic regions of the state—the Dallas-Fort Worth Metroplex, the Houston area, and Central Texas—are closely divided. In 2008, McCain won each of the three regions, but the margins were within five percentage points or less.[21]

Place of Residence

Although the Democrats do well in big-city Texas, the Republicans carry the suburbs, small towns, and rural areas of the state. In 2008, Obama outpolled McCain in cities with a population greater than 500,000 by 55 percent to 44 percent, carrying Travis, Dallas, El Paso, Bexar, and Harris Counties. However, McCain won Texas by racking up large margins in the suburbs (61 percent to 37 percent) and the small town and rural areas of the state (63 percent to 36 percent).[22] McCain's strongest counties in terms of vote margin were Montgomery County, which is just north of Houston, and Collin County, which is just north of Dallas.[23]

Interest Group–Political Party Alliances

Political parties and interest groups form informal alliances. Interest groups assist political parties by providing campaign funds and organizational support to party candidates. Groups endorse candidates and distribute campaign literature to group members and people who would likely sympathize with the group's goals. Interest groups may also provide lobbying support for policies the party favors. In turn, political parties reward their interest group allies by adopting policies that benefit them.

Table 6.2 lists the interest groups generally associated with the Texas Democratic and Republican Parties. Although the list of groups allied with the Democratic Party is longer than the list associated with the GOP, the groups in the Democratic column are not necessarily more effective politically. With the exception of trial lawyers, who support the Democrats, the groups allied with the Republican Party have more money to devote to political action than do the groups who support the Democratic Party. Many of the groups allied with the Democrats, such as teacher organizations and labor unions, have a large membership base, which can be tapped for volunteer campaign support. Their numbers are somewhat offset, however, by the dedication of anti-abortion activists and conservative religious groups supporting the Republican Party.

Although political parties and interest groups form alliances, groups are not wholly owned subsidiaries of parties. For example, not all African Americans, Latinos, and gay men and lesbians support the Democratic Party; some are Republican. Furthermore, groups and group members may not agree with a political party on every issue or endorse all of its candidates.

TABLE 6.2   Political Party and Interest Group Alliances

Groups Allied with the Democratic Party	Groups Allied with the Republican Party
• Organized labor	• Business groups and trade associations
• Environmental organizations	• Most professional organizations, including doctors and realtors
• Consumer groups	
• African American rights organizations	• Farm groups
• Latino rights groups	• Religious conservatives
• Gay and lesbian rights organizations	• National Rifle Association
• Teacher groups	• Pro-life groups
• Pro-choice groups	• Tort reform organizations
• Trial lawyers	• Anti-tax groups
• Women rights groups	

"You can be absolutely certain that every election [to come] in Texas will have a larger percentage of Latino voters."—Sociologist Stephen Klineberg, Rice University

ISSUE ORIENTATION

The two major political parties in Texas agree on the fundamental principles of America's political and economic systems. Neither party wants to rejoin Mexico or establish a monarchy. Both Democrats and Republicans favor good schools, safe streets, healthy families, and a sound economy. However, the two parties disagree on some of the details of policy, particularly on the role of government in society.

Table 6.3 compares the 2008 platforms of the state's two major political parties on selected issues. As the table shows, the two parties agree on some matters.

TABLE 6.3　Texas Democratic and Republican Party Platforms, 2008, Selected Issues

Issue	Democratic Platform Position	Republican Platform Position
State taxes	Says that the franchise tax should be revised to protect small business. Calls for extending property tax relief to renters. Endorses state constitutional amendment to prohibit a sales tax on food and medicine.	Calls for repealing the franchise tax and abolishing the property tax. Calls the sales tax the "simplest and most visible, stable, and equitable" tax.
School finance	Declares that the state should fully fund an exemplary education program in every school district. Favors reducing reliance on the **Robin Hood plan** (a reform of the state's school finance system designed to increase funding for poor school districts by redistributing money from wealthy districts).	Urges state to focus school funding on academics rather than non-academic activities. Opposes tax increases to fund schools.
School choice (an educational reform movement that allows parents to choose the elementary or secondary school their children will attend)	Opposes private school voucher program.	Favors giving parents state funding vouchers and then letting them choose among public, private, or parochial schools, contingent on the passage of a state constitutional amendment exempting private and parochial schools from state regulation.
Other education issues	Rejects effort to destroy **bilingual education** (teaching of academic subjects in both English and a student's native language, usually Spanish). Endorses a comprehensive sex education program. Calls for increasing teacher and support staff pay to the national average. Supports universal access to pre-kindergarten and kindergarten programs.	Calls for the termination of bilingual education programs, preferring instead English emersion programs. Favors abstinence-only sex education. Supports including intelligent design in the science curriculum and allowing teachers to discuss the strength and weaknesses of all scientific theories.

Robin Hood plan A reform of the state's school finance system designed to increase funding for poor school districts by redistributing money from wealthy districts.

School choice An educational reform movement that would allow parents to choose the elementary or secondary school their children will attend.

Bilingual education The teaching of academic subjects in both English and a student's native language, usually Spanish.

TABLE 6.3   Continued

Issue	Democratic Platform Position	Republican Platform Position
Higher education	Calls for increased state funding for higher education coupled with a rollback in the increases in college tuition and fees adopted since 2003. Supports giving high school graduates two years of public college or post-secondary technical education tuition free. Favors expanded grant programs.	Favors the repeal of the **top 10 percent rule** (a state law that grants automatic college admission to public high school graduates who finish in the top 10 percent of their class). Supports charging non-citizens higher tuition and denying non-citizens financial aid.
Illegal immigration	Calls for allocation of sufficient resources to police the border. Supports enforcement of laws against employers who knowingly hire illegal workers at substandard wages. Endorses legislation to create a path to citizenship for undocumented workers living in the United States.	Declares that all necessary means should be employed to control the border, including building a physical barrier. Opposes any form of amnesty for illegal immigrants and calls for their deportation to their home countries.
Healthcare	Calls for the creation of a Texas universal healthcare plan. Calls for government funding of all types of stem cell research. Favors expanding the **State Children's Health Insurance Program (SCHIP),** which is a federal program designed to provide health insurance to children from low-income families whose parents are not poor enough to qualify for Medicaid.	Favors market-based approach to healthcare. Supports government funding for adult stem cell research, but opposes funding research that involves destroying embryos. Calls for passage of a state law that grants healthcare professionals the right to object to participating in medical practices that conflict with their moral or religious beliefs.
Energy	Declares that Texas should reduce global warming pollution by 25 percent below 1990 levels by 2020. Supports the development of renewable energy.	Opposes taxes and regulations imposed to counter the "alleged threat of global warming." Favors domestic energy development, including alternative energy sources.

top 10 percent rule A state law that grants automatic college admission to public high school students who finish in the top 10 percent of their class.

State Children's Health Insurance Program (SCHIP) A federal program designed to provide health insurance to children from low-income families whose parents are not poor enough to qualify for Medicaid.

continued on next page

TABLE 6.3 Continued

Issue	Democratic Platform Position	Republican Platform Position
Privatization (the process that involves the government contracting with private business to implement government programs)	Declares that privatization of social services has been a poor use of tax dollars.	Supports the privatization of government services when beneficial to the taxpayer.
Trans-Texas Corridor	Opposes the Trans-Texas Corridor.	Opposes the Trans-Texas Corridor.
Right-to-work (a law prohibiting a union or closed shop)	Calls for repeal of Texas Right-to-Work Law.	Supports right to work in Texas and calls for a national right-to-work law.
Tort reform (the revision of state laws to limit the ability of plaintiffs in personal injury lawsuits to recover damages in court)	Proposes the reversal of "unjust provisions" of the tort reform legislation passed in 2003 "that have denied Texans who have suffered severe harm the ability to redress their grievances in fair and open courts."	Favors further reform to discourage frivolous lawsuits.
Capital punishment (the death penalty)	Supports the death penalty, but proposes reforms, such as DNA testing, to ensure that it is fairly administered.	Declares that capital punishment, when "properly applied," is a legitimate form of punishment and a deterrent for serious crime. Wants to extend the death penalty to convictions of forcible rape.
Hate crimes legislation (a measure that increases penalties for persons convicted of criminal offenses motivated by prejudice based on race, religion, national origin, gender, or sexual orientation)	Calls for strong enforcement of the Texas Hate Crimes Act.	Calls for the immediate repeal of the Texas Hate Crimes Act.

Privatization The process that involves the government contracting with private business to implement government programs.

Right-to-work A law prohibiting a union or closed shop.

Tort reform The revision of state laws to limit the ability of plaintiffs in personal injury lawsuits to recover damages in court.

Capital punishment The death penalty.

Hate crimes legislation Legislative measures that increase penalties for persons convicted of criminal offenses motivated by prejudice based on race, religion, national origin, gender, or sexual orientation.

TABLE 6.3   Continued

Issue	Democratic Platform Position	Republican Platform Position
Judicial selection	Supports the election of state judges.	Supports the election of state judges.
Role of religion	Declares that the separation of church and state allows religion to flourish.	Declares that the separation of church and state is a myth.
Minimum wage (the lowest hourly wage that an employer can pay covered workers)	Supports increasing the state minimum wage, which applies to farm workers, to keep up with the federal minimum wage.	Calls for the repeal of the minimum wage.
Abortion	Declares that women should decide when and whether to bear children, "in consultation with their family, their physician, personal conscience or their God, rather than having these personal decisions made by politicians."	Declares that the unborn child has an individual fundamental right to life that cannot be infringed. Supports a constitutional amendment to ban abortion.
Divorce	No position.	Calls for repeal of no-fault divorce laws.
Election reform	Opposes requiring prospective voters to produce a photo ID. Supports same-day voter registration.	Favors requiring the re-registration of voters every four years. Says that prospective voters should produce state or federal photo IDs.
Gay and lesbian rights	Supports the passage of the Employment Non-Discrimination Act (ENDA). Opposes discrimination in the state foster care system. Declares that government should honor "family values" through policies that value all families.	Calls for the enactment of a constitutional amendment to protect traditional marriage. Opposes laws granting civil rights protection to gay men and lesbians. Declares that homosexuals should not be allowed to adopt, have custody of children, or have unsupervised visitation with minor children.

Minimum wage
The lowest hourly wage that an employer can pay covered workers.

Trans-Texas Corridor
A proposed network of transportation corridors a quarter mile wide and 370 miles long running from Brownsville to Oklahoma that would include toll roads, railways, and utility lines.

Both the Democrats and the Republicans favor the election of state judges. They both oppose the **Trans-Texas Corridor,** a proposed network of transportation corridors, a quarter mile wide and 370 miles long, running from Brownsville to Oklahoma which would include toll roads, railways, and utility lines. Both parties support better border security to stop drug smuggling and stem the flow of illegal immigration.

On other platform issues, the Democrats and Republicans take positions that are clearly different. Whereas the Democrats support a woman's right to choose, the GOP platform calls for the adoption of a constitutional amendment to outlaw abortion. The Democrats endorse bilingual education; the Republicans reject it. Democrats propose increasing the state minimum wage (the lowest hourly wage that an employer can pay covered workers), whereas Republicans want to repeal it altogether. The Democrats favor creating a path to citizenship for undocumented workers, whereas the Republicans demand their deportation. Democrats endorse the aggressive enforcement of the Texas Hate Crimes Act; the GOP wants it repealed. Democrats favor undoing some of the tort reforms adopted in 2003 whereas Republicans want to expand the reforms.

The party platforms show that the two parties have different perspectives on the role of government. The Democrats believe that government should play a role in addressing social problems. The Democratic platform supports adequate funding for public education, increased state support for higher education, expansion of the State Children's Health Insurance Program (SCHIP), the adoption of a universal healthcare program, and a significant reduction in pollution that causes global warming. On social issues, Democrats support abortion rights and favor the adoption of federal legislation designed to protect gay men and lesbians from job discrimination. In contrast, the Republicans believe that government's primary role is to support traditional family values rather than solving social problems. The GOP platform proposes the repeal of the property tax, which is the major source of tax revenue for local governments in Texas, as well as the franchise tax. The Republican Platform favors private approaches to healthcare and rejects any regulations or taxes adopted to combat global warming, which it calls an "alleged threat." The Republicans believe that government should strengthen traditional marriage by making divorce more difficult, outlawing same-sex marriage, and prohibiting homosexuals from adopting or having the custody of children.

 WHAT IS YOUR OPINION?

Which party's platform more closely matches your political views—the Democratic or the Republican?

THE FUTURE OF PARTY POLITICS IN TEXAS

Recent elections have given Democrats hope that they will soon be able to challenge Republican dominance of state government. The Democrats have gained seats in the Texas House of Representatives and done well in county and judicial contests in many urban areas. Dallas County flipped from Republican control to Democratic dominance in 2006 and the trend continued in 2008. In fact, Democrats won a majority of races on the ballot in Harris County in 2008. Democrats already enjoyed the upper hand in county and judicial contests in Travis County, Bexar County, and El Paso County. With the state's minority population growing and white citizens no longer a majority, the future of the Democratic Party seems promising.

When and if Texas becomes a Democratic state again depends on a number of factors:

- **Latino turnout:** In 2008, Latinos accounted for 36 percent of the state's population[24] but only 20 percent of the electorate.[25] As younger Latinos become adults and older non-citizen Latinos gain their citizenship, the potential Latino electorate will grow. Democratic Party gains hinge on the success of its voter registration efforts and get-out-the-vote drives.

- **Latino voting patterns:** Latinos supported Obama in 2008 by 63 percent to 25 percent for McCain, a considerably greater margin in favor of the Democratic candidate than in 2004, when political analysts estimated that Republican President George W. Bush ran a close race against John Kerry, perhaps even taking the Latino vote in the Lone Star State.[26] Many political observers believe that the Republican Party has alienated many Latino voters by harsh anti-immigrant rhetoric, especially on talk radio.[27] If Latino voters continue to back the Democrats with 60 percent or more of their votes, Texas will almost certainly become a Democratic state in the next decade.

- **White voters:** Although minority residents represent a majority of the state's population, they do not make up a majority of the electorate. In 2008, the Texas electorate was 63 percent white, 20 percent Latino, 13 percent African American, 2 percent Asian, and 2 percent "other."[28] Obama and other Democratic candidates for statewide office lost because they received only about one-fourth of the white vote. McCain trounced Obama among white voters by a 73 percent to 26 percent margin.[29] Although demographic change may eventually lead the Democrats back into power, their success in the near future depends on doing better with white voters. Democrats can take some comfort from exit polls showing that Obama did better with younger white voters than with older whites, although he was still trailing badly in each age bracket. Whereas Obama lost the under 30 white vote to McCain by a sizable 30 percent to 69 percent margin, he lost the over 65 white vote by an even more one-sided margin of 20 percent to 78 percent.[30] As younger white voters mature and older white voters pass away, the overall Democratic share of the white vote will likely improve.

Each political party faces challenges. In the long run, the Democratic Party has the advantage because of demographic change. It can begin winning statewide races again sooner rather than later if it can succeed in turning out its base voters, especially Latinos, with aggressive voter registration efforts and get-out-the-vote drives. Democratic success in the near term also depends on increasing the party's share of the white vote.

The challenge for the Texas Republican Party, meanwhile, is to adapt to demographic change. The Republican base is shrinking. Unless GOP candidates can do better with minority voters, especially Latino voters, they will continue to lose elections in urban centers and will sooner or later lose their statewide majority. Republican leaders recognize the need to extend their party's appeal to minority voters. Recent Republican governors, including Bill Clements, George W. Bush, and Rick Perry, have appointed Latinos and African Americans to high profile positions as secretary of state and to vacancies on the Texas Railroad Commission and the Texas Supreme Court. Bush campaigned hard to win Latino votes, speaking Spanish in campaign appearances and in radio campaign ads. Republicans also hope to attract Latino support by stressing social issues, such as their opposition to abortion and gay marriage.

The dilemma for Republican leaders is that the party's base, especially those voters most likely to participate in Republican primary elections, favors some policy positions that will be a hard sell for minority voters. The 2008 Texas Republican Party platform called for repealing the minimum wage, terminating bilingual education programs, making American English the state's official language, and deporting undocumented workers. The platform opposed raising any state taxes and fees, even to pay for education, and supported abolishing the property tax, which funds schools and other local governments. It even proposed increasing college tuition and denying financial aid for non-citizens, even permanent residents who were in the United States legally. Although those issue positions may appeal to conservative suburban whites, they are unlikely to attract the votes of very many African American, Latino, or Asian voters.[31] Republican officeholders who try to broaden the party's appeal by taking moderate positions on immigration or the SCHIP program may be vulnerable to defeat by more conservative challengers in the Republican primary.

AROUND THE NATION

Party Politics in Kansas

By most measures, Kansas is a very Republican state. In the 2008 presidential election, Republican John McCain easily carried the state, taking 57 percent of the vote against just 42 percent for Democrat Barack Obama. The last Democratic presidential candidate to carry Kansas was Lyndon B. Johnson in 1964. After the 2008 election,

Republicans held both U.S. Senate seats from Kansas and three of the state's four U.S. House seats. The Kansas GOP also enjoyed lopsided majorities in both chambers of the Kansas legislature, outnumbering Democrats 77 to 48 in the Kansas House and 31 to 9 in the Kansas Senate.* Furthermore, a state-by-state assessment of party identification

*Chuck McCutcheon and Christina L. Lyons, eds., *CQ's Politics in America, the 111th Congress* (Washington, DC: Congressional Quarterly Press, 2009), p. 402.

conducted by the Gallup Poll ranked Kansas as the sixth most Republican state in the nation, after Utah, Wyoming, Idaho, Alaska, and Nebraska.** In terms of voter registration, Republicans outnumber Democrats in Kansas by 751,000 to 452,000 (with a large number of independents).[†]

Nonetheless, Kansas has a Democratic governor. Democrat Kathleen Sebelius was elected governor in 2002 and then reelected in 2006. Sebelius won because Kansas Republicans are deeply divided between social conservatives, who focus on abortion clinic protests and teaching creation science in the schools, and business-oriented conservatives, who care primarily about taxes, regulation, and economic development. Sebelius won election and then reelection with the support of some traditional Republican voters and most independents. When Sebelius resigned in early

2008 to become the Secretary of Health and Human Services in President Barack Obama's administration, she was succeeded by another Democrat, Mark Parkinson, who had been lieutenant governor. In fact, Parkinson is a former chair of the Kansas Republican Party who switched parties in order to run for lieutenant governor with Sebelius.[‡]

QUESTIONS TO CONSIDER

1. How similar is party politics in Kansas to party politics in Texas?
2. Is it better to have a governor who has the same party affiliation as the majority in the legislature or not? What is the basis of your answer?
3. Is a divided Republican Party the best hope that Texas Democrats have for winning major office in the Lone Star State? Why or why not?

**Jeffrey M. Jones, "State of the States: Political Party Affiliation," January 28, 2009, available at www .gallup.com
[†]Andrea Stone, "Kansas Politics Bleeds Two Shades of Red," October 22, 2008, *USA Today*, available at www.usatoday.com.
[‡]Chris Moon, "Parkinson's Party Switch Causes Debate," June 2, 2006, *Topeka Capital-Journal*, available at www.cjonline.com.

WHAT WE HAVE LEARNED

1. **What is the party system in the United States?**

   A political party is a group of individuals who join together to seek public office in order to influence public policy. Although the United States has had a two-party system for most of its history, many states, including Texas, have experienced long periods of one-party dominance. In those states, political conflicts were fought between party factions.

2. **How are the two major parties organized at the national and state level in Texas?**

   A national committee and a national chair head the national party organization. The

national political party organizations support party candidates at the state level by spending money on their behalf and providing them with various services. Political parties in Texas have both temporary and permanent party organizations. The temporary party organization allows rank-and-file party supporters a chance to participate in the party's decision-making process in election years by selecting delegates to district, county, and state party conventions. Each party has a permanent organization including a state chairperson and a state executive committee.

3. **What is the history of political party competition in Texas?**

   Texas was a one-party Democratic state from the late nineteenth century through the mid-twentieth century because most native white southerners were alienated from the Republican Party by its association with the Civil War and Reconstruction. Eventually, identifiable liberal and conservative factions developed within the Democratic Party to contend for political power, with the conservative Democrats usually enjoying the upper hand. Beginning in the 1950s, the Texas Republican Party began to come back to life because the legacy of the Civil War began to fade, some conservative Democrats began voting Republican, and the Texas GOP benefited from the migration of white-collar workers from the north. From 1978 to 1994, party politics was closely competitive in Texas between the two major political parties, and between the liberal and conservative factions within the Democratic Party. Since 1994, the Republican Party has become the dominant party in Texas. Although Republicans are still in control today, the Democratic Party has begun to make inroads.

4. **How do the Texas Democratic and Republican Parties compare with one another in terms of voter support and offices held?**

   Surveys indicate that the Texas electorate is closely divided between Democrats and Republicans, with independents as numerous as either set of party identifiers. Surveys of party identification do not necessarily predict election outcomes, however, because Republicans are more likely to vote than are Democrats and because independents in Texas lean Republican, especially in national elections. Republicans also benefit from Texas having a relatively conservative electorate. After the 2008 election, the Texas GOP held every statewide elected office, as well as a majority of state legislative seats and U.S. congressional seats from Texas.

5. **What groups of voters generally support each of the major political parties in terms of income, race and ethnicity, age, gender, region, and place of residence?**

   The Texas Republican Party typically attracts the support of upper-income voters, whites, older people, men, people living in West Texas and East Texas, suburban residents, and the residents of small towns and rural areas. In contrast, the Democrats run more strongly among lower-income voters, minority citizens, younger voters, women, people living in South Texas, and inner-city residents.

6. **What interest groups are allied with each of the state's major political parties?**

   Business and trade groups, most professional organizations, farm groups, religious conservatives, the NRA, pro-life groups, tort reform organizations, and anti-tax groups back the GOP. In contrast, labor groups, environmental organizations, consumer groups, minority-rights groups, teacher organizations, pro-choice groups, trial lawyers, and women's groups are allied with the Democratic Party.

7. **How do the issue orientations of the state's two major political parties compare and contrast with one another?**

   The Texas Democratic and Republican Parties disagree on some of the details of policy, particularly on government's role in society. The Democratic platform is pro-choice, endorses bilingual education, favors increasing the state minimum wage, and supports comprehensive immigration reform. The Republican platform is pro-life, opposes bilingual education, wants to repeal the minimum wage, and calls for deporting illegal immigrants. Whereas the Democrats believe that government should play a role in addressing social problems, the Republicans contend that government's primary role is to support traditional family values rather than solving social problems.

8. **What factors are most likely to affect the future of party politics in Texas and what are the challenges facing both major parties in the state?**

Recent elections have given Democrats hope that they will soon be able to challenge Republican dominance of state government because the Latino population is increasing and the older white population is decreasing. The challenge for the Democrats is to increase voter registration and voter turnout among Latino citizens and younger people. In the short run, however, Democrats will make gains only if they can increase their share of the white vote. The challenge for Republicans, meanwhile, is to adapt to demographic change by appealing to younger voters and minority citizens while satisfying the policy demands of their base, which is composed primarily of conservative suburban whites.

KEY TERMS

bilingual education

capital punishment

conservatism

Electoral College

gender gap

Grand Old Party (GOP)

hate crimes legislation

liberalism

minimum wage

New Deal program

party faction

party platform

political party

privatization

right-to-work

Robin Hood plan

school choice

Solid South

State Children's Health Insurance Program (SCHIP)

top 10 percent rule

tort reform

Trans-Texas Corridor

two-party system

Yellow Dog Democrat

NOTES

1. "Election Results 2008—Texas," *New York Times*, December 9, 2008, available at www.nytimes.com.
2. Wayne Slater, "GOP's Solid Hold in Texas Is Slipping," *Dallas Morning News*, February 20, 2009, available at www.dallasnews.com.
3. Center for Responsive Politics, "2008 Race, Texas District 22, Independent Expenditures," available at www.opensecrets.org.
4. James A. Dyer, Arnold Vedlitz, and David B. Hill, "New Voters, Switchers, and Political Party Realignment in Texas," *Western Political Quarterly* 41 (March 1988): 156.
5. Clay Robison, "Texas GOP Beats Dems in Key Areas," *Houston Chronicle*, November 28, 1989, p. 16A.
6. *Texas Weekly*, July 15, 1991, p. 5.
7. "The Two Souths," *National Journal*, September 20, 1986, pp. 2218–2220.
8. Jeffrey M. Jones, "Political Party Affiliation: 30 States Blue, 4 Red in '09 So Far," August 3, 2009, available at www.gallup.com.
9. "Election Results 2008—Texas."
10. Ibid.
11. Ibid.
12. Ibid.

13. Jeffrey M. Jones, "Ideology: Three Deep South States Are the Most Conservative," February 3, 2010, available at www.gallup.com.

14. Texas Secretary of State, available at www.sos.state.tx.us.

15. National Institute on Money in State Politics, "State at a Glance: Texas 2008," available at www.followthemoney.org.

16. Jay Root, "Texas Democrats at Crossroads in 2010 Elections," March 20, 2009, *El Paso Times*, available at www.elpasotimes.com.

17. "Election Results 2008—Texas."

18. Ibid.

19. Ibid.

20. Ibid.

21. Ibid.

22. Ibid.

23. *Texas Weekly*, November 17, 2008, available at www.texasweekly.com.

24. U.S. Census Bureau, "Resident Population by Race, Hispanic or Latino Origin, and State," August 11, 2005, *The 2009 Statistical Abstract*, available at www.census.gov.

25. "Election Results 2008—Texas."

26. David L. Leal, Matt A. Barreto, Jongho Lee, and Rodolfo O. de la Garza, "The Latino Vote in the 2004 Election," *PS: Political Science and Politics* (January 2005), p. 46.

27. Slater, "GOP's Solid Hold in Texas Is Slipping."

28. "Election Results 2008—Texas."

29. Ibid.

30. Ibid.

31. Jonathan Gurwitz, "The Troubled Texas GOP," *Wall Street Journal*, July 8, 2007, available at www.wsj.com.

Chapter 7

Elections

WHAT WE WILL LEARN

After studying Chapter 7, students should be able to answer the following questions:

▸ What are the advantages and disadvantages of the long ballot?

▸ What are the various types of elections held in Texas?

▸ What factors affect the redistricting process in Texas?

▸ What factors affect election campaigns in Texas?

▸ How does each of the following factors affect voter choice: incumbency, political party identification, issues and ideology, campaigns, candidate image, retrospective and prospective voting, and national factors?

Texas Democrats who wanted to do their best to support Barack Obama or Hillary Clinton for the 2008 Democratic presidential nomination had to do the **Texas Two-Step.** This process, used by the Texas Democratic Party to select delegates to the National Democratic Convention, involved participating in a Democratic Primary and a Democratic Caucus. First, Democrats had to vote in the primary election, either on March 4, which was primary election day, or during the early voting period. Second, they had to return to their precinct polling place in the early evening of March 4 to participate in a precinct caucus. Both the primary and the caucus contributed to the delegate selection process in Texas that eventually helped determine who would win the Democratic Party presidential nomination.

Texas Two-Step The nickname for the process used by the Texas Democratic Party to select delegates to the National Democratic Convention that involved participating in a Democratic Primary and a Democratic Caucus.

Explaining the Texas Two-Step and discussing its role in the 2008 Democratic presidential nomination contest is one of the goals of this chapter on elections. The chapter begins by identifying the long list of officials that are elected in Texas. It discusses the types of elections in which Texas voters have the opportunity to participate, including the presidential delegate selection process. The chapter examines districts and redistricting before turning to a discussion of election campaigns. It concludes by looking at the reasons voters make the choices they do.

This chapter on elections is the last in a set of four chapters examining the political environment for policymaking. Chapter 4 dealt with participation while Chapter 5 addressed the topic of interest groups in Texas. Chapter 6 focused on political parties.

THE LONG BALLOT

Long ballot An election system that provides for the election of nearly every public official of any significance.

Texas has the **long ballot,** which is an election system that provides for the election of nearly every public official of any significance. A conscientious Texas voter who never misses an election has the opportunity to cast a ballot for each of the following public officials:

- The president and vice president
- Two U.S. senators
- One member of the U.S. House of Representatives
- The governor of Texas and five other state executive officials
- Three railroad commissioners
- One member of the State Board of Education (SBOE)
- One state senator
- One state representative
- Nine members of the Texas Supreme Court
- Nine members of the Texas Court of Criminal Appeals
- At least two, and perhaps as many as 60 or more, state appellate and district court judges
- Numerous local officials, including county executives, county judges, city officials, and members of school district boards of trustees.

The ballot is especially long in the state's urban counties, where a large number of state district court judges must stand for election. In 2010, Harris County voters faced a ballot with more than 60 contested races.

The long ballot is not unusual in America, but few states vote on as many officials as Texas. Only four states elect more statewide executive officeholders than Texas; in contrast, three states select only a governor statewide.[1] Considering the number of candidates and constitutional amendments facing Texas voters, the Lone Star State may well have the longest, most complicated election ballot in the nation.

The long ballot is controversial. Its defenders believe that the electoral process is the best way to ensure that public officials remain accountable to the people. If citizens grow unhappy with some aspect of state government, they can simply vote the responsible officials out of office. In contrast, critics of the long ballot argue that most Texans lack the information necessary to make intelligent voting choices on many down-ballot races. Not knowing the qualifications of the candidates, voters may cast ballots for persons with familiar or catchy names who may be unqualified for the offices they seek.

 WHAT IS YOUR OPINION?

Is the ballot too long for Texas voters to be able to make informed choices?

TYPES OF ELECTIONS

Texans have the opportunity to cast ballots in different types of elections held at various times throughout the year.

General Elections

General election A statewide election to fill national and state offices, which is held on the first Tuesday after the first Monday in November of even-numbered years.

The **general election** is a statewide election to fill national and state offices, held on the Tuesday after the first Monday in November of even-numbered years. In recent years, the Texas statewide general election ballot has included candidates for the Republican Party, Democratic Party, and Libertarian Party. To qualify for the ballot, independents and candidates affiliated with other political parties, such as the Green Party, must gather signatures equivalent to 1 percent of all the votes cast for governor in the last general election. In 2006, Carole Keeton Strayhorn and Kinky Friedman, who each ran for governor as independent candidates, had to collect the signatures of 45,540 registered voters who had not participated in the March primary. Not only that, they had to complete the process within a 60-day period in order to qualify for the general election ballot. Only Texas and North Carolina make it so difficult for independents and third-party candidates to get on the ballot.[2] A party can hold its ballot slot as long as one of its candidates receives at least 5 percent of the statewide vote in at least one race.

Straight-ticket voting Citizens casting their ballots only for the candidates of one party.

Texas is one of 16 states that allow **straight-ticket voting,** the practice of voting for candidates of the same political party for all positions on the ballot. The general-election ballot includes a straight ticket box to enable voters to cast straight ticket ballots by marking a single box rather than having to vote individually on all of a party's candidates. In 2008, a record number of Texans, more than 57 percent of voters, cast a straight ticket ballot, with slightly more Republicans voting a straight ticket than Democrats.[3] Citizens who do not cast a straight ticket vote a split ticket. **Split-ticket voting** refers to citizens casting their ballots for candidates of two or more parties for different offices during the same election.

Split-ticket voting Citizens casting their ballots for candidates of two or more parties for different offices during the same election.

The candidate with the most votes wins the general election, regardless of whether that candidate has a majority (more than 50 percent) of the ballots cast. There are no runoffs. The 2006 governor's race featured four major candidates—Republican Rick Perry, Democrat Chris Bell, and independents Strayhorn and Friedman. The outcome of the election was as follows:

Perry	39 percent
Bell	30 percent
Strayhorn	18 percent
Friedman	12 percent

Under the state's election laws, Perry won despite having taken less than a majority of the total votes cast in the election because the candidate with the most votes wins the general election.

Primary Elections

Primary election An intra-party election during which a party's candidates for the general election are chosen.

Although minor parties may select their general election candidates at a state convention, Texas law requires that major parties choose their candidates in a **primary election,** which is an intra-party election at which a party's candidates for the general election are chosen. Democrats compete against other Democrats, and Republicans compete against Republicans. In Texas, primary elections take place on the first Tuesday in March of even-numbered years.

Closed primary An election system that limits primary election participation to registered party members.

The two basic kinds of primary election methods are the closed primary and the open primary. A **closed primary** is an election system that limits primary election participation to registered party members. Many party leaders favor the closed primary because they believe that it prevents the supporters of the opposition party from influencing the selection of candidates for their party. After all, why should Democrats be allowed to help select Republican nominees and vice versa? In contrast, an **open primary** is an election system that allows voters to pick the party primary of their choice without disclosing their party affiliation. Some party leaders favor the open primary because they believe that it will produce nominees who can appeal to independent voters and supporters of the other party more than the closed primary can. Candidates with broad appeal are more likely to win the general election than are candidates who can attract only the votes of other Democrats or Republicans.

Open primary An election system that allows voters to pick the party primary of their choice without disclosing their party affiliation.

The Texas primary system is a cross between an open primary and a closed primary. In contrast to the practice in many states, Texas does not require that citizens disclose their party affiliation when they register to vote. On primary election day, however, voters must publicly choose the party in whose primary they wish to

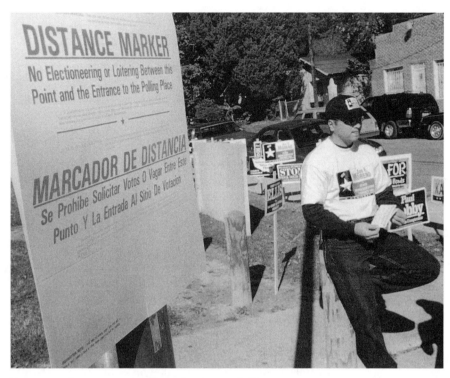

Texas voters choose among candidates for dozens of offices.

participate. They cannot vote in both primaries. Once a voter declares a choice, the election judge stamps the voter registration card with the following phrase: "Voted in the Republican (Democratic) primary."

Figure 7.1 compares Democratic and Republican primary election turnout in statewide (nonpresidential) election years from 1978 to 2010. In 1978, Democratic primary voters outnumbered GOP primary participants by a better than ten to one margin. Subsequently, the Democratic primary electorate has shrunk while the number of people voting in the Republican primary has increased. In 2010, more than twice as many people voted in the Republican primary than participated in the Democratic primary. Republican primary turnout in 2010 was exceptional because voters were drawn to the polls by a hotly contested battle for the Republican gubernatorial nomination between Governor Perry, U.S. Senator Kay Bailey Hutchison, and conservative activist Debra Medina.

Primary turnout in presidential years varies, depending on the level of interest in each party's presidential nomination contest. In 2008, Democratic primary voters outnumbered Republican primary voters 2,874,986 to 1,362,322.[4] The difference in turnout reflected the high level of interest in the Obama–Clinton race on the Democratic side compared with the level of interest in the Republican contest. By

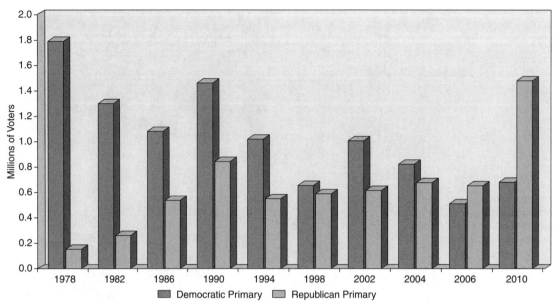

FIGURE 7.1   Primary Turnout, 1978–2010.

the time of the Texas primary, John McCain had essentially wrapped up the Republican presidential nomination.

To win a primary election, a candidate must receive a majority of the votes cast (50 percent plus one vote). If no one receives a majority in a multi-candidate race, the two highest finishers meet in a runoff. For example, suppose that Joe Nava, Elizabeth Jackson, and Lee Chen are running for the Democratic nomination for the office of county sheriff and the vote totals are as follows:

Nava	4,102
Jackson	2,888
Chen	2,009

Nava and Jackson would face one another in the primary runoff because neither received a majority of the votes cast. Chen is eliminated because he finished third.

Runoff primary election An election between the two top finishers in a primary election when no candidate received a majority of the vote in the initial primary.

A **runoff primary election** is an election between the two top finishers in a primary election when no candidate received a majority of the vote in the initial primary. In Texas, the primary runoff takes place on the second Tuesday in April, a little more than a month after the initial primary. People who voted in the March primary may only vote in the same party's runoff election. They cannot switch parties for the runoff. However, citizens who failed to vote in March can vote in either party's runoff primary. The winner of the runoff is the party's official nominee for the fall general election.

Runoff turnout depends on the level of interest in the contests remaining on the ballot. If the voters have the opportunity to decide a runoff between two high-profile candidates for governor or U.S. senator, turnout will be high, perhaps exceeding turnout in the March primary. In contrast, turnout could be quite low if the only races facing runoffs are low-profile judicial contests or county office.

The Presidential Delegate Selection Process

Every four years, Texans have the opportunity to participate in the process through which the Democratic and Republican Parties choose their presidential candidates by selecting delegates to attend the national conventions of the two major parties. The procedure for selecting delegates to the national party conventions varies from state to state. About two-thirds of the states select delegates by means of a **presidential preference primary election,** an election in which party voters cast ballots for the presidential candidate they favor and in so doing help determine the number of convention delegates that candidate will receive. Other states choose national convention delegates by the **caucus method of delegate selection,** a procedure for choosing national party convention delegates that involves party voters participating in a series of precinct and district or county political meetings. The process begins with party members attending precinct conventions, where they elect delegates to district meetings. The district meetings in turn select delegates to the state convention. Finally, the state party convention chooses national convention delegates.

In Texas, the state Republican Party chooses delegates to the national party convention through a presidential preference primary. To receive any delegates, a presidential candidate has to win at least 20 percent of the vote in one or more U.S. congressional districts. Any candidate who gets a majority of the vote in a congressional district claims all of that district's delegates. A candidate who gets more than 20 percent but less than a majority receives a share of the delegates allotted to that district (as long as no other candidate has a majority). In 2008, Senator John McCain won the Republican presidential primary in Texas by taking 51 percent of the total vote compared with 38 percent for former Arkansas Governor Mike Huckabee and 5 percent for Texas Congressman Ron Paul. McCain received 121 delegates; Huckabee was awarded 16.[5]

The Texas Democratic Party selects national convention delegates through a system that combines the primary and the caucus methods—the so-called Texas Two-Step. More than half the state's Democratic delegates are awarded based on the results of the presidential preference primary. Candidates are awarded delegates in rough proportion to the percentage of votes they receive as long as a candidate qualifies by winning at least 15 percent of the statewide vote. Candidates also win delegates based on the results of a caucus process. Finally, the party reserves a number of delegate positions for **super delegates,** which are Democratic officeholders and party officials who attend the national party convention as delegates who are not officially pledged to support any candidate.

The Texas legislature has periodically tinkered with the timing of the spring primary in hopes of increasing the state's influence in the presidential selection process. Despite its size, Texas had enjoyed relatively little influence in presidential nomination

Presidential preference primary election
An election in which party voters cast ballots for the presidential candidate they favor and in so doing help determine the number of convention delegates that candidate will receive.

Caucus method of delegate selection
A procedure for choosing national party convention delegates that involves party voters participating in a series of precinct and district or county political meetings.

Super delegates
Democratic officeholders and party officials who attend the national party convention as delegates who are not officially pledged to support any candidate.

contests because each party's presidential nomination was long decided by the time Texas got around to selecting its convention delegates. In 1987, the legislature moved the spring primary date from May to March. The legislature hoped that, by moving the state's presidential delegate selection process up by a couple of months, presidential candidates would be forced to campaign in the Lone Star State and appeal to Texas voters. The scheme failed, however, because other states moved their primaries and caucuses as well. In 2003, the Texas legislature tried once again to increase the state's role in the presidential selection process by moving the primary up another week, from the second to the first Tuesday in March. The plan was unsuccessful in 2004 because the party nominations were settled before Texans went to the polls. In 2007, some legislators and party leaders proposed moving the 2008 presidential preference primary up to early February in hopes of regaining influence in the nomination process, but the proposal failed to pass the legislature.

In 2008, however, the race for the Democratic presidential nomination between Obama and Clinton continued for so long that Texas became a major battleground despite the relatively late date of its delegate selection process. Obama and Clinton traded victories in the early primary and caucus states, almost evenly dividing the delegates between them. Going into the March 2 primary in Texas, Obama had a small delegate lead, but it was by no means large enough to ensure his eventual victory. Consequently, for the first time in modern presidential primary history, Texas was a major focus of campaign activity. Both Clinton and Obama campaigned personally in the Lone Star State and spent heavily on advertising. The excitement of the race produced a record primary turnout, with more than 2.8 million Texans participating in the Democratic primary, the first stage of the Texas Two-Step. Clinton won the primary, earning 51 percent of the votes compared with 48 percent for Obama. Clinton was awarded 65 delegates compared with 61 delegates awarded to her opponent. Meanwhile, Obama won the caucus, the second stage of the Texas Two-Step, with 56 percent of the votes compared with 44 percent for Clinton, giving him 38 delegates compared with 29 for Clinton. Altogether, Obama received 99 Texas delegates, whereas Clinton won 94.[6]

AROUND THE NATION

The Blanket Primary in Louisiana

Louisiana has a unique primary system. Every candidate competes for votes in a blanket primary, regardless of party affiliation. If one candidate wins a majority of the vote, that candidate is elected. Otherwise, the two top finishers face each other in a runoff election, regardless of party affiliation. In theory, the runoff could involve two Democrats, two Republicans, or one candidate from each party. In 2007, for example, 12 candidates competed in the blanket primary for governor, including one Republican, five Democrats, one Libertarian, and five independents. Bobby Jindahl, the Republican, won without a runoff because he received more than 50 percent of the vote. Louisiana uses the blanket primary, which is also called a jungle primary, in partisan elections for state and local office. However, the state uses the traditional party primary followed by a general election in races for the U.S. Congress and the U.S. Senate. The proponents of the blanket primary argue that it gives voters more options, whereas opponents of the system contend that it weakens political parties by discouraging party loyalty.

Democratic Governor Edwin Edwards invented the blanket primary and got the state's Democratic-controlled legislature to adopt it as a device to slow the rise of the state's Republican Party. To win office, Democrats had to survive a bruising Democratic primary election and then defeat a Republican opponent in the general election who had usually won the Republican primary without strong opposition. Edwards figured that the blanket primary would erase the Republican advantage by forcing all the candidates into the same set of elections.

Although the open primary has not prevented Republicans from making substantial inroads in Louisiana politics, it probably was responsible for Edwards winning a fourth non-consecutive term as governor in 1991. The three main contenders—Edwards, Republican state legislator David Duke, and incumbent Republican Governor Buddy Roemer—carried considerable political baggage into the race. Many Louisiana voters thought that Edwards was a crook because he had spent most of his career fighting off corruption charges. (They were apparently right about Edwards because the former governor is currently serving a ten-year prison sentence for racketeering.) Duke was notorious as a former Nazi sympathizer and leader of the Ku Klux Klan. Finally, Roemer had angered many voters because he broke his promise not to raise taxes. Most experts on Louisiana politics believed that Roemer would have been able to defeat either Edwards or Duke in a runoff, but he finished third. (Raising taxes was apparently a worse political liability than either charges of corruption or ties to the Ku Klux Klan!) Edwards easily defeated Duke in the runoff and became governor of Louisiana once again.

QUESTIONS TO CONSIDER

1. What are the advantages of a blanket primary system such as the one in Louisiana?
2. What are the disadvantages of a blanket primary?
3. Would you like to see Texas adopt a blanket primary system? Why or why not?

Local Elections

Under state law, local elections for city, school district, and special district officials must be held on either the second Saturday in May or the Tuesday after the first Monday in November. Local governments usually conduct their elections in odd-numbered years so they will not coincide with general elections for president, senator, and governor. Most city governments choose officials by majority vote, with a runoff election if no one candidate receives a majority in a multi-candidate field. Most school districts choose the members of their boards of trustees by plurality vote—the candidate who receives the most votes wins, regardless of whether it is a majority. The state constitution *requires* majority election for terms of office greater than two years. State law allows cities and school districts to cancel elections if all candidates are running unopposed and no other issues are on the ballot.

Nonpartisan elections Election contests in which the names of the candidates appear on the ballot but not their party affiliations.

Most local races in Texas are **nonpartisan elections,** which are election contests in which the names of the candidates, but not their party affiliations, appear on the ballot. The supporters of nonpartisan elections argue that the elimination of political parties from local elections reduces corruption. Furthermore, they say that nonpartisan elections free local politics from state and national political controversies. In contrast, critics of nonpartisan elections believe they work to the advantage of upper-income groups because they reduce the amount of information available to voters about candidates. In partisan elections, the single most important piece of information voters have about candidates is the party label. In nonpartisan elections, voters do not know the party attachments of the candidates. They must study the positions of the candidates if they are going to vote in their own best interest. Upper-income persons are in a better position to determine which candidates best represent their interests because they are better able to learn about candidates than low-income people.

Scholarly research largely supports the critics of nonpartisan elections. Turnout for nonpartisan elections is generally lower than turnout for partisan elections. Without party labels on the ballot to guide their choice, some potential voters stay home because they are unable to distinguish among the candidates. Furthermore, some people who do cast ballots base their voting decisions on such factors as incumbency, gender, and the perceived ethnicity of the candidates based on their names.[7]

Special Elections

A **special election** is an election called outside the normal election calendar. Special elections may be used to approve local bond issues, which are discussed in the next section, or to fill unexpected vacancies in the legislature or the state's congressional delegation. Vacancies in executive and judicial offices are generally filled by gubernatorial appointment. When a vacancy occurs, the governor calls a special election. Special elections are nonpartisan although party organizations often get involved. A candidate must receive a majority of the votes cast (50 percent plus one) to win a special election. Otherwise, the two leading candidates meet in a runoff.

Non-Candidate Elections

Texas voters have the opportunity to participate in a number of non-candidate elections, including bond elections, recall elections, and referenda. A **bond** is a certificate of indebtedness issued to investors who loan money for interest income; in lay terms, a bond is an IOU. A **bond election** is an election for the purpose of obtaining voter approval for a local government going into debt. Approval for state government indebtedness is obtained through the adoption of a constitutional amendment.

Recall is a procedure allowing voters to remove elected officials from office before the expiration of their terms. If enough signatures can be gathered on petitions, disgruntled citizens can force a recall election to remove the targeted official and let voters decide whether to keep the officeholder or declare the office vacant. The vacancy is then filled in a special election. In 2003, California voters recalled Governor Gray Davis and replaced him with Hollywood actor Arnold Schwarzenegger, but that sort of action could not happen in the Lone Star State because state officials are not subject to recall. In Texas, the power of recall is limited to the citizens of some city governments.

Many cities (but not the state government) provide for the **initiative process,** a procedure whereby citizens can propose legislation by gathering a certain number of signatures on a petition. Election officials then place the measure on the ballot for approval by the voters. Some cities also allow citizens to repeal ordinances passed by the city council through a similar process. In some municipalities, city officials may place non-binding referenda on the ballot. Furthermore, the executive committees

Special election An election called at a time outside the normal election calendar.

Bond A certificate of indebtedness issued to investors who loan money for interest income; in lay terms, a bond is an IOU.

Bond election An election for the purpose of obtaining voter approval for a local government going into debt.

Recall A procedure allowing voters to remove elected officials from office before the expiration of their terms.

Initiative process A procedure whereby citizens can propose the adoption of a policy measure by gathering a prerequisite number of signatures. Voters must then approve the measure before it can take effect.

of the state Republican and Democratic Parties sometimes include non-binding referendum proposals on their spring primary ballots.

Texans vote on other measures as well. For example, voters must approve amendments to the state constitution. The legislature typically places amendments on the November ballot, usually in odd-numbered years, so that they will not share the ballot with a general election. Voters must also approve the establishment and dissolution of special districts, such as hospital districts or municipal utility districts. Finally, **local-option (wet-dry) elections** are held to determine whether an area will legalize the sale of alcoholic beverages.

Local-option (wet-dry) elections Elections held to determine whether an area legalizes the sale of alcoholic beverages.

 WHAT IS YOUR OPINION?

Does Texas have too many elections?

ELECTION DISTRICTS AND REDISTRICTING

Texas voters select public officials in a combination of at-large and district elections. An **at-large election** is a method for choosing public officials in which every citizen of a political subdivision, such as a state or county, votes to select a public official. The president and vice president, two U.S. senators, the governor, the lieutenant governor, the comptroller of public accounts, the land commissioner, the attorney general, the agricultural commissioner, three railroad commissioners, nine justices of the Texas Supreme Court, and nine justices of the Texas Court of Criminal Appeals are all elected in at-large, statewide elections. Furthermore, a number of local officials, including county and district judges, sheriffs, city mayors, some city council members, and some school district trustees are elected in local at-large elections.

At-large election A method for choosing public officials in which every citizen of a political subdivision, such as a state or county, votes to select a public official.

A **district election** is a method for choosing public officials in which a political subdivision, such as a state or county, is divided into districts and each district elects one official. Members of the Texas legislature, U.S. Congress, and State Board of Education (SBOE) are elected from districts. For example, the 150 members of the Texas House of Representatives are elected one each from 150 state representative districts. The state's 31 state senators are chosen from 31 state senatorial districts. A number of local officials, including county commissioners, city council members in some cities, and the members of boards of trustees in some school districts, are also elected from single-member districts.

District election A method for choosing public officials in which a political subdivision, such as a state or county, is divided into districts and each district elects one official.

Election districts must be redrawn every ten years to adjust for changes in population. The process of redrawing the boundaries of legislative districts is known as **redistricting.** The Texas legislature is responsible for redrawing Texas House districts, Texas Senate districts, U.S. congressional districts, and the districts for the SBOE. Local governing bodies, such as city councils and commissioner courts, redraw the districts of local officials. The national census, which is taken every ten years, provides the population data for redistricting.

Redistricting The process of redrawing the boundaries of legislative districts.

Texas Democrats doing the Texas Two-Step, participating in a precinct caucus after first voting in the presidential preference primary.

One Person, One Vote

State legislatures have not always been conscientious about redistricting. During the first half of the twentieth century, the legislatures of a number of states, including Texas, failed to redistrict despite dramatic population movement from rural to urban areas because rural legislators did not want to relinquish control. As a result, the population size of legislative districts sometimes varied dramatically. In 1961, the ratio between the most populous and the least populous U.S. congressional district in Texas was 4.4 to 1. The ratio was eight to one for state senate districts and two to one for state house districts.[8]

The U.S. Supreme Court addressed this issue in a series of cases that established the doctrine of **one person, one vote.** This judicial ruling states that the Equal Protection Clause of the Fourteenth Amendment to the U.S. Constitution requires legislative districts to be apportioned on the basis of population.[9] If one legislative district has substantially more people than another district, then the people living in the less populous district have more political influence than do the residents of the larger district. Suppose an urban district has ten times more people than a rural district. The people in the rural district then have ten times the influence in the election of a legislator or a member of Congress. Compared with the citizens living in the large urban district, the voters in the smaller rural district effectively have ten votes. The Supreme Court ruled that the Constitution requires that citizens have equal political influence regardless of where they live. Consequently, district boundaries have to be drawn to ensure nearly equal population size. Although the Court

One person, one vote The judicial ruling that the Equal Protection Clause of the Fourteenth Amendment to the U.S. Constitution requires that legislative districts be apportioned on the basis of population.

allows some leeway in state legislative and local district size, it requires that U.S. congressional districts have almost exactly the same number of people. In 2002, for example, a federal court overturned Pennsylvania's redistricting plan because two U.S. House districts varied in size by 19 people—646,361 compared with 646,380![10]

The Supreme Court's one-person, one-vote doctrine had a significant impact on policymaking in Texas. Because of the Court's ruling, urban areas gained representation, whereas rural interests lost ground. The legislative delegation for Harris County, the state's most populous county, increased from one state senator and 12 members of the Texas House to four senators and 19 house members.[11] African Americans, Latinos, and Republicans, all groups that are numerous in urban areas, increased their representation in legislative bodies. Urban problems such as education, transportation, race relations, crime, and healthcare won a more prominent place on the state's policy agenda.[12]

The Voting Rights Act (VRA)

Voting Rights Act (VRA) A federal law designed to protect the voting rights of racial and ethnic minorities.

The **Voting Rights Act (VRA)** is a federal law designed to protect the voting rights of racial and ethnic minorities. The VRA makes it illegal for state and local governments to enact and enforce election rules and procedures that diminish minority voting power. Furthermore, the pre-clearance provision of the VRA requires that state and local governments in areas with a history of voting discrimination submit redistricting plans to the U.S. Department of Justice for approval *before* they can go into effect. Congress and the president included the pre-clearance requirement in the law in order to stay one step ahead of local officials who would adopt new discriminatory electoral procedures as soon as the federal courts threw out an old procedure. The pre-clearance provision of the VRA applies only to states and parts of states that have substantial racial and language minority populations with relatively low rates of voter participation. Texas is covered, along with all or part of 15 other states: Alaska, Alabama, Arizona, California, Florida, Georgia, Louisiana, Michigan, Mississippi, New Hampshire, New York, North Carolina, South Carolina, South Dakota, and Virginia.

In the late 1980s and early 1990s, the Justice Department in the George H. W. Bush administration interpreted amendments to the VRA adopted in 1982 to require that state legislatures go beyond nondiscrimination to drawing districts designed to maximize minority representation. If a legislature *could* draw a district that would likely elect an African American or Latino candidate, then the legislature *must* draw the district. In other words, state legislatures would have to maximize the number of legislative districts with populations that were more than 50 percent minority.[13]

Why would a Republican administration choose to implement the VRA to increase African American and Latino representation in Congress and state legislatures when most minority lawmakers are Democrats? The reason was simple: The policy also helped the Republican Party gain legislative seats.[14] To construct majority African American and Latino districts, state legislatures redrew district lines to shift minority voters away from adjacent districts into new districts designed to elect minority officeholders. Because most African American and Latino voters are

Democrats, the redistricting reduced Democratic voting strength in surrounding districts, threatening the political survival of some white Democratic members of Congress. The Georgia congressional delegation, for example, went from one African American Democrat, eight white Democrats, and one white Republican before redistricting in 1991 to three African American Democrats and eight white Republicans after the 1994 election. Nationwide, the creation of minority districts after the 1990 census helped white Republicans pick up about ten seats in Congress, defeating white Democrats who were stripped of some of their minority voter support.[15]

In the mid-1990s, the U.S. Supreme Court overruled the Justice Department's interpretation of the VRA. Responding to legal challenges filed against minority districts created in Louisiana, Georgia, and other southern states, the Court declared that state governments cannot use race as the predominant, overriding factor in drawing district lines unless they have a "compelling" reason. The goal of maximizing the number of minority districts was not sufficient to justify race-based redistricting, the Court said, because Congress enacted the VRA to prevent discrimination rather than maximize the number of districts that would elect African American and Latino candidates.[16]

 WHAT IS YOUR OPINION?

Should state legislatures consider race and ethnicity in drawing legislative districts?

The role of the VRA in the redistricting process changed considerably during the 1990s. At the beginning of the decade, the VRA forced legislatures to focus on race and ethnicity during redistricting, and legislatures throughout the South created minority districts whenever possible. By the end of the decade, however, the U.S. Supreme Court had made it clear that legislatures could not use race and ethnicity as the primary basis for redistricting unless they had a compelling reason. State legislatures could not regress; that is, they could not legally create legislative districts that would diminish the political influence of minority voters, but neither did they have to increase the number of minority districts.

The Politics of Redistricting

Redistricting is a highly political process. Legislative districts can be drawn to the advantage of one political party over another or one candidate over another. The drawing of legislative district lines for political advantage is known as **gerrymandering.** In the 1991 redistricting, for example, Democratic State Senator (now U.S. Representative) Eddie Bernice Johnson of Dallas used her position as chair of the Texas Senate redistricting committee to enhance her own chances of winning a seat in Congress. The congressional district she created not only included much of her old state Senate district but also excluded the residences of potential opponents.[17]

Gerrymandering can affect election outcomes. After redistricting in 1980, the political parties that drew the lines usually won more seats than they did before redistricting and almost always held the seats created for them throughout the decade.

Gerrymandering
The drawing of legislative district lines for political advantage.

Furthermore, they generally won a higher percentage of seats than votes.[18] On average, a political party with complete control of the redistricting process could gerrymander legislative districts to allow the party's candidates to win 54 percent of legislative seats while capturing only 50 percent of the total vote.[19]

Democrats controlled the redistricting process in Texas following the 1990 Census because they held a majority of seats in both chambers of the Texas legislature and Democrat Ann Richards was governor. Republicans accused the Democrats of using their power to create congressional and legislative districts that were unfair to Republican candidates. In 1992, Democratic candidates for the U.S. House won 21 of the state's 30 congressional seats even though they received only 50 percent of the votes cast. Two years later, Republican congressional candidates carried the popular vote 56 percent to 42 percent, but Democrats still won 19 of 30 seats. Similarly, Democrats captured 17 of the 30 seats at stake in 1996 despite once again losing the popular vote, this time by 54 percent to 44 percent.[20]

The political landscape in Texas after the 2000 Census was considerably different than it was ten years earlier because neither party enjoyed clear control of the redistricting process. Although Democrats still held a majority of seats in the Texas House, Republicans enjoyed a 16 to 15 advantage in the Texas Senate. In addition, Governor Rick Perry was a Republican. The result was a legislative stalemate. The 2001 session of the Texas legislature ended without passage of a redistricting plan for either the two houses of the legislature or the Congress.

Legislative Redistricting Board (LRB) An agency composed of the speaker, lieutenant governor, comptroller, land commissioner, and attorney general that draws the boundaries of Texas House and Senate seats when the legislature is unable to agree on a redistricting plan.

When the legislature and the governor failed to adopt redistricting plans, the responsibility for drawing new district lines for the Texas legislature fell to the **Legislative Redistricting Board (LRB),** an agency composed of the speaker, lieutenant governor, comptroller, land commissioner, and attorney general that draws the boundaries of Texas House and Texas Senate seats when the legislature is unable to agree on a redistricting plan. In 2001, Republicans held four of the five seats on the LRB and they adopted a plan designed to increase Republican strength in the legislature. As a result, the GOP won a majority of seats in the Texas House for the first time in more than a century and increased its majority in the Texas Senate.

Whereas the Republicans were pleased with the results of legislative redistricting, the Democrats were relieved at the outcome of congressional redistricting. Because the LRB has jurisdiction only over redistricting the legislature, a federal court drew the lines for the state's congressional districts. The court redrew the state's existing 30 congressional districts in such a fashion that incumbent members of Congress from both parties would likely win reelection. It then put one of the state's two new congressional districts in Central Texas and the other in the Dallas suburbs. Although Republicans easily captured the two new congressional districts, the Democrats clung to a 17–15 majority in the state's congressional delegation because Democratic incumbents were able to retain their seats.

The Republican Party attempted to increase its strength in the U.S. House of Representatives by revisiting the issue of redistricting in 2003. Republican Congressman Tom DeLay of Sugar Land, Texas, the House Majority Leader, presented the GOP leadership in the Texas House with a congressional redistricting plan that could produce a congressional delegation from the Lone Star State of 22 Republicans and

10 Democrats. When Tom Craddick, the Speaker of the Texas House, pushed for a vote on the plan in the closing days of the legislative session, more than 50 Democratic members of the Texas House of Representatives secretly traveled to Ardmore, Oklahoma, where they would be outside the jurisdiction of Texas law enforcement officials who had been sent to find them and bring them back to Austin. The strategy for the Democrats was to prevent the Texas House from having a quorum, which is the number of members that must be present for the chamber to conduct official business. Because the rules of the Texas House set a quorum at two-thirds of the 150-member body, the absence of more than 50 Democratic legislators blocked the redistricting bill, at least for the time being. Once the deadline for passing legislation expired in the Texas House, the Democrats returned to the state and the legislature resumed its business.

DeLay's redistricting proposal was highly controversial. Republicans said that redrawing the state's congressional district lines to increase the number of Republicans in Congress was fair because Texas is a Republican state. In 2002, Democrats won 17 of the state's 32 U.S. House seats even though 57 percent of Texas voters supported Republicans for Congress. If most Texans vote Republican, DeLay said, most Texas members of Congress should be Republican as well. In contrast, Democrats pointed out that redistricting anytime other than the session after the U.S. Census is both unusual and unnecessary. They accused DeLay of a power grab aimed at preserving Republican control of the U.S. House of Representatives. Democrats hold a majority of the state's congressional delegation, they said, because Texas voters in a number of districts split their tickets to vote Republican for statewide office while backing Democrats for Congress.

Shortly after the end of the 2003 regular session of the legislature, Governor Perry called a 30-day special session to consider congressional redistricting. The Texas House quickly passed a redistricting plan, but it ran into trouble in the Texas Senate because Senate Democrats held together to block consideration of the plan. A longstanding practice in the Texas Senate was to require a two-thirds vote before a measure could be considered on the floor. With 11 Senate Democrats refusing to agree to debate, the redistricting bill failed. The first special session ended without accomplishing anything.

As the first special session ended, the Republican leadership set a trap for the Democrats. Lieutenant Governor Dewhurst declared that he would not honor the two-thirds rule in a second special session, therefore ensuring that the Republican majority would be able to vote a redistricting plan out of the Senate. While Democrats caucused in the capital, Governor Perry called a second special session and Dewhurst ordered the doors locked to trap the Democrats inside. Unfortunately for Dewhurst and Perry, the Democrats got word of the scheme just in time and slipped out a side door. They drove to the airport and flew to Albuquerque, New Mexico, out of the reach of Texas authorities. With 11 Democrats in Albuquerque, the Senate lacked the quorum necessary to conduct official business. The second special session accomplished nothing as well.

Before Governor Perry could call a third special session, the Senate Democrats in Albuquerque broke ranks. Senator John Whitmire returned to Texas, declaring that he and his fellow Democrats had made their point and that he would be on the Senate floor when the governor called the next special session, ensuring a quorum.

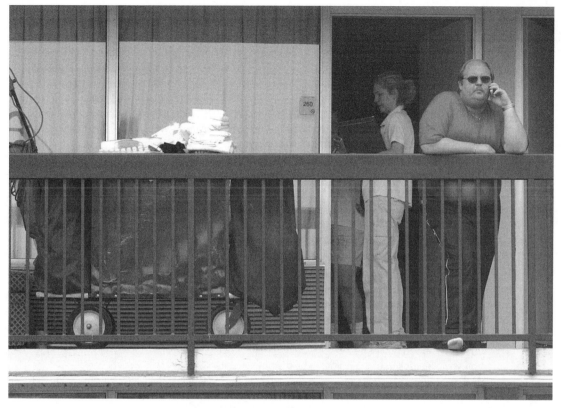

More than 50 Democratic legislators spent several days in Ardmore, Oklahoma, in May 2003 in hopes of defeating a congressional redistricting plan that would favor the Republicans.

Although the other Democrats were furious with Whitmire, they had no choice but to end their boycott and return to Texas.

Whitmire's return did not mean a quick end to the redistricting battle because Texas House and Texas Senate Republicans could not agree on a new map. After several weeks of wrangling, Congressman DeLay flew to Texas to broker an agreement. The Texas House and Texas Senate passed, and Governor Perry signed, a redistricting plan that many observers believed would increase the number of Republicans in the U.S. House from 15 to at least 20 and maybe 22.

The predictions proved true. The GOP picked up one seat in the U.S. House even before the next election when Democratic Congressman Ralph Hall of East Texas switched parties. The Republicans added five more seats in the 2004 election, defeating every targeted Democratic incumbent except for Congressman Chet Edwards of West Texas, who barely hung on to his seat with 51 percent of the vote. In 2005, the state's congressional delegation included 21 Republicans and 11 Democrats.[21]

INTERNET RESEARCH   ## Legislative Districts and State House Elections

The Texas House of Representatives has 150 members elected from 150 districts called state House districts. The districts are numbered from 1 to 150, with each district electing one person to the Texas House. In 2009, for example, Veronica Gonzalez represented District 41, which is located in McAllen.

Students of Texas government can learn a good deal about legislative districts and elections from online resources, especially those located at the website of the Texas legislature: **www.legis.state.tx.us/**. Answer the following questions based on the information in the textbook and your research online:

1. In which state House district is your home located? (Go to the website of the Texas legislature and find the link: "Who Represents Me?" Click on the link and enter your complete address. The district type is "House.")
2. Who represents the district in which you live?
3. The website displays a map of the district. Describe where it is located by making reference to major streets, neighborhoods, bodies of water, or other landmarks.
4. Write a paragraph in which you describe the district's population. Is it urban or rural? Is its population older or younger than the state average? Is its population better educated or less well educated than the state average? Is the average income in the district above or below the state average? Is the population predominantly white, black, Latino, or mixed? (All of this information can be found at the website. Click on the tab at the top of the page labeled "District Information." Indicate that the district type is "Texas House" and enter the number for the district in which you live. Use the pull-down menu to display tables containing the data needed to answer the preceding questions.)
5. Based on your description of the district, would you expect it to typically vote Republican or Democrat, or would you anticipate it to be a swing district? Explain the basis for your answer. (Before you attempt to answer this question, you may wish to review the information in Chapter 6 that describes the voter base for each of the two major political parties.)
6. Is your analysis on the party leanings of the district correct? Use the drop-down menu to review the district election report. It displays the vote breakdown in the district for state, county, and district elections. Do the figures indicate that the district trends Republican or Democratic? Discuss the information you considered in reaching your conclusion.

Reforming the Redistricting Process

Critics believe that the modern redistricting process undermines the quality of democracy in the United States because it reduces electoral competition. The redistricting process typically produces legislative districts that are safe for one party or the other, depriving voters of the opportunity to participate in competitive elections for Congress or state legislatures. In the first election after redistricting following the 2000 Census, the number of elections for seats in the U.S. House nationwide that were decided by less than 10 percentage points fell by 11; the number of seats decided by less than 5 percentage points fell by 15.[22] If elected officials do not have to worry about a serious electoral challenge, critics warn, they have little incentive to represent the interests of their constituents.

State legislators have always tried to create districts that would be safe for their party. Democrats want to draw Democratic districts, whereas Republicans prefer to create Republican districts. No one in the legislature has an incentive to design a competitive district. Computer technology has enabled legislators to accomplish their goals more efficiently than ever before. As a result, relatively few legislative seats are competitive between the two parties.

The critics of redistricting also believe that it produces legislators who represent the extremes of the political spectrum. Republican primary voters are somewhat more conservative than Republicans in general and much more conservative than the electorate as a whole. Democratic primary voters, meanwhile, are somewhat more liberal than Democrats in general and much more liberal than the electorate as a whole. In competitive districts, candidates recognize the value of appealing to a broad spectrum of voters because they understand that they must win not just the primary election but the general election as well. Primary voters also have an incentive to select more moderate candidates because they have a better chance of winning the general election than do candidates whose views are more extreme. Legislative bodies dominated by members representing the extremes of either party may have difficulty reaching compromise on complex policy issues, instead dissolving into partisan gridlock.

Reformers want to change the redistricting process to make it less political. In Iowa, for example, a bipartisan redistricting commission creates a redistricting plan, which the legislature must accept or reject but not amend. If the legislature rejects the plan, the commission tries a second and even a third time. If the legislature fails to approve any of the commission's plans, a court redistricts for the state. After the 2000 Census, four of the state's five U.S. congressional districts were fairly evenly divided between the two parties. The other district was heavily Republican. After the 2006 election, the Iowa congressional delegation included three Democrats and two Republicans. A bill designed to change the redistricting process in Texas to resemble the Iowa system was introduced in a recent session of the legislature, but it has gotten nowhere.

ELECTION CAMPAIGNS

election campaign
An attempt to get information to voters that will persuade them to elect a certain candidate or not elect the candidate's opponent.

An **election campaign** is an attempt to get information to voters that will persuade them to elect a certain candidate or not elect that candidate's opponent. Campaigns educate voters about issues and candidates and increase interest in the election process. The more familiar citizens are with the candidates, the more likely they are to vote.[23]

The Role of Money

Election campaigns are expensive. The total cost of the campaigns for governor, other statewide executive offices, and the legislature in 2006 was nearly $180 million. Campaign spending in 2008 reached $147 million even without major statewide races for governor, lieutenant governor, attorney general, and so on, on the ballot. The median campaign cost for successful candidates for the Texas House in 2008 was $248,790, ranging from $50,000 on the low end to $1.5 million on the high end. Competitive campaigns for the Texas Senate are costlier because Texas Senate districts are larger than Texas House districts. In 2008, Wendy Davis of Fort Worth, the winner of the most expensive Texas Senate contest, spent nearly $2.2 million on her campaign.[24] Local contests in large metropolitan areas are expensive as well. Candidates for mayor in the state's major cities often spend well in excess of a million dollars on their campaigns.

Candidates need money to hire a campaign staff, cover overhead expenses, and purchase advertising. They hire consultants to plan strategy, pollsters to assess public reaction to candidates and issues, media consultants to develop an advertising campaign, field organizers to get out the vote, opposition research experts to dig for dirt on opponents, Internet consultants to design websites, and fundraisers to find the cash to pay for it all. Other money goes for campaign literature, office space, postage, telephones, polling, and consulting fees. The largest single item in the big-time campaign budget is media, especially television. A week's worth of television advertising that covers all of the state's major markets costs around $1 million.[25]

Advertising costs vary by medium and market size. The average charge for running a 30-second television ad during the late night news in Dallas is about $5,000. A 60-second radio spot during drive time in a major market is much less expensive, only around $600, but the audience for radio is only a fraction of what television reaches.[26] Candidates for statewide office buy advertising on both radio and television throughout the state if they have the money available. In contrast, candidates for local office or the legislature may focus their efforts on less expensive approaches, such as radio, cable television, billboards, and direct mail.

Candidates who are wealthy can bankroll their own campaigns. In 2002, David Dewhurst invested $24.2 million in his successful campaign for lieutenant governor, counting both contributions and personal loans.[27] Candidates who loan money to their campaigns can often raise money after the election to cover their loans, especially if they win. State law caps the amount of reimbursement for personal loans to $500,000 for candidates for governor and $250,000 for candidates for other statewide offices. Because the law puts no limit on reimbursement for third-party loans personally guaranteed by candidates, none of Dewhurst's loans were subject to the cap.[28]

 ### WHAT IS YOUR OPINION?

Should wealthy individuals be allowed to finance their own political campaigns?

political action committees (PACs)
Organizations created to raise and distribute money in political campaigns.

Campaign money comes from a relatively small number of contributors. In 2008, most political money in Texas came from individuals and **political action committees (PACs),** organizations created to raise and distribute money in political campaigns. Bob Perry, a Houston homebuilder, was the top individual donor, contributing $2.9 million, mostly to Republican candidates and campaign committees.[29] The Texas Democratic Trust, which is a PAC funded primarily by trial lawyers, gave

$6 million, mostly to support Democratic candidates. In contrast, Texans for Lawsuit Reform, a PAC advocating tort reform, contributed $4.3 million, primarily to Republicans.[30]

Most states restrict the amount of money individuals and groups can contribute to candidates for office, but not Texas. Two-thirds of the states limit campaign contributions and one-third provide public funding for campaigns in exchange for voluntary spending limits.[31] In contrast, Texas law places no limits on campaign contributions or campaign expenditures for candidates for executive or legislative office. Contribution and expenditure limits on judicial races are voluntary. In short, candidates for executive and legislative office in Texas can raise an unlimited amount of money from individuals or PACs as long as they report the names, occupations, and employers of people who give them $500 or more in campaign contributions. Labor unions and corporations may not contribute directly to candidates for office, although they can fund nonpartisan voter registration drives and get-out-the-vote campaigns.

Money is indispensable to major campaign efforts. In general, candidates who spend the most money get the most votes.[32] Money is especially important for challengers and first-term incumbents who usually are not as well known as long-term officeholders. Once a challenger reaches a certain threshold, the amount of money the incumbent spends is irrelevant.[33] Raising money early in the campaign is particularly important because it gives candidates credibility with potential contributors, making it easier to raise money later in the campaign season. Candidates who amass campaign war chests often scare away potential serious challengers.

WHAT IS YOUR OPINION?

Would you support using taxpayer money to finance election campaigns in order to reduce the role of private contributions?

Nonetheless, money does not guarantee victory. In 2002, for example, Democrat Tony Sanchez spent more than $60 million of his family fortune in his campaign for governor and barely received 40 percent of the vote. Furthermore, studies suggest that a law of diminishing returns may apply to campaign spending.[34] The marginal difference between spending $15 million and spending $13 million is not nearly as great as that between spending $2 million and spending $4 million. After all, if the average Texas voter sees a candidate's commercial 15 times, will it make much difference to see it once or twice more?

The relationship between money and electoral success is complex. Although it is true that well-funded candidates are usually successful, it is perhaps more accurate to say that successful candidates are well funded. Major campaign contributors give money to candidates they believe are likely to win because they hope to gain access to elected officials. Money makes strong candidates stronger; likewise, the lack of money makes weak candidates weaker. In 1998, for example, Governor George W. Bush raised more than $25 million for his reelection campaign, even though no one believed that his main opponent, Democrat Gary Mauro, had a serious chance of winning the election.[35] Individuals and groups gave generously to Governor Bush because he was almost a sure bet for reelection. Bush was also someone prominently mentioned as a likely presidential candidate in 2000. Major money players were eager to write big checks to the Bush campaign in hopes of gaining influence not just with the governor of Texas but also with someone who might become president of the United States.

Campaign Organization and Strategy

Political campaigns vary in their size and intensity. Many local contests are modest affairs. The candidates, their families, and a few friends shake some hands, knock on a few doors, put up some signs, create a website, and perhaps raise enough money to buy an ad in the local newspaper. The contest may be hard fought, but the stakes are not high enough to support a major-league campaign effort. Not so, however, with statewide races, local elections in big cities, and contests for Congress and the state legislature. These elections feature professional campaign consultants, well-oiled organizations, and big money.

Big-time campaigns are long, drawn-out affairs, beginning years before voters go to the polls. Candidates spend the early months of a race raising money, building an organization, and planning a strategy. Candidates who successfully raise money and

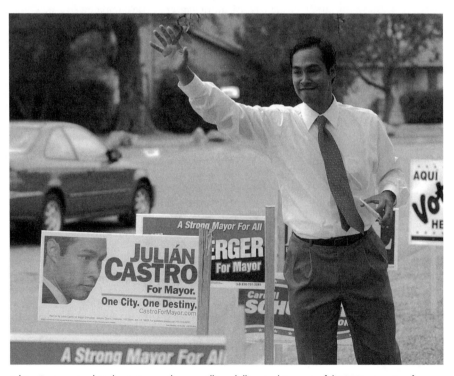

Julián Castro raised and spent more than a million dollars on his successful 2009 campaign for mayor of San Antonio.

create a professional organization well before Election Day establish a reputation as serious candidates. In contrast, candidates who fail to raise money and build an organization early in the political season will probably never seriously contend.

An important goal for many campaigns is to improve the candidate's name recognition, especially if a candidate is a challenger who is not already well known. Races for low profile offices may never move beyond the name-recognition stage. It helps if voters are already familiar with the candidate, or at least the candidate's name. A man named Bruce Wettman once ran for state district judge in Harris County by posting billboards picturing his name written on an umbrella; the strategy must have worked because he won easily.

Sometimes candidates borrow name recognition from better-known namesakes. In 1990, a San Antonio attorney named Gene Kelly won the Democratic nomination for a seat on the Texas Supreme Court despite spending almost no money on the race. Primary voters apparently associated Kelly with the famous entertainer of the same name. "If I had been Fred Astaire, I might have won," joked Kelly's defeated opponent. Kelly's luck ran out in the general election, however, when he lost to Republican nominee John Cornyn. Cornyn spent heavily on media advertising that attacked Kelly as unqualified. Ten years later, Kelly repeated his primary success by winning the Democratic nomination for the U.S. Senate to oppose Senator Kay Bailey Hutchison. Once again, Kelly failed to mount a serious general election campaign and Hutchison easily won reelection.

Besides building name recognition, campaigns attempt to create a favorable image for the candidate. In the fall of 1989, advertising firms hired by Clayton Williams ran a series of political commercials that turned Williams from a virtually unknown candidate into the frontrunner for the Republican nomination for governor. Riding on horseback, wearing a white hat, and bathed in golden light, Williams promised to get tough on illegal drugs by teaching teenagers who use drugs "the joys of bustin' rocks."

Campaigns also attempt to create unfavorable impressions of their opponents. In 2002, for example, Governor Perry ran radio and television ads that attempted to link his Democratic opponent, Tony Sanchez, to the 1985 murder of Enrique "Kiki" Camarena, a federal narcotics officer, because the gang responsible for the murder had earlier done banking business with a savings and loan owned by Sanchez. The ads featured a pair of former drug agents who advised voters to "just say no to Tony Sanchez." Research on negative campaigning reveals that challengers are more likely to use it than are incumbents; in addition, Republicans are more inclined to go negative than Democrats. Negative campaigns by challengers are somewhat effective, especially if they are based on policy rather than personality. However, going negative may backfire on incumbents unless they are attacked first. Negative campaigning stimulates election turnout among party loyalists but depresses it among independents.[36]

The last, but perhaps most important, task for each campaign is to get supporters to the polls. The most popular candidate will not win if his or her supporters stay home on Election Day. Well-organized campaigns identify likely voters and remind them to vote. The campaign distributes early voting materials and telephones likely supporters to urge them to cast their ballots. Getting out the vote is usually more important for Democrats than Republicans. Republicans tend to be better educated and more affluent than Democrats and thus are more likely to participate in elections. Turning out likely Democratic voters, especially African Americans and Latinos, often requires an organized effort.

THE VOTERS DECIDE

Why do voters decide as they do? Political scientists identify a number of factors influencing voter choice.

Incumbency

Incumbent Current officeholder.

In most election contests, an **incumbent** (current officeholder) enjoys a distinct advantage over a challenger. Nationwide, incumbent members of the U.S. Congress win reelection at a rate that typically exceeds 90 percent, and incumbent state legislators seeking reelection do nearly as well. Furthermore, the advantages of incumbency are apparently growing. The number of incumbents winning reelection has increased and a substantial number of incumbents win without facing opposition in either the party primary or the general election. Many potential candidates decide not to run against an incumbent because they believe the incumbent will be difficult to beat.[37]

Incumbent success rates are based on several factors. Incumbents have more name recognition than most challengers and they are usually able to raise more money than their opponents can. Incumbent officeholders can often use their positions to generate favorable publicity for themselves through press releases, whereas most challengers, especially in down-ballot races, struggle to generate a meaningful amount of press coverage. Incumbents can make friends by providing services to individual constituents or groups of constituents. Incumbents also benefit from districting schemes that stack most legislative districts for one party or the other.

Political Party Identification

Political party identification is closely related to voter choice.[38] Democrats vote for Democratic candidates; Republicans back Republicans. On average, 75 percent of voters cast their ballots for the candidate of the party with which they identify.[39] In 2008, 89 percent of Democratic voters in Texas supported Democrat Barack Obama for president, whereas 93 percent of the Republicans cast their ballots for John McCain.[40] Nonetheless, party identification is a complex phenomenon. People identify with a party because they agree with its issue positions, have confidence in its leaders, or feel comfortable with groups associated with the party. When citizens decide to vote for Candidate A because Candidate A is a Democrat (or Republican), their choice is more than blind allegiance to a party label. It is also a response to the perceived issue positions and image of the party.

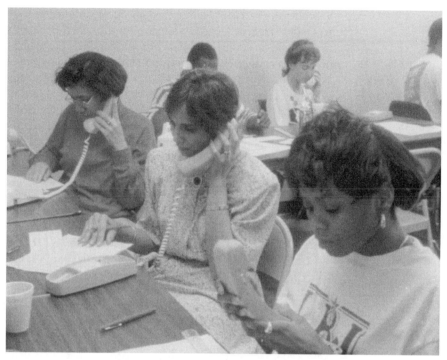

Campaign volunteers staff phone banks to get out the vote for their candidate.

Issues and Ideology

A significant number of voters, perhaps as high as 30 percent, hold ambivalent partisan attitudes. They agree with Democrats on some issues, Republicans on other issues. On still other issues, they may be torn, embracing core elements of both sides of a debate. On the issue of abortion, for example, they may be opposed to a woman deciding to end a pregnancy but still be uncomfortable with government involvement in such a personal decision. People who lack a clear party allegiance will vote on grounds other than partisanship. Well-informed voters will evaluate candidates on their issue stands or political ideology. Less-informed voters will consider other factors, such as the state of the economy, voting for incumbents in good times and against them in bad times.[41]

Campaigns

Campaigns matter because they make it easier for voters to obtain information about candidates and issues. Candidates attempt to raise the visibility of issues that benefit them and weaken their opponents.[42] In the 2006 race for governor, for example, Governor Perry positioned himself as a successful governor willing and able to address important issues. He took credit for cutting property taxes and promised to take action to improve border security. In contrast, Chris Bell, the Democratic candidate, accused the governor of failing to improve education and healthcare. He endorsed a pay raise for teachers and promised to cut the red tape that was preventing hundreds of thousands of youngsters in low-income families from qualifying for the State Children's Health Insurance Program (SCHIP). In the meantime, Carole Keeton Strayhorn and Kinky Friedman, the two independents in the race, declared that they would be constructive alternatives to the politics-as-usual approach of the major party candidates. Strayhorn promised to provide two years of free college education to the state's high school graduates, whereas Friedman said that Texas should legalize casino gambling because the revenues would enable the state to better fund education while cutting taxes.

Candidate Image

Voter perceptions of the personal images of candidates influence candidate choice. This does not mean that most voters are primarily concerned with a candidate's age, hairstyle, and wardrobe, at least not explicitly. Instead, they focus on qualities related to performance in office. Research on presidential voting concludes that voters evaluate candidates on the basis on their model of what a president should be like. This study found that voters regard competence, integrity, and reliability as qualities they desire in a president. On Election Day, voters pick the candidate they believe best matches the qualities the office requires.[43] Although political scientists have yet to conduct similar studies on state and local elections, it is reasonable to expect that voters approach state and local election voting decisions in a similar fashion.

Retrospective and Prospective Voting

Retrospective voting The concept that voters choose candidates based on their perception of an incumbent candidate's past performance in office or the performance of the incumbent party.

Prospective voting The concept that voters evaluate the incumbent officeholder and the incumbent's party based on their expectations of future developments.

Citizens make voting decisions based on their evaluations of the past and expectations for the future. **Retrospective voting** is the concept that voters choose candidates based on their perception of an incumbent candidate's past performance in office or the performance of the incumbent party. If voters perceive that things are going well, incumbent officeholders and their party usually get the credit. In contrast, they get the blame if voters believe that the state or country is on the wrong track. Political science research indicates that the state of the nation's economy is a key element of voter evaluations of incumbent performance. As economic conditions worsen, citizens are more likely to vote against the incumbent party, and vice versa.[44] Similarly, research shows that voters evaluate governors on the state unemployment rate compared with the national average.[45] Voter evaluations have a prospective as well as a retrospective component. **Prospective voting** is the concept that voters evaluate the incumbent officeholder and the incumbent's party based on their expectations of future developments. One study finds, for example, that voter expectations of economic performance have a strong influence on voter choice.[46]

National Factors

National factors can affect voting decisions in Texas. For example, presidential popularity and economic conditions can influence the outcome of races in nonpresidential election years. Texas candidates can also be helped by popular national

Coattail effect A political phenomenon in which a strong candidate for one office gives a boost to fellow party members on the same ballot seeking other offices.

figures. In a presidential election year, for example, a popular presidential candidate can sometimes provide coattails to boost candidates of the same party in other races. The **coattail effect** is a political phenomenon in which a strong candidate for one office gives a boost to fellow party members on the same ballot seeking other offices. In 2008, for example, Texas Democrats may have benefited from an unusually high turnout of core Democratic voters, especially African American voters, because of the Obama candidacy.

GETTING INVOLVED

Campaigning

People who volunteer to work in an election campaign can have more of an impact on the outcome than they would by just voting. An individual controls one vote and it is rare for a single vote to swing the outcome of an election. In contrast, a hard-working campaign volunteer can affect enough votes to make the difference in a close election, especially a low-profile down-ballot race or a local election contest.

Select a candidate to support and contact the candidate's campaign to inquire about volunteering. All major campaigns and some candidates for local office have websites with contact information for prospective volunteers. Every well-organized campaign will have a telephone number. Contact directory assistance to get the number of the campaign office, call, and volunteer your services. Not only will you have the chance to make a difference in the outcome of the race but your instructor may also give you extra credit for your volunteer work.

It's your government—Get involved!

WHAT WE HAVE LEARNED

1. **What are the advantages and disadvantages of the long ballot?**

   Texas has the long ballot, a system that provides for the election of nearly every public official of any significance. Defenders of the long ballot believe that the electoral process is the best way to ensure that public officials remain accountable to the people. In contrast, critics of the long ballot argue that most Texans lack the information necessary to make intelligent voting choices on many down-ballot races.

2. **What are the various types of elections held in Texas?**

   Texans have the opportunity to participate in several different types of elections. The general election is a statewide election to fill national and state offices, held in November of even-numbered years. A primary election is an intra-party election at which a party's candidates for the general election are chosen. If no candidate receives a majority in the primary, the two leading contenders meet in a primary runoff. Every four years, Texans have the opportunity to participate in the process through which the Democratic and Republican Parties choose their presidential candidates by selecting delegates to attend the national conventions of the two major parties. Most local elections, which are usually nonpartisan, are held in odd-numbered years. Special elections are held outside the regular election calendar. Texas voters can also participate in a number of non-candidate elections, including constitutional amendment, bond, recall, initiative, and local-option (wet-dry) elections.

3. **What factors affect the redistricting process in Texas?**

Texas voters select public officials in a combination of at-large and district elections. Election districts must be redrawn every ten years to account for population changes as measured by the U.S. Census. The U.S. Supreme Court held in its one-person, one-vote rulings that legislative districts must be drawn on the basis of population and must be nearly equal in population size. States must also adhere to the VRA, which makes it illegal for state and local governments to enact and enforce election rules and procedures that diminish minority voting power. Even with the limitations of one person, one vote and the VRA, redistricting is highly political. The drawing of legislative district lines for political advantage is known as gerrymandering. If the governor and legislature are unable to agree on redistricting plans, the LRB is charged with redistricting state legislative seats. A federal court draws congressional district lines. In 2000, the Republican Party controlled legislative redistricting through the LRB and used its position to create legislative districts that enabled the Republican Party to win a majority of members in the Texas legislature. The legislature then redrew the state's U.S. congressional districts to add more Republicans to Congress. Critics believe that the modern redistricting process undermines the quality of democracy in the United States because it reduces electoral competition. State legislatures draw districts that are safe for one party or the other, and these districts tend to produce legislators who represent the extremes of the political spectrum. Reformers want to change the redistricting process to make it less political.

4. **What factors affect election campaigns in Texas?**

An election campaign is an attempt to get information to voters that will persuade them to elect a certain candidate or not elect that candidate's opponent. Above all else, campaigns are expensive. Candidates need money to hire a campaign staff, cover overhead expenses, and purchase advertising, especially television advertising, which is often the single largest campaign expenditure. Wealthy candidates can fund their own campaigns. Other candidates raise money from PACs and individual contributors. Texas places no restrictions on how much individuals and groups can contribute to candidates for state legislative and executive offices. Although money is usually necessary for campaign success, it does not guarantee victory. Major campaigns are long, drawn-out affairs. An important goal of a campaign is to improve the candidate's name recognition. Campaigns seek to build a favorable image for their candidate while creating an unfavorable image of the opponent. Finally, campaigns work to get supporters to the polls.

5. **How does each of the following factors affect voter choice: incumbency, political party identification, issues and ideology, campaigns, candidate image, retrospective and prospective voting, and national factors?**

A number of factors affect voter choice. In most elections, the incumbent enjoys a distinct advantage. Party identification is closely related to voter choice. People lacking a clear partisan identification may vote on the basis of issues. Campaigns shape the vote by informing voters about candidates and issues. Voter perceptions of the personal images of candidates influence candidate choice. Citizens make voting decisions based on their evaluations of the past (retrospective voting) and expectations for the future (prospective voting). National factors, such as the coattail effect, can influence Texas election results as well.

KEY TERMS

at-large election

bond

bond election

caucus method of delegate selection

closed primary

coattail effect

district election

election campaign

general election

gerrymandering

incumbent

initiative process

Legislative Redistricting Board (LRB)

local-option (wet-dry) elections

long ballot

nonpartisan elections

one person, one vote

open primary

political action committees (PACs)

presidential preference primary election

primary election

prospective voting

recall

redistricting

retrospective voting

runoff primary election

special election

split-ticket voting

straight-ticket voting

super delegates

Texas Two-Step

Voting Rights Act (VRA)

NOTES

1. Thad L. Beyle, ed., *State Government: CQ's Guide to Current Issues and Activities 1985–86* (Washington, DC: Congressional Quarterly Press, 1985), p. 93.

2. Christy Hoppe, "Independents' 1st Hurdle: Getting on the Ballot," *Dallas Morning News*, February 6, 2005, available at www.dallasnews.com.

3. *Capitol Update*, January 22, 2009, available at www.txdirectory.com.

4. Texas Secretary of State, "Turnout and Voter Registration Figures (1970–Present)," available at www.sos.state.tx.us.

5. CNN, "Election Center 2008, Primary Results for Texas," available at www.cnnpolitics.com.

6. Ibid.

7. Marsha Matson and Terri Susan Fine, "Gender, Ethnicity, and Ballot Information: Ballot Cues in Low-Information Elections," *State Politics and Policy Quarterly* 6 (Spring 2006): 49–72.

8. Steve Bickerstaff, "State Legislative and Congressional Reapportionment in Texas: A Historical Perspective," *Public Affairs Comment* 37 (Winter 1991): 2.

9. *Wesberry v. Sanders*, 376 U.S. 1 (1964) and *Reynolds v. Sims*, 377 U.S. 533 (1964).

10. *Vieth v. Commonwealth of Pennsylvania*, 195 F. Supp. 2d 672 (M.D. Pa. 2002).

11. Victor L. Mote, "The Geographical Consequences of Politics in the United States and Texas," in Kent L. Tedin, Donald S. Lutz, and Edward P. Fuchs, *Perspectives on Texas and American Politics*, 4th ed. (Dubuque, IA: Kendall/Hunt, 1994), p. 10.

12. Mathew D. McCubbins and Thomas Schwartz, "Congress, the Courts, and Public Policy: Consequences of the One Man, One Vote Rule," *American Journal of Political Science* 32 (May 1988): 388–415.

13. Mark Monmonier, *Bushmanders and Bullwinkles: How Politicians Manipulate Electronic Maps and Census Data to Win Elections* (Chicago, IL: University of Chicago Press, 2001), p. 62.

14. David Lublin and D. Stephen Voss, "Racial Redistricting and Realignment in Southern State Legislatures," *American Journal of Political Science* 44 (October 2000): 792–810.

15. David T. Canon, *Race, Redistricting, and Representation: The Unintended Consequences of Black Majority Districts* (Chicago, IL: University of Chicago Press, 1999), p. 257.

16. *Shaw v. Reno*, 509 U.S. 630 (1993) and *Miller v. Johnson*, 515 U.S. 900 (1995).

17. *Texas Government Newsletter*, July 11, 1994, p. 1.

18. Peverill Squire, "The Partisan Consequences of Congressional Redistricting," *American Politics Quarterly* 23 (April 1995): 229–240.

19. Richard G. Niemi and Simon Jackman, "Bias and Responsiveness in State Legislative Districting," *Legislative Studies Quarterly* 16 (May 1991): 183–202.

20. Michael Barone and Grant Ujifusa, *The Almanac of American Politics 1998* (Washington, DC: National Journal, 1997), p. 1,339.

21. Seth C. McKee, Jeremy M. Teigen, and Mathieu Turgeon, "The Partisan Impact of Congressional Redistricting: The Case of Texas, 2001–2003," *Social Science Quarterly* 87 (June 2006): 308–317.

22. Michael P. McDonald, "Redistricting and Competitive Districts," in Michael P. McDonald and John Samples, ed.,

The Marketplace of Democracy: Electoral Competition and American Politics (Washington, DC: Cato Institute, 2006), p. 225.

23. Paul Freedman, Michael Franz, and Kenneth Goldstein, "Campaign Advertising and Democratic Citizenship," *American Journal of Political Science* 48 (October 2004): 723–741.

24. National Institute on Money in State Politics, available at www.followthemoney.org.

25. W. Gardner Selby, "Perry, Strayhorn Poised to Blast off TV Ads," *Austin American-Statesman*, September 3, 2006, available at www.statesman.com.

26. *Texas Weekly*, August 15, 2005, available at www.texasweekly.com.

27. R. G. Ratcliffe, "GOP Winners' Coffers Fattened After Election," *Houston Chronicle*, January 16, 2003, available at www.houstonchronicle.com.

28. *Capitol Update*, December 13, 2002, p. 1.

29. National Institute on Money in State Politics, available at www.followthemoney.org.

30. Texans for Public Justice, "Texas PACs: 2008 Election Cycle Spending," available at www.tpj.org.

31. Malcolm E. Jewell and Sarah M. Morehouse, *Political Parties and Elections in American States*, 4th ed. (Washington, DC: CQ Press, 2001), pp. 67–69.

32. Randall W. Partin, "Assessing the Impact of Campaign Spending in Governors' Races," *Political Research Quarterly* 55 (March 2002): 213–233.

33. Gary C. Jacobson, "Competition in U.S. Congressional Elections," in McDonald and Samples, eds., *The Marketplace of Democracy*, p. 41.

34. Anthony Gierzynski and David A. Breaux, "Money and the Party Vote in State House Elections," *Legislative Studies Quarterly* 18 (November 1993): 515–533.

35. The National Institute on Money in State Politics, available at www.followthemoney.org.

36. Richard R. Lau and Gerald M. Pomper, *Negative Campaigning: An Analysis of U.S. Senate Elections* (Lanham, MD: Rowman & Littlefield, 2004), pp. 30–88.

37. Richard G. Niemi, Lynda W. Powell, William D. Berry, Thomas M. Carsey, and James M. Snyder, Jr., "Competition in State Legislative Elections, 1992–2002," in McDonald and Samples, eds., *The Marketplace of Democracy*, p. 70.

38. Warren E. Miller, "Party Identification, Realignment, and Party Voting: Back to the Basics," *American Political Science Review* 85 (June 1991): 557–568.

39. John R. Petrocik, "Reporting Campaigns: Reforming the Press," in James A. Thurber and Candice J. Nelson, eds., *Campaigns and Elections American Style* (Boulder, CO: Westview, 1995), p. 128.

40. "Election Results 2008—Texas," *New York Times*, December 9, 2008, available at www.nytimes.com.

41. Scott J. Basinger and Howard Lavine, "Ambivalence, Information, and Electoral Choice," *American Political Science Review* 99 (May 2005): 169–184.

42. James N. Druckman, Lawrence R. Jacobs, and Eric Ostermeier, "Candidate Strategies to Prime Issues and Image," *Journal of Politics* 66 (November 2004): 1180–1202.

43. Arthur H. Miller, Martin P. Wattenberg, and Oksana Malachuk, "Schematic Assessments of Presidential Candidates," *American Political Science Review* 80 (June 1986): 521–540.

44. Alan I. Abramowitz, "Can McCain Overcome the Triple Whammy?" May 29, 2008, Larry J. Sabato's Crystal Ball 2008, available at www.centerforpolitics.org.

45. Jeffrey E. Cohen and James D. King, "Relative Unemployment and Gubernatorial Popularity," *Journal of Politics* 66 (November 2004): 1180–1202.

46. Brad Lockerbie, "Prospective Voting in Presidential Elections, 1956–1988," *American Politics Quarterly* 20 (July 1992): 308–325.

Chapter 8

The Texas Legislature

WHAT WE WILL LEARN

After studying Chapter 8, students should be able to answer the following questions:

▸ What effects do bicameralism, biennial sessions, and limited session length have on legislative policymaking in Texas?

▸ What is the job description of a member of the Texas legislature, considering qualifications, background, compensation, turnover, and term limits?

▸ How is the Texas legislature organized in terms of leadership, committee organization, and legislative assistance?

▸ What are the steps of the legislative process?

▸ What effects do the following factors have on the legislative process: legislative leadership, interest groups, constituency, political parties, and political ideology?

Global warming
The gradual warming of the Earth's atmosphere reportedly caused by the burning of fossil fuels and industrial pollution.

In 2009, the Texas legislature cautiously began to address the issue of **global warming,** the gradual warming of the Earth's atmosphere, which is reportedly caused by the burning of fossil fuels and industrial pollutants. The legislature passed a bill authored by Senator Kirk Watson, a Democrat from Austin, which called for the Texas Commission on Environmental Quality (TCEQ) to identify ways to reduce greenhouse gas emissions that either would save money for business and consumers or cost nothing to implement.[1] A second bill authored by Senator Watson would have required utility companies to develop non-wind renewable energy from solar, biomass, or geothermal sources.[2] (The measure focused on renewable energy sources other than the wind because Texas is already a leader in wind energy development.) Another measure, authored by Senator Troy Fraser, a Republican from Horseshoe Bay, would have created a rebate program to help fund the installation of solar panels and other renewable energy devices on the roofs of homes, businesses, and other structures statewide.[3] Meanwhile, measures authored by Senator Kip Averitt, a Republican from Waco, would have provided financial incentives for the development of clean energy projects and emission control technologies.[4] The second measure authored by Watson and the bills authored by Fraser and Averitt all apparently enjoyed sufficient support to pass the legislature. However, they died in the last days of the session, caught up in the end-of-session crunch, which in 2009 was exacerbated by a political tussle over an unrelated issue.

The environmental bills authored by Watson, Fraser, and Averitt enjoyed strong support because they were business friendly. Instead of cracking down on polluters, they offered businesses and industries financial incentives to reduce emissions. Watson described the measure he authored that did pass as a "no regrets" greenhouse gas emissions reduction strategy because it imposed no cost on either taxpayers or business. The other environmentally friendly measures, which also enjoyed sufficient support to pass, could be described as "no regrets" legislation as well. In contrast, proposed bills designed to punish industry for polluting got nowhere in the legislature.[5]

Legislative efforts to enact environmentally friendly legislation illustrate both legislative politics and the legislative process. Since business organizations are the most powerful interest groups in Texas politics, legislation seldom moves forward in the face of business opposition. As noted previously, whereas business friendly environmental legislation made progress in the legislature in 2009, bills designed to punish polluters got nowhere. The effort to pass environmental measures in the legislature also demonstrated the difficulty of the legislative process in Texas. Even measures that enjoy strong support sometimes fail because supporters run out of time in a short legislative session. We examine both legislative politics and the legislative process in detail in this chapter.

This chapter on the legislature is the first of a series of five chapters dealing with the policymaking institutions of Texas government. Chapter 9 focuses on the executive branch of Texas government; Chapter 10 studies the judicial branch. Chapters 11 and 12 examine local government: Chapter 11 considers city government, whereas Chapter 12 discusses the other units of local government in the state—counties, school districts, and special districts.

STRUCTURE

The Texas Constitution provides for a bicameral legislature to meet in biennial regular sessions of 140 days in length. The legislative sessions are numbered consecutively, dating from the 1840s, when Texas became a state. The 81st legislature was elected in 2008 and met in regular session in 2009. The legislature that meets in regular session in 2011 will be the 82nd legislature.

Bicameralism

Bicameral legislature
A legislative body with two chambers.

Texas has a **bicameral** (two-chamber) **legislature** consisting of a House of Representatives and a Senate. The Texas House has 150 members elected from various districts to serve two-year terms, whereas the Texas Senate consists of 31 senators elected from various districts to serve four-year terms. Senate four-year terms overlap, so half the senators run for reelection at one time, with the other half running for reelection two years later. The exception to this pattern occurs in the first election after redistricting when the entire Senate must stand for election. In 2012, for example, all 31 Senate seats will be up for election under new district lines drawn after the 2010 Census. The newly elected senators will then draw lots to determine whether they will have to run for election again in 2014 or 2016.

The Texas Constitution assigns each legislative chamber certain powers and responsibilities. The Texas Senate, for example, has sole authority to confirm or reject the governor's appointments by a two-thirds vote. Only the Texas House may initiate legislation to raise taxes, even though both chambers must agree before any tax bill can pass. The House alone, by majority vote, has the power of **impeachment,** which is a formal accusation against an executive or judicial officeholder. However, the Senate tries the impeached official, with a two-thirds vote needed for conviction and removal from office.

Impeachment
A formal accusation against an executive or judicial officeholder.

The Texas Constitution requires that the two legislative chambers share certain responsibilities. Both the House and Senate must concur before any measure can pass the legislature. Both must vote by a two-thirds margin to propose constitutional amendments. Also, two-thirds of the members of each chamber must agree to override a governor's veto.

The Texas House and Texas Senate often approach policy issues differently because of structural differences in the two legislative chambers. Compare, for example, Texas House and Texas Senate districts. Each House member represents approximately 139,000 people, whereas the population of each state Senate district is 673,000. Because state Senate districts are roughly five times larger than House districts, they will probably be more diverse than the smaller House districts. Since they need to please a more diverse constituency, senators may prove more moderate than House members, whose districts are more homogeneous. In Texas, the two legislative chambers also differ in the length of their members' terms of office. House members must stand for election every two years, whereas senators serve four-year terms (staggered, as previously mentioned, so that half the Senate is up for reelection every two years). As a result, senators can evaluate policy issues from a longer-range perspective than House members, whose next reelection campaign is always just around the corner.

Bicameralism has supporters and critics. Its defenders believe that bicameralism allows one chamber to correct the mistakes of the other. In contrast, the critics of bicameralism believe that a single-chamber legislature is more economical and efficient. Every state has a bicameral legislature except Nebraska, which has a **unicameral** (one-chamber) **legislature.** Nebraska adopted a state constitutional amendment in 1937 to create a unicameral legislature whose members would be chosen in **nonpartisan elections.** In these contests, the names of the candidates, but not their party affiliations, appear on the ballot. The 49 members of the Nebraska legislature serve four-year overlapping terms.

The conventional wisdom is that bicameralism has a conservative effect on the policymaking process because two chambers must approve a measure before it can clear the legislature. Nonetheless, Professor James R. Rogers believes that bicameralism is as likely to increase legislative output as to decrease it because both chambers can initiate legislation as well as reject it. Furthermore, he says, the historical evidence from legislative bodies that have switched from unicameral to bicameral or vice versa fails to support the conventional view.[6]

Unicameral legislature
A legislative body with one chamber.

Nonpartisan elections
Election contests in which the names of the candidates appear on the ballot but not their party affiliations.

 WHAT IS YOUR OPINION?

Should Texas replace its bicameral legislature with a unicameral legislature?

Session Frequency

The Texas Constitution provides that the legislature meet in regular session every other year, in odd calendar years (2009, 2011, etc.), with sessions beginning on the second Tuesday in January. In the late nineteenth century, when the Texas Constitution was written, biennial legislative sessions were standard practice in most American states. As recently as 1960, 32 states still had biennial sessions. Today, Texas is one of only six states (Arkansas, Montana, Nevada, North Dakota, Oregon, and Texas) whose legislatures do not meet in regular session every year. The Arizona legislature, for example, meets every year for 100 days. The California legislature is in session nearly year-round every year.[7] However, the Texas Constitution empowers the governor to call special sessions of the legislature if needed, which may last a maximum of 30 calendar days. Although most state legislatures may call themselves into special session, the Texas legislature has no such power.

Annual legislative sessions are near the top of the list of constitutional reforms proposed by those who would like to see a more streamlined state government. Reformers believe that the affairs of state government are too complex to handle in biennial sessions. Budget issues are particularly difficult to address in biennial sessions because the legislature can neither anticipate state spending needs nor estimate tax revenues over so long a period. The most popular proposal for annual sessions would maintain the current 140-day session in odd-numbered years and add a shorter, 60-day session in even years. The 140-day sessions would write a one-year budget and deal with general legislative concerns, whereas the 60-day sessions would be limited to writing a budget, plus any additional matters the governor would want to submit for legislative consideration.

Nonetheless, biennial legislative sessions have their defenders. Give the legislature more time, they say, and Texas will have more laws, more regulations, more spending, and more taxes. Although observers often blame biennial sessions for legislative logjams at the end of a session, research shows that legislatures that have annual sessions have worse logjams than legislatures with biennial sessions.[8] For example, the New York legislature, which meets annually, has been ridiculed for years because of its inability to pass a budget on time. Furthermore, the citizens of Texas have expressed their support for biennial sessions every time they have had a chance to vote on the issue. In 1930, 1949, 1958, 1969, 1973, and 1975, voters rejected constitutional amendments that would have provided for annual legislative sessions.

Session Length

Constitutional reformers would also like to increase the length of legislative sessions in the Lone Star State. With sessions limited to 140 calendar days, the legislature may not have time to do the state's business. The legislature often falls behind and has to act on a flood of bills in the last few weeks of the session before time runs out. In 2009, for example, the legislature failed to pass measures to continue the operation of the Texas Department of Transportation and the Texas Department of Insurance. Had Governor Rick Perry not called a special session to extend the life of the two agencies, they would have been forced to go out of business in 2010.

The membership of the Texas legislature is more diverse today than at any time in its history.

Defenders of the 140-day session point out that legislative session limits are common among the states and a useful device for forcing legislators to get down to business. Political scientist Malcolm Jewell believes that session limits force lawmakers to make decisions because they set a deadline for wrapping up business. "When there's no limit," he says, "it drags on. They [legislators] postpone compromise to the last minute; they bargain; they play games."[9]

Research shows that the legislative workload in Texas is not as congested as conventional wisdom suggests. Legislative activity in Texas tends to concentrate at certain times, such as the deadline for submitting bills and the end of the session, but lawmakers work on legislation throughout the session. Although 80 percent of the votes for the final passage of bills come in the last two weeks of the session, most of the measures passed have been under legislative consideration for months.[10] Furthermore, the Texas House and Texas Senate have adopted rules to prevent a last minute rush of legislative activity.

A legislative logjam at the end of the 2009 session of the legislature led to the failure of thousands of House bills, including the Watson, Fraser, and Averitt environmental measures. However, that event had more to do with the politics of voter ID than the legislative calendar. With five days to go before the May 26 deadline for passing bills, a voter ID bill appeared on the House calendar. Whereas almost every Republican member of the legislature favored voter ID legislation as a necessary measure to ensure the integrity of elections, almost every Democrat in the legislature was equally convinced that the real purpose of voter ID was to keep older minority voters, who tend to vote Democratic, from casting a ballot. In order to prevent voter ID from moving forward, House Democrats adopted the strategy of spending the maximum allowable time debating each of the 200 mostly non-controversial local bills on the calendar scheduled ahead of the voter ID bill. Under House rules, local bills die if debate last more than ten minutes, so Democratic legislators would talk for nine minutes or so and then allow the bill to pass. The strategy worked in that it prevented consideration of voter ID, but it also doomed thousands of other pieces of legislation by preventing them from coming to a vote.[11]

WHAT IS YOUR OPINION?

Should the Texas legislature meet in annual sessions?

MEMBERSHIP

In 2009, the combined membership of the Texas House and Texas Senate included 43 women, 37 Latinos, 16 African Americans, and 2 Asian Americans among 181 total members. Although the Texas legislature is a more diverse body than at any time in its history, it does not provide an accurate cross-section of the state's population. As Figure 8.1 indicates, the legislature is whiter and has more male members than the state of Texas as a whole. Most members of the legislature hold college degrees. The most common career fields among House members and senators are business and law.[12]

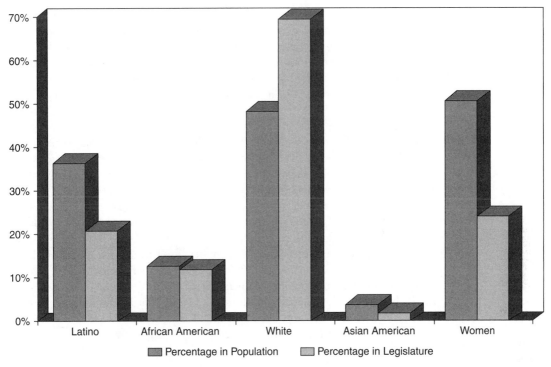

70%

60%

50%

40%

30%

20%

10%

0%

| Latino | African American | White | Asian American | Women |

■ Percentage in Population   ☐ Percentage in Legislature

FIGURE 8.1   Representation in the 81st Legislature.

Compensation

The official salary for members of the legislature, whether they serve in the Texas House or the Texas Senate, is set by the Texas Constitution at $600 a month, or $7,200 a year. Compared with other states, this figure is low. In fact, legislative pay in Texas is the lowest among the ten largest states.[13] Several states have full-time, professional legislatures and pay their lawmakers accordingly. Legislators in California, for example, earn $110,880 a year. Even most states whose legislatures meet for limited periods pay their lawmakers more than Texas pays its legislators. For example, members of the Oklahoma legislature receive $38,400 a year. The pay for Louisiana lawmakers is $16,800 a year. Florida legislators earn $29,916 annually.[14]

Should Texas legislators be paid more? The proponents of higher legislative salaries believe that better pay would allow a wide cross-section of Texans to seek office, not just people who are independently wealthy or have careers that permit them time off to attend legislative sessions. Furthermore, higher salaries would help keep legislators independent of interest groups. In contrast, defenders of the current salary structure argue that low salaries ensure the continuation of a citizen-legislature whose members are relatively immune from outside pressures. Because lawmakers are not dependent on legislative salaries, they are more willing to take political chances to do the right thing than they would be if their salaries were higher.

Non-salary compensation for Texas legislators is relatively generous. When the legislature is in session, lawmakers receive a daily expense allowance of $139. The allowance enables legislators to increase their earnings by $19,460 for each regular session and $4,170 for each 30-day special session. Furthermore, legislators have provided themselves with one of the most generous pension plans in the nation. When State Senator Gonzalo Barrientos retired in January 2007 after serving 32 years in the legislature, he immediately began collecting an annual pension of $92,000. Members who serve a minimum of eight years can qualify for a pension of $23,000 a year at age 60. Members serving 12 or more years can begin collecting at 50 years of age. For each year of legislative service, a member receives an annual pension equal to 2.3 percent of the salary of a state district judge, which was $125,000 in 2010. State lawmakers also receive full healthcare benefits, both as active members and in retirement.[15]

Many legislators use excess campaign funds to supplement their incomes and enrich their families. According to a study conducted by the *Dallas Morning News*, more than one-third of the campaign spending of North Texas lawmakers goes for non-campaign expenditures, including money for travel, entertainment, living expenses, food, charitable donations, and campaign contributions to other legislators.[16] Critics accuse legislators of using campaign donations as a slush fund. "They're using the lobby's money to enhance their lifestyles, a perk that is technically legal but a clear conflict of interest," says Craig McDonald, the executive director of Texans for Public Justice, a citizen group that focuses on campaign finance reform.[17]

Legislative Turnover

Legislative turnover

The replacement of individual members of a legislature from one session to the next.

Legislative turnover refers to the replacement of individual members of a legislature from one session to the next. Legislative turnover peaks in the first election after redistricting because the redistricting process changes the geography of legislative districts. When this happens, some legislators retire rather than attempt reelection from new, less hospitable districts, whereas others are defeated for reelection. The 78th legislature, the first legislature elected from lines drawn after the 2000 Census, included 43 new members—five senators and 38 members of the House. In contrast, legislative turnover declines as redistricting approaches. Incumbents become entrenched and potential challengers often choose to wait until after redistricting before deciding whether to run. The 81st legislature, which was elected in 2008, included only 19 new faces out of 181 members. Legislative turnover rates in Texas are below the national average. During the 1990s, the percentage of new members in each session for the Texas House was 17 percent, and the percentage was only 16 percent for the Texas Senate. The comparable figures for state houses and state senates nationwide were 25 percent and 23 percent, respectively.[18]

Legislative turnover in Texas is more often the result of voluntary retirement than election defeat. More than half of the first-term legislators in the 81st session of the legislature replaced members who retired or resigned to run for higher office. In addition, some members leave because they know they cannot win reelection,

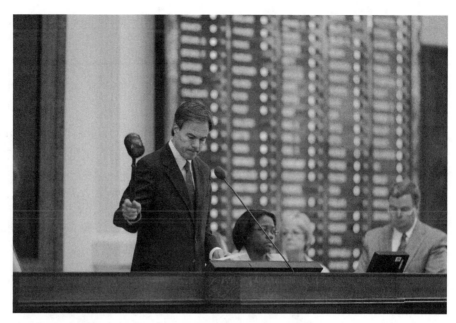

Joe Straus was elected speaker of the Texas House in January 2009.

whereas others quit out of frustration. They complain about low pay, poor staff support, little public appreciation for their efforts, the hectic pace of legislative sessions, and pressure from interest groups and constituents. House members, in particular, often grow cynical about their ability to accomplish their goals. Not all reasons for leaving are negative, however. Some legislators attempt to move up the political ladder by running for higher office. Others choose to leave because their law practice has picked up or they receive a business offer they cannot refuse. Some resign to become well-paid lobbyists. Although many states impose a waiting period between the time legislators leave office and the time they can become lobbyists (usually a year), Texas has no such limitation. Members can begin working for interest groups as registered lobbyists the day they leave office, and many do. In fact, 78 former legislators are registered lobbyists in Texas, more than in any other state.[19] Moreover, lobbyists earn considerably higher incomes than legislators. The average lobbyist in Texas has contracts worth up to half a million dollars a year.[20]

Term Limits

Term limitation
The movement to restrict the number of terms public officials may serve.

Term limitation is the movement to restrict the number of terms public officials may serve. Fifteen states (but not Texas) limit the terms of state legislators. The limits for members of the House in states that have term limits range from 6 to 12 years. They vary from 8 to 12 years for state senators. In only one of the states that has a legislative term limit did the legislature enact term limits.[21] In every other state, the voters

Initiative process
A procedure whereby citizens can propose the adoption of a policy measure by gathering a prerequisite number of signatures. Voters must then approve the measure before it can take effect.

adopted term limitation through the **initiative process,** a procedure whereby citizens can propose the adoption of a policy measure by gathering a prerequisite number of signatures. State officials then place the measure on the ballot for approval by the voters. Because Texas does not have an initiative process, most observers think it is unlikely that the state will adopt term limitation. Although polls show that term limits are popular with the voters, many members of the legislature are unwilling to vote themselves out of a job.

The advocates of term limits believe that they improve the capacity of the legislature to do work. They offer the following arguments on behalf of term limitation:

- Members who are not career-oriented can focus on solving the state's problems rather than entrenching themselves in office.
- By forcing veteran lawmakers from office, term limits give new people with fresh ideas an opportunity to have an impact on public policy.
- Term limits reduce the power of interest groups by forcing their favorite lawmakers from office.
- Legislators who know they are term limited are more likely to represent the interests of the voters rather than entrenched interest groups.

In contrast, the opponents of term limitation are convinced that term limits make legislatures less effective. They offer the following arguments against term limitation:

- Term limits interfere with the voters' right to elect the individuals they favor.
- Legislators with valuable experience and expertise will be forced from office.
- Bureaucrats and lobbyists will be more powerful because it will be easier for them to outwit inexperienced lawmakers than it was for the veteran legislators who were forced to retire.
- Legislators will concern themselves only with short-run problems because they serve for limited periods of time.[22]

In practice, term limits have been neither as beneficial as their advocates have hoped nor as harmful as their opponents have warned. On the positive side, state legislators who are term limited place a greater emphasis on the needs of the state as a whole relative to the interests of the districts they represent. In addition, term-limited legislators are less focused on obtaining special benefits for their districts than are other legislators. On the negative side, term limits strengthen the governor and possibly legislative staffers while weakening legislative leaders. Because term-limited legislators are relatively inexperienced, they have not developed the personal relationships that form the basis for legislative compromise and cooperation. Consequently, influence slips away from the legislature toward other political actors, especially executive branch officials and legislative staffers.[23] Furthermore, rather than focusing on legislative business, many term-limited legislators concentrate on lining up their next job as elected officials in local government or as lobbyists.[24]

AROUND THE NATION

Repealing Term Limits in Idaho

In 1994, Idaho voters adopted the most sweeping term-limits law in the country. The measure, which received nearly 60 percent of the vote, restricted the terms of every elected state official from the governor down to county commissioners and school board members. It limited most state and local officials to eight years in office over any 15-year period; county commissioners and school board members could serve no more than six years out of 11. Because the term-limit clock did not begin ticking until 1996, term limits would not apply to officials in major offices until 2004; it would not impact local officeholders until 2002.

Opposition to term limits grew as the date for their implementation approached. The Republican Party, which is the majority party in Idaho, declared its opposition to term limits because many of its officials, including the legislative leadership, would be forced from office. Party leaders worked behind the scenes to convince Republican legislators to vote to repeal term limits. Local officials and business leaders in rural areas opposed term limits as well because of their potential impact on local government. In sparsely populated rural areas, relatively few people would be willing to serve in low-pay or no-pay positions as county officials and school board members.

If long-term incumbents were forced from office by term limits, perhaps no one would be willing to take their places.

In 2002, Idaho became the first state to repeal term limits. (Utah became the second in 2003.) Early in the year, the Idaho legislature voted for repeal, overriding the governor's veto. Term-limit supporters gathered sufficient signatures to put the issue on the ballot to give the voters the chance to "repeal the repeal" in the November 2002 election. By the narrow margin of 1,889 votes of more than 400,000 ballots cast, Idahoans approved the legislature's action and sustained the repeal of term limits, with rural voters providing the margin of victory.*

QUESTIONS TO CONSIDER

1. When the idea of legislative term limits was introduced more than a decade ago, Republicans supported the concept. Now, however, they oppose term limits, at least in Idaho. Why do you think many Republicans switched sides?
2. Do you think that Idaho voters would support term limits if local governments were exempted?
3. For which level of government are term limits the most appropriate (if any)?

*Daniel A. Smith, "Overturning Term Limits: The Legislature's Own Private Idaho?" *P.S. Political Science and Politics*, April 2003, pp. 215–220.

ORGANIZATION

Modern legislatures choose leaders, establish committees, and hire staff assistance in order to facilitate their work.

Leadership

The lieutenant governor and speaker of the House are the presiding officers and foremost political leaders of the Texas legislature. The speaker, who presides in the House, is a state representative who is selected by the members of the House to serve as speaker. The lieutenant governor, who presides in the Senate, is elected statewide for a four-year term in the same general election year in which the governor is chosen. In contrast to the president and vice president of the United States, the governor and lieutenant governor do not run as a formal ticket. Voters cast ballots for the two offices separately and may choose individuals from different political parties. In 1994, when Republican George W. Bush was initially elected governor, Bob Bullock, a Democrat, was reelected lieutenant governor.

If the office of lieutenant governor becomes vacant, the Senate chooses a successor. For example, when Bush resigned as governor to move to the White House in 2001, Lieutenant Governor Rick Perry moved up to become governor, leaving the office of lieutenant governor vacant. The 31 members of the Texas Senate selected fellow senator Bill Ratliff to replace Perry by majority vote. Ratliff served the remainder of Perry's term as lieutenant governor without resigning his Senate seat. He chose not to stand for election as lieutenant governor in 2002, preferring to run for reelection to the Senate.

The speaker, who presides in the House, is a state representative who is selected by the members of the House to serve as speaker. Because the speaker's powers are extraordinary, the race for the position may be intense. State representatives who hope to become speaker gather signed pledges of support from other House members in hopes of obtaining majority backing well ahead of the actual vote. Usually one candidate wraps up the race early, months or even years ahead of the vote. Because representatives do not want to be on the speaker's bad side, members quickly climb on the bandwagon as soon as it becomes clear that one candidate has the edge. Voting for speaker is done publicly rather than by secret ballot, so members who vote against the speaker may fear retaliation. Consequently, the actual vote for speaker is usually lopsided.

The 81st session of the legislature began with a speaker fight. Republican Tom Craddick of Midland, the incumbent, had held the position since 2003, the year the Republicans became the majority in the House. Craddick won the position with the support of most Republican members of the House and some Democrats, the so-called Craddick Ds who backed Craddick not because they agreed with him philosophically but because they wanted to be part of his leadership team. Over time, Craddick's support diminished. The opponents of Craddick, including some Republicans and most Democrats, accused the speaker of being dictatorial; in other words, concentrating power in his office rather than sharing it with committee chairs. Many members were particularly unhappy with the speaker for forcing votes on controversial issues that could be used against them when they ran for reelection. Moreover, Craddick sometimes supported primary challengers against Republican legislators who dared to vote against the speaker's policy agenda.[25]

Several members of the House declared their intent to seek the office of speaker in 2009. Craddick, who was seeking reelection, had the most signed pledges, but not a majority. In early January, 11 moderate Republicans (the so-called Anybody But Craddick Republicans) met privately to unite behind a speaker candidate. They chose a member of their group, Representative Joe Straus of San Antonio, who was first elected to the House in 2005. Straus promised to run the House in an open, fair manner, dispersing power to the membership, especially committee chairs. Within days, 70 Democrats joined 15 Republicans in pledging their votes to Straus, giving him more than enough support to ensure election as speaker.[26]

The speaker and lieutenant governor are two of the most powerful public officials in the state, exercising extraordinary authority in their respective chambers. The speaker and lieutenant governor control many of the legislative procedures of the House and Senate. They assign bills to committee, and once committees have done their work the speaker and lieutenant governor have considerable influence over which bills are scheduled for debate. As presiding officers in their respective chambers, the speaker and lieutenant governor recognize members for debate, rule on points of order, and interpret rules.

The speaker and lieutenant governor rarely participate directly in the official deliberations of their respective chambers. As an elected member of the House, the speaker is entitled to participate in debate and vote on every issue before the chamber. In practice, though, the speaker seldom engages in floor discussions and votes only on those matters for which he or she wishes to register strong support. With the exception of Ratliff, who was a state senator, the lieutenant governor is technically not a member of the Senate and may vote only to break a tie.

The speaker and lieutenant governor serve on, and make appointments to, some of the state's most important policymaking bodies, including the Legislative Budget Board (LBB) and the Legislative Redistricting Board (LRB). The **Legislative Budget Board (LBB)** is an agency created by the legislature to study state revenue and budgetary needs between legislative sessions and prepare budget and appropriation bills to submit to the legislature. The **Legislative Redistricting Board (LRB),** which is composed of the speaker, lieutenant governor, comptroller, land commissioner, and attorney general, is responsible for redrawing the boundaries of Texas House and Texas Senate seats when the legislature is unable to agree on a redistricting plan. Finally, the speaker and lieutenant governor exercise considerable control over committee membership. They appoint legislative committee chairs, vice chairs, subcommittee chairs, most committee members, and some subcommittee members.

Although the lieutenant governor and the speaker have extraordinary powers, they seldom act in an arbitrary or dictatorial fashion. For the most part, the powers of the speaker and lieutenant governor are not spelled out in the Texas Constitution, and as recently as the 1930s their authority extended little beyond presiding. The powers of the leadership have grown because of changes in House and Senate rules adopted by majority vote in each chamber that could just as easily be withdrawn. The offices of speaker and lieutenant governor have acquired and maintained such broad authority because the people who have held the posts have generally exercised power in a fashion that a majority of legislators approve. Speaker Craddick lost his position because a majority of House members believed that he had abused his power.

The speaker and lieutenant governor base their authority on their ability to keep most members of the legislature happy. Both the speaker and the lieutenant governor are in a position to bestow favors on their friends. These favors can be as small as giving a legislator a larger office or as great as appointing a member to chair a prestigious committee. In either case, the lawmaker owes a favor, which the speaker or lieutenant governor can cash when the time is right. If enough members are unhappy

Legislative Budget Board (LBB)
An agency created by the legislature to study state revenue and budgetary needs between legislative sessions and prepare budget and appropriations bills to submit to the legislature.

Legislative Redistricting Board (LRB)
An agency composed of the speaker, lieutenant governor, comptroller, land commissioner, and attorney general that draws the boundaries of Texas House and Senate seats when the legislature is unable to agree on a redistricting plan.

with the speaker or lieutenant governor, they can face trouble from the membership, as Speaker Craddick discovered. House members have the authority to change leadership. Although senators cannot replace the lieutenant governor, they can strip the lieutenant governor of authority.

The leadership of the speaker and lieutenant governor is collective rather than individual. Each official heads a leadership team made up of supporters in the chamber. This is especially true in the House, where the speaker must first win the backing of a majority of members of the chamber. Both the speaker and the lieutenant governor have a corps of supporters in the chamber that makes up their leadership team. The members of the leadership team advise the speaker or lieutenant governor and work to organize the full chamber to support the leadership's position. The speaker and lieutenant governor reward their team leaders by appointing them to chair the most important committees. In 2009, Speaker Straus rewarded the ten Republicans who were his initial supporters for speaker by appointing each of them to chair a committee, including the most important committees in the House. He named Jim Pitts of Waxahachie to chair the Appropriations Committee, Brian McCall of Plano to head the Calendars Committee, and Burt Solomons of Carrollton to chair the State Affairs Committee. Straus replaced all but five of the 31 committee chairs who had served when Craddick was speaker.[27]

Committees

Standing committee
A permanent committee established to handle legislation in a certain field.

Some of the legislature's most important work takes place in committee. A **standing committee** is a permanent committee. The Texas House had 34 standing committees in 2009, ranging in size from 5 to 27 members. The most common size for House committees was nine members. The Texas Senate had 18 committees, ranging from 5 to 15 members.

Standing committees are important because they enable members to divide the legislative workload. More than 5,000 bills may be introduced in a regular session, far too many for each member to consider in depth. Committees allow small groups of legislators to examine a bill in detail and then report their evaluation to the full chamber. Committees also permit members to specialize in particular policy areas. Most committees deal with particular substantive policy areas, such as higher education, criminal justice, or agriculture.

Legislators usually have strong preferences regarding committee assignments. In the House, the most coveted committee assignments are the Appropriations, State Affairs, Calendars, and Ways and Means Committees. The committees of choice in the Senate are the Finance, State Affairs, and Jurisprudence Committees. The committees dealing with business interests (Business and Industry in the House, Business and Commerce in the Senate) are popular as well. Legislators may also prefer a particular committee assignment because of personal preference or constituency interest. A state representative from Houston or Dallas, for example, may favor service on the Urban Affairs Committee.

House and Senate rules limit the number of standing committees on which legislators may serve to three. Senators are restricted to membership on no more than two of the three most influential committees: Finance, State Affairs, and Jurisprudence. No House member may serve on more than two of the following three committees: Ways and Means, Appropriations, and State Affairs. No legislator may chair more than one committee.

State senators typically serve on more committees than do state representatives. Because the Senate has only 31 members, individual members typically serve on three or four committees. In 2009, for example, State Senator Rodney Ellis of Houston chaired the Government Organization Committee and served on the Criminal Justice, State Affairs, and Transportation and Homeland Security Committees. Because the House is larger with 150 members, individual representatives have more opportunities to specialize on committee assignments. In 2009, most House members served on only one or two committees. Representative Diane Patrick of Arlington, for example, served on the Public Education Committee and the Higher Education Committee.

The lieutenant governor and speaker make most committee assignments. In the Senate, the lieutenant governor appoints all committee chairs, vice chairs, and committee members at the beginning of each legislative session. The only restriction on the lieutenant governor's assignment power is that three members of each committee with ten or fewer members, and four members of each committee with more than ten members, must be senators who served on the committee during the last regular session.

In the House, the speaker appoints committee chairs, vice chairs, and all of the members of the Appropriations Committee and the Calendars Committee. The speaker also names at least half of the members of each of the other standing committees. House rules allow representatives, in order of seniority, to select one committee assignment, provided that the committee is not already half staffed. **Seniority** refers to the length of continuous service a member has with a legislative body.

An **interim committee** is established to study a particular policy issue between legislative sessions, such as higher education or public school finance. Frequently, an interim committee is also a **select,** or **special, committee,** which is established for a limited period of time to address a specific problem. Interim committees may include private citizens as well as legislators. The speaker, lieutenant governor, and governor may appoint interim committees. Legislative leaders use interim committees as a way to compensate for biennial legislative sessions of limited duration. Because interim committees have more time to study issues and formulate policies than do standing committees, they can lay the groundwork for legislation before the regular session begins.

Legislative Assistance

Staff assistance is important to the Texas legislature because legislators are essentially part-time employees asked to perform a monumental legislative task in a limited period of time. Legislative staff members improve the quantity and quality of information available to legislators, bring insight to issues, and help solve constituent problems. Texas legislators have sufficient funds to employ staff assistance in Austin and their

Seniority
The length of continuous service a member has with a legislative body.

Interim committee
A committee established to study a particular policy issue between legislative sessions, such as higher education or public school finance.

Select, or **special, committee**
A committee that is established for a limited period of time to address a specific problem.

home districts. In 2009, the permanent staff of the Texas legislature numbered 2,090, placing the Texas legislature third in the nation in terms of staff resources, after Pennsylvania and New York. Even though the Texas legislature has biennial sessions of limited length, it has staff support equivalent to full-time legislatures in other large states.[28]

The legislature provides members with some institutional assistance as well. Before each session, the Legislative Council conducts a brief orientation for new legislators. During sessions, the staff of the Legislative Council helps members draft bills and assists committees. The Legislative Reference Library fulfills routine requests for research assistance. The House Research Organization (HRO) and Senate Research Center (SRC) research issues, help draft legislation, and prepare technical analyses of bills pending in the legislature. The HRO and SRC also publish daily floor reports explaining and presenting arguments for and against proposed legislation. Standing committees have permanent staffs as well, ranging in size from 2 to 15 staff members in the Senate and from one to six in the House.[29]

THE LEGISLATIVE PROCESS

The Texas legislative process resembles that of the U.S. Congress but with important differences that affect policy.

Introduction

Bill
A proposed law.

Resolution
A legislative statement of opinion on a certain matter, such as a measure congratulating a Texas sports team for winning a championship.

Joint resolution
A resolution that must be passed by a two-thirds vote of each chamber.

During each legislative session, members introduce thousands of bills and hundreds of resolutions. A **bill** is a proposed law, such as a measure to prohibit small children from riding in the open bed of a pickup truck. A **resolution** is a legislative statement of opinion on a certain matter, such as a measure congratulating a Texas sports team for winning a championship. An amendment to the Texas Constitution takes the form of a **joint resolution,** a resolution that must be passed by a two-thirds vote of each chamber.

Introducing bills and resolutions into the legislative process is fairly straightforward. Members of the Texas House or Texas Senate may officially introduce legislation by filing copies in their own chamber with the secretary of the Senate or the chief clerk of the House during a period that begins on the first Monday after the November general election. After the first 60 days of a session, members can introduce only local bills or measures declared an emergency by the governor unless they obtain the approval of four-fifths of the members of their chamber. Once a bill is introduced, the secretary of the Senate or the chief clerk of the House assigns the measure a number, indicating the chamber of origin and order of introduction. HB 45, for example, indicates that the measure is the 45th bill introduced in the House during the session. SR 102 is the 102nd resolution introduced in the Senate.

Committee Action

The lieutenant governor and the speaker, in consultation with the chamber parliamentarian, assign newly introduced measures to committee. With important exceptions, the legislative leadership matches a bill with the committee that specializes in the subject matter it addresses. The exception to the general practice of matching legislation to the committee that deals with its subject matter involves the House Committee on State Affairs and the Senate Committee on State Affairs, which are general-purpose committees to which the speaker and lieutenant governor regularly assign major pieces of legislation regardless of their subject matter.

Committees do the detailed work of the legislative process. They begin their consideration of proposed legislation by holding public hearings. After the hearings are complete, the committee meets for **mark up,** the process in which legislators go over a piece of legislation line-by-line to revise, amend, or rewrite it. Major legislation is almost always rewritten in committee, with the final product reflecting a compromise among the various groups and interests involved. Eventually, committee members vote whether to recommend the revised measure to the entire House or Senate for passage. If a majority of the committee votes in the affirmative, the measure emerges from committee with a favorable report. The report includes the revised text of the measure, a detailed analysis of the bill, and a **fiscal note,** which is an analysis indicating the legislative measure's cost to state government, if any. If the majority of the committee votes against the measure, the legislation is probably dead.

Mark up
The process in which legislators go over a piece of legislation line by line, revising, amending, or rewriting it.

Fiscal note
An analysis of a legislative measure indicating its cost to state government, if any.

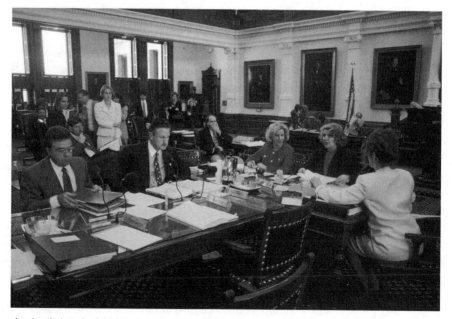

The detailed work of the legislature takes place in committees.

Floor Action

The procedure by which legislation moves from committee to the floor differs in the two chambers of the Texas legislature. In the Texas House, measures recommended favorably by a standing committee go to the Calendars Committee for assignment to a House calendar, which sets the order of priority for considering legislation. In 2009, the House calendars were, in order of priority, the following:

- **Emergency calendar:** This calendar is reserved for legislation declared an emergency by the governor and other measures deemed by the Calendars Committee to merit immediate attention. Tax bills and the **appropriation bill,** which is a legislative authorization to spend money for particular purposes, are usually assigned to the emergency calendar as well.
- **Major state calendar:** This calendar includes measures of statewide effect that do not merit emergency designation.
- **Constitutional amendment calendar:** This calendar is for proposed amendments to the Texas Constitution or ratification of amendments to the U.S. Constitution.
- **General state calendar:** This calendar is for bills of statewide impact, but secondary significance.
- **Local, consent, and resolution calendar:** This calendar includes bills and resolutions that are not controversial as well as **local bills,** which are proposed laws that affect only a single unit of local government.
- **Resolutions calendar:** This calendar is reserved for resolutions.
- **Congratulatory and memorial resolutions calendar:** This calendar contains resolutions congratulating people, places, and organizations for various accomplishments or honoring individuals who have died.

Although House rules provide for the consideration of measures in order of priority as set by the calendar system, the House may vote by a two-thirds margin to consider a measure outside the sequence established by the calendar system. On Mondays, which are known as Calendar Mondays, members can suspend the rules by a simple majority vote. House members may also suspend the rules on other days to sandwich time for items on the last three calendars between other measures.

The House calendar system becomes more important as a legislative session wears on. During the early months of a session, relatively few bills pass committee for assignment to a calendar and the House typically considers every measure before ending its legislative day. Toward the end of the session, however, the legislative pace quickens and the number of measures on the calendar grows. By the end of the session, measures placed on low-priority calendars risk failure for lack of action.

The standard practice in the Texas Senate is to require a two-thirds vote to consider legislation on the floor. Although official Senate rules stipulate that bills emerging from committee must be considered on the floor in the order in which they are received from committee, the official procedure is almost never followed. The first bill reported out of committee at the beginning of a session is invariably a "blocking bill," introduced not to be passed but to rest atop the Senate calendar, blocking

Appropriation bill
A legislative authorization to spend money for particular purposes.

Local bills
Proposed laws that affect only a single unit of local government.

consideration of other measures. In 2009, the blocking bill, SB 621, proposed the creation of a county park beautification and improvement program. The blocking bill ensures that legislation cannot reach the floor unless the Senate votes by a two-thirds margin to suspend the rules to consider a measure out of order. With the blocking bill firmly in place, the lieutenant governor and other Senate leadership decide which bills to consider on the floor and the order in which to consider them. By prearrangement, the lieutenant governor recognizes a particular senator who then moves that the rules be suspended to allow consideration by the full Senate of a particular bill. The rule suspension requires a two-thirds vote. An important feature of this practice is that 11 senators (one-third plus one) can block Senate action on a bill they oppose. Consequently, measures without the support of at least two-thirds of the members of the Senate do not even come to a vote in the chamber because they are never approved for consideration on the floor.

Lieutenant Governor David Dewhurst and most Republicans in the Senate have made exceptions to the two-thirds procedure for certain highly partisan issues. During a special session in 2003, Dewhurst refused to honor the two-thirds rule to allow congressional redistricting legislation to come to a vote in the Senate. At the beginning of the 2009 legislative session, the Senate membership decided by majority vote to exclude voter ID legislation from the two-thirds rule. As a result, the measure passed the Senate despite unanimous Democratic opposition. Many observers expect that the Senate will similarly suspend the two-thirds rule for legislative and congressional redistricting in 2011.

Once a bill reaches the floor of either chamber, members debate its merits and perhaps offer amendments. Because House rules limit debate, the measure eventually comes to a vote unless the session ends before action can be taken. In the Senate, members may speak as long as they please, and occasionally senators attempt to defeat a bill through prolonged debate, a practice known as a **filibuster.** Because debate can be ended by majority vote, however, the filibuster is not as potent a weapon in the Texas Senate as it is in the U.S. Senate, where 60 of 100 votes are needed to shut off debate. The only time a filibuster can be effective in the Texas Senate is near the end of the session, right before a deadline for passing legislation, when an individual senator can literally run out the clock.

Filibuster
An attempt to defeat a bill through prolonged debate.

Both the Texas Senate and Texas House set deadlines for the consideration of measures several days in advance of the constitutional end of the session. Senate rules declare that no bill can be considered unless it is reported from committee at least 15 days before final adjournment. In addition, no votes can be taken on the last day of the session except to correct errors. The House has comparable rules.

Ordinary legislation passes the Texas House and Texas Senate by majority vote of those members present and voting. If all 150 House members participate, 76 votes constitute a majority. In the Senate, 16 of 31 senators are a majority if every senator participates. Constitutional amendments require a two-thirds vote of each chamber. Members of the House vote electronically and a scoreboard displays each vote. In the smaller Senate, the clerk calls the roll and members shout their preference. The names of members voting for or against a measure are printed in the journal for each chamber. Citizens who are interested in how their representatives voted on a particular measure can find the information online at the website of the Texas legislature (www.legis.state.tx.us/). The website provides a link to the journal page showing the vote breakdown on particular pieces of legislation.

Conference Committee Action

A measure has not cleared the Texas legislature until it has passed both the House and Senate in identical form. Sometimes legislation passes one chamber and then goes to the other for consideration. At other times, legislators introduce similar or identical measures simultaneously in the House and Senate. Legislation that passes one chamber of the legislature may be rewritten in the other chamber, either during committee markup or on the floor. By the time a measure that has passed the House has made its way through the Senate (or vice versa), it may differ considerably from the measure originally passed by the other chamber.

What happens when the House and Senate pass similar, but not identical, measures? Frequently, the chamber that initially passed the legislation agrees to the changes adopted by the other chamber. When agreement cannot be reached, and this is often true with major pieces of legislation, the House and Senate form a conference committee to work out the differences. A **conference committee** is a special committee created to negotiate differences on similar pieces of legislation passed by the House and Senate. Separate conference committees are formed to deal with each bill in dispute. In the Texas legislature, conference committees include five members from each chamber, appointed by the presiding officers. A majority of conference members from each house must concur before the conference committee has finished its work.

Conference committee
A special committee created to negotiate differences on similar pieces of legislation passed by the House and Senate.

Once conference committee members have reached an agreement, the conference committee returns it to the floors of the House and Senate for another vote. Each chamber has the option of voting the legislation up or down or returning it to the conference committee for further negotiation. The House and Senate may not amend the measure at this point; rather, legislators must accept or reject the piece of legislation in its entirety.

The legislature passes only a fraction of the measures introduced during a session. In the 2009 regular session, for example, the legislature approved 1,459 bills of 7,419 measures that were introduced, for a passage rate of 20 percent.[30] Many of the measures that passed were local bills or other non-controversial pieces of legislation.

Action by the Governor

Once a bill passes the legislature, it goes to the governor, who has three options. First, the governor may do nothing. If the legislature remains in session, the bill becomes law after 10 days. If the measure reaches the governor's desk within 10 days of adjournment, it becomes law 20 days after the legislative session has ended. Governors generally use this option for bills about which they have mixed feelings. Although they are willing for the measures to become law, they do not want to go on record in favor of them. Second, the governor can sign the bill into law. Governors often sign politically popular bills with great fanfare, staging televised bill-signing ceremonies. Finally, the governor can issue a **veto,** an action in which the chief executive of a

Veto
An action by the chief executive of a state or nation refusing to approve a bill passed by the legislature.

state or nation refuses to approve a bill passed by the legislature. In 2009, Governor Perry vetoed 35 bills. Except for appropriation bills, the governor must choose to veto all of a bill or none of it. For appropriation bills, however, the governor has the **line-item veto,** which is the power to veto sections or items of an appropriation bill while signing the remainder of the bill into law. In 2009, Governor Perry used the line-item veto to cut $289 million from the state budget of $182 billion.[31]

Line-item veto
The power of the governor to veto sections or items of an appropriation bill while signing the remainder of the bill into law.

If the legislature is still in session, it can override the governor's veto by a two-thirds vote of each chamber and the bill becomes law despite the governor's opposition. Nonetheless, overrides are rare in Texas. Because most bills that clear the legislature pass in the last two weeks of the session, the governor can wait until the legislature has adjourned before casting a veto, meaning the veto stands unchallenged. In 2009, the legislature debated a constitutional amendment that would have allowed the legislature to call itself into special session to consider overriding the governor's vetoes. The amendment easily cleared the House, but the Senate failed to vote on the measure. Republican Senator Jeff Wentworth of San Antonio, the measure's author, accused Lieutenant Governor Dewhurst of refusing to recognize him to bring the measure to the floor for a vote, even though it had the support of more than two-thirds of the senators.[32]

Laws take effect at different times. The Texas Constitution declares that all laws except the appropriation bill go into effect 90 days after the legislature adjourns unless the legislature, by a two-thirds vote, designates another date. The appropriation bill takes effect on October 1, the beginning of the state budget year. Sometimes the legislature specifies that a measure take effect immediately upon signature of the governor. At other times the legislature directs that legislation go into effect on September 1.

INTERNET RESEARCH

Tracking Legislation Online

Begin by identifying the people who represent you in the Texas legislature at the following website: **www.legis.state.tx.us/**. Look for the link "Who Represents Me" on the left-column panel. Click on the link and enter your complete address. Take note of the name of your Texas state representative and your Texas state senator. Click on the name of either legislator to go to his or her personal website. The website includes a good deal of information about the legislator, including a link to the bills he or she authored in the last session of the legislature. Click on that link and answer the following questions:

1. What are the names of the people who represent you in the Texas House and Texas Senate?

2. Select a bill to research that was authored by either your Texas state senator or your Texas state representative in the last legislative session. What is the number of the bill? Who is its author?

3. Click on the bill number and you will be taken to a page that includes links to detailed information about the bill, including the bill's complete text. When was the bill introduced?

4. What would the measure do if it became law? (Write in your own words. Do not copy the brief description at the website.)

5. Did the measure become law? If not, at what stage of the legislative process was it halted?

6. Had you been a member of the legislature, would you have voted for the bill? Why or why not?

LEGISLATIVE POLICYMAKING

A number of factors affect the legislative process in Texas.

Legislative Leadership

The speaker of the House and the lieutenant governor are the most powerful figures in the Texas legislature. They appoint members of their leadership team to chair committees and stack key standing committees and conference committees with members who share their political perspectives. They have the power to reward their friends in the legislature and punish their enemies. Their support greatly enhances any measure's chances for passage; their opposition almost certainly dooms a bill to defeat. Environmental legislation made little progress in the legislature prior to 2009 because of the opposition of Speaker Craddick. Speaker Straus, however, was more sympathetic to the issue and appointed a new chair of the House Environmental Regulation Committee that was open to the adoption of business-friendly environmental measures.[33]

The centralization of legislative power in the hands of the leadership offers both advantages and disadvantages for the policymaking process in the legislature. On the one hand, the centralization of legislative power enables the legislature to act on a fair amount of legislation in a relatively short period of time. Leaders with power are in position to make things happen. On the other hand, the disadvantage of a centralized power structure is that members who are not part of the leadership team may be left out of the legislative policymaking process. Texas is a diverse state, but that diversity has not always been represented in the outcomes of the legislative process. Historically, the poor, minorities, organized labor, consumers, and other groups not part of the conservative legislative majority have often had little impact on the outcome of policy debates.

Nonetheless, it would be a mistake to regard the speaker and lieutenant governor as legislative dictators. Their considerable powers have been freely given to them by the members of the legislature and could just as easily be withdrawn by majority vote of the membership by simply changing the rules of the House or the rules of the Senate. Historically, the most effective legislative leaders have exercised their authority in a fashion that most members consider fair. The members of the legislature want the opportunity to pass legislation important to their constituents. They also want to avoid, whenever possible, having to cast a vote on controversial issues that could be used against them in the next election.

Speaker Craddick lost his leadership position in 2009 because most members believed that he neglected their needs in order to advance his policy agenda. They faulted the speaker for failing to share power with the membership, especially the committee chairs, and they resented having to vote on controversial issues that would likely fail in the Senate anyway. The chamber elected Joe Straus as the new speaker because they believed that he would lead fairly without trying to impose his personal policy agenda on the body.[34]

Interest Groups

Interest groups lay the groundwork for influencing the legislative process by contributing money to candidates. Groups give money to legislative candidates because they want **legislative access,** an open door through which an interest group hopes to influence the details of policy. Consequently, interest groups target their contributions to the legislature's most powerful members, including the leadership and members of important committees. The speaker, lieutenant governor, and key committee chairs are able to raise huge amounts of money because they hold positions of influence.

Legislative access
An open door through which an interest group hopes to influence the details of policy.

Interest groups attempt to affect the legislative process through **lobbying,** which is the communication of information by a representative of an interest group to a government official for the purpose of influencing a policy decision. Some lobbyists represent a single firm or organization whereas others contract to lobby on behalf of several clients. In 2009, for example, former state senator David Sibley was a registered lobbyist for 36 interests. Sibley's clients included the Association of Electric Companies of Texas, AT&T, Cingular Wireless, City of Harlingen, Direct Energy LP, El Paso Electric Co., Independent Insurance Agents of Texas, State Farm Insurance, Texans for Lawsuit Reform, and Wholesale Beer Distributors.[35]

Lobbying
The communication of information by a representative of an interest group to a government official for the purpose of influencing a policy decision.

Interest groups are often able to achieve their policy goals by working behind the scenes away from the public spotlight. In 2009, for example, the tobacco industry succeeded in killing a statewide smoking ban even though the measure enjoyed what appeared to be overwhelming support in the legislature. When the session began, the Texas Medical Association (TMA) and other health groups were optimistic that the smoking prohibition would pass. Lance Armstrong, the famous road racing cyclist, had signed on as a celebrity spokesperson for the cause. Even the Texas Restaurant Association (TRA) backed the measure because a statewide smoking prohibition would level the playing field between restaurants in Houston, Dallas, El Paso, and the 25 other cities that have local smoking ordinances and competitors outside the city limits where smoking bans do not apply.[36] The tobacco industry fought back quietly, hiring 40 lobbyists who went to work behind the scenes to kill the bill. The industry's strategy was to convince key lawmakers to slow the process, thus preventing the smoking ban from coming to a floor vote in either chamber. In the Senate, for example, Sen. Jane Nelson, a Republican from Flower Mound who chaired the Health and Human Services Committee, put off holding a hearing on the bill until the last couple of weeks of the legislative session, too late for it to make it through the legislative process. Ironically, Nelson was on record in favor of the bill and even attended Lance Armstrong's press conference to pledge her support for the measure. Because the smoking ban never came up for an official vote, none of the legislators had to go on record against it.[37]

Constituency

To what extent do the actions of legislators reflect the wishes of their constituents? The traditional model of representation is that candidates make promises during the election campaign and then keep (or fail to keep) those promises once in office.

In this approach to representation, citizens hold legislators accountable for keeping their promises. A second model of representation contends that lawmakers do what they think their constituents will approve at the next election. This approach to representation recognizes that legislators may sometimes address issues that were not discussed during the last election. It also implies that voters worry more about performance than promises. A third model of representation holds that legislators use common sense and good judgment to do what is best for their constituents and the state as a whole. Finally, another model of representation suggests that lawmakers sometimes represent constituents outside their districts, such as campaign contributors. From this perspective, big money campaign contributors may have as much or more influence over legislative decision making as do the voters. In practice, legislative behavior mixes several forms of representation, depending on the issue. Lawmakers are more likely to vote what they perceive as the preferences of their constituents on high-profile issues, but high-profile issues are rare, especially in state government. On most policy matters, legislators have the leeway to make their decisions on other bases.[38]

Some of the most important constituency-based legislative divisions in the Texas legislature reflect whether a district is predominantly inner city, suburban, or rural. Inner-city residents worry about crime, public school quality, neighborhood restoration, and opportunities for minorities. Suburban voters are concerned about property taxes, crime, annexation, and neighborhood preservation. Rural residents

The Texas legislature failed to approve a statewide smoking prohibition despite the high-profile support of Lance Armstrong.

focus on agricultural issues, natural-resource development, and property rights. Consider the controversy over the **top 10 percent rule,** a state law that grants automatic college admission to public high school graduates who finish in the top 10 percent of their class. The legislature passed the measure in hopes of increasing minority enrollment at the state's two flagship universities—the University of Texas at Austin and Texas A&M University at College Station. Inner-city minority legislators typically defend the rule as a symbol of racial integration and they are joined by white legislators from small towns and rural areas whose constituents also benefit from the provision.[39] In contrast, suburban lawmakers representing areas with highly competitive high schools have pushed to modify the rule because many of their constituents believe that it limits the opportunity for their youngsters to get into UT-Austin. In 2009, the legislature amended the top 10 percent rule to allow UT-Austin to limit the percentage of top 10 percent students in its freshman class to 75 percent in response to complaints from UT officials that the rule too severely limited their flexibility in making admissions decisions. In 2008, 80 percent of the students in UT's freshman class were admitted under the law.[40]

Political Parties

For most of the state's history, Texas had a **nonpartisan legislature,** a legislative body in which political parties played little or no role. Nearly every legislator was a Democrat. As recently as 1970, only two Republicans served in the Senate, whereas ten Republicans sat in the House. Neither the Democrats nor the Republicans in the Texas legislature organized formally, nor did they elect party leaders or meet regularly as party groups. Even as the Republican contingent in the legislature grew, partisanship generally remained in the background. The speaker and lieutenant governor included both Republicans and Democrats in their leadership teams and appointed legislators of both parties to chair important committees. In 2001, for example, Republican Lieutenant Governor Bill Ratliff appointed a Democrat, Rodney Ellis of Houston, to chair the important Finance Committee, whereas Democratic House Speaker Pete Laney named a Republican, Delwin Jones of Lubbock, to chair the critical Redistricting Committee.

In contrast, the U.S. Congress is a **partisan legislature,** a legislative body in which political parties play a defining role. The members of Congress organize along party lines. The political parties choose committee leaders and floor leaders, with the majority party holding every leadership position both on the floor and in committee. The party leadership acts to advance the party's agenda, and the voting on most pieces of major legislation breaks down along party lines, with a majority of Democrats voting on one side of the issue and a majority of Republicans voting on the other side. Interest group allies and party activists outside of Congress work with the congressional leadership to promote the party's agenda on major issues.

The 78th legislature, which met in 2003, marked the beginning of a turn toward a more partisan legislature, especially in the Texas House. The redistricting plan adopted by the LRB after the 2000 Census produced legislative districts that were clearly tilted to the advantage of one party or the other. Consequently, most legislators

Top 10 percent rule
A state law that grants automatic college admission to public high school graduates who finish in the top 10 percent of their class.

Nonpartisan legislature
A legislative body in which political parties play little or no role.

Partisan legislature
A legislative body in which political parties play a defining role.

School choice
An educational reform movement that would allow parents to choose the elementary or secondary school their children will attend.

Liberalism
The political view that seeks to change the political, economic, or social institutions of society to foster the development of the individual. Liberals believe that the government can (and should) advance social progress by promoting political equality, social justice, and economic prosperity. Liberals usually favor government regulation and high levels of government spending for social programs. Liberals value social and cultural diversity and defend the right of individual adult choice on issues such as access to abortion.

Conservatism
The political view that seeks to preserve the political, economic, and social institutions of society against abrupt change. Conservatives generally oppose most government economic regulation and heavy government spending while favoring low taxes and traditional values.

owed their election to primary voters, forcing Democrats to appeal to their liberal base while Republicans targeted their conservative base.[41]

Craddick, who became speaker in 2003, was a partisan speaker. He used his power to promote Republican positions on a series of controversial issues, including congressional redistricting, reduced spending for the State Children's Health Insurance (SCHIP) program, a constitutional amendment to outlaw gay marriage, voter ID legislation, and **school choice,** an educational reform movement that would allow parents to choose the elementary or secondary school their children will attend. Although most Republican members of the House embraced the party's position on these issues, some members resented being pressured by the speaker to support the party position on issues that would be controversial in their districts. Craddick lost his job in 2009 to Joe Straus primarily because Straus promised to be fair and relatively nonpartisan.

Partisanship remains important in the Texas legislature despite the election of a new speaker. Perhaps the biggest legislative drama of the 2009 regular session was the highly partisan battle over voter ID that pitted almost every Democratic legislator against almost every Republican lawmaker. Although few issues are as polarizing as voter ID and taxes, many issues divide members along party lines, with most Democrats on one side and most Republicans on the other. Party members in a legislature vote together because they have similar beliefs and represent similar constituents. Lawmakers from the same political party also have an incentive to work together to promote their party's success because they want their party to have a positive brand identification come election time.[42]

Political Ideology

Political ideology (liberalism/conservatism) influences the legislative process. **Liberalism** is the political view that seeks to change the political, economic, or social institutions of society to foster the development and well-being of the individual. Liberals believe that government should promote social justice, political equality, and economic prosperity. Liberals usually favor government regulation and high levels of spending for social programs. On social issues, such as abortion, liberals tend to support the right of adult free choice against government interference. In contrast, **conservatism** is the political view that seeks to preserve the political, economic, and social institutions of society against abrupt change. Conservatives generally oppose most government economic regulation and heavy government spending while favoring low taxes and traditional values.

Historically, conservatives have dominated the Texas legislature and legislative policies have reflected their political values. The legislature has enacted regulatory and tax policies designed to promote business expansion while adopting social welfare policies that stress personal responsibility. Few states spend less money on welfare than Texas. The legislature has been tough on crime, building the nation's largest prison system. The legislature has also created the nation's most prolific capital punishment system, executing more convicted murderers than any other state.

GETTING INVOLVED

Contacting Your State Legislators

Two people represent you in the Texas legislature—a state senator and a state representative. You can learn their names and find their e-mail addresses online at the following website: **www.legis.state.tx.us/**. Every session, the legislature deals with issues that affect ordinary citizens in general and college students in particular, including university tuition, college admission requirements, and higher education funding. Write your state legislators about these and other issues. Find out where they stand and let them know how you feel. They represent you, so they need to hear what you have to say.

It's your state—Get involved!

WHAT WE HAVE LEARNED

1. What effects do bicameralism, biennial sessions, and limited session length have on legislative policymaking in Texas?

Texas has a bicameral legislature consisting of a 150-member House of Representatives and a 31-member Senate. Members of the House serve two-year terms; senators serve four-year terms. The Senate is solely responsible for confirming gubernatorial appointments. The House must initiate legislation to raise taxes. The House has the power to impeach, whereas the Senate has the power to remove. Legislation must be passed in identical form by both chambers before it can go to the governor. The Texas Constitution provides that the legislature meets in regular session every other year for no more than 140 calendar days. The governor can call special sessions, which are limited to 30 days. Critics charge that the legislature meets too infrequently and too briefly to do the state's business effectively. In contrast, defenders of the current system say that the current system forces legislators to get down to business.

2. What is the job description of a member of the Texas legislature, considering qualifications, background, compensation, turnover, and term limits?

Although the membership of the legislature is more diverse today than ever before, white males remain overrepresented while other demographic groups are underrepresented. Legislators earn $7,200 a year, a relatively low salary in comparison with other state lawmakers. However, they have given themselves a generous pension plan and other benefits, including the ability to pay some personal expenses from campaign funds. Legislative turnover in Texas, which is below the national average, is more often the result of voluntary retirement than election defeat. Some states have adopted legislative term limits, usually through the initiative process. However, without an initiative process, Texas has not.

3. How is the Texas legislature organized in terms of leadership, committee organization, and legislative assistance?

Modern legislatures choose leaders, establish committees, and hire staff assistance in order to facilitate their work. The lieutenant governor and speaker of the House are the presiding officers and foremost political leaders of the Texas legislature. The speaker, who presides in the House, is a state representative who is selected by the members of the House to serve as speaker. The lieutenant governor, who presides in the Senate, is elected statewide for a four-year term in the same general election year in which the governor is chosen. The speaker and lieutenant governor are two of the most powerful public officials in the state, exercising extraordinary authority in their respective chambers. Some of the legislature's most important work takes place in committee. Committee chairs and most committee members are appointed by the speaker in the House and the lieutenant governor in the Senate. Standing committees enable the legislature to divide the legislative workload. Interim committees are established to consider policy issues between legislative sessions. Staff assistance is important to the Texas legislature because legislators are essentially part-time employees asked to perform a monumental legislative task in a limited period of time. Support agencies include the Legislative Council, Legislative Reference Library, House Research Organization (HRO), and Senate Research Center (SRC).

4. **What are the steps of the legislative process?**

The legislative process begins when a legislator introduces a bill or resolution. The lieutenant governor and the speaker assign newly introduced measures to committee. Committees then do the detailed work of the legislative process, conducting hearings and marking up legislative proposals. Bills that pass standing committee in the House go to the Calendars Committee for assignment to a House calendar, which sets the order of priority for considering legislation. In the Senate, the standard procedure to consider bills on the floor that have passed committee is for the chamber to vote by a two-thirds margin to suspend the rules. Ordinary legislation passes the Texas House and Texas Senate by majority vote of those members present and voting. When the House and Senate pass similar but not identical measures, the leadership appoints members to a conference committee to negotiate a compromise measure which must be voted on again by the two chambers before it has passed the legislature. Once a bill passes the legislature, it goes to the governor. If the governor does nothing, the measure eventually becomes law. The governor can also sign the measure into law or veto it. For appropriations measures, the governor has the line-item veto. The legislature can override a veto with a two-thirds vote, but that is rare, primarily because most vetoes are issued post-adjournment.

5. **What effects do the following factors have on the legislative process: legislative leadership, interest groups, constituency, political parties, and political ideology?**

A number of factors affect the legislative process in Texas. The support of the speaker and lieutenant governor greatly enhances any measure's chances for passage; their opposition almost certainly dooms a bill to defeat. Interest groups lay the groundwork for influencing the legislative process by contributing money to candidates and then attempt to shape the details of legislation through lobbying. Lawmakers are more likely to vote what they perceive as the preferences of their constituents on high-profile issues, but high-profile issues are rare, especially in state government. Although the Texas legislature is not as partisan a body as is the U.S. Congress, it is no longer a nonpartisan body. Historically, conservatives have dominated the Texas legislature and legislative policies have reflected their political values.

KEY TERMS

appropriation bill	conservatism	impeachment
bicameral legislature	filibuster	initiative process
bill	fiscal note	interim committee
conference committee	global warming	joint resolution

NOTES

1. SB 184 (2009), available at www.legis.state.tx.us/.
2. SB 541 (2009), available at www.legis.state.tx.us/.
3. SB 545 (2009), available at www.legis.state.tx.us/.
4. SB 16 and SB 2111 (2009), available at www.legis.state .tx.us/.
5. Susan Peterson and Forrest Wilder, "No Green Sweep," *Texas Observer*, June 26, 2009, pp. 24–25.
6. James R. Rogers, "The Impact of Bicameralism on Legislative Production," *Legislative Studies Quarterly* 28 (November 2003): 509–528.
7. "Texas Legislature Should Meet Every Year," *El Paso Times*, May 22, 2007, available at www.elpasotimes.com.
8. Harvey J. Tucker, "Legislative Logjams: A Comparative State Analysis," *Western Political Quarterly* 38 (September 1985): 432–446.
9. Quoted in Ellen Perlman, "The Gold-Plated Legislature," *Governing*, February 1998, p. 40.
10. Harvey J. Tucker, "Legislative Workload Congestion in Texas," *Journal of Politics* 49 (May 1987): 565–578.
11. Reeve Hamilton, "Five Days of Chub," *Texas Observer*, June 26, 2009, pp. 21–23.
12. "The Texas Legislature by the Numbers," *Texas Observer*, January 23, 2009, pp. 8–9.
13. W. Gardner Selby, "Another Special Session Gives Rise to Legislative Pay Chatter," *Austin American-Statesman*, April 11, 2006, available at www.statesman.com.
14. Empire Center for New York State Policy, "Legislative Salaries per State," available at www.empirecenter.org.
15. Jay Root, "But the Perks Sure Are Nice," *Fort Worth Star-Telegram*, February 4, 2007, available at www.dfw.com.
16. Emily Ramshaw and Marcus Funk, "For Some Dallas-Area Legislators, Donations Fund the Good Life," *Dallas Morning News*, February 1, 2009, available at www.dallasnews.com.
17. Quoted in Ramshaw and Funk, "For Some Dallas-Area Legislators, Donations Fund the Good Life."
18. Gary F. Moncrief, Richard G. Niemi, and Lynda W. Powell, "Time, Term Limits, and Turnover: Trends in Membership

Stability in U.S. State Legislatures," *Legislative Studies Quarterly* 29 (August 2004): 365.
19. *Texas Observer*, January 23, 2009, p. 9.
20. Karen Brooks, "Texas No. 1 in Legislators-Turned-Lobbyists," *Dallas Morning News*, October 13, 2006, available at www .dallasnews.com.
21. U.S. Term Limits, "State Legislative Term Limits," available at www.termlimits.org.
22. Karl T. Kurtz, Bruce Cain, and Richard G. Niemi, *Institutional Change in American Politics: The Case of Term Limits* (Ann Arbor, MI: University of Michigan Press, 2007), pp. 185–192.
23. John M. Carey, Richard G. Niemi, and Lynda W. Powell, *Term Limits in the State Legislatures* (Ann Arbor, MI: University of Michigan Press, 2000), pp. 123–127.
24. Alan Greenblatt, "Term Limits Aren't Working," *Governing*, April 2005, pp. 13–14.
25. Hastings Wyman, "Texas: House Speaker Craddick Gets Runoff Boosts," *Southern Political Report*, April 14, 2008, available at www.southernpoliticalreport.com.
26. Dave Mann, "Fall of the House of Craddick," *Texas Observer*, January 23, 2009, pp. 21–23.
27. Jason Embry, "Straus Rewards GOP Backers in House Posts," *Austin American-Statesman*, February 13, 2009, available at www.statesman.com.
28. National Conference of State Legislatures, "Size of State Legislative Staff: 1979, 1988, 1996, 2003, 2009," available at www.ncsl.org.
29. National Conference of State Legislatures, "Committee Staffing," available at www.ncsl.org.
30. Texas Legislature Online, "Legislative Reports," available at www.legis.state.tx.us/.
31. Office of the Governor, Bills Vetoed by Governor Perry, 81st Legislature, available at www.governor.state.tx.us.
32. Christy Hoppe, "Senator Says that Veto-Override Bill Faces Perry-Dewhurst Conspiracy," *Dallas Morning News*, May 27, 2009, available at www.dallasnews.com.

33. Peterson and Wilder, "No Green Sweep," pp. 24–25.

34. Jason Embry, "Straus Steered House with a Light Hand," *Austin-American Statesman*, June 7, 2009, available at www.statesman.com.

35. Texas Ethics Commission, "Lobby Lists," available at www.ethics.state.tx.us.

36. Emily Ramshaw, "Texas Restaurant Association Backs Statewide Smoking Ban," *Dallas Morning News*, February 17, 2009, available at www.dallasnews.com.

37. Melissa del Bosque, "Snuffed: How Big Tobacco Fended Off a Statewide Smoking Ban," *Texas Observer*, June 26, 2009, pp. 14–15.

38. Jane Mansbridge, "Rethinking Representation," *American Political Science Review* 97 (November 2003): 515–528.

39. Polly Ross Hughes and Matthew Tresaugue, "Small-Town GOP Behind Survival of Top 10% Rule," *Houston Chronicle*, May 30, 2007, pp. B1–B2.

40. James C. McKinley Jr., "Texas Vote Curbs a College Admission Guarantee Meant to Bolster Diversity," *New York Times*, May 31, 2009, available at www.nytimes.com.

41. Bill Bishop, "A Steady Slide Towards a More Partisan Union," *Austin American-Statesman*, May 30, 2004, available at www.statesman.com.

42. Shannon Jenkins, "Party Influence on Roll Call Voting: A View from the U.S. States," *State Politics and Policy Quarterly* 8 (Fall 2008): 239–262.

Chapter 9

Executive Branch

WHAT WE WILL LEARN

After studying Chapter 9, students should be able to answer the following questions:

▸ What is the job description for the governor of Texas, including formal qualifications, length of term, impeachment and removal, compensation, staff assistance, powers and responsibilities, strength of office, and role in the policymaking process?

▸ How is the executive branch of Texas government structured?

▸ How effective are the tools available to the legislature and the governor for overseeing the state's administrative bureaucracy?

Texas homeowners pay more for home insurance than anyone else in the country. In 2006, the average Texas homeowner paid $1,409 in insurance premiums compared with a national average of $804.[1] Texas insurance premiums are even higher than premiums in Florida and California, despite those states having significant exposure to catastrophic weather, wildfires, and, in California, earthquakes. Home values in Florida and California are also substantially higher than home values in Texas.

Consumer organizations and the insurance industry disagree about the reasons for high insurance rates in the Lone Star State. Consumer groups, such as Texas Watch, believe that the insurance industry is gouging consumers. Between 2003 and 2007, insurance companies operating in Texas collected $23 billion in premiums while paying out only $9.6 billion in claims, a loss ratio of 42 percent. That was substantially better for the companies than the 59 percent national loss average for the period.[2] The insurance industry, meanwhile, blames the unpredictable weather for high rates. Hurricanes, tornadoes, hailstorms, floods, and high winds all drive up the cost of insurance in the Lone Star State. Although insurance companies made money between 2003 and 2007, they note that the industry lost money in 2008 because of Hurricane Ike and Hurricane Dolly, paying claims worth $6.3 billion compared with collecting premiums of only $5.2 billion. Companies make a profit in good years, they say, so they can afford to cover losses in bad years.[3]

The Texas Department of Insurance (TDI), the state agency responsible for regulating the insurance industry in the state, has limited authority to control rates. Since 2003, Texas has operated under a file-and-use regulatory system. If an insurance company decides to increase rates, it submits the proposed increase to the TDI and begins collecting the higher premiums from consumers immediately. Although the TDI has the authority to disapprove the increase and order the company to issue refunds, companies can challenge the TDI's action in state court. For example, when the TDI ordered Allstate and State Farm to roll back rates, the two big insurance companies disagreed and took the agency to court rather than reduce their rates and refund premiums to consumers. After four years of legal wrangling, Allstate agreed to a partial refund to consumers. The State Farm lawsuit is ongoing.

The insurance industry and consumer groups disagree about the effectiveness of insurance regulation. Industry spokespersons argue that the file-and-use system is consumer friendly because it encourages insurance companies to do business in Texas. Consumers benefit from competition. Furthermore, under insurance reform legislation adopted in 2003, insurance companies have the freedom to offer a wide range of insurance policies rather than a small set of standardized policies, thus giving consumers the opportunity to shop for a policy that fits their needs at a price they can afford. In contrast, consumer groups believe that insurance regulation in Texas benefits the industry at the expense of homeowners. They favor a prior approval regulatory system in which an insurance company requests a rate increase from the TDI, but cannot begin collecting additional premiums until the increase is approved. Consumer groups also complain that insurance companies offer too many choices. Insurance policies have become so complicated, they say, that consumers are unable to comparison shop. Moreover, many insurance policies written since the 2003 reforms were adopted to cover the cash value of a loss rather than replacement costs, giving consumers insufficient money to rebuild after they suffer a loss.[4]

The controversy over homeowner insurance regulation introduces this chapter on the executive branch of state government. State agencies, such as the TDI, play an important role in implementing policies adopted by the legislature and the governor. The first part of the chapter examines the office of governor, considering the qualifications and background of the state's chief executive. The chapter identifies the powers and responsibilities of the governor and assesses the strength of the office in Texas in comparison with governors in other states. The chapter then studies the role of the governor in the policymaking process. The second part of the chapter describes the various agencies and departments that constitute the executive branch of state government. It discusses the elected executive officials other than the governor, appointed executive officials, elected boards and commissions, and appointed boards and commissions. The chapter concludes by discussing the tools available to the governor and legislature for overseeing administrative agencies and assessing their effectiveness.

This chapter is the second in a series of five chapters dealing with the policymaking institutions of state and local government. The first three chapters in the series—Chapters 8, 9, and 10—examine the legislative, executive, and judicial branches of state government. The final two chapters in the series focus on units of local government. Chapter 11 discusses city government whereas Chapter 12 studies counties, school districts, and special districts.

THE GOVERNOR

The governor is the chief executive officer of the state with important powers to influence the policymaking process.

Qualifications and Background

The Texas Constitution declares that the governor must be an American citizen, a resident of Texas for five years preceding election, and at least 30 years of age. In practice, most of the state's chief executives have come from narrow social circles. Every governor has been a white, Anglo-Saxon Protestant. Only two (Miriam Ferguson and Ann Richards) were women. Most governors have been well-to-do, middle-aged lawyers or business executives with prior experience in public affairs. They have also had fairly common, easy-to-pronounce names, such as Perry, Bush, Richards, White, Clements, Briscoe, Smith, and Connally.

Although most recent governors have conformed fairly closely to the traditional image, the election of Ann Richards showed that Texas voters were willing to consider candidates who did not fit the mold in all respects. Not only was

Richards a woman, but her political career was based on her own efforts rather than those of her husband. Richards, a divorcee, was a schoolteacher before winning election as a county commissioner in Travis County (which includes the city of Austin). In 1982, Richards was elected state treasurer, holding that post until her election as governor in 1990.

Term of Office, Selection, and Removal

The governor's term of office is four years, increased from two years by a constitutional amendment adopted in 1972. This is the norm nationwide, as only two of the 50 states currently elect their governors for two-year terms instead of four.[5] Elections for governor and other elective state executive officials are held in even-numbered years, timed so that they will not coincide with national presidential elections (e.g., 2010, 2014). The Texas Constitution sets no limit on the number of terms a governor can serve. Rick Perry, who assumed office when George W. Bush resigned in 2001 to become president, will hold the record for longest service if he completes the term he began in January 2007.

A governor can be removed from office before his or her term is ended through the process of impeachment and removal by the legislature. **Impeachment** is the formal process through which the Texas House accuses an executive or judicial branch official of misconduct serious enough to warrant removal from office. The House votes to impeach the governor by majority vote. The Senate then conducts a trial and may vote to remove the governor by a two-thirds margin. In 1917, for example, the House impeached Governor James Ferguson and the Senate removed him from office over the alleged misuse of public funds. Ferguson is the only Texas governor to date to be impeached. Many of the state's voters apparently did not share the legislature's opinion of Ferguson because they twice elected his wife, Miriam Ferguson, to serve as the state's chief executive.

Impeachment A formal accusation against an executive or judicial officeholder.

Staff Support

The governor has a full-time professional staff of 137 people with a two-year office budget of $17 million, including the governor's salary of $115,345. In addition, programs assigned to the governor's office employ 136 full-time staff members with a two-year budget of more than $500 million.[6] The governor appoints staff members without need of Senate confirmation and they serve at the governor's pleasure. The governor has a chief of staff, general counsel, and press secretary. The governor's office also includes administrative units dealing with legislative matters, communications, budgeting and planning, and criminal justice. The size of the governor's staff has increased over the years because state government has grown larger and more complex. In addition, today's governor has become a more visible and active participant in the state policy process. Furthermore, federal grant programs often require gubernatorial participation in, and coordination of, program planning and implementation.

GETTING INVOLVED

Forming a Study Group

A study group is an excellent way for students to learn and retain course material. Studying in a group is more efficient than individual study because the collective knowledge of the group almost always exceeds the knowledge of even the best prepared student in the class. Consequently, students are less likely to be stumped for an answer to a question and have to waste time looking it up. Study groups are also more fun than studying alone and they motivate students to succeed.

Take the initiative to organize a study group for this course. Identify students who seem serious about their education based on their class attendance and participation and schedule a group study session at a mutually agreed time and place. Coffee shops are a traditional hangout for students preparing for exams. Use the materials in the study guide or the various learning resources in the textbook (review questions, key terms, etc.) to organize your session. It's your education—Get involved!

Powers and Responsibilities

Although the Texas Constitution grants the governor authority to act in a broad range of policy areas, most of the governor's powers are coupled with limitations.

Legislative Powers The governor's strongest constitutional powers are those used for influencing the legislative process. The Texas Constitution requires that the governor deliver a message to the legislature at the beginning of each legislative session on the condition of the state. The State of the State address, which is comparable to the State of the Union speech the president makes to Congress, enables the governor to focus attention on issues he or she considers the state's most serious policy needs and offer proposals to meet those needs. The governor can send messages to the legislature at other times as well, both formally and informally. Of course, any legislative measure that the governor proposes must be introduced by a member of the legislature and passed by the Texas House and Texas Senate before it can become a law. The governor can also influence legislative priorities by declaring certain pieces of legislation emergency measures. In the House, emergency measures receive priority attention on the floor. Furthermore, members of the legislature can introduce legislation after the deadline for bill filing if the governor designates the measure as emergency legislation.

Veto An action by the chief executive of a state or nation refusing to approve a bill passed by the legislature.

The governor has the power to **veto,** an action by the chief executive of a state or nation who refuses to approve a measure passed by the legislature. If the governor objects to a bill passed by the legislature, the governor has ten days to act unless the legislature adjourns during that time. In that case, the governor has 20 days from adjournment in which to decide to issue a veto.

Line-item veto The power of the governor to veto sections or items of an appropriation bill while signing the remainder of the bill into law.

The governor also enjoys the power of the **line-item veto,** which is the authority to veto sections or items of an appropriation bill while signing the remainder of the bill into law. Keep in mind that the governor's power to issue the line-item veto is limited to the **appropriation bill,** a legislative authorization to spend money for particular purposes. On other pieces of legislation, the governor's options are limited to either accepting or rejecting the measure in its entirety.

Appropriation bill A legislative authorization to spend money for particular purposes.

The Texas legislature can override the governor's veto by a two-thirds vote of each chamber, voting separately. Since Texas became a state, the legislature has successfully overridden only 52 of more than 1,600 gubernatorial vetoes (not counting item vetoes), for an override rate of 3 percent. Furthermore, since 1941 the legislature has overridden only one veto—a veto cast by Governor Bill Clements in 1979 of a local bill exempting Comal County from the state's game laws.

Why has the legislature so seldom reversed the governor's vetoes? Two-thirds majorities are difficult to attain, of course. More important, most gubernatorial vetoes in Texas come after adjournment when overriding is impossible. Because much of the legislation introduced during a regular session does not pass until the session's final days, the governor can simply wait until adjournment to issue a veto. With the legislature gone home, a veto stands unchallenged. Although a number of state constitutions allow the legislature to call itself back into session to consider overriding vetoes, the Texas Constitution does not.

A final legislative power the governor enjoys is the authority to call special sessions. The Texas Constitution empowers the governor to convene the legislature in special sessions that may last no longer than 30 days. Furthermore, the Texas Constitution places no limit on the number of special sessions a governor can call. Between May 2003 and January 2007, Governor Perry called seven special sessions to deal with either legislative redistricting or school finance and property tax rates. The constitution declares that in a special session the "legislature may consider only those matters that the governor specifies in the call or subsequently presents to the legislature." The governor can use the power to set the agenda for special sessions as a bargaining tool in negotiations with legislators. In exchange for support on other matters, the governor can offer to expand the call to include issues of particular interest to individual legislators or groups of lawmakers.

Appointive Powers The governor has extensive powers of appointment. The governor is responsible for staffing positions on more than 150 state administrative boards and commissions that set policy for state agencies under their authority. For example, the governor appoints the Commissioner of Insurance, who is the head of the TDI. Furthermore, the Texas Constitution empowers the governor to fill vacancies in many otherwise elective positions, including district and appellate judgeships, should openings occur between elections. A governor makes about 3,000 appointments during a four-year term.[7]

The power of appointment gives the governor an opportunity to influence policy and score political points. As the state's population has grown more diverse, governors of both political parties have sought a diverse set of appointees. Governor Richards named more women and minorities to office than any governor in the history of the state. In fact, 41 percent of her appointees were women, 32 percent were Latino, and 12 percent were African American. Governor Bush and Governor Perry continued to diversify state government. Among Bush's appointees, 9 percent were African American, 13 percent were Latino, and 37 percent were women. During Perry's first four years in office, his list of appointments was 11 percent African American, 16 percent Latino, and 36 percent women.[8]

The appointive powers of the governor are limited. Because most administrative board members serve six-year overlapping terms, new governors must work with an

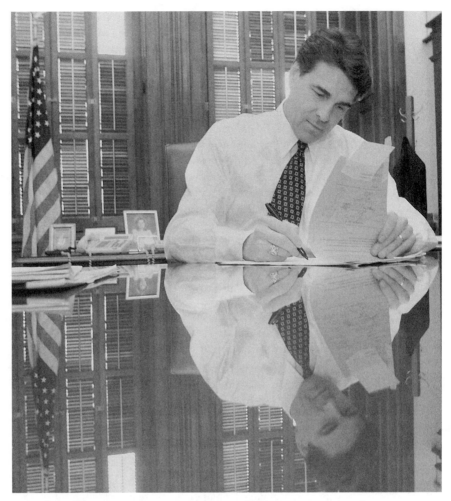

Since taking office in 2001, Governor Perry has issued 238 vetoes, more vetoes than any governor in the history of the state.

administrative structure that was put in place by a predecessor. Although new governors can fill about one-third of administrative positions when they first assume office, they do not have the opportunity to name their own people to a majority of posts for another two years.

The governor has little official removal power. Although the Texas Constitution gives governors the authority to remove their *own* appointees (but not those of a predecessor) with a two-thirds vote of approval by the Texas Senate, this limited procedure has not been used. An incoming governor cannot force the resignation of holdover administrators.

State law allows the governor to appoint a conservator to take over a wayward agency; however, the governor can act only on the recommendation of the Legislative

Audit Commission based on a finding that the agency is guilty of gross fiscal misman-agement. In 2007, the procedure was used to take control of the Texas Youth Com-mission (TYC), the state agency responsible for housing juveniles convicted of criminal offenses. The legislature and the governor acted after media reports surfaced that TYC officials ignored signs that administrators at a West Texas juvenile prison were sexually abusing inmates.[9]

The governor's appointive powers are often restricted by technical, legal require-ments. Consider the makeup of the Texas Racing Commission, which oversees the op-eration of pari-mutuel wagering on horse and dog racing in the state. The legislature reserved two of the eight positions on the commission for the state comptroller and the chair of the Texas Department of Public Safety (DPS). The governor can appoint the other six members, but only within strict guidelines. Two members of the commission must be experienced in horse racing and two others must be experienced at racing grey-hounds. The other two commission members must be veterinarians, one specializing in large animals and the other in small animals. Furthermore, the legislature specified that all members of the commission must be residents of Texas for at least ten years and file detailed financial statements. Persons with a financial interest in a racetrack or who are closely related to someone with such an interest would be ineligible to serve.

Finally, the governor's appointees must be confirmed by a two-thirds vote of the Texas Senate. In contrast, presidential appointees require only a majority vote of approval in the U.S. Senate. Furthermore, the tradition of senatorial courtesy en-sures that the governor's appointees must pass political inspection by their home-area senator or face rejection. **Senatorial courtesy** is a custom of the Texas Senate that allows individual senators a veto over nominees who live in their districts. By tradition, senators will vote against a nominee if the senator from the district in which the nominee lives declares opposition to the nomination.

Gubernatorial appointees who get their positions between legislative sessions serve until the legislature meets again. Then, if the Senate rejects or simply fails to vote on the appointment, the individual loses the position and the governor makes another selection. In 2009, for example, the Texas Senate rejected the nomination of Don McLeroy as chair of the State Board of Education (SBOE) by a vote of 19 in favor to 11 against, just short of the two-thirds vote needed for confirmation. Gov-ernor Perry waited until the legislature adjourned and then appointed Cynthia Dunbar to chair the agency. Dunbar will serve until 2011 when the Senate will have the chance to vote on her confirmation.

Judicial Powers The Texas Constitution gives the governor some authority in the judi-cial process. On the recommendation of the Board of Pardons and Paroles, the gover-nor may grant reprieves, commutations, and pardons. A **reprieve** is the postponement of the implementation of punishment for a criminal offense; a **commutation** is the re-duction of punishment for a criminal offense. A **pardon** is the exemption from pun-ishment for a criminal offense. In a **capital punishment** (death penalty) case, the governor has authority to grant one 30-day reprieve independently, without recom-mendation by Pardons and Paroles, thus postponing a condemned person's execution.

Probably the most effective tool the governor has for influencing judicial policy is the power of appointment. Although judges are elected in Texas, the state constitution

Senatorial courtesy A custom of the Texas Senate that allows individual senators a veto over nominees who live in their districts.

Reprieve A postponement of the implementation of punishment for a criminal offense.

Commutation A reduction of punishment for a criminal offense.

Pardon The exemption from punishment for a criminal offense.

Capital punishment The death penalty.

empowers the governor to appoint a new judge when appellate and district judges die, retire, or resign during the midst of a term. These appointees serve until the next election. In 2008, 53 percent of the state's appellate judges and 40 percent of the district judges had initially taken office through gubernatorial appointment rather than election.[10]

Budgetary Powers The president of the United States and the governors of 47 states enjoy budget-making authority (i.e., preparing a budget to submit to the legislative branch).[11] Although the final budget is invariably a negotiated document between the legislative and executive branches of government, the chief executive has the advantage of proposing the initial document. Consequently, the budget debate in the legislature at least begins with the governor's budgetary priorities and policy proposals.

The governor of Texas has no such advantage. Although the Texas Constitution requires the governor to submit budget proposals to the legislature, the Legislative Budget Board (LBB) prepares a budget as well, and its ideas generally carry more weight. The **Legislative Budget Board (LBB)** is an agency created by the legislature to study state revenue and budgetary needs between legislative sessions and prepare budget and appropriation bills to submit to the legislature. As the legislature debates the budget, the point of departure is not the governor's budget but rather the budget proposed by the LBB. In 2009, Governor Perry decided against preparing a budget, choosing instead to use the LBB document as the starting point.

The most important power the Texas governor has for influencing budget priorities is the line-item veto. In contrast to the president, whose only option on an appropriation bill is to accept or reject the measure in its entirety, most state governors can selectively eliminate items while signing the rest into law. This veto and the threat of its use allow a politically skilled governor the opportunity to exercise considerable influence over the final budget document.

Budget execution authority refers to the power to cut agency spending or transfer money between agencies during the period when the legislature is not in session. Much can happen in the two-year interval between legislative sessions. Because of unforeseen events, such as a hurricane striking the coast or declining welfare rolls, some budget categories may run short of money, whereas others may have excess cash. Budget execution authority is the power to transfer funds among accounts between legislative sessions. The Texas Constitution allows either the governor or the LBB to propose a reduction in spending or a shift in state funds. Both the governor and the LBB must concur on proposed spending reductions or money transfers before they can take place.

Law Enforcement and Military Powers The governor has some peripheral authority in law enforcement. The governor appoints the three-member board that heads the Department of Public Safety and is empowered to assume command of the Texas Rangers should circumstances warrant, which is rare. The governor is also commander-in-chief of the Texas National Guard, which the governor can call out to assist in situations beyond the control of local law enforcement agencies, such as a natural disaster or civil disorder. In 2005, for example, Governor Perry called several units of the Texas State Guard to active duty to help with people evacuated to Texas from Louisiana after Hurricane Katrina. Guard units subsequently assisted with disaster relief in Texas after Hurricane Rita struck the upper Texas coast. Governor Perry has also ordered several hundred National Guard

Legislative Budget Board (LBB) An agency created by the legislature to study state revenue and budgetary needs between legislative sessions and prepare budget and appropriations bills to submit to the legislature.

Budget execution authority The power to cut agency spending or transfer money between agencies during the period when the legislature is not in session.

troops to deploy along the border to assist local police and federal agents in securing the border against drug smuggling and illegal immigration.

Ceremonial Powers In addition to official powers, the governor is the ceremonial leader of the state. The governor greets foreign leaders, speaks at local chamber of commerce luncheons, issues proclamations on state holidays, and shakes hands with visiting scout troops. Ceremonial activities allow the governor the opportunity to give the appearance of leadership, which can be helpful for a governor attempting to influence the policy process. Leadership depends on the perceptions of the public and other political leaders as much as it depends on official powers.

Governors sometimes use their leadership position to recruit out-of-state companies to relocate to the state. Governor Perry, for example, helped convince Toyota to select San Antonio as the site of a new auto-assembly plant. The legislature also did its part by approving the expenditure of state funds to build rail tracks to connect the plant to major rail lines. State and local governments also covered the cost of training 2,000 full-time workers for the plant.[12]

Political Party Leadership The governor is the unofficial leader of his or her political party in the state. The governor sometimes speaks out on partisan controversies and usually campaigns for the party's candidates in state and national elections. Furthermore, as the most visible elected official in a large state, the governor of Texas is often a national political figure. Governor Richards was a prominent figure in Democratic national politics. Her successor, Governor Bush, was elected president of the United States in 2000.

Governor Ann Richards, who died in 2006, was a prominent figure in national Democratic Party politics.

Plural executive
The division of
executive power
among several
elected officials.

Administrative Powers The governor of Texas is probably weakest in the area of administration because of the **plural executive,** the division of executive power among several elected officials. Because the land commissioner, attorney general, comptroller, lieutenant governor, and commissioner of agriculture are all elected, they answer not to the governor but to the voters. Elected executive officials may not share the governor's party affiliation and may be political rivals, even when they have the same political party affiliation. Comptroller Carole Keeton Strayhorn, for example, challenged Governor Perry for reelection in 2006. Both Strayhorn and Perry were Republicans, although Strayhorn chose to run for governor as an independent.

Nonetheless, a determined governor, especially one who serves more than one term in office, can have an influence over state agencies. By the end of one four-year term, a typical governor has appointed two-thirds of administrative officials. After six years in office, the governor has had the opportunity to staff the entire executive branch except for those agencies with elected administrators. Many of these officials, especially administrators serving in the most important agencies, are political allies of the governor. As such, they are inclined to listen to the governor's point of view on policy matters and take direction from the governor if the governor wishes to be assertive. Even if the governor cannot force an official out of office, few appointed administrators can withstand the pressure if the governor calls for resignation. For example, every member of the troubled TYC resigned in the face of demands from the governor and legislative leaders to step down.

Governor Perry has struggled to assert influence over the executive branch of state government. He asked the legislature for authority to appoint agency heads, but it turned him down. It also turned down his request to appoint the heads of all the governing boards. Perry then acted on his own to create the Governor's Management Council, which includes the heads of the state's 11 largest agencies and representatives of small and medium-size agencies. The purpose of the council, which the governor chairs, is to coordinate the operation of the executive branch.[13]

Executive order A
directive issued by the
governor to an
administrative agency
or executive
department.

Perry has also tried to expand his authority to issue executive orders. (An **executive order** is a directive issued by the governor to an administrative agency or executive department.) Historically, Texas governors have used executive orders to create task forces or advisory groups, or simply to express an opinion on a policy issue. Governors have not used executive orders to make policy.[14] In contrast, Perry has used executive orders as a tool for achieving his policy goals. In 2005, Perry ordered the Texas Education Agency (TEA) to change the state reporting system for school districts to require that districts spend at least 65 percent of their funds on classroom instruction. Education Commissioner Shirley Neely indicated that the agency would implement the governor's order.[15] The governor also directed the TEA to create a limited merit pay plan for teachers using $10 million in federal grant money that would financially reward teachers in the 100 campuses that had the most improvement in student performance.[16] In addition to the orders dealing with education, the governor also issued an executive order requiring all Texas girls entering the sixth grade to be vaccinated against the human papillomavirus (HPV), which is the major cause of a sexually transmitted virus that leads to cervical cancer. Furthermore, Governor Perry issued an executive order to the State Office of Administrative Hearings directing it to speed up the permitting process to allow utility companies to build coal-fired power plants in the state.

Governor Perry's efforts to expand the powers of his office through executive orders have met considerable resistance from the legislature, the courts, and other executive officials. The legislature voted overwhelmingly to reverse the governor's effort to mandate HPV vaccinations and a state district judge ruled that Perry exceeded his constitutional authority by ordering faster consideration of power plant permits. Even the Texas Attorney General Greg Abbott weighed in on the matter, at least unofficially. Although the attorney general did not issue a formal opinion, he did indicate to members of the legislature that the governor cannot authorize an agency to do something through an executive order that the agency does not have authority to do and that, in any event, the agency is not obligated to carry out the executive order. In other words, executive orders are advisory opinions without legal weight.[17]

Measuring Gubernatorial Powers

Observers have long held that the constitutional/legal powers of the governor of Texas are among the weakest in the nation. Political scientist Thad Beyle has created an index to measure the official powers of state governors based on the following factors: the number of separately elected officials in the state, the number of years the governor serves and whether the governor can be reelected, the governor's powers of appointment, the governor's power over the state budget, the extent of the governor's veto power, and the governor's authority to reorganize the bureaucracy. Professor Beyle gives the governor of Texas a score of 3.2 on a 5-point scale, placing the powers of the Texas governor in the bottom one-third among the 50 states. The average score is 3.5. The Texas governor scores well on the length of term and opportunity for reelection, the veto, and the governor's power to reorganize the bureaucracy. However, the Texas chief executive scores low on the other measures.

Formal, official powers are an incomplete measure of a governor's authority. Beyle augments his index of official powers with an index measuring each governor's personal power. This index includes the size of the governor's margin of victory in the last election, whether the governor has previously served in lower office and is on an upward career track, whether the governor is early or late in a term, whether the governor can run for reelection, and the governor's standing in public opinion polls. For example, a newly elected governor who won office by a large margin and is perceived as a rising political star is in a better position to be influential than is an unpopular governor nearing the end of a term who is perceived as heading toward retirement. In 2007, Beyle gave Governor Perry a score of 3.8 of a possible 5. The average score for governors nationwide was 3.9.[18]

Governor Bush's experience in dealing with the legislature illustrates the governor's ability to use unofficial, informal powers to achieve policy influence. In 1995, when Bush first took office, he targeted four policy areas—public education, juvenile justice, welfare, and tort reform. The legislature enacted major reforms in each of these areas. With the exception of welfare policy, the legislature adopted policies that closely reflected the governor's policy preferences.

Governor Bush succeeded because he set limited goals for himself and communicated regularly with legislators. Bush targeted policy areas already high on the official policy agenda because of media attention, the efforts of interest groups, and the recent election campaign. He staked out policy positions on the issues that already enjoyed a good deal of support in the legislature and were popular with the electorate. Bush and his staff communicated directly with individual members of the Texas House and Senate, and the governor spoke regularly with Speaker of the House Pete Laney and Lieutenant Governor Bob Bullock.

Eminent domain
The right of the government to take private property for public use.

Governor Perry has been less skilled in dealing with the legislature than his predecessor, however. Perry has failed to establish personal relationships with individual legislators, as Bush had done. By and large, Perry has ignored the legislative process until bills have reached his desk. Consequently, the governor has little influence on the details of legislation. Furthermore, Perry's numerous vetoes have angered legislators and other officials who were blindsided by the governor's opposition. In 2007, for example, the legislature passed a politically popular measure dealing with **eminent domain,** which is the right of the government to take private property for public use. The bill, which passed the House 143–0 and the Senate 29–1, would have limited a city's ability to use eminent domain to take private property for purposes of economic development. Perry surprised almost everyone by vetoing the bill, declaring it would have exposed cities to the possibility of lawsuits. In 2009, legislators bypassed the governor on the eminent domain issue by drafting it in the form of a constitutional amendment, which does not require the governor's approval. They also considered a constitutional amendment that would have empowered the legislature to call itself into special session to consider overriding the governor's vetoes. The proposal easily passed the House and would probably have passed the Senate had it come to a vote in the waning days of the session.[19]

The Governor of Texas and the Policymaking Process

Theodore Roosevelt once said that the presidency was a "bully pulpit." By that phrase, he meant that the office provided its occupants with an excellent platform for making their views widely known. In today's age of modern communications, the phrase "big microphone" might be a more appropriate metaphor. No figure in American politics is better positioned than the president to call public attention to an issue and offer policy proposals to address it.

Similar to the president, the governor is well positioned to influence the official policy agenda. Texas governors are required by the state constitution to make recommendations to the legislature and are empowered to call the legislature into special session for the sole purpose of considering gubernatorial proposals. The governor is the most visible public official in the state and today's mass media provide the governor ample opportunity to get messages across to the people.

The governor's powers to affect policy formulation, policy adoption, and policy legitimation are considerable as well. The governor presents a budget to the legislature and may offer policy initiatives on any subject. As the legislature debates policy proposals, the governor can be an effective lobbyist. The governor's veto power, especially the item veto for appropriation measures, puts the governor in a powerful position to bargain on behalf of his or her program. At the very least, the veto virtually ensures that the governor can defeat legislation he or she opposes. Governors have the visibility to sell the merits of a policy to the public after it has been adopted.

The governor is weakest in the areas of policy implementation and evaluation. In Texas, public policies are implemented by departments headed by elected executives or appointed boards, all of which are largely independent of direct gubernatorial control. Although the state constitution calls the governor the state's "chief executive," it offers the governor little power to fulfill that role. Furthermore, the governor has no formal mechanism for policy evaluation. Instead, the governor must rely on policy analyses conducted by others, including legislative committees, the LBB, the comptroller, the Sunset Advisory Commission, and the press. Nonetheless, the governor has the visibility to effectively promote for policy change.

Although scholars have frequently described the office of governor of Texas as politically weak, the governor has sufficient power to play an important policymaking role. Governors who set realistic policy goals can often achieve them if they are willing to use the resources at their disposal. Governor Bush demonstrated that a politically skillful governor could have influence on at least a range of policy issues. The governor lacks the official powers to coordinate policy implementation effectively, but he or she has ample tools to be a successful leader in agenda setting, policy formulation, and policy adoption.

THE EXECUTIVE BUREAUCRACY

Jacksonian democracy The philosophy (associated with President Andrew Jackson) that the right to vote should be extended to all adult male citizens and that all government offices of any importance should be filled by election.

The executive bureaucracy of Texas government includes more than 150 boards, agencies, offices, departments, committees, councils, and commissions. Some parts of the bureaucracy, such as the Office of the Attorney General and the Railroad Commission, are constitutionally established. The legislature and the governor have created the rest of the state bureaucracy through the legislative process. State government employs 365,700 people.[20]

The executive bureaucracy in Texas is decentralized. In other words, no one official is in charge of the entire structure. Agencies directed by elected executives or elected boards are virtually independent of direction by the governor or other state officials. They respond to the voters, not other officials. Agencies directed by appointed boards operate with a good deal of autonomy as well.

Bureaucratic fragmentation in Texas is a legacy of Jacksonian democracy and the post-Reconstruction distrust of central authority. **Jacksonian democracy** is the view (associated with President Andrew Jackson) that the right to vote should be extended to all adult male citizens and that all government offices of any importance should be filled by election. The influence of Jacksonian democracy in the South led to the creation of the plural executive, in which state executive power was divided among several elected executive branch officials. The framers of the Texas Constitution distrusted central control of government because of their experience with it during Reconstruction. Therefore, they created a decentralized executive branch to guard against the excessive concentration of power in any one person or department.

Elected Executives

In addition to the governor, voters elect five state executive officials: the lieutenant governor, attorney general, comptroller of public accounts, commissioner of agriculture, and commissioner of the General Land Office. These officials are elected simultaneously with the governor to serve four-year terms. States differ in how many executive positions they fill by election. Three states (Tennessee, Maine, and New Hampshire) elect only a governor. Most states also elect an attorney general, a lieutenant governor, and a treasurer. Only about one-fourth of the states elect agriculture commissioners or comptrollers and only one-tenth elect land commissioners.[21] North Dakota leads the nation in elected executive officials with 11.[22]

Lieutenant Governor The lieutenant governor is first in line of succession to the governor's office, should the governor die, resign, or be removed from office. When Governor George W. Bush resigned to become president, Lieutenant Governor Perry moved up to the office of governor. The lieutenant governor also becomes temporary governor whenever the governor is absent from the state. In practice, the foremost responsibilities of the office lie in the Texas Senate, where the lieutenant governor presides, votes in case of a tie, appoints members of standing and conference committees, helps determine the order of business on the floor, and enforces Senate rules. In addition, the lieutenant governor is a member of several boards and councils, including the LBB and the Legislative Redistricting Board. The **Legislative Redistricting Board (LRB),** an agency composed of the speaker, lieutenant governor, comptroller, land commissioner, and attorney general, is responsible for redrawing the boundaries of Texas House and Texas Senate seats when the legislature is unable to agree on a redistricting plan. These responsibilities make the lieutenant governor one of the most visible and important figures in state government. When the legislature is in town, the lieutenant governor is arguably the most powerful official in the state, more powerful even than the governor.

Legislative Redistricting Board (LRB) An agency composed of the speaker, lieutenant governor, comptroller, land commissioner, and attorney general that draws the boundaries of Texas House and Senate seats when the legislature is unable to agree on a redistricting plan.

 WHAT IS YOUR OPINION?

Who is more powerful, the governor or lieutenant governor?

Attorney General Sometimes candidates for attorney general broadcast political advertisements touting their law-and-order credentials and their determination to get tough on crime. Although these kinds of campaign pitches may be politically effective, they are factually misleading. Other than representing Texas in lawsuits challenging the constitutionality of state criminal laws, the attorney general has relatively little to do with fighting crime. That job is primarily the responsibility of city and county law enforcement agencies and county district attorneys.

The attorney general is the state's lawyer, representing state government and its various components in court. In recent years, the attorney general's office has defended the state in federal court against lawsuits over bilingual education, prison overcrowding, the death penalty, and congressional redistricting. The attorney general has broad authority to initiate legal action on behalf of the state. In the late 1990s, for example, Texas Attorney General Dan Morales filed a lawsuit against the tobacco industry to recover the cost of smoking-related illnesses covered by the Medicaid program. Before the case could go to trial, however, the tobacco industry and the attorney general agreed on a $17.3 billion settlement to be paid out over the next 25 years. The industry also agreed to remove all tobacco billboards in Texas, as well as tobacco advertising on buses, bus stops, taxis, and taxi stands.[23]

Attorney general's opinion A written interpretation of existing law.

The attorney general gives legal advice to state and local officials and agencies in the form of opinions. An **attorney general's opinion** is a written interpretation of existing law. The attorney general issues opinions in response to a written request from certain state officials who are authorized by law to ask for an opinion. In 2007, for example, Attorney General Gregg Abbott responded to a request from State Senator Jane Nelson (R., Lewisville) by issuing an opinion holding that cities can legally pass ordinances prohibiting registered sex offenders from living near schools, parks, or other locations where children typically congregate. State law requires sex offenders to register with authorities but it does not limit where they can live.[24] An attorney general's opinion is not binding on the court system, but in the absence of a court ruling it stands as the highest existing interpretation of law or the Texas Constitution.

Comptroller of Public Accounts The comptroller is the state's chief tax administrator and accountant. The comptroller monitors compliance with state tax laws and collects taxes on behalf of the state. Texans who operate retail businesses work closely with the comptroller's office to collect the state sales tax from their customers and remit tax receipts to the state. If a retailer fails to pass along sales tax receipts to the state, the comptroller has the power to shut it down and sell off its assets to pay back taxes.

The comptroller is also the state's banker, receiving funds, assuming responsibility for their safekeeping, and paying the state's bills. When tax revenues flow in more rapidly than the state expends funds, the comptroller deposits the money in interest-bearing accounts to generate additional revenue for the state. When the rate of revenue collection lags behind the rate of expenditure, the comptroller

Attorney General Abbott issued an opinion holding that cities can legally pass ordinances prohibiting registered sex offenders from living near schools, parks, or other locations where children typically congregate.

borrows money on a short-term basis to ensure that the state will have enough cash on hand to pay its bills.

The comptroller's most publicized task involves the state budget. The Texas Constitution requires the comptroller to estimate state revenues for the next biennium at the beginning of each legislative session. The comptroller may update the revenue estimate during a session to take account of revisions in state tax laws and changing economic conditions. The constitution specifies that no appropriation bill may become law without the comptroller's certification that it falls within the revenue estimate unless the legislature votes by a four-fifths margin to adopt an unbalanced budget.

Commissioner of Agriculture The commissioner of agriculture administers all statutes relating to agriculture and enforces the state's weights and measures law. The agency inspects and regulates a variety of items, including seeds, gasoline pumps, meat market scales, flower and plant nurseries, and the use of pesticides. The commissioner of agriculture promotes the sale of Texas agricultural products. The agency also administers the **School Lunch Program,** a federal program that provides free or reduced-cost lunches to children from poor families.

Commissioner of the General Land Office The treaty of annexation that added Texas to the Union in 1845 allowed the Lone Star State to retain its state lands. Although much of that land was eventually sold, the state still owns at least the mineral rights on more than 20 million acres. The land commissioner is responsible for managing the

School Lunch Program A federal program that provides free or reduced-cost lunches to children from poor families.

land, leasing it for mineral exploration and production as well as for agricultural purposes. In 2008, state lands generated a billion dollars, more than 1 percent of total state revenue.[25] That money goes into the **Permanent School Fund (PSF),** a fund established in the Texas Constitution as an endowment to finance public elementary and secondary education. The SBOE invests the money in the PSF to generate investment income known as the Available School Fund (ASF), which is distributed annually to Texas school districts on a per-student basis under laws passed by the legislature. The land commissioner also manages the Veterans' Land Program, which provides low-interest loans to the state's military veterans to purchase land, and the Texas Open Beaches Act, which is designed to ensure public access to the state's beaches.

Permanent School Fund (PSF) A fund established in the Texas Constitution as an endowment to finance public elementary and secondary education.

Appointed Executives

One measure of a governor's power over administration is the number of officials he or she can appoint. In Texas, the most important executive officials are elected, leaving only a handful of executive positions to be filled by the governor, subject to a two-thirds Senate confirmation vote. The most significant of these officials is the Texas secretary of state, who is the state's chief election officer. As such, he or she is responsible for the uniform application, implementation, and interpretation of election laws. On election night, the office of the secretary of state gathers election returns from around the state, compiles them, and releases running vote totals to the press. Later, the office tabulates and releases final, official returns. In addition to its electoral responsibilities, the secretary of state's office serves as a depository of various agreements, reports, and records of state agencies. The governor appoints a number of other agency heads, including the commissioner of education, who heads the Texas Education Agency (TEA), the adjutant general who heads the Texas National Guard, and the commissioner of insurance.

Elected Boards and Commissions

The Railroad Commission and the State Board of Education (SBOE) are executive agencies headed by elected boards.

The Railroad Commission The Texas Railroad Commission was originally established to enforce state laws concerning railroads. Today, the Railroad Commission regulates the Texas oil and natural gas industry, gas utilities, pipeline transporters, the surface mining of coal and uranium, and the liquefied petroleum (LP) gas industry. Ironically, the Railroad Commission no longer regulates railroads, which are now under the jurisdiction of the Texas Department of Transportation. The Railroad Commission is composed of three members elected for six-year overlapping terms. In practice, most commission members initially assume office through gubernatorial appointment. When a commission member resigns before the end of a six-year term, the governor names a replacement subject to a two-thirds confirmation vote by the Texas Senate. Although appointed railroad commissioners must face the voters at the next general election, their initial appointment gives them a significant advantage in name recognition and fundraising capability.

INTERNET RESEARCH

Profile of a State Agency

Your assignment is to research an agency of state government. The agency assigned to you depends on the last digit of your Social Security number. If, for example, your Social Security number is 346-70-1379, your assignment is number 9:

0. Racing Commission
1. Department of Parks and Wildlife
2. Board of Pardons and Paroles
3. Commission on Environmental Quality
4. Department of Public Safety
5. Department of Insurance
6. Department of Criminal Justice
7. Alcoholic Beverage Commission
8. Funeral Service Commission
9. State Board of Athletic Trainers

You can learn a good deal about the agency online. Begin your research at the following website:

www2.tsl.state.tx.us/trail/agencies.jsp

Once you have read about the agency and reviewed its homepage, answer the following questions:

1. Your textbook classifies state agencies. In which category would you place the agency you have been assigned?

2. What is the title of the person (or persons) who heads the agency? What is that person's name?

3. How is the head of the agency chosen? Does the agency head serve a fixed term?

4. What does the agency do? (Answer in your own words. Do not copy the agency's mission statement.)

5. What (if any) are the major administrative units of the agency?

6. What current issues or events affect the agency?

7. What power does the legislature have to influence the operation of the agency?

8. What power does the governor have to influence the operation of the agency?

9. Give an example of an interest group that would be concerned with the activities of the agency.

10. How do the activities of this agency affect ordinary citizens?

Allowable The maximum permissible rate of production for oil and gas wells in Texas as set by the Railroad Commission.

The Railroad Commission's regulatory policies fall into three broad categories. First, the commission is a conservation agency. To prevent the waste of natural resources, the commission establishes what is called an allowable for each oil and gas well in the state. The **allowable** is the maximum permissible rate of production for oil and gas wells in Texas as set by the Railroad Commission. This rate, which is determined by technical engineering and geological considerations, maximizes current production without jeopardizing long-term output. The Railroad Commission also regulates the drilling, storage, and pipeline transmission of oil and gas to protect the environment.

Second, the commission historically has prorated oil production to conform to market demand. Every month, the commission establishes a percentage of allowable that each well may produce. For example, if a well's allowable is 100 barrels a day and the commission prorates production to 80 percent of allowable, the well can pump only 80 barrels a day for that month. From the 1930s to the 1970s, the Railroad Commission used this method to limit the supply of oil to an amount sufficient to fill market demand *at the current price*. If a new oil field came on line, the commission prevented oversupply by reducing the percentage allowable for wells across Texas. Because Texas oil was such a big proportion of the national and world oil supply, the commission effectively controlled oil supplies and, consequently, oil prices worldwide. Since the early 1970s, the worldwide demand for petroleum has been so great that the Railroad Commission no longer prorates oil production below the 100 percent allowable.

Third, the Railroad Commission protects the rights of producers and royalty owners, particularly smaller operators. In the early years, the commission established rules on well spacing, transportation, and oil production quotas that generally benefited small producers at the expense of major oil companies.[26] More recently, however, hostile court decisions and personnel changes have led the commission to adopt more evenhanded rules.[27]

The Railroad Commission regulates the Texas oil industry.

State Board of Education (SBOE) The SBOE coordinates education activities and services below the college level. A 15-member elected board heads the agency. Each member of the board runs for election from a district to serve a four-year term. The terms of the board members are staggered, with roughly half the members facing the voters each general-election year. The SBOE oversees the investment of the money in the Permanent School Fund to generate income for the Available School Fund. It sets standards for teacher certification and school accreditation. The SBOE also approves curricula and selects textbooks for use in the state's public schools.

The SBOE is divided between social conservatives and political moderates. Before the 2010 election, seven of the ten Republican SBOE members were considered to be social conservatives, closely tied to the conservative Christian wing of the Texas Republican Party. The other three Republican board members, along with four of the five Democrats on the board, composed the moderate wing of the SBOE. A fifth Democrat was the swing vote, sometimes siding with the social conservatives and other times joining the moderate members of the board.[28]

The SBOE's most controversial decisions involve the adoption of curriculum standards and their impact on textbook selection. Even though board members are not required to be professional educators or have subject matter expertise, they have the authority to determine the content of the state's textbooks. In 2009, for example, the board debated high school science curriculum standards, focusing on how science teachers should approach the theory of evolution. Most scientists and science teachers wanted the curriculum to focus exclusively on the theory of evolution as the basis of modern biological science. In contrast, social conservatives favored the inclusion of a requirement that students be taught the "strengths and weaknesses" of scientific theories. Whereas the social conservatives on the board argued that the approach would promote critical thinking, scientists and advocates for religious freedom asserted that the real purpose of the "strengths and weaknesses" provision was "an attempt to bring false weaknesses into the classroom in an attempt to get students to reject evolution."[29] Ultimately, the SBOE omitted the "strengths and weaknesses" phrase from the science curriculum standards, instead including a requirement to have teachers scrutinize "all sides" of scientific theories. Although the final language was a compromise, social conservatives were happier with the outcome than was the state's scientific community.[30] Similarly, in 2010, the SBOE drew national attention to itself by rewriting the social studies curriculum to emphasize the role of Christianity in American history, deemphasize the negative aspects of American history, and portray conservatives in a positive light.[31]

Curriculum and textbook battles in the Lone Star State were once thought to have national implications because publishing companies, eager to sell to the big Texas market, would create textbooks to meet Texas curriculum standards and then market them nationwide. Today's technology, however, enables publishers to create a standard text and then tailor it to particular markets. The publisher can market a conservative text in Texas, as well as a liberal text in California. Furthermore, the Texas approach is out of step with the push toward national curriculum standards, which every state except Texas and Alaska have chosen to join. In the future, publishing companies will likely create textbooks to match national curriculum standards and then modify them for the Texas market.[32]

WHAT IS YOUR OPINION?

What approach should high school science classes take to teaching the theory of evolution?

Appointed Commissions

Appointed commissions comprise a substantial part of the executive branch of state government. An unpaid board of three, six, nine, or 18 members heads most of the commissions (which may also be called departments, boards, councils, offices, systems, or authorities). The governor appoints board members with two-thirds Senate approval to serve fixed, overlapping terms of six years. Boards meet periodically to set policy. An executive director, who is either appointed by the governor or hired by the board (depending on the agency), manages the professional staff, which does the agency's day-to-day work. The nine-member board of the Texas Department of Parks and Wildlife, for example, hires an executive director who heads a professional staff that carries out the work of the agency.

Agencies perform such a wide variety of functions that they are a challenge to classify. Nonetheless, it is possible to group many of the agencies by form or function.

Administrative Departments The executive branch of Texas government includes a number of administrative departments, which are responsible for implementing policy and carrying out basic state functions. The Texas Department of Criminal Justice operates the state prison system. The General Land Office manages state lands. The Texas Department of Agriculture implements state agricultural policy. The Lottery Commission operates the state lottery. The Texas Department of Transportation is responsible for financing, constructing, and maintaining highways, rail stations, airports, and other facilities of public transportation. Other state administrative departments include Parks and Wildlife, State Health Services, and Public Safety.

College and University Boards Appointed boards of regents oversee each of the state's public colleges and university systems. University boards consist of nine members selected by the governor with Senate concurrence to serve overlapping six-year terms. University regents are considered prestige appointments, eagerly sought by well-to-do alumni and often awarded to the governor's major financial backers during the last election campaign. The members of the board of regents of the University of Texas and the Texas A&M University systems in particular read like a "Who's Who" of major political supporters of recent governors. Since taking office, Governor Perry has accepted nearly $2.5 million in campaign contributions from individuals he has named to be regents of college and university boards.[33] For example,

Phil Adams, a businessman from Bryan who serves on the Board of Regents of the Texas A&M University System, has given Perry more than $210,000 in political contributions. Steven Hicks, the chair of an investment company in Austin and a member of the Board of Regents of the University of Texas System, has contributed more than $200,000 to Perry.[34] Similarly, Larry Anders and L. Frederick "Rick" Francis, both appointed by Governor Perry to the Texas Tech University Board of Regents, have contributed more than $400,000 and $300,000, respectively, to the governor's political campaigns.[35]

Critics suggest that politically connected boards sometimes make political decisions that can lead to the politicization of higher education. The Board of Regents of Texas Tech University System, for example, chose Kent Hance as Chancellor of the Texas Tech System. Hance had no background in higher education, but he was a former congressman, former railroad commissioner, and former unsuccessful Republican candidate for governor. In 2009, Hance hired former Bush administration Attorney General Alberto Gonzalez for $100,000 a year to teach a class in the political science department and recruit Latino students. Gonzales, an attorney, had no experience in either field. However, he had trouble finding a full-time legal position because he resigned under an ethical cloud. Faculty critics at Texas Tech accused Hance of bestowing a political favor rather than acting in the best interests of the university.[36]

Similarly, the Board of Regents of the Texas A&M University System named former state representative Mike McKinney as chancellor of the system. McKinney was a former chief of staff for Governor Perry. Texas A&M University faculty members charged McKinney with playing politics in forcing the resignation of Elsa Moreno, the president of Texas A&M University at College Station, at least in part over a dispute concerning control of the research budget.[37] Critics accuse McKinney of steering millions of dollars in contracts to companies owned and operated by big-money contributors to Governor Perry. Journalist Paul Burka warns against politicizing the university system: "The management structure of Texas A&M is of the politicians, by the politicians, for the politicians. The governor's reach into the A&M system is the sort of thing that can make it impossible for A&M to recruit top faculty and administrators."[38]

Licensing Boards A number of boards and commissions are responsible for licensing and regulating various professions. Some of these include the Department of Licensing and Regulation, Advisory Board of Athletic Trainers, Board of Chiropractic Examiners, Polygraph Examiners Board, and Funeral Service Commission. State law generally requires that licensing boards include members of the professions they are charged with regulating, as well as lay members. The Funeral Service Commission, for example, includes morticians and cemetery owners.

Regulatory Boards Other state agencies regulate various areas of business and industry. For example, the Public Utility Commission (PUC) regulates telephone and electric utilities. The TDI licenses and regulates insurance companies. The Finance Commission regulates banks and savings and loan institutions. The Texas

AROUND THE NATION

California Addresses Global Warming

California has taken the lead in the effort to address **global warming**, which is the gradual warming of the Earth's atmosphere reportedly caused by the burning of fossil fuels and industrial pollutants. In 2006, the California legislature passed, and Governor Arnold Schwarzenegger signed, legislation to reduce carbon dioxide emissions by 25 percent by 2020. The measure included incentives for alternative energy production and penalties for companies that failed to meet the standard. The legislation calling for a reduction in carbon dioxide emissions was only the most recent attempt by the state to control harmful emissions. California has adopted legislation requiring automobile manufacturers to reduce automobile tailpipe emissions and to mandate that 20 percent of energy sold in the state come from renewable sources, such as wind and geothermal. The state also requires that homebuilders offer buyers the option to have roofs with tiles that convert sunlight into energy.

California political leaders decided to take action to curb greenhouse gas emissions because the federal government had failed to respond to the problem. California is so big that it produces 2.5 percent of the world's total emissions of carbon dioxide. Among the 50 states, only Texas produces more. The California economy is so large that energy companies,

automobile manufacturers, appliance manufacturers, and others cannot afford to ignore the California requirements.* Furthermore, California officials hoped that other states would follow California's lead, and some have done just that. A number of states have adopted energy efficiency requirements for light bulbs and household appliances. Seven states have also agreed on a regional plan to restrict power plant emissions.[†]

Nonetheless, critics warn that the state is taking a huge gamble that it can cut emissions without wrecking the state's economy. Because of the new regulations, California consumers may well have to pay more for energy than consumers in other states and they may face an energy shortage. The new regulations may also place California companies at a competitive disadvantage against firms based in other states without similar environmental regulations.[‡]

QUESTIONS TO CONSIDER

1. Are you worried about the impact of global warming in your lifetime?
2. Would you be willing to pay more for energy in order to curb emissions that cause global warming?
3. Do you think states should take the lead on issues such as global warming if the federal government fails to act?

---

*Jad Mouadwad and Jeremy W. Peters, "California Plan to Cut Gases Splits Industry," *New York Times*, September 1, 2006, available at www.nytimes.com.
[†]Justin Blum, "Stepping in Where Uncle Sam Refuses to Tread," *Washington Post National Weekly Edition*, January 30–February 5, 2006, p. 18.
[‡]Felicity Barringer, "In Gamble, California Tries to Curb Greenhouse Gases," *New York Times*, September 15, 2006, available at www.nytimes.com.

Global warming
The gradual warming of the Earth's atmosphere reportedly caused by the burning of fossil fuels and industrial pollutants.

Alcoholic Beverage Commission regulates the manufacture, transportation, and sale of alcoholic beverages in the state. The Texas Racing Commission oversees horse and dog racing.

State regulatory agencies make **rules,** which are legally binding regulations adopted by a regulatory agency. Whenever the PUC sets telephone rates, for example, it does so through **rulemaking,** a regulatory process used by government agencies to enact legally binding regulations. In Texas, the formal rulemaking process has

Rules Legally
binding regulations
adopted by a
regulatory agency.

Rulemaking A
regulatory process
used by government
agencies to enact
legally binding
regulations.

several steps. When a board or commission considers the adoption of a rule, it must first publish the text of that rule in the *Texas Register*. Interested parties may then comment on the rule. State law requires regulatory agencies to hold public hearings if as many as 25 people request one. After a hearing (if one is held), the board votes to adopt or reject the proposed rule. If the rule is adopted, it goes into effect no sooner than 20 days after the agency files two certified copies with the Texas secretary of state.

The rulemaking process in Texas often involves only a minimal amount of public input. Although some regulatory agency actions, such as the adoption of new telephone rates, receive a great deal of media attention, most rulemaking decisions escape notice of all but those parties most directly involved with the particular agency's action. In practice, most proposed rules generate little comment and public hearings are rare.

Agencies have no inherent constitutional power to make rules. Instead, the legislature delegates authority to agencies to make regulations to implement legislative policy. If the legislature is unhappy with an agency's actions, it can overturn a rule. It can also enact legislation to restrict or even eliminate the agency's rulemaking authority.

Social Service Agencies The legislature has created a number of agencies to facilitate the receipt of federal funds and promote the interests of particular groups in society. The Governor's Committee on People with Disabilities advises state government on disability issues. Other social service agencies include the Texas Department on Aging and Disability Services, Diabetes Council, Council for Developmental Disabilities, and Cancer Prevention and Research Institute. Appointed boards head social service agencies. Board members are appointed by the governor pending Senate confirmation to serve fixed terms.

Promotional and Preservation Agencies Several state agencies are charged with either promoting economic development or preserving the state's historical heritage. The Texas Film Commission, for example, seeks to attract major motion picture and video production to the state. Likewise, the Texas Historical Commission works to preserve the state's architectural, archeological, and cultural landmarks.

Privatization

Privatization The
process that involves
the government
contracting with
private business to
implement
government
programs.

Not all public services are delivered by state agencies. Texas is a national leader in **privatization,** a process that involves the government contracting with private business to implement government programs. For example, thousands of the state's prison inmates are housed in private correction facilities rather than state prisons. Private agencies also manage the state's foster care system, and private contractors build and repair many state highways.

Privatization is controversial. The advocates of privatization believe that it saves taxpayers money because private companies operate more efficiently than government bureaucracies. Furthermore, privatization enables the government to gear up or gear down rapidly because private companies do not have to deal with government personnel policies that make it difficult to hire and fire workers. In contrast, the critics of privatization argue that private companies may cut corners at the expense of public service because they are less interested in serving the public than they are in making a profit. The opponents of privatization also worry that elected officials may award contracts to campaign contributors and political cronies rather than to the companies best qualified to deliver government services.

The state's effort to privatize some aspects of the welfare programs administered by the Texas Health and Human Services Commission (HHSC) has stumbled. In 2003, the Texas legislature decided that the state could save hundreds of millions of dollars by outsourcing most of the customer-service functions of the HHSC. Instead of going to a welfare office to meet in person with a case worker, needy Texans would contact a call center to sign up for Medicaid, the Supplemental Nutrition Assistance Program (which was once called the Food Stamp program), the State Children's Health Insurance Program (SCHIP), and other programs. In theory, privatization would save money by allowing the state to close hundreds of government offices, lay off thousands of state workers, and replace them with four call centers staffed by lower paid privately employed workers hired by the Texas Access Alliance. In practice, the privatization effort was a disaster. Calls were dropped, applications were lost, technology malfunctioned, and thousands of people who qualified for benefits were turned away. The state canceled the contract in 2007 and began hiring state workers to staff the call centers. Instead of saving money, the privatization effort cost the state more than $30 million to pick up the pieces and fix the problems caused by the failed experiment. Despite the setback, the state has not given up on privatization, instead hiring another private company, Maximus, to handle the overall operations of the call centers.[39]

ADMINISTRATIVE OVERSIGHT

State agencies operate with relatively little oversight from the legislature or the governor. Agencies headed by elected executives or commissions are somewhat isolated from legislative or gubernatorial control. Although the legislature determines their budget and can change the laws under which they operate, they are generally free to set policy with no obligation to coordinate their activities with the governor or other agencies. The ballot box provides some accountability, however. Because the elected officials who head the agencies must periodically face the voters, they have an incentive to ensure that the agencies they head avoid scandal and at least appear to be well run.

The agencies led by appointed boards and commissions are even more independent than agencies headed by elected executives. The multi-member boards that typically head these agencies are composed of laypeople selected on the basis of their political ties to the governor rather than their policy expertise. They meet several times a year for a few hours to set basic policy for the agency. In practice, boards typically defer to the leadership of the professional staff.

Legislative Oversight

In theory, the legislature has ultimate authority over most administrative agencies. It can restructure or eliminate a state agency if it chooses or adopt legislation directing an agency to take, or refrain from taking, particular actions. In practice, however, the legislature sometimes struggles to exert control because of its brief, infrequent sessions. Consequently, the legislature has adopted a number of procedures to provide ongoing oversight and administrative control, including sunset review, committee oversight, and LBB supervision.

Sunset review is the periodic evaluation of state agencies by the legislature to determine whether they should be reauthorized. More than 150 agencies are subject to sunset review. Each agency undergoes sunset review every 12 years, with 20 to 30 agencies facing review each legislative session. The list of state agencies facing sunset review in 2011 included the Texas Commission on Environmental Quality (TCEQ), Texas Department of Insurance (TDI), Public Utility Commission (PUC), Texas Racing Commission, and Texas Railroad Commission.[40]

The sunset review process involves the agency facing review, the Sunset Advisory Commission, the legislature, and, to a lesser degree, the governor. The Sunset Advisory Commission includes five members of the Texas House, five members of the Texas Senate, and two citizens. The speaker of the House appoints the House members and one citizen representative, whereas the lieutenant governor names the state senators and the other citizen representative.

Both the agency under review and the staff of the Sunset Advisory Commission evaluate the agency's operation and performance. The agency conducts a self-study while the Commission staff prepares an independent evaluation. Commission members review the two documents and hold hearings at which agency officials, interest-group spokespersons, and interested parties present testimony. After the hearings are complete, the commission recommends whether the agency should be kept as it is, reformed, or abolished. These steps take place before the legislature meets in regular session.

Once the legislative session convenes, lawmakers consider the Sunset Advisory Commission's recommendations and decide the agency's fate. The key feature of the process is that the legislature must reauthorize each agency under review. The reauthorization legislation then goes to the governor for signature or veto. If the legislature fails to act or the governor vetoes the reauthorization measure, the agency dies unless it is a constitutionally created agency, such as the SBOE or the Railroad Commission. Constitutional agencies are subject to review but not abolition. Since the legislature began the sunset process in 1979, it has eliminated 54 agencies and consolidated 12 others. The Sunset Advisory Commission estimates that its recommendations have saved taxpayers nearly $800 million compared with a cost of $25 million to operate the commission and conduct reviews.[41] In practice, the legislature reauthorizes most state agencies while mandating reforms in their procedures. The legislature has added public representation to governing boards, provided for more public input into agency decision-making, imposed conflict-of-interest restrictions on board members, and

Sunset review The periodic evaluation of state agencies by the legislature to determine whether they should be authorized.

mandated closer legislative review of agency expenditures. In 2009, for example, the legislature used the sunset review process to reform the Department of Public Safety (DPS). It ordered the modernization of the driver's license and vehicle inspection divisions, setting goals for shorter lines at licensing offices and less hold time at call centers. Furthermore, the legislature responded to complaints about the agency's personnel policies by creating an inspector general to investigate complaints.[42]

In addition to the sunset process, the legislature uses the committee system and the Legislative Budget Board (LBB) to oversee the executive bureaucracy. During legislative sessions, standing committees may evaluate agency operations and hold hearings to investigate agency performance. Interim committees may oversee agency operations between sessions. An **interim committee** is established to study a particular policy issue between legislative sessions. The LBB influences agency operations through its role in budget execution. Between legislative sessions, the LBB may propose moving funds from one budget category to another, pending the governor's approval. In practice, budget execution authority gives the LBB power to act as a board of directors for the state bureaucracy. The LBB sets goals for agencies, reviews whether the goals are met, and fine-tunes the budget between legislative sessions to reward (or punish) agencies based on their support of LBB goals.

Interim committee
A committee established to study a particular policy issue between legislative sessions, such as higher education or public school finance.

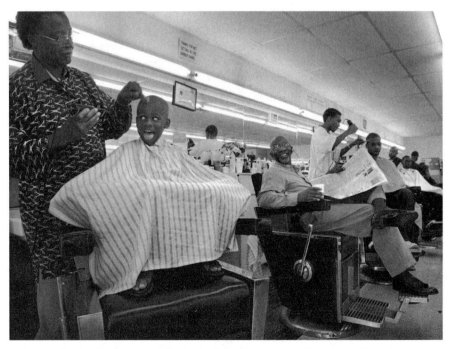

Barbers and barbershops are regulated by the Texas Department of Licensing and Regulation.

Gubernatorial Oversight

The Texas governor's legal/constitutional powers for influencing administrative policymaking are relatively weak. Although the line-item veto (and the threat of its use) can be an effective weapon at times, the governor's powers over administration are otherwise limited. The heads of a number of state agencies are independently elected and thus immune from direct gubernatorial control. Although the governor appoints the members of most state boards, because members serve fixed, multi-year terms, a new governor does not usually get to name a majority of the members of any particular agency for several years. Furthermore, board members are not legally obliged to consult with the governor on policy matters or necessarily follow the governor's lead.

Over time, a governor can influence the administrative bureaucracy through the appointment process. A governor can shape an agency's policy perspectives by appointing men and women to agency boards that share a particular point of view. Governor Bush and Governor Perry both tended to name business-oriented conservatives to serve on most boards, especially boards that directly impacted business interests.

WHAT WE HAVE LEARNED

1. **What is the job description for the governor of Texas, including formal qualifications, length of term, impeachment and removal, compensation, staff assistance, powers and responsibilities, strength of office, and role in the policymaking process?**

The Texas Constitution declares that the governor must be an American citizen, a resident of Texas for five years preceding election, and at least 30 years of age. Although not a requirement, all Texas governors to this point have been white Anglo-Saxon Protestant Christians and all but two have been male. The governor is elected to serve a four-year term without term limits and enjoys staff support. A governor is subject to impeachment by the Texas House and removal by the Texas Senate.

The governor has important powers and responsibilities. The governor can focus legislative attention on policy measures in the State of the State address and by designating a measure as an emergency. The governor can also call special sessions and enjoys the veto power, including the line-item veto for appropriation measures. In addition, the governor is responsible for staffing positions on more than 150 state administrative boards and commissions by appointment subject to a two-thirds confirmation vote by the Texas Senate. However, the governor has limited removal power. The governor may grant reprieves, commutations, and pardons, but only on the recommendation of the Board of Pardons and Paroles. Although the governor makes appointments to fill judicial vacancies, appointees must subsequently run for election. The governor can submit a budget to the legislature, but legislators typically ignore it in favor of the budget document prepared by the LBB. The governor's chief budget power is the line-item veto. The governor, along with the speaker and lieutenant governor, plays a role in budget execution. The governor is commander-in-chief of the Texas National Guard and serves as the ceremonial leader of the state. The governor also serves as the unofficial head of his or her political party in the state, and some go on to become national political figures. The governor's administrative powers are limited because of the plural executive and weak appointive and removal powers. Governor Perry tried to assert influence over the executive branch of state government through appointments and executive orders. However, his efforts met considerable resistance from the legislature, the courts, and other executive officials.

Observers have long held that the constitutional/legal powers of the governor of Texas are among the weakest in the nation. Nonetheless, formal, official powers are an incomplete measure of a governor's authority. Governor Bush's experience in dealing with the legislature illustrates the governor's ability to use unofficial, informal powers to achieve policy influence. Bush succeeded because he set limited goals for himself and communicated regularly with legislators. In contrast, Governor Perry was less successful than his predecessor because he failed to establish positive relationships with members of the legislature.

The governor is an important participant in the state's policymaking process. Similar to the president, the governor is well-positioned to influence the official policy agenda. For example, the governor affects policy formulation by lobbying the legislature. The governor's authority to veto measures, including the line-item veto, also enables the governor to affect policy adoption. The governor participates in policy legitimation by using his or her position to explain and defend policies to the public. Although the governor is weakest in the areas of policy implementation and evaluation, he or she has the visibility to promote policy change.

2. **How is the executive branch of Texas government structured?**

In addition to the governor, voters elect five state executive officials: the lieutenant governor, attorney general, comptroller of public accounts, commissioner of agriculture, and commissioner of the General Land Office. Although the lieutenant governor becomes governor if that office becomes vacant, his or her most important role is to lead the Texas Senate. The attorney general represents the state in court and issues written interpretations of state law called attorney general's opinions. The comptroller monitors compliance with state tax laws and collects taxes on behalf of the state. The comptroller is also the state's banker. In that role, he or she receives funds, assumes responsibility for their safekeeping, and pays the state's bills. The commissioner of agriculture administers all statutes relating to agriculture and enforces the state's weights and measures law. The land commissioner is responsible for managing the land and enforcing the Open Beaches Act. The governor can appoint a limited number of executive officials, including the Texas Secretary of State (the state's chief elections official).

The Railroad Commission and the State Board of Education (SBOE) are executive agencies headed by elected boards. The Railroad Commission, which is led by a three-member elected board, regulates the Texas oil and natural gas industry, gas utilities, pipeline transporters, the surface mining of coal and uranium, and the liquefied petroleum (LP) gas industry. The SBOE, which is a 15-member elected board, oversees the investment of the money in the Permanent School Fund, sets standards for teacher certification and school accreditation, approves curricula, and selects textbooks for use in the state's public schools.

Appointed commissions comprise a substantial part of the executive branch of state government. Most commissions are led by 3-, 6-, 9-, or 18–member unpaid boards appointed by the governor with Senate confirmation. Boards meet periodically to set policy, leaving the daily administration of the agency to a professional staff headed by a professional administrator. The appointed commissions include administrative departments such as the Texas Department of Criminal Justice, college and university boards such as the Board of Regents of the University of

Texas, licensing boards such as the Board of Chiropractic Examiners, regulatory boards such as the Public Utility Commission (PUC), social service agencies such as the Texas Department on Aging and Disability Services, and promotional and preservation agencies, such as the Texas Film Commission.

Texas is a national leader in privatization, a process that involves the government contracting with private business to implement government programs. The advocates of privatization believe that it saves taxpayers money because private companies operate more efficiently than government bureaucracies. In contrast, the critics of privatization argue that private companies may cut corners at the expense of public service because they are less interested in serving the public than they are in making a profit.

3. **How effective are the tools available to the legislature and the governor for overseeing the state's administrative bureaucracy?**

State agencies operate with relatively little oversight from the legislature or the governor. Agencies headed by elected officials are accountable to the voters, at least in theory. In practice, however, most officials below the level of governor are invisible to most voters unless they are involved in some high-profile issue or controversy. Appointed officials are only somewhat accountable to the legislature and governor. The legislature meets too infrequently and too briefly to provide oversight, although it has instituted the sunset review process to assert some control. The governor's legal/constitutional powers for influencing administrative policymaking are relatively weak because of the number of separately elected officials and because the governor has weak removal powers.

KEY TERMS

allowable	impeachment	plural executive
appropriation bill	interim committee	privatization
attorney general's opinion	Jacksonian democracy	reprieve
budget execution authority	Legislative Budget Board (LBB)	rulemaking
capital punishment	Legislative Redistricting	rules
commutation	Board (LRB)	School Lunch Program
eminent domain	line-item veto	senatorial courtesy
executive order	pardon	sunset review
global warming	Permanent School Fund (PSF)	veto

NOTES

1. Terrence Stutz, "Texans Still Pay Highest Insurance Rates for Homeowner Policies," *Dallas Morning News*, March 3, 2009, available at www.dallasnews.com.
2. Jennifer LaFleur and Ed Timms, "State of Neglect: Homeowners Pay Higher Insurance Premiums, Yet Many Policies Limited," *Dallas Morning News*, February 15, 2009, available at www.dallasnews.com.
3. Ibid.
4. Dave Mann, "Are You in Good Hands?" *Texas Observer*, December 12, 2008, available at www.texasobserver.org.
5. David M. Hedge, *Governance and the Changing American States* (Boulder, CO: Westview, 1998), p. 93.
6. "The Imperial Governor," *Texas Observer*, April 20, 2007, p. 3.
7. Governor's Appointment Office, available at www.governor.state.tx.us.

8. Kelly Shannon, "27% of Perry Appointees Are Minorities," *Houston Chronicle*, November 28, 2003, p. 1A.

9. Clay Robinson, "No Shortage of Blame for TYC's Woes," *Houston Chronicle*, March 5, 2007, available at www.chron.com.

10. "Profile of Appellate and Trial Judges," *Texas Judicial System Annual Report—Fiscal Year 2008*, available at www.courts.state.tx.us.

11. Glen Abney and Thomas P. Lauth, "The Executive Budget in the States: Normative Idea and Empirical Observation," *Policy Studies Journal* 17 (Summer 1989): 829–862.

12. "Perry Signs Toyota Rail Legislation," *San Antonio Business Journal*, April 11, 2003, available at www.bizjournals.com/sanantonio.

13. Mike Ward, "A Quiet Revolution in Governor's Office," *Austin American-Statesman*, January 18, 2005, available at www.statesman.com.

14. Kelly Shannon, "Perry Says He's Not Overstepping His Bounds," *Bryan-College Station Eagle*, February 25, 2007, available at www.theeagle.com.

15. "You're Doing What?" *Fort Worth Star-Telegram*, August 24, 2005, available at www.dfw.com.

16. Janet Elliott, "Gov. Perry Institutes Teacher Merit Pay," *Houston Chronicle*, November 3, 2005, p. A1.

17. *Texas Weekly*, March 19, 2007, available at www.texasweekly.com.

18. Thad Beyle, "Gubernatorial Power: The Institutional Power Ratings of the 50 Governors of the United States, 2007 Updates," available at www.unc.edu~beyle.

19. Christy Hoppe, "Republican Lawmakers Resisting Perry Repeatedly," *Dallas Morning News*, April 8, 2009, available at www.dallasnews.com.

20. *Governing*, "State and Local Sourcebook," available at http://sourcebook.governing.com.

21. Council of State Governments, available at www.csg.org.

22. Alan Ehrenhalt, "A Deep Bench," *Governing*, July 2009, p. 10.

23. *Texas Weekly*, February 2, 1998, p. 6.

24. Opinion #GA-0526, available at www.oag.state.tx.us.

25. Comptroller of Public Accounts, "Texas Net Revenue by Source—Fiscal 2008," available at www.window.state.tx.us.

26. William R. Childs, *The Texas Railroad Commission: Understanding Regulation in America to the Mid-Twentieth Century* (College Station, TX: Texas A&M University Press, 2005).

27. Texas Railroad Commission, available at www.rrc.state.tx.us/.

28. *Texas Weekly*, August 24, 2009, available at www.texasweekly.com.

29. Kevin Fisher, past president of the Science Teachers Association of Texas, quoted in James C. McKinley Jr., "In Texas, a Line in the Curriculum Revives Evolution Debate," *New York Times*, January 22, 2009, available at www.nytimes.com.

30. Laura Heinauer, "State Education Board Approves Science Standards," *Austin American-Statesman*, March 28, 2009, available at www.statesman.com.

31. James C. McKinley, Jr., "Texas Conservatives Seek Deeper Stamp on Texts," *New York Times*, March 10, 2010, available at www.nytimes.com.

32. Brian Thevenot, "The Textbook Myth," *Texas Tribune*, March 26, 2010, available at www.texastribune.org.

33. Matt Stiles, "Appointees Have Given Governor Millions," *San Antonio Express News*, May 4, 2009, available at www.mysanantonio.com.

34. Clay Robison, "Do Political Contributions Equal Choice Appointments?" *San Antonio Express News*, February 15, 2009, available at www.mysanantonio.com.

35. Enrique Rangel, "Three Tech Regents Big Perry Donors," *Lubbock Avalanche-Journal*, September 20, 2009, available at www.lubbockonline.com.

36. Rick Casey, "Former AG Humiliated Once Again," *Houston Chronicle*, August 2, 2009, pp. B1, B6.

37. Holly K. Hacker, "A&M Power Struggle Raises Questions About Fallout," *Dallas Morning News*, June 22, 2009, available at www.dallasnews.com.

38. Loren Steffy, "Politics Infect A&M Research," *Houston Chronicle*, August 2, 2009, pp. D1, D5.

39. Jonathan Walters, "The Struggle to Streamline," *Governing*, September 2007, pp. 45–48.

40. Sunset Advisory Commission, available at www.sunset.state.tx.us.

41. Sunset Advisory Commission, "Guide to the Sunset Process," January 2008, available at www.sunset.state.tx.us.

42. Victoria Rossi, "Reconstruction," *Texas Observer*, June 26, 2009, p. 16.

Judicial Branch

WHAT WE WILL LEARN

After studying Chapter 10, students should be able to answer the following questions:

▸ What types of legal disputes do Texas courts address?

▸ What are the procedures followed by trial and appellate courts in Texas?

▸ What are the various courts in Texas and what types of cases does each court hear?

▸ What are the terms of office, method of selection, and qualifications for judges in Texas?

▸ How are judges chosen in Texas and why is judicial selection in the state controversial?

The Culls can be forgiven if they have lost faith in the Texas system of justice. In 1996, Bob and Jane Cull of Mansfield purchased a house from Perry Homes for $233,730. They hoped it would be their retirement home, but the house soon developed structural and foundation problems. When Perry Homes failed to repair the house to their satisfaction, the Culls filed suit against the builder and the warranty company, charging that the structural defects in the house caused its value to fall to $41,000 in 2001. Before the case went to trial the Culls, wanting to avoid a long legal battle, asked to have the dispute settled by an independent arbiter and Perry Homes agreed. The arbiter ruled in favor of the Culls and directed Perry Homes to pay them $800,000, including the cost of the house, legal fees, and **punitive damages,** which are monetary awards given in a lawsuit to punish a defendant for a particularly evil, malicious, or fraudulent act. Perry Homes refused to pay, arguing that the Culls had waived their right to arbitration by filing suit. The arbiter, a district court, and a court of appeals all disagreed with that position. Perry Homes then filed an appeal with the Texas Supreme Court. By a 5–4 vote, the court ruled for Perry Homes, holding that the Culls potentially benefited unfairly from initially filing a lawsuit and should not have been allowed to go to arbitration.[1] The Culls, who were in their 70s, would have to start over, eight years after they originally began the process, by filing a suit against Perry Homes in district court.

Punitive damages
Monetary awards given in a lawsuit to punish a defendant for a particularly evil, malicious, or fraudulent act.

The Texas Supreme Court ruling in the case of *Perry Homes v. Cull* was controversial because Bob Perry, the owner of Perry Homes, was a major campaign donor. Between 2000 and 2008 when the Supreme Court issued its ruling, Perry contributed $263,000 to the nine justices serving on the Texas Supreme Court, giving at least the appearance that the court was biased in his favor. Jane Cull called it a sad day for Texas homeowners. "All we ever wanted was a home with a good foundation, built properly, that could serve as our retirement home," she said. "The little guy just can't win, and that's what's so devastating about it."[2]

The Culls went back to court and won again. In 2010, a jury ruled in their favor against both Perry Homes and the warranty company. It awarded them $14.2 million in actual damages and another $44 million in punitive damages. Nonetheless, the Culls had no expectation that they would see the money, at least not any time soon. Perry Homes was considering an appeal.[3]

Is justice for sale in Texas? The Culls and, according to public opinion polls, more than 80 percent of Texans believe that campaign contributions influence court decisions.[4] Alex Winslow of Texas Watch, a consumer-oriented advocacy group, said that the Supreme Court's decision in *Perry Homes v. Cull* is "little more than a bailout for a major political moneyman."[5] In contrast, a spokesperson for Perry Homes argued that Perry's political contributions may actually have worked against the home builder in the case because the justices, concerned over media scrutiny, would be especially conscientious to be fair to the Culls.[6]

The controversy over *Perry Homes v. Cull* introduces Chapter 10, which focuses on the judicial branch of Texas government. The chapter identifies the types of disputes heard in Texas courts, discusses court procedures, and describes the Texas court system. It profiles the state's judges and discusses judicial selection. In particular, the chapter explores the question raised by *Perry Homes v. Cull:* Is justice for sale in Texas?

This chapter is the third in a series of five chapters examining the policymaking units of state and local government in Texas. Chapter 8 focused on the Texas legislature and Chapter 9 examined the executive branch. The next two chapters deal with the units of local government. Chapter 11 studies city government, whereas Chapter 12 considers counties, school districts, and special districts.

TYPES OF LEGAL DISPUTES

The courts administer justice by settling criminal and civil disputes.

Criminal case
A legal dispute dealing with an alleged violation of a penal law.

Criminal defendant The party charged with a criminal offense.

Prosecutor The attorney who tries a criminal case on behalf of the government.

Burden of proof The legal obligation of one party in a lawsuit to prove its position to a court.

Misdemeanor A relatively minor criminal offense, such as a traffic violation.

Felony A serious criminal offense, such as murder, sexual assault, or burglary.

Capital punishment The death penalty.

Criminal Cases

A **criminal case** is a legal dispute dealing with an alleged violation of a penal law. A **criminal defendant** is the party charged with a criminal offense, whereas the **prosecutor** is the attorney who tries a criminal case on behalf of the government. The role of the court in a criminal case is to guide and referee the dispute. Ultimately, a judge or jury rules on the defendant's guilt or innocence and, if the verdict is guilty, assesses punishment.

 WHAT IS YOUR OPINION?

Did the Culls get a fair hearing in the Texas Supreme Court? Why or why not?

The **burden of proof** is the legal obligation of one party in a lawsuit to prove its position to a court. The prosecutor has the burden of proof in a criminal case. In other words, the prosecutor must show that the defendant is guilty; the defendant need not demonstrate innocence. Texas law requires that the government prove the defendant's guilt "beyond a reasonable doubt." Unless the evidence clearly points to the defendant's guilt, the law requires that the defendant be found not guilty.

The penal code classifies criminal cases according to their severity. A **misdemeanor** is a relatively minor criminal offense, such as a traffic violation. Texas law classifies misdemeanor offenses as Class A, B, or C. Class A misdemeanors are the most serious, Class C the least serious. Class A misdemeanors can be punishable by a fine not to exceed $3,000 and/or a jail term of a year or less. In contrast, the maximum punishment for a Class C misdemeanor is a fine of $500.

A **felony** is a serious criminal offense, such as murder, sexual assault, or burglary. Texas law divides felony offenses into five categories—capital, and first-, second-, third-, and fourth-degree (state jail) felonies—with a fourth-degree felony being the least serious category of offenses. Convicted felons may be fined heavily and sentenced to as many as 99 years in prison. In Texas and 36 other states, convicted capital murderers may be sentenced to death. The death penalty is known as **capital punishment.**

Civil case A legal dispute concerning a private conflict between two or more parties—individuals, corporations, or government agencies.

Plaintiff The party initiating a civil suit.

Civil defendant The responding party in a civil suit.

Property case A civil suit over the ownership of real estate or personal possessions, such as land, jewlery, or an automobile.

Probate case A civil suit dealing with the disposition of the property of a deceased individual.

Domestic-relations case A civil suit based on the law involving the relationships between husband and wife, and between parents and children, such as divorce and child custody cases.

Contract case A civil suit dealing with disputes over written or implied legal agreements, such as a suit over a faulty roof repair job.

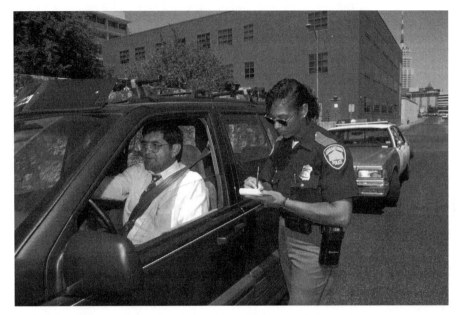

A relatively minor criminal offense, such as a traffic violation, is called a misdemeanor.

Civil Disputes

Courts also settle civil disputes. A **civil case** is a legal dispute concerning a private conflict between two or more parties—individuals, corporations, or government agencies. In this type of legal dispute, the party initiating the lawsuit is called the **plaintiff;** the **civil defendant** is the responding party. The burden of proof in civil cases is on the plaintiff, but it is not as heavy as it is in criminal disputes. With the exception of lawsuits filed to terminate parental rights, the plaintiff is required to prove the case "by a preponderance of the evidence." For the plaintiff's side to win a lawsuit, it need only demonstrate that the weight of evidence in the case is slightly more in its favor. If a judge or jury believes that the evidence is evenly balanced between the plaintiff and the defendant, the defendant prevails because the plaintiff has the burden of proof. For example, a lawsuit to terminate parental rights is a civil action filed by Child Protective Services to ask a court to end a parent–child relationship. The plaintiff has the burden of proof to show by clear and convincing evidence that an individual's parental rights should be terminated because he or she is not a fit parent.

Civil disputes include property, probate, domestic-relations, contract, and tort cases. A **property case** is a civil suit over the ownership of real estate or personal possessions, such as land, jewelry, or an automobile. A **probate case** is a civil suit dealing with the disposition of the property of a deceased individual. A **domestic-relations case** is a civil suit based on the law involving the relationship between husband and wife, as well as between parents and children, such as divorce and child custody cases. A **contract case** is a civil suit dealing with disputes over written or

Tort case A civil suit involving personal injury or damage to property, such as a lawsuit stemming from an automobile accident.

implied legal agreements, such as a suit over a faulty roof repair job. For example, *Perry Homes v. Cull* was a contract case because it dealt with a dispute over the alleged failure of Perry Homes to provide the Culls with a properly constructed house and then to repair any defects that were covered under warranty. Finally, a **tort case** is a civil suit involving personal injury or damage to property, such as a lawsuit stemming from an automobile accident.

COURT PROCEDURES

Litigants The parties in a lawsuit.

The typical image of a court at work is that of a trial with a judge, a jury, witnesses, and evidence. The parties in the lawsuit, the **litigants,** are represented by counsel engaging in an **adversary proceeding,** a legal procedure in which each side presents evidence and arguments to bolster its position while rebutting evidence that might support the other side. Theoretically, the process helps the judge or jury determine the facts in the case.

Adversary proceeding A legal procedure in which each side presents evidence and arguments to bolster its position while rebutting evidence that might support the other side.

In practice, most legal disputes are settled not by trials but through a process of negotiation and compromise between the parties involved. In civil cases, litigants usually decide that it is quicker and less costly to settle out of court than to go through the trial process. They agree on a settlement either before the case goes to trial or during the early stages of the trial. Similarly, most criminal cases are resolved through a **plea bargain,** a procedure in which a defendant agrees to plead guilty in order to receive punishment less than the maximum for an offense. On occasion, defendants may plead guilty to lesser offenses than the crime with which they were originally charged.

Plea bargain A procedure in which a defendant agrees to plead guilty in order to receive punishment less than the maximum for an offense.

Judicial procedures are divided into trials and appeals. A **trial** is the formal examination of a civil or criminal action in accordance with law before a single judge who has jurisdiction to hear the dispute. Trials involve attorneys, witnesses, testimony, evidence, judges, and occasionally juries. In civil cases, the verdict determines which party in the lawsuit prevails. A criminal verdict decides whether the defendant is guilty or not guilty as charged. In general, the outcome of a trial can be appealed to a higher court for review.

Trial The formal examination of a civil or criminal action in accordance with law before a single judge who has jurisdiction to hear the dispute.

Criminal defendants have a constitutional right to trial by jury. The U.S. Supreme Court has held that the U.S. Constitution obliges state governments to offer jury trials to persons charged with felony offenses.[7] The Texas Constitution goes further, granting accused persons the right to trial by jury in *all* cases, misdemeanor and felony, although defendants may waive the right to a jury trial and be tried by a judge alone. Litigants in civil cases have the option of having their case heard by a judge alone or by a jury.

Prospective trial jurors are selected from county voter registration rolls and lists of persons holding Texas driver's licenses and Department of Public Safety (DPS) identification cards. Jurors must be American citizens. Persons who are convicted felons or are under felony indictment are ineligible to serve on a jury. Some groups of people are exempt from jury service if they wish, including full-time students, individuals over 70 years of age, and persons with custody of small children whose absence would leave the children without proper supervision.

Appeal The taking of a case from a lower court to a higher court by the losing party in a lower-court decision.

Reversible error A mistake committed by a trial court that is serious enough to warrant a new trial because the mistake could have affected the outcome of the original trial.

Harmless error A mistake committed by a trial court that is not serious enough to warrant a new trial because it could not have affected the outcome of the original trial.

Double jeopardy The constitutional principle that an individual may not be tried a second time by the same unit of government for a single offense if acquitted in the first trial.

An **appeal** is the taking of a case from a lower court to a higher court by the losing party in a lower-court decision. Civil litigants argue that the trial court failed to follow proper procedures or incorrectly applied the law. They hope that an appellate court will reverse or at least temper the decision of the trial court. Parties who lose tort cases, for example, may ask an appellate court to reduce the amount of damages awarded. Criminal defendants who appeal their convictions contend that the trial court committed **reversible error,** which is a mistake committed by a trial court that is serious enough to warrant a new trial because the mistake could have affected the outcome of the original trial. In contrast, **harmless error** is a mistake committed by a trial court that is not serious enough to warrant a new trial because it could not have affected the outcome of the original trial. The right to appeal criminal court verdicts extends only to the defendant; the prosecution does not have the right to appeal an acquittal. The constitutional principle that an individual may not be tried a second time by the same unit of government for a single offense if acquitted in the first trial is known as the prohibition against **double jeopardy.**

The procedures of appeals courts differ notably from those of trial courts. In general, trial courts are concerned with questions of fact and the law as it applies to those facts. In contrast, appeals are based on issues of law and procedure. Appellate courts do not retry cases appealed to them. Instead, appeals court justices (juries do not participate in appellate proceedings) make decisions based on the law and the constitution, the written and oral arguments presented by attorneys for the litigants in the lawsuit, and the written record of the lower-court proceedings. Also, appellate court justices usually make decisions collectively in panels of three or more judges rather than singly, as do trial court judges. Appeals court decisions are themselves subject to appeal. Both the prosecution and the defendant have the right to appeal the decisions of appellate courts in criminal cases. However, the constitutional protection against double jeopardy applies only to trial proceedings.

Appeals courts may uphold, reverse, or modify lower-court decisions. An appeals court may direct a trial court to reconsider a case in light of the appellate court's ruling on certain legal issues. However, if an appeals court overturns a criminal conviction, the defendant does not necessarily go free. The district attorney who initially prosecuted the case has the option either to retry the case or to release the defendant. In practice, many defendants are retried, convicted, and sentenced once again. Ignacio Cuevas, for example, was tried three times for capital murder, convicted three times, and sentenced to death three times. Twice the Texas Court of Criminal Appeals overturned Cuevas's conviction, but not a third time. Cuevas was ultimately executed.

THE TEXAS COURT SYSTEM

The Texas court system has three levels:

- **Local courts:** Municipal courts, justice of the peace (JP) courts, and county courts hear relatively minor civil cases and misdemeanor criminal disputes.
- **District courts:** State district courts, the general trial courts of the state, hear major civil disputes and try felony criminal cases.

- **Appellate courts:** The Texas Court of Appeals, Texas Court of Criminal Appeals, and Texas Supreme Court constitute the state's appellate court system.

Local Courts

Municipal, JP, and county courts are local courts operated by cities and county governments.

Municipal Courts The Texas legislature has created municipal courts in every incorporated city in the state. Municipal courts operate in 913 cities, staffed by 1,458 judges.[8] Smaller cities have one municipal court with a single judge; larger cities operate several courtrooms, each with its own judge.

City ordinances
Laws enacted by the governing body of a municipality.

Most municipal court cases involve relatively minor criminal matters. Municipal courts have exclusive jurisdiction over cases involving violations of **city ordinances,** which are laws enacted by the governing body of a municipality. In general, persons convicted of violating city ordinances may be fined no more than $500, except for violators of ordinances relating to litter, fire safety, zoning, public health, and sanitation, who may be fined as much as $2,000. Municipal courts share jurisdiction with JP courts in misdemeanor cases involving violations of Class C misdemeanors within city limits. The maximum fine for a Class C misdemeanor is $500. Municipal courts also have the power to award limited civil monetary penalties in cases involving dangerous dogs.

Traffic cases account for more than 80 percent of the workload of municipal courts. Most municipal court defendants plead guilty and pay a relatively small fine. Almost all of the defendants requesting a trial either before a judge alone or with a jury are found guilty as well. Under state law, municipal court proceedings in all but a handful of the state's largest cities (including Houston, Dallas, Fort Worth, San Antonio, and Austin) are not recorded. Consequently, municipal court defendants in most cities are entitled to a new trial called trial *de novo*, usually in county court, if they appeal a conviction. In cities whose municipal courts are courts of record, the

SHOE

appeal is done by the record only and is not a trial *de novo*. Nonetheless, less than 1 percent of municipal court defendants found guilty appeal their conviction.[9] Few defendants appeal because the cost of hiring an attorney to handle the appeal usually exceeds the amount of the fine.

Magistrates
Judicial officers.

Municipal court judges serve as **magistrates** (judicial officers) for the state in a range of proceedings involving both misdemeanor and felony offenses. They may issue search and arrest warrants, set bail for criminal defendants, and hold preliminary hearings. Municipal court judges may also conduct driver's license suspension hearings and emergency mental commitment hearings.

Justice of the Peace (JP) Courts The Texas Constitution requires each county to operate at least one JP court and allows larger counties to have as many as 16. In 2009, 822 JP courts operated in counties statewide.[10] JP courts hear both criminal and civil cases, with criminal disputes comprising nearly 90 percent of their caseloads. Most criminal cases heard in JP court involve Class C misdemeanor traffic offenses, with the rest concerning non-traffic Class C misdemeanors, such as game law violations, public intoxication, disorderly conduct, and some thefts. Justice of the peace courts have a civil jurisdiction. Individuals with civil disputes valued at no more than $10,000 can file suit in JP court and present their case to the justice of the peace without aid of an attorney. JP courts also conduct civil proceedings dealing with mortgage foreclosures, property liens, and forcible entry and detainer suits. A **property lien** is a financial claim against property for payment of debt. A **forcible entry and detainer suit** is an effort by a landlord to evict a tenant (usually for failure to pay rent).

Property lien
A financial claim against property for payment of debt.

Forcible entry and detainer suit
An effort by a landlord to evict a tenant (usually for failure to pay rent).

JP court proceedings, similar to most municipal court proceedings, are not recorded. As a result, a person who files an appeal of a JP court decision is entitled to a new trial, generally in county court. In practice, most cases appealed from JP courts are settled by plea bargains or dismissed by county court judges. Appeals of justice court decisions are rare, involving less than 1 percent of the cases disposed by trial in a JP court.[11]

Similar to municipal court judges, justices of the peace are state magistrates. They may issue search and arrest warrants in both misdemeanor and felony cases, set bail for criminal defendants, and conduct preliminary hearings. They also hold driver's license suspension hearings and conduct emergency mental commitment hearings.

County Courts Each of the state's 254 counties has a constitutional county court, so called because it is required by the Texas Constitution. These courts have both criminal and civil jurisdiction. County courts try criminal cases involving violations of Class A and Class B misdemeanors. In practice, criminal cases constitute more than 85 percent of the cases heard by county courts, with theft, worthless checks, and driving while intoxicated or under the influence of drugs (DWI/DUID) the most common offenses. County courts also try Class C misdemeanor cases appealed from JP or municipal courts.

The civil jurisdiction of the constitutional county courts extends to disputes in which the amount of money at stake is between $200 and $5,000, although these courts may also hear cases involving lesser amounts that are appealed from JP court. The constitutional county courts share their civil jurisdiction with both JP and district courts. An individual bringing a lawsuit for $1,000, for example, can legally file in JP, district, or county court. Lawsuits over debts and personal injury or damage are the most commonly heard civil cases in constitutional county courts.

In addition to their basic civil and criminal jurisdictions, the constitutional county courts fulfill a number of other functions. They probate uncontested wills, appoint guardians for minors, and conduct mental health competency/commitment hearings. The decisions of county courts on mental competency and probate may be appealed to district courts, but all other appeals from county court are taken to the courts of appeals.

The Texas legislature has created 227 additional county courts known as statutory county courts (because they are established by statute) and 18 statutory probate courts to supplement the constitutional county courts.[12] These courts, which are sometimes called county courts at law, operate primarily in urban areas where the caseload of the constitutional county court is overwhelming, and the county judge, who presides in the constitutional county court, is busy with the affairs of county government. Some statutory county courts concentrate on civil matters and some handle only criminal cases. The legislature allows many of the statutory county courts to hear civil cases involving as much as $100,000. Appeals from the statutory county courts proceed in the same manner as appeals from constitutional county courts.[13]

District Courts

Texas has 449 district courts.[14] Each court serves a specific geographic area, which, in rural areas, may encompass several counties. In urban counties, the legislature has created multiple courts, many of which specialize in particular areas of the law. Harris County alone has nearly 60 district courts, including civil, criminal, family, and juvenile district courts.

District courts are the basic trial courts of the state of Texas. They hear all felony cases and have jurisdiction in civil matters involving $200 or more, while sharing jurisdiction on smaller sums with JP and county courts. Civil cases comprise nearly 70 percent of the caseload for district courts. Family law disputes, including divorce and child custody cases, are the civil matters most frequently handled by district courts. Personal injury cases, tax cases, and disputes over debts are important as well. The most frequently heard criminal cases are felony drug offenses, thefts, assaults, and burglary.[15] District courts may also issue a number of **legal writs,** which are written orders issued by a court directing the performance of an act or prohibiting some act. Appeals from district court decisions are taken to the courts of appeals, except capital murder cases in which the death penalty is assessed. These cases are appealed directly and automatically to the Texas Court of Criminal Appeals.

Legal writs
Written orders issued by a court directing the performance of an act or prohibiting some act.

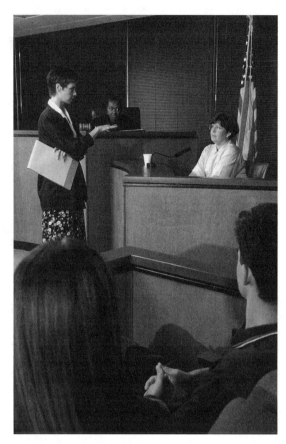

The plaintiff has the burden of proof in a civil trial.

Appellate Courts

The courts of appeals, Texas Court of Criminal Appeals, and Texas Supreme Court constitute the state's appellate court system, which considers appeals filed by litigants who lose in lower courts. With the exception of capital murder cases in which the death penalty has been assessed, appellate courts need not hold hearings in every case. After reading **legal briefs,** which are written legal arguments, and reviewing the trial-court record, appeals court justices may simply **affirm** (uphold) the lower-court ruling without holding a hearing to consider formal arguments. In practice, appellate courts reject the overwhelming majority of appeals based solely on the legal briefs filed in the case.

When an appeals court decides to accept a case on appeal, the court generally schedules a hearing at which attorneys for the two sides in the dispute present oral arguments and answer questions posed by the justices. Appeals courts do not retry cases. Instead, they review the trial-court record and consider legal arguments raised

Legal briefs
Written legal arguments.

Affirm
Uphold.

by the attorneys in the case. After hearing oral arguments and studying legal briefs, appeals court justices discuss the case and eventually vote on a decision, with a majority vote of the justices required to decide a case. The court may affirm the lower-court decision, reverse it, modify it, or affirm part of the lower-court ruling while reversing or modifying the rest. Frequently, an appeals court will **remand** (return) a case to the trial court for reconsideration in light of the appeals court decision. The Texas Supreme Court resolved *Perry Homes v. Cull* by remanding the case to district court to be tried on the merits. The Culls could still win the case and recover damages, but not before the time and expense necessary for a trial and possible appeals.

When the court announces its decision, it may issue a **majority** or **deciding opinion,** which is the official written statement of a court that explains and justifies its ruling and serves as a guideline for lower courts when similar legal issues arise in the future. For example, Justice Scott Brister wrote the majority opinion in *Perry Homes v. Cull*. In addition to the court's majority opinion, members of an appellate court may release dissenting or concurring opinions. A **dissenting opinion** is a written judicial statement that disagrees with the decision of the court's majority. It presents the viewpoint of one or more justices who disagree with the court's decision. A **concurring opinion** is a written judicial statement that agrees with the court ruling but disagrees with the reasoning of the majority. Justices who voted in favor of the court's decision for reasons other than those stated in the majority opinion may file concurring opinions. In fact, several justices filed concurrences or dissents in *Perry Homes v. Cull*.

Courts of Appeals Texas has 14 courts of appeals, each serving a specific geographic area called a court of appeals district. The Court of Appeals for the Second District, which meets in Fort Worth, heard *Perry Homes v. Cull* before it was appealed to the Texas Supreme Court. The number of justices in each court varies from 3 to 13, depending on the workload. Altogether, 80 justices staff the 14 courts of appeals. The justices on each court hear cases in panels of at least three justices, with decisions made by majority vote.

Each of the courts of appeals has jurisdiction on appeals from trial courts located in its district. The courts of appeals hear both civil and criminal appeals, except death penalty appeals, which are considered by the Texas Court of Criminal Appeals. The courts of appeals dealt with 11,000 cases in 2008, with criminal cases outnumbering civil cases by a narrow margin. The courts of appeals reversed the decision of the trial court in whole or in part in 7 percent of the cases it heard.[16] The rulings of the courts of appeals may be appealed either to the Texas Court of Criminal Appeals for criminal matters or to the Texas Supreme Court for civil cases.

Texas Court of Criminal Appeals Texas is one of two states (Oklahoma is the other) with two supreme courts—the Texas Supreme Court for civil disputes and the Texas Court of Criminal Appeals for criminal matters. The Texas Court of Criminal Appeals, which meets in Austin, is the court of last resort for all criminal cases in the state. It has nine judges—one presiding judge and eight additional judges. They sit *en banc* (as a group), with all nine judges hearing a case. As in other appellate courts,

Remand An appellate court returning a case to a trial court for further consideration.

Majority or **deciding opinion** An official written statement of a court that explains and justifies its ruling and serves as a guideline for lower courts when similar legal issues arise in the future.

Dissenting opinion A written judicial statement that disagrees with the decision of the court's majority.

Concurring opinion A written judicial statement that agrees with the court's ruling but disagrees with the reasoning of the majority.

the judges of the Texas Court of Criminal Appeals decide cases by majority vote. Decisions of the Texas Court of Criminal Appeals may be appealed to the U.S. Supreme Court when they involve matters of federal law or the U.S. Constitution. However, the Texas Court of Criminal Appeals is the highest court on issues of state criminal law and the state constitution. The U.S. Supreme Court will not accept appeals on state matters unless they involve federal issues.

The Texas Court of Criminal Appeals considers appeals brought from the courts of appeals and death penalty cases appealed directly from district courts. In 2008, the Texas Court of Criminal Appeals disposed of more than 2,200 cases, including 16 death penalty appeals. Although the court is required to review death penalty cases, other appeals are discretionary—the justices have the option to review the lower-court decision or to allow it to stand without review. In 2008, the Texas Court of Criminal Appeals agreed to consider about 7 percent of the cases appealed to it. The court reversed the decision of the lower court in 55 percent of the cases it reviewed.[17]

writ of *habeas corpus* A court order requiring a government official to show cause why a person is being held in custody.

The Texas Court of Criminal Appeals is empowered to issue a number of writs. The most important of these is the **writ of *habeas corpus,*** a court order requiring a government official to explain why a person is being held in custody. Persons serving sentences in the state's prisons who believe that their rights have been violated may petition the Texas Court of Criminal Appeals for a writ of *habeas corpus* as a means of reopening their case. If the court grants the petition, the state must respond to the prisoner's charges in court. In 2008, the Texas Court of Criminal Appeals granted 350 writs of *habeas corpus* out of 5,290 petitions filed.[18]

Texas Supreme Court The Texas Supreme Court, which sits in Austin, has nine members—one chief justice and eight associate justices—who decide cases *en banc* by majority vote. The Texas Supreme Court decided *Perry Homes v. Cull* by a 5–4 vote. The Texas Supreme Court is the civil court of highest authority on matters of state law, although losers in cases decided by the Texas Supreme Court may appeal to the U.S. Supreme Court *if* they can demonstrate that an issue under federal law or the U.S. Constitution is involved. The U.S. Supreme Court will not review state court interpretations of state law or the state constitution.

The Texas Supreme Court hears civil matters only. Most of its cases come from the courts of appeals, although appeals may be taken directly to the Texas Supreme Court whenever any state court rules on the validity of a state law or an administrative action under the Texas Constitution. The court is also empowered to issue writs of *mandamus* to compel public officials to fulfill their duties and/or follow the law. A **writ of *mandamus*** is a court order directing a public official to perform a specific act or duty. In 2008, the court acted on a total of 3,226 matters.[19]

writ of *mandamus* A court order directing a public official to perform a specific act or duty.

The Texas Supreme Court reviews lower-court decisions on a discretionary basis; that is, the justices choose which cases they will consider. In 2008, the Texas Supreme Court granted review to 11 percent of the cases appealed to it. If the court refuses to grant review, then the lower-court decision stands. The Texas Supreme Court reversed the decision of the lower court in whole or in part in more than 60 percent of the cases it agreed to hear.[20]

INTERNET RESEARCH

Shirley Neeley v. West Orange-Cove Consolidated Independent School District

In 2004, State District Judge John Dietz declared that the Texas school finance system was unconstitutional because it failed to provide enough money to ensure that students receive an adequate education as required by the Texas Constitution. The judge also ruled that the state's property tax cap amounted to an unconstitutional statewide property tax because school districts were effectively required to tax at the maximum rate. Dietz ordered the state to devise a new system for funding public education that would satisfy the requirements of the Texas Constitution. The state appealed the decision to the Texas Supreme Court. (Because Judge Dietz ruled on the constitutionality of a state law, the case could be appealed directly to the Texas Supreme Court rather than having to go through the courts of appeals.)

Students can research the case online at the website of the Texas Supreme Court: **www.supreme.courts.state.tx.us/**. Point the mouse to the "Case Information" link in the panel on the right and then click on "Case Search." In the style box, type in the word *Neeley* and the computer will take you to an information page with multiple links. Review the information and click on some of the links to read about the case. In particular, look for the opinion of the court. Use the information you find online (and your good judgment) to answer the following questions:

1. When the case was filed, it was styled (or titled) *West Orange-Cove Consolidated ISD v. Neeley*. On appeal to the Texas Supreme Court, the litigant names were reversed and the case became *Neeley v. West Orange-Cove Consolidated ISD*. Why would the title of the case change? (This is not a question you can answer from online research, at least not directly. Think through the answer based on the progression of the case through the court system.)

2. In what trial court did the case originate? Identify the court by number and by judge.

3. Who is Shirley Neeley and why is her name attached to the case? (You may need to do an Internet search to answer this question, using a search engine such as **www.google.com**.)

4. When did the Texas Supreme Court issue its decision?

5. Who wrote the opinion of the court?

6. What was the vote of the court?

7. Did every member of the court participate in the decision? If not, why not?

8. In your own words, what did the Texas Supreme Court decide in the case? Did the Supreme Court agree with Judge Dietz or overrule his decision?

In addition to its judicial functions, the Texas Supreme Court plays an important role in administering the judicial branch of state government. It sets the rules of administration and civil procedure for the state court system (as long as those rules do not conflict with state law). It has the authority to approve law schools in the state and appoints the Board of Law Examiners, which administers the bar exam to prospective attorneys. The court also has final authority over the involuntary retirement or removal of all judges in the state.

JUDGES

Table 10.1 summarizes the length of term, method of selection, and qualifications for the more than 3,200 judges who staff Texas courts. As the table shows, the term of office for Texas judges ranges from two to six years. Although municipal court judges in some cities serve two-year terms, most trial court judges are elected for four years. Appellate court judges serve six-year terms.

Except for some municipal court judges who are appointed, Texas judges are chosen by a **partisan election,** which is an election contest in which both the names of the candidates and their party affiliations appear on the ballot. Elected municipal court judges run citywide, generally in nonpartisan city elections. Justices of the peace are elected from JP precincts. Counties with a population of 18,000 to 30,000 people have two to five JP precincts; larger counties have between four and eight JP precincts. Each JP precinct elects either one or two justices of the peace, depending on the size of the county. County court judges are elected countywide. District court judges and courts of appeals justices run from districts ranging in size from countywide for district courts in metropolitan areas to geographically large,

Partisan election
An election contest in which both the names and the party affiliations of candidates appear on the ballot.

TABLE 10.1   Texas Judges

Court	Length of Term	Method of Selection	Qualifications
Municipal courts	Two or four years, depending on the city	Election or appointment, depending on the city	Set by city government
Justice of the peace (JP) courts	Four years	Partisan election from precincts	Qualified voter
Constitutional county courts	Four years	Partisan election countywide	"Well-informed in the law of the state"
Statutory county courts	Four years	Partisan election countywide	Licensed to practice law; other qualifications vary
District courts	Four years	Partisan election countywide or from multi-county districts, with vacancies filled by gubernatorial appointment	Citizen, resident of district for two years, licensed to practice law in Texas, and a practicing attorney or judge for four years
Courts of Appeals	Six-year overlapping terms	Partisan election from a courts of appeals district, with vacancies filled by gubernatorial appointment	Citizen, 35 years of age, practicing attorney or judge of a court of record for ten years
Texas Court of Criminal Appeals	Six-year overlapping terms	Partisan election statewide, with vacancies filled by gubernatorial appointment	Citizen, 35 years of age, practicing attorney or judge of a court of record for 10 years
Texas Supreme Court	Six-year overlapping terms	Partisan election statewide, with vacancies filled by gubernatorial appointment	Citizen, 35 years of age, practicing attorney or judge of a court of record for 10 years

multi-county districts for courts of appeals and district court judges in rural areas. Judges on the Texas Court of Criminal Appeals and the Texas Supreme Court are elected statewide.

The qualifications of judges in Texas depend on the court. The requirements to serve as a municipal court judge vary from city to city, with many municipalities requiring prospective judges to be experienced attorneys. The qualifications of JPs and constitutional county court judges are set in the state constitution. Justices of the peace and constitutional county court judges must be qualified voters, but they need not be attorneys. In fact, most have not even attended law school. Although the Texas Constitution requires that constitutional county court judges "shall be well-informed in the law of the state," it gives no standard for measuring that requirement. Less than 20 percent of the state's county court judges and JPs are lawyers.[21] State law does require, however, that individuals who are elected as judges but who are not attorneys complete a course in legal training before they can serve. The qualifications of statutory county court judges vary, with many courts requiring two to five years of experience as a practicing attorney.

The Texas Constitution establishes the requirements for judges serving on district and appellate courts. District court judges must be citizens and residents of the district for two years. In addition, they must be licensed to practice law in Texas and have at least four years experience as a practicing attorney or a judge in a court of record. Appellate court judges are required to be citizens at least 35 years of age and must be practicing lawyers or judges in a court of record for at least ten years.

JUDICIAL SELECTION

Texas and seven other states elect judges on the partisan ballot.[22] Except for municipal court judges, Texas judges are chosen in a fashion that is formally the same as that for electing officials to the legislative and executive branches of government. People who want to become judges run in either the Democratic or the Republican primary, with the primary election winners representing their party on the general-election ballot. The candidate with the most votes in November becomes judge.

Research on judicial elections in Texas shows that the outcome of judicial contests depends on political party strength, money, and whether a candidate is involved in a high-profile scandal. Many voters know nothing about judicial candidates other than their party affiliation, so they often back the candidates of their favored party. The Texas Republican Party has consequently held every seat on the Texas Supreme Court and the Texas Court of Criminal Appeals for years as well as many judgeships at the county level. Democrats have won most judicial contests in Travis County (Austin) and in South Texas, and have begun to win again in Dallas County and Harris County after more than a decade of Republican dominance. In 2006 and 2008, Democrats prevailed in every judicial contest in Dallas County. In 2008, Democrats won a majority of judicial races in Harris County. Research indicates that well-funded candidates can sometimes overcome a partisan disadvantage and a high-profile scandal can often cause a judicial candidate to lose despite a partisan advantage. In contrast, incumbency, gender, and race/ethnicity have little effect on the outcome of judicial elections.[23]

Despite the formality of an election system, a substantial number of the state's district and appellate judges first reach the bench through appointment. The Texas Constitution empowers the governor (with Senate confirmation) to staff newly created courts at the appellate and district levels and fill judicial vacancies on those courts caused by deaths, retirements, or resignations. In 2008, 53 percent of the state's appellate judges and 40 percent of district judges had initially taken office through gubernatorial appointment rather than election.[24] When a vacancy occurs on a county or JP court, the commissioners court of that county fills the vacancy. Although appointed judges must face the voters at the next election, they enjoy the advantage of incumbency.

Is Justice for Sale in Texas?

Critics of the judicial selection system in Texas believe that money plays too prominent a role in the process. Sitting judges and candidates for judicial office raise and spend money in amounts comparable to candidates for other down-ballot statewide and local offices. Successful candidates for the Texas Supreme Court typically raise at least $800,000. Even candidates for district judgeships may raise and spend sums well in excess of $30,000 on their campaigns, especially candidates running in urban counties.

Although Texas law limits campaign expenditures in judicial elections, the limits are ineffective. Candidates for statewide judicial office may spend no more than $2 million for each election. Candidates seeking seats on the courts of appeals or district court judgeships have lower spending limits. In practice, however, the spending limits are too high to have a meaningful impact on judicial elections. Supreme Court candidates, for example, can raise $2 million for the primary election, $2 million more for the primary runoff (if there is one), and another $2 million for the general election. The limits are voluntary. Furthermore, candidates who pledge to adhere to the spending limits are not bound if an opponent exceeds the limits.[25]

Candidates for judicial office in Texas collect campaign contributions from individuals and groups who have a stake in the outcome of cases. From 2000 through the end of the 2008 election season, the nine incumbent members of the Texas Supreme Court collectively raised $11.8 million in campaign contributions. Chief Justice Wallace B. Jefferson led the way with $2.8 million in contributions. Most of the money came from lawyers, many of whom practice before the court, and business interests with a stake in the outcomes of cases heard by the court.[26]

Ironically, races for seats on the state's other supreme court, the Texas Court of Criminal Appeals, involve less money than many contests for local judicial office. In 2008, no candidate for a seat on the Texas Court of Criminal Appeals raised more than $50,000. In fact, the three winning candidates raised less than $5,000 apiece.[27] Races for the Texas Court of Criminal Appeals are low-budget affairs because the litigants who appear before the court are not as wealthy as the business interests and lawyers whose cases are heard by the Texas Supreme Court. Most criminal defendants have no money and prosecuting attorneys are not especially well paid. Although some criminal defense attorneys earn a good living, they have little incentive to contribute generously to candidates for the Texas Court of Criminal Appeals because, in contrast to trial lawyers, they get paid regardless of whether their clients win or lose.

In 2009, the U.S. Supreme Court weighed in on the issue of campaign contributions and state judicial decision-making in a dispute involving a lawsuit between two coal companies in West Virginia. The smaller company, owned by Hugh Caperton, sued the larger company, A. T. Massey Coal Co., charging that the big company unlawfully drove it out of business. A jury agreed and awarded Caperton $50 million. Massey Coal prepared an appeal, but first its chief executive officer spent $3 million to persuade voters to replace one of the members of the West Virginia Supreme Court with someone more to his liking. The newly elected justice, Brent Benjamin, then cast the deciding vote in a 3–2 decision in favor of Massey Coal, overturning the $50 million in damages awarded to Caperton. The U.S. Supreme Court held that Benjamin should not have participated in the case because the extraordinary amount of money spent by a litigant on his behalf created an "unconstitutional potential for bias." The U.S. Supreme Court ordered the West Virginia Supreme Court to rehear the case without Justice Benjamin participating in the decision.[28]

The impact of the Caperton case on judicial elections in Texas remains to be seen. Although some proponents of reform are using the case to bolster their argument in favor of changing the way Texas selects judges, the ruling may be too narrow to have any practical impact in the state. The U.S. Supreme Court decided the dispute by the narrowest of margins, 5–4, and the majority opinion was careful to note that the circumstances of the West Virginia case were extreme. The amount of money contributed by the owner of the large coal company exceeded all other contributions to both candidates in the race combined. Furthermore, the money was also given during the period between the jury verdict in the case and the time when the West Virginia Supreme Court heard the appeal. Texas politics features few if any campaign contribution scenarios that are so extreme.[29]

 WHAT IS YOUR OPINION?

Should judicial candidates and sitting judges be prevented from accepting campaign contributions from potential litigants?

Do Voters Know the Candidates?

Critics believe that many voters are unable to intelligently evaluate the qualifications of judicial candidates. This problem has worsened, they say, as the number of judgeships has increased. In November 2006, for example, the election ballot in Dallas County included more than 40 contested judicial races. Many Dallas County voters apparently based their voting decision on the one piece of information they

GETTING INVOLVED

Volunteer to Become a Court-Appointed Special Advocate

A court-appointed special advocate is a trained volunteer appointed by a juvenile or family court judge to represent the interests of children who appear before the court. A majority of cases involving an advocate concern children who are removed from their homes because of abuse or neglect. The advocate meets with the child, the child's parents, prospective foster parents, social service caseworkers, and other people involved in the child's life to determine what course of action is in the best interest of the child. The advocate makes recommendations to the court and assists the child in making a transition to a new living situation.

Although the court-appointed special advocacy program is extremely rewarding, it requires a major time commitment and should not be taken lightly.

Volunteers must be at least 21 years old, mature enough to handle difficult situations, and willing to complete a 30-hour training course. They must have their own transportation and be willing to commit to a year or more of volunteer work to see a case through to its resolution.

You can learn more about the Texas child advocacy program at the following website: **www.texascasa.org/**. The website discusses the program and provides contact information for potential volunteers in most of the state's counties. Contact the local organization in your community and inquire about participating in the program. It is your opportunity to play a positive role in the life of a child who needs help.

It's your community—Get involved!

---

knew about the candidates—their party affiliation—because every Democratic judicial candidate defeated every Republican judicial candidate on the ballot. Partisan sweeps for one party or the other have taken place in judicial races in most of the state's large urban counties over the last 20 years.

The election of Steve Mansfield in 1994 to the Texas Court of Criminal Appeals suggests that voters are often uninformed about judicial candidates even in statewide judicial races. Mansfield admitted having lied in his campaign literature about his place of birth, legal experience, and political background. Nonetheless, the message apparently did not reach many of the voters because they chose the Republican Mansfield over the incumbent Democratic Judge Chuck Campbell. After the election, the press discovered that Mansfield previously had been charged in Massachusetts with the use of marijuana and, in Florida, with the unauthorized practice of law.[30]

Is the Texas Judiciary Representative of the State's Population?

Critics of Texas's system of judicial selection note that it has produced a judiciary that does not reflect the ethnic and racial diversity of the state's population. As Figure 10.1 shows, whites are over-represented on the Texas bench, whereas Latinos, African Americans, and people of other ethnicities are under-represented. More than 80 percent of Texas judges are men and the average age is mid-50s.[31]

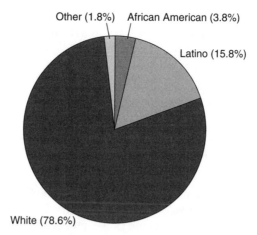

Other (1.8%)   African American (3.8%)

Latino (15.8%)

White (78.6%)

FIGURE 10.1   Profile of Texas Judges.

Is Partisan Politics Incompatible with Judicial Impartiality?

Can a Republican defendant receive a fair trial from a Democratic judge (and vice versa)? Before going to trial for violating state campaign finance regulations, Republican Congressman Tom DeLay asked that the Travis County district judge assigned to hear the case be removed because the judge was a Democrat who had contributed money to groups that oppose DeLay. After a court granted DeLay's request to change judges, the district attorney responded by challenging the impartiality of the administrative judge appointed to name a new trial judge because the administrative judge had ties to a fundraising group associated with DeLay. When that judge withdrew from the case, the chief justice of the Texas Supreme Court ended the fight over judges by appointing a Democratic judge from San Antonio to hear the case. The new judge was acceptable to both sides because of his reputation for fairness and his relative dissociation from partisan politics.

Every judge in Texas is either a Republican or a Democrat. If partisan figures, such as Tom DeLay, face trial or if court cases deal with high-profile political issues, such as school finance or abortion, the judges hearing the disputes and deciding the issues will be Democrats or Republicans, elected in the same fashion as executive branch officials or members of the legislature. As long as Texas elects judges on the partisan ballot, at least some people will believe that party politics will determine the outcomes of cases rather than the law and the constitution.

Reforming the Judicial Selection Process

Reformers offer a number of options for changing the state's method for choosing judges. Some reformers propose that the state adopt the so-called Merit Selection (or Missouri Plan) system of judicial selection, which originated in the state

Merit Selection (or the Missouri Plan)
A method for selecting judges that combines gubernatorial appointment with voter approval in a retention election.

of Missouri in 1941. **Merit Selection (or the Missouri Plan)** is a method for selecting judges that combines gubernatorial appointment with voter approval in a retention election. Twenty-five states use Merit Selection to fill a significant number of judgeships.[32]

 ## ? WHAT IS YOUR OPINION?

How important is it that Texas judges reflect the racial and ethnic diversity of the state?

Former Chief Justice John Hill offered the most detailed proposal for implementing Merit Selection in Texas. Under Hill's plan, the governor, lieutenant governor, speaker of the House, president of the Texas Bar Association, and chairs of the state Democratic and Republican Parties each choose one or more individuals to serve on a 15-member nominating commission. These 15 individuals include nine lawyers and six non-lawyers who serve six-year staggered terms. When an opening occurs on one of the state's appellate or trial courts, the commission draws up a list of three to five qualified persons from which the governor fills the vacancy, subject to a two-thirds confirmation vote by the state Senate. The newly appointed judge faces the voters in a retention (or confirmation) election in the next general election. The ballot reads as follows: "Should Judge _____ be retained in office?" If a majority of voters approve, the judge continues in office for a full term before facing another retention election. Judges failing to win majority support at a retention election lose their seats. Replacements are selected through the initial procedure of nomination by commission and gubernatorial appointment. Merit Selection can be used to choose all or part of a state's judges. Hill proposed separate nominating commissions for appellate and trial courts. He would also permit individual counties to opt out of the plan and continue electing local trial judges if they wished. Other proposals would limit Merit Selection to appellate justices.

The proponents of Merit Selection believe that it is an ideal compromise between a system of appointing judges and the election method. Although the governor is able to select the state's judges under Merit Selection, the bipartisan nominating commission limits the governor's choices to qualified individuals rather than political cronies. Retention (or confirmation) elections allow voters to participate in the process while removing judicial selection from party politics.

Not all Texans favor Merit Selection, however. Critics dispute the notion that Merit Selection takes the politics out of judicial selection. Political Scientist David M. O'Brien believes that all methods of choosing judges are political. The difference between election and appointment is that electoral politics are out in the open. In contrast, he says, the selection of appointed judges can be influenced by political considerations and cronyism that are hidden from public view.[33]

The critics of Merit Selection argue that the system fails to take politics out of the judicial selection process. Lawyers on both sides of the tort reform controversy jockey to influence the selection of people who serve on the nominating

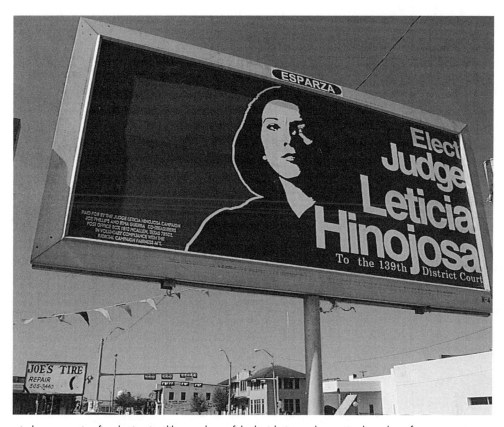

In Texas, judges campaign for election just like members of the legislative and executive branches of government.

commission. The governor and other officials who make appointments to the nomination commission usually choose their political allies. At least some commission members and the governor may play favorites in the final selection process. Typically, the individuals selected as judges in Merit Selection states have at least some ties to the governor making the appointment.[34]

Many minority rights advocates prefer the election of district judges from relatively small sub-county districts, perhaps even single-member districts. A **district election** is a method for choosing public officials in which a political subdivision, such as a state or county, is divided into districts, with each district electing one official. The proponents of district elections believe they increase representation for ethnic/racial minorities, make judges more responsive to citizens, and lessen the importance of money in judicial elections. In contrast, opponents of district elections warn that judges chosen from relatively small districts might be partial to litigants from their districts. Furthermore, they point out that many minority judges who now hold office would be defeated under a district system because they live in

District election
A method for choosing public officials in which a political subdivision, such as a state or county, is divided into districts and each district elects one official.

upper-income neighborhoods that would be unlikely to elect African American or Latino judicial candidates.

 WHAT IS YOUR OPINION?

Should the current system of judicial selection replaced?

Nonpartisan elections Election contests in which the names of the candidates appear on the ballot but not their party affiliations.

Straight-ticket voting Citizens casting their ballots only for the candidates of one party.

Other proposed reforms of the judicial selection process in Texas involve ballot modifications. Some reformers believe that judges should be chosen through **nonpartisan elections,** in which candidates run without party labels. Other reformers propose preventing voters from casting a straight ticket ballot for judicial races. **Straight-ticket voting** is the practice of voting for candidates of the same political party for all positions on the ballot. The advocates of these ballot reforms argue that they reduce the likelihood of partisan sweeps, such as the Democratic sweep in Dallas County in 2006. Furthermore, some research indicates that African American and Latino judicial candidates lose not because of their race but because they usually run as Democrats in counties that are leaning Republican.[35] If party labels are removed from the ballot or straight ticket voting is made more difficult, minority candidates may have more success. In contrast, other observers point out that these limited reforms do little to lessen the role of money in judicial elections and do nothing to solve the problem of poorly informed voters. In fact, nonpartisan elections reduce the amount of information readily available to voters about the candidates because they remove party labels from the ballot.

Not all Texans oppose the current system of electing judges, however. Many political leaders, elected officials, both major political parties, and judges (including some of the justices on the state Supreme Court) favor retaining the current system of partisan election of judges. Texans who want to preserve the state's current system of judicial selection argue that election is the democratic way for choosing public officials. Elected judges are more likely to reflect the will of the community than appointed judges. Furthermore, most of the criticisms made against the election of judges could also be made against the election of legislators and executive branch officials. They feel the best way to improve the judicial election process (and the election process in general) is better voter education.

Judicial Retirement and Removal

Judges leave the bench for a variety of reasons. Some die, some are defeated for re-election, and some retire. State law requires district and appellate judges to retire at age 75. However, judges who reach retirement age before the end of a term can finish that term before retiring. In addition, judges can qualify for an increased pension if they retire before reaching age 70.

Judges may be disciplined and removed from office for incompetence or unethical conduct. The Texas Constitution empowers the Commission on Judicial Conduct, a body composed of judges, lawyers, and laypersons, to investigate

AROUND THE NATION

Drug Courts in Florida

Over the last decade, states around the nation have been creating a new type of court called a problem-solving court to deal with criminal offenses such as drug use and possession, prostitution, shoplifting, and domestic violence. In contrast to a traditional court, which focuses on facts and legal issues, a **problem-solving court** is a judicial body that attempts to change the future behavior of litigants and promote the welfare of the community. The goal of a problem-solving court is not just to punish offenders but also to prevent future harm.*

The oldest problem-solving court in the nation is the drug court of Dade County (Miami), Florida. The Florida legislature created the drug court in 1989 because of the ineffectiveness of traditional judicial approaches to drug crime. The legislature hoped that the drug court would achieve better results for victims, defendants, and the community than traditional courts had achieved. The drug court sentences addicted defendants to long-term drug treatment instead of prison. The judge monitors the defendant's drug treatment and responds to his or her progress or failure with a system of rewards or punishments, including short-term jail sentences. If a defendant completes treatment successfully, the judge reduces the charges or even dismisses the case altogether.

Research shows that drug courts reduce **recidivism,** which is the tendency of offenders released from prison to commit additional crimes and return to prison. Defendants who go through drug court are less likely to be rearrested than are defendants whose cases are heard by a traditional court. Drug court defendants are also more likely to complete treatment than are defendants who enter drug rehabilitation voluntarily.[†]

Drug courts are now in use in every state.[‡] In 2001, the Texas legislature passed, and the governor signed, a measure requiring counties of more than 550,000 people to set up drug courts and meet minimum enrollment figures in treatment programs. Texas officials hope not only to reduce drug offenses but also to save the state money because it is less expensive to sentence drug defendants to drug rehabilitation than it is to send them to prison.[§]

QUESTIONS TO CONSIDER

1. Are drug courts soft on crime?
2. Would you favor the use of a problem-solving court for other sorts of crimes, such as robbery and assault? Why or why not?
3. Are you for or against using drug courts in Texas?

---

*Jeffrey A. Butts, "Introduction: Problem-Solving Courts," *Law & Policy* 23 (April 2001): 121–124.

[†]Greg Berman and John Feinblatt, "Problem-Solving Courts: A Brief Primer," *Law & Policy* 23 (April 2001): 125–132.

[‡]Erik Eckholm, "Courts Give Some Addicts Chance to Straighten Out," *New York Times*, October 15, 2008, available at **www.nytimes.com**.

[§]Pam Wagner, "Drug Courts on Trial," *Fiscal Notes*, June 2002, pp. 8–9.

Problem-solving court A judicial body that attempts to change the future behavior of litigants and promote the welfare of the community.

complaints against judges and recommend discipline. The commission may take any of the following disciplinary actions:

- An admonition is the least serious sanction the commission can impose. It consists of a letter to a judge suggesting that a given action was inappropriate or that another action might have been better. Admonitions may be either private or public.

Recidivism The tendency of offenders released from prison to commit additional crimes and return to prison.

- A warning is stronger than an admonition. It may be issued privately or publicly.

- A reprimand is more serious than either an admonition or a warning. The Commission on Judicial Conduct issues a reprimand, either publicly or privately, when it believes a judge has committed serious misconduct.

- Recommendation to remove from office is the strongest action the commission may take. When this happens, the chief justice of the Texas Supreme Court selects a seven-judge panel chosen by lot from justices sitting on the various courts of appeals. The panel reviews the report and makes a recommendation to the Supreme Court, which may then remove the offending judge from office.

Address from office A procedure for removing judicial officials that is initiated by the governor and requires a two-thirds vote by the legislature.

In addition to removal by the Supreme Court, Texas judges may be removed through the impeachment process or by a procedure known as address from office. Judges may be impeached by majority vote in the Texas House and removed by a two-thirds vote of the Senate. **Address from office** is a procedure for removing judicial officials that is initiated by the governor and requires a two-thirds vote by the legislature. Neither impeachment nor address from office is used with any frequency. Judges in trouble usually choose to resign rather than undergo the public humiliation of removal.

Visiting Judges

Retirement or election defeat does not necessarily spell the end of a Texas judge's career on the bench. Many judges who have retired or been defeated for reelection continue working as visiting judges, the judicial equivalent of temporary workers. Visiting judges are especially in demand in the state's rapidly growing urban areas where the number of district courts has not increased fast enough to keep pace with growing caseloads.[36]

The visiting judge system is controversial. The defenders of the practice declare that temporary judges are needed to keep up with crowded court dockets. However, unless the legislature is willing to create dozens of new courts with their own full-time judges, the only alternative to visiting judges is a hopelessly overloaded court system. In contrast, critics charge that visiting judges are unaccountable to the voters, especially visiting judges who were defeated for reelection.

WHAT WE HAVE LEARNED

1. What types of legal disputes do Texas courts address?

Courts administer justice by settling criminal and civil disputes. A criminal case is a legal dispute dealing with an alleged violation of a penal law. Criminal cases are divided into felonies and misdemeanors. In criminal cases in Texas, the prosecutor must prove the defendant's guilt beyond a reasonable doubt. A civil case is a legal dispute concerning a private conflict between two or more parties—individuals, corporations, or government agencies. Civil cases are classified as property, probate, domestic-relations, contract, and tort cases. In civil cases in Texas, the plaintiff must prove his or her case by a preponderance of the evidence.

2. **What are the procedures followed by trial and appellate courts in Texas?**

The typical image of a court at work is that of a trial with a judge, jury, witnesses, and evidence. In practice, most legal disputes are resolved by plea bargains (for criminal cases) or out of court settlements (for civil cases). Judicial procedures are classified as either trials or appeals. A trial is the formal examination of a civil or criminal action in accordance with law before a single judge who has jurisdiction to hear the dispute. An appeal is the taking of a case from a lower court to a higher court by the losing party in a lower-court decision.

3. **What are the various courts in Texas and what types of cases does each court hear?**

The Texas court system has three levels: local courts, district courts, and appellate courts. Municipal courts, justice of the peace (JP) courts, and county courts are local courts with limited jurisdiction. Municipal courts hear cases involving violations of city ordinances and Class C misdemeanors. JP courts also hear Class C misdemeanor cases and serve as small claims courts for civil matters involving $10,000 or less. County courts, which include constitutional county courts and county courts at law, hear Class A and B criminal cases, as well as civil disputes involving larger amounts of money. District courts try all felony criminal cases and hear larger civil cases. The civil jurisdiction of JP, county, and district courts somewhat overlap. With the exception of capital murder cases in which the death penalty is assessed, all trial court appeals go to one of the state courts of appeals. Death penalty cases are appealed directly and automatically to the Texas Court of Criminal Appeals, which also hears all criminal appeals brought from the courts of appeals. Civil cases appealed from the courts of appeals are taken to the Texas Supreme Court.

4. **What are the terms of office, method of selection, and qualifications for judges in Texas?**

Although some municipal court judges serve two-year terms, most trial court judges have four-year terms. Appellate judges serve six-year terms. Except for some municipal court judges who are appointed, Texas judges are chosen by partisan election. Judicial qualifications vary by court, but all judges must be attorneys except for justices of the peace, county court judges, and some municipal court judges.

5. **How are judges chosen in Texas and why is judicial selection in the state controversial?**

Except for municipal court judges, Texas judges are chosen in a fashion that is formally the same as that for electing officials to the legislative and executive branches of government. The outcome of judicial contests depends on political party strength, money, and whether a candidate is involved in a high-profile scandal. Despite the election system, many district and appellate court judges initially reach the bench through appointment. Critics of the judicial selection system in Texas believe that money plays too prominent a role in the process because campaign contributors to judicial candidates are typically individuals and groups who have a stake in the outcomes of court cases. Critics also believe that many voters are unable to evaluate intelligently the qualifications of judicial candidates. Finally, they note that the state's system of judicial selection has produced a judiciary that does not reflect the ethnic and racial diversity of the state's population. Reformers propose a number of alternative systems of judicial selection, including merit selection or the Missouri Plan, nonpartisan judicial elections, or prohibiting the straight ticket in judicial races. Judges leave the bench for a variety of reasons, including death, election defeat, and retirement. Judges may be disciplined and removed from office for incompetence or unethical conduct. Texas judges may also be removed through the impeachment process or by a procedure known as address from office. However, many judges who have retired or been defeated for reelection continue working as visiting judges.

KEY TERMS

address from office

adversary proceeding

affirm

appeal

burden of proof

capital punishment

city ordinances

civil case

civil defendant

concurring opinion

contract case

criminal case

criminal defendant

dissenting opinion

district election

domestic-relations case

double jeopardy

felony

forcible entry and detainer suit

harmless error

legal briefs

legal writs

litigants

magistrates

majority or deciding opinion

Merit Selection (or the Missouri Plan)

misdemeanor

nonpartisan elections

partisan election

plaintiff

plea bargain

probate case

problem-solving court

property case

property lien

prosecutor

punitive damages

recidivism

remand

reversible error

straight-ticket voting

tort case

trial

writ of *habeas corpus*

writ of *mandamus*

NOTES

1. *Perry Homes v. Cull*, No. 05-0882 (2008).
2. Quoted in Wayne Slater, "Texas Supreme Court Rules Against Mansfield Couple in Battle with Homebuilder," *Dallas Morning News*, May 3, 2008, available at www.dallasnews.com.
3. Sandra Baker, "Jury Awards $58 Million to Mansfield Couple in Home Builder Lawsuit," *Fort Worth Star-Telegram*, March 2, 2010, available at www.star-telegram.com.
4. Chuck Lindell, "Chief Justice Seeks to Abolish Judicial Elections," *Austin American-Statesman*, February 12, 2009, available at www.statesman.com.
5. Quoted in Slater, "Texas Supreme Court Rules Against Mansfield Couple in Battle with Homebuilder."
6. Janet Elliott, "Court Tosses Award Against Perry Homes," *Houston Chronicle*, May 3, 2008, p. B6.
7. *Duncan v. Louisiana*, 391 U.S. 145 (1968).
8. Office of Court Administration, "2009 Texas Judicial System Directory," available at www.courts.state.tx.us.
9. "Activity Report for Municipal Courts," *Annual Report of the Texas Judicial System*, Fiscal Year 2008, available at www.courts.state.tx.us.
10. Office of Court Administration, "2009 Texas Judicial System Directory."
11. "Activity Report for Justice Courts," *Annual Report of the Texas Judicial System*, Fiscal Year 2008.
12. Office of Court Administration, "2009 Texas Judicial System Directory."
13. "Court Structure of Texas," *Annual Report of the Texas Judicial System*, Fiscal Year 2008, available at www.courts.state.tx.us.
14. Office of Court Administration, "2009 Texas Judicial System Directory."
15. "District Courts: Summary Activity by Case Type," *Annual Report of the Texas Judicial System*, Fiscal Year 2008.
16. "Activity for the Fiscal Year Ended August 31, 2008," *Annual Report of the Texas Judicial System*, Fiscal Year 2008.
17. "Court of Criminal Appeals Activity: FY 2008," *Annual Report of the Texas Judicial System*, Fiscal Year 2008.
18. Ibid.
19. "Supreme Court Activity: FY 2004–2008," *Annual Report of the Texas Judicial System*, Fiscal Year 2008.
20. Ibid.
21. "Profile of Appellate and Trial Judges," *Annual Report of the Texas Judicial System*, Fiscal Year 2008.
22. American Judicature Society, "Judicial Selection in the States: Appellate and General Jurisdiction Courts," available at www.ajs.org.

23. Kyle Cheek and Anthony Champagne, *Judicial Politics in Texas: Partisanship, Money, and Politics in State Courts* (New York, NY: Peter Lang, 2005), pp. 79–80.

24. "Profile of Appellate and Trial Judges."

25. Sam Kinch, Jr., *Too Much Money Is Not Enough: Big Money and Political Power in Texas* (Austin, TX: Campaign for People, 2000), p. 14.

26. Randy Lee Loftis and Ryan McNeill, "Drive to Choose Texas Judges on Merit Intensifies," *Dallas Morning News*, March 2, 2009, available at www.dallasnews.com.

27. National Institute on Money in State Politics, available at www.followthemoney.com.

28. *Caperton v. A.T. Massey Coal Co.*, No. 08-22 (2009).

29. Tony Mauro and John Council, "Texas's Campaign Finance Laws Could Mute *Caperton*'s Impact," *Texas Lawyer*, June 15, 2009, available at www.law.com/jsp/tx.

30. *Texas Weekly*, December 12, 1994, p. 4.

31. "Profile of Appellate and Trial Judges."

32. American Judicature Society, "Judicial Selection in the States: Appellate and General Jurisdiction Courts."

33. Quoted in Adam Liptak, "Rendering Justice, With One Eye on Re-Election," *New York Times*, May 25, 2008, available at www.nytimes.com.

34. David W. Neubauer and Stephen S. Meinhold, *Judicial Process: Law, Courts, and Politics in the United States*, 4th ed. (Boston, MA: Wadsworth, 2007), pp. 188–189.

35. Delbert A. Taebel, "On the Way to Midland: Race or Partisanship? A Research Note on Comparative Voting in Urban Counties in Judicial Elections," *Texas Journal of Political Studies* 12 (Fall/Winter 1989/90): 5–23.

36. Mark Smith, "Business Good for Visiting Judges," *Houston Chronicle*, September 20, 1998, p. 23A.

Chapter 11

City Government

WHAT WE WILL LEARN

After studying Chapter 11, students should be able to answer the following questions:

▸ What is the legal status of city governments in Texas?

▸ What are the different forms of city government in Texas?

▸ What election systems do Texas cities use?

▸ What are the most important policies adopted by Texas cities in terms of budgets, annexation, and land use?

▸ How has big-city politics in Texas evolved since the 1950s?

Electoral politics in big-city Texas involves coalition building. Houston, Dallas, San Antonio, El Paso, Austin, Fort Worth, and the state's other large cities are multiethnic and multiracial urban centers with numerous interests competing for political influence. Even though most city elections are officially nonpartisan, political parties often operate just behind the scenes. Consequently, candidates for office in big-city Texas have to assemble a diverse coalition of supporters to be successful.

Consider the dynamics of the 2009 mayoral campaign in Houston, the state's largest city. The race was wide open because Bill White, the incumbent mayor, was term limited. The leading contenders to succeed him were Annise Parker, the city controller (which is the city's financial auditor), and Gene Locke, a former city attorney. Parker was the better known of the two candidates. She had won six consecutive citywide elections, serving on the city council for six years before serving another six years as controller. She was also an experienced community activist, serving two terms as president of the Houston Gay and Lesbian Political Caucus, among other activities.[1] Gene Locke, meanwhile, could be described as a former African American student civil rights activist turned corporate lawyer. During the 1970s he was arrested along with another young man for allegedly inciting a riot at Texas Southern University. However, a jury failed to convict him and the charges were dismissed. He subsequently earned a law degree, worked as a congressional staffer, and served as city attorney for former mayor Bob Lanier. After leaving city government, Locke took a job as a partner in a prominent Houston law firm, representing Metro (the transit authority) and the Port of Houston Authority.[2]

The challenge for both Parker and Locke was to consolidate their bases of support and reach out to other segments of the community. White liberal Democrats were Parker's primary base, especially inner-city neighborhood activists, members of women's groups, people in the arts community, and the Houston Gay and Lesbian Political Caucus. Locke hoped to build a base among African American voters to augment his supporters in the business community who knew him from his work as city attorney and as a partner in a major law firm. The winner of the race would be the candidate most successful at gaining the support of voters that were not part of either candidate's base, especially Hispanic voters and white conservatives.

This chapter is the fourth of five chapters examining the policymaking institutions of state and local government. Chapters 8, 9, and 10 considered the legislative, executive, and judicial branches of state government, whereas Chapter 12 will focus on counties, school districts, and special districts. This chapter deals with the role of cities in the policymaking process. It examines the legal status of Texas cities and describes their political structures and election systems. The chapter discusses three areas of urban policymaking: budgetary policy, annexation and suburban development, and land use regulation. It concludes by examining big-city politics in Texas.

LEGAL STATUS OF TEXAS CITIES

City governments in Texas have broad authority to provide public services, enact regulations, and levy taxes. Texas cities may provide hospitals, libraries, parks, paved streets, police protection, airports, water and sewer service, health clinics, and fire

City ordinances
Laws enacted by the governing body of a municipality.

protection for their residents. They may adopt **city ordinances,** laws enacted by a municipality's governing body to regulate such matters as building construction, land use practices, and driving habits. Cities fund their operations by levying property taxes, sales taxes, and a variety of other taxes, fees, and service charges.

Nonetheless, cities and other units of local government are subordinate units of government, subject to the constitutions and laws of the United States and the state of Texas. Federal laws take precedence over city ordinances and regulations. Cities are dependent on state constitutions and state laws for their creation, organization, and authority. State law controls such matters as city tax rates and exemptions; wages, hours, benefits, and promotion policies for city employees; and annexation procedures.

The Texas legislature and the governor frequently adopt legislation designed to define and limit the policymaking authority of city government. For example, Texas is one of 40 states that prohibits cities from suing the firearms industry.[3] A number of cities in other states have sued gun manufacturers to hold them accountable for manufacturing guns with inadequate safety features that would prevent unauthorized and unintentional shootings, as well as for negligent distribution and marketing practices that contribute to the illegal gun market. The legislature and the governor have also adopted legislation prohibiting city governments from establishing their own **minimum wage,** which is the lowest hourly wage that an employer can pay covered workers.

Minimum wage
The lowest hourly wage that an employer can pay covered workers.

Interest groups, as well as individual citizens, who are unhappy with the decisions of a city government can ask the legislature to intervene. Moreover, the legislature and the governor have grown increasingly willing to override the policy decisions of city governments because of a shift in partisanship. Even though most city elections are officially nonpartisan (party labels are not on the ballot), most officials in the state's major cities are Democrats. For example, Parker and Locke, the two major candidates for Houston mayor in 2009, were both Democrats. In contrast, the Republican Party controls both chambers of the Texas legislature and the governorship. On issues that pit city governments against interests usually aligned with the Republican Party, such as suburban residents and developers, the legislature and the governor more often than not intervene against the city.

Incorporation

Incorporated municipality A city under the laws of the state.

Unincorporated area Territory not part of a legal city.

State law sets the requirements and procedures under which an unincorporated urban area in Texas can become an **incorporated municipality,** which is a city under the laws of the state. An **unincorporated area,** a territory which is not part of a legal city, must have a population of at least 200 people to form a municipality. It must also be outside the legal jurisdiction of other incorporated municipalities unless it receives permission to incorporate from the established city. The proponents of incorporation begin the process by collecting signatures on an incorporation petition. After they have gathered the required number of names, perhaps as many as 10 percent of the registered voters in the prospective municipality, they present their petition to the county judge. The judge then calls an election in which the area's voters may choose either to incorporate or remain unincorporated. The residents of an incorporated city can follow the same procedure if they wish to disincorporate.

City charter The basic law of a city that defines its powers, responsibilities, and organization.

The voters of a newly incorporated municipality must also approve a **city charter,** which is the basic law of a city that defines its powers, responsibilities, and organization. Changes in a city charter must receive voter approval as well.

General Law and Home Rule Cities

General law city A municipality that is limited to those governmental structures and powers specifically granted by state law.

Texas cities are classified as either general law or home rule cities. A **general law city** is a municipality that is limited to those governmental structures and powers specifically granted by state law. Municipalities with fewer than 5,000 people must be general law cities.

Dillon's rule The legal principle that a city can exercise only those powers expressly allowed by state law.

General law cities are bound by **Dillon's rule,** the legal principle that states a city can exercise only those powers expressly allowed by state law. Dillon's rule is named after Judge J. F. Dillon, a member of the Iowa Supreme Court, who wrote an opinion in 1868 concerning the legal status of cities. Dillon concluded that municipalities owe their origins to, and derive their power from, the state legislature. Therefore, they are totally dependent on, and subservient to, the legislature. Courts in Texas and in other states have followed Dillon's rule in defining the authority of general law cities. If a general law city wants to offer a service or adopt a structure of government not provided in state law, it must first obtain specific authorization from the legislature.

Home rule city A municipality that can take any actions not prohibited by state or federal law or the constitutions of the United States or the state of Texas.

In 1913, the Texas legislature proposed, and the voters approved, an amendment to the state constitution to allow a municipality with 5,000 or more people to become a **home rule city,** which is a municipality that can take any actions not prohibited by state or federal law or the constitutions of the United States or the state of Texas. In contrast to general law cities, home rule cities are not burdened by the limitations of Dillon's rule. A home rule city can do anything that qualifies as a "public purpose" that does not violate the Texas Constitution or the laws of the state. Compared with general law cities, home rule cities enjoy more freedom in the following areas:

- **Organizational structure:** Home rule cities can adopt any structure of municipal government they choose, whereas general law cities are limited to a narrow range of options.

Annexation The authority of a city to increase its geographic size by extending its boundaries to take in adjacent unincorporated areas.

- **Annexation:** Home rule cities can annex without the approval of the people living in the annexed area. General law cities, in contrast, cannot annex unless the residents of the targeted area vote to accept annexation. (**Annexation** is the authority of a city to increase its geographic size by extending its boundaries to take in adjacent unincorporated areas.)

- **Ordinance-making authority:** Home rule cities have broader authority to adopt ordinances than do general law municipalities.

Recall A procedure allowing voters to remove elected officials from office before the expiration of their terms.

- **Election processes:** Home rule cities may include both recall and the initiative process in their charters. More than 90 percent of home rule cities allow citizens the power of **recall,** which is a procedure for allowing voters to remove elected officials from office before the expiration of their terms. In addition, 85 percent of home rule cities have the **initiative process,** a procedure available

Initiative process
A procedure whereby citizens can propose the adoption of a policy measure by gathering a prerequisite number of signatures. Voters must then approve the measure before it can take effect.

Population bracket laws
State laws designed to target particular cities based on their population.

in some states and cities whereby citizens can propose the adoption of a policy measure by gathering a prerequisite number of signatures. Voters must then approve the measure before it can take effect.[4]

More than 340 Texas cities are home rule, including all of the state's big cities. Only 19 cities larger than 5,000 people have chosen to remain general law cities. Even if a home rule city falls below the 5,000-population threshold, it maintains its home rule status.[5]

The legislature has the power to pass laws limiting home rule authority. For example, the legislature has established uniform election dates, limiting most local elections to either the second Saturday in May or the Tuesday after the first Monday in November. Although the Texas Constitution prevents the legislature from passing local laws regulating the affairs of individual cities, the legislature gets around the restriction by enacting **population bracket laws,** state laws designed to target particular cities based on their population. Houston and Austin are the most frequent targets of population bracket legislation. For example, the legislature could pass a measure that applies to all Texas cities with a population larger than 1.9 million. It so happens that only one city meets that criterion—Houston. If the legislature wanted to target Austin, it could adopt a bill aimed at cities with populations between 650,000 and 660,000 in 2000. That description applies only to Austin.

FORMS OF CITY GOVERNMENT

The mayor–council and council–manager forms of city government are the basic structures of municipal government in Texas.

Mayor–Council Form

Mayor–council form of city government
A structure of municipal government in which the voters elect a mayor as the chief executive officer of the city and a council that serves as a legislative body.

The **mayor–council form of city government** is a structure of municipal government in which the voters elect a mayor as the chief executive officer of the city and a council that serves as a legislative body. In the mayor–council form of city government, the mayor and council together make policy for the city. They are responsible for raising and spending city revenue, passing local ordinances, and supervising the city's administrative departments.

Being mayor or serving on city council is a full-time job in big cities using the mayor–council form of government, but not in small towns. In Houston, for example, the mayor runs the city government full-time and earns a salary of $187,500 a year. Although most members of the Houston city council have other jobs, they, too, spend many hours a week on city business, making $50,000 a year. In contrast, mayors and council members in small towns using the mayor–council form of city government usually earn only a small salary for a job that normally takes just a few hours a week.

Cities using the mayor–council form of city government differ in the amount of power the mayor enjoys. Figures 11.1 and 11.2 diagram the strong mayor and weak mayor variations of the mayor–council form of city government. In the strong mayor variation (Figure 11.1), the mayor is the foremost figure in city

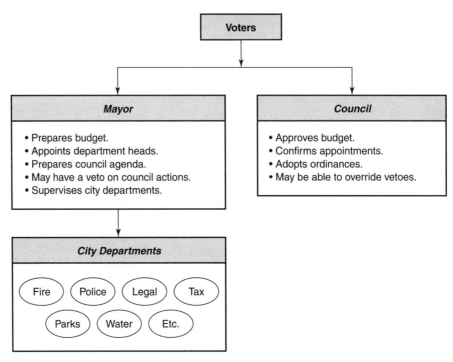

FIGURE 11.1   Strong Mayor–Council Form of City Government.

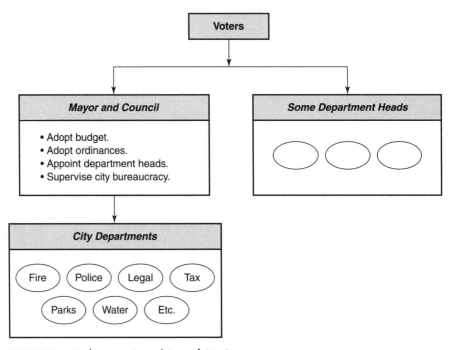

FIGURE 11.2   Weak Mayor–Council Form of City Government.

government, acting as both a political leader and the city's chief administrative officer. The mayor prepares the budget, enjoys a veto over council actions (with or without possibility of a council override), hires and fires department heads, and essentially runs city government. Although the city council must approve (and thus may reject) many of the mayor's actions, politically skillful mayors can usually win approval of most of their initiatives and appointments. Council members elected from districts will want to stay in the mayor's favor because the mayor oversees the provision of public services to their districts. Furthermore, the mayor and the mayor's financial backers may get involved in council races to elect individuals to council who will be part of the "mayor's team" and to defeat the mayor's opponents on council. Bob Lanier, who was mayor of Houston in the 1990s, lost only three council votes during his six years in office.[6] Former Houston City Council Member Vince Ryan described the strong mayor system in Houston as "King Kong and the 14 chimps" because of the relative imbalance of power between the mayor and the 14 council members.[7]

The advocates of the strong mayor variation of the mayor–council form of city government believe that the system provides for efficient city government because it concentrates power and responsibility for policy leadership and policy implementation in the hands of a single elected official, the mayor. The mayor can take the lead in agenda setting, policy formulation, policy adoption, and policy implementation. The voters can then evaluate the mayor on performance. In contrast, the critics of the mayor–council form of city government contend that the strong mayor variation gives the mayor too much power. They worry that the mayor will build a personal empire and become a political boss. Although the voters elect council members to represent neighborhoods and communities, they have relatively little influence on major policy decisions in the strong mayor variation. Instead, council members focus on the most mundane details of urban policy implementation, such as abandoned houses, overgrown vacant lots, potholes, and stray dogs.[8]

In contrast to the strong mayor system, the weak mayor variation of the mayor–council form of city government (Figure 11.2) fragments political authority by forcing the mayor to share power with the council and other elected officials. These officials may include a tax assessor, treasurer, and even a police chief. The mayor and council together appoint administrative officials, supervise city administration, and adopt the budget. The proponents of the weak mayor system contend that it prevents the mayor from becoming too powerful by creating a check-and-balance system. Critics of the weak mayor variation say that it invites corruption and dilutes accountability because it fails to assign policymaking authority to any single official.

The mayor–council system is the traditional form of city government in America, and it is still found in most of the nation's larger cities.[9] In Texas, however, Houston is the only large city to use the mayor–council system. The state's other big cities—including Dallas, San Antonio, Fort Worth, Austin, Corpus Christi, and El Paso—have adopted the council–manager form instead.[10]

Council–Manager Form

The **council–manager form of city government** is a structure of municipal government in which the city council/mayor appoints a professional administrator, called a city manager, to act as the municipality's chief executive officer. In this form of city government, the mayor's power is limited to performing ceremonial duties and presiding at council meetings. In fact, in some smaller council–manager cities, voters do not directly choose a mayor at all. Instead, the office may go to the at-large council member receiving the most votes. Alternatively, the council may choose one of its members to serve as mayor. In such cases, the mayor's ability to act as a policy leader depends on personal leadership skills rather than official powers.

The major difference between the mayor–council and council–manager forms of city government concerns the implementation of policy. In both systems, the mayor and council make basic policy decisions. However, in the council–manager form, policy implementation is the responsibility of a professional administrator hired by the city council—a **city manager.** Figure 11.3 diagrams this form of city government. The city manager is the city's chief administrative officer and is generally

FIGURE 11.3   Council–Manager Form of City Government.

responsible for hiring and firing department heads, preparing the budget, and overseeing policy implementation. In council–manager cities, the mayor and council members are usually considered part-time officials and are paid accordingly. In Fort Worth, for example, the mayor and council members each receive $75 for every week they attend one or more official meetings. In contrast, the Fort Worth city manager earns $186,513 a year.[11]

The council–manager form of city government has both supporters and detractors. Its advocates believe that it is an efficient system that keeps politics out of administration and administrators out of politics. They argue that a professional city manager can provide more efficient policy administration than a mayor with no administrative experience. Nonetheless, most political scientists believe that city managers inevitably become involved in politics, even in the sense of participating extensively in policy formulation and adoption. Furthermore, policy implementation is inherently political because it determines how the power of government is exercised. City managers act politically when they make recommendations to elected officials and seek to develop support for their positions among public officials and interest groups influential in city politics.

 WHAT IS YOUR OPINION?

Would you rather be the mayor of a big city or its city manager? Why?

Critics of the council–manager form of city government argue that it may work fine for mid-size, uncomplicated cities but not for larger cities. They believe that big cities with diverse populations need the policy leadership of a strong mayor. The city manager system is designed to ensure the efficient implementation of policy. What happens, they ask, when city residents and the city council are deeply divided over policy alternatives? Neither the city manager nor the mayor in the council–manager form of government has the political strength to forge a consensus among competing political forces. Critics of city government in Dallas, for example, charge that the city suffers from a council that is divided along ethnic, ideological, and geographic lines and that the mayor has too little power to provide leadership. Nonetheless, Dallas voters turned down a proposal to scrap the council–manager system and replace it with the mayor–council form of city government. The mayor argued that the reform would provide for a more efficient city government, but council members countered that it would give the mayor too much power without checks and balances.

Hybrid Structures

In practice, the structures of city government seldom match the classic mayor–council or council–manager form of municipal government. Many mayor–council cities have added chief administrative officers or deputy mayors who function much as city managers do. Furthermore, many council–manager cities have increased the mayor's power to provide greater accountability.[12]

What are the issues on the agenda of big-city governments in Texas today? The homepages of the state's largest cities can be found at the following Internet addresses:

Austin: **www.ci.austin.tx.us/**

Dallas: **www.dallascityhall.com**

El Paso: **www.ci.el-paso.tx.us/**

Fort Worth: **www.fortworthgov.org/**

Houston: **www.houstontx.gov/**

San Antonio: **www.ci.sat.tx.us/**

Identify the city nearest you, study its website, and answer the following questions:

1. What form of government does the city have?

2. Who is the mayor of the city?

3. How many members does the city council have? Are they elected from districts or at-large?

4. What is the city's property tax rate?

5. What would be the annual tax bill for a piece of business property valued at $500,000?

ELECTION SYSTEMS

At-large election
A method for choosing public officials in which every citizen of a political subdivision, such as a state or county, votes to select a public official.

The most popular system for choosing council members in Texas is the **at-large election** system, a method for choosing public officials in which every citizen of a political subdivision, such as a state or county, votes to select a public official. As Table 11.1 indicates, 131 cities use a place system. Candidates must declare for particular seats (or places) on council and voters then select among the candidates for each council seat. Thirty-six cities elect council members at-large without the use of a place system. On Election Day, voters select as many candidates as seats on council. If the city has five council members, for example, a voter chooses five candidates from among the list of people running for council.

District election
A method for choosing public officials in which a political subdivision, such as a state or county, is divided into districts and each district elects one official.

In contrast to the at-large election method, a **district election** is another method for choosing public officials in which a political subdivision, such as a state or city, is divided into districts, with each district electing one official. Currently 74 Texas cities use district election systems. El Paso, for example, elects eight council members from districts.

Not all Texas cities use either at-large or district election systems, however. Forty-eight cities have a combination of at-large and district seats. The Houston city council, for example, has 14 members—nine members chosen from districts and five elected at large. Finally, one Texas home rule city has

TABLE 11.1   Methods of Council Election in Texas Home Rule Cities

Method of Election	No. of Cities Using System
At-large election by place	131
At-large election	36
District election	74
Combination of district and at-large seats	48
Cumulative voting	1
Total	**290**

Source: Terrell Blodget, "Municipal Home Rule Charters in Texas," *Public Affairs Comment* 41 (1996): 4.

Cumulative voting system An election system that allows individual voters to cast more than one ballot in the simultaneous election of several officials.

Political machines Entrenched political organizations headed by a boss or small group of leaders who held power through such techniques as patronage, control over nominations, and bribery.

Political patronage The power of an officeholder to award favors, such as government jobs, to political allies.

Nonpartisan elections Election contests in which the names of the candidates appear on the ballot but not their party affiliations.

a **cumulative voting system,** an election system that allows individual voters to cast more than one ballot in the simultaneous election of several officials. The difference between at-large and cumulative voting is that the cumulative system allows voters to cast all of their votes for a single candidate.

Both district and at-large election systems have their proponents. Supporters of district elections believe that they make government more responsive to citizens and increase participation. District elections reduce the role of money in city politics, they say, because candidates need less money to campaign in a district than they would to run a campaign citywide. Furthermore, the advocates of district elections argue that they produce a council that more closely reflects the city's racial and ethnic diversity because they enable geographically concentrated minorities to elect group members to public office.

In contrast, defenders of at-large elections believe that council members chosen at-large consider policy issues from a broader perspective than do district council members. Whereas district representatives focus on the particular concerns of their districts, at-large council members must consider what is best for the city as a whole. Furthermore, the supporters of at-large elections believe that citywide campaigns produce better quality officials than do district elections.

Historically, district (or ward) election systems were associated with big-city **political machines,** which were entrenched political organizations headed by a boss or small group of leaders who held power through patronage, control over nominations, and bribery. **Political patronage** is the power of an officeholder to award favors, such as government jobs, to political allies. In the late nineteenth century, machine politicians in New York City, St. Louis, Cleveland, Chicago, and other big cities won election from districts with the support of geographically concentrated white ethnic minorities, especially Italian, Irish, and Polish Americans.

Well-to-do white Anglo-Saxon business groups who opposed the political machines attacked district elections as corrupt, proposing instead the adoption of nonpartisan at-large council election systems. **Nonpartisan elections** are elections in which candidates run without party labels. Although the business leaders packaged their proposal as a good government reform, it was actually designed to favor the interests of affluent business groups who would have more money to fund candidates for citywide seats than would the working-class ethnic minority groups who supported the political machine.

Although most large industrialized cities, including Chicago, St. Louis, and Cleveland, did not adopt nonpartisan at-large election systems, many of the new cities in the South and West did, including most cities in Texas. Dallas, for example, created a nine-member city council with each member elected at-large. Houston's eight-member council was chosen at-large as well.

The adoption of at-large council elections in Texas cities limited the political influence of ethnic and racial minorities, primarily African Americans and Latinos. Under the at-large council system in Dallas, no African Americans and only one Latino won election to council, and the successful Hispanic candidate was a North Dallas businessman who was endorsed and financed by wealthy white business groups.[13] Similarly, the only minority candidate elected to the Houston city council under that city's at-large election system was an African American real estate investor who had the support of downtown business interests.

Voting Rights Act (VRA) A federal law designed to protect the voting rights of racial and ethnic minorities.

The **Voting Rights Act (VRA),** a federal law designed to protect the voting rights of racial and ethnic minorities, provides a means that minority rights groups can use to attack election systems they consider discriminatory. The act allows voters to file lawsuits in federal court challenging local election laws and procedures they believe discriminate against minority voters.[14] In 2007, for example, Manuel Benavidez, a longtime resident of Irving, filed suit against the city under the VRA, arguing that Irving's at-large election system prevented Latino residents from winning seats on city council. Even though 40 percent of the population of Irving was Latino, the eight-member city council was all white. Two years later, a federal judge ruled in favor of Benavidez and ordered the city to change its election system. The city responded by creating a mixed election system with six district and two at-large council seats. The majority population of one of the districts was Latino.[15]

In the late 1970s and early 1980s, minority rights groups used the VRA to force Dallas, Houston, San Antonio, El Paso, Fort Worth, and other cities in the state to abandon at-large election systems. Some cities, such as San Antonio, El Paso, and Fort Worth, began electing all council members from districts; other cities adopted mixed systems that combined district seats with at-large positions. Dallas adopted a system with eight district seats and two at-large positions, with the mayor elected at-large. In 1991, Dallas settled a VRA lawsuit by changing its city election to provide for a 14-member council, all chosen from districts. Only the mayor was elected at-large.[16]

The introduction of district election systems led to the selection of city councils in most of the state's big cities that were more ethnically and racially diverse than ever before. In the first election after the implementation of single-member districts, Houston voters chose three African Americans and one Latino to serve on council. In San Antonio, Latinos and African Americans together won a majority on that city's ten-member council. A study of ten Texas cities found that the change from

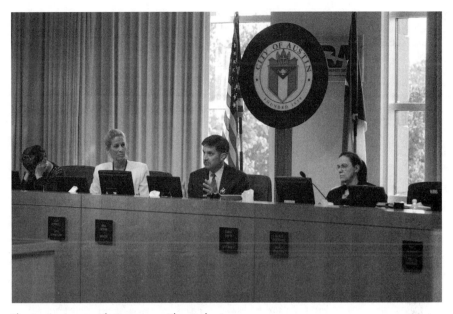

The Austin city council meets to consider city business.

at-large to district election systems led to increases in the number of Latino council candidates, Latinos elected to office, and Latino council members living in predominantly Latino neighborhoods.[17]

 WHAT IS YOUR OPINION?

What sort of city election system is the best—district, at-large, or a mixed system?

PUBLIC POLICIES IN TEXAS CITIES

Developmental urban policies
Local programs that enhance the economic position of a community in its competition with other communities.

Political scientist Paul E. Peterson divides urban public policies into three categories: developmental, redistributive, and allocational. **Developmental urban policies** are local programs that enhance a community's economic position in its competition with other communities. They strengthen the local economy, expand the tax base, and generate additional tax revenues for the city. New sports stadiums, highway expansion, and civic centers are examples of projects that would be part of a developmental urban policy because they could be justified as an investment in the community's economic vitality.

Redistributive urban policies are local programs that benefit low-income residents of an area. These include such programs as the provision of low-income

Redistributive urban policies
Local programs that benefit low-income residents of an area.

Allocational urban policies
Local programs that are more or less neutral in their impact on the local economy.

housing and food assistance to poor families. Although redistributive programs may be desirable from a humanitarian point of view, Peterson says that they retard economic development. Consider the provision of city health clinics for low-income families. City-funded health clinics may discourage businesses and middle-income taxpayers from relocating to the city because they will have to pay more in taxes for this service than they will receive in benefits. Health clinics may encourage the migration of low-income families to the city to take advantage of the service, especially if neighboring ("competing") cities choose not to provide their residents health clinics, instead keeping their tax rates low.

Allocational urban policies are local programs that are more or less neutral in their impact on the local economy. The best examples of allocational policies are urban housekeeping programs such as police and fire protection, garbage pickup, and routine street maintenance. Allocational programs are neither developmental nor redistributive in nature because all members of the community benefit from them without regard for economic status.[18]

Economic factors influence the adoption of urban public policies. Cities concentrate on developmental and allocational programs in order to enhance their tax bases and protect the local economy. Research shows that levels of municipal services and tax rates tend to be lower in cities bordered by other municipalities than they are in cities that are relatively isolated. The study concludes that city officials are forced to keep taxes down and, of course, services low because businesses and middle-income taxpayers have the option of moving to a neighboring municipality with lower tax rates.[19]

City governments frequently adopt developmental policies that entail building entertainment centers, such as sports stadiums and convention centers designed to attract visitors from out of town and the suburbs. Houston, Dallas, San Antonio, and Arlington have all used tax money to build new sports arenas to keep or attract professional sports teams. Although city officials promise that expensive new sports and entertainment facilities generate tax revenue and increase employment, research indicates that projects do not pay for themselves. Economists note that most people have fixed entertainment budgets. People who spend money at new sports stadiums would have spent the money on entertainment elsewhere in the city if the stadium had not been built. Furthermore, new stadiums do little to revitalize neighborhoods. Although new stadiums may be symbols of mayoral leadership, they seldom contribute to economic development.[20]

Political factors also play an important role in urban policymaking. Developmental and allocational policies are often characterized by conflict as political forces compete over policy alternatives. In Houston, for example, two sets of business groups opposed one another over the location of a new convention center, whether it would be built east or west of the downtown business district. Similarly, neighborhoods fought over the timing of the construction of new decentralized police command stations, with each region of town wanting its command station built first.

City officials must balance economic concerns with political demands. Groups representing the interests of disadvantaged constituents in the state's big cities call for the adoption of redistributive programs. They demand home rehabilitation loans, low-interest mortgage loans, small business loans, technical assistance to new businesses, public housing, affirmative action, public transportation in low-income areas, and hiring goals for women and minorities. Research shows that cities become more responsive to the concerns of minority residents as minorities increase their elected representation in city government. One study finds that, after city councils experience an increase in minority representation, city governments hire more minorities, award more contracts to minority-owned businesses, and enact programs favored by minority groups.[21]

Budgetary Policy

The state's largest cities are big enterprises with annual budgets greater than a billion dollars. In fiscal (budget) year 2009, for example, the general fund budget for Houston was $2.1 billion.[22] The state's largest cities offer their residents a broad range of services, including police protection, street repair, garbage pickup, libraries, recreational facilities, health clinics, fire protection, emergency medical services (EMS), water and sewer service, airports, sidewalks, and street lighting. In contrast, small towns may provide only a limited number of basic services. Public safety—police, fire, and municipal courts—is typically the largest item in all city budgets because it is labor intensive.

AROUND THE NATION

Healthcare in San Francisco

The city of San Francisco has a healthcare program designed to provide basic medical services to every city resident without regard for income. The program, which is known as Healthy San Francisco, offers participants comprehensive primary care at any of the city's public and private clinics and hospitals, including lab work, prescription medication, X-rays, hospitalization, and surgeries. The enrollment fee ranges from $3 to $201 a month, depending on an individual's income. People earning less than 300 percent of the poverty level have their enrollment subsidized. The $200 million annual cost of the program is covered by savings in city funds that are no longer needed to provide emergency room care for the uninsured, enrollment fees, and mandatory contributions from city businesses. All businesses with 20 or more employees are required to contribute to the program if they do not provide healthcare coverage for their employees.*

Healthy San Francisco has been at least reasonably successful. It has covered 45,000 of the estimated 60,000 uninsured adults living in the city. Furthermore, fears that it would hurt the city's economy have not been fulfilled because employment growth in San Francisco has not lagged behind employment growth in surrounding communities not covered by the program.†

QUESTIONS TO CONSIDER

1. Is Healthy San Francisco a good idea? Why or why not?
2. Is this an example of a redistributive, developmental, or allocational urban program?
3. Would you expect a city in Texas to adopt something similar anytime soon? Why or why not?

* Laura A. Locke, "San Francisco's Latest Innovation: Universal Healthcare," *Time*, January 23, 2006, available at www.time.com.

† Health Access Blog, August 24, 2009, available at http://blog.health-access.org/.

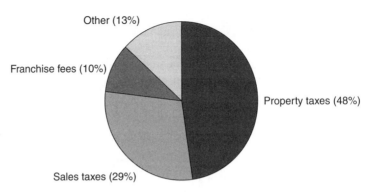

FIGURE 11.4   General Fund Revenues, Houston 2009.

Texas cities generate revenue from property taxes, sales taxes, franchise fees, and other sources. Figure 11.4 shows the relative importance of the various revenue sources for Houston in 2009. As the figure shows, property and sales taxes combined accounted for 77 percent of city revenue. Franchise fees represented 10 percent of revenues, with a variety of other sources supplying the remaining 13 percent.

**Property tax,
or *ad valorem*
property tax** A tax
levied on the value of
real property, such as
land and buildings.

The **property tax,** also known as the ***ad valorem* property tax,** is a levy assessed on real property, such as houses, land, business inventory, and industrial plants. State law sets a maximum property tax rate of $1.50 per $100 of valuation for general law cities and $2.50 per $100 for home rule cities. In practice, the property tax rates in most cities are well below the maximum. In 2009, the property tax rate for Dallas was $0.7479. It was $0.63875 for Houston, $0.56714 for San Antonio, $0.855 for Fort Worth, and $0.4012 for Austin.[23]

City governments may grant property tax breaks, called exemptions, to certain categories of taxpayers, such as homeowners, elderly residents, and veterans with disabilities. Fort Worth, for example, grants exemptions for homeowners, senior citizens, disabled persons, property that is a historic site, and transitional housing for indigent persons. The most common exemption is the **homestead exemption,** which is a property tax reduction granted to homeowners on their principal residence. State law stipulates that property tax exemptions must be at least $5,000 but not more than 20 percent of the property value (unless that figure is less than $5,000).

**Homestead
exemption** A
property tax reduction
granted homeowners
on their principal
residence.

Figuring a property tax bill is relatively easy. Assume, for example, that a home is assessed at $150,000, the city tax rate is $0.60 per $100 valuation, and the city grants a 20 percent homestead exemption. The homeowner's annual property tax bill to the city would be figured as follows:

$150,000	Assessed value
−$30,000	Homestead exemption (20 percent of $150,000)
$120,000	Taxable value
× 0.60 per $100	Municipal tax rate
$720	Municipal tax due

A property owner's tax bill depends on both the tax rate and the valuation of the property. Property taxes go up (and down) when the local government raises (or lowers) tax rates. Taxes also change when property values change. Texas is not one of the 22 states that have **truth in taxation laws,** which are laws that block local governments from raising the total amount of property taxes they collect from one year to the next when assessed values go up. When property values increase in these states, local officials have to vote to increase their total tax revenues and advertise their action in the newspaper. Otherwise, the tax rate falls automatically to compensate for rising property values.[24] In contrast, local governments in Texas benefit from rising property values without elected officials having to go on record in favor of raising additional revenue.

The sales tax is the other major tax source for municipal government in Texas. A **sales tax** is a levy on the retail sale of taxable items. State law allows cities to piggyback an extra 1 percent onto the state's general sales tax rate of 6.25 percent. All of the state's larger cities and many smaller towns take advantage of the sales tax option. Cities without transit authorities may seek voter approval to levy a ½ percent additional sales tax to reduce city or county property taxes or help fund law enforcement. Cities of 56,000 or more population that do not want to swap property taxes for sales taxes can ask voter approval for a ¼ percent sales tax to use for mass transit.

In addition to property and sales taxes, city governments in Texas raise revenue from franchise fees, licenses, permits, fines, and various other sources. Telephone, gas, cable TV, and electric utility companies pay annual franchise fees to city governments for the right to use public rights of way to string wires or lay cable. Cities generate revenue from service charges, such as fees for water and sewer service. Fines for traffic infractions and violations of city ordinances provide cities with revenues as well. Cities raise money from hotel and motel occupancy taxes, rental car taxes, and burglar and fire alarm fees. Federal grant programs offer assistance to municipalities to build sewage treatment plants, acquire parkland, construct airports, treat drug addiction, rehabilitate economically depressed neighborhoods, and provide housing to low-income families.

City governments borrow money by issuing bonds to cover the cost of capital expenditures, such as the construction of buildings, airports, roads, and utility plants. A **bond** is a certificate of indebtedness. A **capital expenditure** is the purchase by government of a permanent, fixed asset, such as a new city hall or highway overpass. City governments levy property taxes to pay back the money they borrow plus interest. In 2008, for example, the property tax rate for the city of Austin was $0.2749 for general purposes and $0.1263 for debt service.[25]

Budgetary policies in urban Texas have historically been allocational and developmental. Police and fire protection, sanitation, and street maintenance—the largest expenditure items for municipal government in the state—are allocational programs. Other allocational expenditures include money for libraries, parkland acquisition, and traffic management. In the meantime, capital expenditures for street construction, sewer trunk line replacement, and new police and fire stations are developmental because they provide infrastructure improvements essential to economic growth.

Truth in taxation laws Laws that block local governments from raising the total amount of property taxes they collect from one year to the next when assessed values go up.

Sales tax A levy on the retail sale of taxable items.

Bond A certificate of indebtedness issued to investors who loan money for interest income; in lay terms, a bond is an IOU.

Capital expenditure The purchase by government of a permanent, fixed asset, such as a new city hall or highway overpass.

Tax increment financing
A program in which a local government promises to earmark increased property tax revenues generated by development in a designated area called a tax increment financing district to fund improvements in the area, such as roads, parks, sidewalks, and street lighting.

Tax abatement
A program that exempts property owners from local property taxes on new construction and improvements in a designated tax abatement district for a set period of time.

Enterprise zones
A state program that allows local governments to designate certain areas called enterprise zones in which private investors can receive property tax abatements, local sales tax rebates (refunds), and government-backed low-interest loans.

City governments use tax incentives to promote economic growth, including tax increment financing, tax abatements, and enterprise zones. **Tax increment financing** is a program in which a local government promises to earmark increased property tax revenues generated by development in a designated area called a tax increment reinvestment zone (TIRZ) to fund improvements in the area, such as roads, parks, sidewalks, and street lighting. A city hopes to encourage private investment by promising that any additional tax revenues generated from higher property values resulting from private development in the district will be spent by the city in the area under development. **Tax abatement** is a program that exempts property owners from local property taxes on new construction and improvements in a designated tax abatement district for a set period of time. San Antonio, for example, granted the Sino Swearingen Aircraft Corporation a series of tax abatements to lure the company into agreeing to manufacture a new business jet in San Antonio, a decision that would bring 850 new jobs to the city.[26] **Enterprise zones** are part of a state program that allows local governments to designate certain areas called enterprise zones in which private investors can receive property tax abatements, local sales tax rebates (refunds), and government-backed low-interest loans.

Local officials argue that tax incentives are an important economic development tool. They believe that tax breaks may make the difference between a company deciding to build a plant in Texas or locating it in another state. When businesses establish new facilities in the state, they create jobs that fuel economic growth because their employees purchase goods and services from established businesses. Local governments benefit as well because the increased economic activity generates added tax revenues, which may be sufficient to make up for the revenues lost by the tax incentives.

 WHAT IS YOUR OPINION?

Should city governments use tax incentives to promote economic development?

The critics of tax incentives charge that they are unnecessary and unfair. Tax breaks are unnecessary, they say, because business managers seldom, if ever, base their relocation decisions on taxes. Businesses decide to expand or relocate based primarily on such factors as transportation and the availability of an educated workforce. Critics charge that tax breaks for new firms are unfair because they shift the cost of government to other taxpayers, including homeowners and established businesses. Business people, in particular, strongly oppose the use of tax incentives to attract potential competitors.

Consider the controversy over the decision made by city leaders in Houston to provide millions of dollars in tax breaks to the Embassy Suites hotel chain. The city agreed to rebate up to $1.4 million a year in hotel occupancy taxes for seven years if Embassy Suites built a hotel near the George R. Brown Convention Center and set aside most of the rooms for convention business. The goal of city government was to attract more convention business to Houston, but critics questioned the need for the tax rebate. If building another hotel downtown made business sense, they asked, then why did the city have to provide a big tax break that competitor hotels did not receive?[27]

Furthermore, research shows that the developmental policies of city government have little, if any, impact on the location decisions of investors and business managers. One study of the factors influencing the location of manufacturing plants in Texas found that local taxes had little effect on plant location decisions. The research discovered that the availability of skilled labor and the presence of strong colleges and universities were important to **high-technology industries,** those industries based on the latest in modern technology. Some of the other factors important to economic development were the presence of port facilities and the concentration in the area of firms in a similar line of work.[28] Some scholars believe that local officials grant tax incentives because of the political pressure to create jobs. Tax incentive programs give the *appearance* that local officials are doing something to help the economy, even if they have little real impact on economic development. Businesses that accept economic development money typically exaggerate the number of jobs they plan to create and actually expand more slowly than companies that do not accept government subsidies.[29]

> **High-technology industries** Industries that are based on the latest in modern technology.

Annexation and Suburban Development

Traditionally, cities annex to protect their tax bases. Big cities across America have been caught in a financial squeeze as revenues have fallen while demand for services has risen. For decades, the tax bases of the nation's largest cities have declined. Middle-class taxpayers and business establishments have moved to the suburbs in search of safer streets, better schools, and more desirable housing. In contrast, poor people, seriously ill persons who do not have health insurance, and people without places to live have moved into the city to take advantage of health clinics, shelters, and other social services not available in the suburbs. Texas cities have used their power to annex to maintain their tax bases and financial health. The Texas Municipal League, a nonprofit organization that represents Texas cities, calculates that if San Antonio did not have the ability to annex adjacent suburban development—that is, if it still had the same boundaries that it had in 1945—then it would have more poverty and unemployment than Newark, New Jersey.[30]

Another reason for annexation is the desire of city officials to prevent encirclement by other incorporated municipalities. Because state law prohibits cities from annexing other cities without their consent, a big city surrounded by smaller incorporated municipalities cannot grow. Many cities located in the Northeast and Midwest find themselves in just such a position. Dallas allowed itself to become ringed by small towns during the early years of its development. In 1976, Dallas broke out of its encirclement by convincing the town of Renner to agree to become part of Dallas. Since the Renner annexation, Dallas has pushed its city limits to the north into Collin and Denton Counties. Other Texas cities have avoided a similar predicament by annexing adjacent unincorporated areas before they could incorporate and by annexing the land around neighboring small towns to prevent their expansion. In Harris County, for example, the municipalities of Bellaire and West University Place are completely surrounded by Houston.

Finally, cities annex in order to reap the political benefits of a larger population. Federal grant money is often awarded on the basis of formulas that include population. The more people living within a city, the more federal grant money it receives. Because legislative districts are drawn on the basis of population size, increased population also leads to additional representation in Congress and the Texas legislature.

State law permits a city to increase its total land area by as much as 10 percent in any one year. A city that does not annex its full allotment in a year may carry the remaining amount forward to be used in later years, as long as the city does not increase its geographic size by more than 30 percent in any one year. A city of 100 square miles, for example, could add another 10 square miles to its land area this year. Because state law allows municipalities to carry forward unused annexation authority, the city of 100 square miles could wait a few years and then annex up to 30 square miles.

A city government typically annexes an entire **utility district,** which is a special district that provides utilities, such as water and sewer service, to residents living in

Utility district
A special district that provides utilities such as water and sewer service to residents living in unincorporated urban areas.

Most city governments provide garbage collection services for their residents.

unincorporated urban areas. When a city annexes a subdivision, it annexes the utility district that services the subdivision, rather than the development itself. The annexing city takes over the operation of the utility district, similar to a large corporation taking over a small business. The city takes possession of the utility district's physical assets, such as its water and sewer facilities, and assumes its financial assets and liabilities. The city brings police, fire, solid waste, and emergency medical services (EMS) to the area while contracting with a private company to operate the old utility district's water and sewer system.

Historically, Texas cities have annexed aggressively. Between 1950 and 1980, Houston added more than 370 square miles, Dallas more than 230, San Antonio nearly 200, El Paso over 200, Fort Worth nearly 150, Corpus Christi more than 150, and Austin more than 80. During the 1970s alone, Texas cities annexed 1,472 square miles containing 456,000 people. That is an area bigger than Rhode Island and a population almost as large as Wyoming.[31]

Since the early 1980s, the pace of annexation by Texas cities has slowed. The annexations of the 1970s produced a political backlash from newly annexed residents who were determined to do their best to vote incumbent mayors and council members out of office. Subsequently, local officeholders grew cautious about adding more angry constituents to their cities. Furthermore, the Texas legislature and the governor have responded to complaints from people living in unincorporated areas near major cities by adopting legislation forcing cities to better accommodate the interests of suburban residents living in unincorporated areas.

In 1999, the legislature passed, and the governor signed, a measure overhauling annexation policy to require that cities adopt an annexation plan that specifically identifies the areas to be annexed and details how the city will provide those areas with services. The county government may appoint a panel of citizens to negotiate with the city on behalf of area residents. The city cannot complete the actual annexation until the third anniversary of the adoption of the annexation plan, and then it must act within 31 days or lose the opportunity to annex the identified areas for five years. The city must provide police, fire, EMS, solid waste, street repair, water and sewer, and park maintenance services immediately. It has two and a half years to provide full services comparable to those offered to other city residents. If a majority of residents in the newly annexed area believe that the city has failed to provide them with full services, they may petition the city to be disannexed. If the city fails to act, residents may file suit in district court to ask a judge to order disannexation.

 WHAT IS YOUR OPINION?

Do you favor changing state law to require that the people in an area to be annexed must approve before the annexation can take place?

The legislation also gave cities and utility districts the authority to negotiate Strategic Partnership Agreements (SPAs) to provide for limited-purpose annexation. In this case, the utility district gives the city permission to collect sales taxes—but not property taxes—at retail businesses within the district. In exchange, the city provides the district with some city services, such as police and fire service, and a portion of the sales tax revenue collected within its borders. The city also pledges to postpone annexing the district during the period of the partnership.[32] Both units of government benefit from the additional tax revenues, whereas utility district residents avoid annexation, at least in the short run. Houston has moved more aggressively than other cities in the state to negotiate partnership agreements with surrounding utility districts, signing more than 100 agreements. In fact, SPAs have become so popular that some utility districts have approached the city about establishing partnerships in order to share in the sales tax revenue and stave off the possibility of annexation.[33] For example, Houston and The Woodlands signed an agreement in 2007 that would enable the suburban community to eventually incorporate in exchange for a share of local sales tax revenues that would be deposited in a special fund to be used for regional development.[34]

Extraterritorial jurisdiction (ETJ)
The authority of a city to require conformity with city ordinances and regulations affecting streets, parks, alleys, utility easements, sanitary sewers, and the like in a ring of land extending from one half to five miles beyond the city-limits line.

In addition to reforming annexation procedures, the legislature and the governor have revised state laws dealing with **extraterritorial jurisdiction (ETJ),** the authority of a city to require conformity with city ordinances and regulations affecting streets, parks, alleys, utility easements, sanitary sewers, and the like in a ring of land extending from one-half to five miles beyond the city limits line. The width of an ETJ depends on the population of the city. Within the extraterritorial area, no new cities may be incorporated without the consent of the existing city. The ETJ is not part of the city; its residents do not pay property or sales taxes to city government and receive no services.

The original purpose of extraterritoriality was to enable a city to control development within the ETJ, thus preparing it for future annexation. When the city eventually annexed subdivisions in the ETJ, they would already conform to city building standards. If the ETJs of two cities overlapped, the cities generally apportioned the area between them.

In 2001, the legislature passed, and the governor signed, legislation requiring cities and counties to create a single office for dealing with development in the ETJ; it would be run by the city, the county, or cooperatively by both units of local government. The legislature acted in response to complaints from developers that they were sometimes caught between conflicting county and city regulations. In practice, most cities and counties have created a joint office, with a city office the next most popular option.[35]

Land Use Regulation

Historically, land use policies in Texas cities have been developmental. Instead of regulating land use, municipalities in the Lone Star State have promoted private development through street construction and the provision of streetlights, drainage, and water and sewer services in undeveloped areas. In the process, city governments have left decisions about land use policy to private interests—developers, investors, builders, realtors, and architects.

Land use policy in Texas cities is undergoing a transformation. The introduction of single-member districts has increased the political strength of neighborhood groups concerned about quality-of-life issues, such as traffic congestion, air pollution, and neighborhood revitalization. Neighborhood groups in low-income areas have demanded that city government focus on land use policies affecting their neighborhoods, such as low-cost housing and urban redevelopment.

Building and Housing Codes Building and housing codes are established by city ordinance to set minimum standards for the construction and maintenance of buildings. **Building codes** are municipal ordinances that set minimum standards for the types of materials used in construction, building design, and construction methods employed in all buildings within the city. Building permits are required for all construction covered by the code. **Housing codes** are local ordinances requiring all dwelling places in a city to meet certain standards of upkeep and structural integrity. City officials enforce the housing codes by making systematic inspections and investigating complaints. Property owners are responsible for structural integrity. Owners and occupants share the responsibility for upkeep. Violators of building codes and housing codes may be fined.

Building and housing codes are designed to promote the health, safety, and welfare of the community, but the results often fall short of the ideal. Critics say that codes are frequently outdated and inconsistent across cities. They believe that enforcement is often lax and too frequently accompanied by graft. The opponents of building codes also charge that they increase building costs, thus encouraging construction outside a city's ETJ, beyond the reach of city authority. Furthermore, the opponents of building and housing codes argue that property owners sometimes fail to repair old, run-down structures because improvements would place them under the building codes, thus forcing owners to undertake more expensive work than they desire and can afford.

Compared with cities in other states, Texas municipalities have been slow to establish code standards. Many Texas cities did not adopt building codes until after 1954 when the federal government made them a condition for obtaining federal funds for public housing, FHA, and urban renewal programs. Houston did not even adopt fire codes until the 1970s.

Zoning and Planning The governmental designation of tracts of land for industrial, commercial, or residential use is known as **zoning.** In 1927, the Texas legislature authorized municipalities to adopt zoning ordinances to restrict the use of privately owned land. Subsequently, many Texas cities adopted local zoning ordinances.

How does zoning work? Once a city decides it wishes to control land use within its boundaries, it creates a zoning commission. The commission studies land use in the area and makes recommendations concerning appropriate uses of land and the location of commercial and residential districts. After public hearings, the city council considers the proposal and adopts a zoning ordinance based on the commission's recommendation. After the ordinance goes into effect, property owners may not build structures or put property to any use that conflicts with the zoning ordinance applicable to their district.

Building codes
Municipal ordinances that set minimum standards for the types of materials used in construction, building design, and construction methods employed in all buildings within the city.

Housing codes
Local ordinances requiring all dwelling places in a city to meet certain standards of upkeep and structural integrity.

Zoning The governmental designation of tracts of land for industrial, commercial, or residential use.

Proponents of zoning and other types of land use regulation believe that they help create an orderly city. They say that zoning enables city government to separate districts for residential, commercial, and industrial uses, thus preventing nuisances from developing in residential areas, such as strip shopping centers and trailer parks. Careful planning, they argue, can prevent street congestion, the overcrowding of land, and the overconcentration of population by allowing city officials to plan adequately for the provision of transportation, water, sewage, schools, parks, drainage, and other public requirements.

Opponents of zoning and other types of land use restrictions believe that city planning is inefficient and potentially corrupt because it substitutes the judgment of government bureaucrats for free enterprise development. Without government controls, they say, cities develop and change in accordance with the dictates of the marketplace. Zoning shifts the basis for deciding how land will be used from economics to politics. As a result, land use decisions become political, with decisions made on the basis of which developers have made the largest campaign contributions.

Urban land use policies reflect political conflict between the owners of developed land and the owners of undeveloped property. Homeowners and commercial property owners favor the imposition of strict land use controls to manage further development in their neighborhoods in order to maintain and enhance their property values. In contrast, persons who own undeveloped tracts of land prefer few land use restrictions, so that they can develop their property unhindered. Throughout much of the twentieth century, developers held the upper hand politically in big-city Texas and used their influence to limit land use controls. Over the last decade or so, however, the political balance has changed in most of the state's large cities. As cities have matured and development has slowed, the owners of developed land have gained political influence. Furthermore, the introduction of single-member districts has enhanced the political influence of neighborhood civic associations concerned about property values.

WHAT IS YOUR OPINION?

Are you in favor of zoning?

Deed restrictions
Private contractual agreements that limit what residential property owners can do with their houses and land. Almost every modern residential subdivision in the state has deed restrictions.

Deed Restrictions The opponents of zoning sometimes argue that deed restrictions are preferable to government regulation. **Deed restrictions** are private contractual agreements that limit what residential property owners can do with their houses and land. Almost every modern residential subdivision in the state has deed restrictions. Developers, and sometimes the mortgage company, draw up deed restrictions to spell out in detail what lot owners may or may not do. Deed restrictions differ from zoning in that they are the result of voluntary contractual agreements between private parties, whereas zoning involves the enactment of city ordinances.

Deed restrictions typically allow owners to use their property only for specified purposes. They force property owners to observe certain standards and refrain from altering their property without the written approval of the neighborhood civic association's architectural control committee. Deed restrictions cover such issues as where residents can park their vehicles, the color they can paint their homes, and the type of shingles they can put on their roofs. If someone violates the restrictions, the civic association can get a court order commanding the offender to stop the violation. Property owners who disobey a court order can be fined or jailed for contempt of court. Deed restrictions that are not enforced may terminate or become unenforceable. This is most likely to occur, of course, in older neighborhoods.

Deed restrictions accomplish some but not all of the goals of zoning. At its best, zoning represents an attempt by government to ensure orderly development. In contrast, deed restrictions provide piecemeal zoning by private developers without resorting to a comprehensive plan. People who live in the suburbs benefit, whereas the residents of older neighborhoods without zoning must live with changes wrought by market forces.

Emergency medical services are also provided by city governments.

GETTING INVOLVED   Contacting City Officials

City governments deal with issues that are close to home—police and fire protection, street repair, garbage pickup, water and sewer service, EMS, parks, libraries, airports, animal control, and local taxes. You can find the name and contact information for the mayor and council members of your city at its homepage, which can be found at the following website: www.statelocalgov.net/state-tx.cfm. Contact the people who represent you at city hall and let them know how you feel about city services, taxes, and regulations.

It's your city—Get involved!

CITY POLITICS IN TEXAS

Elite theory (or elitism) The view that political power is held by a small group of people who dominate politics by controlling economic resources.

Boosters People who promote local economic development.

Before the mid-1970s, a small group of business people controlled political power in big-city Texas. **Elite theory (or elitism)** is the view that political power is held by a small group of people who dominate politics by controlling economic resources. Growth-oriented business leaders in each of the state's major cities used their economic power to dominate the local policymaking process. In Houston, the elite were a small group of business leaders called the 8-F Crowd because of their practice of meeting informally in Suite 8-F of a downtown hotel. The members of the 8-F Crowd were all wealthy businessmen with interests in real estate, construction, oil and gas, banking, law, and insurance.[36]

The overriding goal of the business groups who dominated city politics was economic growth and development. They were **boosters** (people who promote local economic development) who believed that whatever was good for business was also good for their city. The business leaders favored low tax rates, aggressive annexation, and few restrictions on land use. When the occasion arose, they did what was necessary to boost their cities. During the 1930s, for example, Dallas business leaders convinced the legislature to make their city the site for the official celebration of the Texas Centennial, even though Dallas did not exist during the Texas Revolution. In Houston, business leaders promoted the construction of the Ship Channel and the creation of the Johnson Spacecraft Center (JSC).

Business leaders frequently exerted their influence through the vehicle of nonpartisan good government groups, such as the Citizens' Charter Association (CCA) in Dallas, Good Government League (GGL) in San Antonio, Seventh Street in Fort Worth, Citizens for Better Government in Abilene, and Citizens' Committee for Good Government in Wichita Falls. These groups recruited slates of candidates sympathetic with their goals and backed them financially in the at-large nonpartisan elections that were then the norm in most Texas cities. In San Antonio, the GGL won 85 of 97 contested council races between 1955 and 1975. In Dallas, the CCA captured 181 of 211 seats between 1931 and 1975.[37]

Most of the candidates supported by business groups were white businessmen. For example, in Fort Worth, no African Americans were elected to city council

In 2009, Annise Parker was elected mayor of Houston using a deracialization strategy that encompassed not just race and ethnicity but also sexual orientation.

before 1967; no Latinos won election before 1977. In fact, most Fort Worth council members lived within blocks of one another on the city's affluent southwest side.[38] In Houston, no women, no Latinos, and only one African American were elected to council before 1981.

Texas cities grew rapidly, but the growth came with social costs. Texas cities developed serious air and water pollution problems. The Environmental Protection Agency (EPA), the federal agency responsible for enforcing the nation's environmental laws, identified four major areas of the state that had failed to meet federal air quality standards for ozone: Dallas–Fort Worth, Houston–Galveston, Beaumont–Port Arthur, and El Paso. In the meantime, air quality in Austin, San Antonio, and Tyler barely met the standard.[39] Texas cities also suffered from traffic congestion, overcrowded schools, and flooding brought on by **subsidence,** the sinking of the surface of the land caused by the too-rapid extraction of subsurface water.

The costs of rapid development mobilized opposition to the growth-oriented business groups that had long dominated city politics. The business community split between those industries that benefited from development and those that were more concerned with quality of life issues. Real estate developers, construction contractors, and other firms that depend on development favored continuing growth-oriented public policies. In contrast, the tourist industry and high-technology firms that employed middle-class professionals were more concerned with the quality of urban life. Neighborhood groups and minority interests demanded that city governments respond to their needs.

By the mid-1970s, the rules of the political game had changed sufficiently to allow the new forces to have an impact on the policy process. The elimination of the poll tax and the liberalization of Texas's once highly restrictive voter registration

Subsidence The sinking of the surface of the land caused by the too-rapid extraction of subsurface water.

procedures opened the door to greater political participation by African Americans and Latinos. Furthermore, the extension of the VRA in 1975 to include Texas led to the introduction of single-member districts in most of the state's largest cities, including Houston, Dallas, San Antonio, El Paso, Lubbock, Corpus Christi, Waco, and, most recently, Irving.

The new voter registration procedures and single-member district elections enabled minority and neighborhood groups to gain a real share of political power in big-city Texas. More African Americans and Latinos won city council seats than ever before, and some Asian Americans won seats on councils as well. The number of women serving on city councils increased and both Houston and Dallas elected city officials who were openly gay or lesbian. African Americans, Latinos, and women served as mayor in the state's major cities.[40]

The nature of business groups in big-city Texas also changed. During the 1950s, each city's business establishment was dominated by a fairly small group of strong-willed, fiercely independent, wealthy entrepreneurs, such as Eric Jonsson in Dallas and George Brown in Houston. By the 1980s, the business community in big-city Texas had grown too diverse for any one individual or small group of individuals to speak on its behalf. Furthermore, the days of the individual entrepreneur were past, as management teams now ran the state's major corporations. Before local managers could agree to support a development project, they would have to obtain approval from a corporate board of directors based in New York, San Francisco, or Tokyo.

Pluralist theory (or pluralism) The view that diverse groups of elites with differing interests compete with one another to control policy in various issue areas.

Contemporary urban politics in Texas reflects **pluralist theory (or pluralism),** which is the view that diverse groups of elites with differing interests compete with one another to control policy in various issue areas. In big-city Texas today, different groups are active on different issues, but no one group is able to dominate policymaking across issue areas. Business groups may control policymaking in one issue area, whereas neighborhood or minority rights groups may have more influence in another issue area.

Deracialization The attempt of political candidates to de-emphasize racially divisive themes in order to garner crossover support from voters of other races/ethnicities while also receiving the overwhelming majority of support from voters of the candidate's own racial/ethnic group.

Political scientists use the term "deracialization" to describe contemporary urban politics. **Deracialization** is the attempt by political candidates to de-emphasize racially divisive themes in order to garner crossover support from voters of other races/ethnicities while also receiving the overwhelming majority of support from voters of the candidate's own racial/ethnic group.[41] To be successful, candidates running for citywide office in the state's major cities know that they have to attract voters from more than one racial/ethnic group because no one group has an electoral majority. They promote images of themselves that other racial/ethnic groups will perceive as nonthreatening and avoid issues that divide voters along racial/ethnic lines, such as bilingual education, affirmative action, and immigration. In the meantime, they work aggressively to mobilize their own base of support. Political scientist Christian Collet uses the term "toggling" to describe the approach that candidates take to city politics. "Toggling," Collet says, "is a strategy that seeks to build or maintain a victorious electoral coalition in a politically polarized, multicultural environment through the balanced communication of broad- and narrow-cast messages, symbols, issue positions, personal characteristics, and socio-cultural cues to specific racial and ethnic groups."[42] Candidates emphasize broad themes to the general community in order to appeal to as many groups as possible while highlighting points designed to mobilize their own base of support. For example, a candidate can talk about being tough on crime while also promising better representation on the police force for racial and ethnic minority groups.[43]

The 2009 Houston city election illustrated deracialization in Texas urban politics. Annise Parker and Gene Locke, the two leading contenders for mayor, each had strengths and weaknesses. Parker was the better known of the two, having won three consecutive citywide elections for city council and then another three elections for controller. Because of her experience, she had a better grasp of the issues than her opponent. She could also count on a small army of campaign volunteers, especially members of the gay and lesbian community. Parker was unable to raise as much money as Locke, however, and some observers questioned whether Houston voters would be willing to elect an openly lesbian mayor.[44] Locke, with strong business backing, was better funded than Parker. Furthermore, as an African American, he could expect majority support from the city's largest voting bloc. The combination of downtown business money and African American voters had historically been a formidable partnership in Houston politics. Locke's weakness was that, having never run for election before, he was an inexperienced candidate who was not well-known among Houston voters, not even among African American voters.

The initial challenge for the Parker and Locke campaigns was to do well enough in the November election to make the December runoff. Houston city elections are held in November of odd-numbered years. If no candidate wins a majority of the vote in the first round of voting, the two top finishers meet in a December runoff. As two other serious candidates were in the field in addition to Parker and Locke, a runoff was likely. The Parker campaign used volunteers to identify supporters and encourage them to vote, using phone banks, direct mail, Facebook, and Twitter. Meanwhile, Locke used his financial advantage to build name recognition through radio and television advertising. In particular, Locke wanted to increase his visibility among African American voters.

The November election set the stage for a December runoff. Parker led with 31 percent of the vote, followed by Locke with 26 percent. Each campaign performed best with its core supporters. Parker led among liberal white voters while Locke performed best among African Americans. Most of the remainder of the vote was divided between liberal City Councilman Peter Brown and conservative activist Roy Morales. Brown ran second to Parker in liberal white neighborhoods and second to Locke in African American neighborhoods. Most observers expected his vote would split along racial lines in the runoff, with Brown's white voters backing Parker and his African American supporters voting for Locke. If so, the outcome of the runoff election would hinge on the voting decisions of the white conservative voters who supported Morales in the first round. Would they support Parker, the openly gay city controller, or Locke, an African American attorney who was a former civil rights activist?

Both runoff candidates worked to turn out their bases of support while appealing to the conservative voters who initially voted for Morales. Parker said that her experience working with city finances better prepared her to guide the city through tough economic times. Locke promised to increase the number of police officers on patrol. Meanwhile, Steven Hotze, an anti-gay political activist, made sexual orientation an issue by mailing fliers to conservative voters warning about a "gay takeover" of city government and endorsing Locke. Even though Locke was on record as a strong supporter of gay and lesbian rights, he did not reject Hotze's support. In fact, the *Houston Chronicle* newspaper revealed a few days before the runoff election that the chairman and another member of Locke's finance committee had funded the Hotze mailer attacking Parker and endorsing Locke.[45]

Houston voters made history in the runoff by electing Annise Parker mayor, 54 percent to 46 percent for Locke. Parker led among voters in every area of the city except for African American neighborhoods, which Locke carried. Her success was built on a deracialization strategy that encompassed not just race and ethnicity but also sexual orientation. Parker had always been upfront about her sexual orientation throughout her political career, but she focused on issues of concern to Houstonians in general. She was a gay candidate but not *the* gay candidate. Whereas many gay and lesbian Houstonians were strongly motivated to contribute money and volunteer their time for her campaign, other Houstonians, including many relatively conservative voters, were not threatened by her. Parker won because most Houston voters viewed her as the safe choice—at least, a safer choice than Gene Locke.

WHAT WE HAVE LEARNED

1. **What is the legal status of city governments in Texas?**

   Cities are subordinate units of government, subject to the constitutions and laws of the United States and the state of Texas. State law sets the requirements and procedures under which an unincorporated urban area in Texas can become an incorporated municipality. A general law city is a municipality that is limited to those governmental structures and powers specifically granted by state law. It must follow Dillon's Rule. Larger cities may choose home rule, giving them more flexibility than general law cities in such matters as organizational structure, annexation, ordinance-making authority, and election processes.

2. **What are the different forms of city government in Texas?**

   The mayor–council and council–manager forms of city government are the basic structures of municipal government in Texas. The mayor–council form of city government is a municipal government structure in which the voters elect a mayor as the city's chief executive officer as well as a council that serves as a legislative body. Cities with the mayor–council form of city government vary in the mayor's strength. Some cities have a strong-mayor variation, others a weak-mayor variation. Although the mayor–council form of city government is the traditional form for large cities in the United States, Houston is the only big city in Texas that uses it. The state's other large cities have the council–manager form, a municipal government structure in which the city council/mayor appoints a professional administrator, called a city manager, to act as the municipality's chief executive officer. In both systems, the mayor and council make basic policy decisions. In the council–manager form, however, policy implementation is the responsibility of a professional administrator hired by the city council—a city manager.

3. **What election systems do Texas cities use?**

The at-large election system is the most popular election system Texas cities use to select their city councils. District elections are the next most popular. Historically, district election systems were associated with big-city political machines. For much of the twentieth century, Texas cities elected city councils using nonpartisan at-large election systems, which limited the political influence of ethnic and racial minorities, primarily African Americans and Latinos. The VRA enabled minority rights groups to attack the at-large election systems in court. As a result, many Texas cities adopted district election systems or systems that combined both district and at-large council seats. The introduction of district election systems led to the selection of city councils in most of the state's big cities that were more ethnically and racially diverse than ever before.

4. **What are the most important policies adopted by Texas cities in terms of budgets, annexation, and land use?**

Political scientist Paul E. Peterson divides urban public policies into three categories: developmental, redistributive, and allocational. Developmental urban policies are local programs that enhance a community's economic position in its competition with other communities. Redistributive urban policies are local programs that benefit low-income residents of an area. Allocational urban policies are local programs that are more or less neutral in their impact on the local economy.

The state's largest cities are big enterprises with annual budgets greater than a billion dollars. Texas cities generate revenue from property taxes, sales taxes, franchise fees, and other sources. City governments borrow money by issuing bonds to cover the cost of capital expenditures. Budgetary policies in urban Texas have historically been allocational and developmental. City governments use tax incentives to promote economic growth, including tax increment financing, tax abatements, and enterprise zones.

Traditionally, cities annex to protect their tax bases. Another reason for annexation is the desire of city officials to prevent encirclement by other incorporated municipalities. Finally, cities annex in order to reap the political benefits of a larger population. Historically, Texas cities have annexed aggressively; however, the pace of annexation has recently slowed because of changes in state laws and because of a political backlash from newly annexed residents. Recently passed legislation gives cities and utility districts the authority to negotiate Strategic Partnership Agreements (SPAs) to provide for limited-purpose annexation. State law also gives cities the authority to control development just beyond their city limits, a power known as extraterritoriality.

Historically, land use policies in Texas cities have been developmental. Building and housing codes are established by city ordinance to set minimum standards for the construction and maintenance of buildings. Many Texas cities (but not Houston) have zoning, which is the governmental designation of tracts of land for industrial, commercial, or residential use. The opponents of zoning sometimes argue that private deed restrictions are preferable to government regulation.

5. **How has big-city politics in Texas evolved since the 1950s?**

Before the mid-1970s, big-city politics in Texas was best explained by the elite theory. In one city after another, a small group of wealthy business people dominated politics by controlling economic resources. The overriding goals of the business groups were economic growth and development. Most of the candidates they supported were white businessmen. Economic development and rapid population growth mobilized opposition to the growth-oriented business groups that had long controlled city politics. By the mid-1970s, the rules of the political game had changed sufficiently to allow the new forces to have an impact on the policy process. In particular, the introduction of district elections increased representation for women, minorities, and council members rooted in communities. Contemporary urban politics in Texas reflects pluralist theory or pluralism. Meanwhile, political scientists use the term "deracialization" to describe big-city politics. It is the attempt by political candidates to de-emphasize racially divisive themes in order to garner crossover support from voters of other races/ethnicities while also receiving the over-whelming majority of support from voters of the candidate's own racial/ethnic group. In 2009, for example, Annise Parker was elected mayor of Houston using a deracialization strategy that encompassed not just race and ethnicity but also sexual orientation.

KEY TERMS

allocational urban policies

annexation

at-large election system

bond

boosters

building codes

capital expenditure

city charter

city manager

city ordinances

council–manager form of city government

cumulative voting system

deed restrictions

deracialization

developmental urban policies

Dillon's rule

district election

elite theory (or elitism)

enterprise zones

extraterritorial jurisdiction (ETJ)

general law city

high-technology industries

home rule city

homestead exemption

housing codes

incorporated municipality

initiative process

mayor–council form of city government

minimum wage

nonpartisan elections

pluralist theory (or pluralism)

political machines

political patronage

population bracket laws

property tax (or *ad valorem* property tax)

recall

redistributive urban policies

sales tax

subsidence

tax abatement

tax increment financing

truth in taxation laws

unincorporated area

utility district

Voting Rights Act (VRA)

zoning

NOTES

1. Annise Parker for Houston, available at www.anniseparker .com.
2. Gene Locke for Mayor, available at www.genelocke.com.
3. David R. Berman, *Local Government and the States: Autonomy, Politics, and Policy* (Armonk, NY: M.E. Sharpe, 2003), p. 84.
4. Terrell Blodget, "Municipal Home-Rule Charters in Texas," *Public Affairs Comment* 41 (1996): 2.
5. Texas Municipal League, "Local Governments in Texas," available at www.tml.org.
6. Rachel Graves, "In Need of Repairs," *Houston Chronicle*, July 8, 2001, p. 23A.
7. Quoted in T. J. Milling, "'King Kong, 14 Chimps,'" *Houston Chronicle*, October 8, 1995, p. 38A.
8. Rob Gurwitt, "Are City Councils a Relic of the Past?" *Governing*, April 2003, pp. 20–24.
9. Emily Ramshaw, "Strong Mayor Foes Are Diverse," *Dallas Morning News*, January 8, 2005, available at www .dallasnews.com.
10. Texas Municipal League, "Local Governments in Texas."
11. Wayne Lee Gay, "The Salary Survey," *Fort Worth Star-Telegram*, September 12, 2002, available at www.dfw .com.

12. H. George Frederickson, Gary A. Johnson, and Curtis H. Wood, *The Adapted City: Institutional Dynamics and Structural Change* (Armonk, NY: M. E. Sharpe, 2004), pp. 163–167.

13. Steven R. Reed, "Dallas: A City at a Crucial Crossroads," *Houston Chronicle*, December 3, 1990, p. 11A.

14. Joshua G. Behr, *Race, Ethnicity, and the Politics of City Redistricting* (Albany, NY: State University of New York Press, 2000), pp. 97–114.

15. Brandon Formby, "Irving's Single-Member District Plan Unseats Two Officeholders," *Dallas Morning News*, August 21, 2009, available at www.dallasnews.com.

16. Ruth P. Morgan, *Governance by Decree: The Impact of the Voting Rights Act in Dallas* (Lawrence, KS: University of Kansas Press, 2004), pp. 270–273.

17. Jerry L. Polinard, Robert D. Wrinkle, and Tomás Longoria, Jr., "The Impact of District Elections on the Mexican American Community: The Electoral Perspective," *Social Science Quarterly* 72 (September 1991): 608–614.

18. Paul E. Peterson, *City Limits* (Chicago, IL: University of Chicago Press, 1981), Ch. 3.

19. Kenneth K. Wong, "Economic Constraint and Political Choice in Urban Policymaking," *American Journal of Political Science* 32 (February 1988): 1–18.

20. Josh Goodman, "Skybox Skeptics," *Governing*, March 2006, pp. 41–43.

21. *Texas Town and City*, March 1990, pp. 17–35.

22. City of Houston, "Fiscal Year 2009 Budget," available at www.houstontx.gov.

23. Various municipal websites.

24. Alan Greenblatt, "The Loathsome Local Levy," *Governing*, October 2001, p. 36.

25. Travis Central Appraisal District, available at www.traviscad.org.

26. Sean M. Wood, "Jet Maker to Bring 850 New Jobs to S.A.," *San Antonio Express-News*, June 30, 2006, available at www.mysanantonio.com.

27. Bradley Olson, "Hotel Could Get a Tax Deal," *Houston Chronicle*, April 22, 2009, pp. B1, B3.

28. Helen F. Ladd and John Yinger, *America's Ailing Cities: Fiscal Health and the Design of Urban Policy* (Baltimore, MD: Johns Hopkins University Press, 1989), pp. 287–293.

29. Todd M. Gabe and David S. Kraybill, "The Effect of State Economic Development Incentives on Employment Growth of Establishments," *Journal of Regional Science* 42 (November 2002): 703–730.

30. Texas Municipal League, "Annexation: It Isn't a Four-Letter Word," available at www.tml.org.

31. Arnold P. Fleischmann, "Balancing New Skylines," *Texas Humanist* 6 (January/February 1984): 28–31.

32. Terry Kliewer, "Anxiety Over Annexation," *Houston Chronicle*, July 15, 2002, pp. A13–A14.

33. Josh Goodman, "The Tax Grab Game," *Governing*, April 2007, p. 48.

34. Carolyn Feibel and Renee C. Lee, "Council Approves Woodlands Deal," *Houston Chronicle*, October 25, 2007, pp. B1, B4.

35. Jeremy Schwartz, "Cities, Counties Grapple with New Law," *Austin American-Statesman*, April 29, 2002, available at www.statesman.com.

36. Robert D. Thomas and Richard W. Murray, *Pro-growth Politics: Change and Governance in Houston* (Berkeley, CA: Institute of Government Studies Press, 1991), p. 13.

37. Chandler Davidson and Luis Ricardo Fraga, "Slating Groups as Parties in a 'Nonpartisan' Setting," *Western Political Quarterly* 41 (June 1988): 373–390.

38. Judy Fitzgerald and Melanie Miller, "Fort Worth," in Robert Stewart, ed., *Local Government Election Systems*, Vol. II (Austin, TX: Lyndon B. Johnson School of Public Affairs, 1984), pp. 12–21.

39. Texas Commission on Environmental Quality, "The Quest for Clean Air," available at www.tceq.state.tx.us.

40. Karen M. Kaufmann, *The Urban Voter: Group Conflict and Mayoral Voting Behavior in American Cities* (Ann Arbor, MI: University of Michigan Press, 2004), pp. 197–205.

41. Huey L. Perry, ed., *Race, Politics, and Governance in the United States* (Gainesville, FL: University of Florida Press, 1996), pp. 1–7.

42. Christian Collet, "Minority Candidates, Alternative Media, and Multiethnic America: Deracialization or Toggling?" *Perspectives on Politics* 6 (December 2008): 4.

43. Ibid.

44. Rick Casey, "His Advisers Gave Locke Wrong Key," *Houston Chronicle*, December 13, 2009, pp. A1, A22.

45. Bradley Olson, "Key Locke Backers Gave to Anti-Gay Group," *Houston Chronicle*, December 7, 2009, available at www.chron.com.

Counties, School Districts, and Special Districts

WHAT WE WILL LEARN

After studying Chapter 12, students should be able to answer the following questions:

‣ What is the constitutional/legal status of counties in Texas, how are they structured, how are they funded, what services do they provide, and what issues do they face?

‣ How are school districts governed, how are they funded, what issues do they face, and how well do they perform?

‣ How are special districts created, organized, operated, and funded, and what are their benefits and liabilities?

Texas has the largest merit pay program for teachers in the nation. In 2009, the Texas legislature appropriated $400 million for merit pay, divided between the 2009–2010 and 2010–2011 school years. The program, which is called District Awards for Teacher Excellence (DATE), provides money for districts that choose to participate. In 2008–2009, one in five districts took part in the program. Although districts establish their own reward criteria, the state requires that at least 60 percent of the funds must be used for bonuses based on student performance. The rest of the money can be used as stipends for teachers working in hard-to-staff schools or in high-demand subjects, such as math and science.[1]

Merit pay has both defenders and critics. The advocates of merit pay believe that teachers who work hard and produce positive results should be rewarded financially for their good performance. Merit pay gives all teachers an incentive to do their best and encourages the most effective teachers to remain on the job, rather than leaving the field for higher-paying jobs. The Texas merit pay program also provides districts with money that can be used to reward the best, most experienced teachers for working in schools with large numbers of low-income and minority students.[2] In contrast, teacher unions and other critics of merit pay complain that merit pay is too often based on simplistic measures of performance that fail to grasp the essence of good teaching. Instead of incentive bonuses, the opponents of merit pay favor raising teacher salaries across the board.[3]

Merit pay in Texas has been slow to produce measurable results. Most districts chose not to participate in the program in 2008–2009 because the state required them to put up 15 percent of the program cost at a time when school district budgets were tight. Furthermore, most participating districts paid bonuses between $1,000 and $1,500, well below the $3,000 minimum bonus recommended by the state and arguably too small to make a difference in performance.[4]

The controversy over merit pay for teachers illustrates the sorts of issues facing local government in Texas. Local government is important, affecting the daily lives of all of the state's residents. This chapter on county, school district, and special district government is the last in a series of chapters dealing with the institutions of state and local government in Texas. Chapters 8, 9, and 10 dealt with the legislative, executive, and judicial branches of state government, respectively. Chapter 11 focused on city government.

 WHAT IS YOUR OPINION?

If you were a teacher, would merit pay motivate you to work harder?

COUNTY GOVERNMENT

Texas has 254 counties, ranging in population size from Harris County, with nearly 4 million people, to tiny Loving County, with a population of less than a hundred.[5] Some counties are dominated by large cities, such as Harris (Houston), Bexar

General law units of local government Units of local government that are limited to those structures and powers specifically granted by state law.

Home rule The authority of a unit of local government to take actions not prohibited by the laws or constitutions of the United States or the state.

(San Antonio), Travis (Austin), Tarrant (Fort Worth), El Paso, and Dallas counties. Other counties are predominantly rural, with only a few small towns and no large cities.

Legal Status

Texas counties are **general law units of local government;** that is, units of local government that are limited to those structures and powers specifically granted by state law. In contrast to Texas cities and the counties in most other states, Texas counties may not adopt home rule status, which would allow them greater discretion in choosing governmental structures, functions, and tax systems. **Home rule** refers to a unit of local government's authority to take actions not prohibited by the laws or constitutions of the United States or the state. If county officials want to respond to local problems by taking an action not specifically allowed by state law, they must first obtain authorization from the Texas legislature.

Edwards County Courthouse in Rocksprings, Texas.

Responsibilities

County governments in Texas play a dual role of implementing state policies and providing services to residents.

- **Law enforcement:** Counties enforce state laws. The county sheriff's office is the primary law enforcement agency for Texans living in unincorporated areas. Counties also operate county jails, which house people who are awaiting trial and persons convicted of misdemeanor offenses.
- **Courts:** Counties operate justice of the peace, county, and district courts. With the exception of cases tried in municipal court, every state trial that takes place in Texas, both criminal and civil, is held in a court operated by county government.
- **Health:** Counties enforce the state's health laws and provide healthcare services for indigent residents. Under Texas law, counties are required to cover the healthcare costs of residents at or below 21 percent of the federal poverty level ($4,630 a year for a family of four in 2009) if those residents do not qualify for other healthcare programs.[6]
- **Records:** County governments collect and maintain records of births, deaths, marriages, divorces, and deeds.
- **Tax collection:** County governments collect a number of taxes and fees on behalf of the state, including charges for license plates and certificates-of-title for motor vehicles.
- **Elections:** County governments register voters and conduct both primary and general elections for the state.
- **Roads and bridges:** Counties build and maintain roads and bridges.
- **Other services:** State law allows counties to provide a range of additional services. Some counties operate airports or seaports. Counties may also provide their residents with libraries, parks, and recreational facilities. In Houston, for example, Harris County owns and operates Reliant Stadium, the home of the Houston Texans National Football League team.

Commissioners court The board of directors for county government composed of four county commissioners and the county judge.

Organization

Figure 12.1 is the organizational chart of county government in Texas. In many respects, county government is a miniature version of state government in that no single official is in charge. Instead, executive functions are divided among a sizable number of elected and appointed officials.

Partisan election Election contest in which both the names and the party affiliations of candidates appear on the ballot.

Commissioners Court The **commissioners court,** the board of directors for county government, is composed of four county commissioners and the county judge. The members are chosen in partisan elections held concurrently with the biennial statewide general elections. A **partisan election** is an election contest in which both the names and the party affiliation of candidates appear on the ballot. County voters elect the four commissioners, one each from the four districts called county

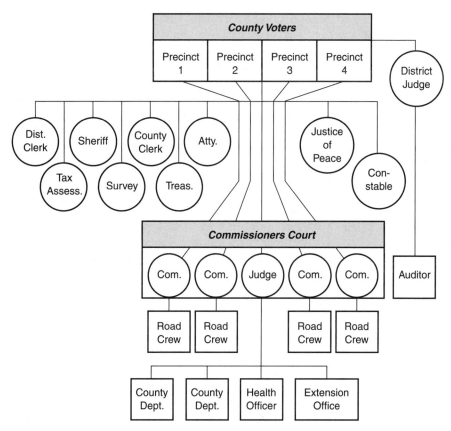

FIGURE 12.1   County Government in Texas.

commissioner precincts, to serve four-year staggered terms. They elect the county judge countywide to serve a four-year term as well.

Individual commissioners essentially run county government within their precincts. In most counties, the commissioners oversee road repair and construction in their precincts. In fact, roadwork is such an important part of the county commissioners' job in rural counties that residents often refer to them as road commissioners. The commissioners control large road budgets and pick contractors to do county work. Meanwhile, they hire their own crews to do routine maintenance on county roads and in county facilities, such as parks and recreation centers. In Harris County, the state's largest county, the budgets for each of the four commissioners range in size from $40 million to $80 million. They employ full-time staffs of 280 to 380 workers, depending on the geographic size of the precincts.[7] The commissioners also select vendors for the purchase of equipment and supplies.

The responsibilities of the county judge vary, depending on the size of the county. In rural counties, the county judge is the presiding judge in the constitutional county court. In urban counties, the county judge devotes most, if not all, of his or her time to county business and leaves the work of trying cases to the county courts at law. In smaller counties, those with fewer than 225,000 people, the judge is also the county's chief budget officer. In larger counties, an auditor appointed by the district court judge(s) drafts the budget and oversees county finances.

The powers of the county judge more closely resemble those of a mayor in the council–manager form of city government than a mayor in the mayor–council form of city government with the strong mayor variation. The county judge presides in commissioners court but has only one vote and no veto. As the most visible figure in county government, the county judge often serves as the spokesperson for county government. The county judge's ability to provide policy leadership, however, depends more on political skill than official power because the judge lacks the authority to run commissioners court and has no executive power to manage county government.

Commissioners court has limited authority. Commissioners court can set the county property tax rate, but it does not have general ordinance-making power. An **ordinance** is a law enacted by the governing body of a unit of local government. Most of the power of commissioners court comes from its budget-making authority and its power to choose among the optional services county government has available to offer county residents. The commissioners court is empowered to adopt the county budget. This authority gives it an important tool to influence policy in county departments not directly under the court's supervision. Also, state law gives the commissioners court authority to determine whether the county will offer residents such local programs/services as parks, libraries, airports, hospitals, and recreation facilities. In counties that choose to implement these optional programs, the commissioners court appoints administrators to head them. These appointed officials may include a county agricultural agent, home demonstration agent, fire marshal, county health officer, county welfare officer, medical examiner, librarian, county engineer, and, in more populous counties, county purchasing agent.

Other Elected County Officials The county courthouse contains numerous elected officials in addition to the members of commissioners court. These officials are chosen in partisan elections to serve staggered four-year terms. All but justices of the peace and constables are elected countywide.

After the county judge, the most visible official is the county sheriff, who is the chief law enforcement officer for the county. The sheriff's department has jurisdiction over the entire county; however, in urban areas city governments and the county usually agree on a division of responsibilities. City police departments patrol within their cities, whereas the sheriff enforces the law in unincorporated areas. The sheriff also operates the county jail, which holds prisoners awaiting trial for felony offenses and people serving sentences for misdemeanor convictions. In urban counties, in particular, managing the jail consumes a significant proportion of the sheriff department's budget and personnel. Finally, the sheriff assists county courts and state district courts within the county by serving arrest warrants and subpoenas, as well as providing deputies to serve as bailiffs. A **subpoena** is a legal order compelling a person's attendance at an official proceeding, such as a trial.

Ordinance A law enacted by the governing body of a unit of local government.

Subpoena A legal order compelling the attendance of a person at an official proceeding, such as a trial.

Larger counties elect both a district attorney and a county attorney. In smaller counties and in Bexar County (San Antonio), the district attorney performs both roles. In counties with both officials, the district attorney's office prosecutes felony criminal cases in state district courts. The county attorney advises the commissioners court and other county officials on legal issues and represents the county in court, mostly in cases of lawsuits to collect delinquent property taxes. The county attorney's office also prosecutes misdemeanor cases in JP and county court, except in Harris County, where the district attorney prosecutes both felony and misdemeanor cases.

Two other offices whose titles frequently confuse voters are those of county clerk and district clerk. The county clerk records legal documents, such as deeds, mortgages, and contracts, and keeps vital statistics on births, deaths, marriages, and divorces. The county clerk is also the county election official. He or she conducts early voting, instructs precinct election workers, certifies election returns, and forwards election results to the office of the Texas secretary of state. In a few counties, the county clerk registers voters. The district clerk, meanwhile, maintains legal records for the district courts. In small counties, the county clerk performs the functions of the district clerk.

Justices of the peace (JPs) try Class C misdemeanor cases and hear small claims civil suits. Depending on its population, a county may be divided into as many as eight JP precincts, with each precinct electing one or two JPs. In addition to their judicial duties, JPs in small counties may assume the responsibilities of the county clerk. The JP may also serve as county coroner (although few justices of the peace have medical backgrounds).

Each county elects as many constables as it has justices of the peace. Although constables are certified law enforcement officers, their primary chore in most counties is to assist the JP court(s) by serving legal papers, such as subpoenas and warrants. Constables also handle evictions, execute judgments, and provide bailiffs for the justice courts. In some urban counties, particularly Harris County, constables provide for-hire law enforcement services to subdivisions in unincorporated areas through contract deputy programs.

The tax assessor-collector is the county's chief tax official. The tax assessor collects the county's property taxes, collects fees for automobile license plates, and issues certificates-of-title for motor vehicles. Despite the title of the office, the tax assessor-collector no longer assesses the value of county property for tax purposes. The legislature has assigned that duty to a county tax appraisal district in each county. In small counties, those with fewer than 10,000 people, the sheriff performs the duties of the tax assessor.

Poll tax A tax that prospective voters had to pay in order to register to vote.

In most counties, the tax assessor-collector directs voter registration. This duty is a holdover from the era of the **poll tax,** which was a tax that prospective voters had to pay in order to register to vote. State law allows the commissioners court to transfer voter registration and/or election administration duties to another official, and a number of urban counties have assigned those responsibilities to the county clerk or to an appointed election administrator.

The county treasurer is responsible for receiving funds and making authorized expenditures. In recent years, the state legislature has proposed, and voters have passed, constitutional amendments to allow several counties to abolish the office of county treasurer and transfer its duties to the auditor, who is appointed by the district judge(s) in the county.

Two counties, Harris and Dallas, still have county departments of education. These agencies are governed by five-member boards of trustees, with one trustee elected countywide and the other four trustees chosen from the four commissioners court precincts. Historically, county departments of education coordinated relations among the common school districts within the county. Common school districts have now been replaced by independent school districts, and in 1978 the legislature abolished all county education departments except those in Harris and Dallas counties, which successfully argued that they provided important services to county residents. Critics charge that these agencies are expensive bureaucracies whose services can and should be provided by independent school districts.

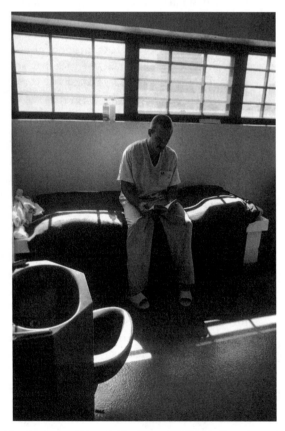

The county jail holds prisoners awaiting trial for felony offenses and people serving sentences for misdemeanor convictions.

Finances

Property taxes are the main source of tax revenue for county government. The county tax rate is limited to $0.80 per $100 of valuation, although state law allows county voters to approve as much as $0.15 more for road and bridge operations and up to $0.30 more to build and maintain farm-to-market (FM) roads. In practice, most county governments set their tax rates well below the allowed maximum. Table 12.1 compares the property tax rates of the six largest counties in Texas.

County governments can expand their taxing authority by creating separate but closely allied special districts to provide such costly services as healthcare, flood control, and toll road construction and maintenance. In Harris County, for example, the commissioners court controls three special districts—the Harris County Flood Control District, Hospital District, and Port of Houston Authority. If the property tax rates for these districts were added to the Harris County tax rate, it would jump from $0.38923 to $0.62998. Although that figure would still be well below the state-approved maximum rate for counties, members of the commissioners court find it politically beneficial to spread taxes and occasional tax increases among special districts with their own separate boards of directors, rather than consolidate them under the taxing authority of county government.

Property taxes are not the only revenue source for county governments. Counties that do not have transit authorities or incorporated cities within their boundaries can levy sales taxes. Other revenue sources for county governments include fees for motor vehicle licenses, service charges, and federal aid.

The relative importance of county expenditures varies considerably among counties. Road and bridge construction and maintenance is a major budget item for all counties, but it is particularly prominent in geographically large counties. Rural, sparsely populated counties do little more than maintain the roads, enforce the law, operate a county court, and carry out the basic administrative functions of county government, such as recording deeds and registering voters. In contrast, county governments in metropolitan areas provide a wide range of services, especially if the county has a large population living in unincorporated areas. Although the largest single item in the budget for Harris County is road and bridge construction and maintenance, Harris County government and its related special districts also spend

TABLE 12.1   Tax Rates in Selected Counties, 2008

County	Tax Rate per $100 Valuation
Bexar (San Antonio)	$0.289399
Dallas	$0.2281
El Paso	$0.342437
Harris (Houston)	$0.38923
Tarrant (Fort Worth)	$0.264
Travis (Austin)	$0.4122

Source: Various county appraisal district websites.

millions of dollars for law enforcement, jail operation, indigent healthcare, the operation of county and district courts, flood control, and parks.

Legislative budget decisions sometimes impact county government. In 2001, the Texas legislature passed, and the governor signed, legislation requiring counties to establish indigent defense programs to ensure that indigent criminal defendants receive competent legal representation. Although the legislature provided for some funding, county governments were forced to cover more than 90 percent of the program's cost.[8] Similarly, legislative cuts in the State Children's Health Insurance Program increased healthcare costs for counties. The **State Children's Health Insurance Program (SCHIP)** is a federal program designed to provide health insurance to children from low-income families whose parents are not poor enough to qualify for Medicaid. In 2003, legislative cuts in the program left several hundred thousand youngsters from low-income families without health insurance. Without SCHIP coverage, parents often took their ill children to county hospital emergency rooms, forcing county governments to pick up the cost of their healthcare.[9]

State Children's Health Insurance Program (SCHIP) A federal program designed to provide health insurance to children from low-income families whose parents are not poor enough to qualify for Medicaid.

Issues in County Government

County government has both staunch defenders and harsh critics. The proponents of county government declare that counties are the unit of local government that is closest and most responsive to the people. Counties provide basic government services that citizens want and need. In contrast, critics charge that county government is a relic of the nineteenth century. They believe that county government is inefficient and often corrupt.

To a substantial degree, the validity of the criticism against county government depends on the county's size. For the most part, county government functions effectively in rural and small-town Texas. In rural areas, counties are the primary units of local government. Citizens are aware of county services and know county officials well. In contrast, county governments are almost invisible governments in urban Texas despite employing thousands of persons and spending millions of dollars. Counties operate with little accountability because the media and most citizens are focused primarily on other units and levels of government.

The Long Ballot and Accountability to the Voters The critics of county government believe that the long ballot makes it difficult for county voters to intelligently choose qualified officeholders, at least in urban areas. The **long ballot** is an election system that provides for the election of nearly every public official of any significance. County elections coincide with state and national primary and general elections held in even-numbered years. Considering all the other races on the ballot in those years, especially in urban counties, many voters may be uninformed about the relative merits of candidates for county clerk, district clerk, or many other county offices. For that matter, most urban voters probably cannot even distinguish between the county clerk and the district clerk.

The theory of democracy is that elections make public officials responsive to the citizens. Public officials do what the voters want because, if they do not, they face

Long ballot An election system that provides for the election of nearly every public official of any significance.

defeat at the ballot box. However, democracy does not work—or at least does not work well—if the voters are unaware of public officials. Furthermore, elected officials have no incentive to serve the public if the public is unaware of their work. The danger is that public officials who are not likely to be held accountable to the voters will act instead to further their own personal interests and the interests of the individuals and groups who support them politically.

The critics of county government would like to reform the system to make county officials more accountable, at least in urban areas. Reformers would like to reduce the number of elected county officials, either by consolidating positions into a smaller number of offices or providing for the appointment of officials by a single county executive who would be accountable to the voters. Reformers would also like to minimize the role of organized interests in county policymaking.

 WHAT IS YOUR OPINION?

Are too many county officials elected for voters to keep track of the offices and the candidates?

Conflict of interest
A situation in which the personal interests of a public official may clash with that official's professional responsibilities.

Hiring, Purchasing, Contracting, and Conflict of Interest **Conflict of interest** refers to a situation in which the personal interests of a public official may clash with that official's professional responsibilities. For example, a public official faces a conflict of interest in determining whether to award a government contract to a firm owned by family members, as opposed to a company whose management has no personal connection to the official. Public policy analysts generally believe that government works better when public officials avoid decisions in which their personal interests are at stake.

The critics of county government believe that county operations make conflict of interest inevitable. In general, county commissioners and elected department heads hire and fire employees as they see fit. County governments lack a merit-hiring system and county employees do not enjoy civil service protection. Critics say that county officials often hire and fire employees for political reasons. Furthermore, county employees have an incentive to become campaign workers for their bosses at election time, perhaps even on county time.

Another problem is the absence of centralized purchasing in most counties. Each department contracts for goods and services on its own, often without the benefit of competitive bids. At a minimum, this practice prevents the county from taking advantage of quantity discounts. More seriously, it increases opportunities for corruption by county officials who may be tempted to do business with their friends and political supporters.

The contracting process presents similar problems. County governments contract for services from engineers, accountants, surveyors, architects, and attorneys. Most of these services are provided in connection with road construction projects. Although rural counties are small businesses, urban counties are big businesses. In 2009, general fund expenditures for Harris County totaled $1.4 billion.[10]

Because state law prohibits competitive bidding, individual commissioners decide which firms receive the contracts for work in their precincts, whereas the commissioners court as a whole awards contracts for the entire county. In practice, the firms who win the contracts are also the major election campaign supporters of the commissioners court members. Between 2003 and 2007, for example, the five members of the commissioners court in Harris County raised more than $10 million in campaign contributions, with most of the money coming from contractors, engineering firms, law firms, and architects that received millions of dollars in no-bid contracts from the county. The single largest campaign donor, James Dannenbaum of Dannenbaum Engineering, contributed $160,000, while receiving $6.6 million in county contracts.[11]

The contracting process is highly controversial. County commissioners declare that they select the firms best able to provide the services to their constituents. Political contributions have no impact on their decisions, they say, because state law makes it illegal for public officials to accept campaign contributions or anything else of value in return for a contract. In contrast, critics charge that the contracting process is inherently corrupt. Furthermore, they say, the system helps insulate county commissioners from electoral accountability. County commissioners receive so much campaign money from firms doing business with the county that incumbent commissioners are virtually impossible to defeat for reelection, at least in urban areas.

Some counties use a unit road system, which is a centralized system for maintaining county roads and bridges under the authority of the county engineer. The proponents of the unit road system argue that it allows county government to operate more efficiently and less politically. In contrast, county commissioners, who would suffer a loss of political influence under a unit road system, contend that it would weaken local control of road and bridge maintenance.

Decentralization and Accountability Critics believe that the decentralization of county government makes it difficult for county officials to fulfill the responsibilities of their offices and impossible for voters to accurately evaluate their performance. In many instances, the people who raise revenue and write the budget—the commissioners court—have no direct control over the people who administer county programs—the elected department heads. The sheriff, for example, is the county's chief law enforcement official but does not directly control the budget for law enforcement. If county residents are unhappy with the operation of the county jail, whom do they blame—the commissioners court for not putting enough money in the budget or the sheriff for being a poor administrator?

 WHAT IS YOUR OPINION?

Is county government too decentralized to operate efficiently?

Structural Inflexibility and the Twenty-First Century Is county government able to respond to contemporary policy problems, especially in urban areas? Anyone driving through an urban county can easily distinguish where a city's jurisdiction ends and the county jurisdiction begins by the proliferation of roadside vendors, fireworks stands, outsized billboards, portable signs, and automobile junkyards. Cities can pass ordinances to regulate such matters, but counties cannot. Some reformers favor granting county governments ordinance-making power, especially county governments in urban areas. If counties could make ordinances, they could better address issues of development in unincorporated areas, such as land use, flood control, environmental protection, and neighborhood integrity. In contrast, the opponents of ordinance-making power for county government are against allowing yet another unit of government the power to regulate people's lives.

County Politics

The nature of county politics depends on the county. In rural and small-town Texas, county government is high-profile because counties are the primary units of local government. The population is small enough that public officials and county residents often know one another personally. Officials in some counties hold office for decades without facing electoral challenge, sometimes because they are personally popular and sometimes because no one else wants the job. In other counties, political factions form, often on the basis of personalities, and compete for control, usually in the Democratic Party primary. (Despite the growth of the Republican Party in state politics, most rural county courthouses remain Democratic.) The issues of county government in rural Texas are relatively minor; nonetheless, they are important to the people involved. Fixing potholes and paving county roads may not be the most important policy issues facing government in Texas, but they are important issues to the people who live in the region.

In urban areas, county governments are big business but low-profile. Most residents of the state's big cities are unaware of county issues and ignorant of county government. The local media typically ignore county issues, preferring instead to cover crime, automobile accidents, and natural disasters. When local media outlets do cover local government, they typically focus on city government and, occasionally, school district politics, but they seldom address county issues.

County government in urban areas is important, especially to selected segments of the population. People without health insurance rely on county health clinics and charity hospitals for healthcare. Residents of unincorporated areas depend on the county sheriff for police protection. Land developers benefit from road construction that provides access to their property. Engineers, contractors, attorneys, surveyors, and other professionals do substantial business with county government.

SCHOOL DISTRICTS

Many Texans consider school districts the most important unit of local government. Public education is the single largest budget expenditure for state and local government in Texas. In fact, many homeowners pay more money in school property taxes than they do in county and city property taxes combined. School districts are major employers, and school activities, especially high school football, are the focus of social life in many communities. Good schools are the foundation for economic growth in a community and the instrument for training young people for success in college and the workforce.

Administration

Independent School Districts (ISDs) Units of local government that provide public education services to district residents from kindergarten through the twelfth grade.

Independent School Districts (ISDs) are units of local government that provide public education services to district residents from kindergarten through the twelfth grade. The state has more than a thousand school districts, ranging in size from the Houston ISD with 200,000 students, to several hundred districts that have fewer than 500 students. In 2008–2009, 4.7 million students attended public schools in Texas.[12]

The governing body for ISDs is the board of trustees, generally composed of seven members (although some of the larger districts have nine members). Trustees may be elected either at-large or from districts to serve terms of two, three, four, or six years. Two-year terms are the most common. School trustee elections, which are nonpartisan, are usually held at times that do not coincide with statewide spring primaries and general elections. **Nonpartisan elections** are elections in which candidates run without party labels. In many urban areas, city elections and school trustee elections take place on the same day, usually the second Saturday in May in odd-numbered years.

Nonpartisan elections Election contests in which the names of the candidates appear on the ballot but not their party affiliations.

The board of trustees is a body of ordinary citizens that meets periodically to set policy for the district. The members of the board of trustees receive no salary for their services; they are laypeople rather than professional educators. The board approves the budget, sets the property tax rate, and arranges financial audits. It makes personnel decisions, involving such matters as setting the salary schedule and approving personnel contracts. Other board decisions concern the letting of contracts for the expansion and repair of the district's physical plant.

Perhaps the board's most important decision is the hiring of a superintendent. The superintendent is a professional school administrator who manages the day-to-day operation of the district and ensures that the board's policy decisions are implemented effectively. Board members tend to defer to the superintendent on the basic outline of education policy. Nonetheless, board members, especially in urban districts, frequently make political demands on a superintendent regarding contracts and jobs, especially when it comes to responding to the needs of particular ethnic groups or constituencies. In large urban districts, boards of trustees are sometimes split along racial and ethnic lines, as well as between members representing inner-city areas and members from the suburbs. Consequently, superintendents of urban districts may find themselves caught in the crossfire of a divided board. Nationwide, the average tenure for superintendents in large urban districts is about three years.[13] Texas is no exception to the pattern of conflict between school boards and superintendents. The Dallas ISD, for example, had five superintendents between 1996 and 2000.[14]

Public schools in Texas educate 4.7 million students.

Education Finance

The federal government, state government, and local taxpayers fund public education in Texas. Figure 12.2 shows the relative importance of the three revenue sources for school districts. In 2008, the average ISD received 52.4 percent of its funds from local tax sources, 37.8 percent from the state, and 9.8 percent in federal grant money.[15]

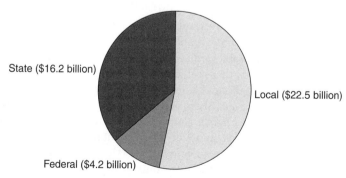

FIGURE 12.2   Education Funding Sources, 2008.
Source: Texas Education Agency.

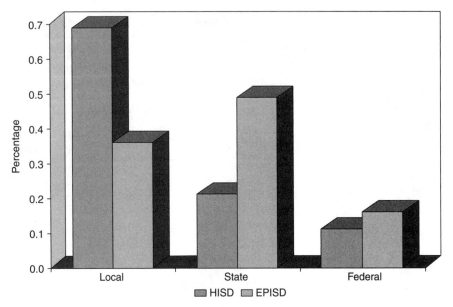

FIGURE 12.3   Funding Comparison, Houston and El Paso.
Source: Texas Education Agency.

The relative importance of funding sources varies dramatically among school districts. Figure 12.3 compares funding sources for two large, big-city school districts: Houston Independent School District (HISD) and El Paso Independent School District (EPISD). The HISD raises most of its money from local property taxes, whereas the EPISD gets more of its funding from the state than from any other source. Both districts receive some money from the federal government.

District funding reflects differences in the way the money is raised or awarded. The federal government awards money to school districts through a **federal grant program,** a program through which the national government gives money to state and local governments to spend in accordance with set standards and conditions. Federal grant money targets economically disadvantaged students and students with disabilities. Federal dollars also support the **School Lunch Program,** a federal program that provides free or inexpensive lunches to children from poor families. The amount of federal money a school district receives depends on such factors as the number of district students who are economically disadvantaged or who have limited English-language proficiency. Both the HISD and the EPISD qualify for substantial amounts of federal money under those criteria because a large proportion of their students are poor, have limited English-language proficiency, or need special education. In contrast to the HISD and EPISD, school districts that serve an affluent population, such as the Highland Park ISD in Dallas, receive almost no federal grant money.

Federal grant program A program through which the national government gives money to state and local governments to spend in accordance with set standards and conditions.

School Lunch Program A federal program that provides free or reduced-cost lunches to children from poor families.

Foundation School Program The basic funding program for public education in the state of Texas.

The **Foundation School Program** is the basic funding program for public education in the state of Texas. The legislature establishes certain minimum standards that school districts must meet in such areas as teacher compensation and student transportation. The actual amount of money a district receives depends on district wealth, local property tax rates, and a host of other factors. Wealthy districts, such as Highland Park ISD, receive relatively little state money, whereas poor districts, such as the Edgewood ISD in San Antonio, receive most of their money from the state. Because the El Paso ISD is relatively poorer than the Houston ISD, it receives a greater share of its funding from the state than does the HISD.

The state distributes other money to school districts from the Available School Fund. In the 1850s, the legislature set aside a large block of state land to create a trust fund for public education. Income from the sale and lease of that land and from royalties earned from oil and gas production on it goes into the **Permanent School Fund (PSF),** a fund constitutionally established as an endowment to finance public elementary and secondary education. The PSF principal of $25 billion cannot be spent.[16] Instead, it must be invested to earn interest and dividends, which go into the Available School Fund (ASF). The ASF is also supported by one-fourth of the taxes collected on motor fuels and natural resources. The state distributes ASF money to school districts based on the number of students in average daily attendance.

Permanent School Fund (PSF) A fund established in the Texas Constitution as an endowment to finance public elementary and secondary education.

Public education in Texas is also funded through local property taxes. School districts use local tax money to participate in the Foundation School Program and for "local enrichment," that is, to pay for services that go beyond the state-mandated minimum standards. Local money pays for building and maintaining school facilities as well as to pay off debt incurred when schools and other district facilities were built.

School tax rates tend to be higher than the property tax rates assessed by counties and cities. A school district's property tax rate includes a maintenance and operations (M & O) rate, as well as an interest and sinking fund (I & S) rate. The M & O rate applies to the district's general operating expenses, whereas the I & S rate is used to pay off the district's bond debt. Before 2006, the legislature limited the M & O rate to $1.50 per $100 valuation. It capped the I & S rate at $0.50 for debt incurred since 1992 plus whatever rate was needed to pay off debts incurred before 1992.[17] In 2006, the legislature passed, and the governor signed, a measure that reduced the maximum M & O rate to $1.00 in 2007. Local school boards could add another 4 cents to the rate for local enrichment if they wished. Faced with increased enrollment and the rising cost of student transportation, almost every district exercised that option.[18] If local school districts wished to generate more money, they could increase their M & O tax rate as high as $1.17 with voter approval. In 2008, 120 districts asked for voter approval to raise their tax caps above the $1.04 ceiling and voters in three-fourths of the districts approved.[19] The cap for the I & S rate remained unchanged.[20]

School districts grant property tax breaks to homeowners and people over 65 years of age. The Texas Constitution provides for a $15,000 homestead exemption, reducing the taxable value of a home for school tax purposes. Most school districts grant additional exemptions for persons with disabilities and people over 65 years of age. Furthermore, a homeowner's school property taxes are frozen at age 65. Regardless of increases in tax rates, elderly Texans are assessed the same tax rate they were charged on their current home when they reach their sixty-fifth birthday.

The state's system of financing public education has long been controversial because districts with wealthy property tax bases can raise more money than districts that are less affluent, even with lower property tax rates. The Glen Rose ISD in Somervell County benefits from having a nuclear power plant in its taxing district. As a result, the taxable value of property located in the Glen Rose ISD is nearly $1.7 million per student. With a relatively modest tax rate of $0.878, Glen Rose ISD generates $11,071 a year per student locally. In contrast, Crystal City ISD in Zavala County includes no refineries or power plants within its boundaries. The taxable value of property in Crystal City ISD is only $123,386 per student. Even with a relatively hefty property tax rate of $1.404, Crystal City ISD raises just $2,603 per pupil in local revenue. Left to its own financial resources, the Glen Rose ISD would have substantially more money to spend to provide a quality education to its 1,678 students than Crystal City ISD would have to support the education of its 1,951 students.[21]

In 1989, the Texas Supreme Court ruled in the case of *Edgewood v. Kirby* that the state's system of financing public education violated the Texas Constitution. The court ordered the legislature to create a system whereby districts with the same tax rate would have roughly the same amount of money to spend per student.[22] The court focused on equality of tax revenues rather than equality of expenditures. It ordered the state to adopt a system of school funding that ensured that districts would generate similar revenue per student at similar levels of tax effort. If Glen Rose ISD and Crystal City ISD had the same property tax rate, then they would be able to raise the same amount of money per student. The court did not require expenditure equality because it did not force districts to have the same tax rate. The citizens of Crystal City ISD (or Glen Rose ISD) could choose to fund their schools more (or less) generously by adopting a higher (or lower) tax rate than most other districts.

Robin Hood Plan
A reform of the state's school finance system designed to increase funding for poor school districts by redistributing money from wealthy districts.

The legislature responded to *Edgewood v. Kirby* by adopting the **Robin Hood Plan,** a reform of the state's school finance system designed to equalize funding among school districts by redistributing money from wealthy districts. Districts that are able to generate more property tax revenue per student than allowed by the state have several choices, but most wealthy districts have complied with the law by either sending money to the state or transferring it to one of the state's poor school districts. In 2008–2009, districts with more than $476,500 in property valuation per student had to return money to the state or share their wealth with poorer districts.[23] Two hundred districts qualified as wealthy and were forced to redistribute more than $1 billion in revenue because of the Robin Hood Plan.[24] Glenn Rose, for example, sent the state more than $10 million out of local property tax revenue of $29 million.[25]

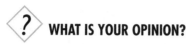

WHAT IS YOUR OPINION?

Is the Robin Hood school-finance reform plan fair?

Texas may soon face another lawsuit over education funding equity.[26] Although the Robin Hood Plan initially closed the funding gap between property-poor and property-rich school districts, the legislature has tinkered with the school funding system and disparities have reemerged. Consider the data in Table 12.2 comparing the Highland Park ISD in Dallas, one of the state's wealthiest school districts, with the Edgewood ISD in San Antonio, one of the state's poorest school districts. The Highland Park ISD has more than 20 times the taxable value per student than the Edgewood ISD ($1,803,002 per student compared with just $75,178 per student in the Edgewood ISD). The principle of the *Edgewood* case is that districts with similar tax rates should have similar amounts of money to spend per student regardless of property wealth. To close the funding gap, the state provides more money to property poor districts and, in accordance with the Robin Hood Plan, requires wealthy districts to write a check to the state or share revenues with poorer districts. As Table 12.2 shows, Edgewood received 67 percent of its revenue from the state in 2008, whereas the Highland Park ISD got only 16 percent of its money from the state. Furthermore, the Highland Park ISD had to reduce its local revenue by transferring $66.2 million to the state. Nonetheless, the Edgewood ISD had less money to spend per student than the Highland Park ISD ($4,760 compared with $4,815), despite having a substantially higher tax rate. Property owners in the Edgewood ISD paid a tax rate of $1.405 compared with a tax rate for property owners in Highland Park of $1.037.

Another equity issue involves a disparity in funding between rapidly growing school districts and districts with stable student populations. State funding has failed to keep up with enrollment growth in suburban districts that have experienced rapid enrollment growth. In 2008, for example, Cypress-Fairbanks ISD, which is located in a rapidly growing area in Northwest Houston, received $4,606 per student from the state. In contrast, nearby Tomball ISD, whose enrollment is not growing as rapidly, received $5,903 per student.[27]

Chapter 13 continues an examination of education funding in Texas.

TABLE 12.2   Financial Information: Highland Park ISD and Edgewood ISD, 2008

Financial Criteria	Highland Park ISD	Edgewood ISD
Taxable value per student	$1,803,002	$75,178
Property tax rate per $100	$1.037	$1.405
Percentage total revenue from the state	16 percent	67 percent
Instructional expenditures per pupil	$4,815	$4,760
Equity transfers (funds returned to the state)	$66.2 million	$0

Source: Texas Education Agency, www.tea.state.tx.us.

INTERNET RESEARCH

Comparing School Districts

The largest school districts in the state are the Aldine ISD (Harris County), Arlington ISD, Austin ISD, Cypress-Fairbanks ISD (Harris County), Dallas ISD, El Paso ISD, Fort Bend ISD, Fort Worth ISD, Garland ISD, Houston ISD, North East ISD (Bexar County), Northside ISD (Bexar County), and San Antonio ISD. Each of these districts has 50,000 or more students. Your assignment is to select two of the state's largest school districts and write an essay in which you compare and contrast the two districts. You can find a great deal of data about the state's school districts by reviewing the Texas Education Agency (TEA) school report cards, which can be found at the following Internet address:

http://ritter.tea.state.tx.us/perfreport/snapshot/2008/district.srch.html

Indicate that you wish to search by district name and then type the name of the district for which you wish to find data. The website includes a good deal of information.

Your essay should cover the following topics:

- **A demographic profile of each district.** How do the two districts compare in terms of size? What is each district's racial/ethnic profile? What proportion of each district's student body has special needs of one sort or another?

- **A funding profile of each district.** How do the districts compare in terms of tax base? What are their tax rates? How much revenue does each district raise per student? How much state aid does each district receive?

- **A profile of each district's teachers.** How experienced are the two faculties? Does each district have a diverse group of faculty? How well paid are each district's teachers?

- **A performance evaluation.** How well do the students of each district perform on TAKS and other tests? What is each district's accountability rating?

Conclude your essay with a discussion of the strengths and weaknesses of each district. Consider whether it is possible to determine which district is more effective. Keep in mind that the challenges facing the two districts are not the same and the resources available may not be identical, either.

Issues in Education Policy

Education issues are an important part of the official Texas policy agenda. We will discuss five of the more prominent contemporary educational issues: charter schools, school choice, class size, bilingual education, and basic skills testing.

Charter school A publicly funded but privately managed school that operates under the terms of a formal contract or charter with the state.

Charter Schools A **charter school** is a publicly funded but privately managed school that operates under the terms of a formal contract, or charter, with the state. Parents, teachers, private companies, and nonprofit organizations may petition the state for a charter to create a school. The charter spells out the school's educational programs, targets the student population the school intends to serve, defines the school's management style, and identifies its educational goals. Each charter school is independent in that it is not part of an ISD and parents from any district may voluntarily choose to send their children to a particular charter. Charter schools may not discriminate on the basis of race, ethnicity, gender, disability, or educational need, but they may refuse to accept a student who has a history of misbehavior. A charter school may not charge tuition or levy taxes. The state funds charter schools through the Foundation School Program, awarding the same amount of money per student that it gives to traditional public schools. It provides no funding for facilities. In 2009, more than 90,000 students attended one of the state's 460 chapter campuses.[28]

Charter schools are exempt from most state education regulations. Although they must conform to health and safety codes and teach the state-mandated curriculum, they do not have to follow state regulations concerning class sizes, teacher qualifications, and the school calendar. Nonetheless, the state evaluates charter schools on the same basis as other schools, including TAKS (Texas Assessment of Knowledge and Skills), and on the basis of the goals the schools set for themselves. If a charter school performs poorly and fails to meet its goals, it risks losing its charter and having to close its doors.

Charter schools are controversial. Their supporters believe that each charter school is an opportunity for educational innovation. Teachers can better do their jobs when freed of red tape, they say. Moreover, the competition from charter schools will force public schools to perform better. In contrast, the critics of charter schools argue that they are a back-door method for funneling taxpayer dollars from public schools to private schools. They feel state funds should be used to improve the existing schools, rather than support an unproven educational experiment.

The performance of charter schools has been uneven. Although some charter schools—mostly small, college-preparatory schools—have excelled, other charter schools have failed to make the grade because of poor test scores, financial mismanagement, or both. A national study of charter school performance conducted by Stanford University found that 17 percent of charters provide outstanding educational opportunities for their students and nearly half of charters achieve results no different from the local public school option. Over one-third of charter schools perform worse than their traditional school counterparts. Furthermore, the report singles out Texas for doing a particularly poor job of holding poorly run charter schools accountable.[29]

School choice An educational reform movement that would allow parents to choose the elementary or secondary school their children will attend.

School Choice The educational reform movement that would allow parents to choose the elementary or secondary school their children will attend is known as **school choice.** Under a parental choice program, the state would give parents a voucher that would provide a type of scholarship to be paid to the school that the parents select for their child to attend. Some proponents of parental choice would allow parents to choose not only from among public schools but also from among private schools.

School choice is controversial. The proponents of school choice believe that competition for funding will force schools to improve. If low-quality public schools did not upgrade the quality of their educational programs, they would have to shut down for lack of funding. In contrast, the opponents of school choice question whether lack of competition is the main problem with public schools, believing

AROUND THE NATION

Cash for Grades in the District of Columbia

Students in the District of Columbia (DC) can earn money by making good grades. The program, which targets low-income middle school pupils, allows students to collect as much as $100 every two weeks if they behave themselves, wear their school uniforms, go to class, complete their homework, and get good grades. During the fall term of 2008, the average DC student earned $406 of a possible $1,000.*

Cash for grades is controversial. The program's advocates see it as a way to close the performance gap between low-income and middle-class young-sters. Although wealthy families may reward their children with trips, parties, and even cash for doing well in school, low-income families do not have the option. In contrast, the opponents of the program contend that students should value learning for learning's sake, not because of a financial reward. Furthermore, the program is expensive to implement.

Research on the effectiveness of cash incentive programs is mixed at best. Studies show that student performance improves during the program, but then falls back after the program ends and the money goes away. Studies find no evidence that cash rewards have a lasting effect on student learning. In fact, cash incentive programs may actually undercut interest in learning.[†]

QUESTIONS TO CONSIDER

1. Would you do better in this course if you were promised cash if you did well?
2. Are cash-for-grade programs a good use of tax-payer dollars? Why or why not?
3. Do the arguments used in favor of merit pay for teachers also apply to financial incentive pro-grams for students (and vice versa)?

*Theresa Vargas, "Cash Incentives Create Competition," *Washington Post*, March 22, 2009, available at www.washingtonpost.com.
†Zach Patton, "Wage Learners," *Governing*, August 2009, pp. 25–28.

instead that poverty, lack of parental involvement, and inadequate funding are the primary causes of poor school performance. They fear that vouchers would enable middle-class parents to take their children from public schools, leaving the children of poor families behind in public schools with even less funding. Public schools would get worse, they say, not better.

Texas has a limited school choice program. The parents of students in schools that are judged as low-performing schools for two consecutive years can transfer their children to any other public school in the district that will agree to receive them, including charter schools. The parents of students in low-performing schools are also eligible for free tutoring. In practice, however, few parents and students take advan-tage of their opportunities. In 2006, for example, 19,000 students in the Houston ISD were eligible to transfer or to receive free tutoring. Only 122 chose to transfer while only 1,185 accepted the free tutoring.[30]

 WHAT IS YOUR OPINION?

If you were a parent of a student in a low-performing public school, would you transfer your child to another school?

GETTING INVOLVED   **Helping a Child Learn**

Nothing is more rewarding than helping a child learn. Most school districts have tutoring programs, in which volunteers assist students who are trying to learn to read or understand mathematics.

Call your local school district (the number is in the telephone book) and volunteer to tutor.
It's your community—Get involved!

Class Size Does class size matter? Some advocates of education reform believe that the key to improving education is to have smaller classes. The concept is fairly simple: Teachers can do a better job if they have fewer students in a class. In recent years, some state legislatures have mandated smaller class sizes, especially in the early grades. Texas law caps the size of classes in kindergarten through the fourth grade at 22 students, although districts may request a waiver if a school is struggling with rapid growth or lacks facilities. In general, however, if a class exceeds 22 students, the district must hire another teacher and split the class or assign students to another class to ensure that no class exceeds the cap.[31]

Critics argue that the movement to reduce class size may not be a good use of resources. Reducing class size is an expensive reform because it requires school districts to hire additional teachers. Furthermore, research on the effect of smaller class sizes is unclear. Studies show that class sizes must drop to 15–17 to make much difference, and even then smaller classes seem to make a difference only in student performance in the lowest grades. Critics of the smaller-class movement believe that the money could be better spent on teacher training.

Bilingual education The teaching of academic subjects in both English and a student's native language, usually Spanish.

Bilingual Education **Bilingual education** is the teaching of academic subjects in both English and the student's native language, usually Spanish. About one-sixth of the state's public school children have limited proficiency in the English language, including 33 percent in the Dallas ISD, 30 percent in the Houston ISD, and 29 percent in the El Paso ISD.[32] Spanish is by far the most common language spoken by Texas children who have limited English-language ability.

Bilingual education is a controversial education policy issue. The advocates of bilingual education believe that it enables students whose primary language is not English to learn academic subjects in their own language while they work on their English. Otherwise, they would fall behind, grow frustrated with school, and potentially drop out. Students enrolled in bilingual education programs typically take several years to learn to read, write, and speak English well enough to enter mainstream classes. In contrast, the opponents of bilingual education argue that it retards the English-language development of non-English-speaking students. They believe that students with limited English-language proficiency are better served by a period of intensive English instruction, after which they enter regular academic classes.

Texas schools use a mixture of bilingual education and English-language immersion programs. The legislature has neither mandated bilingual education nor prohibited its use. Instead, each district decides how it can best meet the educational needs of students with limited English-language proficiency.

No Child Left Behind Act A federal law that requires state governments and local school districts to institute basic skills testing as a condition for receiving federal aid.

Basic Skills Testing The **No Child Left Behind Act** is a federal law that requires state governments and local school districts to institute basic skills testing as a condition for receiving federal aid. The results of the tests must be used to assess school performance and track the progress of individual students. Poor-performing schools that fail to improve will eventually lose federal aid money.

Texas Assessment of Knowledge and Skills (TAKS) A state mandated basic-skills test designed to measure student progress and school performance.

Texas uses the **Texas Assessment of Knowledge and Skills (TAKS),** a state-mandated basic skills test designed to measure student progress and school performance. TAKS testing begins in the third grade and continues through high school. Ninth-grade students take TAKS tests in reading and math. Tenth and eleventh graders test in English, math, science, and social sciences. Eleventh graders must pass all four subjects to earn a diploma, regardless of their course grades. Students who fail in the eleventh grade have several more opportunities to pass the test in their senior year and even during the summer after graduation. Students who fail to pass the graduation TAKS can still participate in their high school's graduation ceremony, but they receive a certificate of attendance rather than a diploma, unless they eventually pass the test. In 2009, one in seven high school seniors, nearly 37,000 students, failed the TAKS and were prevented from graduating.[33] The Texas Education Agency (TEA) uses TAKS scores along with four-year high school graduation rates to rate schools and school districts as exemplary, recognized, academically acceptable, or academically unacceptable. In 2008, 3007 districts were rated exemplary or recognized[34] compared with 87 districts that were academically unacceptable.[35]

The proponents of basic skills tests, such as TAKS, believe that testing improves public education by holding students, teachers, and school administrators accountable. Students in elementary and middle school must pass TAKS before they can be promoted to higher grades unless they are granted a waiver (and many are). High school students must pass TAKS in order to graduate. Teachers may face reassignment and school administrators may lose their jobs if their students do poorly on the test. In contrast, the critics of basic skills testing argue that tests actually undermine educational quality because they force schools to focus on the test rather than student learning. Schools neglect other subjects for weeks before the test is given so they can prepare. Much of their work focuses not on basic skills but on test-taking techniques. Instead of learning to read, write, and do math, students learn how to take multiple-choice exams. Furthermore, critics charge that TAKS standards are too low to be meaningful. Students taking the eleventh-grade social studies exam only need to correctly answer 28 of 55 multiple-choice questions to pass. The passing standard for the eleventh-grade science exam is 30 correct of 55 questions.[36]

The Texas legislature and the governor adopted legislation in 2007 to replace high school TAKS testing with end-of-course exams. Beginning with high school freshmen in 2011–2012, students in the ninth, tenth, and eleventh grades will take end-of-course exams in English, math, science, and social sciences each year for a total of 12 tests. The new test will be called the State of Texas Assessment of Academic Readiness (STAAR). Students will have to average passing scores in the four subjects in order to earn their high school diplomas. Testing in grades three through eight will remain unchanged.[37]

Educational Performance

Independent assessments of the performance of Texas schools indicate that the state's students are less well prepared for college and the workforce than students in many other states. Consider the performance of Texas students on the SAT, which is a standardized exam taken by students planning to apply for admission to a university. In 2009, the composite SAT score for Texas students was 1,467 compared with a national average of 1,509.[38]

Texas suffers from a relatively high dropout rate. The 2007–2008 high school graduation class started with more than 370,000 students and ended with 237,000 high school graduates, or 64 percent. Although not all the missing students are dropouts (some may have left Texas public schools and graduated elsewhere), the dropout rate is nonetheless considerable. An estimate, using a formula called the Cumulative Promotion Index, sets the Texas high school graduation rate at 65 percent.[39] Latino and African American youngsters are considerably more likely

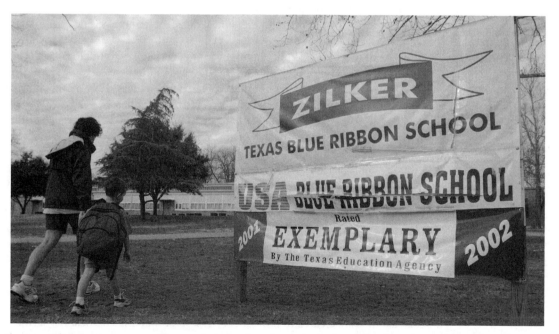

The Texas Education Agency uses test scores and other factors to rate schools as exemplary, recognized, academically acceptable, or academically unacceptable.

to drop out of high school than are white students. The dropout rate for Latino and African American high school students is 45 percent and 40 percent, respectively, compared with a dropout rate of 20 percent for whites.[40] Because of the state's high dropout rate, the proportion of Texas residents without high school diplomas is expected to rise 11 percentage points to 30 percent by 2040.[41]

Texas does an average job at best in preparing students for college. Half the students entering public colleges and universities in the state are unprepared for college-level work in math, reading, or writing and therefore must take at least one remedial course. Colleges and universities spend more than $90 million a year teaching college students the basic skills that they did not learn in high school.[42] Moreover, students who enter college unprepared for college work are much less likely to graduate than are students who have college-level skills. Just 16 percent of students who require remediation earn a degree or certificate in six years compared to 47 percent of college-ready students.[43]

SPECIAL DISTRICTS

Special district A unit of local government created to perform specific functions.

Subsidence The sinking of the surface of the land caused by the too-rapid extraction of subsurface water.

Utility district A special district that provides utilities such as water and sewer service to residents living in unincorporated urban areas.

Hospital district A special district that provides emergency medical services, indigent healthcare, and community health services.

A **special district** is a unit of local government created to perform specific functions. Soil and water conservation districts, for example, work to prevent soil erosion and preserve water resources. Levee improvement districts build and maintain levees. Coastal subsidence districts regulate the use of subsurface water resources in order to minimize **subsidence**, which is the sinking of the surface of the land caused by the too-rapid extraction of subsurface water. Mosquito control districts spray for mosquitoes to control annoying pests and reduce the danger of encephalitis and other diseases spread by mosquitoes.

Special districts provide important governmental services to millions of Texans. A **utility district** is a special district that provides utilities, such as water and sewer service, to residents living in unincorporated urban areas. Texas has more than 1,100 utility districts, going by such names as Fresh Water Supply Districts (FWSDs), Water Control and Improvement Districts (WCIDs), and Municipal Utility Districts (MUDs), which are the most numerous. In addition to water and sewer services, utility districts may also provide their residents with solid waste collection, fire protection, drainage, parks, and recreation facilities. A **hospital district** is a special district that provides emergency medical services, indigent healthcare, and community health services. The Harris County Hospital District, for example, is the primary medical provider for nearly a million residents in Harris County who do not have health insurance. Its operating budget exceeds $1.3 billion a year.[44] Community/junior college districts enroll more students in higher education than do the state's public universities. Flood control districts are responsible for flood control in many areas of the state.

Reasons for Special Districts

Special districts are created to provide services that other units of local government cannot or will not provide. For example, state law specifies a maximum property tax rate for counties and cities. Local governments can overcome the property tax ceiling by creating special districts with their own taxing authority. Harris County has a flood control district, hospital district, and port authority. Although these districts are separate units of government with their own taxing authority, Harris County Commissioners Court controls them. Transit authorities and port authorities are other big-budget special districts whose operations could not easily be financed within the budget constraints of existing city and county governments.

Sometimes special districts are an advantageous approach to solving problems that transcend the boundaries of existing units of local government. Flooding, for example, is seldom confined to a single county or city. A countywide or area-wide flood control district offers a regional approach to a regional problem. Similarly, transportation problems may affect several cities and counties. In each of these cases, it is often easier to create a special district that includes the whole area affected by the problem than it is to coordinate the efforts of existing governments.

Other motivations for the establishment of special districts include political expediency and financial gain. At times, existing units of local government refuse to provide certain services because of the opposition of individual officeholders. Special districts can be an effective means of outflanking that opposition. Some problems, such as flood control or mass transit, may become so difficult or controversial that local officials may choose to ignore them. The creation of a special district allows officials to pass the buck while taking credit for having taken the problem "out of politics."

Utility districts enable developers to build subdivisions in rural areas, outside of the coverage of municipal water and sewer services. The utility district borrows money to build water and sewer systems for the development. Homeowners pay off the debt over time through service charges and property taxes. By using a utility district to defer the construction cost of a water and sewer system, developers are able to reduce their upfront construction expenditures, and consumers can buy new homes less expensively than if the utility costs were built into the purchase price.[45] In Denton County, for example, a developer named Realty Capital Belmont Corp. is using two freshwater supply districts to help fund a 4,000-home development near Argyle and Northlake. In 2006, the developer parked three mobile homes on the property and rented them to employees. The renters filed the necessary paperwork to establish residency and then requested an election to create two freshwater supply districts. In 2007, the seven registered voters living in the three mobile homes cast their ballots to approve the creation of the districts which would borrow money to pay for roads, water pipes, and a sewage treatment system. The development's future homeowners will pay off the debt with a property tax whose rate could be as high as $1.00 per $100 of valuation.[46]

Creation, Organization, and Operation

Special districts are created through a variety of procedures. Hospital districts require the adoption of a constitutional amendment. The State Soil and Water Conservation Board creates soil and water conservation districts. The legislature, the Texas Commission on Environmental Quality (TCEQ), or a county commissioners court can establish utility districts. Utility districts that are to be located in a city's extraterritorial

Transit authorities, such as Metro in Houston, provide transportation services to area residents.

jurisdiction must first be approved by that city. The Texas legislature authorizes community/junior college districts, transit authorities, port authorities, and sports authorities.

Most districts require voter approval of area residents before they begin operations. After the legislature authorizes the creation of a utility district, for example, the measure goes on the ballot for approval by voters living within the boundaries of the proposed district. At the same election, voters may also be asked to grant the district authority to sell bonds (that is, to borrow money) and to tax. Utility districts generally issue bonds to finance the construction of sewage treatment plants. Flood control districts use them to pay for drainage improvements. Likewise, airport authorities use bond money to build runways and terminals. Sports authorities issue bonds to finance the construction of sports stadiums.

A board of directors, usually consisting of five members, is the governing body for most special districts. The board may be either appointed or elected. District voters elect most water district and community/junior college boards, whereas city mayors appoint housing authority boards. The governor names the directors of river authorities. County commissioners courts select hospital, noxious weed control, and rural fire prevention district boards. In most cases, district board members are unsalaried. They set basic policy but leave the day-to-day operation of the district to a professional staff. Perhaps the most important task for the board of trustees of a community/junior college district, for example, is to hire a chancellor or president to manage the daily affairs of the college.

Funding

Special districts receive funding from a variety of sources. Many districts levy taxes. Utility districts, port authorities, hospital districts, flood control districts, and community/junior college districts all levy property taxes. Suburban utility districts often assess higher property tax rates than do nearby incorporated municipalities. The funding for sports authorities may come from sales taxes, hotel/motel occupancy taxes, property taxes, or taxes on rental cars. Transit authorities levy sales taxes.

Special districts raise revenues from service charges. Utility districts charge residents for water and sewer usage and for garbage pickup. Students in community/junior college districts pay tuition and fees for the classes they take. Transit authorities raise revenues from ticket charges. Toll road authorities collect tolls from drivers. Funding for coastal subsidence districts comes from fees charged for permits to drill water wells. Finally, special districts receive funding from other units of government. Federal mass transit aid supports the state's transit authorities. Community/junior college districts benefit from state funding and federal grant money. Hospital districts receive both federal and state funding to support their programs, including funding from the two huge federal healthcare programs, Medicare and Medicaid.

Evaluation of Special Districts

Special districts have both defenders and critics. Their supporters argue that they provide services that otherwise would not be available. In contrast, critics identify several problem areas. First, special districts often operate in the shadows, with little state supervision and even less public participation. For example, fewer than a dozen voters may participate in utility district authorization elections. Second, special districts generally operate less efficiently than general-purpose units of local government, such as cities and counties.[47] Small districts, particularly utility districts, can be uneconomical. Their operations are often run amateurishly and they are too small to take advantage of economies of scale. Finally, the multiplicity of special districts in Texas complicates the problems of urban government. For example, many observers believe that utility districts are a major cause of land subsidence in the Houston–Galveston area because of their extensive use of subsurface water resources.

WHAT WE HAVE LEARNED

1. **What is the constitutional/legal status of counties in Texas, how are they structured, how are they funded, what services do they provide, and what issues do they face?**

Texas has 254 counties, ranging in size from sparsely populated counties to large urban counties with millions of people. As general law units

of local government, counties are limited to the structures of government and powers set by state law. Counties play a dual role in that they provide services to county residents as well as implement state policies. County governments enforce state laws, operate state and county courts, provide some health services, keep records, collect certain taxes, administer elections, build and maintain roads and bridges, and provide other services.

Counties have numerous elected officials. The commissioners court, consisting of a county judge and four commissioners, is the board of directors for county government. Although commissioners court sets the property tax rate and adopts a budget, it does not have general ordinance-making power. Other elected county officials, depending somewhat on the size of the county (i.e., large counties have more officials than smaller counties), include the sheriff, district attorney, county attorney, district clerk, county clerk, justices of the peace, constables, tax assessor-collector, county treasurer, and—in Harris and Dallas Counties—county boards of education.

Property taxes are the main source of tax revenue for county governments. County governments can expand their taxing capacity by creating separate but closely allied special districts to provide such costly services as healthcare, flood control, and toll road construction and maintenance. Other revenue sources for county governments include fees for motor vehicle licenses, service charges, and federal aid.

Although road and bridge construction is a major budget item in all counties, it is especially significant in geographically large counties. County governments in metropolitan areas provide a wide range of services, especially if the county has a large population living in unincorporated areas. These services include law enforcement, jail operation, indigent healthcare, the operation of county and district courts, flood control, and parks.

The issues facing county government depend on the size of the county. In rural areas, county governments are the local governments closest to the people. In urban areas, county governments are almost invisible governments despite employing thousands of persons and spending millions of dollars. Issues include the long ballot and accountability to the voters; hiring, purchasing, contracting, and conflict of interest; decentralization

and accountability; and problems created because of structural decentralization.

2. **How are school districts governed, how are they funded, what issues do they face, and how well do they perform?**

Independent school districts (ISDs) are units of local government that provide public education services to district residents from kindergarten through the twelfth grade. Each ISD is governed by an elected board of trustees, which is a body of ordinary citizens that meets periodically to set policy for the district. The board hires a professional administrator called a superintendent to run the day-to-day affairs of the district.

School districts receive money from the federal government, state government, and from local property taxes. The federal government gives money to school districts through grant programs, such as the School Lunch Program. The Foundation School Program is the basic funding program for K–12 education in Texas. The state's system of financing public education has long been controversial because districts with wealthy property tax bases can raise more money than districts that are less affluent, even if the wealthy districts have lower property tax rates. In *Edgewood v. Kirby*, the Texas Supreme Court ordered the legislature to create a system whereby districts with the same tax rate would have roughly the same amount of money to spend per student. The legislature responded by adopting the Robin Hood Plan, a reform of the state's school finance system designed to equalize funding among school districts by redistributing money from wealthy districts.

Texas school districts face a number of important issues, involving charter schools, school choice, class size, bilingual education, and basic skills testing. A charter school is a publicly funded but privately managed school that operates under the terms of a formal contract, or charter, with the state. Whereas supporters believe that charter schools are an opportunity for innovation, critics charge that they are a back-door method for funneling taxpayer money from public schools to private schools. School choice is the educational reform movement that would allow parents to choose the elementary or secondary school their children will attend. The proponents of school choice believe that competition for funding will force schools to improve, but critics warn that choice will weaken public schools by taking funding away from them. Education reformers also debate the merits of class size. Bilingual education, the teaching of academic subjects in both English and the student's native language (usually Spanish), is controversial as well. No Child Left Behind (NCLB) is a federal law that requires state governments and local school districts to institute basic skills testing as a condition for receiving federal aid. Texas currently uses the TAKS, which will eventually be replaced with the STAAR. The proponents of basic skills tests believe that testing improves public education by holding students, teachers, and school administrators accountable. In contrast, the critics argue that tests actually undermine educational quality because they force schools to focus on the test rather than student learning.

Independent assessments of the performance of Texas schools indicate that the state's students are less well prepared for college and the workforce than students in many other states. Average SAT scores in Texas are below the national average whereas the dropout rate exceeds the national average. Texas does an average job at best in preparing students for college.

3. **How are special districts created, organized, operated, and funded, and what are their benefits and liabilities?**

A special district is a unit of local government created to perform specific functions. Special districts include transit authorities, mosquito control districts, hospital districts, community college districts, flood control districts, port authorities, utility districts, and many more. Special districts are created to provide services that other units of government cannot or will not provide. They are created through a variety of procedures, including the adoption of amendments to the Texas Constitution or the actions of the Texas legislature, TCEQ, or county commissioners court. Most districts require voter approval of area residents before they begin operations. Special districts receive funding from a variety of sources, including taxes and service charges. The supporters of special districts argue that they provide services that otherwise would not be available. Critics charge that they often operate inefficiently and uneconomically, and that they complicate the problems of local government.

KEY TERMS

bilingual education

charter school

commissioners court

conflict of interest

federal grant program

Foundation School Program

general law units of local government

home rule

hospital district

Independent School Districts (ISDs)

long ballot

No Child Left Behind Act

nonpartisan elections

ordinance

partisan election

Permanent School Fund (PSF)

poll tax

Robin Hood Plan

school choice

School Lunch Program

special district

State Children's Health Insurance Program (SCHIP)

subpoena

subsidence

Texas Assessment of Knowledge and Skills (TAKS)

utility district

NOTES

1. Terrence Stutz, "Texas Takes Another Crack at Merit Pay," *Dallas Morning News*, August 24, 2009, available at www.dallasnews.com.

2. Kate Alexander, "Experienced Teachers Not in Neediest Schools, Report Shows," *Austin American-Statesman*, August 5, 2008, available at www.statesman.com.

3. Alan Greenblatt, "Merit Pay Moves Forward," *Governing*, January 2007, p. 51.

4. Terrence Stutz, "Many Texas School Districts Reject Merit Pay for Teachers," *Dallas Morning News*, March 10, 2008, available at www.dallasnews.com.

5. U.S. Bureau of the Census, available at www.census.gov.

6. Melissa del Bosque, "Sick and Tired: How Texas' Healthcare System Bleeds County Coffers and Sends Some to Early Graves," *Texas Observer*, September 4, 2009, pp. 8–14.

7. Rick Casey, "Why Run for Judge if You're King," *Houston Chronicle*, July 8, 2005, p. B1.

8. Equal Justice Center, "Texas Indigent Defense Spending," available at www.equaljusticecenter.org.

9. Glenn Evans, "Counties Concerned Over Too Much Control Coming Out of Austin," *Longview News-Journal*, April 4, 2004, available at www.news-journal.com.

10. Harris County, FY 2009–2010 Budget, available at www.co.harris.tx.us.

11. Chase David, "Few Rivals But Plenty of Donors," *Houston Chronicle*, November 24, 2007, pp. A1, A9.

12. Texas Education Agency, available at www.tea.state.tx.us.

13. Council of Great City Schools, available at www.cgcs.org.

14. Jim Henderson, "Dallas School Trustees Left Holding Bag Again," *Houston Chronicle*, July 9, 2000, pp. 1A, 21A.

15. *Texas Directory*, January 22, 2009, available at www.txdirectory.com.

16. Office of the Permanent School Fund, *Texas Permanent School Fund, Annual Report, Fiscal Year Ending August 31, 2008*, available at www.tea.state.tx.us.

17. *Financing Public Education in Texas*, 2nd ed., available at www.lbb.state.tx.us.

18. Terrence Stutz, "New Study Shows Texas School Property Tax Relief Largely Wiped Out," *Dallas Morning News*, August 14, 2008, available at www.dallasnews.com.

19. Terrence Stutz, "Vote to Raise Property Taxes Failed to Pass in More than Half of Texas' School Districts," *Dallas Morning News*, November 6, 2008, available at www.dallasnews.com.

20. House Research Organization, Focus Report, "Schools and Taxes: A Summary of Legislation of the 2006 Special Session," available at www.hro.house.state.tx.us.

21. Texas Education Agency, available at www.tea.state.tx.us.

22. *Edgewood v. Kirby*, 777 S.W.2d 391 (1989).

23. Terrence Stutz, "Lawmakers Tackle Teacher Pay, Tests but Leave School Finance for 2011," *Dallas Morning News*, June 2, 2009, available at www.dallasnews.com.

24. Ericka Mellon, "For 1st Time, HISD Must Pay the State," *Houston Chronicle*, March 7, 2008, pp. A1, A6.

25. Texas Education Agency, available at www.tea.state.tx.us.

26. Gary Scharrer, "Could Another School Funding Lawsuit Be Brewing?" *San Antonio Express-News*, June 21, 2009, available at www.mysanantonio.com.

27. Ericka Mellon, "Cy-Fair ISD Considering Major Tax Increase," *Houston Chronicle*, June 9, 2009, available at www.chron.com.

28. Shirley Jinkins, "Texas Charter School Students Lag Behind, Study Says," *Fort Worth Star-Telegram*, June 16, 2009, available at www.star-telegram.com.

29. Sam Dillon, "Education Chief to Warn Advocates That Inferior Charter Schools Harm the Effort," *New York Times*, June 22, 2009, available at www.nytimes.com.

30. Jennifer Radcliffe and Ericka Mellon, "More HISD Schools Miss Federal Mark," *Houston Chronicle*, August 16, 2007, pp. A1, A8.

31. Terrence Stutz, "Lawmakers May Modify Class Size Cap," *Dallas Morning News*, April 4, 2004, available at www.dallasnews.com.

32. Texas Education Agency, "2006 District AEIS+ Report," available at www.tea.state.tx.us.

33. Terrence Stutz, "1 in 7 Seniors Failed Part of TAKS Exam, Texas Education Agency Says," *Dallas Morning News*, June 5, 2009, available at www.dallasnews.com.

34. Linda Stewart Ball, "Student Achievement Rising in Urban Texas Schools," *Fort Worth Star-Telegram*, February 25, 2009, available at www.star-telegram.com.

35. Kate Alexander, "Good News, Bad News in School Accountability Ratings," *Austin American-Statesman*, August 1, 2009, available at www.statesman.com.

36. Holly K. Hacker and Kent Fischer, "Dispelling 7 TAKS Myths with a Healthy Dose of Reality," *Dallas Morning News*, March 3, 2009, available at www.dallasnews.com.

37. Jenny LaCoste-Caputo, "TAKS on Its Way Out, But It's Not History Yet," *San Antonio Express-News*, August 17, 2007, available at www.mysanantonio.com.

38. Terrence Stutz, "Texas Students Improve SAT Math Scores but Slip in Reading, Writing," *Dallas Morning News*, August 25, 2009, available at www.dallasnews.com.

39. Abby Rapoport and Brian Thevenot, "Dropout Problem Drags Texas Down," *Texas Tribune*, November 4, 2009, available at www.texastribune.org.

40. Michele Angél, "Gap Widens Between Hispanic and Anglo Dropout Rates," *Rio Grande Guardian*, November 1, 2007, available at www.riograndeguardian.com.

41. Raven L. Hill and Laura Heinauer, "Texas' Dropout Problem Probably Worse than Reported," *Austin American-Statesman*, May 27, 2007, available at www.statesman.com.

42. Melanie Markley, "Scores on TAAS Rose as SATs Fell," *Houston Chronicle*, June 6, 2004, p. A35.

43. Ralph K. M. Haurwitz and Laura Heinauer, "Half of Students Entering Public Colleges Need Remedial Courses," *Austin American-Statesman*, May 15, 2005, available at www.statesman.com.

44. Harris County Hospital District, "Changing Lives Through Health and Wellness: 2009 Annual Report," available at www.hchdonline.com.

45. Paula Lavigne, "Will Sprouting of MUDs Make Mess?" *Dallas Morning News*, October 26, 2003, available at www.dallasnews.com.

46. Dan X. McGraw, "Special Districts Get Voter Approval," *Denton Record-Chronicle*, November 12, 2007, available at www.dentonrc.com.

47. Kathryn A. Foster, *The Political Economy of Special-Purpose Government* (Washington, DC: Georgetown University Press, 1997), pp. 174–183.

State Budget Policy

WHAT WE WILL LEARN

After studying Chapter 13, students should be able to answer the following questions:

▸ What are the most important revenue sources for the state of Texas, including both tax and non-tax sources, and how has the relative importance of those sources changed over the last 20 years?

▸ What important revenue issues face state government in Texas?

▸ What policy options have been proposed for reforming the state's revenue structure?

▸ How do spending levels in Texas compare and contrast with those of other states?

▸ What are the most important budget priorities in Texas and how are those priorities reflected in budget policy?

▸ What are the primary steps in the state budgetary process?

▸ How are budget policies made in Texas?

Recession An economic slowdown characterized by dealing economic output and rising unemployment.

Texas government is facing a budget crisis. In the short run, the problem is the severe recession that began in late 2008 and extended through most of 2009. A **recession** is an economic slowdown characterized by declining economic output and rising unemployment. State revenues fall during a recession because people make fewer purchases that are subject to the state sales tax and motor vehicle sales and rental tax. Meanwhile, state spending increases during a recession because more people can qualify for unemployment benefits and welfare payments. The Texas legislature was able to balance the budget for 2009–2011 even though it had less state tax money to spend than it had in the previous budget period by using $12.1 billion in federal funds, which were part of an $877 billion stimulus package. Congress passed, and President Barack Obama signed, the stimulus legislation, which was known as the American Recovery and Reinvestment Act, in order to reduce the impact of the recession.[1] Although the legislature will have a Rainy Day Fund worth as much as $9 billion to spend when it meets in 2011, the federal money will not be available. The **Rainy Day Fund** is an emergency reserve set aside by the state to cover future budget shortfalls.

Rainy Day Fund An emergency reserve set aside by the state to cover future budget shortfalls.

In the long run, the state faces a structural problem caused by its effort to reduce school property taxes. In 2006, the legislature responded to homeowner complaints about rising school property taxes by enacting a tax shift. The legislature reduced the maximum school property tax rate by nearly one-third. It then revised the state's business tax, which is called the franchise tax, and increased some other taxes to make up the shortfall. Unfortunately for legislative leaders, the revised franchise tax generated $1.4 billion less than projected, leaving the state with an ongoing shortfall.[2]

The legislature and the governor have limited options for addressing the state's short-term and long-term budget shortfalls. They can raise taxes, but tax increases are unpopular and many legislators ran for office promising never to vote to raise taxes. Although they can cut spending, Texas already ranks last in the nation in state spending **per capita** (per person). Finally, they can look for revenue alternatives, such as casino gambling, but that too is controversial.

Per capita Per person.

The looming budget crisis and the debate over how to address it illustrate the nature of the budgetary policymaking process. Budgetary policymaking involves deciding what societal needs to address and where to find the funds to address them. The chapter begins with a section examining state revenues and then turns to a discussion of expenditures. The chapter reviews the budgetary process before concluding with an overview of budgetary policymaking. This is the first of two chapters dealing with the nature of public policy in particular policy areas. This chapter addresses budgetary policymaking, whereas Chapter 14 focuses on criminal justice.

STATE REVENUES

Fiscal year Budget year.

During the 2009 **fiscal year** (i.e., budget year), the state of Texas generated $97 billion in revenue from all sources, including both taxes and non-tax sources of revenue. Table 13.1 identifies the various sources of state revenue and indicates their relative importance. Because the table includes data for fiscal years 1989, 1999, and 2009, it also shows changes in the relative importance of each revenue source across time.

TABLE 13.1   State Revenues by Source, Fiscal Years 1989, 1999, and 2009

Tax Sources of State Revenue as a Percentage of Total Revenue			
Source	**1989**	**1999**	**2009**
General sales tax	31.9 percent	27.2 percent	21.7 percent
Franchise tax	3.1 percent	4.3 percent	4.4 percent
Motor fuels tax	6.9 percent	5.4 percent	3.1 percent
Motor vehicle sales and rental	4.7 percent	5.2 percent	2.7 percent
Severance taxes on oil and gas production	5.4 percent	1.4 percent	2.4 percent
Taxes on alcohol and tobacco products	3.5 percent	2.3 percent	2.4 percent
Insurance company tax	2.0 percent	1.7 percent	1.3 percent
Utility taxes	0.9 percent	0.6 percent	0.5 percent
Other taxes	1.2 percent	1.1 percent	1.7 percent
Total taxes	**59.6** percent	**49.2** percent	**40.2** percent
Non-Tax Sources of State Revenue as a Percentage of Total Revenue			
Federal funds	23.0 percent	29 percent	33.6 percent
Licenses and fees	6.8 percent	8.7 percent	7.7 percent
Interest and investment income	7.0 percent	3.3 percent	1.8 percent
Net lottery proceeds	–	3.0 percent	1.6 percent
Land income	1.3 percent	0.5 percent	0.1 percent
Other non-tax revenue	2.3 percent	6.3 percent	15.0 percent
Total non-tax sources of revenue	**40.4** percent	**50.8** percent	**59.8** percent
Total net revenue (tax and non-tax sources combined)	**100 percent** **($20.5 billion)**	**100 percent** **($48 billion)**	**100 percent** **($97 billion)**

Source: Texas Comptroller of Public Accounts, "Revenue by Source," various years, available at www.cpa.state.tx.us.

Taxes

The state of Texas raises 40.2 percent of its total revenue from taxes. The general sales tax is by far the most important state tax source, generating substantially more money than any other tax. The other major state taxes include a business franchise tax, a motor fuels tax, a tax on motor vehicle sales and rental, and severance taxes on oil and natural gas production.

The relative importance of taxes to the state's revenue picture has declined over the last 20 years. As Table 13.1 indicates, the proportion of state revenue generated by taxes fell from nearly 60 percent in 1989 to just over 40 percent in 2009. However, the trend does not reflect a decline in tax revenues. The legislature and the governor have increased various tax rates, and most tax revenues have also risen because of economic growth. Taxes have declined as a source of state revenue relative to total revenues because of the rapid growth of non-tax sources of revenue, especially federal funds. Since 1989, federal funds have increased from 23 percent of state revenues to 33.6 percent. Most of the growth in federal funds has been through **Medicaid,** a federal program designed to provide health insurance coverage to the poor, people with disabilities, and elderly Americans who are impoverished.

Medicaid A federal program designed to provide health insurance coverage to low-income persons, people with disabilities, and elderly people who are impoverished. A federally funded health insurance program for the elderly.

Sales tax A levy on the retail sale of taxable items.

General Sales Tax A **sales tax** is a levy on the retail sale of taxable items. Texas has a relatively high sales tax rate. In 2006, the average Texan paid $1,457 in sales taxes, the thirteenth-highest sales tax bite in the nation.[3] The state levies a sales tax of 6.25 percent on the retail purchase of taxable items. Cities and other units of local government may add as much as 2 percent more to the state tax rate, bringing the total sales tax in many areas of the state to 8.25 percent.

Not all sales are subject to taxation. Although restaurant meals are taxable, food purchased at a grocery store is tax exempt (except for ready-to-eat items). The sale of most agricultural items is tax exempt, including the sale of agricultural machinery and parts, fertilizer, feed for animals, and seed. Drugs and medicine are exempt as well, whether sold over the counter or by prescription. Only some services are taxable. The list of taxable services includes charges for laundry, dry cleaning, cable television service, credit reporting, data processing, debt collection, landscaping, security, telecommunications, car repair, and janitorial services. The sales tax does not apply, however, to charges and fees for many other services, including legal retainers, accounting services, builder and contractor fees, real estate commissions, brokerage fees, and healthcare charges.

The growth of Internet sales is undermining the state sales tax base. State governments cannot legally compel an Internet or mail order retailer to collect its sales tax unless the retailer has a physical presence in the state. Sears, for example, charges sales tax on Internet purchases made by Texas consumers because Sears has stores throughout the state, but LL Bean, an Internet and mail order retailer based in Maine, does not because it has no outlets located in the Lone Star State. By 2011, Texas may lose as much as 10 percent of its total expected sales tax collection to Internet sales.[4]

Franchise tax A tax on businesses chartered or organized in Texas and doing business in the state.

Franchise Tax A **franchise tax** is a tax on businesses chartered or organized in Texas and doing business in the state. It is the primary tax assessed by state government on business, but it is not the *only* tax businesses pay because local governments also levy property taxes on business property, such as land, warehouses, manufacturing plants, stores, inventory, and office buildings. In 2006, the legislature increased the franchise tax rate and expanded its coverage in order to replace the revenue lost by cutting school property taxes. The new franchise tax generated 4.4 percent of state revenue in 2009 compared with 3.6 percent of state revenue in 2006, the year the new tax was adopted.[5]

Severance tax A tax imposed on the extraction of natural resources, such as oil, coal, and gas.

Severance Taxes on Oil and Natural Gas Production A tax levied on natural resources at the time they are taken from the land or water is known as a **severance tax.** The most important severance taxes in Texas are levied on the production of oil and natural gas. The state collects a 4.6 percent tax on the value of oil produced and 7.5 percent on natural gas, rates that are comparable to those charged by other energy-producing states. Texas also levies severance taxes on the production of cement and the extraction of sulfur. The relative importance of severance taxes has changed because of declining production levels and the variability of oil and gas prices. The role of severance taxes in the state's revenue picture has generally been falling because oil production has been in decline for decades. In 2008, Texas wells produced 352 million barrels of

Texans pay one of the highest sales taxes in the nation.

oil compared with 651 million barrels in 1989.[6] Severance tax collections also fluctuate with the price of oil and gas. In recent years, severance tax collections have increased as the price of oil has risen. In 2009, severance taxes accounted for 2.4 percent of state revenues, which was up from 1999, but considerably lower than 1989, when severance tax revenues represented 5.4 percent of state revenues.

Excise tax A tax levied on the manufacture, transportation, sale, or consumption of a particular item or set of related items.

Excise Taxes An **excise tax** is a tax levied on the manufacture, transportation, sale, or consumption of a particular item or set of related items. It is a selective sales tax. Texas state government levies excise taxes on motor vehicle sales and rentals, motor fuels, alcohol, and tobacco. In 2008, the state's various excise taxes collectively generated 8.2 percent of state revenue. Excise taxes of alcohol and tobacco products are called sin taxes.

Sin tax A levy on an activity that some people consider morally objectionable, such as smoking or drinking.

A **sin tax** is a levy on an activity that some people consider morally objectionable, such as smoking or drinking. Sin taxes are designed not just to raise revenue but also to discourage the behavior. In 2006, for example, the legislature increased the state's cigarette tax by $1.00 a pack to $1.41, moving the Texas tax rate up to the top one-third among states nationwide. The goal of the tax increase was both to raise revenue to use to fund school property tax cuts and to discourage smoking. The measure is apparently achieving both goals because tobacco tax revenues are up and smoking is down.[7]

WHAT IS YOUR OPINION?

Should the government increase taxes on tobacco products and alcohol to discourage smoking and drinking?

Other Taxes In addition to the general sales tax, franchise tax, severance taxes on oil and gas production, and excise taxes, the state of Texas collects a number of other levies. These other taxes include an insurance company tax, utility taxes, and an inheritance tax. Not one of these taxes accounts for as much as 2 percent of the state's total revenue, but collectively they are an important part of the state's revenue picture.

Pari-mutuel wagering A system for gambling on horse and dog racing.

The state's tax revenue sources also include taxes on **pari-mutuel wagering,** a system for gambling on horse and dog racing. In this system, the total amount of money wagered on a horse or dog race is pooled and then divided among those who bet on one of the top three finishers, minus percentages that go to the owners of the winning animals, track management, and the government. In 1987, the legislature authorized pari-mutuel gambling on horse and dog racing pending voter approval in a statewide referendum, which passed by a good margin. The legislature permitted the construction of major horse tracks in the Dallas, Houston, San Antonio, and Fort Worth areas, with smaller tracks allowed in other counties pending local voter approval. The legislature permitted the construction of greyhound racetracks in only three counties—Galveston, Nueces (Corpus Christi), and Cameron (Brownsville). Although some observers predicted that taxes on pari-mutuel wagering would eventually produce as much as $100 million a year, the payoff for the state has been insignificant. In 2008, pari-mutuel wagering generated $4 million in state revenue, well less than 0.10 percent of total state revenues.[8]

WHAT IS YOUR OPINION?

Should Texas allow gambling on dog and horse racing?

Non-Tax Sources of Revenue

Non-tax sources of revenue account for a majority of total state revenues.

Federal Funds The federal government is a major funding source for state government in Texas, accounting for more than one-third of state revenues. Medicaid is the largest single source of federal financial aid to state government. Federal money also supports highway construction, a number of welfare programs, and a broad range of other state activities.

Licenses and Fees Texas state government raises money through the sale of licenses and the collection of fees. Texans who wish to drive a motor vehicle, operate a

Taxes on pari-mutuel wagering have so far generated relatively little revenue for the state.

business, practice a profession, go hunting and fishing, attend a state university, or sell alcoholic beverages must purchase licenses or pay a fee for the privilege. In 2009, licenses and fees accounted for 7.7 percent of state revenue.

Interest and Investment Income The state of Texas holds billions of dollars in cash and securities that generate dividend and interest income from their investment. The largest pool of money is the **Texas Teacher Retirement System (TRS) Trust Fund,** a pension fund for the state's public school teachers. The TRS Trust Fund held $91.4 billion in assets in 2009. Similarly, the **Employees Retirement System (ERS) Trust Fund,** a pension fund for state employees, was worth $23.5 billion in 2009.[9] The TRS and ERS trust funds provide retirement, disability, and death or survivor benefits to their members. Both funds declined in value in late 2008 and early 2009 when the stock market suffered heavy losses.

Although the TRS and ERS trust funds seem flush with cash, they lack sufficient assets to cover future liabilities. The two trust funds are billion of dollars short of having enough money to cover promised retirement benefits for current and future retirees. The legislature has begun to address the problem by increasing state contributions to the TRS Trust Fund and by making it difficult for teachers and state employees to take early retirement.[10]

Texas Teacher Retirement System (TRS) Trust Fund A pension fund for the state's public school teachers.

Employees Retirement System (ERS) Trust Fund A pension fund for state employees.

Permanent School Fund (PSF) A fund established in the Texas Constitution as an endowment to finance public elementary and secondary education.

Permanent University Fund (PUF) Money constitutionally set aside as an endowment to finance construction, maintenance, and some other activities at the University of Texas, Texas A&M University, and other institutions in those two university systems.

General Fund The state treasury account that supports state programs and services without restriction.

The Permanent School Fund (PSF) and the Permanent University Fund (PUF) support education. The **Permanent School Fund (PSF)** is a fund established in the Texas Constitution as an endowment to finance public elementary and secondary education. At the end of 2008, the market value of PSF bonds and securities stood at $30.2 billion. The **Permanent University Fund (PUF)** is a fund established in the Texas Constitution as an endowment to finance construction, maintenance, and some other activities at the University of Texas and Texas A&M University. The value of the PUF in 2008 was $14.6 billion.[11] The state's interest and investment income varies, depending on the investment climate. In 2009, interest and investment income accounted for 1.8 percent of state revenue.

Land Income The state of Texas owns more than 20 million acres of land that produce revenue for the state from leases for agricultural use and for oil and gas production. The PSF and PUF hold the largest blocks of land—13 million acres and 2.1 million acres, respectively.[12] Income from land held by the PSF and PUF is invested in stocks, bonds, and other securities, which, in turn, generate interest and investment income. In 2009, land income accounted for 0.8 percent of state revenue.

Lottery Revenue Since the Texas Lottery began operation in 1992 it has generated more than $16 billion for the state.[13] Although that is a great deal of money, it is a relatively small part of the state's total revenue picture. In fact, lottery revenues accounted for just 1.6 percent of state revenues in 2009. Furthermore, most of the money the lottery generates goes not for education but for marketing, vendor commissions, and prizes. Figure 13.1 shows the distribution of money spent on the lottery. More than 60 percent of the money that Texans pay for lottery tickets goes for prizes. After subtracting money for administration and for compensation to retailers for selling lottery tickets, the state realizes 28 percent in revenue for every dollar spent on the lottery.

Lottery proceeds go into the Foundation School Program. When the lottery was created, the legislature funneled lottery earnings into the **General Fund,** the state treasury account that supports state programs and services without restriction. In 1997, the legislature amended the law to dedicate lottery proceeds to public

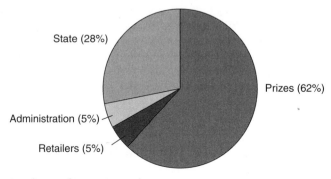

FIGURE 13.1   Distribution of Lottery Proceeds.

education. Because the legislature reduced education spending by a sum equal to the amount of anticipated lottery proceeds, the dedication had no impact on the total amount of money spent for education in Texas.

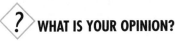 **WHAT IS YOUR OPINION?**

Is it morally wrong for the government to use gambling to raise money?

The history of lotteries nationwide is that they start strong but then decline as the novelty wears off. States attempt to slow or reverse the decline by introducing new or different games and by manipulating how jackpots pile up.[14] Texas is no exception to this pattern. In 1998, Texas Lottery sales dropped after the legislature reduced prizes in order to increase the amount of money going to the state. The Lottery Commission reacted to the situation by making the lottery more difficult to win. Instead of having to pick six numbers correctly from 1 to 50, players had to pick six numbers from 1 to 54. This increased the odds of winning from 15.8 million to 1 to 25.8 million to 1. By making the lottery more difficult to win, the state hoped to increase the size of the jackpots, which would entice more people to spend money on lottery tickets. The strategy worked for a while because lottery sales increased temporarily. When ticket sales slumped again, the state made it even more difficult to win by adding a Bonus Ball, reducing the odds of winning to 47.7 million to 1.[15]

In 2003, the legislature passed, and the governor signed, legislation authorizing the state's participation in a multi-state lottery in hopes of generating additional gambling revenue. The Lottery Commission has decided to participate in both Mega Millions and Powerball, games that are offered in a number of states. Mega Millions and Powerball are attractive to bettors because the long odds of winning, more than 100 million to 1, have produced some giant jackpots, including a payout of more than $360 million.[16]

Other Non-Tax Revenue The "other non-tax revenue" category in Table 13.1 groups a number of miscellaneous revenue sources, which in 2009 collectively generated 15 percent of total state revenue. For example, the category includes employee benefit contributions, which is money withheld from the paychecks of state workers to cover health insurance for their families and other benefits. Although the money is technically revenue to the state, the funds are earmarked for employee benefits.

The category also contains revenue from the tobacco lawsuit settlement. In 1996, Texas brought suit against eight large tobacco companies, their public relations companies, and their research firms, accusing them of violating state and federal law by marketing tobacco products to children and adjusting the nicotine levels in tobacco to cause mass addiction. The suit asked for money to cover the state's share of the healthcare costs of Medicaid recipients suffering from smoking-related illnesses. Rather than go to trial, the tobacco industry agreed to a $17.3 billion settlement to be paid out over 25 years.[17]

The Texas Lottery generates 1.6 percent of total state revenue.

ISSUES IN STATE FINANCE

Texas policymakers face a number of issues in government finance.

State Revenue Adequacy

Do state and local governments in Texas generate enough money to meet the needs of the state's large and rapidly growing population? Liberals believe that state and local governments generate insufficient revenue to address pressing state needs in education, healthcare, and transportation. In contrast, conservatives favor limiting the capacity of government to raise revenue because they believe that small government promotes economic growth.

Table 13.2 presents data comparing and contrasting government revenue in Texas with the national average. The table includes both tax revenues and non-tax sources of revenue, including fees, service charges, and federal aid money. As the table shows, state and local governments in Texas receive less revenue from taxes and other sources than does the average state. In 2006, total state and local revenue per capita in Texas was $7,661 compared with a national average of $9,171. Texas ranked forty-first among the 50 states. On average, government revenue in Texas represented 20.2 percent of personal income compared with a national average of 23.5 percent.

State and local governments in Texas generate less revenue per capita than do their counterparts in other states primarily because Texas is one of only seven states (Alaska, Florida, Nevada, South Dakota, Washington, and Wyoming are the others) without a personal income tax. The average state income tax generates $899 per capita annually compared with nothing in Texas. However, most other state and local taxes in Texas are relatively high. As Table 13.2 indicates, Texas has the thirteenth-highest sales tax burden in the nation and the twelfth-heaviest property tax burden.

TABLE 13.2   Government Finance in Texas and the United States, FY 2006

Measure	Texas	National Average	Texas's National Rank
State and local revenue per capita	$7,661	$9,171	41
State and local revenue as a percentage of personal income	20.2 percent	23.5 percent	43
Personal income taxes per capita	0	$899	–
State and local sales taxes per capita	$1,457	$1,379	13
State and local property taxes per capita	$1,388	$1,202	12
State and local fees and other charges per capita	$1,626	$1,803	32
Federal aid to states and localities per capita	$1,328	$1,514	39

Source: *Governing*, State and Local Source Book, available at www.governing.com.

Tax Incidence

Tax incidence The point at which the actual cost of a tax falls.

The term **tax incidence** refers to the point at which the actual cost of a tax falls. When social scientists and policymakers consider the incidence of a tax, they are focusing on who actually pays the tax. Sometimes the people who write the check to the government are not the only people who bear the burden of a tax. Consider the franchise tax. Although businesses pay the tax, the actual expense of the tax is borne by people—stockholders who earn smaller dividends, customers who pay higher prices for the company's products, or employees who receive lower wages. Taxes on alcohol and tobacco fall not only on those people who drink and smoke but also on tobacco and liquor companies because higher prices caused by the tax will reduce consumer demand for their products. Tobacco companies oppose efforts to increase cigarette taxes not because they want to shelter their customers from higher prices but because they know that fewer people will smoke if cigarettes cost more.

Progressive tax A levy whose burden weighs more heavily on persons earning higher incomes than it does on individuals making less money.

Proportional tax A levy that weighs equally on all persons, regardless of their income.

Regressive tax A levy whose burden weighs more heavily on low-income groups than wealthy taxpayers.

Social scientists use the terms "progressive," "proportional," and "regressive" to discuss the impact of taxation on different income groups. A **progressive tax** is a levy whose burden weighs more heavily on persons earning higher incomes than it does on individuals making less money. A luxury tax on expensive yachts and jewelry is an example of a progressive tax. If we assume that members of the upper-income groups are the primary people who purchase luxury items, then the tax would obviously represent a greater proportion of the incomes of wealthier individuals than it would the incomes of low-income people. A **proportional tax** is a levy that weighs equally on all persons, regardless of their income. An income tax that charged everyone the same percentage amount without deductions or exemptions would be a proportional tax because each income group would pay the same percentage of its earnings in tax. A **regressive tax** is a levy whose burden weighs more heavily on low-income groups than wealthy taxpayers. Economists generally classify sales and excise taxes as regressive because lower-income persons spend a greater proportion of their earnings on items subject to taxation than do upper-income persons. People in upper-income groups pay more in sales and excise taxes because they purchase more taxable items and the items they purchase tend to be more expensive. However, sales and excise taxes are regressive because lower-income individuals spend a greater proportion of their incomes on taxable items than do members of middle- and upper-income groups.[18]

WHAT IS YOUR OPINION?

Do you favor reforming the tax system in Texas to make it more progressive?

The Texas tax structure is regressive because of its heavy reliance on property, sales, and excise taxes. A family earning $12,100 a year pays 14.2 percent of its income in state and local taxes. In contrast, a family with an annual income of $177,800 pays just 5.1 percent of its income in taxes. All of the major taxes in Texas are regressive, but some are more regressive than others. The property tax is the least regressive, whereas the gasoline tax is the most regressive. Texas has the fifth most regressive tax system of the 50 states.[19]

Even the lottery falls more heavily on lower income groups. Texans earning less than $20,000 a year spend on average nearly twice as much on the lottery as those people who earn $50,000 to $59,000—$76.50 compared with $39.24 a month. Ironically, considering that the lottery helps fund education, high school dropouts spend more than three times as much on the lottery as Texans with college degrees—$173.17 a month compared with $48.61 a month.[20] Furthermore, the state's most expensive lottery tickets, those costing $10, $20, $25, $30, and $50 a game, sell better on a per capita basis in the state's lowest income areas than they do in the wealthiest neighborhoods.[21]

Tax Fairness

Ability-to-pay theory of taxation
The approach to government finance that holds that taxes should be based on an individual's financial resources.

Although everyone agrees that taxes should be fair, observers define fairness in different ways. Some people favor a tax system based on the **ability-to-pay theory of taxation.** This approach to government finance holds that taxes should be based on an individual's financial resources. They argue that people who earn relatively high incomes should pay more in taxes because well-to-do persons can better afford to pay taxes than can people who make less money. The advocates of the ability-to-pay theory of taxation are critical of the tax system in the state of Texas because it is regressive. They favor the adoption of progressive taxes, such as the personal income tax.

In contrast, some experts on public finance favor a tax system that encourages economic growth. They think that government should keep taxes low, especially taxes on business, in order to encourage investment and business expansion. The advocates of growth-oriented tax systems believe that progressive taxes, such as the personal income tax, are harmful because they reduce the amount of money that middle- and upper-income individuals have to invest in economic development. They also oppose high property taxes because of their impact on business. Instead, they prefer the use of consumer taxes, such as sales and excise taxes. The supporters of growth-oriented tax structures give the Texas tax system mixed reviews. Although they applaud the absence of an individual income tax, they worry that local property taxes are so high that they discourage business expansion. They advocate reducing or even repealing the property tax in favor of an expanded sales tax.

 WHAT IS YOUR OPINION?

What sort of tax system is the best? Why?

Tax Elasticity

Tax elasticity The extent to which tax revenues increase as personal income rises.

The term **tax elasticity** refers to the extent to which tax revenues increase as personal income rises. It is a measure of the ability of tax revenues to keep up with economic growth. If tax revenues increase in pace with economic growth, then the government has the funds to address the increased demand for services generated by growth, such as new schools and additional roads. If tax revenues fail to keep up with growth, then state government will lack the resources necessary to meet the demand for services unless the government raises tax rates. The Texas tax system is relatively inelastic.

- The general sales tax is somewhat elastic because retail sales generally increase as personal income rises. Nonetheless, the sales tax is not perfectly elastic because not all goods and services are taxable. As average income rises, people may purchase goods and services that are not taxable, such as stocks, bonds, real estate, accounting services, and legal services. Furthermore, the growth of sales over the Internet is lessening the elasticity of the sales tax.

- Excise taxes on gasoline, alcohol, and tobacco products are inelastic because sales of those products do not necessarily rise as incomes increase. In fact, gasoline tax revenues may fall as income rises because people may trade in their old vehicles for newer model cars that get better gasoline mileage.

- Severance taxes are inelastic as well. Rising personal income is unrelated to oil and gas production.

- The franchise tax may be elastic if business growth keeps up with the growth in personal income.

- Property taxes are only mildly elastic because property values do not necessarily rise as rapidly as personal income.

Many economists believe that the state's relatively inelastic tax system will be increasingly unable to meet the needs of state government. Texas can no longer count on raising substantial tax revenues from severance taxes on oil and gas production because of falling production. Furthermore, the healthiest, most rapidly growing sectors of the state's economy are largely exempt from the general sales tax. The sales tax does not cover many service industries, including accounting, legal, medical, and brokerage services. Personal income growth from salaries and investment gains escapes direct taxation as well because Texas does not have a personal income tax.

POLICY OPTIONS FOR REFORMING THE STATE REVENUE SYSTEM

Critics of the Texas tax system offer a number of policy options designed to make the state's tax structure more equitable, efficient, or productive.

A Personal Income Tax

Most discussions of tax reform in Texas include an examination of the wisdom of a personal income tax. Income tax advocates argue that the state's tax system, which relies heavily on consumer taxes, is incapable of generating sufficient revenue to meet the growing demand for state services. Although some segments of the state's economy are taxed heavily, other sectors of the economy escape taxation almost entirely. As a result, the legislature periodically faces a budget shortfall because the cost of healthcare, public education, criminal justice, higher education, highway construction, and other state services has gone up faster than the revenues have grown to pay for them. Income tax supporters believe that a personal income tax would more accurately mirror growth in the economy, thus producing more revenue for state government.[22]

Tax reformers believe that a personal income tax would be a fairer way to raise revenue than the state's current tax system. The state of Kansas levies a personal income tax with three brackets ranging from 3.5 percent to 6.45 percent of adjusted gross income minus exemptions and deductions. A family of four pays no tax on an income of $24,400. Were Texas to adopt an income tax based on the Kansas model, it would generate $16.4 billion a year.[23] The adoption of an income tax would also make the state's tax system less regressive.

Income tax opponents question its fairness. Because of loopholes and deductions, they say, wealthy individuals have often avoided paying federal income taxes, leaving the tax burden on the backs of middle- and lower-income people. Who would guarantee that a state income tax would be implemented fairly? Most important, the opponents of a state income tax believe that the real goal of its supporters is to raise revenue to pay for a bigger, more intrusive state government. Instead of replacing or reducing the state sales tax or local property taxes, they predict that a personal income tax would merely supplement other taxes. In the long run, they warn, the adoption of a state income tax would lead to higher taxes for *all* Texans, not just the wealthy.

Conservative economists argue that taxes retard economic growth—the more taxes the government collects, the slower the rate of economic growth. Income taxes are particularly harmful because they discourage people from making the sorts of investments on which business growth depends. High taxes also retard population growth because people generally choose to live and do business in states with lower tax rates.[24]

The Texas Constitution prohibits the legislative adoption of a personal income tax without voter approval. The constitution declares that no personal income tax can take effect unless enacted through the legislative process and then approved by the voters in a referendum election. Furthermore, revenues generated by the tax can be used only for education and for reducing local property taxes for schools.

Broadened Sales Tax Base

Another proposal for reforming the state tax system is to enlarge the sales tax base to include more services than are currently taxed. Although the legislature broadened the tax base somewhat in the 1980s, many services, including most of the services provided by architects, lawyers, interior designers, advertising agents, insurance companies, investment counselors, accountants, brokers, and physicians, remain untaxed. Eliminating exemptions for all services would have added another $5.4 billion in sales tax revenue in 2009.[25] The advocates of a widened tax base believe that it would spread the sales tax burden more fairly than it is now. It would also make the tax system more elastic because the service sector is one of the most rapidly growing elements of the state economy. In contrast, critics charge that broadening the sales tax base is just another means of increasing the tax burden on consumers. Regardless of the rhetoric, taxes on services are taxes on people who use the services. Businesses will inevitably pass the tax along to the consumers who purchase their services. Furthermore, extending the sales tax to cover services that are not taxed in other states might make Texas firms less competitive nationwide.

Expanded Legalized Gambling

Some states rely far more heavily on revenues generated by legalized gambling than does Texas. Revenues from taxes on casino gambling, slot machines at racetracks, and lotteries account for more than 10 percent of state revenue in Nevada, South Dakota, Rhode Island, Louisiana, and Oregon. Nevada is by far the state most dependent on gambling revenue, with taxes on games of chance accounting for 27.5 percent of state revenue.[26] In contrast, gambling proceeds account for less than 2 percent of state revenues in Texas.

Gambling is controversial. The proponents of legalized gambling believe that the legalization of casino gambling or the introduction of slot machines (called video lottery terminals) at racetracks would produce billions in additional state revenue, which could be used to fund education and reduce property tax rates. Gambling is a voluntary tax, they argue; no one pays unless he or she chooses to play. Legalized gambling creates jobs and attracts visitors with money to the state. It also provides a local alternative for Texans who have been traveling to neighboring states to visit casinos. In contrast, the opponents of legalized gambling argue that it creates a morally corrupting climate that is associated with social problems, such as crime, bankruptcy, and gambling addiction. Furthermore, the introduction of casinos and other gambling establishments into an area hurts small businesses because people spend their money gambling rather than purchasing goods and services.[27]

The fate of proposals to expand organized gambling in Texas is uncertain. Although many legislators would prefer an expansion of gambling to a tax increase, opposition to casino gambling and slot machines is substantial. Furthermore, any measure to expand legalized gambling would have to come in the form of a constitutional amendment, requiring a two-thirds vote of the Texas House and Texas

Senate, as well as voter approval, a significantly higher hurdle than required for the passage of ordinary legislation.

Selling Assets

Some state and local governments have sold assets in order to raise money to fund public services. The city of Chicago, for example, sold four downtown parking garages to Morgan Stanley, an investment bank, for more than $500 million. Indiana leased the Indiana Toll Road to private investors for nearly $4 billion. In recent years, pension funds, banks, and other investors have decided that toll roads, lotteries, airports, and other government assets are good long-term investments because they produce steady revenue streams.[28] State and local governments then use the money to finance government operations without having to raise taxes. Governor Perry has proposed selling the Texas Lottery to private investors, but the legislature has not acted on his proposal.[29]

AROUND THE NATION

Toll Road Privatization in Indiana

In 2006, Indiana leased the 157-mile Indiana Toll Road, which runs east and west between Ohio and Illinois, to a private consortium comprised of Cintra, a Spanish company, and Macquarie, an Australian firm. The consortium gave the state $3.8 billion up front in exchange for the right to collect tolls for the next 75 years. At the end of the lease, the toll road would revert back to the state of Indiana. The state has invested the $3.8 billion and is using the interest to augment its road construction budget. The consortium, meanwhile, has begun increasing tolls in order to earn a return on its investment.*

The Indiana toll road privatization is controversial. Its supporters, including Indiana Governor Mitch Daniels, argue that the state would never have been able to generate nearly as much cash had its operation remained public because legislators lack the resolve needed to pass regular increases in toll rates. The upfront money from the consortium enabled the state to increase its highway budget without increasing taxes. In contrast, opponents criticize the state for turning over control of the toll road to private firms that are accountable to their shareholders rather than the public interest. They argue that the consortium will increase tolls and neglect maintenance in order to maximize its profit.†

QUESTIONS TO CONSIDER

1. Should state government in Texas consider selling assets, such as toll roads and the lottery, to make money that can be used to finance government services?

2. Would you expect tolls to rise faster if a toll road is controlled by a private firm as opposed to being publicly owned and controlled?

3. Which is preferable—the government selling assets to raise money or increasing taxes?

*Theodore Kim, "After Privatization, Indiana Toll Road's Biggest Difference Is the Price," *Dallas Morning News*, October 19, 2008, available at www.dallasnews.com.

†Tom Coyne, "Indiana Lawmakers at Odds Over Toll Road," *Washington Post*, June 27, 2007, available at www.washingtonpost.com.

Tax Relief to Low-Income Families

Some states have enacted special tax exemptions and credits for low-income individuals, so that their state tax systems are less regressive. A number of states allow property owners a partial rebate on their property taxes if the taxes exceed a certain percentage of income (as certified on IRS tax forms). Iowa, for example, grants property tax relief to those people who are eligible (mostly senior citizens and persons with disabilities) on a sliding scale based on income. New Mexico and Kansas give a sales tax rebate to low-income people.

In Texas, the legislature and the governor have created a sales tax holiday for the third weekend in August. For three days, consumers can purchase clothing, footwear, backpacks, and other back-to-school items costing less than $100 without paying the state sales tax. Most local governments drop their sales tax as well although they are not required to participate in the tax holiday.

STATE EXPENDITURES

Biennuium The state's two-year budget program.

The state budget for 2010–2011 was $182.2 billion. Because the Texas legislature meets in regular session only once every two years, the legislature and the governor appropriate money for a two-year budget period, which is known as the **biennium.** The eighty-first legislature, which met in regular session in 2009, approved spending $92.7 billion for 2010 and $89.5 billion for 2011.[30]

Table 13.3 identifies the most important items in the state budget and compares spending priorities in 1989, 1999, and 2009. The largest expenditure categories for state government are health and human services, education, transportation, and public safety and corrections. In 2009, those four categories accounted for more than 80 percent of total state spending. Since 1989, the share of state spending going for health and human services has increased by nearly 70 percent. No major expenditure category has grown as rapidly. In contrast, the relative importance of education and transportation to the budget has declined.

TABLE 13.3   State Expenditures for Selected Government Functions, 1989, 1999, and 2009

Expenditure	1989	1999	2009
Health and human services	22.2 percent	35.1 percent	37.4 percent
Education	46.6 percent	37.7 percent	32.6 percent
Transportation	12.3 percent	8.1 percent	6.7 percent
Public safety and corrections	4.1 percent	6.3 percent	4.9 percent
General government administration	4.9 percent	3.6 percent	6.5 percent
Natural resources/recreational services	1.1 percent	1.6 percent	2.0 percent
Other	8.8 percent	7.6 percent	9.9 percent
Total expenditures	**100 percent**	**100 percent**	**100 percent**
	($20.7 billion)	**($45.6 billion)**	**($102.2 billion)**

Source: Texas Comptroller of Public Accounts, "Texas Revenue History by Function," various years, available at www.cpa.state.tx.us.

TABLE 13.4   State and Local Government Spending, Texas and the United States, FY 2006

Criterion	Texas	National Average	Texas Rank Among the States
Total state and local government expenditures per capita	$6,845	$8,393	46
State and local government expenditures as a percentage of personal income	20.2 percent	23.5 percent	45
Elementary and secondary education expenditures per capita	$1,848	$1,763	11
Higher education expenditures per capita	$668	$642	26
Welfare expenditures per capita	$870	$1,240	48
Health and hospital expenditures per capita	$458	$608	34
Highway expenditures per capita	$471	$453	23
Parks and recreation expenditures per capita	$71	$116	41
Environmental expenditures per capita	$204	$292	44
Fire protection expenditures per capita	$87	$114	30
Police protection expenditures per capita	$208	$265	32
Corrections expenditures per capita	$189	$210	21

Source: Governing, State and Local Source Book, available at www.governing.com.

Table 13.4 compares and contrasts Texas with other states in terms of state and local government spending. Government expenditures in Texas are well below the national average, $6,845 per capita compared with the national figure of $8,393. Texas is forty-sixth among the 50 states in total government spending per capita. It is forty-fifth in spending as a percentage of personal income.

Few public services in Texas are well-funded, at least in comparison with their funding levels in other states. For example, state and local government expenditures per capita for welfare, health and hospitals, parks and recreation, the environment, fire protection, and police protection are all below the national average. Higher education and highway expenditures per capita are near the national average. The only expenditure category in which Texas is above the national average is per capita expenditures for elementary and secondary education. Furthermore, the high rank for education expenditures is misleading because it reflects the size of the state's population of school-age children rather than a generous commitment to funding education. Per capita expenditures for education are relatively high in Texas because the state has a comparatively large population of school-age children. School-age children represent 19.1 percent of the population of Texas compared with only 16.2 percent of the population nationwide. Only Alaska has a larger percentage of school-age youngsters than Texas. In fact, on a per-student basis, funding for elementary and secondary education in the Lone Star State lags behind the national average, $8,048 per student compared with a national average of $9,557 per student. Texas ranks forty-first among the 50 states.[31]

Texans disagree about the appropriate level of government expenditures. Conservatives favor limited government with low tax rates and low levels of government expenditures. They believe that low tax rates promote economic growth because they leave money in the hands of individual investors and business owners who generate business activity and create jobs. Although government expenditures stimulate economic activity as well, private spending is more economically efficient because of the profit motive. Whereas private employers have an incentive to reduce payrolls and cut costs in order to increase profit margins, government bureaucrats want to enlarge their staffs and increase their budgets. Conservatives favor limiting the growth in state taxes and spending to ensure continued economic prosperity.

In contrast, liberals argue that the state's low-tax, low-spend philosophy fails to address basic social problems. They believe that economic prosperity is built on the presence of an educated workforce whose basic needs are met. Liberals note that the Lone Star State has one of the lowest high school graduation rates in the country and it trails the national average in the proportion of adults holding bachelor's degrees.[32] In addition, the poverty rate in Texas is 16.9 percent compared with a rate of 13.3 percent for the nation as a whole.[33] Texas has the highest percentage of residents without health insurance in the country, and trails the national average in the percentage of children without health insurance coverage as well.[34] Texas liberals advocate tax increases to fund enhanced public services to improve the quality of life for the state's large and diverse population.

BUDGET PRIORITIES

The foremost budget priorities for state government in Texas are healthcare, elementary and secondary education, higher education, welfare, and transportation.

Healthcare

Medicaid and the State Children's Health Insurance Program (SCHIP) are the state's major health programs.

Medicaid The Texas Medicaid program provides medical services to 2.8 million residents of the state who are poor or disabled. It covers such services as inpatient and outpatient hospital care, health screening, dental care, hearing evaluations, physician services, family-planning services, laboratory fees, x-ray work, and prescription drugs. Although two-thirds of the state's Medicaid recipients are children from low-income families, most Medicaid expenditures go to provide services for the blind, persons with disabilities, and impoverished elderly people because their medical needs are greater and therefore more expensive to meet.[35]

Federal grant program A program through which the national government gives money to state and local governments to spend in accordance with set standards and conditions.

Medicaid is a **federal grant program,** a program through which the national government gives money to state and local governments for expenditure in accordance with set standards and conditions. Medicaid is now the nation's largest healthcare program, bigger even than the **Medicare program,** a federally funded healthcare program for the elderly. Medicaid covers the cost of two-thirds of nursing home residents and one-third of all births.[36] The states and the federal government share the cost of Medicaid, with the size of the state share depending on the state's personal income. The federal government covers 61 percent of the cost of the Texas Medicaid program, with the state paying the other 39 percent.

Medicare program A federally funded health insurance program for the elderly.

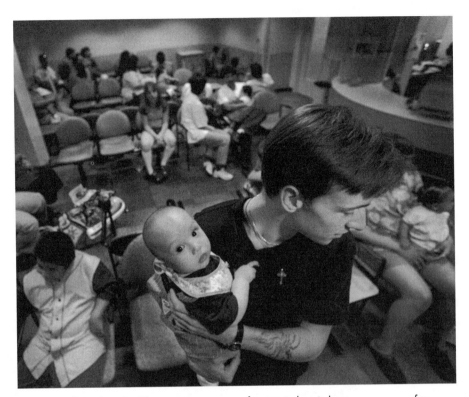

People who do not have health insurance coverage often turn to hospital emergency rooms for healthcare.

States enjoy considerable flexibility to design their own Medicaid programs and Texas has created one of the least generous programs in the nation. Only pregnant women, people with disabilities, and children from low-income families are ineligible for Medicaid benefits in Texas. Just 17 percent of Texans are enrolled in Medicaid, compared with 27 percent in New York and 29 percent in California.[37] Furthermore, nursing home reimbursements for Medicaid patients in Texas are the second lowest in the country—$112.79 per patient per day, which is 30 percent below the national average. Industry experts contend that the low reimbursement rate means that nursing homes in Texas are unable to pay competitive wages. That leads to high staff turnover, which can hurt patient care. About two-thirds of the 90,000 nursing home residents in Texas are on Medicaid.[38]

Medicaid is a large and rapidly growing component of state spending. Medicaid funding accounted for 26 percent of state spending in 2007, up from 20.5 percent in 1996.[39] Medicaid expenditures have increased because the cost of healthcare services has been going up and the number of recipients has been growing. Prescription drug costs, in particular, have been increasing rapidly, as have long-term care costs for the elderly and people with disabilities.

State governments nationwide are struggling to cover Medicaid costs. During the early years of the 2000s, Medicaid spending rose by 10 percent or more each year, much faster than the growth in government revenues.[40] If states cannot control the growth in Medicaid spending, they will have difficulty paying for education, transportation, homeland security, and other budget priorities.

The healthcare reform legislation passed by Congress and signed into law by President Barack Obama will add a million Texans to the Medicaid program. Beginning in 2014, anyone whose income is below 133 percent of the federal poverty level, or $29,300 for a family of four, will be eligible for Medicaid. This total includes childless adults, who are currently not covered in Texas.[41] Although the federal government will initially pay the entire cost of the additional enrollees, state governments will be required to pick up 5 percent of the extra cost in 2017, 7 percent by 2019, and then 10 percent from 2020 going forward. In Texas, the additional expense to state government of the Medicaid expansion will be $185 million in 2017, $259 million in 2019, and then $370 million a year beginning in 2020.[42]

State Children's Health Insurance Program (SCHIP) A federal program designed to provide health insurance to children from low-income families whose parents are not poor enough to qualify for Medicaid.

State Children's Health Insurance Program (SCHIP) The **State Children's Health Insurance Program (SCHIP)** is a federal program designed to provide health insurance to children from low-income families whose parents are not poor enough to qualify for Medicaid. The Texas SCHIP provides health insurance to children and young adults under the age of 19 whose family income does not exceed twice the poverty level.[43] SCHIP is relatively cost effective for the states because the federal government picks up more than 70 percent of the cost, leaving the rest to the states. Furthermore, SCHIP saves the government money because it reduces emergency care costs. Families with health insurance have fewer visits to hospital emergency rooms. One billion dollars in SCHIP spending over a decade saves $4.4 billion in reduced emergency care, hospital stays, and charity care. SCHIP also reduces school absences.[44]

Matching funds requirement A legislative provision that the national government will provide grant money for a particular activity only on condition that the state or local government involved supply a certain percentage of the total money required for the project or program.

Texas has consistently failed to take advantage of all the SCHIP money available. Between 1998 and 2003, Texas passed up more than $600 million in federal funds because it failed to meet the federal **matching funds requirement,** a legislative provision in which the national government will provide grant money for a particular activity only on the condition that the state or local government involved supplies a certain percentage of the total money required for the project or program. The state passed up another $550 million in federal funds during the 2004–2005 biennium because the legislature and the governor cut SCHIP funding, so that they could balance the budget without raising taxes. As Figure 13.2 shows, SCHIP enrollment dropped from more than 500,000 in 2003 to less than 350,000 in 2005, 2006, and 2007 before picking up again in 2008 after the legislature relaxed some of the enrollment restrictions added to the program in 2003. By 2010, Texas SCHIP enrollment had finally returned to its 2003 level.

Elementary and Secondary Education

Foundation School Program The basic funding program for public education in the state of Texas.

As noted in Chapter 12, state government distributes money to independent school districts through the **Foundation School Program,** the basic funding program for public education in the state of Texas. The amount of money each district receives depends on a complex set of formulas that account for the variable costs of educating different types of students. For example, students with learning disabilities or with limited English proficiency are more expensive to educate than other students.

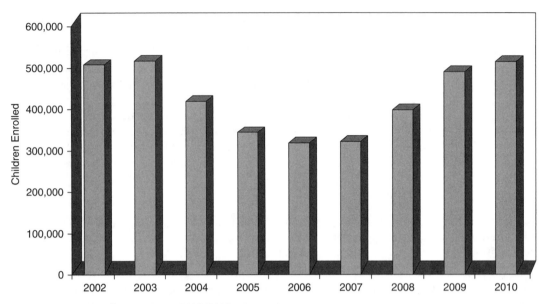

FIGURE 13.2   SCHIP Enrollment in Texas, 2002–2010.

Robin Hood Plan
A reform of the state's school finance system designed to increase funding for poor school districts by redistributing money from wealthy districts.

The amount of state funding each district receives also depends on the **Robin Hood Plan,** a reform of the state's school finance system designed to increase funding for poor school districts by redistributing money from wealthy districts. The state guarantees that a district will generate a set amount of money per student for each penny of property tax it assesses. The state also provides additional aid to districts that are relatively poor in order to bring them up to the guaranteed yield while forcing wealthy school districts to remit money to the state for redistribution to relatively poor districts.[45]

Although education is the single largest expenditure category in the state budget, its importance has declined. As Table 13.3 shows, education's share of state spending fell from nearly 50 percent in 1989 to less than one-third in 2009. In part, the change in the relative position of education in the budget reflects the dramatic growth of the Medicaid program. Even though the state spends more money on education than ever before, its relative importance has shrunk because of the explosion in Medicaid expenditures. The decline in the budget share devoted to public education also reflects the failure of state funding to keep pace with the rising cost of public education.

The education finance reforms adopted in 2006 increased the state's share of education spending without significantly increasing total education funding. As discussed in Chapter 12, the legislature cut school property tax rates and increased state funding to make up the difference. To cover the increased state share, the legislature expanded the franchise tax and increased the cigarette tax. It also changed the method for reporting sales taxes on private used car purchases to increase state revenue.

Nonetheless, many school districts soon faced a financial crisis. The legislature froze spending at 2005–2006 levels, failing to take into account the rising costs of transportation and technology. In fact, the state reimbursement rate to districts for student transportation has not changed in 25 years despite a significant increase in fuel costs. Similarly, state technology funding has been $30 per student for the last 20 years, too little to cover the cost of computers and software needed for instruction.[46] In 2009, the legislature provided an additional $1.9 billion in state aid for schools spread over the following two years; however, with an average funding increase of less than 3 percent per district, the amount barely kept pace with inflation. Legislative leaders predicted that the legislature would have to address education funding once again in its 2011 session.[47]

Higher Education

More than 1.1 million students attend one of the state's 35 public universities, three colleges, 50 community college districts, nine health-related campuses, and four technical colleges. Only California has more publicly supported colleges and universities than Texas, or more students enrolled in higher education. The University of Texas at Austin is the largest center of higher education in the state, registering more than 51,000 students in 2009.[48] Enrollment at Texas A&M University is close, exceeding 48,000 students.[49] More students attend community colleges in Texas than attend universities. Furthermore, Latino and African American students are more likely to attend community colleges than universities.[50]

Higher education governance in Texas is a hodgepodge. Eleven boards of regents appointed by the governor with Texas Senate confirmation oversee management of the state's colleges and universities. The Board of Regents of the University of Texas and the Texas A&M University Board of Regents manage large university systems with campuses located throughout the state. In contrast, Midwestern State University has its own board of regents, even though it has only one campus (in Wichita Falls) and just more than 6,000 students. Each community college district has its own, locally elected board of trustees.

Texas has no clear policy on which institutions can offer which degrees. As a result, the education system has a proliferation of doctoral programs. Of the 35 state universities in Texas, 25 offer doctoral degrees, more than any other state. The Texas Higher Education Coordinating Board (THECB) faces considerable pressure from universities to grant requests for doctoral programs because campus administrators, state legislators, and local communities regard them as a sign of prestige. In contrast, higher education specialists generally agree that reserving doctoral education to a relatively small number of campuses ensures depth and quality. In contrast, spreading doctoral programs around the state fosters mediocrity because state government lacks adequate financial resources to fund them all sufficiently.[51]

Higher education funding in Texas is near the national average. In 2008, Texas spent $668 per capita on higher education compared with a national average of $642.[52] Colleges and universities in Texas receive funding from a number of sources in addition to the state. Money to support community/junior colleges comes from state funding, student tuition and fees, and local tax support. The state provides 44 percent of the average community college's budget, with local property taxes (30 percent) and student tuition and fees (26 percent) supplying most of the rest. Less than one-half the funding for state universities in Texas comes from state appropriations, with student tuition and fees, research grants, and private donations making up the rest.[53]

The relative importance of higher education spending in state budgets nationwide has been in decline for years, primarily because the growth of Medicaid has been overwhelming most other budget categories. Since 1990, for example, state funding for the University of Texas has declined by about 1 percent annually when adjusted for inflation.[54] Many states also cut higher education funding in 2008 and 2009 because the recession reduced available revenues for funding state government in general. As the relative importance of state funding for higher education has declined, tuition and fees have soared and community colleges have raised their tax rates. Between fall 2003 and fall 2007, Texas public universities increased their tuition by 112 percent, from an average of $625 for 15 semester credit hours in 2003 to $1,330 in 2007.[55] Higher education in Texas used to be a bargain compared with its cost in other states, but tuition and fees at public four-year colleges and universities in Texas now exceed the national average.[56] State education leaders worry that the rising cost of a higher education will prevent many low-income Texas students from earning college degrees. Community college districts, meanwhile, have not only raised their tuition but have increased their tax rates as well. The largest state source of financial aid for students enrolling in public colleges is the Toward Excellence, Access & Success (TEXAS) grant program, which is available to high school graduates whose families earn less than $40,000 a year. Because the legislature has failed to fully fund the program, only about 40 percent of students who qualify receive aid.[57]

The University of Texas (UT) at Austin and Texas A&M University at College Station benefit from the Permanent University Fund (PUF). In 1876, the framers of the Texas Constitution set aside a million acres of grassland in West Texas to finance "a university of the first class," including "an agricultural and mechanical branch." A few years later, the legislature added another 1.1 million acres. Income from mineral development on the land and agricultural leasing goes into a Permanent University Fund similar to the Permanent School Fund. The PUF may not be spent but is invested to earn dividends and interest. These earnings constitute the Available University Fund (AUF), two-thirds of which is distributed to the University of Texas with the other one-third distributed to Texas A&M University. The PUF money is used to guarantee bonds for capital improvements at schools in the UT and A&M University Systems. Funds from the AUF cover debt service, including payments on principal and interest. Surplus AUF funds can be used at the University of Texas in Austin, Texas A&M in College Station, and Prairie View A&M for "excellence programs," including scholarships, library improvements, and lab equipment.

In 2009, the legislature and the voters approved measures to provide funding aimed at increasing the number of Tier One universities in Texas. A Tier One university is measured by the amount of research it conducts and by membership in the prestigious Association of American Universities. Tier One universities attract the

GETTING INVOLVED

Appealing a Property Appraisal

The amount of property tax homeowners owe depends on the tax rate and the appraised value of their property. Although property owners can do little about the tax rate, they can appeal their appraisal if they believe that it is inaccurate or unfair. If you think that your assessment is too high based on the value of similar property in the area, you should file a written protest with your county appraisal district. Contact your county appraisal district (the telephone number will be in the government pages of the telephone book) to determine the procedure in your county for appeal. In general, you will need to prove that the assessed value for your property is incorrect. As evidence, you can present the sales contract for your property if it was recently purchased, an independent appraisal, or lower appraisals for comparable pieces of property.

It's your government—get involved!

best students and the most research money. In 2006, Texas universities received 5.5 percent of federal funding for research and development in science and engineering compared with 13.6 percent received by schools in California.[58] Whereas California has nine Tier One institutions and New York has seven, Texas has only three—the University of Texas at Austin, Texas A&M University, and Rice University, which is private. The measures set aside more than half a billion dollars in incentive grants that seven state universities can draw upon as they move toward Tier One status. The institutions are the University of Houston, Texas Tech University, University of Texas at Dallas, University of Texas at San Antonio, University of Texas at Arlington, University of Texas El Paso, and the University of North Texas.[59]

Welfare

The philosophy underlying the nation's welfare system has changed. Before 1996, the unofficial goal of welfare policy was to provide recipients with a minimal standard of living. Low-income families and individuals who met the eligibility requirements could qualify for various federal programs providing healthcare, food vouchers, and cash. In 1996, Congress passed, and President Bill Clinton signed, sweeping welfare reform legislation that explicitly changed the underlying philosophy of government policy from welfare to work. Instead of attempting to supply low-income individuals and families with cash and in-kind benefits sufficient to meet basic human needs, the new goal of welfare reform was to move recipients from the welfare rolls to the workforce. Able-bodied welfare recipients would have to find work and/or participate in job training programs in order to receive welfare assistance. Furthermore, the government placed lifetime limits on the amount of time welfare recipients could collect benefits before having to leave the welfare rolls forever.

 WHAT IS YOUR OPINION?

Do you agree with placing lifetime limits on the amount of time an individual can collect welfare benefits?

Temporary Assistance for Needy Families (TANF) A federal block grant program that provides temporary financial assistance and work opportunities to needy families.

The welfare reform legislation created **Temporary Assistance for Needy Families (TANF),** a federal program that provides temporary financial assistance and work opportunities to needy families. Low-income families and individuals who meet eligibility requirements receive cash and qualify for other benefits. To maintain eligibility, recipients must comply with a Personal Responsibility Agreement (PRA). The PRA requires recipients to agree to stay free of alcohol or illegal drug use, participate in parenting skills if referred, obtain medical screenings for their children, and ensure that their children are immunized and attending school. They also agree not to quit a job voluntarily. People who fail to comply with their PRA may suffer loss of benefits.

Welfare benefits in Texas are among the least generous in the nation. In 2008, Texas ranked forty-eighth in welfare spending per capita ($870), compared with a national average of $1,240.[60] The average TANF recipient in Texas is a 30-year-old African American or Latino woman caring for one or two children under the age of 11. She has neither a high school education nor job training and does not have reliable transportation. Her only income is a TANF grant of $223 a month or less.[61]

Welfare reform has helped reduce the welfare rolls, but it has not eliminated poverty. Although the number of people in Texas receiving a TANF check has declined by more than 30 percent just since 2005, the poverty rate in the state has not fallen. Today, only 2.5 percent of the state's 4.1 million poor children and adults receive checks. The average monthly benefit for the state's 103,076 TANF recipients, 86 percent of whom are children, is only $68 a month.[62] The state has succeeded in moving thousands of single mothers into the workforce, but their average wage is only $7.19 an hour, not enough to lift them out of poverty.[63]

Many low-income Texans qualify for the Supplemental Nutrition Assistance Program (SNAP), which is the new name for the program previously known as the Food Stamp Program. In October 2009, 2.8 million Texans received SNAP assistance, with an average monthly benefit of $312 per family paid to recipients through a Lone Star Card, which resembles a debit card. More than one-half of SNAP recipients were children. To qualify for SNAP, families and individuals needed to be low income and have less than $5,000 in assets, including cash, savings accounts, stocks, bonds, retirement, and even prepaid burial plots. Adults under the age of 50 were limited to three months of benefits unless they had a child living at home.[64]

Texas has one of the worst-administered food assistance programs in the nation. Whereas the federal government covers the cost of the food and one-half the administrative costs, state governments implement the program and pay the other half of administrative costs. The U.S. Department of Agriculture, the federal agency in charge of the program, estimates that 650,000 Texans qualify for food assistance but are not receiving it, which costs Texas grocers nearly $1 billion a year in food sales. The state routinely fails to process applications within the 30-day federal deadline, leaving many Texas families waiting months for assistance.[65]

Transportation

The Texas Good Roads Amendment has been the foundation of Texas transportation funding for more than 60 years. In 1946, the legislature proposed, and the voters

Dedicated Highway Fund A constitutionally earmarked account containing money set aside for building, maintaining, and policing state highways.

ratified, an amendment to the Texas Constitution creating the **Dedicated Highway Fund,** a constitutionally earmarked account containing money set aside for building, maintaining, and policing state highways. The amendment specified that three-fourths of the motor fuels and lubricants tax be set aside for the construction, policing, and maintenance of state highways.[66] Vehicle license fees support road construction as well. A subsequent amendment to the Texas Constitution allowed the Texas Department of Transportation (TxDOT) to issue bonds secured by future revenue to raise money to support highway construction and expansion. Federal grant money accounts for nearly 40 percent of state transportation funding, with the rest almost evenly divided between the Highway Fund and bond money secured by future revenues.[67]

Texas transportation officials and legislative leaders agree that current funding streams are inadequate to meet the state's transportation needs. Although Texas highway expenditures are about average ($471 per capita compared with a national average of $453), Texas has more highway mileage than any other state and its population is growing rapidly. Although gasoline tax revenues have been rising because the number of cars on the road has been increasing steadily, gasoline tax revenues have not kept up with the cost of highway construction, especially the cost of building freeways in urban centers. Because automobile engines are more fuel efficient, they use less gasoline per mile driven than they did in 1991 when the legislature and governor set the current gasoline tax rate of $0.20 a gallon.[68] Texas transportation officials estimate that without additional funding the state will be unable to build additional roads beyond 2012 and will soon lack sufficient funds to maintain existing roads.[69]

State officials are turning to toll roads to address the state's transportation needs. The advantage of toll roads is that they provide funding without raising taxes, an action that legislators and the governor have been unwilling to do, especially considering that TxDOT officials estimate it would take a 17-cent a gallon increase in gasoline taxes to meet the state's highway needs.[70] Unlike the gasoline tax, toll revenues do not have to be shared with the Texas Education Agency (TEA). Nonetheless, public opposition to toll roads has been building, especially to toll roads built by private companies that may not be accountable to the public interest. Texas residents also complain about proposals to convert formerly free roads into toll roads.

Trans-Texas Corridor A proposed network of transportation corridors a quarter mile wide and 370 miles long running from Brownsville to Oklahoma that would include toll roads, railways, and utility lines.

Consider the fate of the **Trans-Texas Corridor,** a proposed network of transportation corridors stretching from Brownsville to Oklahoma. The state planned to grant rights-of-way as much as a quarter mile wide to private developers who would construct a network of transportation corridors. Each corridor would contain separate lanes for automobiles, trucks, and rail lines, as well as additional space for pipelines and utility lines. The private developers would recoup their investment by charging tolls to drivers and other users of the corridor. Its supporters, including Governor Rick Perry, saw the Trans-Texas Corridor as an innovative solution to the state's transportation needs because private developers, rather than taxpayers, would bear the cost and the risk. Nonetheless, public opposition to the Trans-Texas Corridor was overwhelming. Opponents charged that the corridor was a boondoggle that would benefit private developers and harm the public interest. Environmentalists warned that it would consume vast stretches of open land and harm sensitive ecosystems. Property rights advocates opposed the project because private landowners would be forced to sell their land to private developers.[71] The legislature initially supported the Trans-Texas Corridor, but its enthusiasm waned in the face of public opposition. As a result, the TxDOT eventually abandoned the project. The state would have to find another way to meet its transportation needs.

 WHAT IS YOUR OPINION?

Are toll roads or higher gasoline taxes the better option for funding the state's transportation needs?

THE BUDGET PROCESS

Performance-based budgeting
A system of budget preparation and evaluation in which policymakers identify specific policy goals, set performance targets for agencies, and measure results.

The state of Texas uses **performance-based budgeting,** a system of budget preparation and evaluation in which policymakers identify specific policy goals, set performance targets for agencies, and measure results. The governor begins the budget process in the spring of the year before the legislature meets by defining the mission of state government, setting goals, and identifying priorities. Each state agency develops a strategic plan for accomplishing one or more of the goals. A strategic plan defines the mission of the agency, states its philosophy, and presents a strategy for achieving the goal. The agency also creates a budget to support its strategic plan. In June, July, and August, agencies submit their strategic plans and budgets to the

Building toll roads is an alternative to increasing the gasoline tax.

governor and the **Legislative Budget Board (LBB),** an agency created by the legislature to study state revenue and budgetary needs between legislative sessions and prepare budget and appropriation bills to submit to the legislature. Agencies must submit budget requests by the beginning of August.

The philosophy behind performance-based budgeting is that agency budgets are tied to measurable goals. Agencies establish goals, identify quantitative measures to assess progress, and prepare a budget designed to support their efforts. In 2009, for example, the performance measures used by the Texas Higher Education Coordinating Board (THECB) included the number of community college students who transfer to a university. Even though most college students in Texas begin their studies at a community college, the transfer rate has remained at 20 percent for several years. If Texas universities are going to increase the number of bachelor's degrees they award, the transfer rate between community colleges and universities will need to improve.[72] The state rewards managers who achieve their goals by giving them more discretion in the use of funds or allowing them to carry over part of a budget surplus from one budget period to the next.

Professor Thomas Anton identifies three "rules of the budget game" that government agencies follow in making budget requests:

1. Agencies ask for more money than they received the year before and more money than they expect to get, so that they will have room to cut their budget requests later.

2. Agencies insert some items into their budgets that are obvious targets for spending cuts, in hopes that the items they really want included in the budget will survive the cuts.

3. When agencies want large amounts of additional money, they present the requests as extensions of existing programs because it is easier to justify expanding a current program than it is to begin a new initiative.[73]

We could add a fourth rule: When asked to recommend spending reductions, agencies propose cutting programs that are politically popular. Once when the LBB asked the state bureaucracy to prepare budget requests that could be funded without a tax increase, agencies proposed cutting 23,000 poor children from welfare rolls, kicking 12,000 elderly Texans out of nursing homes, and leaving newly built prisons stand unopened.[74] Agency heads wanted to convince state budget makers that it was wiser politically to look elsewhere for budget cuts than to trim their particular piece of the budget pie.

After agencies submit their budgets, the LBB and the governor's staff hold hearings, at which agency administrators explain and defend their requests. During the last few months of the year, the LBB drafts an **appropriation bill,** a legislative authorization to spend money for particular purposes. Legislators introduce the LBB draft in the Texas House and Texas Senate as the basis for legislative deliberations on the budget for the upcoming biennium. The governor usually submits budget recommendations as well, but because the legislative leadership—the speaker and lieutenant governor—control the LBB, its budget serves as the starting point for the legislature, rather than the proposals offered by the governor.

The Texas Constitution, similar to most other state constitutions, prohibits the adoption of a budget that is in deficit. A **budget deficit** is the amount by which

---

Legislative Budget Board (LBB) An agency created by the legislature to study state revenue and budgetary needs between legislative sessions and prepare budget and appropriations bills to submit to the legislature.

Appropriation bill A legislative authorization to spend money for particular purposes; are usually assigned to the emergency calendar as well.

Budget deficit The amount of money by which annual budget expenditures exceed annual budget receipts.

budget expenditures exceed budget receipts. The state comptroller estimates state revenues for the upcoming biennium at the beginning of each legislative session. The comptroller may issue periodic updates during the session to reflect changing economic conditions or revisions in tax laws. Any spending bill the legislature approves must fall within the comptroller's revenue projections unless the legislature votes by a four-fifths majority to run a deficit, which, of course, is unlikely.

The Texas Constitution also caps state spending to the rate of economic growth. At the beginning of a legislative session, the comptroller projects the rate of economic growth in the state for the next two-year period. The rate of growth in state spending may be no greater than the projected rate of economic growth unless a majority of legislators agree that an emergency exists that warrants additional spending. The limit does not affect the expenditure of federal funds or money generated through dedicated funds.

Most spending decisions are predetermined by federal requirements, court orders, or dedicated funds. The U.S. Congress stipulates that most federal dollars fund particular activities, such as highway construction, healthcare for low-income families and children, and vocational education. In order to participate in federal programs, the state must satisfy a matching funds requirement. The national government will provide grant money for a particular activity only on the condition that the state or local government involved supplies a certain percentage of the total money required for the project or program.

The state must also spend money to respond to court orders issued by both federal and state courts. The legislature has appropriated billions of dollars in response to court rulings concerning state hospitals, prisons, public education, higher education in South Texas, and for people who are mentally ill or mentally retarded. The legislature spent hundreds of millions of dollars to expand educational opportunities in South Texas, for example, because of a lawsuit charging that state higher education funding unconstitutionally discriminated against Latinos living along the border with Mexico. The Texas Supreme Court eventually ruled in favor of the state, at least in part because of the efforts of the legislature to upgrade and expand higher education in South Texas.

Dedicated funds
Constitutional or statutory provisions that set aside revenue for particular purposes.

The legislature's budgetary discretion is also limited by **dedicated funds,** such as the Dedicated Highway Fund and the PUF, which are constitutional or statutory provisions that set aside revenue for particular purposes. The state has more than a hundred dedicated funds setting aside money for highways, parks, university construction, public schools, retirement funds, and other purposes. Constitutional or statutory dedications accounted for 49 percent of general revenue appropriations in the 2008–2009 budget.[75] The advocates of dedicated funds contend that they enable the state to make long-term commitments to goals. Earmarking revenue is also a means of generating public support for a tax increase because it makes budgeting comprehensible to ordinary people and gives the public confidence that tax money will be used as promised. In contrast, critics believe that earmarking contributes to state budget crises by limiting legislative discretion. Dedicated funds deny legislators the option of cutting certain programs, such as the highway construction budget, in order to avoid a tax increase or to find money for other priorities, such as public education or healthcare. Furthermore, dedicated funds, especially those contained in the state constitution, restrict the legislature's ability to modify budget priorities to reflect the state's changing needs.

The budget must pass the legislature in a fashion similar to other bills. In the Texas Senate, the Finance Committee deals with both appropriation and tax bills, making recommendations to the Senate floor. In the House, the Appropriations Committee drafts the budget, whereas the Ways and Means Committee deals with tax measures. In most instances, the final details of the state appropriation bill and most tax packages have to be ironed out by a House–Senate **conference committee,** a special committee created to negotiate differences on similar pieces of legislation passed by the Texas House and Texas Senate. Once legislation receives final legislative approval, it goes to the governor.

On appropriation bills, the governor of Texas (and the governors of most states) has the **line-item veto,** the power to veto sections or items of an appropriation bill while signing the remainder of the bill into law. Although the line-item veto (and the threat of its use) is a potentially potent weapon for influencing the state budget, research shows that it has a relatively small impact on total state spending.[76] In 2009, Governor Perry used the line-item veto to cut $289 million from the state budget of $182 billion.[77] In practice, the legislature has limited the governor's ability to knock out objectionable items by lumping millions of dollars of expenditures together in a single line item. In 1941, for example, the appropriation for the University of Texas at Austin included 1,528 line items.[78] Today, the legislature funds each institution of higher education through a single line item or lump-sum appropriation. Governor Perry has criticized this approach to budgeting because it limits his ability to impact the budget process.

Political scientists who study budgeting have developed models to understand the process. The most common approach is the **incremental model of budgeting,** a theoretical effort to explain the budget process on the basis of small (incremental) changes in budget categories from one budget period to the next. Scholars who favor this approach to understanding the budget process believe that agency heads, legislators, and governors all regard an agency's current budget share as its base. Increases or decreases in that base must be justified, whereas maintaining current levels need not be. Consequently, changes in individual budget items tend to be small. Another explanation for incremental budgeting is that an agency's current budget reflects its political strength relative to the strength of other agencies competing for money. Because the relative political influence of various claimants on the state budget is unlikely to change dramatically from one budget period to the next, budget figures are unlikely to change dramatically, either.

Although incremental budgeting may be the norm, not all budget changes are incremental. Between 1989 and 2009, for example, the share of the budget devoted to health and human services grew by more than half, increasing from 22.2 percent to 37.4 percent of state spending. Spending for health and human services increased because of the growth in Medicaid spending. In contrast, the transportation share of the budget fell by nearly half, from 12.3 percent of spending to 6.7 percent.

The governor and the LBB share **budget execution authority,** which is the power to cut agency spending or transfer money between agencies during the period when the legislature is not in session. Between legislative sessions, either the LBB or the governor may propose reductions or shifts in state spending. If the LBB proposes a change, the governor must approve the transfer before it can take effect, and vice versa.

Conference committee A special committee created to negotiate differences on similar pieces of legislation passed by the House and Senate.

Line-item veto The power of the governor to veto sections or items of an appropriation bill while signing the remainder of the bill into law.

Incremental model of budgeting A theoretical effort to explain the budget process on the basis of small (incremental) changes in budget categories from one budget period to the next.

Budget execution authority The power to cut agency spending or transfer money between agencies during the period when the legislature is not in session.

MAKING BUDGETARY POLICY

The public policy approach offers a useful mechanism for analyzing budgetary policymaking in Texas.

The Context of Budgetary Policymaking

Environmental and political factors provide the context for budgetary policymaking. Economic development is the single most important factor for explaining state budgetary policies. States with greater levels of personal income have higher tax rates and higher levels of spending for transportation, education, healthcare, criminal justice, and welfare than do states with lower levels of personal income. In short, wealthy states tax their residents more heavily and provide more generous levels of public services than do poor states.[79] Budgetary policies in Texas are consistent with the state's status as a relatively poor state. Compared with other states, tax rates in the Lone Star State are low and spending programs are poorly funded.

States adopt budgetary policies to respond to competition from other states. States offer tax breaks and other subsidies to businesses to encourage them to relocate to the state. In Texas, the legislature has created a multimillion dollar fund that the governor can use to lure companies to the state, either by providing them with cash subsidies or benefits, such as job training for workers or improved transportation to plant sites. Citgo Petroleum, BP Chemical, Home Depot, Sematech, and Tyson Foods have all benefited from state subsidies.[80] In the meantime, state governments hesitate to increase welfare benefits because they do not want to become welfare magnets, attracting low-income people from other states. Although states attempt to attract companies that create jobs and generate economic activity, they want to repel low-income people who would be a drain on public services.[81]

Short-term economic factors affect budgetary policymaking as well. Economic expansion improves the state's budget picture by fueling the growth of sales tax and excise tax revenues. In the late 1990s, the economy boomed and state officials were able to cut taxes and increase spending at the same time. In contrast, state tax revenues decline during a recession. The recession of 2008–2009 helped produce a budget shortfall that would have forced the legislature to make some difficult decisions involving spending and state revenues were it not for the federal stimulus money. The addition of billions of dollars in federal funds to the 2010–2011 budget allowed the legislature and governor to avoid (or at least postpone) some painful decisions involving spending and taxation.

 WHAT IS YOUR OPINION?

Do you favor a small state government that provides relatively modest services but holds down taxes or a larger state government that provides more services but costs more?

Political culture The widely held, deeply rooted political values of a society.

Individualistic political culture An approach to government and politics that emphasizes private initiative with a minimum of government interference.

Texas's budgetary policies of relatively low tax rates coupled with poorly funded public services reflect the state's political culture, interest group environment, and political party balance. **Political culture** is the widely held, deeply rooted political values of a society. Texas's low-tax/low-spend budgetary philosophy is consistent with the state's **individualistic political culture,** which is an approach to government and politics that emphasizes private initiative with a minimum of government interference. Many Texans believe in small government. When given a choice between higher taxes with more government services and lower taxes with fewer services, they prefer the latter.

The interest group configuration in Texas is consistent with a low-tax/low-spend government. Interest groups that would favor higher taxes to support better-funded public services, such as labor unions, consumer groups, and racial and ethnic minority organizations, are relatively weak in the Lone Star State. In contrast, business organizations, which typically prefer lower tax rates and less generously funded services, are especially strong in Texas. In particular, business interests favor low welfare benefits and strict limits on the amount of time an individual can collect benefits. Low welfare spending not only saves money and helps hold down tax rates, but it also helps to hold down wage rates by pushing welfare recipients into the job market and making them more willing to accept low-paying jobs.[82]

The current party balance also supports the state's low-tax/low-spend budgetary policies. The Republican Party, which now controls all three branches of Texas state government, advocates limited government. When faced with a substantial budget shortfall in 2003, Republican leaders in the legislature and the executive branch favored cutting services rather than raising taxes to balance the budget. In 2007, Republican leaders chose to save most of the state's budget surplus in a Rainy Day Fund so that it could be used to pay for future property tax reductions rather than increase spending for health, education, and welfare. The Democratic Party, which tends to favor a more active government, has limited influence in the state's policy-making process.

Demographic change may eventually affect the environment for budgetary policy-making in Texas. The Latino population is young and growing rapidly, whereas the white population is aging. Population growth will invariably lead to political influence. Because Latinos as a group are more likely to be poor, they are more dependent on public services for healthcare, education, transportation, job training, and welfare than the white population. As the political influence of Latino voters grows, the state may adopt budgetary policies that shift the tax burden away from consumers and low-income families while increasing spending for government services.

Agenda Setting

Budgetary issues are always near the forefront of the state's official policy agenda because of the biennial budget cycle. Adopting a balanced budget that will meet the state's needs is typically the overriding issue of each legislative session. Whether legislators will have sufficient funds to enact new initiatives or consider a tax cut or whether they will have to cut programs and raise taxes depends on economic conditions. Boom times produce budget surpluses that can be spent, whereas a recession causes a shortfall that must be addressed.

Public officials and interest groups raise budgetary issues because they hope to see their concerns included in the state's official policy agenda. Public school administrators want the legislature to reform school finance to increase state funding for education. Business interests favor the use of tax breaks and government subsidies to promote business expansion. Medical professionals advocate an increase in the state cigarette tax in hopes of discouraging young people from taking up the smoking habit.

Budgetary issues sometimes arise because of external pressures. For example, Texas absorbed hundreds of thousands of evacuees after Hurricane Katrina. Although the federal government covered some of their food, housing, healthcare, transportation, and other living expenses, state and local governments had to pick up much of the cost. School districts, in particular, faced millions of dollars of unexpected expenses to cover the cost of educating thousands of children from Louisiana. Court decisions can also force budgetary issues on state government. The legislature and governor have had to address school finance in numerous regular and special sessions because of court rulings in *Edgewood v. Kirby* and *Neeley v. West Orange-Cove Consolidated ISD*.

Policy Formulation, Adoption, and Legitimation

A broad range of political actors participate in budgetary policy formulation. State agencies make budget proposals and lobby for their adoption. For example, the THECB lobbies for increased funding for higher education. The agency's strategy is to focus on the gap in educational attainment between whites and the state's two largest minority populations, African Americans and Latinos. THECB officials, joined by allies in higher education and minority rights organizations, argue that closing the educational gap is essential to the state's future. To achieve that goal, they declare, the state must fund higher education more generously.

The members of the legislative leadership are the key players in drafting a budget and formulating tax policy. The speaker and lieutenant governor control the LBB, which prepares the initial budget document. Their closest political allies chair the Texas House and Texas Senate committees that formulate the details of budget policy. The speaker and the lieutenant governor control the conference committee that prepares the final budget document.

The governor's role in formulating budgetary policy depends on the interest and the skills of the state's chief executive. In 2003, Governor Perry made clear his opposition to raising taxes, calling instead for the legislature to cut spending to eliminate the budget shortfall. Nonetheless, the governor did not want to become deeply involved in the budget process. When given the opportunity to submit a balanced budget without new taxes at the beginning of the 2003 legislative session, Perry offered a document filled with zeros. Perry explained that his budget symbolized the importance of carefully examining every budgetary item to set priorities and make cuts; his critics accused him of zero leadership.

The federal government has a significant impact on policy formulation in Texas because of federal programs. Some of the most important items in the budget rely heavily on federal funds, including welfare, healthcare, transportation, and public education. Federal money, however, comes with strings attached. To ensure the continued flow of federal dollars, state budgetary policies must conform to federal guidelines. They must also appropriate billions of dollars in state money as matching funds.

The legislature and the governor adopt budgetary policies through the legislative process. The appropriation bill and tax bills must be passed by majority vote of both the Texas House and the Texas Senate. The governor must sign them or allow them to become law without signature. If the governor issues a veto, it can be overridden by a two-thirds vote of both chambers of the legislature. In practice, gubernatorial vetoes of tax and spending bills are seldom, if ever, overridden because the legislature invariably gets them to the governor's desk late in the session and the governor allows the legislature to go home before issuing vetoes.

The Texas Constitution establishes special rules for budgetary policymaking that create an atmosphere of budgetary caution. The constitution stipulates that the legislature adopt a balanced budget unless lawmakers agree by a four-fifths majority to run a deficit. The constitution also demands that state spending grow no more rapidly than economic growth unless both chambers vote in favor of greater spending. These two provisions create a bias in favor of spending restraint. The clear message of the Texas Constitution is that public officials should focus on limiting the growth of government rather than providing enough spending to meet the needs of the state and its people.

The governor plays a special role in budgetary policymaking because of the line-item veto. On most legislative measures, including tax bills, the governor faces a take-it-or-leave-it choice. The governor can sign the bill, allow it to become law without signature, or veto it. On appropriation measures, however, the governor can pick out individual provisions to veto while allowing the rest to become law. As a result, the governor can play a more active role in budgetary policymaking than in other sorts of policy issues.

The state officials, interest groups, and political parties that support the adoption of budgetary policies also promote their legitimation. After the 2003 legislative session when lawmakers cut spending rather than increase taxes, Governor Perry and legislative leaders defended the action as evidence of the state's wise budget management. Business groups and Republican officials attribute the state's relatively strong economy to its low-tax/low-spend policies. In contrast, Democrats and their interest group allies warn that the state's economic future is jeopardized by the failure of state government to adequately fund education, healthcare, and transportation.

Policy Implementation, Evaluation, and Change

Private companies, local governments, and state agencies implement budgetary policies. Retail business establishments collect sales taxes and many excise taxes on behalf of the state. State law requires that retailers obtain a sales tax permit from the comptroller, collect taxes on the retail purchase of taxable items, keep records, and remit tax receipts to the state. In return for acting as the state's tax collector, retail establishments can keep a small portion of the money they collect as compensation for their work.

Local governments play a role in administering the state's programs. Most of the state's spending for education goes to independent school districts, which provide educational services for kindergarten through high school. Community/junior colleges implement higher education policies, whereas hospital districts participate in the implementation of the state's healthcare policies. County governments collect a number of taxes and fees on behalf of the state, including charges for license plates and certificates-of-title for motor vehicles.

State agencies implement budgetary policies as well. The comptroller is the state's chief tax collector, sometimes collecting taxes directly and sometimes working through intermediaries, such as retail merchants. The Texas Department of Corrections (TDC) administers the state's correctional programs. The Health and Human Services Commission implements welfare policies. The Texas Department of State Health Services operates mental health facilities. The state's public universities provide higher education services to the state's residents.

Performance-based budgeting ensures that state agencies evaluate at least some aspects of their programs. Agencies set goals, plan strategies, and identify measures to determine whether they are achieving their goals. Each year they produce a report showing their progress at achieving their goals.

The comptroller, LBB, and legislative committees evaluate state programs as well. The websites of the comptroller (www.cpa.state.tx.us) and the LBB (www.lbb.state.tx.us) include a number of reports evaluating the state tax system and various programs, such as the state's health programs and the Foundation School Program. Legislative committees evaluate state agencies and programs under their jurisdiction. The legislature also evaluates agencies and programs through **sunset review,** the periodic evaluation of state agencies by the legislature to determine whether they should be reauthorized.

Sunset review The periodic evaluation of state agencies by the legislature to determine whether they should be reauthorized.

Budgetary policies change because of changing economic conditions, federal action, and political change. Budgetary policies change as economic conditions change. Whereas a strong economy produces money to fund new programs or expand old ones, a weak economy makes for a tight budget. Some changes in state budget policy occur because of the federal government. Over the next few years, the Texas Medicaid program will expand to cover a million additional Texans because of the federal healthcare reform law adopted in 2010. Finally, policy changes follow political change. The election of a Democratic governor along with Democratic majorities in the legislature would likely lead to an increase in funding for public services along with a reformed tax system that relies less on taxes that affect low- and middle-income residents and more on taxes levied on business and upper-income groups.

WHAT WE HAVE LEARNED

1. What are the most important revenue sources for the state of Texas, including both tax and non-tax sources, and how has the relative importance of those sources changed over the last 20 years?

The general sales tax is by far the most important state tax source, generating substantially more money than any other tax. The state sales tax rate is 6.25 percent and local governments can add 2 percent more. The other major state taxes include a business franchise tax, a motor fuels tax, a tax on motor vehicle sales and rental, and severance taxes on oil and natural gas production. The franchise tax is a tax on businesses chartered or organized in Texas and doing business in the state. Severance taxes are taxes levied on natural resources such as oil and gas at the time they are taken from the land or water. Excise taxes are selective sales taxes. The proportion of state revenues generated by tax sources

has declined over the last 20 years whereas non-tax sources, especially federal funds, have grown in importance. Federal money, which represents one-third of state spending, helps fund healthcare, welfare, highway construction, and a broad range of other state activities. Other non-tax sources of revenue include licenses and fees, interest and investment income, land income, and lottery revenue.

2. What important revenue issues face state government in Texas?

Texas policymakers face a number of issues in government finance. Does the government generate enough money to meet the needs of the state's large and rapidly growing population? Liberals believe that state government generates insufficient funds to address the state's needs whereas conservatives argue that high taxes limit economic growth. What is the incidence of taxation in Texas? The term "tax incidence" refers to the point at which the actual cost of a tax falls, that is, who actually pays the tax. Tax systems are classified as progressive, regressive, or proportional, depending on the incidence of taxation. The Texas tax structure is regressive because of its heavy reliance on property, sales, and excise taxes. Is the tax system fair? Although everyone agrees that taxes should be fair, observers define fairness in different ways. Some favor income taxes because they reflect the ability-to-pay theory of taxation. In contrast, other experts on public finance believe that government should keep taxes low and focus on consumer taxes, such as the sales tax, in order to encourage economic growth. Finally, to what extent do tax revenues increase as the economy grows (a concept known as tax elasticity)? The Texas tax system is relatively inelastic because of its reliance on excise taxes, severance taxes, and property taxes.

3. **What policy options have been proposed for reforming the state's revenue structure?**

Critics of the Texas tax system offer a number of policy options designed to make the state's tax structure more equitable, efficient, or productive. Most discussions of tax reform in Texas include an examination of the wisdom of a personal income tax. Another proposal for reforming the state tax system is to enlarge the sales tax base to include more services than are currently taxed. Some members of the legislature want to increase revenue by expanding legalized gambling. The state could also raise money by selling assets, such as the lottery, to private investors. A number of states have enacted special tax exemptions and credits for low-income individuals, such as the August sales tax holiday.

4. **How do spending levels in Texas compare and contrast with those of other states?**

The state budget for the 2010–2011 biennium was $182.2 billion. The largest expenditure categories for state government were health and human services, education, transportation, and public safety and corrections. State government expenditures in Texas are well below the national average. Few public services in Texas are well-funded, at least in comparison with their funding levels in other states.

5. **What are the most important budget priorities in Texas and how are those priorities reflected in budget policy?**

The foremost budget priorities for state government in Texas are healthcare, elementary and secondary education, higher education, welfare, and transportation. Medicaid and the State Children's Health Insurance Program (SCHIP) are the state's major health programs. Even though Texas has one of the least generous Medicaid programs in the country, it consumes more than one-fourth of total state spending and is growing rapidly. Furthermore, federal healthcare reform legislation adopted in 2010 will expand Medicaid dramatically, eventually increasing the cost to Texas government. SCHIP is a federal program designed to provide health insurance to children from low-income families whose parents are not poor enough to qualify for Medicaid. Texas has consistently failed to take advantage of all the SCHIP money available because it has not met the federal matching funds requirement.

State government distributes money to public schools through the Foundation School Program. The amount of money each district receives depends on a complex set of formulas, including the Robin Hood Plan, which is designed to equalize funding. In 2006, the legislature cut school property tax rates and increased state funding to make up the difference. Nonetheless, many districts soon faced a financial crisis because the legislature froze spending at 2005–2006 levels without taking account of rising costs. The legislature provided additional funding in its 2009 session, but the new money barely kept pace with inflation, leaving many school districts financially strapped.

Higher education funding in Texas is near the national average. As the relative importance of state funding for higher education has declined, tuition and fees have soared and community colleges have raised their local property tax rates. The University of Texas (UT) at Austin, Texas A&M University at College Station, and some other schools in the UT and A&M systems benefit from the Permanent University Fund (PUF). In 2009, the legislature and the voters approved measures to provide funding aimed at increasing the number of Tier One universities in Texas.

The philosophy underlying the nation's welfare system has changed from providing recipients with a minimal standard of living to moving recipients to the workforce. Welfare benefits in Texas are among the least generous in the nation. TANF grants average just $223 a month. Although welfare reform has reduced the welfare rolls, it has not eliminated poverty. Many low-income Texans qualify for the Supplemental Nutrition Assistance Program (SNAP), which was formerly called the Food Stamp Program. Texas has one of the worst-administered food assistance programs in the country.

The Texas Constitution dedicates a majority of the motor fuels tax to construction and maintenance of highways. Nonetheless, Texas transportation officials indicate that current funding is inadequate to meet the state's transportation needs. The state's efforts to address the problem through toll roads have met resistance from the general public and the legislature.

6. What are the primary steps in the state budgetary process?

Texas uses performance-based budgeting. The LBB begins the budget process in the year before the legislature meets in regular session by asking agencies to submit their strategic plans and budgets. The LBB drafts an appropriation bill for submission to the legislature by the end of the year.

Although the governor may offer a bill as well, the LBB document is the starting point for legislative deliberation. The comptroller presents legislators with an estimate of anticipated revenue for the upcoming two-year budget period and the legislature must stay within that estimate unless it votes by a four-fifths margin to run a budget deficit. Most spending decisions are predetermined by federal requirements, court orders, or dedicated funds. The budget must pass the legislature in a fashion similar to other bills. The governor has the line-item veto for appropriations measures. Although some political scientists explain the budget process using the incremental model of budgeting, not all budget changes are incremental. The governor and the LBB share budget execution authority.

7. How are budget policies made in Texas?

Environmental and political factors provide the context for budgetary policymaking. Texas' budgetary policies of relatively low tax rates coupled with poorly funded public services reflect the state's political culture, interest group environment, and political party balance. Budgetary issues are always near the forefront of the state's official policy agenda because of the biennial budget cycle. A broad range of political actors participate in budgetary policy formulation, including state agencies, legislative leaders, the governor, and the federal government. The legislature and the governor adopt budgetary policies through the legislative process. The state officials, interest groups, and political parties that support the adoption of budgetary policies also promote their legitimation. Private companies, local governments, and state agencies implement budgetary policies. Performance-based budgeting ensures that state agencies evaluate at least some aspects of their programs. The comptroller, LBB, and legislative committees evaluate state programs as well. Budgetary policies change because of changing economic conditions, federal action, and political change.

KEY TERMS

ability-to-pay theory of taxation

appropriation bill

biennium

budget deficit

budget execution authority

conference committee

dedicated funds

Dedicated Highway Fund

Employees Retirement System (ERS) Trust Fund

excise tax

federal grant program

fiscal year

Foundation School Program

franchise tax

General Fund

incremental model of budgeting

individualistic political culture

Legislative Budget Board (LBB)

line-item veto

matching funds requirement

Medicaid

Medicare program

pari-mutuel wagering

per capita

performance-based budgeting

Permanent School Fund (PSF)

Permanent University Fund (PUF)

political culture

progressive tax

proportional tax

Rainy Day Fund

recession

regressive tax

Robin Hood Plan

sales tax

severance tax

sin tax

State Children's Health Insurance Program (SCHIP)

sunset review

tax elasticity

tax incidence

Temporary Assistance for Needy Families (TANF)

Texas Teacher Retirement System (TRS) Trust Fund

Trans-Texas Corridor

NOTES

1. Darren Barbee, "Texas Legislature Used Stimulus Funds to Help Balance Budget," *Fort Worth Star-Telegram*, September 18, 2009, available at www.star-telegram.com.
2. Gary Scharrer, "Could Another School Funding Lawsuit Be Brewing?" *San Antonio Express-News*, June 21, 2009, available at www.mysanantonio.com.
3. *Governing*, State and Local Source Book, available at www.governing.com.
4. Penelope Lemov, "The Untaxables," *Governing*, July 2002, p. 36.
5. Texas Comptroller of Public Accounts, "Revenue by Source," available at www.windows.state.tx.us.
6. Texas Railroad Commission, available at www.rrc.state.tx.us.
7. "Cigarette Tax Increase Pushes Revenue Up, But Sales Are Down," *Dallas Morning News*, March 10, 2007, available at www.dallasnews.com.
8. Texas Racing Commission, *Year 2009 Annual Report*, available at www.txrc.state.tx.us.
9. Texas Comptroller of Public Accounts, "State of Texas 2009 Annual Cash Report," available at www.cpa.state.tx.us.
10. "Abbott Calls for Stricter Oversight of Texas Public Pensions," *Austin American-Statesman*, June 26, 2007, available at www.statesman.com.
11. Texas Comptroller of Public Accounts, "State of Texas 2008 Annual Cash Report."
12. "Solid Ground for Education," *Fiscal Notes*, May 1996, pp. 12–13.
13. Texas Lottery Commission, available at www.txlottery.org.
14. Ellen Perlman, "Losing Numbers," *Governing*, September 2001, pp. 46–47.
15. "Lotto Texas Jackpot Gets Longer Odds," *Houston Chronicle*, March 27, 2003, available at www.houstonchronicle.com.
16. Mega Millions, available at www.megamillions.com.
17. David W. Winder and James T. LaPlant, "State Lawsuits Against 'Big Tobacco': A Test of Diffusion Theory," *State and Local Government Review* 32 (Spring 2000): 132–141.
18. Comptroller of Public Accounts, "Tax Exemptions and Tax Incidence, 2009," available at www.window.state.tx.us.
19. Dick Lavine, "Who Pays Texas Taxes?" Center for Public Policy Priorities, March 20, 2007, available at www.cppp.org.
20. Ken Rodriguez, "'Pro-Education' Lottery Quietly Fleeces the Poor, Not-So-Educated," *San Antonio Express-News*, September 29, 2006, available at www.mysanantonio.com.
21. Lisa Sandberg and Julie Domel, "So Who's Buying the $50 Scratch-Offs?" *San Antonio Express News*, June 11, 2007, available at www.mysanantonio.com.

22. Dave Mann, "The Best Idea They Won't Talk About," *Texas Observer*, April 21, 2006, pp. 6–7, 18.

23. Dick Lavine, "The Best Choice for a Prosperous Texas," Center for Public Policy Priorities, March 1, 2005, available at www.cppp.org.

24. Richard Vedder, "Taxing Texans," Texas Public Policy Foundation, available at www.texaspolicy.com.

25. Texas Comptroller of Public Accounts, "Tax Exemptions and Tax Incidence 2009."

26. Nevada Department of Administration, "General Fund Revenues by Source, 2007–2009," available at http://budget.state.nv.us.

27. Ian Pulsipher, "Counting on Gambling," *State Legislatures*, February 2005, pp. 24–26.

28. Christopher Swope, "Unloading Assets," *Governing*, January 2007, pp. 36–40.

29. John Moritz, "Perry Still Backs Sale of Lottery," *Fort Worth Star-Telegram*, March 27, 2008, available at www.star-telegram.com.

30. "General Appropriation Act for the 2010–2011 Biennium," available at www.lbb.tx.us.

31. *Governing*, State and Local Source Book, available at www.governing.com.

32. U.S. Census Bureau, "Educational Attainment by State," *The 2009 Statistical Abstract*, available at www.census.gov.

33. U.S. Census Bureau, "Individuals and Families Below Poverty Level—Number and Rate by State," *The 2009 Statistical Abstract*, available at www.census.gov.

34. U.S. Census Bureau, "Income, Poverty, and Health Insurance Coverage in the United States: 2008."

35. "Texas Medicaid in Perspective," January 2009, Texas Health and Human Services Commission, available at www.hhsc.state.tx.us.

36. Donald F. Kettl, "Looking for a Real Crisis: Try Medicaid," *Governing*, April 2005, p. 20.

37. Dave Michaels, "Texas Ranks Nearly Last in Getting Stimulus Funds," *Dallas Morning News*, September 28, 2009, available at www.dallasnews.com.

38. Bob Moos, "Texas Nursing Homes in a Tight Fix on Medicaid," *Dallas Morning News*, March 4, 2009, available at www.dallasnews.com.

39. "Texas Medicaid in Perspective."

40. Ibid.

41. Michael Luo, "Some States Find Burdens in Health Law," *New York Times*, March 26, 2010, available at www.nytimes.com.

42. "Cheap at First, Expensive Later," *Texas Weekly*, March 29, 2010, available at www.texasweekly.com.

43. U.S. Department of Health and Human Services, "The 2009 HHS Poverty Guidelines," available at www.hhs.gov.

44. Hy Gia Park and Leah Oliver, "Is SCHIP Shipshape?" *State Legislatures*, May 2004, pp. 16–18.

45. House Research Organization, "State Finance Report," April 4, 2005, available at www.capitol.state.tx.us.

46. John Moritz, "Budget Crunch Coming for Texas School Districts," *Fort Worth Star-Telegram*, July 30, 2008, available at www.star-telegram.com.

47. Terrence Stutz, "Lawmakers Tackle Teacher Pay, Tests but Leave School Finance for 2011," *Dallas Morning News*, June 2, 2009, available at www.dallasnews.com.

48. University of Texas News, available at www.utexas.edu.

49. Texas A&M News, available at http://tamunews.tamu.edu.

50. Texas Higher Education Coordinating Board, "Closing the Gaps Progress Report 2007," available at www.thecb.state.tx.us.

51. Ralph K. M. Haurwitz, "Spread of Doctoral Programs in Texas Raises Concerns," *Austin American-Statesman*, June 3, 2008, available at www.statesman.com.

52. *Governing*, State and Local Source Book, available at www.governing.com.

53. Texas Higher Education Coordinating Board, "Facts on Higher Education," available at www.thecb.state.tx.us.

54. *Capitol Update*, October 2, 2008, available at www.txdirectory.com.

55. John Austin, "Texas Public University Tuition up 112% Since Deregulation," *Fort Worth Star-Telegram*, June 4, 2008, available at www.star-telegram.com.

56. Holly K. Hacker, "Report Shows College Costs More in Texas," *Dallas Morning News*, October 23, 2007, available at www.dallasnews.com.

57. "Priced Out of College," *Texas Observer*, May 1, 2009, p. 4.

58. Katherine Leal Unmuth, "Texas Colleges' Math-Science Push Falling Short, Board Says," *Dallas Morning News*, August 3, 2009, available at www.dallasnews.com.

59. Holly K. Hacker, "Tier One University Bill Is Signed, Uniting Old Foes," *Dallas Morning News*, June 18, 2009, available at www.dallasnews.com.

60. *Governing*, State and Local Source Book, available at www.governing.com.

61. Texas Health and Human Services Commission, "Temporary Assistance for Needy Families," available at www.hhsc.state.tx.us.

62. "Texas TANF and SNAP Enrollment Statistics," Texas Health and Human Services Commission, available at www.hhsc.state.tx.us.

63. Janet Elliott and Terri Langford, "The Cost of Cutting Welfare," *Houston Chronicle*, January 28, 2007, available at www.chron.com.

64. Texas Health and Human Services Commission, available at www.hhsc.state.tx.us.

65. Corrie MacLaggan, "U.S. Food Stamp Official: State Could Be Aiding More Texans," *Austin American Statesman*, January 12, 2010, available at www.statesman.com.

66. Article 8, Section 7a, Texas Constitution.

67. Texas Department of Transportation, available at www.dot .state.tx.us.

68. Matt Sundeen, "States Shift Gears," *State Legislatures*, December 2006, pp. 22–24.

69. Josh Baugh, "Legislators Debate Road Funding," *San Antonio Express-News*, February 1, 2010, available at www .mysanantonio.com.

70. Ben Wear, "State: No Tolls Would Mean 17-Cent Gas Tax," *Austin American-Statesman*, September 12, 2006, available at www.statesman.com.

71. Cathy Booth Thomas, "A Big, Fat Texas Boondoggle?" *Time*, December 6, 2004, pp. 40–42.

72. Legislative Budget Board, "Performance Measures for Higher Education," available at www.lbb.state.tx.us.

73. Thomas J. Anton, *The Politics of State Expenditures in Illinois* (Urbana, IL: University of Illinois Press, 1966).

74. Mary Lenz, "$52 Billion State Budget Clears Board," *Houston Post*, December 15, 1990, p. A-1.

75. House Research Organization, "Writing the State Budget, 81st Legislature," available at www.capitol.state.tx.us/ hrofr/.

76. James W. Enderaby and Michael J. Towle, "Effects of Constitutional and Political Controls on State Expenditures," *Publius: The Journal of Federalism* 27 (Winter 1997): 83–98.

77. Office of the Governor, Bills Vetoed by Governor Perry, Eighty-first Legislature, available at www.governor.state.tx.us.

78. Pat Thompson and Steven P. Boyd, "Use of the Item Veto in Texas, 1940–1990," *State and Local Government Review* 26 (Winter 1994): 38–45.

79. Thomas R. Dye, *Politics, Economics, and the Public* (Chicago, IL: Rand McNally, 1966).

80. Paul Sweeney, "Texas: The Corporate Welfare State," *Texas Observer*, April 15, 2005, pp. 6–9, 28.

81. Michael A. Bailey and Mark Carl Rom, "A Wider Race? Interstate Competition Across Health and Welfare Programs," *Journal of Politics* 66 (May 2004): 326–347.

82. Carl Klasner, Xiaotong Mao, and Stan Buchanan, "Business Interest Group Power and Temporary Assistance to Needy Families," *Social Science Quarterly* 88 (March 2007): 104–119.

Chapter 14

Criminal Justice

WHAT WE WILL LEARN

After studying Chapter 14, students should be able to answer the following questions:

▶ What methods are used to measure the crime rate, and what do the data indicate about the crime rate in the United States and the state of Texas?

▶ What groups of people are most likely to be the victims of crimes and what groups are most likely to commit crimes?

▶ What are the steps of the criminal prosecution process?

▶ What is the capital punishment law in Texas and how is it implemented?

▶ How does Texas deal with juvenile offenders?

▶ What categories of prisoners are held in county jails, state jails, and state prisons, and how are those facilities managed?

▶ How are criminal justice policies made in Texas?

sobriety checkpoint

A police checkpoint in which officers randomly stop vehicles to investigate the possibility that drivers may be too impaired to drive safely.

A sobriety checkpoint is a police procedure in which officers randomly stop vehicles to investigate the possibility that drivers may be too impaired to drive safely. To accomplish this, law enforcement personnel set up a roadblock on a public highway or city street late at night or on weekends when the proportion of drunken drivers tends to be highest. They then stop every vehicle or, more frequently, every fourth, fifth, or sixth vehicle, and officers question the drivers. If an officer believes that a driver may be impaired, the driver is given a field sobriety test and arrested if he or she fails.

Sobriety checkpoints are controversial. Mothers Against Drunk Driving (MADD) and other groups opposed to drunk driving believe that sobriety checkpoints are an effective weapon against drunk driving. They note that 45 percent of all traffic fatalities in Texas are alcohol related compared with 37 percent nationwide.[1] In contrast, the opponents of sobriety checkpoints, including the Texas Criminal Lawyers Association, argue that they are an invasion of privacy and that they inconvenience law-abiding drivers. Critics contend that law enforcement should use its personnel for roving DWI patrols, looking out for erratic drivers.[2]

Texas is one of 11 states that prohibit sobriety checkpoints. State Senator John Corona, a Republican from Dallas, introduced legislation in the 2009 session of the Texas legislature that would have allowed the use of sobriety checkpoints, but the bill failed to pass.[3] Proponents have indicated that they will introduce the measure again in a future session.

The debate over sobriety checkpoints introduces this chapter on criminal justice in Texas. The chapter reviews the crime rate, traces the criminal justice process, and describes the state's system of jails and prisons. This chapter on criminal justice is the second of two chapters dealing with the nature of public policy in particular policy areas. Chapter 13 addressed budgetary policymaking.

CRIME STATISTICS

Crime is a major policy issue in Texas. Many Texans fear becoming victims of crime, local newscasts feature stories of grisly murders, and politicians run for office promising to get tough on crime. One might wonder, how serious is crime in Texas? Is the crime rate going up or down? Which groups of people are more likely to be victims of crime? Who are the criminals?

 WHAT IS YOUR OPINION?

Are sobriety checkpoints a good idea? Why or why not?

Measuring Crime

Uniform Crime Reports (UCR) A record of offenses known to police compiled by the Federal Bureau of Investigation (FBI) from reports submitted by local law enforcement agencies.

The U.S. Department of Justice uses two complementary measures to assess the incidence of crime in America: the Uniform Crime Reports (UCR) and the National Crime Victim Survey (NCVS). The **Uniform Crime Reports (UCR)** is a record of offenses known to police compiled by the Federal Bureau of Investigation (FBI) from reports submitted by local law enforcement agencies. The UCR includes four violent crimes—murder, forcible rape, robbery, and aggravated assault—and four property crimes—burglary, larceny/theft, motor vehicle theft, and arson. The advantage of the UCR is that it provides crime data for every state and city in the nation, allowing researchers to compare crime rates. The disadvantage of the UCR is that it underestimates the incidence of crime because it only counts offenses known to the police. Some offenses, such as forcible rape, often go unreported because victims may feel ashamed or endangered. Other crimes, such as theft and burglary, may not be reported because victims have little confidence that the police will apprehend the offenders and recover stolen property. In addition, some victims of crime, such as drug dealers or illegal aliens, may not report offenses because they want to avoid contact with the police.

> **National Crime Victim Survey (NCVS)** A measure of the incidence of crime in the United States based on interviews with people in more than 50,000 households.

The **National Crime Victim Survey (NCVS)** is a measure of the incidence of crime in the United States based on interviews with people in more than 50,000 households. It estimates the crime rate on the basis of the number of people in the sample who claim to have been victims of crime during the previous year. Although most social scientists regard the NCVS as a better measure of crime than the UCR, it, too, has shortcomings because it relies on individuals accurately and honestly reporting crimes to an interviewer. Furthermore, the FBI does not break down NCVS data by states and cities because the sample size would be too small.

The Crime Rate

Crime affects many Americans. According to the UCR, the crime rate for the United States in 2008 was 3,667 offenses per 100,000 people, giving the average American one chance in 27 of being the victim of a serious crime. Property crimes occur more frequently than violent crimes. In 2008, the violent crime rate was 454 per 100,000 in population compared with a property crime rate of 3,213 per 100,000. Of the eight categories of crime counted by the UCR, larceny/theft was the most frequent. Murder was the least frequent.[4] The incidence of crime in Texas is higher than the national average. The rate of reported crime in Texas in 2008 was 4,495 per 100,000 in population—23 percent higher than the national average. In other words, the odds of being a victim of a serious crime in Texas were one in 22.[5]

Trends

Figure 14.1 graphs the ups and downs of the crime rate in the United States from 1990 through 2008. As the figure indicates, the crime rate dropped sharply during the 1990s. It then rose briefly in 2001 before beginning to fall again, this time at a slower pace of decline than during the 1990s.

Criminologists offer a number of possible explanations for the recent changes in the crime rate.

- **Prison expansion:** Between 1990 and 2007, the number of people behind bars in the United States nearly tripled, increasing from 773,919 in 1990 to 2,310,980 in 2007.[6] Keeping criminals off the streets holds down the crime rate.
- **Better police work:** Some experts attribute the falling crime rate to better police work, including the introduction of community policing and the implementation

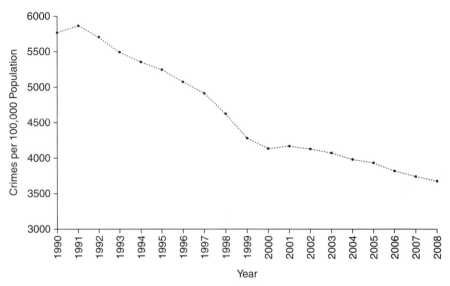

FIGURE 14.1   National Crime Rate, 1990–2008.
Source: FBI, Uniform Crime Reports.

Community policing An approach to law enforcement that seeks to reduce crime by increasing the interaction and cooperation between local law enforcement agencies and the people and neighborhoods they serve.

of zero tolerance policies in high-crime areas. **Community policing** is an approach to law enforcement that seeks to reduce crime by increasing the interaction and cooperation between local law enforcement agencies and the people and neighborhoods they serve. The goal of a zero tolerance policy, meanwhile, is to get lawbreakers off the street by any legitimate means. New York and a number of other cities have aggressively enforced the law in high-crime areas, arresting people not just for serious crimes but also for petty offenses, such as public intoxication, urination in public, traffic law infractions, and vagrancy.

- **High-tech crime fighting tools:** Computer technology is giving police the tools to target specific locations and types of crimes minute by minute so they can attack crime before it happens.[7]

Although crime rates are falling, many Americans do not feel safe. The Gallup Poll regularly asks national samples of Americans the following question: "Is there more crime in your area than there was a year ago or less?" Every year since 1990, more people have said "more" than have said "yes," even though the correct answer has almost always been "yes." In 2009, 74 percent of Americans said there was more crime.[8]

Criminologists identify a number of reasons for the disparity between falling crime rates and public apprehension about crime. Police departments continue to warn about the dangers of crime, even when crime rates are falling, because that is their job and their budgets depend on public support for law enforcement. Politicians focus on crime to win votes. Likewise, the media spotlight crime, especially violent crime, to attract viewers and readers. The adage "if it bleeds, it leads" has become the catch phrase for local television news.

VICTIMS AND CRIMINALS

Who are the victims of crime? Although all of us are threatened, some groups of people are more frequent victims of crime. The incidence of crime in urban areas is more than twice as high as in rural areas and is significantly higher than in the suburbs. In addition, low-income persons are more likely to be victims of violent crime than are middle- and upper-income individuals, who, in turn, are more likely to be victims of property crime. Young people are more frequently victimized than are older persons. Except for the crime of forcible rape, men are more likely to be crime victims than are women. Offenses occur more often against racial and ethnic minority groups than against whites. Renters are more likely to become crime victims than are homeowners.[9]

Most criminals are young, poorly educated men. A majority of the people arrested for property crimes and 46 percent of individuals arrested for violent crimes are under the age of 25. Three-fourths are male.[10] Criminals and victims often know one another. In fact, a majority of violent crimes occur between people who know one another.[11] Furthermore, murder typically stays within racial groups. According to official data, 83 percent of white murder victims nationwide are killed by other whites, whereas 90 percent of black murder victims are killed by other blacks.[12]

Victims of violent crime in Texas may receive up to $75,000 in financial assistance from the Texas Crime Victims' Compensation Fund. This program makes money available to people who are "innocent victims of violent crimes" to cover the loss of earnings, funeral expenses, medical expenses, and the care of minor children.

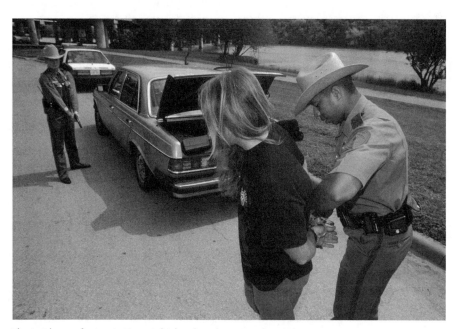

The incidence of crime in Texas is higher than the national average.

However, it does not provide compensation for stolen property. The fund is designed to pay expenses not covered by other sources, such as insurance, sick leave, workers' compensation, or Social Security. The fund is financed through fines paid by convicted felons. To receive compensation, a crime victim must report the crime to police within 72 hours, cooperate with law enforcement officials (crime participants are excluded), and file a claim with the Crime Victims' Compensation Division in the attorney general's office within 180 days.[13]

CRIMINAL PROSECUTION PROCESS

The criminal prosecution process begins with an arrest and proceeds through pretrial actions, trial, and sentencing.

Arrest

Probable cause The reasonable belief that a crime has been committed and that a particular suspect is the likely perpetrator of that crime.

The criminal prosecution process begins with an arrest. Police officers arrest suspects when, in their professional judgment, there is probable cause. **Probable cause** is the reasonable belief that a crime has been committed and that a particular suspect is the likely perpetrator of that crime.

Law enforcement authorities exercise discretion in deciding whether to make an arrest, especially for relatively minor offenses. For example, a police officer may or may not stop a driver traveling at seven miles per hour over the speed limit. Likewise, a city police officer may warn a pet owner for violating the local leash ordinance, rather than issuing a citation.

Clearance rate The proportion of crimes known to authorities for which an arrest is made.

Law enforcement authorities do not solve every serious crime reported to them. The **clearance rate** is the proportion of crimes known to authorities for which an arrest is made. The clearance rate varies, depending on the offense. It is highest for violent crimes against persons, such as murder, aggravated assault, and robbery. It is lowest for nonviolent crimes against property, such as larceny/theft, motor vehicle theft, and burglary. Victims of violent crimes are often able to identify offenders, whereas property crimes usually occur without witnesses. Furthermore, law enforcement authorities concentrate their resources on violent crime.

Pretrial Actions

Booking An administrative procedure in which law enforcement personnel document a suspect's arrest.

After making an arrest, a police officer takes the suspect to a police station or sub-station to be booked. **Booking** is an administrative procedure in which law enforcement personnel document a suspect's arrest. While the suspect is fingerprinted and photographed and the paperwork is completed, officials search the records for outstanding arrest warrants against the suspect for other offenses.

An assistant district attorney then determines whether to press charges. Sometimes people arrested for relatively minor offenses such as public intoxication or gambling are not charged. The assistant district attorney may also order a suspect released because of insufficient evidence.

Arraignment A judicial proceeding at which a suspect is formally charged with a crime and asked to enter a plea.

If charges are filed, suspects are brought before a judge for **arraignment,** a judicial proceeding at which a suspect is formally charged with a crime and asked to enter a plea. The judge tells the accused persons of the charges they face and informs them of their constitutional rights. Criminal suspects have the right to remain silent and to know that anything they say may be used against them. They also have the right to discontinue an interview at any time. In addition, they have the right to an attorney and, if they cannot afford to hire one, they have the right to a lawyer appointed by the state. This procedure is known as the *Miranda* **warning,** which is the judicial stipulation that a criminal defendant's confession cannot be admitted into evidence unless police first inform the defendant of the constitutional right to remain silent and to consult an attorney. Otherwise, any confessions suspects give may not be admitted as evidence at their trials.[14]

Miranda **warning** The judicial stipulation that a criminal defendant's confession cannot be admitted into evidence unless police first inform the defendant of the constitutional right to remain silent and to consult an attorney.

At the arraignment, the accused may plead not guilty, guilty, or *nolo contendere,* which is Latin for "no contest." ***Nolo contendere*** is a plea indicating a defendant's decision not to contest a criminal charge. As far as a criminal case is concerned, a plea of *nolo contendere* is the legal equivalent of a guilty plea. At this stage of the criminal prosecution process, most defendants plead not guilty, including many defendants who will eventually plead guilty.

Nolo contendere A plea indicating a defendant's decision not to contest a criminal charge.

The arraigning judge also sets bail. **Bail** is money or securities posted by accused persons to guarantee their appearance at later proceedings. In general, the amount of bail is based on the seriousness of the criminal offense and the likelihood of the accused returning for trial. If the offense is relatively minor or if the accused has deep roots in the community (a family, job, home, etc.), the judge may release the defendant on personal recognizance (that is, without bail) or at low bail. In contrast, the judge will set a high bond for serious offenses or when there is a strong likelihood that the accused will flee to escape prosecution. In extreme circumstances, the judge may refuse to set bail altogether, requiring the accused to remain in jail until trial. Suspects who make bail are released pending the outcome of their case. In contrast, accused persons without enough money to cover bail must either wait in the county jail or hire a private bail bond company to put up the money for a nonrefundable fee, usually 10 to 15 percent of the bond. If suspects flee, they forfeit their bail and the judge issues a warrant for their arrest. Bail jumping is a crime.

Bail Money or securities posted by accused persons to guarantee their appearance at later proceedings.

Indictment A formal accusation charging an individual with the commission of a crime.

The Texas Constitution requires a grand jury indictment in all felony cases unless the defendant waives that right. An **indictment** is a formal accusation charging an individual with the commission of a crime. A **grand jury** is a body of 12 citizens who hears evidence presented by the prosecuting attorney and decides whether to indict an accused person. Texas has two methods for selecting the members of a grand jury. In the first method, a state district criminal court judge appoints three to five people to serve as jury commissioners. The commissioners, meeting in private, compile a list of 15 to 20 potential grand jurors and present the list to the judge, who selects 12 people to serve as members of a grand jury. In the second method, grand jurors are selected at random from voter registration and driver's license lists, the same pool from which trial jurors are chosen. Grand juries typically meet once or twice a week for a three-month term.

Grand jury A body of 12 citizens that hears evidence presented by the prosecuting attorney and decides whether to indict an accused person.

True bill An indictment issued by a grand jury.

Magistrate Judicial officers.

The grand jury works in secret, investigating criminal matters and hearing evidence brought to it by the district attorney. At least nine of the 12 jurors must agree in order to issue an indictment, also known as a **true bill,** against a defendant. In theory, the grand jury is a screening device that protects innocent persons from unwarranted prosecution by requiring the prosecutor to marshal sufficient evidence to convince a grand jury that there is probable cause of the accused's guilt. Nonetheless, some observers believe that, in contemporary criminal justice systems, grand juries usually act as rubber stamps for the prosecutor. The grand jury hears only the district attorney's view of the case because the defendant does not have the right to present evidence to the grand jury or challenge the information presented by the prosecutor.

Not all states use the grand jury system, however. Many states allow prosecutors to file felony charges directly in the form of an "information." In this method, a judge or a **magistrate** (a judicial official) conducts a hearing to determine if the evidence is sufficient to take the case to trial. Both the prosecutor and the defendant have the opportunity to present evidence to the judge or magistrate, who decides whether the evidence is sufficient to warrant a trial.

The U.S. Supreme Court has ruled that criminal defendants are constitutionally entitled to be represented by an attorney, regardless of their financial status.[15] Texas law empowers district judges to determine whether a defendant is unable to afford an attorney. In practice, judges often assume that a criminal defendant who can afford to make bond has sufficient financial resources to hire an attorney. If the judge determines that a defendant is indigent, the judge assigns the defendant an attorney, who is paid

Accused persons without enough money to cover bail must either wait in the county jail or hire a private bond company to put up the money for a nonrefundable fee.

by the county for representing the defendant both at the trial stage and, if necessary, through one round of appeals. Indigent defendants who wish to continue the appeals process beyond that point must obtain private legal assistance or file legal papers themselves. Ten Texas counties, including El Paso and Dallas counties, have public defender offices that employ attorneys full-time to represent indigent defendants. The advocates of the public defender system believe that it provides indigent defendants with better legal representation at less cost to the government.[16] In counties without a public defender office, district judges appoint lawyers in private practice to represent indigent criminal defendants in return for a fee paid by the county government.

Trials

Accused persons have a constitutional right to trial by jury. The U.S. Supreme Court has held that the U.S. Constitution obliges state governments to offer jury trials to persons charged with felony offenses.[17] A **felony** is a serious criminal offense, such as murder, sexual assault, or burglary. The Texas Constitution goes further, granting accused persons the right to trial by jury in *all* cases, misdemeanor and felony. A **misdemeanor** is a less serious offense than a felony. If defendants choose, they may waive the right to a jury trial and be tried by a judge alone.

Prospective trial jurors are selected from county voter registration rolls, lists of persons holding Texas driver's licenses, and Department of Public Safety identification cards. Only American citizens may serve on juries. Persons who are convicted felons or under felony indictment are ineligible to serve on a jury. Some groups of people are exempt from jury service if they wish, including full-time students, individuals over 70 years of age, and persons with custody of small children whose absence would leave the children without proper supervision. A six-person jury hears misdemeanor cases, whereas a felony-case jury consists of 12 persons.

A criminal trial is an **adversary proceeding,** that is, a legal procedure in which each side may present evidence and arguments to bolster its position, while rebutting evidence that might support the other side. An assistant district attorney prosecutes the case by presenting evidence and testimony in an effort to prove the defendant's guilt. The defense attorney, meanwhile, cross-examines the prosecution's witnesses to undermine the case against the defendant. After the prosecution has presented its side, the defense has a chance to offer evidence and testimony to show that the defendant is not guilty.

The **burden of proof,** the legal obligation of one party in a lawsuit to prove its position to a court, is on the prosecutor, who must demonstrate the defendant's guilt beyond a reasonable doubt. At least in theory, the defendant need not prove his or her innocence. The judge conducts the trial, ruling on points of law and procedure. The jury or the judge, if the defendant has waived the right to a jury trial, decides guilt or innocence. The defendant is free to go if acquitted. If the verdict is guilty, punishment must be assessed.

Relatively few individuals indicted for serious crimes ever have a full-blown trial. As Table 14.1 indicates, 71.5 percent of the 160,792 felony cases disposed of by state district courts in 2008 involved the defendant pleading guilty. Most guilty pleas

Felony A serious criminal offense, such as murder, sexual assault, or burglary.

Misdemeanor A relatively minor criminal offense, such as a traffic violation.

Adversary proceeding A legal procedure in which each side presents evidence and arguments to bolster its position while rebutting evidence that might support the other side.

Burden of proof The legal obligation of one party in a lawsuit to prove its position to a court.

TABLE 14.1   Disposition of Felony Cases in State District Courts, 2008

Disposition	Number of Cases	Percentage
Pled guilty or *nolo contendere*	114,900	71.5 percent
Tried and convicted	3,406	2.1 percent
Tried and acquitted	1,022	0.6 percent
Directed acquittal ordered by judge	26	—
Dismissed	41,438	25.8 percent
Total	160,792	100 percent

Source: Office of Court Administration, *Texas Judicial System Annual Report Fiscal Year 2008,* available at www.courts.state.tx.us.

Plea bargain A procedure in which a defendant agrees to plead guilty in order to receive punishment less than the maximum for an offense.

are the result of a **plea bargain,** a procedure in which a defendant agrees to plead guilty in order to receive a punishment that is less than the maximum for an offense. Prosecutors plea bargain because courts are overcrowded—plea bargaining saves money and valuable court time. Also, a plea bargain ensures a conviction. Defendants plea bargain because they fear a harsher punishment or a conviction on a more serious charge.

Most criminal cases that make it to a courtroom conclude with a conviction, through either plea bargaining or a guilty verdict. As Table 14.1 indicates, less than 1 percent of the felony cases heard in Texas in 2008 resulted in the defendant's acquittal. Most defendants pled guilty. Of those who actually went to trial, most were convicted. Furthermore, only about 2 percent of the total number of cases involved jury trials.[18]

 WHAT IS YOUR OPINION?

Do plea bargains advance the cause of justice?

Sentencing

Except for Class C misdemeanor cases, sentencing is a distinct second phase of the trial proceeding in Texas. Both prosecution and defense may present evidence and arguments in hopes of obtaining a stiffer or lighter sentence for the accused. In jury trials, the defendant may select either the jury or the judge to determine the sentence. In trials without juries, the judge sets the punishment.

Probation The suspension of a sentence, permitting the defendant to remain free under court supervision.

Under Texas law, possible sentences vary, depending on the severity of the crime. For misdemeanor offenses, punishment can include a fine and a period of confinement not exceeding a year in jail. For felonies, the fine can be as high as $10,000 and imprisonment, which can range from 180 days to 99 years in prison. Persons convicted of capital murder may be given the death penalty.

With a few exceptions, Texas law permits the judge or jury to grant **probation,** which is the suspension of a sentence, permitting the defendant to remain free under court supervision. The Texas Department of Corrections (TDC) uses the term "community supervision" rather than probation. Instead of going to prison or jail, convicted persons live and work in the community under the supervision of a county probation officer. In granting probation or community supervision, judges may require convicted defendants to hold jobs, support their families, make restitution for their crimes, and stay out of trouble with the law. Should individuals violate the terms of their probation, it may be revoked, and they will be forced to serve time in the county jail or a state prison. Texas has more than twice as many probationers than it has prison inmates—440,000 offenders in community supervision compared with 156,000 offenders behind bars in 2008.[19]

Persons who plead guilty to relatively minor offenses may be given **deferred adjudication,** a type of probation that can be granted by a judge to a defendant who pleads guilty or *nolo contendere* to certain, relatively less serious offenses. The court defers the judicial proceeding *without* entering the guilty plea in the defendant's record. If the defendant successfully completes the probation, the charges are dismissed and the defendant does not have a conviction on the record, although the defendant will have to file a petition of nondisclosure with a court in order to seal the record of the deferred adjudication from the general public. If the defendant violates probation, the case is resumed and the defendant can be convicted and sentenced as if the probation had never taken place. In 2008, state district courts granted deferred adjudication in nearly 50,000 cases, 30 percent of the total number of convictions.[20]

Deferred adjudication A type of probation that can be granted by a judge to a defendant who pleads guilty or *nolo contendere* to certain relatively less serious offenses.

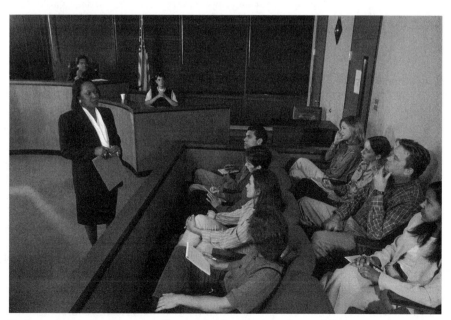

The Texas Constitution guarantees all criminal defendants the right to trial by jury.

CAPITAL PUNISHMENT

The Texas legislature enacted the state's first capital punishment law in 1923. The first executions took place on February 24, 1924, when five young African American men were electrocuted for murder. Between 1924 and 1964, 503 men and three women were sentenced to death in Texas; 361 of the men eventually died in the electric chair. Of those put to death, 229 were African American men, 108 were white men, 23 were Latino men, and one was an American Indian man. None of the three women sentenced to death was executed.[21]

In 1972, the U.S. Supreme Court ruled, in the case of *Furman v. Georgia*, that the death penalty as it was then applied was unconstitutional because it allowed too much discretion to judges and juries, thereby opening the door to discriminatory practices. Getting the death penalty, the Court said, was similar to being struck by lightning.[22] The Court did *not*, however, rule that capital punishment in and of itself was unconstitutional, at least not for the crime of murder.

After the *Furman* decision, many state legislatures adopted new capital punishment laws designed to meet the Supreme Court's objections by reducing discretion in the implementation of the death penalty. The Texas legislature passed a new death penalty statute in 1973 which, with subsequent amendments, defined capital murder to include the following crimes:

- Murdering a peace officer or firefighter, who is acting in the lawful discharge of an official duty and who the person knows is a police officer or firefighter;
- Intentionally committing a murder in the course of committing or attempting to commit kidnapping, burglary, robbery, aggravated sexual assault, or arson;
- Committing a murder for pay or promise to pay or employing another person to commit murder;
- Committing a murder while escaping or attempting to escape from a penal institution;
- Murdering a prison employee while incarcerated;
- Committing a gang-related murder while incarcerated;
- Committing a murder to obstruct justice or in retaliation against a witness in a criminal case;
- Committing serial or mass murder; and
- Murdering a child under the age of six.

The punishment for capital murder is either life imprisonment without possibility of parole or the death penalty. To determine a verdict, the judge or jury must answer three questions:

1. Was the conduct of the defendant that caused the death of the victim committed deliberately and with the reasonable expectation that the victim's death would ensue?
2. Is it probable that the defendant would commit additional criminal acts of violence that would constitute a continuing threat to society?

AROUND THE NATION

Civil Commitment of Sexually Violent Criminals in Kansas

Kansas has adopted a civil commitment procedure to hold sexually violent criminals behind bars after they have completed their prison sentences. In 1994, the Kansas legislature passed, and the governor signed, the Kansas Sexually Violent Predator Act to provide for the involuntary confinement of sexually violent predators beyond the completion of their prison sentences. Under the law, a sexually violent predator is defined as a person convicted or charged with a sexually violent offense who suffers from a "mental abnormality" or "personality disorder" that makes the person likely to engage in repeat acts of sexual violence. Once pedophiles and other sexually violent offenders finish their prison sentences, they must be released unless the state can prove to a judge or jury that they meet the criteria to be declared a sexually violent predator. Persons held under the statute are not released until a court certifies that their mental condition has changed and that they no longer qualify as sexually violent predators.

Civil commitment for sexual predators is controversial. The defenders of the procedure argue that it is necessary to protect the community from individuals who are likely to commit horrific crimes. The recidivism rate for sexual offenders is quite high. In contrast, critics contend that the procedure is an unconstitutional mechanism for continuing to punish people who have already served their criminal sentences. They believe the Kansas law violates the Double Jeopardy Clause of the Constitution, which protects people from being tried twice for the same offense.

The U.S. Supreme Court upheld the constitutionality of the Kansas Sexually Violent Predator Act in *Kansas v. Hendricks.* In a narrow 5-4 decision, the Court compared the civil commitment of sexual predators with the civil commitment of mentally ill persons who are a danger to themselves or others. The Court ruled that the Kansas law does not violate the Double Jeopardy Clause because it is not a criminal penalty. It also ruled that the state is not required to offer treatment for persons held under the statute.*

Nineteen states have adopted civil commitment laws similar to the Kansas statute. In practice, few persons have ever been released because they are no longer considered a threat to offend. Out of 3,000 sexual offenders held in civil commitment facilities nationwide, only 115 have been sent home, most because of technical legal reasons. The program is expensive to operate, especially as the inmates in custody age and require specialized medical care. From 2001 to 2005, the cost of civil commitment in Kansas increased from $1.2 million a year to $6.9 million.†

QUESTIONS TO CONSIDER

1. Should Texas adopt a civil commitment procedure to hold criminally violent sexual offenders in custody after they have completed their prison sentences, similar to the Kansas law?
2. Is it ever safe to release persons convicted of sexually violent crimes from custody?
3. Is civil commitment for violent sexual offenders preferable to longer prison sentences or even the death penalty?

*Kansas v. Hendricks, 521 U.S. 346 (1997).

†Monica Davey and Abby Goodnough, "Doubts Rise as States Hold Sex Offenders After Prison," *New York Times,* March 4, 2007, available at www.nytimes.com.

Parole The conditional release of convicted offenders from prison to serve the remainder of their sentences in the community under supervision.

3. Is there anything in the circumstances of the offense and the defendant's character and background that would warrant a sentence of life imprisonment rather than a death sentence?

The sentence is death if the jury or judge answers *yes, yes,* and *no.* Otherwise, the defendant receives life in prison without **parole,** which is the conditional release of convicted offenders from prison to serve the remainder of their sentences in the community under supervision.

In 1977, the legislature amended the state's capital punishment law to retire "Old Sparky," as the electric chair was nicknamed, and replace it with lethal injection as the means of execution. The law provides that a medically trained individual, whose identity is not revealed, inserts an intravenous catheter into the condemned person's arm. After giving the prisoner the opportunity to make a last statement, the warden orders the introduction of the lethal solution into the catheter. The individual injecting the fatal fluid is visibly separated from the execution chamber by a wall and locked door. A physician makes the final death pronouncement but has no function in the execution. The law allows family members of the convicted murderer and the family of the murder victim to witness the execution.

Because of appeals and other legal delays, no one was executed in Texas from July 1964 until December 1982, when Charlie Brooks, Jr., an African American man convicted of murdering a Fort Worth auto mechanic, died of lethal injection. Between 1982 and November 2009, Texas carried out 442 executions, substantially more than any other state.[23] Today, death row in Livingston houses 325 men and ten women.[24]

Capital punishment remains controversial. The opponents of the death penalty charge that the process of trials and appeals is so flawed that innocent people may face execution. A study published by Columbia University law professor James S. Liebman found that two-thirds of the death sentences given by American courts between 1973 and 1995 were overturned on appeal. When death penalty cases were retried, 7 percent of the defendants were found not guilty.[25] Furthermore, the critics of the death penalty argue that it is inefficient because only 5 percent of death sentences are actually carried out and only then after years of appeal.[26] In contrast, the proponents of capital punishment defend the process, saying that it is scrupulously fair. They point out that people given the death penalty are entitled to an appeals process that lasts for years. In Texas, the interval between sentencing and execution for convicted murderers is 10.6 years, more than enough time for their cases to be thoroughly examined for error.[27]

JUVENILE JUSTICE

The juvenile crime rate has been falling faster than the overall crime rate. In the mid-1990s, juvenile offenders committed about one-quarter of all criminal offenses nationwide. By 2008, the percentage of arrestees under the age of 18 had fallen to 15 percent.[28] In fact, the recent decline in the crime rate can be attributed almost entirely to a decrease in juvenile crime. Between 1999 and 2008, the juvenile crime rate fell by 16 percent, whereas the adult crime rate actually increased by 3 percent.[29]

Texas deals with some juvenile offenders as if they were adults. Some juveniles as young as 14 who are charged with serious crimes may be certified to be tried as adults. Judges decide whether to certify a juvenile as an adult depending on the crime's severity and the youngster's maturity. Juveniles below the age of 14, or older juveniles who are not certified as adults, are dealt with by the juvenile court system.

Juvenile courts are different from adult courts. Cases tried in juvenile court are heard under the family law code, which is a civil law code rather than criminal law. Juvenile court judges hold hearings to determine if an accused juvenile has engaged in delinquent conduct. The district or county attorney represents the state and must prove the case beyond a reasonable doubt. The juvenile has rights similar to those of adult defendants, including the right to an attorney and the right to cross-examine witnesses. Similar to adult court proceedings, many juvenile court proceedings are settled through plea bargains. If a juvenile is determined to be delinquent or in need of supervision, the court holds a disposition hearing to determine how the youngster should be handled. The court considers both the safety of the community and the child's best interests.

Juvenile courts enjoy considerable leeway in deciding how to handle youthful defendants. The court can suspend the driver's license of a juvenile offender, order the juvenile to pay restitution to the crime victim, and require the juvenile and the juvenile's parents to perform community service. The court can also order a juvenile to be sent to a community rehabilitation facility or an alternative school. Repeat offenders or juveniles guilty of serious criminal offenses may be held in a state facility operated by the Texas Youth Commission (TYC). Juveniles guilty of certain violent offenses may be transferred to adult prison when they are between ages 16 and 21.

CORRECTIONS

No country locks up as many people and keeps them behind bars as long as the United States. In the United States, 2.3 million criminals are behind bars. China, with four times the population, imprisons only 1.6 million people. The United States also has the world's highest incarceration rate with 751 inmates for every 100,000 in population. In contrast, the incarceration rate is 151 per 100,000 in the United Kingdom, 88 in Germany, and 63 in Japan.[30]

The Texas prison system houses 156,000 inmates, making it the largest prison system in the United States. The Texas prison system is more than twice as big as the prison system in New York, even though New York's population is only 12 percent smaller than the Texas population. The incarceration rate in Texas is 683 prison inmates per 100,000 people compared with a national rate of 501 per 100,000. Texas has the second highest incarceration rate in the country, after Louisiana.[31]

County Jails

Except for a few small counties, each of the state's 254 counties has a county jail, built by county tax dollars and staffed by the office of the county sheriff. Jails house people accused of felony and misdemeanor criminal offenses who have not made bail, convicted felons who are awaiting transfer to the Texas Department of Criminal Justice (TDCJ), people charged with federal criminal offenses who are awaiting transfer to a federal facility, and persons convicted of misdemeanor offenses who are serving relatively short sentences. Counties with excess capacity rent space to counties with overcrowded jails. The average daily population of Texas jails in 2009 was 70,131, a figure representing 82 percent of total jail capacity.[32]

State Jails

In 1993, the Texas legislature authorized the creation of a state jail system with an eventual capacity of 22,000 to divert certain nonviolent offenders from the state prison system. State jails house persons convicted of fourth-degree (state jail) felonies. Fourth-degree felonies include forgery, fraud, relatively minor theft, possession or delivery of small amounts of certain illegal drugs, car theft (under $20,000 value), burglary of a building that is not a home, and other nonviolent crimes. Persons convicted of fourth-degree felonies can be given as much as five years' probation or be sentenced to serve as much as two years in a state jail. State jails are designed to keep inexperienced criminals away from hardcore criminals, get them off drugs, and help them finish high school equivalency courses. While in state jails, inmates can receive chemical abuse therapy, job training, and family counseling. State jail inmates serve flat time sentences, with no early release for good behavior. In 2008, 15 state jail facilities housed more than 13,000 offenders.[33]

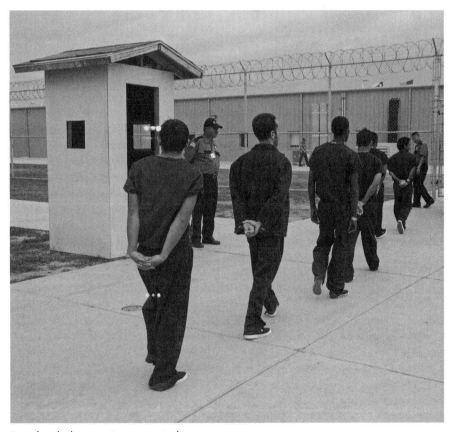

Texas has the largest prison system in the country.

State Prisons

For years, the Texas prison system was widely regarded as one of the most austere in the nation. More than 90 percent of state prisoners were held in maximum-security prisons, where they were prohibited from having any physical contact with visitors. Inmates were even forbidden from talking with one another in dining areas. Critics called Texas prisons both brutal and brutalizing. However, other observers praised the Texas prison system for its efficiency and effectiveness—the best in the country, they said. Inmates were required to work and attend school. Escapes were rare, the reported rate of inmate violence low, and prison riots unheard of. Furthermore, all of this was achieved at a cost per inmate that was lower than in any other state in the nation.[34]

In 1972, a group of prisoners filed suit in federal court, claiming that living and working conditions in Texas prisons constituted "cruel and unusual punishment," forbidden by the Eighth Amendment to the U.S. Constitution. The suit, *Ruiz v. Estelle*, charged that the state's prison system was severely overcrowded, the prison staff was too small to maintain security, working conditions were unsafe, disciplinary procedures were severe and arbitrary, and medical care was inadequate. In particular, the suit attacked the building tender system, in which inmate guards were given authority over their cell blocks to keep them clean and safe. Texas prison officials defended the system for its effectiveness, saying that inmate building tenders were nothing more than glorified janitors. In contrast, critics claimed that inmate guards were dictators who controlled their cell blocks through brute force while guards looked the other way.

In 1980, U.S. District Judge William Wayne Justice ruled against the state of Texas, ordering sweeping changes in the Texas prison system. Although an appeals court later overturned part of Judge Justice's ruling, it agreed with the key points of his decision. Eventually, the state settled the suit by agreeing to limit the inmate population to 95 percent of the prison's capacity, separate hardcore offenders from inmates convicted of nonviolent crimes, improve the guard-to-inmate ratio, upgrade inmate medical treatment, and eliminate the building tender system.[35]

While the state struggled to deal with the impact of *Ruiz v. Estelle*, poor planning by the legislature and the governor made the problem of prison overcrowding considerably worse. During the 1970s and 1980s, the governor and legislature responded to public concerns about crime by getting tough. The legislature passed dozens of anticrime bills, upgrading the seriousness of certain offenses and increasing prison time for offenders. Texas judges and juries began sentencing more people to prison to serve longer terms. The legislature also required that persons convicted of **aggravated offenses** (violent crimes) or crimes using a deadly weapon serve at least one-third of a sentence before becoming eligible for parole. As a result, the prison system stacked up with inmates who could not be paroled. In the meantime, the legislature failed to expand prison capacity sufficiently to accommodate the increase in the number of inmates. During the entire decade of the 1970s, the state built only one prison unit with a mere 600 beds. Although the state added 13,000 more beds in the early 1980s, the increase in capacity failed to keep up with the growth of admissions. Although prison capacity rose by 50 percent, admissions increased 113 percent.[36]

Aggravated offenses Violent crime.

In the late 1980s, the legislature, the governor, and the voters authorized a massive prison construction program to hold the state's rapidly growing prison population. The legislature proposed, and the voters approved, constitutional amendments to borrow money to build new prison units. Meanwhile, the legislature and the governor appropriated funds to operate the new prison units and begin the long-term process of paying for their construction. The state's prison expansion plans also included the privatization of operations and management at some facilities. **Privatization** involves the government contracting with private business to implement government programs. In 2008, Texas housed nearly 20,000 inmates (11.5 percent of its inmate population) at privately managed facilities.[37] The proponents of privatization contend that it saves money, and research indicates that the cost of housing prisoners in privately run facilities is about 10 percent less than it is in state-run facilities. In contrast, the critics of prison privatization argue that the savings are illusory because they result from the use of poorly trained, underpaid personnel who pose a security risk.[38]

Privatization The process that involves the government contracting with private business to implement government programs.

Although spending for corrections is one of the few budget categories in which Texas exceeds the national average, the Texas prison system is not especially well-funded. Despite having the largest prison system in the country, Texas is twenty-first in per capita spending on corrections. New York, with a prison population less than one-third the size of the Texas inmate population, has a larger corrections budget.[39]

Prison Release

Prisoners leave the prison system through parole or by completing their sentences. In theory, parole is a mechanism for reintegrating offenders into the community because it allows the state to release prisoners to the community conditionally, under supervision. In general, parolees must not associate with known criminals, possess firearms, use illegal drugs, or drink to excess. They are required to report regularly to a parole officer and inform that official of any change of residence or a change of jobs. Parole is also cheaper than prison. The cost of parole supervision is $3.74 a day for each offender compared with $47.50 for each day in prison.[40]

Under state law, most prisoners are eligible for parole after serving one-fourth of their sentence or 15 years, whichever is less. The state determines the amount of time served for inmates convicted of nonviolent offenses by adding together the actual days spent behind bars with good time earned. **Good time** is a prison policy that credits inmates with time off for good behavior. Prisoners can earn a maximum of 75 days of good time for every 30 days actually served if they attend school, work in prison, and generally behave themselves. Violent offenders serve flat time without the opportunity to earn good time. Furthermore, persons found guilty of violent crimes or who used a deadly weapon in the course of committing an offense must serve at least half of their sentence before becoming eligible for parole. In theory, both parole and good time are prison management tools because they give inmates an incentive to cooperate with prison officials. Prisoners who attend classes, develop work skills, and stay out of trouble behind bars earn the opportunity for parole. If parolees fail to live up to the conditions of their release, they can be returned to prison.

Good time A prison policy that credits inmates with time off for good behavior.

WHAT IS YOUR OPINION?

Should prison inmates be released early from prison because of good behavior?

Recidivism

Recidivism The tendency of offenders released from prison to commit additional crimes and be returned behind bars.

Many inmates released from prison get in trouble again. **Recidivism** is the tendency of offenders released from prison to commit additional crimes and once again end up behind bars. In Texas, 28 percent of inmates released from prison are rearrested for a serious crime within three years of their release.[41] Recidivism is less a problem in Texas than in many other states, however. The three-year recidivism rate in California, for example, is 57 percent.[42]

MAKING CRIMINAL JUSTICE POLICY

The most important elements of the policymaking environment for criminal justice policymaking are public opinion, federal court rulings, and the budgetary outlook. The general public has strong views about crime. Elected officials all want to be seen as tough on crime. Whereas public opinion in Texas generally supports a "lock 'em up and throw away the key" philosophy, federal court rulings and the state budget impose constraints on policymakers. Federal court rulings establish the ground rules for the criminal justice process and determine the range of punishments that are constitutionally acceptable. Meanwhile, the state's budget outlook determines the resources policymakers will have available to address criminal justice issues. When the budget is tight, state leaders are more generous with probation and parole than they are in good economic times. In 2007, for example, the legislature passed legislation to expand drug treatment programs and revise parole practices with the goal of reducing the number of nonviolent offenders behind bars.[43]

Agenda Setting

A number of political actors set the agenda for criminal justice policymaking. Federal court decisions sometimes force the legislature and the governor to address policy issues. For example, recent decisions of the U.S. Supreme Court on the constitutionality of imposing the death penalty on offenders who were juveniles at the time of their crime[44] or against the mentally retarded[45] have forced the state to revise its capital punishment statute. The legislature and the governor had to address the issue of prison reform because of *Ruiz v. Estelle*, a U.S. District Court decision. Media reports of horrific crimes or the possibility that the state has sent an innocent person to prison or even death row set the agenda as well. The legislature and the governor focused on overhauling the operation of the Texas Youth Commission after the media revealed allegations of sexual abuse by staff members against juvenile offenders held in TYC custody.

Policy Formulation, Adoption, and Legitimation

The legislature, governor, and some interest groups participate in criminal justice policy formulation. Legislators formulate policy with input from the governor and a number of interest groups that focus on criminal justice issues, such as Mothers Against Drunk Driving (MADD), public employee groups representing police officers and corrections employees, death penalty opponents, and victim rights organizations. For example, MADD lobbies in favor of tougher DWI laws. Unions representing prison employees fought against prison privatization and succeeded in limiting the practice to newly built prisons, rather than privatizing existing units, thus saving the jobs of their members.

The legislature and the governor adopt criminal justice policies through the legislative process. Criminal justice bills must pass the Texas House and Texas Senate and then go to the governor for signature. If the governor vetoes a measure, it dies unless both the Texas House and Texas Senate vote to override the veto by a two-thirds vote.

Interest groups, political parties, and elected officials participate in the policy legitimation process. For example, as the legislature has toughened DWI laws, MADD has defended the action. Many state officials defend Texas's status as the nation's leading capital punishment state.

Policy Implementation, Evaluation, and Change

State and local law enforcement, district attorneys, the court system, and the TDCJ implement criminal justice policies. Police officers implement criminal justice policies by arresting suspects. District attorneys decide whether to prosecute, and courts conduct trials. Ordinary citizens also participate in policy implementation by serving on juries. The TDCJ houses prisoners serving their sentences whereas the Board of Pardons and Paroles determines whether to grant parole.

A number of state and federal agencies evaluate criminal justice policies. The Federal Bureau of Investigation (FBI), Federal Bureau of Justice Statistics, Texas Commission on Jail Standards, and the Legislative Budget Board (LBB) all gather criminal justice statistics. The LBB, comptroller, and Texas Sunset Commission prepare analytical reports evaluating the operation of the TDCJ. The legislature and the governor then use these reports as the basis for proposing legislation designed to reform criminal justice policies.

Criminal justice policy change occurs because of the federal government, public opinion, and budget constraints. Many of the state's criminal justice policies have changed because of the actions of the federal government, especially federal court decisions. The decision of lower federal courts in the case of *Ruiz v. Estelle* eventually led to a substantial increase in the state's prison capacity. Public opinion also drives changes in criminal justice policies. During the 1970s, public anger over rising crime rates compelled the legislature to toughen the state's sentencing laws. Finally, budget constraints affect criminal justice policies. Lawmakers in recent sessions of the Texas legislature have reformed sentencing procedures to increase the use of probation and parole in order to save money.

WHAT WE HAVE LEARNED

1. **What methods are used to measure the crime rate, and what do the data indicate about the crime rate in the United States and the state of Texas?**

   The U.S. Department of Justice uses two complementary measures to assess the incidence of crime in America: the Uniform Crime Reports (UCR) and the National Crime Victim Survey (NCVS). According to the UCR, the crime rate for the United States in 2008 was 3,667 offenses per 100,000 people, giving the average American one chance in 27 of being the victim of a serious crime. The rate of reported crime in Texas in 2008 was 4,495 per 100,000 in population—23 percent higher than the national average. The crime rate has been falling, both nationally and in Texas, for well over a decade. Criminologists are not certain why the crime rate has been falling, but possible explanations include prison expansion, better police work, and the use of high-tech crime fighting tools.

2. **What groups of people are most likely to be the victims of crimes and what groups are most likely to commit crimes?**

   The crime rate is higher in urban areas. Low-income people, young people, racial and ethnic minorities, men, and renters are more likely to be victims of crime than other groups. Most criminals are young, poorly educated men.

3. **What are the steps of the criminal prosecution process?**

   The criminal prosecution process begins with an arrest based on probable cause. Arrests are followed by booking and arraignment. Defendants enter a plea—usually "innocent" at this stage—and may be given the opportunity to make bail. The Texas Constitution requires a grand jury indictment in all felony cases unless the defendant waives that right. Although accused persons have a right to trial by jury, many criminal defendants plea bargain rather than go to trial. Criminal trials are adversary proceedings in which the prosecution has the burden of proof. Except for Class C misdemeanor cases, sentencing is a distinct second phase of the trial proceeding in Texas.

4. **What is the capital punishment law in Texas and how is it implemented?**

   The Texas death punishment statute definition of capital murder includes a distinct set of offenses. The punishment for capital murder is either life imprisonment without possibility of parole or the death penalty. Lethal injection is the method of execution in Texas, which leads the nation in carrying out the death penalty.

5. **How does Texas deal with juvenile offenders?**

   The juvenile crime rate has been falling faster than the overall crime rate. A judge can certify juveniles as young as 14 to be tried as adults. Juvenile courts try younger juveniles and juveniles not certified as adults. Juvenile courts enjoy considerable leeway in deciding how to handle youthful defendants, including referral to the Texas Youth Commission.

6. **What categories of prisoners are held in county jails, state jails, and state prisons, and how are those facilities managed?**

   No country locks up as many people and keeps them behind bars as long as the United States. The Texas prison system houses 156,000 inmates, making it the largest prison system in the United States. County jails house people accused of felony and misdemeanor criminal offenses who have not made bail, convicted felons who are awaiting transfer to the TDCJ, people charged with federal criminal offenses who are awaiting transfer to a federal facility, and persons convicted of misdemeanor offenses who are serving relatively short sentences. State jails hold persons convicted of fourth-degree (state jail) felonies. State prisons house persons convicted of all other felonies. *Ruiz v. Estelle* (1972) forced the state to reduce overcrowding, initially by releasing prisoners and subsequently by building additional prisons. The state has contracted with private firms to operate some of the prisons. Prison officials use good time as a prison-management tool. The tendency of offenders released from prison to commit additional crimes and be returned behind bars is known as recidivism.

7. **How are criminal justice policies made in Texas?** The most important elements of the policymaking environment for criminal justice policymaking are public opinion, federal court rulings, and the budgetary outlook. A number of political actors set the agenda for criminal justice policymaking, including federal judges, legislators, the governor, and the media. The legislature, governor, and some interest groups participate in criminal justice policy formulation. The legislature and the governor adopt criminal justice policies through the legislative process. Interest groups, political parties, and elected officials participate in the policy legitimation process. State and local law enforcement, district attorneys, the court system, and the TDCJ implement criminal justice policies. A number of state and federal agencies evaluate criminal justice policies. Criminal justice policies change because of the federal government, public opinion, and budget constraints.

KEY TERMS

adversary proceeding	good time	plea bargain
aggravated offenses	grand jury	privatization
arraignment	indictment	probable cause
bail	magistrate	probation
booking	*Miranda* warning	recidivism
burden of proof	misdemeanor	sobriety checkpoint
clearance rate	National Crime Victim Survey (NCVS)	true bill
community policing		Uniform Crime Reports (UCR)
deferred adjudication	*nolo contendere*	
felony	parole	

NOTES

1. "2006 Drunk Driving Statistics," available at www .alcoholalert.com.
2. Jessica Meyers, "Texas DWI Bills Gain Support After Tragedy," *Dallas Morning News*, October 2, 2008, available at www.dallasnews.com.
3. Alex Branch, "Sobriety Checkpoint Bill Appears Dead in State House," *Fort Worth Star-Telegram*, May 11, 2009, available at www.star-telegram.com.
4. Federal Bureau of Investigation, Uniform Crime Reports, available at www.fbi.gov.
5. Texas Department of Public Safety, "The Texas Crime Report for 2008," available at www.txdps.state.tx.us.
6. Bureau of Justice Statistics, available at www.ojp.usdoj.gov.
7. "Experts Did Not See This Coming at All," *Washington Post National Weekly Edition*, July 27–August 2, 2009, p. 33.
8. "Crime," Gallup Poll, available at www.gallup.com.

9. "Victimization Rates, by Type of Crime and Characteristics of the Victim: 2006," U.S. Census Bureau, *2009 Statistical Abstract*, available at www.census.gov.

10. Federal Bureau of Investigation, "Arrests of Persons 15, 18, 21, and 25 Years of Age, 2005," *Crime in the United States 2008*, available at www.fbi.gov.

11. "Victim-Offender Relationship in Crimes of Violence, by Characteristics of the Criminal Incident," U.S. Census Bureau, *2009 Statistical Abstract*, available at www.census.gov.

12. Federal Bureau of Investigation, "Race and Sex of Victim by Race and Sex of Offender, 2008," *Crime in the United States 2008*, available at www.fbi.gov.

13. Texas Crime Victims' Compensation Fund, available at www.oag.state.tx.us.

14. *Miranda v. Arizona*, 384 U.S. 436 (1966).

15. *Gideon v. Wainwright*, 372 U.S. 335 (1963).

16. Office of Court Administration, "Evidence for the Feasibility of Public Defender Offices in Texas," available at www.courts.state.tx.us.

17. *Duncan v. Louisiana*, 391 U.S. 145 (1968).

18. Office of Court Administration, *Texas Judicial System Annual Report Fiscal Year 2008*, available at www.courts.state.tx.us.

19. Texas Department of Criminal Justice, available at www.tdcj.state.tx.us.

20. Office of Court Administration, *Texas Judicial System Annual Report Fiscal Year 2008*.

21. U.S. Law Enforcement Assistance Administration, *Prisoners in State and Federal Institutions on December 31, 1977*, National Prisoner Statistics Bulletin, SD-NPS-PSF-5 (Washington, DC: U.S. Government Printing Office, 1979); Texas Judicial Council, "Capital Murder Study," in *Forty-Seventh Annual Report 1975* (Austin, TX: Texas Judicial Council, 1976), pp. 89–94; and Rupert C. Koeniger, "Capital Punishment in Texas, 1927–1968," *Crime and Delinquency* 15 (January 1968): 132–141.

22. *Furman v. Georgia*, 408 U.S. 238 (1972).

23. "Executions," Texas Department of Criminal Justice, available at www.tdcj.state.tx.us.

24. "Offenders on Death Row," Texas Department of Criminal Justice, available at www.tdcj.state.tx.us.

25. James S. Leibman, *A Broken System: Error Rates in Capital Cases, 1973–1995*, available at www.thejusticeproject.org.

26. Ibid.

27. "Execution Statistics," Texas Department of Criminal Justice, available at www.tdcj.state.tx.us.

28. Federal Bureau of Investigation, "Arrests by Age," *Crime in the United States 2008*, available at www.fbi.gov.

29. Federal Bureau of Investigation, "Ten-Year Arrest Trends 1999–2008," *Crime in the United States 2008*, available at www.fbi.gov.

30. Adam Liptak, "Inmate Count in U.S. Dwarfs Other Nations'," *New York Times*, April 23, 2008, available at www.nytimes.com.

31. *Governing*, State and Local Source Book, available at www.governing.com.

32. Texas Commission on Jail Standards, "Jail Population Report," available at www.tcjs.state.tx.us.

33. Texas Department of Criminal Justice, *Annual Review 2008*, available at www.tdcj.state.tx.us.

34. John J. DiIulio, Jr., "Judicial Intervention: Lessons from the Past," in Timothy J. Flanagan, James W. Marquart, and Kenneth G. Adams, eds., *Incarcerating Criminals: Prisons and Jails in Social and Organizational Context* (New York, NY: Oxford University Press, 1998), pp. 81–93.

35. *Ruiz v. Estelle*, 503 F. Supp 1265 (S.D. Tex 1980); 679 F 2d 115 (5th Cir. 1982).

36. Dianna Hunt, "Justice Delayed: Our State's Criminal Crisis," *Houston Chronicle*, December 2, 1990, p. 24A.

37. Bureau of Justice Statistics, "Prison and Jail Inmates at Midyear 2008," available at www.ojp.usdoj.gov.

38. Douglas McDonald and Carl Patten, Jr., "Governments' Management of Private Prisons," National Institute of Justice, available at www.ncjrs.gov.

39. *Governing*, State and Local Source Book, available at www.governing.com.

40. Legislative Budget Board, "Criminal Justice Uniform Cost Report Tables," available at www.lbb.state.tx.us.

41. Legislative Budget Board, "Statewide Criminal Justice Recidivism and Revocation Rates," January 2005, available at www.lbb.state.tx.us.

42. Office of Adult Research, California Department of Corrections and Rehabilitation, April 2008, available at www.cdcr.ca.gov.

43. *Capitol Update*, March 6, 2008, available at www.txdirectory.com.

44. *Roper v. Simmons*, 543 U.S. 551 (2005).

45. *Atkins v. Virginia*, 536 U.S. 304 (2002).

Glossary

AARP: An interest group representing the concerns of older Americans. (Ch. 5)

Ability-to-pay theory of taxation: The approach to government finance that holds that taxes should be based on an individual's financial resources. (Ch. 13)

Address from office: A procedure for removing judicial officials that is initiated by the governor and requires a two-thirds vote by the legislature. (Ch. 10)

Adversary proceeding: A legal procedure in which each side presents evidence and arguments to bolster its position while rebutting evidence that might support the other side. (Chs. 10 and 14)

Advocacy groups: Organizations created to seek benefits on behalf of persons who are unable to represent their own interests. (Ch. 5)

Affirm: Uphold. (Ch. 10)

Agenda setting: The process through which issues become matters of public concern and government action. (Introduction)

Aggravated offenses: Violent crime. (Ch. 14)

Allocational urban policies: Local programs that are more or less neutral in their impact on the local economy. (Ch. 11)

Allowable: The maximum permissible rate of production for oil and gas wells in Texas as set by the Railroad Commission. (Ch. 9)

American Federation of Labor–Congress of Industrial Organizations (AFL–CIO): A national association of labor unions. (Ch. 5)

Americans with Disabilities Act (ADA): A federal law intended to end discrimination against disabled persons and eliminate barriers preventing their full participation in American society, imposes a broad range of federal mandates. (Ch. 3)

Annexation: The authority of a city to increase its geographic size by extending its boundaries to take in adjacent unincorporated areas. (Ch. 11)

Appeal: The taking of a case from a lower court to a higher court by the losing party in a lower court decision. (Ch. 10)

Appropriation bill: A legislative authorization to spend money for particular purposes, are usually assigned to the emergency calendar as well. (Ch. 8)

Appropriation process: The procedure through which Congress legislatively provides money for a particular purpose. (Chs. 3 and 9)

Arraignment: A judicial proceeding at which a suspect is formally charged with a crime and asked to enter a plea. (Ch. 14)

At-large election: A method for choosing public officials in which every citizen of a political subdivision, such as a state or county, votes to select a public official. (Ch. 7)

Attorney general's opinion: A written interpretation of existing law. (Ch. 9)

Authorization process: The procedure through which Congress legislatively establishes a program, defines its general purpose, devises procedures for its operation, specifies an agency implementation, and indicates an approximate level of funding. (Ch. 3)

Bail: Money or securities posted by accused persons to guarantee their appearance at later proceedings. (Ch. 14)

Battleground state: A swing state in which the relative strength of the two major party presidential candidates is close enough so that either candidate could conceivably carry the state. (Ch. 4)

Bicameral legislature: A legislative body with two chambers. (Chs. 2 and 8)

Biennium: Two-year budget period. (Ch. 13)

Bilingual education: The teaching of academic subjects in both English and a student's native language, usually Spanish. (Ch. 12)

Bill: A proposed law. (Ch. 8)

Bill of rights: A constitutional document guaranteeing individual rights and liberties. (Ch. 2)

Block grant program: A federal grant-in-aid program that provides money for a program in a broad, general policy area, such as elementary and secondary education, or transportation. (Ch. 3)

Bond: A certificate of indebtedness issued to investors who loan money for interest income; in lay terms, a bond is an IOU. (Chs. 7 and 11)

Bond election: An election for the purpose of obtaining voter approval for a local government going into debt. (Ch. 7)

Booking: An administrative procedure in which law enforcement personnel document a suspect's arrest. (Ch. 14)

Boosters: People who promote local economic development. (Ch. 11)

Branch banking: A business practice whereby a single, large bank conducts business from several locations. (Ch. 2)

Budget deficit: The amount of money by which annual budget expenditures exceed annual budget receipts. (Chs. 2 and 13)

Budget execution authority: The power to cut agency spending or transfer money between agencies during the period when the legislature is not in session. (Chs. 2, 9, and 13)

Building codes: Municipal ordinances that set minimum standards for the types of materials used in construction, building design, and construction methods employed in all building within the city. (Ch. 11)

Burden of proof: The legal obligation of one party in a lawsuit to prove its position to a court. (Chs. 10 and 14)

Capital expenditure: The purchase by government of a permanent, fixed asset, such as a new city hall or highway overpass. (Ch. 11)

Capital punishment: The death penalty. (Introduction, Chs. 9 and 10)

Catching the late train: The practice of giving campaign contributions to a candidate after an election is over and the candidate has won. (Ch. 5)

Categorical grant program: A federal grant-in-aid program that provides funds to state and local governments for a fairly narrow, specific purpose, such as removing asbestos from school buildings or acquiring land for outdoor recreation. (Ch. 3)

Caucus method of delegate selection: A procedure for choosing national party convention delegates that involves party voters participating in a series of precinct and district or county political meetings. (Ch. 7)

Cause groups: Organizations whose members care intensely about a single issue or a group of related issues. (Ch. 5)

Charter school: A publicly funded but privately managed school that operates under the terms of a formal contract or charter with the state. (Ch. 12)

Checks and balances: The overlapping of the powers of the branches of government so that public officials limit the authority of one another. (Ch. 2)

Citizen groups: Organizations created to support government policies that they believe will benefit the public at large. (Ch. 5)

City charter: The basic law of a city that defines its powers, responsibilities, and organization. (Ch. 11)

City manager: A professional administrator hired by city council in the council-manager form of city government to manage the day-to-day affairs of city government. (Ch. 11)

City ordinances: Laws enacted by the governing body of a municipality. (Chs. 10 and 11)

Civic culture: A political culture that is conducive to the development of an efficient, effective government that meets the needs of its citizens in a timely and professional manner. (Ch. 1)

Civil case: A legal dispute concerning a private conflict between two or more parties—individuals, corporations, or government agencies. (Ch. 10)

Civil defendant: The responding party in a civil suit. (Ch. 10)

Civil union: A legal partnership between two men or two women that gives the couple all the benefits, protections, and responsibilities under law as are granted to spouses in a marriage. (Ch. 2)

Class action lawsuit: A suit brought by one or more people on behalf of themselves and others who are similarly situated. (Ch. 5)

Clearance rate: The proportion of crimes known to authorities for which an arrest is made. (Ch. 14)

Closed primary: An election system that limits primary election participation to registered party members. (Ch. 7)

Coattail effect: A political phenomenon in which a strong candidate for one office gives a boost to fellow party members on the same ballot seeking other offices. (Ch. 7)

Commissioners court: The board of directors for county government composed of four county commissioners and the county judge. (Ch. 12)

Community policing: An approach to law enforcement that seeks to reduce crime by increasing the interaction and cooperation between local law enforcement agencies and the people and neighborhoods they serve. (Ch. 14)

Commutation: A reduction of punishment for a criminal offense. (Ch. 9)

Concurring opinion: A written judicial statement that agrees with the court's ruling but disagrees with the reasoning of the majority. (Ch. 10)

Conference committee: A special committee created to negotiate differences on similar pieces of legislation passed by the House and Senate. (Chs. 8 and 13)

Conflict of interest: A situation in which the personal interests of a public official may clash with that official's professional responsibilities. (Ch. 12)

Conservatism: The political view that seeks to preserve the political, economic, and social institutions of society against abrupt change. Conservatives generally oppose most government economic regulation and heavy government spending while favoring low taxes and traditional values. (Chs. 6 and 8)

Constitution: A fundamental law by which a state or nation is organized and governed. (Ch. 2)

Constitutional amendment: A formal, written change or addition to the state's governing document. (Ch. 2)

Constitutional law: Law that involves the interpretation and application of the constitution. (Ch. 2)

Constitutional revision: The process of drafting a new constitution. (Ch. 2)

Contract case: A civil suit dealing with disputes over written or implied legal agreements, such as a suit over a faulty roof repair job. (Ch. 10)

Council–manager form of city government: A structure of municipal government in which the city council/mayor appoints a professional administrator called a city manager to act as the chief executive officer of the municipality. (Ch. 11)

Criminal case: A legal dispute dealing with an alleged violation of a penal law. (Ch. 10)

Criminal defendant: The party charged with a criminal offense. (Ch. 10)

Cumulative voting system: An election system that allows individual voters to cast more than one ballot in the simultaneous election of several officials. (Ch. 11)

Dedicated funds: Constitutional or statutory provisions that set aside revenue for particular purposes. (Chs. 2 and 13)

Dedicated Highway Fund: A constitutionally earmarked account containing money set aside for building, maintaining, and policing state highways. (Chs. 2 and 13)

Deed restrictions: Private contractual agreements that limit what residential property owners can do with their houses and land. Almost every modern residential subdivision in the state has deed restrictions. (Ch. 11)

Deferred adjudication: A type of probation that can be granted by a judge to a defendant who pleads guilty or *nolo contendere* to certain relatively less serious offenses. (Ch. 14)

Deracialization: The attempt of political candidates to de-emphasize racially divisive themes in order to garner crossover support from voters of other races/ethnicities while also receiving the overwhelming majority of support from voters of the candidate's own racial/ethnic group. (Ch. 11)

Developmental urban policies: Local programs that enhance the economic position of a community in its competition with other communities. (Ch. 11)

Dillon's rule: The legal principle that a city can exercise only those powers expressly allowed by state law. (Ch. 11)

Direct democracy: A political system in which the citizens vote directly on matters of public concern. (Ch. 2)

Disfranchisement: The denial of voting rights. (Ch. 4)

Dissenting opinion: A written judicial statement that disagrees with the decision of the court's majority. (Ch. 10)

District election: A method for choosing public officials in which a political subdivision, such as a state or county, is divided into districts and each district elects one official. (Chs. 7 and 10)

Domestic-relations case: A civil suit based on the law involving the relationships between husband and wife, and between parents and children, such as divorce and child custody cases. (Ch. 10)

Double jeopardy: The constitutional principle that an individual may not be tried a second time by the same unit of government for a single offense if acquitted in the first trial. (Ch. 10)

Dual school system: Separate sets of schools for white and African American youngsters. (Ch. 3)

Early voting: A system that allows citizens to cast ballots before Election Day. (Ch. 4)

Election campaign: An attempt to get information to voters that will persuade them to elect a candidate or not elect an opponent. (Ch. 7)

Electoral College: The system established in the U.S. Constitution for the selection of the president and vice president of the United States. (Ch. 6)

Electoral mandate: The expression of popular support for a particular policy demonstrated through the electoral process.

Election precinct: An election district. (Ch. 4)

Elite theory (or **elitism**)**:** The view that political power is held by a small group of people who dominate politics by controlling economic resources. (Ch. 11)

Eminent domain: The right of the government to take private property for public use. (Ch. 9)

Empirical analysis: A method of study that relies on experience and scientific observation. (Introduction)

Employees Retirement System (ERS) Trust Fund: A pension fund for state employees. (Ch. 13)

Enfranchise: To grant the right to vote. (Ch. 4)

Enterprise zones: A state program that allows local governments to designate certain areas called enterprise zones in which private investors can receive property tax abatements, local sales tax rebates (refunds), and government-backed low-interest loans. (Ch. 11)

Entitlement programs: Government programs providing benefits to all persons qualified to receive them under law. (Ch. 3)

Environmental Protection Agency (EPA): The federal agency responsible for enforcing the nation's environmental laws. (Ch. 3)

Equal Protection Clause: The constitutional provision found in the Fourteenth Amendment of the U.S. Constitution that declares that "No State shall . . . deny to any person within its jurisdiction the equal protection of the laws." (Ch. 3)

Equal protection of the law: The legal principle that state laws may not arbitrarily discriminate against persons. (Ch. 2)

Excise tax: A tax levied on the manufacture, transportation, sale, or consumption of a particular item or set of related items. (Ch. 13)

Executive order: A directive issued by the governor to an administrative agency or executive department. (Ch. 9)

Extraterritorial jurisdiction: The authority of a city to require conformity with city ordinances and regulations affecting streets, parks, alleys, utility easements, sanitary sewers, and the like in a ring of land extending from one half to five miles beyond the city-limits line. (Ch. 11)

Federal grant program: A program through which the national government gives money to state and local governments to spend in accordance with set standards and conditions. (Chs. 3, 12, and 13)

Federal mandate: A legal requirement placed on a state or local government by the national government requiring certain policy actions. (Ch. 3)

Federal preemption of state authority: An act of Congress adopting regulatory policies that overrule state policies in a particular regulatory area. (Ch. 3)

Federal system *or* federation: A political system that divides power between a central government, with authority over the whole nation, and a series of state governments. (Ch. 3)

Felony: A serious criminal offense, such as murder, sexual assault, or burglary. (Chs. 10 and 14)

Filibuster: An attempt to defeat a bill through prolonged debate. (Ch. 8)

Fiscal note: An analysis of a legislative measure indicating its cost to state government if any. (Ch. 8)

Fiscal year: Budget year. (Ch. 13)

Forcible entry and detainer suit: An effort by a landlord to evict a tenant (usually for failure to pay rent). (Ch. 10)

Formula grant program: A grant program that awards funding on the basis of a formula established by Congress. (Ch. 3)

Foundation School Program: The basic funding program for public education in the state of Texas. (Chs. 12 and 13)

Franchise: The right to vote. (Ch. 4)

Franchise tax: A tax on businesses chartered or organized in Texas and doing business in the state. (Ch. 13)

Gender gap: Differences in party identification and political attitudes between men and women. (Ch. 6)

General election: A statewide election to fill national and state offices, which is held on the first Tuesday after the first Monday in November of even-numbered years. (Ch. 7)

General Fund: The state treasury account that supports state programs and services without restriction. (Ch. 13)

General law city: A municipality that is limited to those governmental structures and powers specifically granted by state law. (Ch. 11)

General-law units of local government: Units of local government that are limited to those structures and powers specifically granted by state law. (Ch. 12)

General obligation bonds: Certificates of indebtedness that must be repaid from general revenues. (Ch. 2)

Gerrymandering: The drawing of legislative district lines for political advantage. (Ch. 7)

Global warming: The gradual warming of the Earth's atmosphere reportedly caused by the burning of fossil fuels and industrial pollutants. (Chs. 8 and 9)

Good business climate: A political environment in which business would prosper. (Ch. 5)

Good time: A prison policy that credits inmates with time off for good behavior. (Ch. 14)

Grand jury: A body of 12 citizens who hears evidence presented by the prosecuting attorney and decides whether to indict an accused person. (Ch. 14)

Grand Old Party (GOP): Nickname for the Republican Party. (Ch. 6)

Grange: An organization of farmers. (Ch. 2)

Gross State Product (GSP): The total value of goods and services produced in a state in a year. (Ch. 1)

Habeas corpus, writ of: A court order requiring a government official to explain why a person is being held in custody. (Ch. 10)

Harmless error: A mistake committed by a trial court that is not serious enough to warrant a new trial because it could not have affected the outcome of the original trial. (Ch. 10)

Hate crimes legislation: Legislative measures that increase penalties for persons convicted of criminal offenses motivated by prejudice based on race, religion, national origin, gender, or sexual orientation. (Ch. 5)

High-technology industries: Industries that are based on the latest in modern technology. (Chs. 1 and 11)

Home rule: The authority of a unit of local government to take actions not prohibited by the laws or constitutions of the United States or the state. (Ch. 12)

Home rule city: A municipality that can take any actions not prohibited by state or federal law or the constitutions of the United States or the state of Texas. (Ch. 11)

Homestead: Legal residence. (Ch. 2)

Homestead exemption: A property tax reduction granted homeowners on their principal residence. (Ch. 11)

Hospital district: A special district that provides emergency medical services, indigent healthcare, and community health services. (Ch. 12)

Housing codes: Local ordinances requiring all dwelling places in a city to meet certain standards of upkeep and structural integrity. (Ch. 11)

Impeachment: A formal accusation against an executive or judicial officeholder. (Chs. 8 and 9)

Incorporated municipality: A city under the laws of the state. (Chs. 11 and 13)

Incremental model of budgeting: A theoretical effort to explain the budget process on the basis of small (incremental) changes in budget categories from one budget period to the next. (Ch. 13)

Incremental model of policy formulation: An approach to policy formulation that assumes that policymakers, working with imperfect information, continually adjust policies in pursuit of policy goals that are subject to periodic readjustment. (Introduction)

Incumbent: Current officeholder. (Chs. 5 and 7)

Independent School Districts (ISDs): Units of local government that provide public education services to district residents from kindergarten through the twelfth grade. (Ch. 12)

Indictment: A formal accusation charging an individual with the commission of a crime. (Ch. 14)

Individualistic political culture: An approach to government and politics that emphasizes private initiative with a minimum of government interference. (Chs. 1 and 13)

Initiative process: A procedure whereby citizens can propose the adoption of a policy measure by gathering a prerequisite number of signatures. Voters must then approve the measure before it can take effect. (Chs. 2, 7, 8, and 11)

Interest groups: Organizations of people who join together voluntarily on the basis of some interest they share for the purpose of influencing policy. (Ch. 5)

Interim committee: A committee established to study a particular policy issue between legislative sessions, such as higher education or public school finance. (Chs. 8 and 9)

Interstate Commerce Clause: The constitutional provision giving Congress authority to "regulate commerce . . . among the several states." (Ch. 3)

Issue network: A group of political actors that is concerned with some aspect of public policy. (Introduction)

Jacksonian democracy: The philosophy (associated with President Andrew Jackson) that suggested the right to vote should be extended to all adult male citizens and that all government offices of any importance should be filled by election. (Chs. 2 and 9)

Joint and several liability: The legal requirement that a defendant with "deep pockets" held partially liable for a plaintiff's injury must pay the full damage award for those defendants unable to pay. (Ch. 5)

Joint resolution: A resolution that must be passed by a two-thirds vote of each chamber. (Ch. 8)

Judicial review: The authority of courts to declare unconstitutional the actions of the other branches and units of government. (Ch. 10)

League of United Latin American Citizens (LULAC): A Latino interest group. (Chs. 4 and 5)

Legal briefs: Written legal arguments. (Ch. 10)

Legal writs: Written orders issued by a court directing the performance of an act or prohibiting some act. (Ch. 10)

Legislative access: An open door through which an interest group hopes to influence the details of policy. (Chs. 5 and 8)

Legislative Budget Board (LBB): An agency created by the legislature to study state revenue and budgetary needs between legislative sessions and prepare budget and appropriations bills to submit to the legislature. (Chs. 8, 9, and 13)

Legislative Redistricting Board (LBB): An agency composed of the speaker, lieutenant governor, comptroller, land commissioner, and attorney general that draws the boundaries of Texas House and Senate seats when the legislature is unable to agree on a redistricting plan. (Chs. 7, 8, and 9)

Legislative turnover: The replacement of individual members of a legislature from one session to the next. (Ch. 8)

Liberalism: The political view that seeks to change the political, economic, or social institutions of society to foster the development of the individual. Liberals believe that the government can (and should) advance social progress by promoting political equality, social justice, and economic prosperity. Liberals usually favor government regulation and high levels of government spending for social programs. Liberals value social and cultural diversity and defend the right of individual adult choice on issues such as access to abortion. (Chs. 6 and 8)

Line-item veto: The power of the governor to veto sections or items of an appropriation bill while signing the remainder of the bill into law. (Chs. 8, 9, and 13)

Litigants: The parties in a lawsuit. (Ch. 10)

Lobbying: The communication of information by a representative of an interest group to a government official for the purpose of influencing a policy decision. (Ch. 8)

Local bills: Proposed laws that affect only a single unit of local government. (Ch. 8)

Local governments: Subunits of states. (Ch. 3)

Local-option (wet-dry) elections: Elections held to determine whether an area legalizes the sale of alcoholic beverages. (Chs. 2 and 7)

Lone Star State: Nickname for Texas. (Ch. 1)

Long ballot: An election system that provides for the election of nearly every public official of any significance. (Chs. 2, 7, and 11)

Magistrates: Judicial officers. (Chs. 10 and 14)

Majority or deciding opinion: An official written statement of a court that explains and justifies its ruling and serves as a guideline for lower courts when similar legal issues arise in the future. (Ch. 10)

Mandamus, writ of: A court order directing a public official to perform a specific act or duty. (Ch. 10)

Mark up: The process in which legislators go over a piece of legislation line-by-line, revising, amending, or rewriting it. (Ch. 8)

Matching funds requirement: A legislative provision that the national government will provide grant money for a particular activity only on condition that the state or local government involved supply a certain percentage of the total money required for the project or program. (Chs. 3 and 13)

Mayor–council form of city government: A structure of municipal government in which the voters elect a mayor as the chief executive officer of the city and a council that serves as a legislative body. (Ch. 11)

Medicaid: A federal program designed to provide health insurance coverage to low-income persons, people with disabilities, and elderly people who are impoverished. (Chs. 3 and 13)

Medicare program: A federally funded health insurance program for the elderly. (Ch. 13)

Merit selection (or the Missouri Plan): A method for selecting judges that combines gubernatorial appointment with voter approval in a retention election. (Ch. 10)

Minimum wage: The lowest hourly wage that an employer can pay covered workers. (Chs. 1, 5, and 11)

Miranda warning: The judicial stipulation that a criminal defendant's confession can not be admitted into evidence unless police first inform the defendant of the constitutional right to remain silent and to consult an attorney. (Ch. 14)

Misdemeanor: A relatively minor criminal offense, such as a traffic violation. (Chs. 10 and 14)

Moralistic political culture: An approach to government and politics in which people expect government to intervene in the social and economic affairs of the state, promoting the public welfare and advancing the public good. (Ch. 1)

Mothers Against Drunk Driving (MADD): An interest group that supports the reform of laws dealing with drunk driving. (Chs. 4 and 5)

NARAL Pro-Choice Texas: An organization that favors abortion rights. (Ch. 5)

National Association for the Advancement of Colored People (NAACP): An interest group organized to represent the interests of African Americans, the Browns filed suit against the state. (Chs. 3 and 5)

National Crime Victim Survey (NCVS): A measure of the incidence of crime in the United States based on interviews with people in more than 50,000 households. (Ch. 14)

National Organization for Women (NOW): A group that promotes women's rights. (Ch. 5)

National Rifle Association (NRA): An interest group organized to defend the rights of gun owners and defeat efforts at gun control. (Chs. 4 and 5)

National Supremacy Clause: A constitutional provision that declares that the Constitution, the laws made under it, and the treaties of the United States are the supreme law of the land. (Ch. 3)

Natural population increase: The extent to which live births exceed deaths. (Ch. 1)

New Deal program: The name of President Franklin Roosevelt's legislative program for countering the Great Depression. (Ch. 6)

No Child Left Behind Act: A federal law that requires state governments and local school districts to institute basic skills testing as a condition for receiving federal aid. (Ch. 12)

Nolo contendere: A plea indicating a defendant's decision not to contest a criminal charge. (Ch. 14)

Nonpartisan elections: Election contests in which the names of the candidates appear on the ballot but not their party affiliations. (Chs. 7, 8, 10, 11, and 12)

Nonpartisan legislature: A legislative body in which political parties play little or no role. (Ch. 8)

Normative analysis: A method of study that is based on certain values. A normative analysis of the death penalty might consider the morality of the policy and the fairness of its implementation. (Introduction)

Official policy agenda: Those problems that government officials actively consider how to resolve. (Introduction)

One person, one vote: The judicial ruling that the Equal Protection Clause of the Fourteenth Amendment to the U.S. Constitution requires that legislative districts be apportioned on the basis of population. (Ch. 7)

Open primary: An election system that allows voters to pick the party primary of their choice without disclosing their party affiliation. (Ch. 7)

Ordinance: A law enacted by the governing body of a unit of local government. (Ch. 12)

Pardon: The exemption from punishment for a criminal offense. (Ch. 9)

Pari-mutuel wagering: A system for gambling on horse and dog racing. (Ch. 13)

Parole: The conditional release of convicted offenders from prison to serve the remainder of their sentences in the community under supervision. (Chs. 3, 4, and 14)

Partisan election: An election contest in which both the names and the party affiliations of candidates appear on the ballot. (Chs. 10 and 12)

Partisan legislature: A legislative body in which political parties play a defining role. (Ch. 8)

Party faction: An identifiable subgroup within a political party. (Ch. 6)

Party platform: A statement of party principles and issue positions. (Ch. 6)

Per capita: Per person. (Ch. 13)

Performance-based budgeting: A system of budget preparation and evaluation in which policymakers identify specific policy goals, set performance targets for agencies, and measure results. (Ch. 13)

Permanent School Fund (PSF): A fund established in the Texas Constitution as an endowment to finance public elementary and secondary education. (Chs. 9, 12, and 13)

Permanent University Fund (PUF): Money constitutionally set aside as an endowment to finance construction, maintenance, and some other activities at the University of Texas, Texas A&M University, and other institutions in those two university systems. (Chs. 2 and 13)

Plaintiff: The party initiating a civil suit. (Chs. 5 and 10)

Plea bargain: A procedure in which a defendant agrees to plead guilty in order to receive punishment less than the maximum for an offense. (Chs. 10 and 14)

Plural executive: The division of executive power among several elected officials. (Chs. 2 and 9)

Pluralist theory (or pluralism): The view that diverse groups of elites with differing interests compete with one another to control policy in various issue areas. (Ch. 11)

Policy adoption: The official decision of a government body to accept a particular policy and put it into effect. (Introduction)

Policy change: The modification of policy goals and means in light of new information or shifting political environments. (Introduction)

Policy cycle: The passage of an issue through the policy process from agenda building through policy change. (Introduction)

Policy evaluation: The assessment of policy. (Introduction)

Policy formulation: The development of strategies for dealing with the problems on the official policy agenda. (Introduction)

Policy implementation: The stage of the policy process in which policies are carried out. (Introduction)

Policy legitimation: The actions taken by government officials and others to ensure that most citizens regard a policy as a legal and appropriate government response to a problem. (Introduction)

Policymaking process: A logical sequence of activities affecting the development of public policies. (Introduction)

Policy outcomes: The situations that arise as a result of the impact of policy in operation. (Introduction)

Policy outputs: Actual government policies. (Introduction)

Political Action Committees (PACs): Organizations created to raise and distribute money in political campaigns. (Chs. 5 and 7)

Political culture: The widely held, deeply rooted political values of a society. (Chs. 1 and 13)

Political machines: Entrenched political organizations headed by a boss or small group of leaders who held power through such techniques as patronage, control over nominations, and bribery. (Ch. 11)

Political party: A group of individuals who join together to seek public office in order to influence public policy. (Ch. 6)

Political patronage: The power of an officeholder to award favors, such as government jobs, to political allies. (Ch. 11)

Politics: The process that determines who shall occupy the roles of leadership in government and how the power of government shall be exercised. (Introduction)

Poll tax: A tax that prospective voters had to pay in order to register to vote. (Chs. 4 and 12)

Population bracket laws: State laws designed to target particular cities based on their population. (Ch. 11)

Pork barrel spending: Expenditures to fund local projects that are not critically important from a national perspective. (Ch. 3)

Poverty line: The amount of money an individual or family needs to purchase basic necessities, such as food, clothing, health care, shelter, and transportation. (Ch. 1)

Presidential preference primary election: An election in which party voters cast ballots for the presidential candidate they favor and in so doing help determine the number of convention delegates that candidate will receive. (Ch. 7)

Primary election: An intra-party election during which a party's candidates for the general election are chosen. (Chs. 4 and 7)

Privatization: The process that involves the government contracting with private business to implement government programs. (Chs. 9 and 14)

Probable cause: The reasonable belief that a crime has been committed and that a particular suspect is the likely perpetrator of that crime. (Ch. 14)

Probate case: A civil suit dealing with the disposition of the property of a deceased individual. (Ch. 10)

Probation: The suspension of a sentence, permitting the defendant to remain free under court supervision. (Chs. 4 and 14)

Problem-solving court: A judicial body that attempts to change the future behavior of litigants and promote the welfare of the community. (Ch. 10)

Progressive tax: A levy whose burden weighs more heavily on persons earning higher incomes than it does on individuals making less money. (Ch. 13)

Project grant program: A grant program that requires state and local governments to compete for available federal money. (Ch. 3)

Property case: A civil suit over the ownership of real estate or personal possessions, such as land, jewelry, or an automobile. (Ch. 10)

Property lien: A financial claim against property for payment of debt. (Ch. 10)

Property tax (*ad valorem* property tax): A tax levied on the value of real property, such as land and buildings. (Ch. 11)

Proportional tax: A levy that weighs equally on all persons, regardless of their income. (Ch. 13)

Prosecutor: The attorney who tries a criminal case on behalf of the government. (Ch. 10)

Prospective voting: The concept that voters evaluate the incumbent officeholder and the incumbent's party based on their expectations of future developments. (Ch. 7)

Public policy: What government officials choose to do or not to do about public problems. (Introduction)

Punitive damages: Monetary awards given in a lawsuit to punish a defendant for a particularly evil, malicious, or fraudulent act. (Chs. 5 and 10)

Racial profiling: The practice of a police officer targeting individuals as suspected criminals on the basis of their race or ethnicity. (Ch. 5)

Radical Republicans: Members of the Republican Party that wanted sweeping social change to take place in the South after the Civil War. (Ch. 2)

Rainy Day Fund: An emergency reserve set aside by the state to cover future budget shortfalls. (Ch. 13)

Rational comprehensive model of policy formulation: An approach to policy formulation that assumes that policymakers establish goals, identify policy alternatives, estimate the costs and benefits of the alternatives, and then select the policy alternative that produces the greatest net benefit. (Introduction)

Real ID Act: A federal law designed to ensure that states issue driver's licenses only to people who are in the country legally. (Ch. 3)

Recall election: A procedure allowing voters to remove elected officials from office before the expiration of their terms. (Chs. 7 and 11)

Recession: An economic slowdown characterized by declining economic output and rising unemployment. (Chs. 1, 3, 4, and 13)

Recidivism: The tendency of offenders released from prison to commit additional crimes and be returned behind bars. (Chs. 10 and 14)

Redistributive urban policies: Local programs that benefit low-income residents of an area. (Ch. 11)

Redistricting: The process of redrawing the boundaries of legislative districts. (Ch. 7)

Regressive tax: A levy whose burden weighs more heavily on low-income groups than wealthy taxpayers. (Ch. 13)

Religious right: Individuals who hold conservative social views because of their religious beliefs. (Ch. 5)

Remand: An appellate court returning a case to a trial court for further consideration. (Ch. 10)

Representative democracy or republic: A political system in which citizens elect representatives to make policy decisions on their behalf. (Ch. 2)

Reprieve: A postponement of the implementation of punishment for a criminal offense. (Ch. 9)

Resolution: A legislative statement of opinion on a certain matter, such as a measure congratulating a Texas sports team for winning a championship. (Ch. 8)

Retrospective voting: The concept that voters choose candidates based on their perception of an incumbent candidate's past performance in office or the performance of the incumbent party. (Ch. 7)

Reversible error: A mistake committed by a trial court that is serious enough to warrant a new trial because the mistake could have affected the outcome of the original trial. (Ch. 10)

Right-to-work law: A statute prohibiting a union shop. (Ch. 5)

Robin Hood plan: A reform of the state's school finance system designed to increase funding for poor school districts by redistributing money from wealthy districts. (Chs. 12 and 13)

Rulemaking: A regulatory process used by government agencies to enact legally binding regulations. (Ch. 9)

Rules: Legally binding regulations adopted by a regulatory agency. (Ch. 9)

Runoff primary election: An election between the two top finishers in a primary election when no candidate received a majority of the vote in the initial primary. (Ch. 7)

Sales tax: A levy on the retail sale of taxable items. (Chs. 11 and 13)

School choice: An educational reform movement that allows parents to choose the elementary or secondary school their children will attend. (Chs. 8 and 12)

School Lunch Program: A federal program that provides free or reduced-cost lunches to children from poor families. (Chs. 3, 9, and 12)

Select, or special, committee: A committee that is established for a limited period of time to address a specific problem. (Ch. 8)

Senatorial courtesy: A custom of the Texas Senate that allows individual senators a veto over nominees who live in their districts. (Ch. 9)

Seniority: The length of continuous service a member has with a legislative body. (Ch. 8)

Separation of powers: The division of political authority among legislative, executive, and judicial branches of government. (Ch. 2)

Severance tax: A tax imposed on the extraction of natural resources, such as oil, coal, or gas. (Chs. 1 and 13)

Sierra Club: An environmental organization. (Ch. 5)

Sin tax: A levy on an activity that some people consider morally objectionable, such as smoking or drinking. (Ch. 13)

Sobriety checkpoint: A police procedure in which officers randomly stop vehicles to investigate the possibility that drivers may be too impaired to drive safely. (Ch. 14)

Social lobbying: The attempt of lobbyists to influence public policy by cultivating personal, social relationships with policymakers. (Ch. 5)

Solid South: The usual Democratic sweep of southern state electoral votes in presidential election years between the end of the Civil War era and the current party era. (Ch. 6)

Sovereignty: The authority of a state to exercise legitimate powers within its boundaries, free from external interference. (Ch. 3)

Special district: A unit of local government created to perform specific functions. (Ch. 12)

Special election: An election called at a time outside the normal election calendar. (Ch. 7)

Split ticket voting: Citizens casting their ballots for candidates of two or more parties for different offices during the same election. (Ch. 7)

Standing committee: A permanent committee. (Ch. 8)

State Children's Health Insurance Program (SCHIP): A federal program designed to provide health insurance to children from low-income families whose parents are not poor enough to qualify for Medicaid. (Chs. 3, 5, 12, and 13)

Statutory law: Law made by a legislature. (Ch. 2)

Straight ticket voting: The practice of voting for candidates of the same political party for all positions on the ballot. (Chs. 7 and 10)

Subpoena: A legal order compelling the attendance of a person at an official proceeding, such as a trial. (Ch. 12)

Subsidence: The sinking of the surface of the land caused by the too-rapid extraction of subsurface water. (Chs. 11 and 12)

Suffrage: The right to vote. (Chs. 2 and 4)

Sunset review: The periodic evaluation of state agencies by the legislature to determine whether they should be re-authorized. (Chs. 9 and 13)

Super delegates: Democratic officeholders and party officials who attend the national party convention as delegates who are not officially pledged to support any candidate. (Ch. 7)

Tax abatement: A program that exempts property owners from local property taxes on new construction and improvements in a designated tax abatement district for a set period of time. (Ch. 11)

Tax elasticity: The extent to which tax revenues increase as personal income rises. (Ch. 13)

Tax incidence: The point at which the actual cost of a tax falls. (Ch. 13)

Tax increment financing: A program in which a local government promises to earmark increased property tax revenues generated by development in a designated area called a tax increment financing district to fund improvements in the area, such as roads, parks, sidewalks, and street lighting. (Ch. 11)

Tea Party movement: A loose network of conservative activists organized to protest high taxes, excessive government spending, and big government in general. (Ch. 4)

Temporary Assistance for Needy Families (TANF): A federal block grant program that provides temporary financial assistance and work opportunities to needy families. (Chs. 3 and 13)

Term limitation: The movement to restrict the number of terms public officials may serve. (Ch. 8)

Texas Assessment of Knowledge and Skills (TAKS): A state mandated basic-skills test designed to measure student progress and school performance. (Ch. 12)

Texas Association of Business (TAB): An association for business firms ranging from giant corporations to small neighborhood business establishments. (Ch. 5)

Texas Equal Rights Amendment (ERA): A provision in the Texas Constitution that states the following: "Equality under the law shall not be denied or abridged because of sex, race, color, creed, or national origin." (Ch. 2)

Texas Medical Association (TMA): A professional organization of physicians. (Ch. 5)

Texas Right to Life Committee: An organization that opposes abortion. (Ch. 5)

Texas Teacher Retirement System (TRS) Trust Fund: A pension fund for the state's public school teachers. (Ch. 13)

Texas Trial Lawyers Association (TTLA): An organization of attorneys who represent plaintiffs in personal injury lawsuits. (Ch. 5)

Texas Two-Step: The nickname for the process used by the Texas Democratic Party to select delegates to the National Democratic Convention that involved participating in a Democratic Primary and a Democratic Caucus. (Ch. 7)

Top 10 percent rule: A state law that grants automatic college admission to public high school graduates who finish in the top 10 percent of their class. (Ch. 8)

Tort case: A civil suit involving personal injury or damage to property, such as a lawsuit stemming from an automobile accident. (Ch. 10)

Tort reform: The revision of state laws to limit the ability of plaintiffs in personal injury lawsuits to recover damages in court. (Ch. 5)

Trade associations: Organizations representing the interests of firms and professionals in the same general field. (Ch. 5)

Traditionalistic political culture: An approach to government and politics that sees the role of government as the preservation of tradition and the existing social order. (Ch. 1)

Trans-Texas Corridor: A proposed network of transportation corridors stretching from Brownsville to Oklahoma. (Chs. 6 and 13)

Trial: The formal examination of a civil or criminal action in accordance with law before a single judge who has jurisdiction to hear the dispute. (Ch. 10)

True bill: An indictment issued by a grand jury. (Ch. 14)

Truth in taxation laws: Laws that block local governments from raising the total amount of property taxes they collect from one year to the next when assessed values go up. (Ch. 11)

Two-party system: The division of voter loyalties between two major political parties, resulting in the near exclusion of minor parties from seriously competing for a share of political power. (Ch. 6)

Unicameral legislature: A legislative body with one chamber. (Chs. 2 and 8)

Uniform Crime Reports (UCR): A record of offenses known to police compiled by the Federal Bureau of Investigation (FBI) from reports submitted by local law enforcement agencies. (Ch. 14)

Unincorporated area: Territory not part of a legal city. (Ch. 11)

Union shop or closed shop: A workplace in which every employee must be a member of a union. (Ch. 5)

Utility district: A special district that provides utilities such as water and sewer service to residents living in unincorporated urban areas. (Chs. 11 and 12)

Veto: An action by the chief executive of a state or nation refusing to approve a bill passed by the legislature. (Chs. 8 and 9)

Voting age population (VAP): The number of state residents who are 18 years of age or older. (Ch. 4)

Voting eligible population (VEP): The number of state residents who are eligible to vote. (Ch. 4)

Voting Rights Act (VRA): A federal law designed to protect the voting rights of racial and ethnic minorities. (Chs. 7 and 11)

White primary: An election system that prohibited African Americans from voting in Democratic primary elections, ensuring that white voters would control the Democratic Party. (Ch. 4)

Yellow Dog Democrat: A loyal Democratic Party voter. (Ch. 6)

Zoning: The governmental designation of tracts of land for industrial, commercial, or residential use. (Ch. 11)

Index

PRACTICE TESTS

Introduction: The Policymaking Process

NOTE: The first number in parenthesis after each question stem indicates the "What We Will Learn" question associated with the particular multiple-choice question. The second is the page number(s) in the text addressed in the question. For example, multiple-choice question one deals with material covered in the first "What We Will Learn" questions. The information is found on p. 2 of the text.

Circle the correct answer.

1. "What government officials choose to do or not to do about public problems" is the definition for which of the following terms? **(1)** (p. 2)

   (A) Agenda setting
   (B) Policy evaluation
   (C) Public policy
   (D) Feedback

2. The background in which the policymaking process takes place is known as which of the following? **(1)** (p. 3)

   (A) Public policy approach
   (B) Politics
   (C) Context of policymaking
   (D) Feedback

3. Which of the following contextual factors affects capital punishment policymaking in Texas? **(1)** (p. 3)

   (A) Public opinion, which supports the death penalty
   (B) The U.S. Constitution, which sets the legal/constitutional framework for state death penalty laws
   (C) Federal courts, which often rule on death penalty issues
   (D) All of the above

4. The process through which issues become matters of public concern and government action is known as which of the following? **(1)** (p. 4)

   (A) Agenda setting
   (B) Policy formulation
   (C) Policy adoption
   (D) Policy implementation

5. The governor, lieutenant governor, and speaker appoint a committee to consider ways to increase the number of Texans with health insurance. This action would best illustrate which of the following stages of the policymaking process? **(1)** (p. 5)

   (A) Agenda setting
   (B) Policy formulation
   (C) Policy adoption
   (D) Policy implementation

6. The governor gives a speech in which he declares that transportation is a major challenge facing the state of Texas in the twenty-first century. The governor's action best illustrates which of the following stages of the policymaking process? **(1)** (p. 4)

   (A) Agenda setting
   (B) Policy formulation
   (C) Policy adoption
   (D) Policy evaluation

7. The development of strategies for dealing with the problems on the official policy agenda is known as which of the following? **(1)** (p. 5)

   (A) Agenda setting
   (B) Policy formulation
   (C) Policy adoption
   (D) Policy evaluation

8. The Texas House passes legislation to increase business taxes in order to lower local property taxes. This action would best illustrate which of the following stages of the policymaking process? **(1)** (pp. 5–6)

   (A) Agenda setting
   (B) Policy formulation
   (C) Policy adoption
   (D) Policy implementation

9. Which of the following terms can be defined as actions taken by government officials and others to ensure that most citizens regard a policy as a legal and appropriate government response to a problem? **(1)** (p. 6)

   (A) Policy formulation
   (B) Policy adoption
   (C) Policy evaluation
   (D) Policy legitimation

10. The stage of the policy process in which policies are carried out is known as which of the following? **(1)** (pp. 6–8)

    (A) Agenda setting
    (B) Policy formulation
    (C) Policy adoption
    (D) Policy implementation

11. Last year your uncle served on a jury in a capital murder case. That jury trial would best illustrate which of the following stages of the policymaking process? **(1)** (pp. 6–8)

    (A) Agenda setting
    (B) Policy implementation
    (C) Policy formulation
    (D) Policy adoption

12. The assessment of policy is the definition for which of the following terms? **(1)** (pp. 8–9)

    (A) Policy evaluation
    (B) Policy formulation
    (C) Policy adoption
    (D) Policy implementation

13. Research on capital punishment in Texas shows that the average time between conviction and execution is more than ten years. The research report best illustrates which of the following stages of the policymaking process? **(1)** (pp. 8–9)

    (A) Policy formulation
    (B) Policy adoption
    (C) Policy evaluation
    (D) Agenda setting

14. Which of the following would be an example of a normative evaluation of the death penalty in Texas? **(1)** (pp. 8–9)

    (A) An essay entitled "Three Reasons Why the Death Penalty Is Just and Fair"
    (B) A study showing that most death penalty prosecutions take place in relatively few counties
    (C) An assessment of the cost of capital punishment compared with the cost of life in prison without parole
    (D) A roster of the current population of death row along with the crimes for which each inmate was convicted

15. Which of the following factors probably accounts for the decline in death sentences given by Texas juries? **(1)** (p. 10)

    (A) Public opinion in Texas has turned against capital punishment.
    (B) The murder rate in Texas is increasing.
    (C) Texas juries now have the option of life without parole.
    (D) All of the above.

16. Which of the following terms can be defined as the modification of policy goals and means in light of new information or shifting political environments? **(1)** (pp. 9–10)

    (A) Policy change
    (B) Policy legitimation
    (C) Policy evaluation
    (D) Policy implementation

17. The passage of an issue through the policy process from agenda setting through policy change is known as which of the following? **(2)** (p. 10)

    (A) Policy cycle
    (B) Policy output
    (C) Policy outcome
    (D) Issue network

18. A group of political actors that is concerned with some aspect of public policy is known as which of the following? **(2)** (pp. 10–11)

    (A) Policy cycle
    (B) Policy output
    (C) Policy outcome
    (D) Issue network

19. The process that determines who shall occupy the roles of leadership in government and how the power of government shall be exercised is known as which of the following? **(2)** (p. 11)

    (A) Public policymaking process
    (B) Politics
    (C) Political science
    (D) Capital punishment

20. Which of the following is a reason for studying Texas government and politics? **(3)** (pp. 11–12)

    (A) Everyone living in the state pays taxes to state and local governments.
    (B) State law requires that the core curriculum for public colleges and universities include the study of the Texas Constitution.
    (C) State and local governments provide a wide range of services.
    (D) All of the above

Chapter 1: The People, Economy, and Political Culture of Texas

Circle the correct answer.

1. Which of the following statements about population growth in Texas is true? **(1)** (pp. 17–18)

   (A) The population of Texas is growing more rapidly than the population of the United States as a whole.
   (B) The population of Texas is growing more slowly than the population of the United States as a whole.
   (C) The population of Texas is growing at the same rate as the population of the United States as a whole.
   (D) Texas grew more rapidly than the nation as a whole during the 1990s, but since 2000 the state's population growth rate has fallen below the national average.

2. Which of the following is *not* a reason for relatively brisk population growth in Texas? **(1)** (p. 18)

   (A) People live longer in Texas because of outstanding healthcare and near universal health insurance coverage.
   (B) The birthrate in Texas is one of the highest in the nation.
   (C) The population in Texas is relatively young.
   (D) Texas is the destination for a large number of immigrants from other countries.

3. Which of the following statements about illegal immigration is true? **(1)** (pp. 18–19)

   (A) Texas has more illegal immigrants than any other state.
   (B) A majority of illegal immigrants in Texas come from Mexico.
   (C) Illegal immigrants drag down the state's economy because they pay no taxes.
   (D) All of the above

4. According to a report by the Texas Comptroller of Public Accounts, what impact does illegal immigration have on the Texas economy and government? **(1)** (p. 19)

   (A) Illegal immigrants contribute to economic growth.
   (B) Illegal immigrants pay more in state taxes than they receive in state services.
   (C) Illegal immigrants receive more services from local government than they pay in local taxes.
   (D) All of the above

5. Why do demographers believe that Texas will gain seats in the U.S. House after the 2010 Census? **(1)** (p. 20)

   (A) The population of Texas will surpass 26 million.
   (B) The population of Texas will include more than 1.4 million illegal immigrants.
   (C) The population of Texas has been growing more rapidly than the population of the nation as a whole since 2000.
   (D) A majority of Texans will be Latino in 2010.

6. Which of the following statements about the population of Texas is *not* true? **(1)** (p. 20)

   (A) A majority of state residents are Latino.
   (B) The Latino population in Texas is larger than the state's African American population.
   (C) A majority of the Texas population is African American, Latino, or Asian.
   (D) A majority of Latinos in Texas are Mexican American.

7. Which of the following regions is the least densely populated? **(1)** (pp. 21–22)

   (A) West Texas
   (B) South Texas
   (C) North Texas
   (D) Gulf Coast area

8. Which of the following Texas cities is *not* among the ten largest cities in the United States? **(1)** (pp. 21–22)

   (A) Dallas
   (B) Austin
   (C) San Antonio
   (D) Houston

9. Which of the following regions of the state is growing the most rapidly? **(1)** (pp. 21–22)

   (A) Small towns
   (B) Rural areas
   (C) Suburban areas
   (D) Inner-city urban areas

10. Which of the following statements about religious belief and practice in Texas is *not* true? **(1)** (pp. 22–23)

    (A) The percentage of people who say that religion is very important in their lives is greater in Texas than in the nation as a whole.
    (B) The percentage of people who are Catholic is greater in Texas than in the nation as a whole.
    (C) The percentage of people who are evangelical Protestants is greater in Texas than in the nation as a whole.
    (D) The percentage of people who go to church on a weekly basis is greater in Texas than in the nation as a whole.

11. Why is the petroleum industry a less significant component of the Texas economy today than it was 20 or 30 years ago? **(2)** (pp. 23–24)

    (A) Oil production in Texas has been declining for decades.
    (B) The international price of oil has been falling for years.
    (C) Most major oil companies have moved their headquarters from Texas to Louisiana and Oklahoma.
    (D) All of the above

12. Which of the following industries is *more* important now than it was in the first half of the twentieth century? **(2)** (p. 25)

    (A) Cotton
    (B) Computers
    (C) Petroleum
    (D) None of the above

13. Which of the following is *not* an example of a high-technology industry? **(2)** (p. 25)

    (A) Robotics
    (B) Telecommunications
    (C) Computers
    (D) Cosmetology

14. Which of the following statements about the Texas economy is true? **(2)** (p. 25)

    (A) The petroleum industry is the single-largest component of the Texas economy.
    (B) The Texas economy is growing at a faster rate than the national economy.
    (C) Texas has the largest economy in the nation.
    (D) All of the above

15. Which of the following statements about the Texas economy is true? **(2)** (pp. 25–27)

    (A) Texas has the second largest state economy in the nation after California.
    (B) Texas is a relatively poor state at least in terms of individual and family income.
    (C) The poverty rate in Texas exceeds the national average.
    (D) All of the above

16. Which of the following groups of Texans has the highest household income? **(2)** (p. 25)

    (A) African Americans
    (B) Whites
    (C) Latinos
    (D) Household income is roughly the same for all three groups.

17. Which of the following statements is true about income and wealth in Texas? **(2)** (pp. 25–27)

    (A) The income differential between the wealthiest and the poorest families is greater in Texas than it is in most other states.
    (B) The Texas economy is growing more slowly than the economies of most other states.
    (C) The poverty rate in Texas is lower than the national average.
    (D) All of the above

18. Which of the following terms is defined as the widely held, deeply rooted political values of a society? **(3)** (p. 28)

    (A) Political science
    (B) Public policy
    (C) Politics
    (D) Political culture

19. Professor Elazar classifies the political culture of Texas as which of the following? **(3)** (p. 30)

    (A) Moralistic
    (B) Individualistic
    (C) Traditionalistic
    (D) A hybrid, including both traditionalistic and individualistic elements.

20. Which of the following strains of political culture is *not* generally found in Texas? **(3)** (p. 29)

    (A) Individualistic
    (B) Moralistic
    (C) Traditionalistic
    (D) Civic culture

21. Which of the following is a characteristic of a moralistic political culture? **(3)** (p. 29)

    (A) The role of government is limited.
    (B) Political participation by ordinary citizens is low.
    (C) The role of government is to promote the social welfare.
    (D) The role of government is to preserve the social order.

22. Which of the following is a political culture that is conducive to the development of an efficient, effective government that meets the needs of its citizens in a timely and professional manner? **(3)** (p. 30)

    (A) Individualistic
    (B) Moralistic
    (C) Civic culture
    (D) Traditionalistic

23. Which of the following is an element of a civic culture? **(3)** (p. 30)

    (A) Civic engagement
    (B) Political equality
    (C) Social structure of cooperation
    (D) All of the above

24. Where does Texas rank among the 50 states in terms of civic culture? **(3)** (p. 30)

    (A) Texas has the highest level of civic culture in the nation.
    (B) Texas has the lowest level of civic culture in the nation.
    (C) Texas ranks below average in civic culture.
    (D) Texas ranks above average in civic culture.

25. Which of the following is true of a state with a high level of civic culture? **(3)** (p. 30)

    (A) It has an innovative, effective government.
    (B) Citizen participation in the public policymaking process is low.
    (C) Citizens are intolerant of people with different ideas and lifestyles.
    (D) All of the above

Chapter 2: Texas Constitution

Circle the correct answer.

1. Which of the following is a characteristic of both the U.S. Constitution and most state constitutions? **(1)** (pp. 37–38)

   (A) They provide for bicameral legislatures.
   (B) They provide for separation of powers.
   (C) They create a representative democracy.
   (D) All of the above

2. The Texas Constitution creates a legislative branch with a House and a Senate. Which of the following terms best describes this sort of legislature? **(1)** (p. 37)

   (A) Bicameral
   (B) Separation of powers
   (C) Unicameral
   (D) Checks and balances

3. The Texas Constitution creates a government with a legislative branch, an executive branch, and a judicial branch. Which of the following terms best describes this sort of arrangement? **(1)** (p. 37)

   (A) Bicameral
   (B) Separation of powers
   (C) Unicameral
   (D) Federalism

4. In which of the following ways do state constitutions typically differ from the U.S. Constitution? **(1)** (pp. 37–38)

   (A) State constitutions are shorter than the U.S. Constitution.
   (B) State constitutions have been amended less frequently than the U.S. Constitution.
   (C) Most state constitutions provide for the election of judges whereas the U.S. Constitution provides for the appointment of federal judges.
   (D) All of the above

5. The philosophy of Jacksonian democracy is most closely associated with which of the following? **(2)** (p. 39)

   (A) A school system funded with property taxes
   (B) Low election turnout
   (C) The long ballot
   (D) Branch banking

6. In 1850, the Texas Constitution was amended to provide for the election of judges. This development reflected which of the following? **(2)** (p. 39)

   (A) Jacksonian democracy
   (B) Radical Republicanism
   (C) Checks and balances
   (D) Direct democracy

7. Which of the following factors influenced the drafting of the current Texas Constitution? **(2)** (pp. 39–41)

   (A) Reaction to the Reconstruction administration of E. J. Davis
   (B) The Grange
   (C) Jacksonian democracy
   (D) All of the above

8. Which of the following was a goal of the framers of the Texas Constitution of 1875? **(3)** (p. 41)

   (A) To control the excesses of big business
   (B) To limit the power of government
   (C) To reduce the cost of government
   (D) All of the above

9. The Texas Constitution provided for the election of a governor, lieutenant governor, attorney general, land commissioner, comptroller, and other executive officials. Which of the following terms best describes this type of governmental organization? **(3)** (p. 41)

   (A) Separation of powers
   (B) Plural executive
   (C) Checks and balances
   (D) Bicameral legislature

10. Which of the following provisions was included in the Texas Constitution written in 1875? **(3)** (pp. 41–43)

    (A) The Constitution outlawed branch banking.
    (B) The Constitution created a cabinet system of government.
    (C) The Constitution provided for annual legislative sessions.
    (D) None of the above

11. Local-option elections deal with which of the following? **(3)** (p. 42)

    (A) The selection of judges
    (B) The sale of alcoholic beverages
    (C) Branch banking
    (D) School finance

12. How does the Texas Constitution differ from the U.S. Constitution? **(4)** (pp. 44–45)

    (A) The Texas Constitution has a bill of rights whereas the U.S. Constitution does not.
    (B) The Texas Constitution is longer and more detailed than the U.S. Constitution.
    (C) The Texas Constitution creates a unicameral legislature whereas the U.S. Constitution creates a bicameral legislature.
    (D) All of the above

13. How does the Texas Bill of Rights compare with the U.S. Bill of Rights? **(4)** (pp. 44–45)

    (A) The Texas Bill of Rights simply restates the provisions of the U.S. Bill of Rights.
    (B) The Texas Bill of Rights is shorter than the U.S. Bill of Rights.
    (C) The Texas Bill of Rights phrases the protection of rights positively rather than prohibiting government from taking certain actions.
    (D) All of the above

14. Which of the following provisions is included in the Texas Constitution but not found in the U.S. Constitution? **(4)** (pp. 44–45)

    (A) A detailed discussion of local government
    (B) Separation of powers with checks and balances
    (C) A bicameral legislature
    (D) A method for amendment

15. Which of the following is the most important means for changing the Texas Constitution? **(5)** (p. 46)

    (A) Change through amendment
    (B) Change through judicial interpretation
    (C) Change through practical experience
    (D) All three means are equally important.

16. A formal, written change or addition to the state's governing document is known as which of the following? **(5)** (p. 46)

    (A) Constitutional revision
    (B) Judicial review
    (C) Constitutional amendment
    (D) None of the above

17. Which of the following changes has *not* come about because of the adoption of constitutional amendments in Texas? **(5)** (pp. 46–48)

    (A) A four-year term for the governor
    (B) Annual sessions for the legislature
    (C) Budget execution authority for the governor
    (D) Branch banking

18. Why does the state issue general obligation bonds? **(5)** (pp. 46–47)

    (A) To raise taxes
    (B) To amend the Texas Constitution
    (C) To ratify an amendment to the U.S. Constitution
    (D) To borrow money

19. Which of the following is *not* a step in the process of amending the Texas Constitution? **(5)** (p. 47)

    (A) The Texas House proposes an amendment by two-thirds vote.
    (B) The Texas Senate proposes an amendment by two-thirds vote.
    (C) The amendment goes to the governor for signature.
    (D) The voters ratify the amendment at the ballot box.

20. Which of the following statements about constitutional amendment elections is true? **(5)** (pp. 47–48)

    (A) Turnout at amendment elections typically exceeds turnout at candidate elections.
    (B) In recent years, voters have rejected every amendment on the ballot.
    (C) Amendments cannot be ratified unless they receive a two-thirds vote of the electorate.
    (D) None of the above

21. Voter turnout in Texas was lowest in which of the following elections? **(5)** (pp. 47–48)

    (A) Constitutional amendment ratification election
    (B) Governor's election
    (C) Presidential election
    (D) Turnout was the same for all three elections.

22. Which of the following universities does *not* benefit from the Permanent University Fund (PUF)? **(5)** (p. 49)

    (A) Texas A&M University
    (B) University of Texas at Austin
    (C) University of Houston
    (D) All state universities benefit from the PUF.

23. *Edgewood v. Kirby* (1989) dealt with which of the following Texas issues? **(6)** (p. 53)

    (A) Gay marriage
    (B) School finance
    (C) Legalized gambling
    (D) Abortion

24. Can a state grant its residents more rights (such as giving same-sex couples the right to marry) than are guaranteed by the U.S. Constitution? **(6)** (p. 52)

    (A) No. States are limited to granting those rights listed in the U.S. Constitution.
    (B) Yes, but any additional rights must be approved by the U.S. Supreme Court.
    (C) Yes, but any additional rights must be approved by the U.S. Congress.
    (D) Yes. States can grant their residents greater rights protections than are granted by the U.S. Constitution.

25. Which of the following is the legal principle that state laws may not arbitrarily discriminate against persons? **(6)** (p. 53)

    (A) Equal protection of the laws
    (B) Direct democracy
    (C) Representative democracy
    (D) Jacksonian democracy

Circle the correct answer.

1. In Canada, political power is divided between a central government and a series of provincial governments, which are similar to American states. Which of the following terms most accurately describes the Canadian political system? **(1)** (p. 59)

   (A) Representative democracy
   (B) Federal system
   (C) Democracy
   (D) Monarchy

2. In the American federal system, which of the following levels of government enjoy sovereignty? **(1)** (p. 59)

   (A) Only the federal level
   (B) Only the state level
   (C) Both the federal and state levels
   (D) Neither the federal nor state levels

3. Are the states or the national government the dominant partners in the American federal system? **(1)** (p. 59)

   (A) States are the dominant partners.
   (B) States and the national government are equal partners.
   (C) The national government is the dominant partner because of the National Supremacy Clause.
   (D) The Supreme Court determines which level of government takes precedence on a case-by-case basis.

4. Can states adopt laws that conflict with federal laws? **(1)** (p. 59)

   (A) No. Federal laws take precedence over state law.
   (B) Yes. Both states and the national government are sovereign.
   (C) No. State laws can be overruled by the U.S. Constitution but not U.S. law.
   (D) Yes, but Congress would have to adopt new legislation specifically repealing the state measure.

5. Which of the following cases dealt with racial integration of public schools? **(2)** (pp. 61–62)

   (A) *Brown v. Board of Education of Topeka*
   (B) *Ruiz v. Estelle*
   (C) *Roe v. Wade*
   (D) *Edgewood v. Kirby*

6. Which of the following cases dealt with prison overcrowding? **(2)** (p. 62)

   (A) *Brown v. Board of Education of Topeka*
   (B) *Ruiz v. Estelle*
   (C) *Roe v. Wade*
   (D) *Edgewood v. Kirby*

7. Which of the following cases dealt with abortion? **(2)** (p. 63–64)

   (A) *Brown v. Board of Education of Topeka*
   (B) *Ruiz v. Estelle*
   (C) *Roe v. Wade*
   (D) *Edgewood v. Kirby*

8. Texas was forced to eliminate dual school systems because of which of the following? **(2)** (pp. 61–62)

   (A) *Brown v. Board of Education of Topeka*
   (B) *Ruiz v. Estelle*
   (C) *Roe v. Wade*
   (D) *Edgewood v. Kirby*

9. *Ruiz v. Estelle* dealt with which of the following issues? **(2)** (p. 62)

   (A) School funding
   (B) School integration
   (C) Abortion
   (D) Prison overcrowding

10. Which of the following provisions is *not* part of the laws governing abortion in the state of Texas? **(2)** (pp. 64–65)

    (A) A 24-hour waiting period
    (B) Parental consent for minors
    (C) Spousal (or partner) notification
    (D) All of the above—Texas places no restrictions on the availability of abortion services

11. An act of Congress adopting regulatory policies that overrule state policies in a particular regulatory area is known as which of the following? **(3)** (pp. 65–66)

    (A) Federal preemption of state authority
    (B) Federal grant in aid
    (C) Federal matching funds requirement
    (D) Federal mandate

12. A legal requirement placed on a state or local government by the national government requiring certain policy actions is known as which of the following? **(3)** (p. 66)

    (A) Federal preemption of state authority
    (B) Federal mandate
    (C) Federal grant in aid
    (D) Federal matching funds requirement

13. The Americans with Disabilities Act (ADA) requires that state and local governments make public buildings accessible to persons with disabilities. This requirement is an example of which of the following? **(3)** (pp. 66–67)

    (A) Federal mandate
    (B) Federal preemption
    (C) Categorical grant
    (D) Federal grant program

14. The Real ID Act requires that states change the procedures they follow in issuing driver's licenses to ensure that only people who are in the United States legally are able to get licenses. The Real ID Act is an example of which of the following? **(3)** (pp. 66–67)

    (A) Federal preemption
    (B) Federal matching funds requirement
    (C) Federal grant program
    (D) Federal mandate

15. The procedure through which Congress legislatively establishes a program, defines its general purpose, devises procedures for its operation, specifies an agency for implementation, and indicates an approximate level of funding is known as which of the following? **(4)** (p. 68)

    (A) Appropriation process
    (B) Grants process
    (C) Authorization process
    (D) Appeals process

16. The procedure through which Congress legislatively provides money for a particular purpose is known as which of the following? **(4)** (p. 68)

    (A) Appropriation process
    (B) Grants process
    (C) Authorization process
    (D) Appeals process

17. A federal grant program that provides funds to state and local governments for a fairly narrow, specific purpose, such as removing asbestos from school buildings or acquiring land for outdoor recreation, is known as which of the following? **(4)** (p. 69)

    (A) Formula grant program
    (B) Project grant program
    (C) Categorical grant program
    (D) Block grant program

18. A federal grant program that provides money for a program in a broad, general policy area, such as transportation or elementary and secondary education, is known as which of the following? **(4)** (p. 69)

    (A) Formula grant program
    (B) Project grant program
    (C) Categorical grant program
    (D) Block grant program

19. Which of the following is an example of an entitlement program that provides health insurance coverage to low-income individuals? **(4)** (p. 70)

    (A) Medicaid
    (B) School Lunch Program
    (C) Unemployment Compensation
    (D) Temporary Assistance to Needy Families (TANF)

20. A college professor works on a grant proposal to seek funding to support her research on genetic mutations of the influenza virus. The funding is awarded through which of the following types of grant programs? **(4)** (p. 71)

    (A) Formula grant program
    (B) Project grant program
    (C) Categorical grant program
    (D) Block grant program

21. A city government receives federal funding based on its population and level of substandard housing. The funding is awarded through which of the following types of grant programs? **(4)** (p. 71)

    (A) Formula grant program
    (B) Project grant program
    (C) Categorical grant program
    (D) Block grant program

22. On average, the federal government picks up 60 percent of the cost of the Medicaid program with state governments covering the rest. Which of the following terms best describes this arrangement? **(4)** (p. 71)

    (A) Formula grant
    (B) Entitlement program
    (C) Matching fund requirement
    (D) Federal preemption of state authority

23. Federal grant money flows to Texas to help fund which of the following? **(5)** (p. 73)

    (A) Highway construction and maintenance
    (B) Mass transit projects
    (C) Healthcare
    (D) All of the above

24. Federal funds represent what proportion of the state budget? **(5)** (pp. 73–74)

    (A) One-fifth
    (B) One-third
    (C) One-half
    (D) Two-thirds

25. Have federal funds been growing, shrinking, or staying the same as a proportion of the state budget? **(5)** (pp. 73–74)

    (A) Growing
    (B) Shrinking
    (C) Staying the same
    (D) They were growing until the last three years when they began to decline in importance.

Chapter 4: Political Participation

Circle the correct answer.

1. Which of the following groups was able to fully participate in Texas politics when the state joined the Union in 1845? **(1)** (p. 80)

   (A) White males only
   (B) Whites only
   (C) Males only
   (D) All Texans but African Americans

2. Why did some white Texans organize chapters of the Ku Klux Klan after the Civil War? **(1)** (p. 81)

   (A) To intimidate African Americans
   (B) To protect the voting rights of minority Texans
   (C) To fight against the Union forces occupying the state
   (D) To restore law and order

3. The poll tax had a negative impact on voter participation rates by which of the following groups? **(1)** (p. 82)

   (A) African Americans
   (B) Latinos
   (C) Low-income whites
   (D) All of the above

4. Which of the following was *not* used to disfranchise African American Texans? **(1)** (p. 82)

   (A) Primary elections
   (B) Poll tax
   (C) White primary
   (D) All three were used to disfranchise African Americans.

5. The white primary prevented African Americans from voting in which of the following elections? **(1)** (p. 82)

   (A) Republican elections
   (B) General election
   (C) Democratic primary
   (D) All of the above

6. Which of the following elections was most important in late nineteenth century Texas? **(1)** (p. 82)

   (A) Republican primary
   (B) Democratic primary
   (C) General election
   (D) All of the above were equally important.

7. George Parr is associated with which of the following? **(1)** (p. 83)

   (A) Lyndon Johnson's election to the U.S. Senate in 1948
   (B) Duval County
   (C) Box 13 in Jim Wells County
   (D) All of the above

8. *Smith v. Allwright* dealt with which of the following issues? **(1)** (p. 84)

   (A) Poll tax
   (B) Grandfather clauses
   (C) Abolition movement
   (D) White primary

9. Lawrence A. Nixon is remembered for initiating legal challenges to which of the following? **(1)** (pp. 83–84)

   (A) Poll tax
   (B) Grandfather clauses
   (C) White primary
   (D) All of the above

10. Which of the following is *not* a requirement to vote in Texas? **(2)** (p. 86)

    (A) You must be an American citizen.
    (B) You must live in the state for six months.
    (C) You must be at least 18 years of age.
    (D) All of the above are requirements to vote in Texas.

11. Are persons who have been convicted of serious crimes (felonies) eligible to vote in Texas? **(2)** (p. 86)

    (A) No.
    (B) Yes.
    (C) Yes, but only after they have been released from prison.
    (D) Yes, but only after they have fully completed their sentences, including time served on parole and probation.

12. The election is next week and you want to vote, but you realize that you have not registered. What are your options? **(2)** (p. 86)

    (A) You must register immediately because voter registration ends a week before the election.
    (B) You are out of luck because registration ends 30 days before an election.
    (C) You can register at the polls on the day of the election.
    (D) You can register now and vote early, but you cannot vote on the day of the election.

13. Which of the following statements about elections in Texas is/are true? **(2)** (p. 86)

    (A) Newcomers must live in the state 90 days before they can register to vote.
    (B) Texans must register before they can vote.
    (C) Texas has term limits for all of its executive and legislative officials.
    (D) All of the above

14. Which of the following statements about elections in Texas is/are true? **(2)** (pp. 86–87)

    (A) Early voting is limited to people who will be out of town on the day of the election.
    (B) People who are out of town on the day of the election can use the Internet to cast their ballots.
    (C) In order to increase election turnout, the legislature recently changed state law to allow people to register to vote on the day of the election.
    (D) None of the above

15. You hear on the news that early voting has begun for next month's election. Can you vote early if you just want to avoid the rush on the day of the election? **(2)** (p. 87)

   (A) Yes. Anyone can vote early.
   (B) You can vote early if you are elderly or disabled, but otherwise you must vote on the day of the election.
   (C) You are required to vote early if you are over 65 years of age, but other people must vote on the day of the election.
   (D) You can vote early if you have a good reason, but otherwise you must vote on the day of the election.

16. You live in Houston, but you are attending college in Waco. What are your options for voting in the November election? **(2)** (p. 87)

   (A) You can change your voter registration to Waco and vote there.
   (B) You can vote early in Houston if you visit your parents during the early voting period next fall.
   (C) You can vote by mail.
   (D) All of the above

17. Which of the following groups of Texas residents is largest? **(3)** (pp. 89–90)

   (A) The voting age population (VAP)
   (B) The voting eligible population (VEP)
   (C) Registered voters
   (D) People who voted in 2008

18. How does voter turnout in Texas compare to national turnout rates? **(3)** (pp. 90–91)

   (A) Turnout in Texas is about average compared to national turnout rates.
   (B) Turnout in Texas is below average compared to national turnout rates.
   (C) Turnout in Texas is above average compared to national turnout rates.
   (D) Turnout in Texas was once well above average but is now just below the national average.

19. Which of the following Texas elections would produce the highest turnout rate measured as a percentage of the voting eligible population (VEP)? **(3)** (p. 90)

   (A) A presidential election
   (B) A constitutional amendment election
   (C) A governor's election
   (D) A local election

20. Which of the following factors affects voter participation rates? **(3)** (pp. 90–91)

   (A) The average age of the population
   (B) The average level of education of the population
   (C) The average income level of the population
   (D) All of the above

21. Which of the following factors is associated with relatively low voter participation rates in Texas? **(4)** (pp. 90–91)

   (A) Neither political party has mounted a major GOTV campaign because Texas has not been a battleground state.
   (B) The population of Texas is relatively young.
   (C) A disproportionate number of Texans are recent immigrants to the state.
   (D) All of the above

22. Which of the following groups of Texans is underrepresented at the ballot box compared to its representation in the population of the state? **(4)** (p. 92)

   (A) African Americans
   (B) Whites
   (C) Latinos
   (D) None of the above

23. The Texas electorate is representative of the population of the state of Texas in which of the following respects? **(5)** (pp. 94–95)

   (A) Racial/ethnic composition
   (B) Income
   (C) Education
   (D) None of the above

24. Which of the following groups of Texans is underrepresented at the ballot box compared to their representation in the population? **(5)** (p. 95)

   (A) Whites
   (B) African Americans
   (C) Low-income Texans
   (D) All of the above

25. Which of the following groups is better represented among voters than among the population as a whole? **(5)** (p. 95)

   (A) Asians
   (B) Wealthy persons
   (C) Latinos
   (D) All of the above

Chapter 5: Interest Groups

Circle the correct answer.

1. Which of the following is an example of an interest group? **(1)** (p. 102)

   (A) Texas Trial Lawyers Association (TTLA)
   (B) Sierra Club
   (C) League of United Latin American Citizens (LULAC)
   (D) All of the above

2. The most powerful interest groups in Texas politics are which of the following? **(1)** (p. 103)

   (A) Business groups and trade associations
   (B) Racial and ethnic minority groups
   (C) Religious groups
   (D) Organized labor

3. Which of the following interest groups would be most likely to favor the state having a "good business climate"? **(1)** (p. 104)

   (A) Texas AFL-CIO
   (B) TTLA
   (C) Texas Association of Business (TAB)
   (D) LULAC

4. Which of the following factors would a group of business people *not* consider an important factor in the development of a good business climate? **(1)** (p. 104)

   (A) Low taxes on business
   (B) Strong labor unions
   (C) Good transportation system
   (D) Favorable regulation of business

5. Which of the following pairs of interest groups are on opposite sides of the issue of medical malpractice insurance reform? **(1)** (pp. 102 and 104)

   (A) AFL-CIO and TAB
   (B) NRA and Texas Right to Life
   (C) NAACP and LULAC
   (D) TTLA and TMA

6. Right-to-work laws are designed to accomplish which of the following goals? **(1)** (p. 108)

   (A) Limit the amount of money plaintiffs can recover from personal injury lawsuits
   (B) Ensure full employment in the state
   (C) Weaken labor unions
   (D) Guarantee workers the right to join a union

7. The Texas AFL-CIO would be most likely to favor which one of the following policy goals? **(1)** (p. 109)

   (A) Increasing the state minimum wage
   (B) Prohibiting abortion in the state
   (C) Lowering property tax rates
   (D) Limiting punitive damages in medical malpractice lawsuits

8. The Texas Farm Bureau would be most concerned with which of the following issues? **(1)** (pp. 109–110)

   (A) Raising the state minimum wage
   (B) Water development
   (C) Abortion
   (D) Gun control

9. Which of the following organizations would be most likely to advocate for the rights of Latinos? **(1)** (p. 110)

   (A) NAACP
   (B) LULAC
   (C) MADD
   (D) AFL-CIO

10. Which of the following is an organization that supports the interests of African Americans? **(1)** (p. 110)

    (A) NAACP
    (B) AFL-CIO
    (C) MADD
    (D) LULAC

11. Which of the following organizations would be most concerned about the problem of racial profiling? **(1)** (p. 110)

    (A) TMA
    (B) American Federation of State, County, and Municipal Employees (AFSCME)
    (C) LULAC
    (D) Sierra Club

12. Texans for Public Justice (TPJ) is an organization whose goals are to improve the quality of life for ordinary citizens of Texas. It is an example of which of the following types of organizations? **(1)** (p. 112)

    (A) Political action committees
    (B) Cause group
    (C) Advocacy group
    (D) Citizen group

13. An organization created to seek benefits on behalf of persons who are unable to represent their own interests is known as which of the following? **(1)** (p. 112)

    (A) Trade association
    (B) Cause group
    (C) Citizen group
    (D) Advocacy group

14. Which of the following groups is an environmental organization? **(1)** (p. 112)

    (A) TARAL
    (B) NRA
    (C) Sierra Club
    (D) AARP

15. Which pair of interest groups below would be most likely to agree on the issue of abortion? **(1)** (p. 112)

    (A) Sierra Club and Texas Association of Business (TAB)
    (B) LULAC and AARP
    (C) NRA and AFL-CIO
    (D) NOW and NARAL Pro-Choice Texas

16. Which of the following organizations would be most likely to support legislation to allow people with handgun licenses to carry concealed weapons on college campuses? **(1)** (p. 112)

    (A) TTLA
    (B) NRA
    (C) NARAL Pro-Choice Texas
    (D) MADD

17. Which of the following interest groups would be most likely to endorse legislation designed to give older homeowners relief on their property tax bills? **(1)** (p. 112)

    (A) AARP
    (B) Texas Medical Association
    (C) NARAL Pro-Choice Texas
    (D) Sierra Club

18. Which of the following is the most important issue for MADD? **(1)** (pp. 112–113)

    (A) Abortion
    (B) Drunk driving
    (C) Gay marriage
    (D) College admissions

19. An organization created to raise and distribute money in political campaigns is known as which of the following? **(2)** (p. 113)

    (A) Political action committee (PAC)
    (B) Interest group
    (C) Political party
    (D) Trade association

20. What is the limit on the amount of campaign contributions a PAC can give to candidates for statewide executive office or the legislature in Texas? **(2)** (p. 113)

    (A) $5,000 per candidate per election
    (B) $10,000 per candidate and $100,000 overall
    (C) $200,000 overall
    (D) Texas allows unlimited contributions.

21. What does "catching the late train" mean? **(2)** (p. 116)

    (A) Contributing to the winning candidate after an election in which you backed the losing candidate
    (B) Changing political parties after an election defeat
    (C) Forming an interest group after losing a legislative battle
    (D) Changing the name of a PAC after an election defeat

22. What is lobbying? **(2)** (p. 116)

    (A) Forming an organization to raise and distribute money during an election campaign
    (B) The communication of information by a representative of an interest group to a government official for the purpose of influencing a policy decision
    (C) Filing a lawsuit against a government agency that adopts a policy harmful to the position of an interest group
    (D) Endorsing candidates in an election

23. A lobbyist invites a member of the Texas legislature and her staff to a golf outing at which they discuss pending legislation. This action is an example of which of the following? **(2)** (p. 116)

    (A) Catching the late train
    (B) Litigation
    (C) Social lobbying
    (D) Racial profiling

24. Which of the following actions do interest groups take in order to gain legislative access? **(2)** (p. 117)

    (A) File a lawsuit against a member of the legislature.
    (B) Offer a member of the legislature a bribe.
    (C) Threaten to endorse a legislator's opponent in the next election.
    (D) Contribute generously to a legislator's reelection campaign.

25. Which of the following is *not* part of the alliance opposed to tort reform in Texas? **(2)** (p. 118)

    (A) Democratic Party
    (B) TTLA
    (C) Consumer groups
    (D) TMA

Chapter 6: Political Parties

Circle the correct answer.

1. A group of individuals who join together to seek public office in order to influence public policy is known as which of the following? **(1)** (p. 124)

   (A) Political party
   (B) Political action committee
   (C) Interest group
   (D) Issue network

2. An identifiable subgroup within a political party is known as which of the following? **(1)** (p. 125)

   (A) Interest group
   (B) Third party
   (C) Political action committee
   (D) Party faction

3. Which of the following individuals was able to participate in a Democratic precinct caucus held after the March 2010 primary election? **(2)** (p. 126)

   (A) Any citizen
   (B) Any citizen who voted in the primary election
   (C) Any citizen who voted in the Democratic primary
   (D) Only elected party officials

4. Which of the following is *not* one of the purposes of a state political party convention? **(2)** (p. 127)

   (A) To adopt a party platform
   (B) To elect a state party chairperson
   (C) To select party nominees for statewide office
   (D) To select delegates to the national party convention in presidential election years

5. Which of the following statements best describes the nature of party politics in Texas from the Civil War era until the middle of the twentieth century? **(3)** (pp. 128–129)

   (A) Texas was a one-party Republican state.
   (B) Texas was a one-party Democratic state.
   (C) Texas was divided evenly between the two parties.
   (D) Third parties competed equally with Democrats and Republicans for control of state government.

6. Why were most white native Texans loyal members of the Democratic Party after the Civil War era? **(3)** (pp. 128–129)

   (A) They agreed with the Democratic Party on economic issues.
   (B) Most Texans were poor and the Democrats were the party of poor people.
   (C) They were hostile to the Republican Party because of its association with the Union during the Civil War era.
   (D) All of the above

7. The liberal wing of the Democratic Party favored which of the following positions? **(3)** (p. 129)

   (A) Higher taxes on business and industry
   (B) More government spending on healthcare and education

   (C) Voting rights for minority group members
   (D) All of the above

8. Which of the following groups did not support the liberal faction of the Democratic Party? **(3)** (p. 129)

   (A) Business people
   (B) Low-income voters
   (C) African Americans
   (D) Latinos

9. Which of the following political groupings in Texas was helped most by the increased voting participation of minority Texans? **(3)** (p. 131)

   (A) Liberal Democrats
   (B) Conservative Democrats
   (C) Republicans
   (D) Independents

10. John Tower was a U.S. Senator representing which of the following political groupings in Texas? **(3)** (p. 131)

    (A) Conservative Democrats
    (B) Republicans
    (C) Independents
    (D) Liberal Democrats

11. A Yellow Dog Democrat can be best described as which of the following? **(3)** (p. 131)

    (A) Someone who always votes Democratic.
    (B) Someone who switched from the Democratic to the Republican Party.
    (C) Someone who calls him- or herself a Democrat but often votes Republican.
    (D) Someone who switched from the Republican Party to the Democratic Party.

12. Which of the following factors helped the Republican Party emerge as a political force in Texas? **(3)** (pp. 131–132)

    (A) People were attracted to Franklin Roosevelt and the New Deal.
    (B) African Americans switched parties from the Democratic Party to the Republican Party.
    (C) Many conservative white Democrats became disenchanted with the national Democratic Party because they thought it was too liberal.
    (D) All of the above

13. Which of the following factors helps explain the current party balance in Texas? **(4)** (pp. 133–134)

    (A) Significantly more Texans identify with the Republican Party than call themselves Democrats.
    (B) Significantly more Texans identify with the Democratic Party than call themselves Republicans.
    (C) Significantly more Texans consider themselves liberal than call themselves conservative.
    (D) Significantly more Texans consider themselves conservative than call themselves liberal.

14. Which of the following statements was true about the party balance in Texas after the 2008 election? **(4)** (p. 134)

(A) A majority of the members of the Texas House were Republicans.
(B) A majority of the members of the Texas Senate were Republicans.
(C) All statewide elected officials were Republicans.
(D) All of the above

15. Democratic candidates do best with which of the following groups of voters? **(5)** (p. 135)

(A) Upper income voters
(B) White voters
(C) Latino voters
(D) Suburban voters

16. Democratic candidates run the most strongly among which of the following groups of voters? **(5)** (p. 135)

(A) African Americans
(B) Latinos
(C) Whites
(D) Democrats run equally well with each group.

17. Which of the following areas would be most likely to support a Democratic candidate? **(5)** (p. 136)

(A) A rural county in West Texas
(B) A suburban county outside a major city
(C) A small town in Central Texas
(D) An inner-city Houston neighborhood

18. Which of the following groups of voters would you expect to be the strongest support group for the Republican Party in Texas? **(5)** (pp. 135–136)

(A) Younger Latino men
(B) Older white men
(C) Younger white men
(D) Older African American women

19. Which of the following groups is aligned with the Democratic Party? **(6)** (pp. 136–137)

(A) Religious conservatives
(B) Farm groups
(C) Pro-life groups
(D) Organized labor

20. Which of the following groups is allied with the Republican Party? **(6)** (pp. 136–137)

(A) Trial lawyers
(B) Anti-abortion groups
(C) Consumer groups
(D) Minority-rights organizations

21. On which of the following issues do the Texas Republican and Democratic Parties take opposing positions? **(7)** (pp. 137–142)

(A) Minimum wage laws
(B) Gay and lesbian rights
(C) Abortion rights
(D) All of the above

22. Which of the following is *not* a position taken by the Texas Republican Party? **(7)** (pp. 137–142)

(A) Opposition to amnesty for undocumented workers
(B) Opposition to the election of state judges
(C) Opposition to gay marriage
(D) Opposition to bilingual education

23. Which of the following philosophical positions reflect the Texas Democratic platform rather than the Texas Republican platform? **(7)** (pp. 137–142)

(A) Government should reduce regulation in order to enhance economic growth.
(B) Government should take action to strengthen the traditional family.
(C) Government has a role to play in addressing social problems.
(D) All of the above

24. Which of the following groups will be a larger proportion of the Texas electorate in 2020 than it is today? **(8)** (pp. 143–144)

(A) Latinos
(B) Rural residents
(C) Whites
(D) The electorate is not expected to change between now and 2020.

25. Why does the textbook declare that the electoral base of the Texas Republican Party is shrinking? **(8)** (pp. 143–144)

(A) Increased border security has reduced illegal immigration.
(B) Many Latino residents of the state are ineligible to vote because they are non-citizens.
(C) The white population is shrinking.
(D) All of the above

Chapter 7: Elections

Circle the correct answer.

1. An election system that provides for the election of nearly every public official of any significance is known as which of the following? **(1)** (p. 150)

    (A) Straight-ticket voting
    (B) Long ballot
    (C) Split-ticket voting
    (D) Retrospective voting

2. Which of the following elections is always held in November? **(2)** (p. 151)

    (A) Primary election
    (B) Primary runoff election
    (C) General election
    (D) All of the above

3. Which of the following is an election contest between candidates of different political parties? **(2)** (p. 151)

    (A) General election
    (B) Primary election
    (C) Primary runoff election
    (D) All of the above

4. In the fall general election, Republican A won 52 percent of the vote, Democrat B took 45 percent, and Independent C captured the remaining 3 percent. What was the outcome? **(2)** (p. 152)

    (A) Republican A won by having the most votes.
    (B) Republican A and Democrat B faced each other in a runoff because they were the top two candidates.
    (C) Republican A won by having a majority of the vote. Otherwise, a runoff would have been held.
    (D) All three candidates took part in a runoff.

5. In the fall general election, Republican A won 40 percent of the vote, Democrat B took 35 percent, and Independent C captured the remaining 25 percent. What was the outcome? **(2)** (p. 152)

    (A) Republican A won by having the most votes.
    (B) Republican A and Democrat B faced off in a runoff because they were the top two candidates.
    (C) Republican A won by having at least 40 percent of the vote. Otherwise, a runoff would have been held.
    (D) All three candidates took part in a runoff.

6. In 2008, more than twice as many Texas voters participated in the Democratic primary than in the Republican primary. Which of the following reasons is the best explanation for that? **(2)** (p. 153)

    (A) The Democratic Party is the majority party in Texas.
    (B) In Texas, Democratic voters are more likely to turn out than Republican voters in all types of elections.
    (C) Democrats are used to voting in primary elections and Republicans are not.
    (D) The level of interest in the Democratic presidential nomination contest between Obama and Clinton was greater than the interest in the Republican presidential nomination race.

7. In the March primary, Candidate A received 40 percent of the vote, Candidate B received 35 percent, and Candidate C received the remaining 25 percent. What was the outcome? **(2)** (p. 154)

    (A) Candidate A won by having the most votes.
    (B) Candidates A and B faced off in a runoff because they were the top two candidates.
    (C) Candidates A and B faced off in a runoff because no one candidate had a majority and Candidate A and Candidate B were the top two finishers.
    (D) All three candidates took part in a runoff.

8. Voter turnout is typically the greatest in Texas for which of the following elections? **(2)** (pp. 154–155)

    (A) Republican primary
    (B) Democratic primary
    (C) Primary runoff elections combined
    (D) General election

9. What is the purpose of a presidential preference primary? **(2)** (p. 155)

    (A) To award national convention delegates to presidential candidates
    (B) To determine which candidate wins the state's electoral vote
    (C) To select a president and vice president
    (D) To identify the people who will serve as electoral college electors for the state of Texas

10. Who won the Texas Two-Step in 2008? **(2)** (p. 156)

    (A) Hillary Clinton won.
    (B) Hillary Clinton won the primary, but Barack Obama won the caucus and took the most delegates altogether.
    (C) Barack Obama won the primary, but Hillary Clinton won the caucus and took the most delegates altogether.
    (D) John McCain won.

11. Which of the following elections is typically held in odd-numbered years? **(2)** (p. 157)

    (A) Primary election
    (B) Primary runoff
    (C) General election
    (D) Local election

12. Which of the following Texas elections is typically a nonpartisan election? **(2)** (p. 157)

    (A) Election for mayor
    (B) Election for the Texas Supreme Court
    (C) Election for attorney general
    (D) Election for the state legislature

13. What is the purpose of a bond election? **(2)** (p. 158)

    (A) To set the amount of money a criminal defendant must pay to get out of jail
    (B) To ratify constitutional amendments
    (C) To authorize local governments to borrow money
    (D) To remove an elected official from office

14. Which of the following officials is *not* elected in an at-large election? **(3)** (p. 159)

    (A) State senator
    (B) Lieutenant governor
    (C) Attorney general
    (D) U.S. Senator from Texas

15. What is the concept of one person, one vote? **(3)** (p. 160)

    (A) Legislative districts should be drawn to have the same or nearly the same population.
    (B) Everyone should vote in order for democracy to function effectively.
    (C) People voting more than once are guilty of breaking the law.
    (D) Legislative districts must be redrawn every 10 years.

16. What is the purpose of the Voting Rights Act (VRA)? **(3)** (p. 161)

    (A) To ensure that legislative districts have nearly equal population
    (B) To prevent gerrymandering
    (C) To eliminate at-large elections
    (D) To protect the voting rights of racial and ethnic minority groups

17. The VRA has had which of the following effects in Texas? **(3)** (pp. 161–162)

    (A) Increasing the number of minority legislators and members of Congress
    (B) Increasing the number of Republicans in the legislature and in Congress
    (C) Requiring Texas to submit redistricting plans to the Justice Department for approval before they take effect
    (D) All of the above

18. Which of the following is responsible for redrawing state legislative districts every ten years? **(3)** (pp. 162–163)

    (A) U.S. Congress
    (B) State legislature
    (C) Governor
    (D) Federal courts

19. Why did Congressman Tom DeLay and the Republican leadership in the legislature want to redraw congressional districts in 2003? **(3)** (pp. 163–164)

    (A) To increase the number of Latino members of Congress from Texas
    (B) To increase the number of Republican members of Congress from Texas

    (C) To take account of major population shifts since the last census
    (D) To correct errors that took place in the redistricting two years earlier

20. What is the most expensive cost for major statewide election campaigns? **(4)** (p. 168)

    (A) Television
    (B) Polling
    (C) Travel
    (D) Consultants

21. How much money can a wealthy individual spend on his or her own campaign for an office in Texas government? **(4)** (p. 168)

    (A) None
    (B) $5,000
    (C) $500,000
    (D) The amount is unlimited.

22. How much money can a wealthy contributor give to a candidate for governor of Texas? **(4)** (p. 169)

    (A) $5,000
    (B) $500,000
    (C) $1,000,000
    (D) The amount is unlimited.

23. Why do incumbent members of Congress and the state legislature usually win reelection? **(5)** (p. 172)

    (A) They are usually better known than their challengers.
    (B) They can usually raise more money than their challengers.
    (C) Most districts are stacked in favor of one political party or the other, giving most incumbents a free ride in the general election.
    (D) All of the above

24. "I am voting against the governor because I am unhappy about the state's support for higher education and my college tuition keeps going up and up." The above statement is an expression of which of the following concepts? **(5)** (p. 174)

    (A) Retrospective voting
    (B) Electoral mandate
    (C) Coattail effect
    (D) Prospective voting

25. A political phenomenon in which a strong candidate for one office gives a boost to fellow party members on the same ballot seeking other offices is known as which of the following? **(5)** (p. 175)

    (A) Retrospective voting
    (B) Electoral mandate
    (C) Coattail effect
    (D) Prospective voting

Chapter 8: The Texas Legislature

Circle the correct answer.

1. How many members serve in the Texas legislature? **(1)** (p. 181)

   (A) There are 31 members of the Senate and 150 members of the House.
   (B) There are 100 members of the Senate and 435 members of the House.
   (C) There are 150 members of the Senate and 31 members of the House.
   (D) There are 100 members of the House and 435 members of the Senate.

2. In the 2010 election, the last election before redistricting, how many members of the legislature stood for reelection? **(1)** (p. 181)

   (A) All members of the House and Senate
   (B) No members because they all stood for election in 2008 and will not run again until 2012
   (C) All members of the House but only half the Senate
   (D) Half of the members of the House and one-third of the members of the Senate

3. How often does the Texas legislature meet in regular session? **(1)** (p. 182)

   (A) It meets every year for 140 days.
   (B) It meets in odd-numbered years for 140 days.
   (C) It meets in odd-numbered years for 140 days and in even-numbered years for 60 days.
   (D) It meets every year for as long as it takes to complete its work.

4. Who has the authority to call the legislature into special session? **(1)** (p. 182)

   (A) The governor, lieutenant governor, and speaker can call special sessions by majority vote.
   (B) The legislature can call itself into special session by majority vote of each chamber.
   (C) Either the governor, lieutenant governor, or the speaker can call a special session.
   (D) Only the governor can call a special session of the legislature.

5. What controversial issue caused a legislative logjam at the end of the 2009 session and led to the failure of thousands of pieces of legislation? **(1)** (p. 184)

   (A) Voter ID
   (B) Global warming
   (C) Abortion
   (D) Property taxes

6. Which of the following groups is over-represented among the membership of the legislature? **(2)** (pp. 184–185)

   (A) Women
   (B) Latinos
   (C) African Americans
   (D) White men

7. How much money do members of the legislature make? **(2)** (p. 185)

   (A) $7,200 a year
   (B) $15,000 a year
   (C) $35,000 a year
   (D) $100,000 a year

8. How does the Texas legislature compare and contrast with legislatures in other states? **(2)** (pp. 181–186)

   (A) Most state legislatures meet in regular session every year, but the Texas legislature meets every other year.
   (B) Most state legislators are paid more than members of the Texas legislature.
   (C) Most state legislatures are bicameral and so is the Texas legislature.
   (D) All of the above

9. What is the most important reason for turnover in the Texas legislature? **(2)** (pp. 186–187)

   (A) Term limits
   (B) Defeat for reelection
   (C) Voluntary retirement
   (D) Death

10. Which of the following is the most important figure in the Texas Senate? **(3)** (p. 189)

    (A) Speaker
    (B) Lieutenant governor
    (C) Vice president
    (D) Majority leader

11. How is the lieutenant governor normally chosen? **(3)** (p. 189)

    (A) The lieutenant governor is elected by the membership of the Senate.
    (B) The lieutenant governor is appointed by the governor.
    (C) The lieutenant governor is elected in a statewide election.
    (D) The lieutenant governor is elected running on a ticket with the governor.

12. Which of the following is the most important figure in the Texas House? **(3)** (p. 190)

    (A) Lieutenant governor
    (B) Vice president
    (C) Majority leader
    (D) Speaker

13. An individual member of the Texas House is interested in becoming Speaker in the next session of the legislature. What step does that individual take to accomplish his or her goal? **(3)** (p. 190)

  (A) Begin raising money and organizing a campaign for a statewide election
  (B) Lobby the governor for the appointment
  (C) Begin collecting pledge cards from other House members
  (D) None of the above

14. Which of the following agencies plays the greatest role in state budget policy? **(3)** (p. 191)

  (A) Legislative Redistricting Board (LRB)
  (B) Legislative Budget Board (LBB)
  (C) Land Commission
  (D) State Board of Education (SBOE)

15. How are committee chairs chosen in the Texas House? **(3)** (p. 193)

  (A) They are elected by the membership.
  (B) They are appointed by the governor.
  (C) They are chosen on the basis of seniority.
  (D) They are chosen by the Speaker.

16. How are committee chairs chosen in the Texas Senate? **(3)** (p. 193)

  (A) They are chosen by the lieutenant governor.
  (B) They are elected by the membership.
  (C) They are appointed by the governor.
  (D) They are chosen on the basis of seniority.

17. What is HB 201? **(4)** (p. 194)

  (A) A bill introduced in the legislature in 2001
  (B) A bill introduced in the Texas Senate
  (C) The 201st bill introduced in the Texas House
  (D) The 201st bill introduced in the Texas Senate

18. A hearing on a bill is most likely to take place in which of the following? **(4)** (p. 195)

  (A) On the floor
  (B) In standing committee
  (C) In conference committee
  (D) When it reaches the governor's desk

19. What is the purpose of a fiscal note? **(4)** (p. 195)

  (A) To indicate the cost of a measure to the state (if any)
  (B) To indicate whether the measure is consistent with the Texas Constitution
  (C) To measure the level of support for the measure in the legislature
  (D) To indicate whether the governor supports or opposes the measure

20. What is the purpose of the House calendar? **(4)** (p. 196)

  (A) To determine when the legislature adjourns
  (B) To set the priority order for consideration of legislation on the House floor
  (C) To indicate the cost of a measure
  (D) To assign House members to committee

21. What is the two-thirds rule in the Senate? **(4)** (pp. 196–197)

  (A) Legislation cannot reach the floor of the Senate unless two-thirds of the membership agrees to suspend the rules.
  (B) Legislation cannot pass unless two-thirds of the Senate votes for final passage.
  (C) Constitutional amendments must be proposed by a two-thirds vote.
  (D) Two-thirds of the members of the Senate must be present in order to conduct official business.

22. Is the filibuster an effective weapon in the Texas Senate? **(4)** (p. 197)

  (A) Not usually, because it can be halted by majority vote.
  (B) Yes, because it takes a two-thirds vote to halt it.
  (C) No, because Senate rules prevent the filibuster.
  (D) None of the above.

23. On which of the following issues are members of the Texas legislature most likely to vote what they perceive to be the wishes of their constituents? **(5)** (pp. 201–202)

  (A) Issues that are noncontroversial
  (B) Issues involving money
  (C) Issues that are highly complex
  (D) Issues that are high profile

24. Which of the following members of the Texas legislature would be most likely to favor repeal or modification of the top 10 percent rule? **(5)** (pp. 202–203)

  (A) A Republican
  (B) A member representing an inner-city minority district
  (C) A member representing a wealthy suburban district
  (D) A member representing a rural district

25. Which of the following terms most accurately describes the history of policymaking in the Texas legislature? **(5)** (p. 204)

  (A) It has adopted politically liberal policies.
  (B) It has adopted politically conservative policies.
  (C) It has been a highly partisan body.
  (D) It has been politically moderate.

Chapter 9: Executive Branch

Circle the correct answer.

1. Which of the following recent governors *least* fits the traditional image of a Texas governor? **(1)** (pp. 211–212)

    (A) Rick Perry
    (B) George W. Bush
    (C) Ann Richards
    (D) Bill Clements

2. What is the impact of the governor declaring a particular legislative measure an emergency? **(1)** (p. 213)

    (A) Emergency measures receive priority attention on the floor of the House.
    (B) Legislators can introduce emergency measures after the deadline for introducing bills.
    (C) The action focuses legislative and public attention on a particular measure.
    (D) All of the above.

3. The legislature passes a measure to authorize the construction of a medical school in El Paso. Which of the following options does the governor *not* have for dealing with this particular bill? **(1)** (p. 214)

    (A) The governor can sign the bill into law.
    (B) The governor can veto the bill.
    (C) The governor can allow the bill to become law without signature.
    (D) The governor can sign the bill while issuing a line-item veto to remove parts of it that the governor does not like.

4. The legislature passes an appropriation measure that includes funding for the medical school in El Paso. What are the governor's options for dealing with this particular bill? **(1)** (p. 214)

    (A) The governor can sign the bill into law.
    (B) The governor can veto the entire bill.
    (C) The governor can sign the bill while issuing a line-item veto to remove parts of it that the governor does not like.
    (D) All of the above

5. Which of the following statements about special sessions is true? **(1)** (p. 214)

    (A) The governor sets the agenda for special sessions.
    (B) The governor shares the power to call special sessions with the lieutenant governor and the Speaker of the House.
    (C) Special sessions may last no more than 60 days.
    (D) All of the above

6. Which of the following statements about the appointive power of the governor is true? **(1)** (pp. 214–216)

    (A) The governor appoints a cabinet, including an attorney general, secretary of state, comptroller, and commissioner of agriculture.
    (B) The governor appoints the judges of the state's highest courts.

    (C) The governor's appointees must be confirmed by a two-thirds vote of the Texas Senate.
    (D) None of the above

7. Which of the following is true of the judicial powers of the governor? **(1)** (pp. 216–217)

    (A) The governor appoints judges to fill vacancies in state district and appellate courts.
    (B) The governor has the sole authority to pardon individuals convicted of serious criminal offenses.
    (C) Although the members of the Texas Supreme Court are elected, the governor designates one judge as chief justice.
    (D) All of the above

8. Which of the following plays the most important role in drafting the Texas state budget? **(1)** (p. 217)

    (A) Governor
    (B) Legislative Redistricting Board
    (C) Legislative Budget Board
    (D) Comptroller of Public Accounts

9. Which of the following officials participates directly in the budget execution process in Texas? **(1)** (p. 217)

    (A) Comptroller
    (B) Governor
    (C) Attorney general
    (D) Chair of House Appropriations Committee

10. Which of the following executive officials in Texas is appointed by the governor? **(2)** (pp. 219 and 226)

    (A) Attorney general
    (B) Comptroller
    (C) Secretary of state
    (D) Commissioner of agriculture

11. Which of the following officials is elected? **(2)** (p. 226)

    (A) Railroad commissioner
    (B) Secretary of state
    (C) Insurance commissioner
    (D) All of the above

12. Which of the following officials issues written opinions to interpret state laws and the state constitution? **(2)** (p. 224)

    (A) Agriculture commissioner
    (B) Lieutenant governor
    (C) Attorney general
    (D) Comptroller

13. Which of the following officials estimates state revenues for the next biennium at the beginning of each legislative session? **(2)** (p. 225)

    (A) Agriculture commissioner
    (B) Lieutenant governor
    (C) Attorney general
    (D) Comptroller

14. A business person operating a retail store would work closely with which of the following state officials on administering the state's sales tax? **(2)** (p. 224)

    (A) Secretary of state
    (B) Comptroller
    (C) Attorney general
    (D) Land commissioner

15. If you suspect that the gasoline pump at the local service station is shortchanging purchasers, you can report your suspicion to which of the following state officials? **(2)** (p. 225)

    (A) Agriculture commissioner
    (B) Attorney general
    (C) Comptroller
    (D) Land commissioner

16. Students doing research on state election results can find data at the website of which of the following state officials? **(2)** (p. 226)

    (A) Comptroller
    (B) Attorney general
    (C) Secretary of state
    (D) Land commissioner

17. Which of the following agencies regulates oil and gas production in the state? **(2)** (pp. 226–228)

    (A) Public Utility Commission
    (B) Railroad Commission
    (C) Texas Commission on Environmental Quality
    (D) Land Commission

18. Which of the following agencies is led by a 15-member elected board? **(2)** (p. 229)

    (A) State Board of Education
    (B) Railroad Commission
    (C) Texas Higher Education Coordinating Board
    (D) Public Utility Commission

19. A local businessperson has been appointed to serve on the Board of Regents of Texas A&M University. Which description best explains the job? **(2)** (pp. 230–231)

    (A) University regents are responsible for running the daily affairs of the university.
    (B) Serving as a member of a university board of regents is a full-time job.
    (C) University regents earn $100,000 a year.
    (D) The board of regents sets basic university policy, but it does not manage the daily affairs of the university.

20. The process that involves the government contracting with private business to implement government programs is known as which of the following? **(2)** (p. 233)

    (A) Rulemaking
    (B) Privatization
    (C) Budget execution authority
    (D) Impeachment

21. If the governor is unhappy with the policy decisions of the State Board of Education (SBOE), what can he or she do to influence its actions? **(3)** (pp. 234 and 237)

    (A) The governor can remove its members and appoint replacements.
    (B) The governor can remove the members that he or she appointed but only with the approval of the Texas Senate.
    (C) The governor can order the SBOE to change its policy position.
    (D) The governor has little, if any, direct power to influence the SBOE.

22. If the governor is unhappy with the policy decisions of the Texas Department of Parks and Wildlife, what can he or she do to influence its actions? **(3)** (p. 237)

    (A) The governor can appoint new board members as the terms of the old board members expire.
    (B) The governor can remove its board members and appoint new ones.
    (C) The governor can order the agency to change its policy position.
    (D) The governor has little, if any, power to influence the agency.

23. The Public Utility Commission (PUC) is a rulemaking body. When the PUC adopts a rule, what is it doing? **(3)** (pp. 233–234)

    (A) It is overriding a law passed by the legislature.
    (B) It is adopting a legally binding regulation.
    (C) It is recommending a new law to the legislature and the governor.
    (D) It is adopting procedures for its own internal management.

24. An agency is scheduled for sunset review this year, but the legislature takes no action. What is the status of the agency? **(3)** (p. 235)

    (A) It will have to undergo sunset review in the next session of the legislature.
    (B) It will have to shut down operations unless the governor signs an executive order to keep it in operation.
    (C) It will have to shut down operations.
    (D) Nothing.

25. Which of the following powers does the governor of Texas have for influencing administrative policymaking? **(3)** (p. 237)

    (A) The governor appoints most state executives, including the attorney general and the comptroller.
    (B) The governor has the authority to appoint the members of most state boards.
    (C) The governor has the authority to state executives and board members if he or she disagrees with their policy decisions.
    (D) All of the above

Circle the correct answer.

1. Who are the litigants in a criminal case? **(1)** (p. 243)

   (A) Civil defendant and prosecutor
   (B) Criminal defendant and the crime victim
   (C) Prosecutor and the criminal defendant
   (D) Judge and jury

2. Which of the following is a type of criminal dispute? **(1)** (p. 243)

   (A) Misdemeanor case
   (B) Tort case
   (C) Contract case
   (D) All of the above

3. Which of the following would be a misdemeanor as opposed to a felony offense? **(1)** (p. 243)

   (A) Aggravated assault
   (B) Murder
   (C) Robbery
   (D) Speeding through a school zone

4. Who has the burden of proof in a criminal case? **(1)** (p. 243)

   (A) Prosecutor
   (B) Defendant
   (C) Crime victim
   (D) Judge

5. Who has the burden of proof in a civil case? **(1)** (p. 244)

   (A) Defendant
   (B) Plaintiff
   (C) Judge
   (D) Jury

6. Assume that you are a member of a jury in a criminal case. After the evidence is presented, you think it is more likely than not that the defendant is guilty but it is a fairly close call in your judgment. How do you vote as a member of the jury? **(1)** (p. 243)

   (A) You vote to convict the defendant because you think the defendant is guilty.
   (B) You vote to convict because the defendant has failed to prove innocence.
   (C) You vote not guilty because the prosecution has failed to prove guilt beyond a reasonable doubt.
   (D) You vote not guilty because the prosecution has failed to prove the case by a preponderance of the evidence.

7. Which of the following is *not* an example of a civil case? **(1)** (p. 244)

   (A) A dispute over injuries suffered in an automobile accident
   (B) A trial of an individual accused of breaking into a home
   (C) A dispute over a will
   (D) A child custody battle

8. Which of the following is an example of a tort case? **(1)** (p. 245)

   (A) A personal injury
   (B) A divorce proceeding
   (C) A theft of property
   (D) A dispute over the estate of a deceased person

9. A procedure in which a defendant agrees to plead guilty in order to receive punishment less than the maximum for an offense is known as which of the following? **(2)** (p. 245)

   (A) Adversary proceeding
   (B) Trial
   (C) Appeal
   (D) Plea bargain

10. Which of the following is characteristic of a trial but would *not* be characteristic of an appellate proceeding? **(2)** (pp. 245–246)

    (A) A jury weighing guilt or innocence
    (B) A witness presenting testimony
    (C) A prosecuting attorney introducing evidence
    (D) All of the above

11. The taking of a case from a lower court to a higher court by the losing party in a lower court decision is known as which of the following? **(2)** (p. 246)

    (A) Adversary proceeding
    (B) Trial
    (C) Appeal
    (D) Plea bargain

12. A jury acquits a defendant of a criminal charge. New evidence subsequently emerges that indicates that the defendant is guilty after all. What, if anything, could the prosecutor do? **(2)** (p. 246)

    (A) The prosecutor can do nothing because the Constitution protects against double jeopardy.
    (B) The prosecutor can appeal the acquittal to a higher court.
    (C) The prosecutor can ask a grand jury to reconsider the case.
    (D) The prosecutor can ask the judge to reconsider the original verdict.

13. Which of the following courts would be most likely to try a case involving a traffic ticket? **(3)** (p. 247)

    (A) District court
    (B) County court
    (C) Municipal court
    (D) Texas Supreme Court

14. Which of the following courts would try a felony criminal case? (3) (p. 249)

    (A) Municipal court
    (B) Justice of the peace court
    (C) District court
    (D) County court

15. Which of the following courts would try a misdemeanor case involving theft? (3) (pp. 248–249)

    (A) Municipal court
    (B) Justice of the peace court
    (C) District court
    (D) County court

16. Which of the following courts would try a multi-million dollar civil suit? (3) (p. 249)

    (A) District court
    (B) Court of appeals
    (C) Municipal court
    (D) Texas Supreme Court

17. Which of the following courts would neither try nor hear the appeal of an assault case? (3) (pp. 252–263)

    (A) District court
    (B) Court of appeals
    (C) Texas Supreme Court
    (D) Texas Court of Criminal Appeals

18. Which of the following courts would neither try nor hear the appeal of a medical malpractice lawsuit? (3) (pp. 251–252)

    (A) District court
    (B) Court of appeals
    (C) Texas Supreme Court
    (D) Texas Court of Criminal Appeals

19. Which of the following courts decides cases by majority vote of its nine members? (3) (pp. 251–252)

    (A) Court of appeals
    (B) District court
    (C) Texas Court of Criminal Appeals
    (D) Municipal court

20. Which of the following legal proceedings would take place in the Texas Supreme Court? (3) (pp. 252–253)

    (A) A divorce trial
    (B) The appeal of a burglary conviction
    (C) A capital murder trial
    (D) None of the above

21. How long are the terms served by appellate court judges in Texas? (4) (p. 254)

    (A) Eight years
    (B) Six years
    (C) Four years
    (D) Two years

22. How are district court judges chosen in Texas? (4) (p. 255)

    (A) Nonpartisan election
    (B) Missouri Plan
    (C) Partisan election
    (D) Gubernatorial appointment

23. An individual without a law degree would be qualified to serve as a judge on which of the following Texas courts? (4) (p. 255)

    (A) Justice of the peace court
    (B) District court
    (C) Courts of appeals
    (D) None of the above

24. Why are candidates for the Texas Supreme Court typically able to raise more money than candidates for the Texas Court of Criminal Appeals? (5) (pp. 256–257)

    (A) State law limits contributions for candidates for the Texas Court of Criminal Appeals and it does not limit contributions to Supreme Court candidates.
    (B) The Texas Supreme Court hears appeals of cases from the Texas Court of Criminal Appeals, so it is more important.
    (C) The litigants who appear before the Texas Supreme Court (insurance companies, bankers, business people, etc.) have more money than the litigants who appear before the Texas Court of Criminal Appeals.
    (D) All of the above

25. Which of the following steps is not part of Merit Selection or the Missouri Plan method of judicial selection? (5) (pp. 260–261)

    (A) A commission draws up a short list of qualified candidates to fill a judicial vacancy.
    (B) The governor selects an appointee from the list.
    (C) The Texas Senate must confirm the appointment by a two-thirds vote.
    (D) The Texas Supreme Court evaluates the judge's performance every four years and determines whether the judge stays in office.

Chapter 11: City Government

Circle the correct answer.

1. Which of the following is true about the legal authority of Texas cities? **(1)** (p. 271)

   (A) Cities must conform to state law.
   (B) Cities must conform to federal law.
   (C) Cities must conform to the Texas Constitution.
   (D) All of the above

2. Which of the following statements about a general law city is true? **(1)** (pp. 272–273)

   (A) It may only exercise those powers specifically granted under state law.
   (B) It must have a city charter.
   (C) Voters must approve its incorporation.
   (D) All of the above

3. Which of the following statements about home rule cities is true? **(1)** (pp. 272–273)

   (A) It can annex only with the approval of the residents of the area to be annexed.
   (B) It is bound by Dillon's Rule.
   (C) It must have at least 5,000 residents.
   (D) All of the above

4. A structure of municipal government in which the voters elect a mayor as the chief executive officer of the city as well as a council that serves as a legislative body is known as which of the following? **(2)** (p. 273)

   (A) Mayor–council form of city government
   (B) Home rule city
   (C) General law city
   (D) City manager form of city government

5. Which of the following Texas cities uses the mayor–council form of city government? **(2)** (p. 275)

   (A) Dallas
   (B) Houston
   (C) San Antonio
   (D) All of the above

6. Which of the following statements is *not* true about the mayor–council form of city government? **(2)** (pp. 273–275)

   (A) It is the traditional form of city government for large cities in the United States.
   (B) It is found in all the nation's major cities, including Houston, Dallas, and San Antonio.
   (C) In the strong mayor variation, the mayor prepares the budget.
   (D) The city council serves as a legislative body.

7. In which of the following forms of city government does the mayor have the most policymaking influence? **(2)** (pp. 273–274)

   (A) Mayor–council, strong mayor variation
   (B) Mayor–council, weak mayor variation
   (C) Council manager
   (D) The mayor is equally powerful in all three forms of city government.

8. Which of the following election systems is the most popular method for choosing city councils in Texas? **(3)** (p. 278)

   (A) Appointment by the mayor
   (B) District election method
   (C) Cumulative voting method
   (D) At-large election method

9. Which of the following factors led to the election of city councils in most of the state's big cities that were more ethnically and racially diverse than ever before? **(3)** (pp. 280–281)

   (A) The adoption of at-large election systems
   (B) The adoption of mayor–council systems of city government
   (C) The adoption of district election systems
   (D) The adoption of council–manager systems of city government

10. A city opens a series of neighborhood health clinics to provide basic healthcare to low-income families. This action is an example of which of the following? **(4)** (pp. 281–282)

    (A) Developmental urban policy
    (B) Redistributive urban policy
    (C) Allocational urban policy
    (D) None of the above

11. Police and fire protection are examples of which of the following? **(4)** (pp. 281–282)

    (A) Developmental urban policy
    (B) Redistributive urban policy
    (C) Allocational urban policy
    (D) None of the above

12. Texas cities provide all but which one of the following services? **(4)** (p. 283)

    (A) Fire protection
    (B) Libraries
    (C) Garbage pickup
    (D) Public education

13. Which of the following is *not* a revenue source for Texas cities? **(4)** (p. 284)

    (A) Sales tax
    (B) Property tax
    (C) Income tax
    (D) Franchise tax

14. What is the purpose of a homestead exemption? **(4)** (p. 284)

    (A) To exempt homeowners from zoning laws
    (B) To give a property tax break to homeowners
    (C) To permit home-based businesses in a residential area
    (D) To grant homeowners the right to vote on annexation

15. A property owner can claim a homestead exemption on which of the following? (4) (p. 284)

(A) A primary residence
(B) A rented house
(C) A small business establishment
(D) All of the above

16. A program in which a local government promises to earmark increased property tax revenues, generated by development in a designated area called a tax increment financing district, to fund improvements in the area, such as roads, parks, sidewalks, and street lighting, is known as which of the following? (4) (p. 286)

(A) Homestead exemption
(B) Redistributive urban policy
(C) Extraterritoriality
(D) Tax increment financing

17. What is the maximum amount of territory a city of 100 square miles can annex in a single year (assuming that it annexed its full allotment in previous years)? (4) (p. 288)

(A) None
(B) 100 square miles
(C) 10 square miles
(D) An unlimited amount

18. Which of the following is not a reason a city would annex a subdivision? (4) (pp. 287–288)

(A) To expand its property tax base
(B) To increase suburban shopping opportunities for inner-city residents
(C) To prevent the incorporation of surrounding municipalities
(D) To increase the amount of federal grant money it receives

19. Strategic Partnership Agreements are negotiated in regard to which of the following? (4) (pp. 289–290)

(A) Annexation
(B) Zoning
(C) Tax abatement
(D) Enterprise zones

20. You own property in the ETJ of a major city. What impact does the ETJ have on you? (4) (p. 290)

(A) If you build on the property, you must follow city construction ordinances and regulations.
(B) You must pay property taxes to the city.
(C) You can vote in city elections.
(D) All of the above

21. The governmental designation of tracts of land for industrial, commercial, or residential use is known as which of the following? (4) (p. 291)

(A) Zoning
(B) Deed restriction
(C) Capital improvement
(D) Housing code

22. Which of the following is a private agreement as opposed to a governmental ordinance? (4) (pp. 292–293)

(A) Zoning
(B) Deed restriction
(C) Capital improvement
(D) Building code

23. The view that political power is held by a small group of people who dominate politics by controlling economic resources is known as which of the following? (5) (p. 294)

(A) Elite theory
(B) Pluralism
(C) Democracy
(D) Political machine

24. The view that diverse groups of elites with differing interests compete with one another to control policy in various issue areas is known as which of the following? (5) (p. 296)

(A) Elite theory
(B) Democracy
(C) Pluralism
(D) Political machine

25. The attempt of political candidates to de-emphasize racially divisive themes in order to garner crossover support from voters of other races/ethnicities, while also receiving the overwhelming majority of support from voters of the candidate's own racial/ethnic group, is known as which of the following? (5) (p. 296)

(A) Elite theory
(B) Pluralism
(C) Redistributive urban policies
(D) Deracialization

Chapter 12: Counties, School Districts, and Special Districts

Circle the correct answer.

1. Which of the following is *not* a responsibility of county government? **(1)** (p. 306)

   (A) Maintain records, such as birth, death, marriage, and divorce documents
   (B) Enforce laws
   (C) Administer primary and general elections
   (D) Provide public education

2. Which of the following officials is a member of commissioners court? **(1)** (pp. 306–307)

   (A) County judge
   (B) County sheriff
   (C) County clerk
   (D) All of the above

3. Which of the following county officials is elected from a district smaller than the entire county? **(1)** (pp. 306–307)

   (A) County judge
   (B) County commissioner
   (C) County sheriff
   (D) County tax assessor-collector

4. The county judge has which of the following powers and responsibilities? **(1)** (p. 308)

   (A) Veto power over the actions of commissioners court
   (B) Authority to appoint the county sheriff
   (C) A vote on commissioners court
   (D) All of the above

5. Which of the following units of local government has general ordinance-making power? **(1)** (p. 308)

   (A) Counties
   (B) Cities
   (C) Municipal Utility Districts
   (D) All of the above

6. Which of the following officials administers the county jail? **(1)** (p. 308)

   (A) County judge
   (B) County clerk
   (C) Sheriff
   (D) District clerk

7. Which of the following officials records legal documents, such as deeds, mortgages, and contracts? **(1)** (p. 309)

   (A) County clerk
   (B) District clerk
   (C) County attorney
   (D) County tax assessor

8. Which of the following officials is the county election official? **(1)** (p. 309)

   (A) County clerk
   (B) District clerk
   (C) County attorney
   (D) County tax assessor

9. Which of the following officials serves warrants and other legal papers on behalf of the justice of the peace? **(1)** (p. 309)

   (A) Sheriff
   (B) County attorney
   (C) District attorney
   (D) Constable

10. Which of the following officials issues certificates of title for motor vehicles? **(1)** (p. 309)

    (A) District clerk
    (B) Tax assessor-collector
    (C) County clerk
    (D) Justice of the peace

11. Which of the following officials is in charge of voter registration? **(1)** (p. 309)

    (A) Tax assessor-collector
    (B) County clerk
    (C) District clerk
    (D) Sheriff

12. What is the main tax source for county government in Texas? **(1)** (p. 311)

    (A) Sales tax
    (B) Income tax
    (C) Property tax
    (D) Inheritance tax

13. Which of the following county officials is elected? **(1)** (pp. 312–313)

    (A) Tax assessor-collector
    (B) County clerk
    (C) County treasurer
    (D) All of the above

14. Which of the following local officials is *not* elected? **(2)** (p. 316)

    (A) Superintendent of schools
    (B) County tax assessor-collector
    (C) School board trustee
    (D) County sheriff

15. The board of trustees of an independent school district would make which of the following decisions? **(2)** (p. 316)

    (A) Set the property tax rate
    (B) Hire a new superintendent
    (C) Approve a contract to build a new high school facility
    (D) All of the above

16. Which of the following statements accurately reflects the ruling of the Texas Supreme Court in *Edgewood v. Kirby*? **(2)** (p. 320)

   (A) School districts with the same property tax rate should be able to raise the same amount of money per student.
   (B) School districts should all have the same tax rate.
   (C) School districts should all have the same amount of money.
   (D) School districts should all have the same amount of money per student.

17. The Robin Hood Plan requires which of the following? **(2)** (p. 320)

   (A) Giving students in failing schools the opportunity to transfer to other schools, including private schools
   (B) Requiring wealthy property districts to transfer funds either to the state or to other, poorer school districts
   (C) Forcing school districts to balance school enrollment by race and ethnicity
   (D) Basing school funding on TAKS scores

18. Which of the following is a publicly funded but privately managed school that operates under the terms of a formal contract or charter with the state? **(2)** (p. 322)

   (A) Independent school district
   (B) Special district
   (C) Municipal Utility District
   (D) Charter school

19. What is the theory behind the concept of parental choice? **(2)** (pp. 323–324)

   (A) Schools will improve if they have to compete for students.
   (B) Poorly performing schools should be closed.
   (C) Schools with private management will outperform public schools.
   (D) Students will master English better in an English immersion class than a bilingual class.

20. Your child's school is rated exemplary. What does that mean? **(2)** (p. 326)

   (A) It means that many parents chose the school as part of the parental choice program.
   (B) It means that the school has a healthy property tax base.
   (C) It means that the school receives more money from the state than other schools.
   (D) It means that the school's students do well on the TAKS test and have a low dropout rate.

21. A unit of local government created to perform specific functions is known as which of the following? **(3)** (p. 328)

   (A) Charter school
   (B) Special district
   (C) County
   (D) Independent school district

22. A family purchases a home in a subdivision located in an unincorporated area near a large urban center. The family will probably receive its water and sewer service from which of the following? **(3)** (p. 328)

   (A) A Municipal Utility District (MUD)
   (B) The county
   (C) The nearby city
   (D) A water well and septic tank they will dig on their own property

23. How are community/junior colleges governed? **(3)** (p. 330)

   (A) They are part of university systems.
   (B) They are governed by local independent school districts.
   (C) They are special districts headed by elected boards of trustees.
   (D) They are led by boards appointed by the governor.

24. Which of the following is the main tax revenue source for MUDs? **(3)** (p. 331)

   (A) Sales taxes
   (B) Income taxes
   (C) Property taxes
   (D) Inheritance taxes

25. Which of the following special districts is funded by a local sales tax? **(3)** (p. 331)

   (A) Junior/community college
   (B) Municipal Utility District (MUD)
   (C) Transit authority
   (D) Hospital district

Circle the correct answer.

1. What is the most important source of tax revenue for the state? **(1)** (p. 339)

   (A) Personal income tax
   (B) General sales tax
   (C) Excise tax
   (D) Property tax

2. Which federal program accounts for the single largest amount of federal money flowing to the state? **(1)** (p. 339)

   (A) School Lunch Program
   (B) State Children's Health Insurance Program (SCHIP)
   (C) Medicaid
   (D) Temporary Assistance for Needy Families (TANF)

3. Which of the following items is *not* subject to the general sales tax? **(1)** (p. 340)

   (A) Breakfast eaten at the local diner
   (B) A box of cereal purchased at the corner grocery store
   (C) Blood pressure medicine purchased by prescription
   (D) All of the above

4. A tax levied on the manufacture, transportation, sale, or consumption of a particular item or set of related items is known as which of the following? **(1)** (p. 341)

   (A) Sales tax
   (B) Severance tax
   (C) Franchise tax
   (D) Excise tax

5. Which of the following would be an example of a "sin tax"? **(1)** (p. 341)

   (A) Severance tax on oil and gas production
   (B) Motor vehicle sales and use tax
   (C) Cigarette tax
   (D) All of the above

6. Which of the following statements about the Texas Lottery is *not* true? **(1)** (pp. 344–345)

   (A) The lottery raises about 10 percent of total state revenue.
   (B) Lottery proceeds go into the Foundation School Program.
   (C) Lower income people are more likely to purchase lottery tickets than middle- and upper-income people.
   (D) In addition to the Texas Lottery, state residents can participate in the Mega Millions and Powerball lotteries.

7. A levy whose burden weighs more heavily on persons earning higher incomes than it does on individuals earning lower incomes is known as which of the following? **(2)** (p. 347)

   (A) Progressive tax
   (B) Regressive tax

   (C) Proportional tax
   (D) Sin tax

8. How does the tax incidence in Texas compare with that in other states? **(2)** (p. 348)

   (A) Texas has a relatively progressive tax system.
   (B) Texas has one of the most regressive tax systems in the country.
   (C) The Texas tax system is somewhat regressive, but not more so than the tax systems in other states.
   (D) The Texas tax system is proportional because everyone pays the same sales tax rate on each purchase.

9. Which of the following taxes is based on the ability-to-pay theory of taxation? **(2)** (p. 348)

   (A) Sales tax
   (B) Property tax
   (C) Personal income tax
   (D) Excise tax

10. The extent to which tax revenues increase as personal income rises is the definition of which of the following concepts? **(2)** (p. 349)

    (A) Tax incidence
    (B) Performance-based budgeting
    (C) Tax elasticity
    (D) Progressive taxation

11. Conservatives oppose the adoption of a state income tax for which of the following reasons? **(3)** (p. 350)

    (A) They believe that it would make the state tax system less regressive.
    (B) They believe that it would make the state tax system less elastic.
    (C) They believe that it would raise less money than other alternatives, such as broadening the sales tax.
    (D) They believe that it would slow economic growth.

12. When is the Texas Sales Tax Holiday scheduled? **(3)** (p. 353)

    (A) In December before Christmas
    (B) In early January
    (C) In May
    (D) In August before the start of school

13. Which of the following state spending categories has grown the most rapidly over the last two decades? **(4)** (p. 353)

    (A) Public education
    (B) Health and human services
    (C) Criminal justice
    (D) Transportation

14. How do spending levels in Texas compare with spending levels in other states? **(4)** (p. 354)

(A) Texas state spending is below the national average.
(B) Texas state spending is around the national average.
(C) Texas state spending is above the national average.
(D) Texas state spending was once well below the national average but is now above the national average.

15. Which of the following services in Texas is well-funded in comparison with its funding levels in other states? **(4)** (p. 354)

(A) Welfare
(B) Corrections
(C) Higher education
(D) All of the above

16. How will the federal healthcare reform legislation passed by Congress and signed into law by President Obama in 2010 affect Texas? **(5)** (p. 357)

(A) It will add a million people to the Texas Medicaid program.
(B) It will cover low-income childless adults, a group that had not previously been eligible for Medicaid in Texas.
(C) It will eventually increase the cost of Medicaid to Texas state government.
(D) All of the above

17. The Robin Hood Plan is associated with which of the following? **(5)** (p. 358)

(A) Higher education funding
(B) Healthcare funding
(C) Public education funding
(D) Highway funding

18. The PUF is associated with which of the following? **(5)** (p. 360)

(A) Higher education funding
(B) Healthcare funding
(C) Public education funding
(D) Highway funding

19. A Personal Responsibility Agreement (PRA) is part of which of the following programs? **(5)** (p. 362)

(A) Medicaid
(B) Temporary Assistance for Needy Families (TANF)
(C) School Lunch Program
(D) Annexation

20. Which of the following is the main source of funding for the Dedicated Highway Fund? **(5)** (p. 363)

(A) Motor fuels and lubricants tax
(B) Lottery
(C) Sales tax
(D) Driver's license fees

21. A system of budget preparation and evaluation in which policymakers identify specific policy goals, set performance targets for agencies, and measure results is known as which of the following? **(6)** (p. 364)

(A) Incremental budgeting
(B) Performance-based budgeting
(C) Political culture
(D) Sunset review

22. Which of the following officials (or group of officials) plays the most important role in preparing the state's budget? **(6)** (pp. 364–365)

(A) Governor
(B) Comptroller
(C) Legislative Budget Board (LBB)
(D) Secretary of state

23. What impact does the line-item veto have on state spending? **(6)** (p. 367)

(A) None. The governor of Texas seldom issues a line-item veto.
(B) Very little. The governor's vetoes typically account for less than 1 percent of total spending.
(C) A fair amount. The governor's vetoes typically represent about 5 percent of state spending.
(D) A considerable amount. The governor's vetoes typically represent about 10 percent of state spending.

24. Which of the following interest groups typically prefers public policies of low taxes with minimal regulation? **(7)** (p. 369)

(A) Labor unions
(B) Racial and ethnic minority organizations
(C) Consumer groups
(D) Business groups

25. Which of the following factors helps account for Texas's budgetary policies of relatively low tax rates coupled with poorly funded public services? **(7)** (pp. 369–370)

(A) The state's individualistic political culture
(B) The relative strength of business organizations and the relative weakness of labor unions
(C) The dominance of the Republican Party in state politics
(D) All of the above

Circle the correct answer.

1. How does the crime rate in Texas compare with the national crime rate? **(1)** (p. 381)

   (A) The crime rate in Texas is higher than the national crime rate.
   (B) The crime rate in Texas is lower than the national crime rate.
   (C) The crime rate in Texas is about the same as the national crime rate.
   (D) The crime rate in Texas was once higher than the national crime rate but it is now below the national rate.

2. Which of the following statements most accurately describes recent trends in the national crime rate? **(1)** (pp. 381–382)

   (A) The crime rate has been rising fairly steadily since the early 1990s.
   (B) The crime rate has been falling fairly steadily since the early 1990s.
   (C) The crime rate has remained fairly steady since the early 1990s.
   (D) The crime rate fell throughout the 1990s but has been rising steadily since 2000.

3. An approach to law enforcement that seeks to reduce crime by increasing the interaction and cooperation between local law enforcement agencies and the people and neighborhoods they serve is known as which of the following? **(1)** (p. 382)

   (A) Zero tolerance
   (B) Good time
   (C) Community policing
   (D) Adversary proceeding

4. Which of the following statements about the incidence of crime is true? **(2)** (pp. 383–384)

   (A) Homeowners are more likely to become victims than renters.
   (B) Men are more likely to become victims than women.
   (C) Whites are more likely to become victims than African Americans or Latinos.
   (D) All of the above

5. Which of the following descriptions best matches the profile of the typical criminal? **(2)** (pp. 383–384)

   (A) Middle-aged man
   (B) Young, poorly educated man
   (C) Young woman
   (D) Well-educated older man

6. The reasonable belief that a crime has been committed and that a particular suspect is the likely perpetrator of that crime is known as which of the following? **(3)** (p. 384)

   (A) Booking
   (B) Indictment
   (C) Probation
   (D) Probable cause

7. For which of the following crimes is the clearance rate the highest? **(3)** (p. 384)

   (A) Theft
   (B) Burglary
   (C) Arson
   (D) Murder

8. An administrative procedure in which law enforcement personnel document a suspect's arrest is known as which of the following? **(3)** (p. 384)

   (A) Probable cause
   (B) Booking
   (C) True bill
   (D) Indictment

9. What is the purpose of an arraignment? **(3)** (p. 385)

   (A) To determine whether a crime has been committed
   (B) To determine whether an inmate should be released on parole
   (C) To determine whether a guilty defendant should be given probation
   (D) To formally charge a suspect with a crime and ask the suspect to enter a plea

10. What is the purpose of bail? **(3)** (p. 385)

    (A) To ensure that a defendant shows up for later court proceedings
    (B) To raise money for the Texas Crime Victims' Compensation Fund
    (C) To punish an offender for committing a crime
    (D) To provide restitution to the victim of a crime

11. What does a grand jury do? **(3)** (p. 385)

    (A) It hears evidence and decides whether to indict an accused person.
    (B) It decides the guilt or innocence of a person accused of a crime.
    (C) It determines punishment for someone found guilty of a crime.
    (D) All of the above

12. A legal procedure in which each side may present evidence and arguments to bolster its position, while rebutting evidence that might support the other side, is known as which of the following? **(3)** (p. 387)

    (A) Indictment
    (B) Adversary proceeding
    (C) Plea bargain
    (D) Arraignment

13. Who has the burden of proof in a criminal case? **(3)** (p. 387)

    (A) The defendant
    (B) The judge
    (C) The prosecutor
    (D) The jury

14. The suspension of a sentence, permitting the defendant to remain free under court supervision, is known as which of the following? **(3)** (pp. 388–389)

    (A) Parole
    (B) Plea bargain
    (C) Probation
    (D) Good time

15. Which of the following allows a defendant who pleads guilty to avoid having a conviction on his or her record? **(3)** (p. 389)

    (A) Parole
    (B) Good time
    (C) Plea bargain
    (D) Deferred adjudication

16. What issue did *Furman v. Georgia* address? **(4)** (p. 390)

    (A) Death penalty
    (B) Prison overcrowding
    (C) Juvenile justice
    (D) All of the above

17. Which of the following offenses would *not* qualify for the death penalty under Texas law? **(4)** (p. 390)

    (A) Person A is robbing a convenience store with a gun pointed at the clerk. Even though Person A did not intend to use the gun, it accidentally goes off and the clerk is killed.
    (B) Person B hires Hitman X to kill her husband and Hitman X carries out the dirty deed.
    (C) Person C is babysitting his girlfriend's infant child. Person C grows exasperated when the baby cries; he shakes the infant and the baby dies.
    (D) Person D has held a grudge against a coworker for years. One day Person D waits outside the coworker's house and shoots him to death when he comes home.

18. A prison inmate sentenced to 12 years behind bars is released after serving eight years. His release is an example of which of the following? **(4)** (pp. 391–392)

    (A) Probation
    (B) Parole
    (C) Recidivism
    (D) Plea bargain

19. How has the juvenile crime rate changed compared to the overall crime rate? **(5)** (pp. 392–393)

    (A) The juvenile crime rate has been falling faster than the overall crime rate has fallen.
    (B) The juvenile crime rate has been increasing faster than the overall crime rate has risen.
    (C) The juvenile crime rate has been falling while the overall crime rate has been rising.
    (D) The juvenile crime rate has been rising while the overall crime rate has been falling.

20. Which of the following state agencies houses juvenile offenders? **(5)** (p. 393)

    (A) Texas Department of Public Safety
    (B) Texas Department of Criminal Justice
    (C) Texas Youth Commission
    (D) Texas Attorney General

21. Which state has the largest prison system in terms of number of inmates? **(6)** (p. 393)

    (A) Louisiana
    (B) California
    (C) Texas
    (D) New York

22. Which of the following offenders would be most likely to be housed in a state jail? **(6)** (p. 394)

    (A) An inmate convicted of capital murder
    (B) A person accused of robbery and awaiting trial who is unable to make bail
    (C) A juvenile convicted of a serious crime
    (D) An inmate convicted of fraud, a fourth-degree felony

23. A prison policy that credits inmates with time off for good behavior is known as which of the following? **(6)** (p. 396)

    (A) Good time
    (B) Probation
    (C) Parole
    (D) Plea bargain

24. The tendency of offenders released from prison to commit additional crimes and be returned behind bars is known as which of the following? **(6)** (p. 397)

    (A) Adversary proceeding
    (B) Recidivism
    (C) Clearance rate
    (D) Burden of proof

25. Which of the following interest groups would lobby in favor of tougher DWI laws? **(7)** (p. 398)

    (A) MADD
    (B) NRA
    (C) AFL-CIO
    (D) ACLU

ANSWERS TO PRACTICE TEST QUESTIONS

Introduction: The Policymaking Process

1. C	8. C	15. C
2. C	9. D	16. A
3. D	10. D	17. A
4. A	11. B	18. D
5. B	12. A	19. B
6. A	13. C	20. D
7. B	14. A	

Chapter 1: The People, Economy, and Political Culture of Texas

1. A	11. A	21. C
2. A	12. B	22. B
3. B	13. D	23. D
4. D	14. B	24. C
5. C	15. D	25. A
6. A	16. B	
7. A	17. A	
8. B	18. D	
9. C	19. D	
10. B	20. B	

Chapter 2: Texas Constitution

1. D	11. B	21. A
2. A	12. B	22. C
3. B	13. C	23. B
4. C	14. A	24. D
5. C	15. A	25. A
6. A	16. C	
7. D	17. B	
8. D	18. D	
9. B	19. C	
10. A	20. D	

Chapter 3: The Federal Context of Texas Policymaking

1. B	11. A	21. A
2. C	12. B	22. C
3. C	13. A	23. A
4. A	14. D	24. B
5. A	15. C	25. A
6. B	16. A	
7. C	17. C	
8. A	18. D	
9. D	19. A	
10. C	20. B	

Chapter 4: Political Participation

1. A	11. D	21. D
2. A	12. B	22. C
3. D	13. B	23. D
4. A	14. D	24. C
5. C	15. A	25. B
6. B	16. D	
7. D	17. A	
8. D	18. B	
9. C	19. A	
10. B	20. D	

Chapter 5: Interest Groups

1. D	11. C	21. A
2. A	12. D	22. B
3. C	13. D	23. C
4. B	14. C	24. D
5. D	15. D	25. D
6. C	16. B	
7. A	17. A	
8. B	18. B	
9. B	19. A	
10. A	20. D	

Chapter 6: Political Parties

1. A	11. A	21. D
2. D	12. C	22. B
3. C	13. D	23. C
4. C	14. C	24. A
5. B	15. C	25. C
6. C	16. A	
7. D	17. D	
8. A	18. B	
9. A	19. D	
10. B	20. B	

Chapter 7: Elections

1. B	11. D	21. D
2. C	12. A	22. D
3. A	13. C	23. D
4. A	14. A	24. A
5. A	15. A	25. C
6. D	16. D	
7. C	17. D	
8. D	18. B	
9. A	19. B	
10. B	20. A	

Chapter 8: The Texas Legislature

1. A	11. C	21. A
2. C	12. D	22. A
3. B	13. C	23. D
4. D	14. B	24. C
5. A	15. D	25. B
6. D	16. A	
7. A	17. C	
8. D	18. B	
9. C	19. A	
10. B	20. B	

Chapter 9: Executive Branch

1. C	11. A	21. D
2. D	12. C	22. D
3. B	13. D	23. B
4. C	14. B	24. C
5. A	15. A	25. B
6. C	16. C	
7. A	17. B	
8. C	18. B	
9. B	19. D	
10. C	20. B	

Chapter 10: Judicial Branch

1. C	11. C	21. B
2. A	12. A	22. C
3. D	13. C	23. A
4. A	14. C	24. C
5. B	15. D	25. D
6. C	16. A	
7. B	17. C	
8. A	18. D	
9. D	19. C	
10. D	20. D	

Chapter 11: City Government

1. D	11. C	21. A
2. D	12. D	22. B
3. C	13. C	23. A
4. A	14. B	24. C
5. B	15. A	25. D
6. B	16. D	
7. A	17. C	
8. D	18. B	
9. C	19. A	
10. B	20. A	

Chapter 12: Counties, School Districts, and Special Districts

1. D	11. A	21. B
2. A	12. C	22. A
3. B	13. D	23. C
4. C	14. A	24. C
5. B	15. D	25. C
6. C	16. A	
7. A	17. B	
8. A	18. D	
9. D	19. A	
10. B	20. D	

Chapter 13: State Budget Policy

1. B	11. D	21. B
2. C	12. D	22. C
3. D	13. B	23. B
4. D	14. A	24. D
5. C	15. B	25. D
6. A	16. D	
7. A	17. C	
8. B	18. A	
9. C	19. B	
10. C	20. A	

Chapter 14: Criminal Justice

1. A	11. A	21. C
2. B	12. B	22. D
3. C	13. C	23. A
4. B	14. C	24. B
5. B	15. D	25. A
6. D	16. A	
7. D	17. D	
8. B	18. D	
9. D	19. A	
10. A	20. C	